HISTORY OF THE POPES
VOL. XXIV.

PASTOR'S HISTORY OF THE POPES

THE HISTORY OF THE POPES. Translated from the German of LUDWIG, FREIHERR VON PASTOR. Edited, as to Vols. I.-VI., by the late FREDERICK IGNATIUS ANTROBUS, and, as to Vols. VII -XXIV., by RALPH FRANCIS KERR, of the London Oratory. In 24 Volumes.

Vols. I. and II.	A.D. 1305-1458
Vols. III. and IV.	A.D. 1458-1483
Vols. V. and VI.	A.D. 1484-1513
Vols. VII. and VIII	A D. 1513-1521
Vols. IX. and X.	A.D. 1522-1534
Vols XI. and XII.	A.D. 1534-1549
Vols. XIII. and XIV.	A.D. 1550-1559
Vols. XV. and XVI.	A.D. 1559-1565
Vols. XVII. and XVIII.	A D. 1566-1572
Vols. XIX. and XX.	A.D. 1572-1585
Vols. XXI. and XXII	A.D. 1585-1591
Vols. XXIII. and XXIV.	A.D. 1592-1605

The original German text of the *History of the Popes* is published by Herder & Co., Freiburg (Baden).

THE
HISTORY OF THE POPES

FROM THE CLOSE OF THE MIDDLE AGES

DRAWN FROM THE SECRET ARCHIVES OF THE VATICAN AND OTHER
ORIGINAL SOURCES

FROM THE GERMAN OF

LUDWIG, FREIHERR VON PASTOR

EDITED BY

RALPH FRANCIS KERR

OF THE LONDON ORATORY

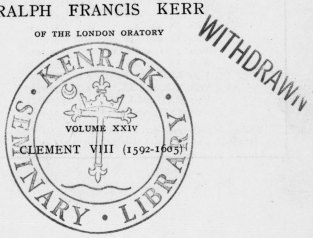

VOLUME XXIV

CLEMENT VIII (1592-1605)

B. HERDER BOOK CO.
15 AND 17 SOUTH BROADWAY,
ST. LOUIS, MO.
1933

1915

PRINTED IN GREAT BRITAIN BY THE DEVONSHIRE PRESS, TORQUAY.

CONTENTS OF VOLUME XXIV.[1]

[1] For Bibliography see Volume XXIII.

TABLE OF CONTENTS OF VOLUME XXIV.

CHAPTER I.

PERSECUTION OF THE CATHOLICS IN HOLLAND AND IN ENGLAND.

CHAPTER II.

PERSECUTION IN SCOTLAND AND IRELAND.—CLEMENT VIII. AND JAMES I.

CHAPTER III.

ATTEMPTED CATHOLIC RESTORATION IN SWEDEN

CHAPTER IV.

PROGRESS OF CATHOLIC RESTORATION IN POLAND.—REUNION
OF THE SCHISMATIC RUTHENIANS.—THE FALSE DEMETRIUS.

CHAPTER V.

CLEMENT VIII. AND THE INTERIOR LIFE OF THE CHURCH.—
THE RELIGIOUS ORDERS.—THE EPISCOPATE.—THE SACRED
COLLEGE.

CHAPTER VI.

THE ROMAN INQUISITION.—GIORDANO BRUNO.—THE INDEX.—
THE VULGATE.

CHAPTER VII.

FOREIGN MISSIONS—THE BEGINNINGS OF PROPAGANDA.

CHAPTER VIII.

THE GREAT JUBILEE OF 1600.

CHAPTER IX.

THE CONTROVERSY ON GRACE.

CHAPTER X.

THE PAPAL STATES.—THE RE-ACQUISITION OF FERRARA.— DEATH OF THE POPE.

LIST OF UNPUBLISHED DOCUMENTS IN APPENDIX.

CHAPTER I.

PERSECUTION OF THE CATHOLICS IN HOLLAND AND IN ENGLAND.

As a result of the schism, the kingdom of Queen Elizabeth and the young republic of the Low Countries had also become missionary countries, and the prohibition of the public exercise of Catholic worship was all the more oppressive in that the number of the Catholics was still very considerable. In the greater part of the provinces of Holland, in Utrecht, Gelderland, Frisia and Oberyssel, the Catholics formed a large majority.[1] In the first years of his pontificate Clement VIII. at once took steps to provide them with spiritual assistance, and in the instructions given to the nuncio Caetani, who was sent to Spain in the autumn of 1592, it may be seen what care the Pope took to deal with the religious difficulties which had sprung up in Holland and Zeeland. Clement's idea was to provide a remedy by sending missionaries of the Society of Jesus, and the Franciscan Order. He had already had much at heart the establishment of the Franciscans in a seminary founded at Tournai in 1592. Caetani was instructed to obtain once more for this institution the subsidy which Philip II. had suspended, and at the same time to secure the continuance of the payment of

[1] This is admitted even by so inveterate an adversary of the Catholics as the author of the " Scriptum A⁰ 1604 " published in the *Neuen Lausitzschen Magazin*, XLI., 157 *seqq.* " when he had left the Popedom and had come hither from Rome," p. 169 (maximus est numerus [catholicorum] in Hollandia, Selandia, Frisia, etc.). *Cf.* also W. KNUTTEL, De toestand der Katholieken onder der Republiek, I., The Hague, 1892.

the contribution for the exiled priests who were living at
Louvain and Douai.[1]

The idea of employing the Jesuits in the mission in Holland
had been suggested to the Pope in 1592 by the Dutch priest
Jan Smith. At the same time another Dutch priest had
approached the provincial of the Jesuits in Belgium, Oliver
Manaraeus.[2] The General of the Society of Jesus, Claudio
Aquaviva, welcomed the proposal, and in October two Dutch
Jesuits of the Belgian province were sent to Holland,[3] and
thus founded the Dutch mission. To them, and to the
Franciscans who were already labouring there is due the
credit for the preservation of the faith in Holland. The
missionaries had no fixed abode, but travelled about the
country as apostles, but as there were severe edicts against
the celebration of mass, and especially a prohibition of giving
hospitality to the Jesuits, the latter were exposed to the
gravest dangers. They had to disguise themselves, and
constantly change their place of residence. As in the days of
the catacombs, the celebration of mass and the administration
of the sacraments could only take place at night, while, in
order to prevent a surprise, it was necessary to set guards.
At dawn the missionary went on to another place.[4]

The mission would have been altogether prevented if the
large number of the Catholics who still remained, and the
greed for money on the part of the officials had not made it

[1] For the *instructions for Caetani (Cod. 468, p. 1 seq., Corsini
Library, Rome) see LÄMMER, Zur Kirchengesch. 121 seq., and
R. MAERE in Bull. de la Commiss. Roy. d'hist., LXXIII., Brussels,
1904, 3 ; there is also mention of the attempt of the Calvinists
secretly to introduce Protestant writings into Spain. For the
seminary at Tournai see Bull., IX., 367 seq. ; WADDING, Annales
Min., XXIII., 414.

[2] See PONCELET, Les Jésuites en Belgique, 32.

[3] See IUVENCIUS, Hist. Soc. Iesu P. V. tom. post. 414 seq.
Cf. OLIV. MANARAEUS, De initiis missionis batavae, in ALLARD,
Eene missiëreis door Nord-Nederland en de 17e eeuw, 's
Hertogenbosch, 1883, 37 seq.

[4] See IUVENCIUS loc. cit., 417 seq. ; PONCELET, loc. cit.

possible to evade the severe ordinances. The right to public worship, which was granted in 1603 to the Mahometan ambassador,[1] was still withheld from the Catholics born in the same land, but by means of bribes it was possible to obtain from the officials entrusted with the carrying out of the edict the power to have mass said in secret.

For this reason the work of the Jesuit and Franciscan missionaries was very arduous. This may clearly be seen from the reports of the Jesuits, who had begun their mission there with two fathers in 1592.[2] These tell of cases where a missionary was forced to change his residence eight times in the course of twelve days. On the other hand the zeal of the Catholics to hear the word of God and receive the sacraments was very consoling, some of them having been deprived of these things for thirty or even forty years. Sometimes the fathers had to preach twice or three times in the day.[3] The head of the mission, Johann Bargius, who came from Amsterdam, describes the labours that they had to undergo. " In Frisia," he writes, " for nine weeks I had to employ the nights as well as the days ; in the evening at dusk I set myself to hearing confessions and baptizing, and then preached and said mass ; after this there again came to me those who wished to confess or communicate, and some whose marriages had to be regularized.[4] Thus there only remained three hours for sleep, for very early in the morning I had to set out for another place." With such labours as this, it is not surprising that Bargius died at the age of forty-eight. " The work increases from day to day," he says in a report of 1604 ; " if only we had greater forces at our command ! "[5]

The direction of the missionaries, as appears from a brief

[1] See Litt. ann. Soc. Iesu, 1603, 646.

[2] See *Tijdschrift voor Utrecht geschied.*, IX., 236, 266 *seq.* ; BROM, Archivalia in Italië, III., 's Gravenhage, 1914, xxxviii.

[3] See Litt. ann. Soc. Iesu, 1597, 283, 285 ; 1598, 258 *seq.* ; 1599, 314 ; 1600, 533 *seq.* ; 1602, 709 ; 1603, 625 *seq.* ; 1604, 702 *seq.*

[4] See *ibid.*, 1600, 532 *seq.*

[5] *Ibid.*, 1604, 703.

of Clement VIII., of 1592,[1] as well as from other documents,[2] was in the hands of Sasbout Vosmeer, as vicar apostolic, who resided almost entirely at Cologne. From a report of Frangipani of April, 1592, it appears that at that date two Catholic priests were secretly giving the Dutch Catholics the consolations of their religion ; at Leyden alone they confessed about a thousand of the faithful, and brought about the conversion of several Protestants.[3] In 1594 there was an idea of appointing a bishop for Holland,[4] but this was abandoned. In 1596 the vicariate apostolic of Holland was placed under the nunciature at Brussels.[5] Vosmeer caused northern Holland to be visited every year from 1594 onwards by Albert Eggis, but when in 1601 Vosmeer appointed Eggis as vicar-general of the former diocese of Haarlem, he met with opposition from the chapter. In this way the government of the Low Countries discovered the existence of a Catholic hierarchy in their own country. It was impossible to reach Vosmeer, because he was abroad, but Eggis was arrested in March, 1602, and proceedings were taken against him, which ended in his banishment.[6] The report which

[1] See N. BROEDERSEN, Tract. hist., I. (1729), 245. This document was missed by Friedrich ; he thought that Vosmeer had hardly become vicar-apostolic in 1602 ; see *Zeitschr. f. Missionswissenechaft*, XI. (1922), 130 *seq.* ; " Holland als Weige der Missionshierarchie."

[2] On April 9, 1592, Frangipani sent Clement VIII. a letter from the " vicar-apostolic " Vosmeer ; see BROM-HENSEN, Romeinsche Bronnen, The Hague, 1922, 425 *seq.*

[3] See *ibid.*, 426.

[4] See in App. No. 5 the *letter of Cardinal Cinzio Aldobrandini to L. Madruzzo, May 2, 1594, Cod. Campori 214 of the Este Library, Modena. *Ibid.* concerning the mission of a Flemish Dominican to Holland, who had received from the Inquisition all the needful faculties.

[5] See MAERE in the *Rev. d'hist. ecclés.*, VII. (1905), 822 ; Corresp. de Frangipani, I., xv.

[6] See HENSEN in Molhuysen-Blok, Nieuw Nederlandsch Biogr. Woorden-boeck, III., Leyden, 1914, 320 *seqq.*, and the literature there cited.

Vosmeer sent to the Pope in 1602,[1] revealed the sad state of the Dutch Catholics. Vosmeer was then given the title of Archbishop of Philippi,[2] but he had to continue to live in exile at Cologne, where he made provision for the training of priests for Holland by the establishment of a college.[3]

The nuncio at Cologne, Ottavio Mirto Frangipani, took the liveliest interest in, and gave every possible assistance to the Catholic missions in Holland ; after 1596 he was in charge of the nunciature at Brussels, established not long before, and was able to help yet more from there than from Cologne.[4] When disputes arose between the vicar apostolic Vosmeer and the Jesuits, in 1598 Frangipani summoned the vicar to Brussels where an agreement was come to, which, unfortunately, was not of long duration.[5]

[1] See *Archief v. geschied. v. h. aartsbisd. Utrecht*, XVII. (1899), 150 *seqq.* *Cf.* FRUIN, Verspriede Geschriften, III., 's Gravenhage, 1901, 249 *seq.*

[2] See Uittreksel uit Francisci Dusseldorpii Annales, 1566-1616, ed. FRUIN, 's Gravenhage, 1893, 316. *Cf. ibid.*, 284 *seq.*, the edict of Clement VIII. of May 26, 1601, extending the indulgence of the holy year to the Dutch Catholics.

[3] For the College of Cologne see *Bijdragen v. d. geschied. v. h. bisd. Haarlem*, VIII., 1 *seqq.* ; XV., 87 *seqq.* ; BROM-HENSEN, Rom. Bronnen, 426, 427, 429. Eggis left the college 16,000 florins ; see HENSEN, *loc. cit.*

[4] The whole correspondence of Frangipani, his reports, and his instructions from the Secretary of State, are to be found in the National Library, Naples. In my account of my journey in 1893 made in the interests of the Nuntiaturberichte (*Hist. Jahrb.*, XV., 712 *seq.*). I once again called the attention of scholars to this material which had so long remained unnoticed. It is pleasant to record that the director of the Dutch Historical Institute in Rome, Mgr. Hensen, will shortly publish all Frangipani's reports concerning his own country. With regard to the publication of the reports of Frangipani by L, v.d. Essen, see Vol. XXIII. of this work, p. 398, While this work was in the press there appeared : L. v. WASSENHOVEN O.M. Frangipani en de Engelsche Katholicken (1596-1606), Baasrode, 1925.

[5] See KNUTTEL, *loc. cit.*, 50 *seq.* *Cf. Archief v.d. geschied. v.h. aartbisd. Utrecht*, XXII., 406 *seq.*

Clement VIII., who prayed daily for the Dutch Catholics,[1] during his last years entertained the hope, on the conclusion of an armistice between the Archduke Albert and the revolted provinces, of obtaining facilities for Catholic worship there. He urgently begged the Archduke and his pious consort, Isabella, not to separate the cause of God from their own, for otherwise they would have reason to fear lest God should abandon them.[2]

The pontificate of Clement VIII. was destined to be of great importance for the situation in England, for the change which had been inaugurated by Sixtus V. attained to its full development under the Aldobrandini Pope. The sacking of Cadiz by the English in 1596, and the failure of the second Spanish Armada in 1597, manifested to the whole world the weakness of the vast Spanish empire. Under Clement VIII. the Papacy definitely and finally renounced all hopes of seeing the ancient religion restored in England by means of Spanish intervention or that of any other foreign power. A return to former religious conditions, or at least to liberty of conscience, could at the utmost be looked for by the Holy See from the accession to the throne of some prince who was not hostile to the Catholics ; in the meantime it limited itself henceforward to an attempt to save and maintain by the peaceful means of preaching and instruction what still remained to be saved and preserved.[3]   The separation from Spain was further facilitated

[1] See the *brief to " Carolus dux Croy et Areschotii " of March 31, 1599 ; Arm. 44, t. 43, n. 198, Papal Secret Archives. *Ibid.*, n. 199 a similar *letter to Philippe de Croy, of the same date.

[2] See the *brief to Albert and Isabella, January 8, 1600, Arm. 44, n. 4, Papal Secret Archives.

[3] " With regard to these (the heretics) the Curia, since Clement VIII. had ascended the throne, had changed its policy ; it was no longer by force, but by negotiations with heretical sovereigns, and missions to the apostate peoples, that it hoped to overcome heresy." F. HILTEBRANDT in *Quellen u. Forsch.*, XV. (1913) ; 307 *seq.* So too, POLLEN in *The Month*, XCIV. (1899), 241 ; COUZARD, Une ambassade à Rome sous Henri IV., septembre 1601–juin 1605 (Philippe de Béthune), Paris, 1901, 103 *seq.*

by the fact that after the conversion of Henry IV. the world-
wide dominion of Charles V. steadily lost its name as the one
Catholic power, and found a serious rival in France.

The changed attitude of the Pope was not immediately
grasped and followed by the Catholics in England of Spanish
sympathies. It was only gradually, and not without a
temporary disagreement among the supporters of the ancient
religion, that this change of front could be brought about.
During the first years of the pontificate of Clement VIII. the
Spanish claims to the succession to the English throne were
still ardently maintained, especially by the Jesuit, Robert
Persons.[1] It may perhaps be looked upon as a further sign
of such sentiments that just at that time there sprang up on
Spanish soil, and with the consent of Clement VIII. a number
of colleges which were to be devoted to the training of English
priests.

In 1589, a few months after the great disaster of the first
armada, Persons, who displayed unwearied courage, went
to Spain in order to obtain from Philip II., among other
things, a larger subsidy for the seminary at Douai.   Soon after
this it seemed to him to be more advantageous to establish a
new college in Spain itself after the model of that at Douai.
A small party of six students was at once transferred from
Allen's great seminary to Valladolid, while many generous
benefactors were found in Spain, who gave abundant alms to
the new institute.   Philip II. too, who had been described as
its " founder " by Clement VIII. in his bull of confirmation
of November 3rd, 1592,[2] assigned to it an annual revenue of
1600 crowns, and on the occasion of a visit to the seminary
was profoundly moved at the sight of these youths who had
left their country for the sake of the faith, in order to face a
life of suffering and persecution ; he thereupon increased his
annual contribution, and took all the debts of the seminary

According to Couzard (*ibid.*) the Pope in this was following the
advice of Henry IV.

[1] For Persons *cf.* Vol. XIX. of this work, pp. 388 *seqq.*

[2] Bull. X., 630 ; *Synopsis*, 170.

upon his own shoulders. In 1592 the establishment had
75 students, though in 1598 there were only 53, the first three
priests being sent to England in 1593.[1] English seminaries
were also established by Persons at Seville[2] and Madrid,[3]
which, however, did not prosper very much. A special
position among the English foundations in the Peninsula was
held by the seminary at Lisbon, which was placed in the
charge of secular priests and of the vicar apostolic of England.
It owed its origin to Nicholas Ashton, who in the time of
Queen Elizabeth had the care of the English at Lisbon, but
was only endowed with sufficient revenues in 1629 by the
Portuguese, Pedro Coutinho.[4]

Even more important than the above-mentioned establishments, which all devoted themselves to the teaching of
theology, was another foundation of Persons in Flanders.
The English Catholics were in need of a school for the teaching
of the classics and preparation for theology. Therefore in
1582 Persons founded such a school at Eu in Normandy,
which at the end of 1592 was transferred to Saint-Omer, after
the murder of its benefactor, the Duke of Guise. In 1595
the number of students was only 38, but in 1601 had risen to

---

[1] *Bellesheim*, Kard. Allen, 237-244, 289-291 (letters of recommendation of the Benedictine abbot Alphonsus and the nuncio
Caetani, September 10 and November 6, 1596).

[2] *Ibid.*, 244. Bull of confirmation by Clement VIII., May 15,
1594. Bull., X., 139, *Synopsis*, 183. A *brief of February 13,
1593, to the Cardinal of Seville " founder of the college " in
Brevia, Arm. 44, t. 38, n. 221, Papal Secret Archives.

[3] BELLESHEIM, Allen, 248. By a pontifical decree of July 7,
1599, to Cardinals Caetani and Borghese, the internal scholastic
organization, which had been adopted for the English College in
Rome, was declared obligatory for the other English institutes
(Bull., X., 521). An ordinance of September 18, 1597 (*ibid.*, 375)
removed certain abuses which had arisen in consequence of the
title of doctor being attained by the English students.

[4] *Ibid.*, 250 ; W. CROFT, Historical account of Lisbon College,
London, 1902 ; BELLESHEIM in *Hist.-pol. Bl.*, CXXXI. (1903),
785 *seqq.*

100, and to 120 in the following year. Philip II. granted it
an annual subsidy of 1920 ducats. At first only those pupils
were taken who wished to devote themselves to the priesthood,
but this restriction was afterwards abandoned, so that
Saint-Omer became a place of education for the English
Catholic aristocracy, and in this way did an important work.[1]
The largest of these establishments were witnesses to numerous
conversions among the English Protestants,[2] while they were
a support and centre for the Catholics.

All these establishments represented steps and attempts to
place the future of the Church in England upon a secure basis.
In other ways too Clement VIII. stood for a new era for the
Catholics in the British Isles, in that they now attempted to
abandon their indefinite position, which in course of time had
become intolerable, and to establish a secure state of affairs.
They were also impelled to these new methods by the death of
Cardinal Allen, which took place on October 16th, 1594.[3]

Allen's piety, learning, gentleness and moderation were
realized by men in Rome, who nevertheless had but a faint
conception of his real powers.[4] But Allen, as Clement VIII.

[1] This still survives in the great Jesuit college at Stonyhurst
near Blackburn. *Cf.* L. WILLAERT in the *American Catholic
Quarterly Review*, October, 1905, 745-758 ; O. BLED, Les Jésuites
anglais à Saint-Omer. Difficultés avec le magistrat à l'occasion
de leur premier établissement, Saint-Omer, 1890 ; BELLESHEIM,
Allen, 251-264, 291 *seq.* (Report of the bishop of Saint-Omer,
1612), 292-294. (Report of the nuncio at Brussels Bentivoglio
October 18, 1609, of the welcome given him at the college).
LECHAT, 215 *seqq.* ; MEYER, 148. For the dangers to which the
students were exposed when they went to the Spanish seminaries
cf. BEDE CAMM, O.S.B. in *The Month*, XCI. (1898), 375 *seqq.* ;
XCII. (1898), 164-177 ; STEVENSON, *ibid.*, 1879 ; II., 535 ;
1880, I., 44, 392 ; II., 395. Description of life at the college,
ibid., XCIV. (1899), 167-170.

[2] BELLESHEIM, *loc. cit.*, 239 *seq.*, 242, 246, 254.

[3] For his death see BELLESHEIM, 199 *seq.*

[4] *Cf.* *Avviso of October 19, 1594 : On Sunday [October 17]
Allen died " santamente col giuditio retto fin all'ultimo sospiro,
lascia nome di religiosissimo altretanto dotto, esemplare, da bene,

informed the Archduke Ernest, was not only a " jewel " of
Catholic England, but had been, as the Pope justly added,
the man who had kept the English Catholics united, and one
whose death had deprived his fellow-countrymen of a strong
support.[1] He was indeed a man " as it were made for the
salvation of England," and the centre round which the English
Catholics gravitated both at home and abroad[2] ; " our Moses "
as the Jesuit, Holt, called him.[3] All turned their eyes to him
as to a father and venerated master, and he had the gift of
communicating to others his unswerving courage, and his
unhesitating confidence in God, and of preventing the worst
forms of discord among the Catholics of his country.

Thus, so long as he was alive, the English clergy did not
feel the lack of a leader armed with episcopal authority and
jurisdiction.[4] Among the Catholic priests in England, who
had gradually become more numerous, there existed a relationship of subordination or superiority only in so far as they
voluntarily accepted advice and instruction from men of
greater spirituality. Thus it came about that the secular
priests took their instructions from the Jesuit Persons, and
the Jesuits from Allen.

The result of this uncertain state of affairs was that everything seemed to fall to pieces when death snatched away the

dolce et di altre belle parti, ma di leggiera armatura, et povero di
partito et di consiglio, senza havere mai nociuto a veruno."
Urb. lat. 1062, p. 608, Vatican Library.

[1] *Letter of October 22, 1594, Brevia, Arm. 44, t. 39, n. 337,
Papal Secret Archives.

[2] *Cf.* the expressions in BELLESHEIM, Allen, iii.

[3] POLLEN in *The Month*, C. (1902), 179.

[4] In 1606 the Spanish ambassador wrote of 160 priests in
England. Other information at that time ranges between 400
and 900 (WILLAERT in the *Revue d'hist. ecclés.*, VI. [1905], 569 *seq.*).
A report of March 9, 1600, maintains that more masses were said
and more frequent sacraments received than in Spain (*ibid.*, 569).
In 1607 it was said that in Holy Week 600 Catholics received the
sacraments at the house of the ambassador in London (*ibid.*, 570).
In 1584 Persons wrote of 300 priests in England (FOLEY, I., 634).

man who had been their rallying point. Many now thought
of asking Clement VIII. to give them a new " Cardinal of
England." But where was the man to be found who could
take the place of Allen ? The Scottish party turned their
thoughts to Owen Lewis, who, after he had been summoned
to Rome by the Pope, had had a share in the foundation of the
English College, had then become vicar-general of Charles
Borromeo, and finally Bishop of Cassano.[1] The Spanish
party among the exiles, on the other hand, asked for Persons
The priests and seminarists took up his cause eagerly, and
letters of recommendation were even obtained from Alessandro
Farnese and others in high places, which paved the way for
the English Jesuit with the Pope and the Cardinals. A
certain Dr. Worthington collected signatures in his favour,
while Philip II. and the Protector of the English nation
seemed to have been won over to his cause. Persons, however,
who by the rules of his Order could neither aspire to the
purple nor accept it voluntarily, and who did not wish to
become a Cardinal, recommended for the position the distinguished Thomas Stapleton, who, from the summer of 1596
onwards was actually invited by the Pope three times to come
to Rome.

The struggle then became acute, especially between the
supporters of Lewis and Persons, until at last the death of
Lewis, on October 14th, 1595, and the exclusion of Persons by
Clement VIII. put an end to the disgraceful disputes. In
May, 1597, Persons himself had come to the conclusion that
there was no one who could replace Allen, and that it was
better for England to have no Cardinal at all than one who
was not fitted.[2] After this the disputes among the exiles

[1] *Cf.* Vol. XIX. of this work, p. 381.

[2] LECHAT, 177-180 ; POLLEN in *The Month*, C. (1902), 180 ;
BELLESHEIM, Allen, 202-206. A *brief to Stapleton of December
2, 1595 (thanking him for sending his " Antidota "). In Brevia,
Arm. 44, t. 40, p. 338, Papal Secret Archives. On January 29
Giulio Cesare Foresto *wrote to Mantua that he expected ere long
the appointment of an English Cardinal. Gonzaga Archives,
Mantua.

from England, between the " Spaniards " and the " Scots "
came to an end as far as this question was concerned, but only
to be rekindled with even greater violence on other matters.

The Scottish group among the English exiles had been in
existence from about 1580 onwards, and had at first been
limited to France, which was ill-disposed towards Spain. It
was only when their leaders, Mary Stuart's agents, Charles
Paget and Thomas Morgan, removed in 1588 to Flanders,
that the Low Countries became the principal focus of the
disputes.[1] Their followers called themselves the " party of
the laity and aristocracy," and spoke of their opponents as
the party of the priests or of the Jesuits. As early as 1581
Allen had had to act as peacemaker between Persons and
William Tresham, who declared that it was unworthy of a
man of noble birth to be guided in matters of politics by
priests.[2] At first the disagreement between the two parties
did not seem to be insuperable : the efforts of Allen at anyrate
brought about a rapprochement, though Paget and Morgan
continued to receive annual subsidies from the Spaniards.[3]
But Allen himself, who was Spanish in his sympathies, became
a subject of dispute, and from the first the " Scots " worked
strongly against his appointment as Cardinal, and sought at
anyrate to oppose to him in the person of Owen Lewis, who
belonged to their party, a rival in the College of Cardinals ;
the " Spaniards " replied by accusing Paget and Morgan of
having betrayed Mary Stuart, and of having brought about
her death. It was a fact that these two, by their impetuous
thoughtlessness, had given assistance to the English government against the unhappy Queen of Scots[4] ; it is also certain
that Paget had on several occasions taken steps to secure the
favour of Elizabeth.[5] In this violent dispute the Scottish
party lost ground all along the line, and Allen and Lewis drew

[1] LECHAT, 157 seqq.
[2] Ibid., 164 seq.
[3] Ibid., 158.
[4] Cf. Vol. XXII, of this work, p. 12.
[5] LECHAT, 158.

up a joint letter in which[1] they declared before the world that they were sincere friends and disclaimed all rivalry ; in February, 1590, Morgan was arrested by Farnese and was banished from Flanders in 1592 ; a search of his house had revealed the fact that he was conspiring against Farnese, in order to substitute for him the Duke of Savoy.[2] Moreover, Allen himself, in spite of his moderation, had expressly asked Farnese in 1590 to banish that disturber of the peace, Morgan.[3]

After the death of the Cardinal of England the attacks of the Scottish party were directed above all against the Jesuits, because they looked upon them as the most ardent champions of the Spaniards. Persons had given grounds for this opinion by publishing, a short time before Allen's death, a work defending the Spanish rights to the English throne.[4] The Jesuits were in every way held in high esteem by the Spanish government in Flanders ; Persons could be said to be the adviser of Philip II. in all English questions, while his confrère William Holt was entrusted with the administration of the Spanish subsidies to the English exiles in the Low Countries. Soon the dispute became even more embittered, and the most incredible accusations were put forward. Denunciations were made on all sides, and an attempt was made to obtain from the government and from the General of the Jesuits the removal from the Low Countries of their hated adversaries.[5] The bitter dispute reached its climax in a denunciation of the Jesuit Holt, which was presented in 1597 to the Archduke Albert, the governor of the Low Countries. In thirty-six articles he was accused of attempts upon the honour, the property, the liberty and even the lives of his adversaries ! By the order of the Archduke, the vice-provincial of the Jesuits in Belgium, Oliver Manaraeus, together with John Baptist Taxis, who did his best in the cause of peace and

[1] Of May 6, 1591, *ibid.*, 162.
[2] *Ibid.*, 162-164.
[3] May 4, 1590, *ibid.*, 163.
[4] See *infra*, p. 43.
[5] LECHAT, 182 *seqq.*

reconciliation, found himself obliged to devote his attention, much against his will, to an examination of the accusations. The verdict of these two was in favour of Holt, and this should have put an end to this lamentable affair. But it was now Holt's turn to demand a discussion of the accusations before the courts, and the excitement only died down when in 1598 Holt was summoned to Spain by the superiors of the Order there, and died there in the following year.[1] One of the principal reasons for Holt's obstinacy lay in his friendship for Hugh Owen, one of the most devoted adherents of Spain among the English in Flanders, for he was unwilling to leave his friend alone to carry on the struggle against the English nobles. Things went so far that, as it would seem, to the great displeasure of Manaraeus, some of these nobles left the Low Countries.[2] The bitterness of the dispute is shown by the accusations which William Gifford, Dean of Lille, and later on a Benedictine and Archbishop of Rheims, who was usually a man of great moderation, made against the Jesuits ; these included even homicide, simony, theft, arrogance and ambition.[3] Gifford for his part withdrew these and asked for pardon,[4] but then the Jesuits committed the error of publishing the withdrawal far and wide.[5]

The agitation against the Jesuits was not limited to the Low Countries. Their prestige, which had reached its height under Gregory XIII., had after that much declined throughout Europe.[6] They were driven out of Paris, while in Madrid they found adversaries in the Duke of Lerma and the Papal nuncio Malvasia. Even more to their disadvantage was the

---

[1] *Ibid.*, 186 *seqq.*

[2] *Ibid.*, 189.

[3] POLLEN in *The Month*, XCIV. (1899), 246.

[4] Letter of the nuncio in Flanders, September 26, 1598, *ibid.*, 236 ; LECHAT, 192 *seqq.*

[5] LECHAT, 113.

[6] For this *cf.* POLLEN, *loc. cit.*, 235-248. For the cause of the change of opinion on account of mistakes made by the Jesuits, *ibid.*, 242 *seqq.* ; for Persons in particular 244 *seqq.* ; for Creswell in Spain 349 *seqq.*

fact that the Pope himself was not well disposed towards them. It is true that Clement VIII. was convinced that the reconstruction and consolidation of the Catholic religion must be based above all on the education of youth, and he therefore favoured the Jesuit colleges, but at the same time he maintained an attitude of coldness towards the Order. His modifications of the constitutions of the Society of Jesus, even though they were only concerned with matters of secondary importance,[1] and his attitude towards the dispute concerning the doctrine of grace, made this very clear.[2] At times he was glad to see his advisers among the Jesuits anywhere else than in Rome ; thus Persons was allowed to recuperate his strength at Naples, Bellarmine was made Archbishop of Capua, and the General of the Jesuits, Aquaviva, was often threatened with a similar promotion.[3] In Spain the Pope's dislike involved certain Jesuits of Alcalà in a severe experience of the prisons of the Inquisition.[4] The marginal notes which he added at that time to the reports of the Spanish nunciature, speak of the " pride and arrogance of those Spaniards who devise new and dangerous doctrines " and of the " need for the public humiliation of such people " ; when the confessor of the Queen of Spain complained to the nuncio of the harm that was being done to his Order on all sides by unfounded attacks, Clement VIII. added the terse marginal note : " God resists the proud."[5]

Naturally such opinions in the most exalted ecclesiastical circles had its influence in the most distant places. The students of the English College in Rome once more complained of their masters and professors ; they were discontented at not receiving before their return to England the same spiritual privileges as were enjoyed by the Jesuits ; they were

[1] Cf. infra, Chapter V., pp. 167-184,
[2] Cf. infra, Chapter IX,
[3] Cf. infra, Chapter V.
[4] For all this see POLLEN, loc. cit., 237 seqq., and infra, Chapter V,, pp, 167 seqq,
[5] POLLEN, loc. cit., 238 seqq.

embittered by the book concerning the succession to the throne, which was generally attributed to Persons ; as they had little love for the Spaniards, they rejoiced at their ill-success, and refused to remove their hats in the presence of the Spanish ambassador.[1] Things went so far that Aquaviva begged the Pope to release the Order from the direction of the English College.[2] A visitation by Cardinal Sega restored peace, at anyrate as far as external appearances went, though only with difficulty, but it was only in 1597, when Persons returned from Spain to Rome, that he was able, by his prudence and moderation, to win over the hearts of the students, who, under his influence, were completely changed in a few days.[3]

The seminaries in Spain were not at that time in a state to experience any such disturbances, but in 1603 the storm burst out there as well. When a disobedient student at the English College at Valladolid was being punished, all his school-fellows ran to his assistance armed with sticks. Out of seventy-one seminarists twenty-five left the college to enter a Benedictine monastery, while it became difficult for a time to provide bread for those who remained, as the benefactors, who had hitherto supported the college, stopped their donations when they heard of the occurrence. A visitation by the Jesuit, Luis de la Puente, and a decree of the Roman Inquisition on December 10th, 1608, restored peace, which had already been inaugurated by pacificatory negotiations between the two Orders. The prudent moderation of Persons also contributed greatly in Spain to the cessation of hostilities.[4]

A principal reason for the discontent among the students was the fact that neither the Spaniards nor the Italians understood the English character, and therefore did not know

[1] Henry Tichborne to Th. Darbyshire, February 2, 1598, in *Foley*, III., 723.

[2] POLLEN in *The Month*, C. (1902), 182 ; IUVENCIUS, I., 13, n. 13.

[3] POLLEN in *The Month*, C. (1902), 183. For the visitation by Sega see GASQUET, English College, 93.

[4] B. CAMM, O.S.B. in *The Month*, XCII. (1898), 364-377 ; POLLEN, *loc. cit.*, XCIV. (1899), 233-248, 348-365.

how to deal with them. When, by Allen's advice, those in Rome were given Englishmen as rectors, the rebellion ceased as though by magic.[1] The exasperation of the youths in Rome may also have been fostered by the hostile feelings towards the Jesuits which prevailed in Flanders, for as early as the year 1597 the Scottish party in the Low Countries was seeking to obtain from the Pope the recall of the Jesuits from England and from the seminaries on the continent.[2] The college at Douai, however, took no part in these attempts ; on the contrary, Allen's successor, Dr. Barrett, went to Rome on purpose to support the continuance of the Jesuits as directors of the seminary in Rome. In September, 1596, Clement VIII. spoke to him of the complaints which had reached him from the Low Countries, and especially of the supposed tyranny and ambition of Holt. Barrett described all this as mere suspicion and jealousy. A document which was circulated in Flanders, and to which were attached many signatures, begged the Pope to pay no attention to the calumnies against the Jesuits, or at anyrate to have the matter inquired into. Barrett was not satisfied at the want of circumspection exercised in obtaining these signatures, but all the same attached his own name to a similar petition which came from the college at Douai.[3]

An even greater disturbance than that of the bitter quarrels in Flanders was occasioned by similar events on English soil, when in the so-called " stirs of Wisbech "[4] disputes broke out between the Jesuits and secular clergy, which contained the germs of even more serious occurrences.

[1] POLLEN in *The Month*, XCIV. (1899), 353 *seqq.*, and C. (1902), 182.

[2] LECHAT, 195.

[3] *Ibid.*, 185 *seqq.*

[4] POLLEN The stirs of Wisbech in *The Month* CXX. (1912) 33–48 (this was the first work written independently of the biassed work of Bagshaw, and on the basis of the papers in the Westminster Archives). Description of Wisbech Castle in FOLEY II. (Ser. 4) 592 *seq.* *Cf.* IUVENCIUS, P.V. tom. post. I., 13, n. 14.

Ever since 1579 the English government had kept shut up in the Castle of Wisbech a number of priests and laymen, whom it was unwilling either to set at liberty or to put to death. At first their imprisonment was very severe, but after the appointment of a new director of prisons in 1593, it assumed a character of leniency quite unusual in England in the case of Catholic priests. The prisoners were no longer supervised at their common meals, and were allowed to visit each other, and to form a library of books which they were even able to lend to other priests outside ; they were also able to receive visits and to accept presents from their visitors. Some Catholics made long journeys in order to be able to breathe once more a purely Catholic atmosphere, as well as to seek advice and receive the sacraments. After one such visit the Jesuit Henry Garnet wrote to the " Confessors of Wisbech " that he had not enjoyed such consolation for seven years, and that during the time he had passed in their midst he had felt as though he were in heaven.

After about two years of this common and comparatively free existence, the disadvantages of this liberty began to make themselves felt. Among the thirty-three prisoners there were certain men of another way of thinking, and not all of them had that intellectual greatness which for the most part distinguished the " Confessors of Wisbech." Three of them later on apostatized, while others, while they were still in the seminaries, had given proof of having intractable and difficult characters. It may be supposed that all of them had the energy and independence which was called for by the life of a missionary in England, but an imprisonment of so many years with the same companions also produced in all of them an abnormal state of tension and nerves. Thus at their meals in common violent disputes broke out ; to those who by their natural disposition and their training were inclined to hold a strict idea of the sacerdotal life it seemed that a too great liberty of thought was creeping in, and they feared, rightly or wrongly, that this might lead in time to real scandal.

This tendency to greater freedom and the tendency to greater strictness found their champions among the prisoners

in two men of great intellect, the Jesuit William Weston and
the secular priest Christopher Bagshaw. The latter, during
his period of study at Oxford, Rheims and Rome, had shown
himself to be possessed of a spirit of turbulence, a defect
which robbed all his other good qualities of their efficacy.
Weston was an austere ascetic, very severe towards himself,
and not over lenient with others. After Christmas, 1594, he
began to withdraw from the common meetings, and took his
meals in his own room.[1] This example was followed by the
majority of his fellow-prisoners, and twenty of them decided
upon leading a kind of community life, for which they drew
up twenty-two rules and asked Weston to be their superior.
Weston declared his readiness to accept this, provided his
superior, Henry Garnet, gave his consent. Garnet expressed
his agreement with this plan of reform, but did not wish
Weston to have the title or position of superior, nor to exercise
any power of punishment ; all that he might do in the name
of his nineteen companions and as their representative, was
to settle certain rules. From that time onward the separation
and division became more and more marked, in spite of the
remonstrances of Bagshaw and his followers, and the attempt
to remove the disunion by calling in a stranger to arbitrate
only made the division more acute. At last on November
6th, 1595, a plan of reconciliation, which was modified more
than twenty times, was accepted, and those who had hitherto
been divided, embraced each other with tears and an emotion
which rendered them incapable of speech. A treasurer and
a steward were chosen ; fines were fixed for any excess which
might lead to a renewed rupture, and a general common rule
was agreed upon, even by those who had hitherto been

[1] IUVENCIUS (*loc. cit.* p. 219) says : " Mota rixa, catholicus
nescio quis [Thomas Bluet] sacerdotem palam graviterque per-
cusserat. Hunc sancita per canones sacros poena teneri, com-
munique consortio, donec absolveretur arcendum sentiebant
ceteri praesertim P. Guillelmus Westonus . . . Dissensit acriter
Bagshaus et alii, principia pauci, mox plures, etc." When the
majority had terminated their confederation " osores pacis primo
Westonum et alios coniunctos e communi triclinis eiecere, etc."

Weston's opponents, by which act the need for some sort of
rule was recognized.

In spite of certain menaces this concord lasted until the
beginning of 1597, when there appeared at Wisbech, Robert
Fisher, who rekindled the flames. Seven of the prisoners,
who were themselves divided into parties, again withdrew
from the common meals, and from that moment men took
sides with one party or the other even beyond the confines of
England. For the disputants it was now no longer a case of
personal sympathies or antipathies, nor a question of the
Jesuit Weston and his supposed arrogance, but it became a
quarrel between the secular clergy and the Jesuits. In the
course of the years a great deal of hatred and jealousy of the
latter had rightly or wrongly grown up ; their labours and
their successes were looked upon as a usurpation of the rights
of the secular clergy, and as an unwarranted attack upon
their good name. All this now became a matter of open
discussion. The Jesuits, it was said, were making their way
into everything ; in their eyes nothing was sacred, orthodox
or lawful if it did not come from themselves ; they tried to
seize upon donations and alms for themselves alone ; in a
word, they aimed at the suppression and subjection of the
secular clergy.[1] These accusations were reproduced in many
pamphlets, some of which were printed and found their way
as far as Rome.[2]

The ill-feeling against the Jesuits found its strongest
expression in the so-called " archpriest controversy."[3]

[1] MEYER, England, 348.

[2] On October 31, 1597, Clement VIII. sent " Anglis catholicis "
a *brief highly praising their perseverance in the faith, but at
the same time exhorting them to the concord against which
Satan was striving in a special way, Brevia, Arm. 44, t. 41, n. 234,
Papal Secret Archives.

[3] THOMAS GRAVES LAW, The Archpriest Controversy. Documents relating to the dissensions of the Roman Catholic Clergy,
1597, 1602, Vol. 1-2, Edinburgh, 1896, 1898. MEYER, 351-396 ;
JOHN GERARD, in The Month, LXXXIX. (1897), 37-53 ; BELLES-
HEIM in Katholik, 1902, II., 481-495.

That the Catholics of England had need of a leader was made clear to everyone by the disturbances which occurred after the death of Allen, while the impossibility of appointing a new English Cardinal, who should direct the affairs of his native land from Rome, lent strength to the proposal, so favourable for England, to set up a new centre of Catholic life on English soil.

In order to put an end, once and for all, to so uncertain a state of affairs, Persons brought all his influence to bear in favour of the appointment of bishops, and as a result of his representations Cardinal Caetani, the Protector of England, spoke to the Pope and the Cardinals of the Inquisition, who had been instructed to discuss the matter. But Clement VIII. refused to accept this view.[1] Persons had asked to have for his country an archbishop with his see in Flanders, who was to be assisted by a bishop living on English soil.[2] Another suggestion was put forward by the secular clergy. They sought before all things to increase their own influence, and especially over the Jseuits, by forming themselves into an association, and proposing the election of one of their number as bishop. The money that was received in alms and from foundations for the support of the English clergy was to be held by a duly appointed administration, and equitably divided, so that none should go in want of necessaries. So far each priest had been a little Pope, and there was no one who could demand an account, or make an admonition, and this state of affairs was all the more deplorable because in recent years there had come to England many priests " who were beardless youths of twenty-four," yet had to go there as priests in lay dress, to live in private houses among men and women, and thus without any of those forms of control, which elsewhere of themselves restrained priests from too great freedom of conduct.[3]

[1] Array to Blackwell, in LAW, 120. *Cf.* GERARD, *loc. cit.*, 52. For the reasons why no bishop was appointed for England, *cf.* IUVENCIUS, I., 13, n. 30.

[2] POLLEN in *The Month*, C. (1902), 183.

[3] MEYER, England, 351, 354. The youth of so many of the

But the authority possessed by a bishop in matters of jurisdiction and orders exposed anyone who had it in the England of those days to death, or at anyrate to a life of imprisonment and concealment. It was probably for this reason that Clement VIII. was unwilling to appoint a bishop for England,[1] and for ten years the nuncios in Flanders were ordered to oppose any suggestions of this kind.[2] An attempt was then made to satisfy the need in another way. Instead of the appointment, as Persons had desired, of an English archbishop in Flanders, the nuncio in Flanders was appointed as his representative by the Cardinal Protector of England, Caetani, with faculties to settle all juridical questions in England as well. Instead of a bishop on English soil, Caetani in 1598 appointed an archpriest, without episcopal consecration, in the person of George Blackwell.[3] English priests who had recently left the seminaries on the continent were to be subject to Douai, in Spain to the superiors they had had hitherto, and in Brussels to the nuncio.[4] The archpriest was given twelve priests as his counsellors ; six of these were to be chosen by the Cardinal Protector, while the other six were to be appointed by Blackwell himself.

secular clergy and their youthful mistakes led to some extent to their dependence on the Jesuits, which was so bitterly resented. Some of the laity for example would have nothing to do with the seminary priests, unless they brought with them the recommendation of some Jesuit. Report of the visitation by Sega, in FOLEY, VI., 50.

[1] Array, loc. cit.

[2] " Perchè altre volte si è tentato di fargli [the archpriest] dare la dignità vescovile, sotto apparenti pretesti di maggior profitto della religione, non si resta di dire a lei che ciò non e stato giudicato espediente da questa Santa Sede, per ragionevolissime cause ; onde se a lei ne fosse mossa nuova prattica, dovrà troncarla come negotio risoluto o rimetterlo a Roma." Instructions to the nuncio Gesualdo, October 23, 1615, in CAUCHIE-MAERE, 50 seq. cf. ibid., 69, 93, the instructions of 1610 and 1635.

[3] According to Cardinal d'Ossat (Lettres, II., 390), the archpriest was sent by the advice (à la suggestion) of Persons.

[4] POLLEN, in The Month, C. (1902), 184,

The brief of appointment of March 7th, 1598, obviously
contains allusions to the recent controversies. The reason
why the office of archpriest was introduced, this states, was to
promote peace and concord among the brethren, and especially
with the Jesuits, who together with the other priests were
labouring in the vineyard of the Lord. They had no
supremacy over the secular priests, nor did they wish for it,
and were therefore in no way an obstacle. The differences
that had arisen, therefore, could only be attributed to the
cunning and deceits of the infernal foe, who wished to destroy
all that had been gained with so great labour, by making
Catholics entertain and propagate feelings of jealousy against
them.[1]

The same desire for harmony and the removal of all
differences had also led to the choice of Blackwell as archpriest. He was a friend of the Jesuits, and the idea was
perhaps entertained in Rome that if a friend of the Order was
placed at the head of the secular clergy, this would guarantee
the restoration and preservation of peace between the two
bodies. But any such idea was greatly mistaken. It is true
that the appointment of an archpriest was hailed with joy by
the great majority of the about three hundred secular priests,
but all the greater was the opposition of the minority, which,
according to contemporary information, did not number, at
anyrate at first, more than ten or twelve persons,[2] but which
for that reason was all the more active. Legally, no attack
was made upon the authority of the Jesuits over the priests
in the seminaries, and any attempt to do so would have been
in itself ridiculous, but it was feared that Persons, who was
then all-powerful in Rome, had sent the complaisant
Blackwell in order through him to govern indirectly the
secular clergy, and to impose upon them his hated Spanish
policy. This suspicion was increased by a passage in the
instructions which were given to Blackwell together with his
brief of appointment.

[1] MEYER, 356 ; IUVENCIUS, I., 13, n. 150.
[2] GERARD, *loc. cit.*, 42 *seq.*

The wish of the Pope, so the Cardinal Protector said, is that there should be the fullest concord between the Jesuits and the secular clergy in the kingdom, and as the superior of the Jesuits, by his experience of English affairs and the reputation which he enjoys among Catholics, can be of great help in all decisions to be made by the clergy, the archpriest must endeavour, in all questions of major importance, to ask for his advice and opinion.[1]   A false interpretation saw in these words a formal order to follow in all matters of importance the advice of the superior of the Jesuits, Henry Garnet, so that, as that blusterer William Watson, put it, in future the Catholics would be dependent upon Blackwell, Blackwell on Garnet, Garnet on Persons, and Persons on the devil, who was the author of all the rebellions, treasons, homicides and disobediences which that cursed Jesuit had raised up against her majesty, her safety, her crown and her life.[2]

It was not all those who made up the minority who thought and spoke thus bitterly.   There were among them priests of the greatest moderation and worthy of all respect, such as William Bishop, the future vicar-apostolic, Colleton, Charnock, Mush and Bluet.   Some of the malcontents had suffered imprisonment, and two of them death, for their faith.   But on the other hand, Watson was not the only one whose words and actions call for our attention.   Bagshaw, who now, as formerly at Wisbech, took a prominent part, later on, in the conspiracy of the Gunpowder Plot, made denunciations to the government against his co-religionists ; another, John Cecil, who was even entrusted with a mission to Rome, was only a tool in the hands of the English statesmen, whose duty it was to spy on the Catholics.[3]   It was soon evident that even the reputable party among the minority held views on many subjects which were anything but Catholic.

Discontent against the new leader of the English Catholics led to a resolve to address complaints to Rome against the

[1] *Ibid.*, 50 *seq.*
[2] *Ibid.*, 50.
[3] *Ibid.*, 45, 46.

appointment of Blackwell, but from the first his opponents were guilty of an almost incredible mistake as to their motives and reasons for such a step. It was not only said that the appointment of the archpriest had been made by order of the Cardinal Protector, whereas such a measure required a Papal brief, but certain entirely Gallican assertions were made. It was stated that the English clergy had not been asked for their opinion before the appointment, and that this was a violation of an ancient English right ; without the consent of the clergy and people, who must give their opinion in a free election, the appointment of Blackwell must be looked upon as null and void. Gallican views were also set forth in a little work by a certain John Bishop, which was printed in London about that time.[1]

The danger of such principles does not seem to have entered the minds of the malcontents, for towards the end of the summer of 1598 they sent William Bishop and Robert Charnock to Rome in order to win over the Pope to their side. The requests that they wished to lay before him privately were concerned with the appointment of a bishop for England, who was to be elected by a majority of the votes of the English clergy, and with the consent of the association of secular priests. The Pope was also to be asked to take away the English College in Rome from the Jesuits, and to make the publication of controversial writings against the queen and the English government dependent upon the approval of the ecclesiastical superiors.[2]

In the meantime the other party had naturally not remained idle. The superior of the Jesuits, Henry Garnet, also had recourse to Rome in a letter bearing the signatures of nineteen Jesuits and secular priests.[3] This asked the Pope to confirm the archpriest in his office and to address a severe admonition to the two appellants, and only to allow them to return to England if they completely changed their views.

[1] MEYER, 362.
[2] MEYER, 363.
[3] On October 30, 1598, *ibid.*, 364.

The two appellants gave yet further proof of their ingenuous confidence in the success of their undertaking when, in December, 1598, they knocked at the gates of the English College, in order to ask the hospitality of Persons, their most dangerous adversary. They very soon realized that they had found lodging in what was their prison. An order for their arrest from the Pope forbade them to leave the seminary, and in February, 1599, they had to appear before Cardinals Caetani and Borghese, the Protector and vice-Protector of England, and submit themselves to legal proceedings. With truly English tenacity Bishop set himself to defend before the Cardinals the plan for an association of priests, though later on (February 20th), he advised his friends in England to abandon this project. In April the sentence was delivered : all the requests of the appellants were rejected. Bishop was sent to live in Paris, and his colleague Charnock was sent to Lorraine ; they were not to return to England, nor make their homeward journey together, nor communicate with each other in any way.[1] They had not succeeded in seeing the Pope, while a Papal brief of April 6th, 1599, which confirmed the dignity of the archpriest, removed all hopes of their obtaining from him a more favourable judgment than they had received from his representatives.

If the appellants did not wish to become open rebels, there remained no course open to them but to submit, which they accordingly did. By the summer of 1599 peace seemed to have been restored. " Thanks be to God," Persons wrote to Bishop at that time, " for now, owing to the wise measures taken by His Holiness, everything is systematized and in order."[2]

But the cure was not very deep, and secret agitations against the Jesuits still continued. The rancour against the Order now led two representatives of the extreme party to a fatal step : abandoned by the Pope, and filled with Gallican ideas they sought the support of the civil authorities. Watson

[1] *Ibid.*, 364 *seq.*
[2] *Ibid*, 366.

denounced them to the English government, and accused them before the King's Proctor of high treason, for having defended the Spanish succession. Charles Paget, Mary Stuart's former agent, got into personal touch with the English ambassador in Paris, and worked upon his feelings against the so greatly hated religious.[1]

The imprudence of Blackwell was the cause of the dispute breaking out in public. The archpriest was convinced that the malcontents were guilty of schism, and had incurred the penalties appointed by the canon law, and that they were therefore obliged to confess their fault and ask for absolution. The accused resisted this unjust supposition, and an opinion of the University of Paris, of May 3rd, 1600, was given in their favour. Blackwell, exceeding his powers, prohibited, under pain of an interdict, any sort of defence of this decision, but his adversaries paid no attention to his prohibition. Blackwell then forbade two of the clergy, who were among the eldest and most deserving, to exercise any of their sacerdotal functions. After this fresh abuse of power, the struggle broke out again all along the line.[2]

Feeling certain that this time they undoubtedly had right on their side, the adversaries of Blackwell had recourse once more to Rome, and a deed of accusation, of November 17th, 1600, summarized in an extremely objective form, and with the addition of proofs, all the accusations against the arch-priest. This document was drawn up at the castle of Wisbech, and bore the signatures of thirty-three priests.[3]

While the reply of the Pope was being long awaited, an embittered literary war broke out in England, in which, even more than against the archpriest, the attacks were made upon the Jesuits, whose instrument and mouthpiece Blackwell was supposed to be. Blackwell had attempted to support his view as to the supposed schismatics by the help of a " Roman decision," that is to say by certain expressions of English

---

[1] *Ibid .* 367.
[2] *Ibid.*, 368 *seqq.*
[3] *Ibid.*, 371.

Jesuits,[1] one of whom, Thomas Lister, defended the view in an intemperate work, which was approved by the archpriest.[2] As Blackwell wrote on October 22nd, 1600, to Clement VIII., the Jesuits had protected him against the disturbers of the peace, and had stood by his side in his danger, both for attack and defence.[3]   All the hatred of Persons and the Society of Jesus which had been accumulating in recent years now broke out in the form of numerous and violent polemical writings, which were almost equalled in the violence of their language by some of the replies of Persons.[4]   This literary warfare was begun by a polemical work of Lister.

The goal at which the malcontents were aiming was the removal and recall of the Society of Jesus from England, and their quarrel with the Jesuits had gradually led them far away from those principles which hitherto had guided the attitude of the Catholics, especially towards the government.   Was it necessary, so the appellants asked themselves, to attach such importance to the bull of excommunication of Pius V. ?   If the question was put to the martyrs :   What would you do if the Pope were to send an Armada to conquer England ?   had it really been necessary to reply with such great caution, and by that exaggerated caution irritate and rouse the suspicions of the government ?   In any case was it not possible now to change their attitude, and seek for a reconciliation with the queen ?   " We ought to act towards her, our true and legitimate queen, and towards our country, very differently from the way adopted by so many Catholics, and above all by

---

[1] *Ibid.*, 368.

[2] Entitled " Adversus factiosos in Ecclesia," *ibid.*, 372.

[3] *Ibid.*, 370.

[4] It must be noted that Persons, at the same time, in letters not intended for publication, expressed himself in a conciliatory way towards his adversaries (GERARD, *loc. cit.*, 47 *seq.*).   With regard to Lister, his superior, Garnet, wrote of him at the same time that he was composing his work against the schismatics, that he was suffering from mental over-excitement, which made him fear for his physical health (*ibid.*, 42, n. 1).   The characteristic part of Persons' reply in MEYER, 373 *seq.*

the Jesuits," was the reply given to such questions in a work by Watson. Elizabeth, Watson insisted, had from the first treated the Catholics with kindness and favour ; all good sense was on her side, and all the wrong on the side of the Catholics ; if the Pope should give orders for the conferring of the crown on an enemy of the country, there would be no obligation to obey him ; the bull of excommunication of Pius V., which John Bishop described as erroneous, was merely treated by Watson as surreptitious.[1]

The Jesuits formed a serious obstacle to any conclusion of peace on the basis of such opinions, and therefore the idea gained more and more ground among their adversaries of suggesting to the government that they should renounce their co-operation in England as the price of the restoration of peace and the toleration of the old religion. The laws that were still in force against the Catholics could be abrogated and changed into laws against the Jesuits.

The statesmen who governed England could not fail to rejoice that the internal quarrels of the Catholics should thus become more and more acute, and the appellants met with the greatest sympathy and ready support from them. One of the prisoners of Wisbech, the secular priest Thomas Bluet, was summoned in the summer of 1601 to present himself before the Bishop of London, Richard Bancroft, to explain his views more fully ; he declared that the Jesuits were a danger to the state, but that the secular clergy, on the contrary, were loyal subjects and were being unjustly persecuted.[2] Further negotiations with the royal councillors followed, and Bluet was even allowed to appear before Elizabeth herself to explain his views. Their complaisance went even further : although, according to the English law, an appeal to the Pope was looked upon as a crime deserving of the stake, Bluet even dared to present a petition that he and certain other secular priests might be allowed to go to Rome in support of the appeal already presented there, or better still to press the

[1] MEYER, 376.
[2] Ibid., 377.

Pope for the recall of the Jesuits.[1]   The government accepted
this proposal ;   the prison doors were thrown open, and,
furnished with English passports,[2] at the beginning of
November, 1601, certain prisoners of state, who had been
declared worthy of death, went to Rome in order to induce
the Pope, who from every pulpit had been declared the greatest
enemy of England, to enter into an alliance with England
against Catholic priests.   The ever astute Elizabeth even
thought it well to allow a few words of adulation from her
sovereign lips to come to his ears : " unlike Pius, Gregory and
Sixtus, those warlike Popes " so she expressed herself to
Bluet, " Clement, as his very name shows, should be a peaceful
Pope."[3]   So as to make the journey of Bluet and his companions less noticeable, they were " banished " from England,
after they had been given the opportunity of collecting the
necessary funds for their journey to Rome.[4]

When they arrived in Belgium the envoys learned that
Rome had already (August 17th, 1601) given its decision on
the dispute.   Blackwell too had received a Papal brief, but he
took the liberty of keeping this secret for several months,

[1] *Ibid.*, 378.

[2] Dated August, October and November, *ibid.*, 379, n.   .

[3] *Ibid.*, 379.   Some further expressions of Elizabeth concerning
" the Pope " (Clement VIII. ?), on December 24, 1597, in PREVOST-
PARADOL, Elizabeth et Henri IV., 170.   He is supposed to have
said to two English gentlemen that Elizabeth was indeed a
heretic, but that she was in other respects the most competent
sovereign in the world, and that he would have been more ready
to place himself at her disposal than many other princes.   On
the other side the queen complained of the fables that were spread
in Rome of her cruelty towards the Catholics ; that she had
never persecuted a Catholic, except in the case of persons who
were a danger to the state.   The differences between the various
religious confessions were not so important after all, for there
was but one Christ and one creed, and that everything else was
a trifle, as to which it would be easy to come to an understanding,
so long as the two principles of good will and courage existed in
Christendom.

[4] LINGARD, VIII., 391.

until January, 1602, when the last of the polemical writings of Persons appeared in print.[1]   This brief, which " unites in the happiest way the two-fold purpose of defending both justice and ecclesiastical discipline," rejected the appeal,[2] but admits the reasonableness of the appellants, in that it rejected the accusation of schism, and threatened with excommunication anyone that dared to make it.   All further polemical writings on the matter were prohibited, as well as those which had appeared so far, among these especially the work of Lister. The brief contained a clear admonition both to Blackwell and his adversaries, and exhorted them to obedience.[3]

If the English envoys had only been sent in support of their appeal, they ought in that case to have returned home.   The nuncio in Flanders, Frangipani, who informed them of the Papal brief, tried in every way to induce them to do so, but only succeeded in the case of one of their number.[4] Frangipani knew perfectly what it was that the appellants were seeking, for on August 22nd, 1602, he had already written to Rome to say that Elizabeth had given them permission to make the journey in order that she might be freed from the Jesuits.[5] But when the latter, in February, 1602, sent a commission of their own to Rome, which arrived there on April 9th,[6] it was only natural to fear a perpetuation of the quarrel, from which Frangipani feared the greatest evils for the Church in England.[7]

But all his attempts at pacification had no effect upon the appellants, who were still full of hope.   " If I, poor worm

---

[1] *Ibid.*, 380 *seq.*

[2] So MEYER (381).

[3] *Ibid.*, 380 *seq.*

[4] *Ibid.*, 382. *Cf.* L. v. WASSENHOVEN, O. M. Frangipani, Nuntius van Flanderen, en de Engelsche Katholicken, 1596–1606, Baesrode, 1925, who gives a detailed account of the efforts of Frangipani to settle the disputes among the English Catholics, and to improve their position.

[5] *Ibid.*, 378, n. 2.

[6] *Ibid.*, 382.

[7] To Aldobrandini, March 8, 1602, *ibid.*, 382, n. 3.

that I am, have obtained so much from the queen," said
Bluet later on in Rome,[1] " how much may not be effected
by the prestige of His Holiness, added to the support of the
King of France, for the relief of the English Catholics ? " [2]
The toleration of the Catholics was at that time a thing so
greatly desired in Rome that there were some who could well
believe that the sacrifice of the Jesuits would count for nothing.

Blackwell had laid his complaints against his adversaries
before the Inquisition in 1601,[3] and this tribunal was given
the charge of inquiring into the matter. The discussions
began in April ; some thought that they were safe in prophesy-
ing that they would be very protracted, as the Pope seemed
determined to have the whole unpleasant affair gone into
this time with all possible completeness.[4] But about a month
later the rumour was spread that Clement VIII. had quickly
settled the matter. Both the Pope and the Cardinals were
weary of the affair, because the noisy complaints of the
appellants had only been caused by unworthy motives, so
that it only required the temporary absence of Persons to
quiet the whole business.[5] The authors of the accusation
had therefore to listen to words of severe admonition from
the Pope, on account of the impatience with which they had
attempted at all costs to relieve themselves of persecution,
as well as on account of their relations with heretics and with
Elizabeth, whom they wrongly looked upon as their queen,
though she was excommunicated and dethroned, as well as
on account of their hostility towards an Order which was
recognized by the Church.[6] It is reported that as to this
last charge the appellants refused altogether to admit in
Rome that they had ever tried to get the Jesuits driven out,

[1] *Ibid.*, 387.

[2] *Ibid.*

[3] MEYER, 372.

[4] " For His Holiness seemeth now to be inclined to have the
matter ripped open from the bottom." Report from Rome,
April 27, 1602, in FOLEY, I., 13.

[5] *Ibid.*, 14.

[6] MEYER, 384.

while they repudiated the writings of Watson and others.[1] They found a powerful supporter in the French ambassador in Rome, while the Spanish ambassador was opposed to them.[2]

But in England in the meantime matters were pursuing their course, and the appellant priests were filled with confidence in the success of their cause.[3] Bancroft, together with certain ministers of state, continued to give them support, while it was said of the queen herself that she gladly welcomed the development of the quarrel, so as thus to introduce discord into the College of Cardinals, to hold back the Pope from making any decision, and to deprive the Spaniards of any hope of finding their party strengthened by the English Catholics.[4] To the disgust expressed by the Puritans at her apparent rapprochement with the Catholics, the queen replied by increasing the persecution and by executing several priests.[5] The written attacks of the appellants on the Jesuits continued,[6] and they were not ashamed to present to the government a detailed list of the hiding places of their hated adversaries.[7] The Protestants watched with joy these disagreements among the Catholics, and the writings of the appellants found eager readers among them.[8]

[1] FOLEY, I., 14, 38. The Venetian ambassador in Rome, Francesco Vendramin, learned that the appellants wished to obtain liberty of conscience by the removal of the Jesuits. Reports of March 9 and 23, 1602, in BROWN, n. 1061, 1066.

[2] BROWN, n. 1061, 1066, 1078.

[3] Letter of the Jesuit Rivers to Persons, in FOLEY, 41.

[4] Ibid., 23.

[5] Ibid., 23, 30.   A Puritan, who had attacked the Lord Treasurer, the Secretary of State, the Bishop of London, and others for their relations with the Catholics, was condemned to the pillory and the loss of his ears.   The judge said to him that Bancroft had rendered his country a much greater service than anyone else by sowing cockle among the priests themselves. Letter of the Jesuit Richard Blount, February 14, 1602, ibid., 18 seq.

[6] Ibid., 37.

[7] FOLEY, I., 38.

[8] Ibid., 39.

On July 20th, 1602, the long expected judgment of the Inquisition was delivered. By this the appellants were justified in so far that the accusation of schism was declared unfounded, while, for the sake of peace, the archpriest was forbidden to take counsel with the Jesuits about the affairs of his office, and Blackwell was advised to refer directly to the Pope or the Cardinal Protector. He was, moreover, warned not again to exceed his powers. But in all other matters the appellants met with no success. They must, when they return home, submit to the reproofs of the English Secretary of State for not having fulfilled their promises, and for not having obtained either the recall of the Jesuits or the removal of the archpriest. Moreover the Jesuits were left in possession of their English colleges on the continent, while all further negotiations with the heretics to the injury of other Catholics were prohibited. Anyone who disobeyed in this matter would *ipso facto* incur excommunication.[1]

Clement VIII. waited for another two months before he gave his final judgment on this unpleasant affair ; in the meantime Persons attempted to obtain a mitigation for Blackwell and his followers, but in vain, and the brief to the archpriest, dated October 5th, 1602, was in all points in accordance with the suggestions of the Inquisition. In two respects it went even further : the faculties of the archpriest were more exactly defined, and he was compelled to appoint three of the appellants to the first three places among his counsellors, which should become vacant. The zeal and piety of the Jesuits were praised,[2] and thus scrupulous care was taken that none of the interested parties was wronged, and no one was given cause for complaint.

In the meantime Elizabeth was preparing a surprise for the appellants at home ; this was her last edict against the Catholics.[3] This distinguished between the Jesuits and their

[1] MEYER, 385.

[2] *Ibid.*, 387 ; FOLEY I., 16–18.

[3] Of November 5 (15), 1602, in LINGARD, VIII., 391. *Cf.* ANDREAS PHILOPATER (Jos. Creswell, S.J.), Responsio ad edictum Elisabethae Reg. Angliae contra catholicos, Rome, 1593.

adherents, and the secular clergy. The former were without exception declared guilty of high treason, because they aroused foreign princes against their country and placed the life of the queen in danger. The secular clergy were spoken of as anti-Jesuit and less perverse, but they too are disobedient and disloyal subjects, who, under a mask of conscience, steal the hearts of the simple and ingenuous people, and attach them to the Pope. The Jesuits and their adherents must therefore leave the country within thirty days, if they do not wish to incur the punishment of the law against Catholic priests. Other priests were allowed a period until January 1st, or at the latest, February 1st, 1603 ; if by that time they had made a formal act of obedience before the queen's court, they would then be proceeded against leniently. The edict complains in strong terms of the audacity of those priests who showed themselves in the streets in full daylight, and who brought the queen under the suspicion of intending to tolerate two religions in the country. God, who can read the hearts of men, knew well that she was not guilty of any such madness, and that none of her advisers had dared to lay any such proposal before her, which would not only disturb the peace of the Church, but would also throw the State into confusion.[1]

This edict had a two-fold purpose ; it was in the first place to exonerate the queen in the eyes of the Protestants from the suspicion of favouring the Catholics, and in the second, it was to be a test as to how far the appellants had progressed along the mistaken course which they had adopted. It had seemed at first that the latter were in no hurry to obey the sentence of the Pope, yet the royal edict only brought one priest to make his act of submission, and induced another to refuse to accept the Papal briefs.[2] Even though there were still as before comings and goings of the appellants to the house of the Bishop of London, and Bluet was even lodged there for a time, there is no reason to see in this a formal act

[1] LINGARD, VIII., 392 ; MEYER, 389 *seq.*
[2] MEYER, 393.

of disobedience, because all relations with the heretics was not forbidden. Such conduct, however, was still a matter for suspicion, as was the fact that the appellants asked, through one of their representatives, for the support of the French government against the Jesuits ; the English ambassador in Paris was kept closely informed of these negotiations. But something more than mere suspicion was aroused by the fact that polemical writings against the Jesuits still continued to appear in print.[1]

It was not, however, possible to be content with half measures if the malcontents intended to remain Catholic priests. On the other hand, the latter did not wish altogether to reject the hand held out to them by the government ; if in an official edict a distinction had been drawn between priests and priests, this marked a step forward and held out a ray of hope. Moreover, a special tribunal had been set up, composed of the archbishop, the Keeper of the Privy Seal, the Lord Treasurer and others, who were to summon each priest before them and decide as to the question of his exile, and as to the manner and terms of its enforcement ;[2] this too seemed to show a tendency to greater leniency, for it was left to the good-will of this tribunal to change, for example, the punishment of perpetual imprisonment for the lesser penalty of exile. Accordingly, on the last day before the expiration of the term allowed, thirteen priests assembled, not to make an act of submission to the government, but merely to declare their loyalty as subjects. The queen, it is stated in a work by William Bishop, has the same authority as her predecessors, and has the right to the same obedience as is paid by Catholic priests to Catholic sovereigns, and no one in this world can dispense them from this duty. In the case of a conspiracy, or of an invasion of England, even in the name of religion, they would be bound to take the part of the queen against all her enemies, and to make known to her all such attempts. The excommunication which might

[1] *Ibid.*, 391 *seq.*
[2] LINGARD, VIII., 392.

in the event be launched against her they judged to be invalid. In the Pope, however, they recognized their supreme ecclesi- astical pastor and the successor of Peter. " Just as we are absolutely ready to shed our blood in the defence of her Majesty and our country, so too would we rather lose our lives than offend against the lawful authority of the Catholic Church of Christ."[1]

In spite of this last phrase there can be no mistaking the fact that these thirteen priests were placing themselves in a position with regard to the Pope, the danger of which was destined to become perfectly clear in the years to come. The attitude of the opposing party was far more logical and in conformity with Catholic principles. When the Papal decision of the question, which had been so long pending, was imminent, the superior of the Jesuits, Henry Garnet, issued a circular to his subjects, calling for a sincere and reverent obedience to the Pope, and exhorting them to peace and concord with the secular clergy.[2] At the very beginning of the dispute, on March 1st, 1598, Garnet had issued a similar document as well as a kind of declaration of loyalty, though this was not addressed to the government but to the whole of the clergy of England. " Eighteen years have gone by," he says in this, " since our Society came to your England to join you, who are labouring so generously in the vineyard of the Lord. During all this time we have experienced the greatest affection on your part towards us, and by the grace of God have lived in such a way as to take every care that every one of you shall receive the honour which is your due, and to assist every one of you with all zeal, rendering to you all the services that were in our power, and thus embracing each of you with all the fervour of charity of which the human soul is capable. Our consciences bear testimony to this, and I have no doubt that more than one of you will confirm it, and that none of you has any just ground for complaint of us. In saying this we do not venture to state that all that we have done has

---

[1] *Ibid.*, VIII., 393 *seq.* ; MEYER, 393 *seq.*
[2] MEYER, 392.

been without blame, for we are but mortal men, and in a situation that is so full of mire, it may well be that perchance some dust has collected on our feet. But however weak and imperfect we may be, we at least desire to be better, and your affection has most certainly preserved us from the fault of having voluntarily offended against any one of you. In spite of all this there has come into our hands a passage from a memorial which was sent to the Holy Father, and which contains things than which nothing more unworthy could have come from your pen, and nothing more monstrous could have been brought against us, not even by the heretics, and this has been presented to His Holiness by two persons, the one a priest and the other a layman,[1] in the name of the English clergy. To you, therefore, priests of England, I have recourse, to you who are the nursery of our renascent Church, the ornament of the Catholic world, and the training ground of heroic martyrs. Tell us if these monstrous accusations really emanate from you."[2]

They had not, indeed, emanated from the majority of the secular clergy, and even if the minority, by reason of its polemical writings, seemed to be speaking for itself, there were not lacking the expressions of those who thought differently. Even at Wisbech, the true hot-bed of the hostility to the Jesuits, and from whence had come the denunciation of Blackwell in 1600, there gathered together in the following year a number of secular priests in order to give to their fellow labourers of the Society of Jesus a shining proof of their friendship. As at that time the old complaints of the arrogance of Weston had been sent even as far as Rome, these gave, in a collective letter to the Pope, a brilliant testimony to the accused.[3]

The minority of the secular clergy were guided by sound reason when they judged that they must not count upon

---

[1] This certainly is an allusion to Gifford and Paget.

[2] GERARD (cf. supra, p. 20, n. 3), 49.

[3] On September 29, 1601 ; extract in BARTOLI, Inghilterra, I., 5, c. 17, p. 227.

violent measures, or look to the foreign princes for any help
for the old religion. In this, they coincided with the ideas
of the Pope himself, and in 1596, in a memorial to Cardinal
Aldobrandini, the nuncio in Flanders, Malvasia, expressed
himself in the same sense.[1] The nuncio was of the opinion
that it would be possible to bring pressure to bear upon
Elizabeth through Henry IV. ; it should be suggested to her
that she should put an end to the fierce persecution of the
Catholics, and, following the example of so many other
princes, who tolerated various forms of religion in their
countries, grant to them, at any rate in their own houses, if
not in public, the right of Catholic worship. The queen would
then have for the future loyal subjects in the English exiles
in Flanders, who were now dependent upon the subsidies of
Spain, which were hardly ever paid, and who often, in their
misery, allowed themselves to be drawn into the most desperate
undertakings ; she would be set free from a thousand dangers,
from the constant fear of conspiracies and treason, and from
the endless expense of defending herself against the King of
Spain.[2] Once she was set free from disturbances of the peace
at home, the queen need no longer fear the slow-moving and
distant foreign enemy, all the more so as jealousy of the mighty
King of Spain would attract many allies to her side, once
religious scruples no longer stood in the way.

Just as in this respect Malvasia partly forestalled the
proposals of the appellants, so was it in another matter. The
nuncio, who was not well disposed towards the Jesuits,
wondered whether it would not be wise to withdraw them
from England, at any rate for the time being, as they were
especially hateful to and suspected by the queen. So as still

---

[1] The edict (with incomplete date) in BELLESHEIM, Schottland,
II., 460--468. According to Cod. Ottob. 2510 the date is " 11
gennaro, 1596." Vatican Library.

[2] Also the report of an English nobleman of the year 1595,
in MEYER, 309, n. 1, says that almost all the exiles " data minima
securitate religionis " and from the extreme need in which they
found themselves, would leave the Spanish service and return
to their country.

further to pacify Elizabeth, it might be well, under pain of ecclesiastical penalties, possibly even of excommunication, to forbid the returned exiles to make any attempts upon the crown, or to take any part in politics.[1]

Clement VIII. was less disposed to make such concessions,[2] and England was, and always remained for him, a child of sorrow. " Cut off though you are from us by space," he wrote on October 31st, 1597, to the English Catholics,[3] but united to us by faith and charity, we ever think of you and rejoice in your steadfastness. All Catholics look to you and thanks to you give praise to God. Persevere therefore in your expectation of an eternal reward."[4] The Pope never abandoned the hope that England would return to the ancient Church, and in the meantime made use of every opportunity of obtaining the mediation, little valuable though it was, of the Catholic princes, on behalf of the persecuted Catholics of England.[5]

---

[1] BELLESHEIM, Schottland, II., 468.

[2] Cf. infra., pp. 59, 73.

[3] *Brevia, Arm. 44, t. 41, n. 234, Papal Secret Archives. The Pope received news from England through the agent, Giovanni degli Effetti, who had gone to England in the suite of the French ambassador, the Duke of Sully, in 1603. Cf. B. CAMM in The Month, LXXXVIII. (1896), 251–258.

[4] Carte Strozz. (September, 1595), I., 2, 248 ; *report of the Venetian ambassador, June 7, 1603, State Archives, Venice.

[5] Francesco Gonzaga wrote to Rudolph II. on July 31, 1601, concerning the joy of Clement VIII. at the mediation of the Emperor, State Archives, Vienna. A *request for the intercession of the King of Poland, August 23, 1594, in Brevia, Arm. 44, t. 39, n. 94, p. 149, Papal Secret Archives ; *to the Emperor, November 23, 1604, ibid., t. 56, p. 339. The Pope also intervened many times on behalf of the English exiles in Flanders, e.g. on March 15, 1593, with Philip II., in order that they might be sent their monthly payments, which had not been paid to them for many months (Brevia, Arm. 44, t. 38, n. 260, loc. cit.) ; on January 20 and May 15, 1594, with the Archduke Ernest (ibid., t. 39, n. 74, 196) ; On May 19, 1596, with Cardinal Archduke Albert (ibid., t. 40, n. 39).

While Elizabeth, deaf to all entreaties, was working for the extermination of the old religion, the signs of her own approaching death became more and more clear. In vain she tried to deceive the world and herself as to the steady failure of her powers, and with the energy that characterized her this woman of more than sixty forced her broken body to take part in balls and hunting-parties,[1] but at the opening of Parliament in 1601, crushed under the weight and splendour of her royal attire, she fell in the arms of the knight who was standing near her ;[2] soon after this a visitor to the court found her worn to a skeleton and plunged in melancholy, an intolerable burden to herself and to those about her.[3]

But even now the queen remained obstinately determined to take no steps to settle the succession to the throne. Anxiety as to this assumed all the greater proportions in England as the whole question had been hopelessly complicated by the caprices of Henry VIII. The whole country had been forced to swear allegiance to Elizabeth when she was still an infant ; when she was three years old her own father had caused her to be declared by Parliament incapable of succeeding to the crown, and by his will he had left Mary Tudor heir to the throne. Mary Stuart, on the other hand, who was legally the next heir, had been completely passed over by Henry in his will ; after the death of Mary Tudor, she could no longer be considered the heir to the throne, because she was looked upon as the future Queen of France, and France was at war with England, and the act of Parliament which, after Elizabeth had ascended the throne, confirmed the will of Henry VIII., once more tacitly excluded her from the succession. From that moment Mary Stuart assumed the arms of England, and this tacit assertion of her rights never again fell into oblivion. After her death it was Mary's son, the King of Scots, to whom English statesmen for the most part turned their eyes, even

[1] LINGARD, VIII., 384 *seq.* *Cf.* the contemporary letters of the Jesuit Rivers in FOLEY 24, 47.

[2] LINGARD, VIII., 379,

[3] *Ibid.*, 394.

though, besides James, many other claimants to the crown
were entitled to aspire to it.[1]

But besides the question of primogeniture, there was
another motive which weighed heavily in the matter of the
succession, according as men were Catholics or Protestants.
Both parties were resolved not to give the crown to anyone
who was not of their own faith. The hopes of the Catholics
had been greatly raised once Henry IV. had made his abjuration, a thing which seemed to secure a preponderance in
Europe to the Catholic powers. After 1591 it seemed that
the Catholics were resolved to uphold the claims of Ferdinand
Stanley, but he, who was Earl of Derby from 1593, definitely
refused the honour, and an English exile who, it is said, had
gone to him with such a proposal, was handed over by him
to the government, and thus to execution, which took place
on November 29th, 1593.[2]

Soon after this another step was taken by the Catholic
party. Two years before (in 1591) the Puritan Peter Wentworth had dared not only to raise the question of the succession
in Parliament, but also to publish a work on the subject ;
he had had to pay for his audacity by imprisonment in the
Tower, from which he was only freed by his death in 1596.[3]
The Jesuit Persons, who had not yet given up hopes of seeing
ia Catholic ascend the English throne, and with him the old
religion, also formed the idea of writing a work, asking for an
impartial examination of the various claims to the succession,
but actually emphasizing the rights of the royal house of
Spain, in that Philip II. counted Edward III. among his
ancestors,[4] and before the setting out of the Armada had asked

[1] Cf. POLLEN, The question of Queen Elizabeth's successor, in
The Month, CI., (1903), 516–532, and especially the genealogical
tree, ibid. 520.

[2] POLLEN, loc. cit., 522 ; LECHAT, 169 seq.

[3] Wentworth at first supported Edward Seymour, Lord
Beauchamp, and later on, when in the Tower, James of Scotland,
as the true heir. POLLEN, loc. cit., 523.

[4] See the genealogical tree, ibid., 520. The claims of the
daughter of Philip II., Isabella Clara Eugenia, are spoken on

Sixtus V. to nominate him as King of England.[1]   The General of the Order, Aquaviva, learned of this intention with dismay ; more far-seeing than his subject, he at once realized that Persons was exposing the whole Order to obvious peril for the sake of an impossible project.   The author of the work could not remain unknown, he wrote to the English Jesuits, and if it was still possible to do so, its publication must be prevented.[2]

This advice of Aquaviva arrived too late, and even before he had received Persons' reply, what he had feared had taken place.   Not all the Catholics took the part of Persons and Spain, and a party among the English exiles in the Low Countries, very hostile to the Jesuits and little scrupulous about their choice of means, had adopted the cause of James of Scotland as successor to the throne.   One of their agents, Charles Paget, had been able to procure from an employé of the printers, for a sum of money, the manuscript of the book, while another member of the party, Dr. Gifford, recognized the handwriting ; the greater part of the book was by Verstegan, with long additions and corrections by Persons.[3] Gifford at once laid accusations against the book before the Papal nuncio Malvasia, who reported it to Rome in accordance with Gifford's ideas ; Paget denounced it to the English authorities.   It would seem, however, that the government refused to take any steps, and the book, which appeared under the pseudonym of "Doleman,"[4] did no harm to anyone except its authors.

elsewhere.   Essex wrote to James of Scotland that of the all-powerful party of the Earl of Nottingham, Cecil, Raleigh and Cobham would press their rights.   Cf. LINGARD, VIII., 362, 269 seq.

[1] Letter to Olivares, February 11, 1587.   Cf. POLLEN, loc. cit., 521.

[2] Letter to Persons, March 30, 1594, ibid., 524 ; Persons' reply, June 4, 1594, ibid.

[3] POLLEN, loc. cit., 525 seq.   Ibid., 526, concerning the authors.

[4] A Conference about the next succession to the Throne, pub. by R. DOLEMAN, and generally entitled : The Book of Titles.

By this injudicious book, the authorship of which was only partly his, though he was entirely responsible for its publication, Persons showed that he was quite out of touch with his own country. The Spaniards had very few partisans in England, while the appearance that the Catholics were pledged to their interests gave their adversaries a welcome opportunity for attacking them. " I cannot see," wrote the Scottish Jesuit Crichton to Persons, " that this book has done the least good, though its disastrous consequences are manifest. The French have a proverb : You cannot catch a hare with a drum. The preachers are hammering incessantly upon this drum of yours, from the English as well as from the Scottish pulpits."[1]

But Persons did not even yet give up his hopes in Spain ; when in June 1596 an English fleet had sacked Cadiz, Philip II. planned a new expedition against England. In the event of this proving successful Persons had obtained a promise from the King of Spain that he would leave England as an independent kingdom, or at any rate under the regency of his daughter Isabella Clara Eugenia.[2] Persons even drew up a memorial[3] as to the manner in which Catholic reform should be effected in England, and went to Rome to get this accepted in accordance with Spanish ideas.

At the Vatican, however, at the beginning of April, 1597, he found a state of affairs that was but ill-disposed both to the Jesuits and the Spaniards ; while France was making every effort to undermine Spanish influence. Nevertheless Persons' skill brought it about that at the end of May the Secretary of State wrote to the legate in France on the subject of the succession to the English throne in a sense that seemed

---

Summary of the contents in LINGARD, VIII., 332. For a partially new reprint of the book by the Puritans in 1647 cf. The Month, 1911, 270.

[1] POLLEN in The Month, CI., 528.

[2] Dispatch from the nuncio in Spain, November 6, 1596. Cf. POLLEN, loc. cit., 528 seq.

[3] " A memorial of the Reformation of England," ibid., 529.

to reflect the ideas of Persons.[1]   It is true that the suggestions were expressed in very vague terms ; there was no mention of definite plans, and no word of agreements or subsidies. Evidently it was intended to await the result of the new Spanish Armada.

When in 1598 the last attack of Philip II. upon England met with an inglorious fate, Spanish prestige came to an end. It was immediately realized that the failure of the great undertaking of 1588 as well could not be attributed to chance, but to the weakness of the Spanish power.   Philip II. now sought to make peace with France, and this was concluded on May 2nd, 1598, at Vervins.

Henceforward the Spanish preponderance passed to France, and even Persons began to lose his confidence in Philip II., and in the very same year, 1598, turned to Henry IV. for support for the English Catholics.[2]   The question of who should obtain the crown of Elizabeth now seemed to depend upon the King of France.   But Henry IV. was very far from wishing to put himself forward as the champion of the Catholic Church ; rather was it his aim to subjugate the Hapsburgs by means of a league of the Protestant powers with France at their head.[3]

Once Henry IV. had decided in favour of James VI. his rights to the succession were assured, in spite of all acts of Parliament.   During the years that followed they still continued to occupy themselves in Rome and Madrid with the important question of the succession to the English throne, but these negotiations were marked with but little clarity or energy.

In Rome Persons still remained the important personality in this matter, and a messenger from England with supposedly important instructions was sent on by the nuncio in Madrid to Rome, as the Pope wished to order the English Jesuit to take this matter into his own hands, notwithstanding the fact that the rules of his Order forbade him to interfere in any

[1] *Ibid.*, 530.
[2] *Ibid.*, 331 *seq.   Cf.* MEYER, 383.
[3] POLLEN, *loc. cit.*, 577.

affairs of state.[1] On July 12th, 1600, the Pope sent three
briefs to the nuncio in Flanders, which he was to keep until
they could be made use of ; one of these exhorted the English
Catholics to concord, and the two others warned the archpriest
and the nuncio not to support any claimant to the throne who
was not a Catholic.[2] Certain letters attached to the briefs and
containing instructions to the nuncio, were composed by
Persons. In one letter to Persons on August 19th, 1600, the
nuncio Frangipani remarked that the briefs in their indefinite
form would probably make very little impression : it was
necessary to decide upon a definite successor to the throne
and give his name. Persons had a conversation with the
Pope as to this on September 12th. It would seem that Rome
would most willingly have supported the claims of the house
of Farnese, which could be strengthened by a marriage with
Arabella Stuart, the niece of Darnley.[3] It was necessary,
however, to take Henry IV. into consideration, and the King
of France replied to his Cardinal, Ossat, by whom these
projects had been reported to him, with a definite refusal.
He wrote that the party which the Pope and the Spaniards
were supporting was so weak that the position of the English
Catholics would become even worse should they have recourse
to force. He added that if the Spaniards tried to obtain a
footing in England, he would oppose them.[4]

In Spain the burning question of the succession to the
English throne was a perpetual subject of discussion, and in

---

[1] *Ibid.,* 572.

[2] *Brevia, Arm. 44, t. 44, n. 190, Papal Secret Archives.

[3] Cardinal d'Ossat to Henry IV., Nov. 26, 1601, Lettres, II.,
501 *seqq.* The claims of Farnese were also maintained in the
Low Countries ; LECHAT, 167–169.

[4] BERGER DE XIVREY, Lettres missives de Henri IV., Vol. V.,
Paris, 1850, 512 ; POLLEN, *loc. cit.* For the position of Henry IV.
cf. PRÉVOST-PARADOL, Elisabeth et Henri IV., 1595–1598, Paris,
1862 ; LAFFLEUR DE KERMAINGANT, L'ambassade de France en
Angleterre sous Henri IV. Mission de Jean de Thumery, sieur
de Boissise, 1598–1602, Paris, 1886 ; Mission de Christ. de Harlay,
comte de Beaumont, 1602–1605, Paris, 1895.

two letters of May 11th and June 12th, 1600, the Spanish ambassador called attention to the importance of the matter. As a result of this the Spanish Privy Council decided that it would be well to put forward the claims of the Infanta Isabella Clara Eugenia, and to place 200,000 ducats at the disposal of the Spanish ambassador in Flanders.   But the matter ended with this decision, and nothing further was done.[1]

It would seem, however, that the matter was dealt with a little more energetically two years later.   Although the greater part of the English Catholics patiently bore the religious persecution, there were among them some who were not averse to violent measures, especially those who, like Lord Monteagle, Tresham, and Catesby, had either once been Protestants, or had been brought up among Protestants. All these names appear among those who had taken part in the rising of Essex, names which later on became so unfortunately celebrated in connexion with the Gunpowder Plot. At the beginning of 1602 Thomas Winter was sent by this group to Spain, to find out what could be hoped for from Spain in the case of a rebellion.   The government at Madrid refused to allow itself to be drawn into making definite promises, though it would seem that it held out certain hopes to the envoy, and even took certain steps in the same direction. In the same year, 1602, the Infanta Isabella, now the wife of the Archduke Albert, Governor of the Low Countries, sent Captain Thomas James to Madrid with orders to say that both she and her husband were absolutely opposed to any claim being made on their behalf to the English crown.   After this renunciation Philip III. gave up all further hopes of the English succession, and declared his readiness to support whatever claimant the Pope preferred.[2]   When Henry IV.

---

[1] POLLEN, *loc. cit.*, 373

[2] *Ibid.*, 581 ; the results of the embassy of Winter were enormously exaggerated in a report from the Jesuit Creswell, as well as in the forensic speeches of Edward Coke on the occasion of the Gunpowder Plot (*cf.* POLLEN, 578-580).   Contemporary documents in the Archives of Simancas show that the Spanish government made no definite promises (*ibid.*, 580).

at last showed signs of a rapprochement with Spain, there was again much discussion of the subject in the Spanish Privy Council in February and March, and it seemed as though something really would be done in the matter of the succession, but certainly nothing was done.[1]

[1] POLLEN, *loc. cit.*, 582 *seq.*

CHAPTER II.

PERSECUTION IN SCOTLAND AND IRELAND.—CLEMENT VIII. AND JAMES I.

AMONG the English Catholics in Rome as well confidence in the Spanish party had waned. This change had been greatly promoted by the embassy of the appellants, sent by the English secular clergy, which had made a stay in Rome during 1602, leaning to the support of France, and working against the interests of Spain.[1] At the same time Persons lost that prestige which he had hitherto enjoyed in high places in Rome. The appellants informed the Pope through the French ambassador, that James of Scotland would be glad to see the English Jesuit sent away from Rome. At that time Persons was ill in bed, but when on his recovery he went for a change of air to Capua, to Cardinal Bellarmine, Clement VIII. forbade him to return.[2]

It was indeed necessary to show every consideration towards the King of Scots, for he had now for some time been the only claimant to the English throne who had any serious prospect of success. He himself had spared no effort to obtain the dazzling crown of the neighbouring country, and would have accepted it from the hands of the devil himself, thought a contemporary, even though this meant the destruction of both Catholic and Protestant preachers.[3] Thus he did not hesitate to hold out to the Pope and the Catholics the hope of his return to the ancient faith, nor to make use of their money and their influence.

---

[1] POLLEN, *loc. cit*, 581.

[2] *Ibid.* 584.

[3] Report for the year 1601 on Scotland by the Jesuit, Alexander MacQuhirrie, in FORBES-LEITH, 270.

It is difficult to say definitely whether at times James really had any inclination towards the old religion ; in any case he detested the Presbyterianism of his own country, and had reintroduced episcopacy there.[1] There were many Catholics among his courtiers ;[2] he knew that his wife Anne had become a Catholic, and exacted no more from her than that she should keep the fact secret.[3] Archbishop James Beaton, who had for many years been his mother's ambassador in Paris, was confirmed by James in this office, as well as in the possession of his honours and titles ;[4] the same was true of John Leslie, the Bishop of Ross.[5]

But whatever may be thought of the sympathetic feeling of James towards the Catholics, any energetic action, based upon a real conviction, was certainly not to be looked for from a prince of such weak character.   As a report of the year 1616 describes him,[6] he was extraordinarily timorous, but at the same time had been even from his youth autocratic in the highest degree. Both his thoughts and his actions were always guided by the opportunism of the moment, and he subjected all else to this ; his conscience, his religion, his friendships, his loyalty, the lives and deaths of his sons and of the aristocracy, as well as the choice of his officials and counsellors. Thus he was not really attached to any particular form of religion, but always favoured the party that was predominant for the moment ; as King of Scots he had been a Calvinist, while later on in England he was an Anglican. He aimed with all his might at the suppression of the Catholic religion, and thought that he would be losing

[1] BELLESHEIM, Schottland, II., 208.

[2] FORBES-LEITH, 266.

[3] BELLESHEIM, II., 200 *seqq.* and the documents 453 *seqq.*   For Anne *cf.* W. PLENKERS in *Stimmen aus Maria-Laach*, XXXV. (1888), 372–390, 494–504 ; W. BLISS in the *Eng. Hist. Rev.*, 1889, 110 (Paul V. spoke to the nuncio in Paris concerning his suspicions of the Catholic sentiments of Anne).

[4] BELLESHEIM, II., 182, 190.

[5] *Ibid.*, 182.

[6] *Ibid.*, 249 *seq.*

half his power should the Pope once more obtain ecclesiastical jurisdiction in Scotland, which might prove to be the case if the number of the Catholics greatly increased. James was a master of deceit and hypocrisy, and it meant nothing to him to break his pledged word or to fail to keep an oath ; he counted it the highest prudence to deceive the world with lies under the appearance of good faith. He was not wanting in astuteness, and as is wont to be the case with weak and timorous natures, was full of cruelty and tyranny which he vented in a horrible way upon the Catholics and upon all those whose vengeance he feared on account of the wrongs that he had done them. When he had filled himself with strong and sweet wine he poured out abominable blasphemies against the Pope, the religious, the Catholic Church, and even against God and the saints, and would not desist until his servants carried him to bed.

Already at the death of his mother in 1587 James had given proof of his want of principle. When on receipt of the news of the tragedy the Scottish nobles had thrown themselves at his feet, and with clashing arms and loud curses had demanded vengeance on Elizabeth, and when a cry of indignation had echoed through the country, it had been the only son of the victim thus disgracefully sacrificed who had readily accepted the excuses of Elizabeth, yet who, purely out of consideration for public opinion, had for a short time professed his willingness to give his assistance to the Armada of Philip II., but who, for the sake of an annual sum of five thousand pounds from England, had shown himself forgetful of the honour of Scotland and of his own crown, and had recently with the support of English gold implicated the Catholic Scottish aristocracy in a rebellion.[1] Yet once again he pretended to be favourable to the Catholics. Thus, after the above-mentioned rising of the Catholic nobles, their property was confiscated, but James refused to have the sentence carried out, as well as the law threatening with loss of property those who gave hospitality to a Catholic priest in their houses.[2]

[1] FORBES-LEITH, 215 seqq.
[2] Ibid., 221 ; cf. 228, 235.

He actually succeeded in getting the adherents of the old religion to rally to him both in Scotland and in England ; his own Catholic subjects were won over by a promise of liberty of conscience, and those of England by the expectation of his conversion.[1] " There are great hopes of universal toleration " runs a letter to Persons, " and the agreement of the Catholics in recognizing the king is so complete, that it seems as though God is about to accomplish great things. All the religious parties are full of expectation and hope, and the Catholics have good reasons to look for special consideration being shown to their aspirations, for the Catholic nobles are working almost to a man on behalf of the king, and have obtained the most far-reaching promises from him."[2]

Nothing shows the duplicity of the king better than his efforts to obtain the good will of the Pope.[3] He had already raised the hopes of Gregory XIII. for his return to the ancient faith, in order to obtain subsidies from Rome.[4] Under Clement VIII. he had once again entered into negotiations, though only through secret intermediaries, who could be disavowed at any moment, and who were eventually thus disavowed.

In the year 1592, we learn that James had sent two Jesuits, the Scotsmen Gordon and Crichton, openly to Rome, to treat of nothing less than the re-establishment of the Catholic religion.[5] In 1594 Clement VIII. sent to the king an envoy with 40,000 ducats, and promised 10,000 ducats as a monthly subsidy if liberty of conscience was given to the Catholics.[6] But even before the Papal envoy Sampiretti set foot in Scotland on July 16th, 1594, James had once again turned

[1] A. O. Meyer in *Quellen u. Forsch.*, VII. (Rome, 1904), 272.

[2] Zimmermann in *Katholik*, 1889, II., 256.

[3] Meyer, *loc. cit.* 268-306 ; G. F. Warner in the *Eng. Hist. Rev.*, XX. (1905), 124-127.

[4] *Cf.* Vol. XIX, of this work, p. 434 *seq.*, ; Brosch, VII., 4.

[5] Forbes-Leith, 222, 355. *Cf.* Bellesheim, II., 452, 461. See also Ranke, Engl. Gesch., I., 494.

[6] Walter Lindsay of Balgawies, Account of the present state of the Catholic religion, 1594, in Forbes-Leith, 355.

to the Protestant preachers, and by an edict of November 12th, 1593, had confronted many thousands of Catholics with the choice between apostasy and exile.[1] The papal envoy and his companions fell into the hands of the heretics, but were rescued by the Earls of Errol and Angus, while the subsidy that had been sent came into the hands of the Catholic nobles.[2] In spite of this, in 1595 and 1596 James sent a fresh envoy, the Catholic Scotsman, John Ogilvy, to Rome and to Spain ; the ends for which Ogilvy was working in Rome during the summer and autumn of 1595, though probably he was going beyond his instructions, were : the appointment of a Cardinal to represent Scotland, annual subsidies for the war against the rebels in his own country, and against the heretics throughout Great Britain, and the excommunication of all the opponents of the Scottish succession in England. This intermediary, however, met with no success, because Clement VIII. did not trust the King of Scots,[3] but great hopes were raised in the Pope's mind when in 1599 Edward Drummond arrived in Rome with a letter in the address of which Clement VIII. was called " Most Holy Father," and the King of Scots signed himself as " his most devoted son."[4] Drummond was instructed to bring pressure to bear upon the Pope, as well as on the Grand Duke of Tuscany and the Duke of Savoy, to obtain the red hat for a Scotsman, this time for the Bishop of Vaison, William Chisholm. Clement VIII. did not grant this request, but

[1] FORBEF-LEITH, 223.

[2] W. LINDSAY, *loc. cit.*, 355 *seq.*

[3] RANKE (Engl. Gesch., I., 494) thinks that this refers to a going beyond of the faculties ; T. G. LAW (Documents illustrating Catholic policy in the reign of James VI., 1596–1598, Edinburgh, 1893, 5) refrains from making any judgment ; according to A. O. MEYER (*loc. cit.*, 271) who perceives in the mission of Ogilvy " the typical features of the negotiations of James with the Catholic powers." For the negotiations of Ogilvy in Venice, Florence and Spain, *cf.* LINGARD, VIII., 345.

[4] " Beatissime Pater . . . Obsequentissimus Filius " (MEYER, *loc. cit.*, 273). For Drummond, *cf.* LINGARD VIII., 346.

he answered the king's letter with great kindness, expressing
the hope that the king would yet find the way of return to
the ancient Church.[1] It is possible that the Papal briefs
to the English Catholics[2] were connected with the letter
of the King of Scots,[3] but Clement VIII. would not
consent to any direct recognition of James' right to the
throne.

The object which the astute King of Scots had principally
had in view in writing his letter had thus not been attained,
and if he thought that his relations with Rome had been
kept secret, he was equally mistaken. Queen Elizabeth
heard of his letter and demanded an explanation ; but he
was quite able to extract himself from the difficulty ; he
flatly denied his relations with Rome. A letter from the
king, addressed to a Scottish gentleman, James Hamilton,
who was at that time in England, charged him to assure all
honest people " on the word of a Christian prince " that
without any vacillation he had held firmly to his faith, and
would always hold firm to it, and that as King of England
he would never permit any other religion.[4] James found
himself in fresh difficulties again in 1608, when, in connexion
with the " Test " oath, Bellarmine reminded the king of his
letter and the signature he had attached to it. Thereupon
James, while he himself remained hidden in an adjoining
room, forced his secretary to confess that it was he who had
forged his signature. This confession had scarcely left the
lips of Balmerino when the king came out from his hiding-
place ; the secretary threw himself at his feet, but was not
able to avert being condemned to death. But in spite of
all this James was not able to free himself from the suspicion
of having staged a comedy of complicity with the servile
secretary.[5]

[1] Letter of April 13, 1600 ; extract in MEYER, loc. cit., 278.
[2] Cf. supra, p.
[3] MEYER, 278.
[4] Ibid., 276.
[5] Cf. BELLESHEIM, II., 192.

That James, despite his emphatic denial, had indeed written to the Pope, is clear from a letter from his wife. This was a letter written in her own hand, ordering Drummond to make the excuses of the king to Clement VIII., and saying that James had not replied in person to the reply which the Pope had sent to the king's letter, because Queen Elizabeth had learned of his relations with the Pope, and had threatened him with the anger of the English Protestants, a thing which might have involved for the King of Scots the loss of the English crown.[1]

The same letter to Drummond[2] further contains orders to profess before the Pope in the queen's name, the Catholic faith in accordance with the decrees of Trent, to swear allegiance to the Apostolic See, and to recommend to the Pope's protection the royal princes, whom their mother, as far as it lay in her power, was bringing up in the Catholic faith. It was necessary, she said, for the king's safety that he should have a bodyguard, and the Pope was asked to grant a subsidy for this purpose, either on his own account or by obtaining it from the King of France, or from the Dukes of Lorraine or Tuscany. James had granted to all his subjects liberty of conscience, so that heresy would disappear of its own accord, but in order to facilitate this action of the king the French ambassador should, at the suggestion of the Pope, ask for liberty of conscience for England as well. This request, which had already been laid before the Curia on several occasions by a Scottish prelate, was renewed by Anne because in this way the quarrel between the secular clergy and the Jesuits could be healed, and in the hands of Elizabeth this

[1] " Excusato quam diligenter regem apud eundem pontificem, quod non rescripserit ; siquidem regina Angliae scriptionem impedivit, quae priorum *quas scripserat* litterarum clanculario admonita nuncio, etiam per epistolas ad regem inscriptas minitata est, si cum pontifice agat, sinistra in protestantium mentibus de eo sparsa opinione, etiam ab Anglici regni spe depulsuram." Instructions for Drummond, in MEYER, *loc. cit.*, 301.

[2] MEYER, 301–303. *Cf.* MARTIN, Clément VIII. et Jacques Stuart, in the *Rev. d'hist. dipl.*, XXV. (1911), 368,

had become a principal means of preventing the conversion
of England. Finally, the Pope must not take it amiss if
James advanced but slowly, and especially if he and the
queen took part in the celebration of Protestant worship.
She was writing all this with the knowledge of James and
with his consent.[1]

Only a short time after her return to the old religion Anne
had had recourse by letter to the Pope as well as to the General
of the Jesuits, who was asked to represent her interests in
Rome. The bearer of her letters, James Wood, Laird of
Boniton, fell, however, into the hands of the Scottish Presbyterians and was executed. King James who, when Elizabeth
had complained of the mission of Ogilvy and Drummond,
had imprisoned the envoys, again on this occasion publicly
boasted of having freed himself from the "archpapists." The
queen's letters escaped the notice of the Presbyterians, but
nevertheless, it would seem, never reached their destination.[2]

The exchange of letters between Edinburgh and Rome
still continued for a time, by means of a new envoy, the
Scottish Catholic, James Lindsay, and also through Lord
Sanquair. One of the queen's letters, presented this time
by Drummond, safely reached the hands of the Pope.
Clement VIII. replied to it on July 16th, 1602,[3] expressing
the hope that Anne would be able to win over her husband
to the Catholic faith. He took a further step in two briefs,
dated August 9th, 1602, which Lindsay took back with him
from Rome;[4] in these he asked of the queen and of the king
the Catholic education of the heir to the crown, Henry (died

---

[1] " Quo sciente et consentiente haec nos omnia praestamus et
postulamus " (MEYER, 302). A *petition (of Drummond) to the
Pope on the basis of Anne's instructions in Borghese II., 348 :
" Viva voce et scriptis apud V.S. egi, ut aliquando de rebus
Scotiae serio cogitaret, etc." Papal Secret Archives.

[2] Alexander MacQuhirrie, The State of Scotland, 1601, in
FORBES-LEITH, 273 ; cf. ibid. 269, and POLLEN, The Month, CI.
(1903), 272.

[3] Published in MEYER, 303.

[4] Published ibid. 304 (brief to James), 305 (brief to Anne).

1612). If the king would follow the Pope's advice in this, then Clement VIII., Lindsay reported orally, would be prepared to assist James with subsidies in money, and would support the king's aspirations to the English throne.

Although this step on the part of the Pope seemed logical, after all that had transpired, it nevertheless greatly embarrassed the deceitful king. He now had to take up a definite attitude, and could no longer continue his double game. James therefore sought to gain time by putting off his reply as long as possible. He was able to do this without fear, as Elizabeth's minister, Robert Cecil, who had formerly opposed the Scottish succession,[1] had now allowed himself to be won over to it, without the knowledge of his sovereign, who was growing old,[2] so that James no longer had any need of the Papists,[3] as he expressed it later on. As a matter of fact his succession to the throne after the death of Elizabeth was accomplished without the least difficulty or disturbance.

Clement VIII. naturally followed this event with great hopefulness, and he addressed to the king a letter of good wishes, in which he begged him to show himself well-disposed towards the Catholics as he had done hitherto.[4] The Pope also had recourse to the Catholic princes, whose influence might have weighed with James, and expressed his desire that they should combine in taking the part of their English co-religionists. Thus on May 31st a brief was sent to the governor of the Low Countries, the Archduke Albert, on June 6th to Duke Charles of Lorraine, and another on

---

[1] LINGARD, VIII., 343, 362.

[2] *Ibid*, 377 *seq.*

[3] *Ibid..* IX. 10 note.

[4] BELLESHEIM, II., 225 ; MEYER, *loc. cit*, 284. *Cf.* *" Discorso scritto lo 20 aprile 1603, in cui si tratta se si debba credere che il nuovo Re d'Inghilterra sia per esser amico del Re di Spagna e se si confedererà con S. M. Catt. o col Re di Francia et se si possa spearare che si faccia cattolico " Urb. 860, p. 272–276, Vatican Library.

December 10th, on August 23rd to the King of Poland, and
on November 25th to the Emperor.[1]

Several times in these letters the request is expressed that
they should induce James, kindly and gently, to join the
Catholic Church.[2] As early as April 12th, 1603, the nuncio
in Paris wrote that he would endeavour to obtain the mediation of Henry IV. for this purpose, and in September he sent
in the Pope's name two letters of good wishes, one to the king
and a special one to the queen, both of which had previously
been approved by Clement VIII.[3] It certainly was not a
mere stereotyped expression when the Pope wrote to the
Archduke Albert that he was tormented day and night by
the thought of England and its new king, and by the question
whether that kingdom, once so celebrated for its defence of
the faith, would return to the Roman Church, a thing for
which he would willingly shed his blood.[4] On May 28th,

---

[1] MEYER, *loc. cit.* *" Preme grandemente ancora alla Santità
Sua l'ambasciata che V. Maestà ha da mandare in Inghilterra,
ne ha discorso più volte col signor cardinale S. Giorgio, dal quale
io sò confidentemente questi et molti particolari." (Paravicini
to Rudolph II., November 22, 1603, State Archives, Vienna,
Hofkorrespondenz, 10). To the Doge of Venice, M. Grimani,
Clement VIII. wrote on June 7, 1603 : " Magna in spe sumus
. . . sub hoc novo Angliae rege res fidei catholicae meliore multo
loco futuras, eumque se mitem et benignem praebiturum catholicis, qui in eius regnis sunt." State Archives, Venice. *Cf.*
Brevia, Arm. 44, t. 47, n. 148, Papal Secret Archives.

[2] *" Quin etiam et rex ipse, si fieri possit . . . ad catholicam
religionem suscipiendam blande et leniter alliciatur " (MEYER,
loc. cit., 285). Meyer translates *Blande . . . alliciatur* by
" schmeichelnd verlocken " *i.e.* " to allure with flatteries," but
allicere does not mean *alletare* (*pellicere*).

[3] BELLESHEIM, II., 224. Two letters of Clement VIII. to
Henry IV., of May 31 and July 14, 1603, concerning the succession
to the throne, and the attitude the Pope meant to take up towards
the new king, in order to bring him back to the Catholic faith,
are summarized in FILLON, 2452, 2453.

[4] The *letter to Albert, May 31, 1603, in Brevia, Arm. 44,
t. 47, n. 145, Papal Secret Archives.

1603, he published a jubilee, in order that the faithful might pray to God for the restoration of the Catholic faith in England, Scotland and Ireland.[1] In Rome itself, on Apirl 27th, 1603, Clement VIII. ordered the Forty Hours to be celebrated in all the churches for England and Scotland.[2] But with all his zeal, he moved with great caution, so as not to excite the suspicions of the king, who was extraordinarily diffident. He rejected the project of the French nuncio to encourage the leaders of the Scottish Catholics by briefs to struggle for religious equality ; the Scottish Catholics were told, on the contrary, to recommend themselves to the good will of their king by their humility, loyalty and peaceful behaviour.[3] When certain of the English exiles wished to avail themselves of the change in the crown in order to return home, and asked for the support of the Pope, Clement VIII. first demanded guarantees that this was not a mere case of restlessness, and he even offered to deliver the king from such folk by pontifical intervention.[4] The sad case in which two Catholic priests, the excitable Watson and Clark, had mixed themselves up in a plot against James, probably gave occasion for this offer.

Special hopes were raised in Rome by a work of the king's, printed privately in 1599, and publicly issued in 1603 ; this was entitled " Basilikon Doron " [5] and laid down for the heir

[1] *Ibid.*, p. 164 *seqq.* ; MEYER, 284.

[2] *Avviso of May 3, 1603, Urb. 1071, Vatican Library.

[3] MEYER, 287.

[4] *Ibid.*, 288 ; A. ZIMMERMANN io *Katholik*, 1899, II., 258.
Paratissimum esse . . . eos omnes (missionaries] e regno evocare, quos sua maiestas rationabiliter indicaverit, regno et statui suo noxios fore." From the instructions to Dr. Gifford, in LINGARD, IX., 21.

[5] βασιλικὸυ Δωρον, Divided into three bookes, Edinburgh, 1599 (only seven copies printed). The first edition which was generally obtainable, Edinburgh, 1603, and London, 1603, French translation, Paris, 1603. A critique of the work in Cod, 680, pp. 64 *seqq.* of the Corsini Library, Rome. *Cf.* LÄMMER, Zur Kirchengesch., 174 (it is here stated that the king was learned, but was not clear as to his principles),

to the throne, Henry, certain rules for the better government
of the kingdom.   This condemned in severe terms the religious
divisions in Scotland ; these were the result of rebellion, and
were the work of men of disaffected spirit and greedy for
power ; every party that weakened the kingdom and threw
it into confusion had encouraged them.   " Be on your guard "
it states, " against Puritans of this kind, who are a pest to
the Church and to society, and who are not to be won over
by gifts, nor feel bound by oaths and promises.   They breathe
treason and calumny.   I profess before Almighty God that
you will not find among the bandits of the mountains or of
the border greater ingratitude, a greater spirit of falsehood,
more brazen perjury, or more hypocritical sentiments, than
among these fanatics."[1]   On the other hand, in the French
translation of the book, which James caused to be sent to
the Pope through the French ambassador, there was not to
be found a single word against the Catholics.   James informed
the Pope that he had purposely toned down such passages,
and had desired the book to be presented to him in order to
demonstrate his feeling of good will towards His Holiness.
Clement VIII. was indeed " enthusiastic:" over this work,
and was on the verge of shedding tears of joy when Persons
informed him of some of the passages in it.[2]   But his
" enthusiasm " was quickly cooled when he received from
London the Latin version of the book, with the passages
about the Pope and the Catholic religion unaltered.   This
translation soon found a place on the Index of prohibited
books.[3]   While the King of Scots was thus encouraging the
Pope by holding out constant hopes to him, the actual state
of affairs in his kingdom was even worse than in the neighbour-

---

[1] BELLESHEIM, II., 210.

[2] " His Holiness, who I assure you could scarce hold tears for
comfort to hear certain passages in favour of virtue and hatred
to vice which I related to him."   Persons to Garnet, May 14,
1603, in TAUNTON, 283.

[3] MEYER, 288-292. *Ibid.*, 291. Comparison of certain texts
of the edition of 1599 with the French and Latin translations of
1603 and 1604.

ing kingdom of England under the rule of Elizabeth. In England anyone who was not a priest, and who did not hold public office, was able to remain of the old religion, even though he had to pay heavy fines ; in Scotland on the other hand, the laws only left the Catholics the choice between apostasy and banishment.[1] In the kingdom of James VI. anyone might arrest the priests of the Society of Jesus, and even kill them in case of resistance.[2] " We live," wrote the Jesuit Abercromby to the General of his Order,[3] " in cellars, hiding-holes and desolate places, always changing our abode like the gypsies, and we never sleep for two nights running in the same place." When Abercromby had gone to the house of a Catholic inn-keeper, the other Catholics did not dare to enter by the door, but climbed up through the windows at the back of the house by night by means of ladders.[4] The situation of the Scottish Catholics was only the better in that the laws were not enforced with the same rigour as in England. But even this apparent leniency had its limits, wherever any determined attachment to the old religion was detected. Among the aristocracy, who were for the most part still Catholics at heart, the three Earls of Huntly, Errol and Angus openly declared themselves for the Church of their fathers, but they were persecuted and threatened until in 1597 they, externally at any rate, and so as to prevent the loss of all their property, signed the profession of faith of the Scottish Church.[5]

In a report on Scotland in 1601,[6] it is stated that the king was the true cause of this sad state of affairs. Whenever he made a speech it was to give utterance to nothing but blasphemies and heresy, and the one thing that his pride aimed at was the crown of England. He hated the Catholics except

---

[1] FORBES-LEITH, 223, 269.
[2] Ibid., 271.
[3] On June 9, 1596, in FORBES-LEITH, 226.
[4] Ibid., 228. Cf. BELLESHEIM, II., 204.
[5] FORBES-LEITH, 233 seqq., 229 seqq.
[6] MacQUHIRRIE, ibid., 270 seq.

when they might prove useful to his designs upon the English throne.   His fears or his hopes might perhaps one day make him a hypocrite, but nothing but a great miracle of the divine omnipotence could make him a Catholic.

In these circumstances it seems an enigma how the Catholics of Great Britain and the Roman Curia can have continued to entertain hopes of the return of James to the ancient Church, and why the king made use of so many subterfuges to win the favour of the Pope.   Both these problems are answered in a memorial drawn up by the Papal nuncio in Brussels, Malvasia.[1]

Malvasia's remarks are above all a proof of the fact that in Rome they were more and more abandoning the point of view of the Catholics who were favourable to Spain.   Above all things they must not seek to better the position of the Catholics by violent measures, for such things would only drive James VI. more and more into the arms of the English queen and the heretics.   The Holy See could not supply its own lack of the necessary armed force even with the assistance of Spain, which would find no support in Scotland itself, but would on the contrary encounter armed opposition from the jealous foreign powers, such as England, Holland, Denmark and France.   No hopes could be placed in the nobles of the Scottish kingdom ; it was true that the Duke of Lennox and about a dozen earls and other great nobles were Catholics at heart, but they would never take up arms, while the three earls who were definitely Catholic, Huntly, Errol and Angus, had been banished.

Moreover, since the king had on several occasions shown his good-will towards the Catholics, it would not be opportune to employ violent measures.   It had only been necessary for him to have given his consent, and they would have been exterminated, but actually James had never done so ; he tolerated those who were of another religion than his own ; he willingly listened to religious discussions ; the Bishop of

---

[1] In BELLESHEIM, II., 460-468.   Cf. LÄMMER, Analecta, 53 and MARTIN in the Rev. d'hist. dipl., XXV., 293.

Dunblane,[1] Colonel Semple,[2] the Jesuits Holt and Morton and others had suffered imprisonment but no more. Moreover he placed confidence in Catholics, since the first president, the master of the household, the captain of the bodyguard, some of the chamberlains and others were Catholics at heart ; he allowed the queen to act in a similar way in the choice of her ladies and courtiers. He had proclaimed the Duke of Lennox as the next claimant to the throne, and had allowed the Earl of Huntly to have mass said in the royal palace itself, though with closed doors.

On the other hand the king was greatly opposed to the preachers, though naturally he did not show this outwardly, because of the populace and Queen Elizabeth, whose protection made such gentry, in spite of their lowly origin, so arrogant and haughty that they tyrannized over the king himself.[3]

The arguments of Malvasia which have been given so far naturally prove nothing more than that James knew very well how to deceive the Pope and the Catholics. The reason, however, why the astute king took so much trouble to win their sympathies, is given by Malvasia as follows : James had need of the Catholics ; if, after the death of Elizabeth, it became a question of ensuring his claims to the English throne, there were none upon whom he could rely except the aristocracy of his own country. But the greater and the more important part of the nobles of the kingdom were either openly Catholics, or were more inclined to Catholicism

---

[1] William Chisholm the younger " who renounced his episcopal see in order to become a Carthusian, and was sent by Sixtus V. to his own country, where he remained in disguise for several months, giving great edification and spiritual help, ending his life in Rome (1593) in the odour of sanctity." Walter Lindsay of Balgawies, in FORBES-LEITH, 353.

[2] Alessandro Farnese attempted by his means to secure an alliance with James ; after the defeat of the Armada the king made him a prisoner, but Semple escaped the death that threatened him by flight. FORBES-LEITH, 369 ; BELLESHEIM, II., 282.

[3] MALVASIA. loc. cit., 462.

than to any other form of religion.[1]   All of them were filled
with hatred and aversion for the preachers.   If, after the
death of Elizabeth, so Malvasia thought, James were to drive
them out and declare himself a Catholic, then all the most
powerful nobles would rally to his support, and since, according to Scottish usage, the vassals were very submissive to
and devoted to their lords, these two would follow the example
of the nobles.

According to Malvasia it was also known on the authority
of James himself that he was very anxious about the intrigues
of Spain.   Even in the time of Sixtus V., Philip II. had sent
an envoy to ask for the excommunication of James VI.,
and in the eyes of the Spaniards and of many others, the King
of Scots was not fitted to wear either the English crown
or that of Scotland.   For this reason James VI. greatly feared
excommunication and therefore strove to keep on good terms
with the Pope.[2]   As the Earl of Huntly said to Malvasia,
a threat or admonition from the Pope would be well received
by the king, because he would then have an excuse for favouring the Catholics, and by their means raising up a
counterweight to the insolence of the preachers.[3]   Huntly
was of the opinion that an envoy should be sent as soon as
possible to ask for toleration and liberty of conscience for
the Catholics, and, should he not obtain this, to threaten
the king with excommunication.   Least disturbance would
be caused if the Duke of Lorraine, who was James' cousin,
were to send an envoy on some pretext ; the envoy could
speak privately to the king about his return to the ancient
faith, while James, out of respect for the Pope, would hear
him very willingly.[4]   Besides this pressure might be brought
to bear upon the king by means of the Catholic nobles, and

---

[1] List of the aristocracy who were still secretly Catholics
(July 1, 1592) in FORBES-LEITH, 361 *seqq.* ; BELLESHEIM, II., 182.

[2] " Della qual scommunica per questi respetti ha tanta paura
il Re di Scotia, ch'egli farà sempre gran conto del Sommo Pontefice." BELLESHEIM, II., 464.

[3] BELLESHEIM, *loc. cit.*

[4] *Ibid.*, 466.

upon the latter by the Jesuit Gordon, who, as Huntly's uncle, had access to the nobles, and who, although he was a mere child in political matters, was learned, well-liked and respected.[1] An attempt should also be made to increase the number of the Scottish Catholics by encouraging the work of the Jesuits,[2] though they must not interfere in affairs of state, either in England or in Scotland, since, on account of their friendship with Spain, they were suspected by the King of Scots, and highly disliked by the alumni of the English College.[3] Finally, priests should be trained for Scotland by the development of the Scots College, the scanty revenues of which had hitherto only sufficed for seven or eight students.[4]

The Scots College of which Malvasia spoke had been founded in 1576 at Tournai by an exiled Scottish parish priest. During the first ten years of its existence the College was successively transferred to Pont-à-Mousson, Douai, Louvain and Antwerp, to find at length a permanent home at Douai in 1612.[5] The poverty of this institute was known in Rome, for the gifts of various Scottish priests were not sufficient, while the annual revenues assigned to it by Gregory XIII. and Mary Stuart were discontinued after the deaths of the donors. Clement VIII. therefore issued a circular in 1593 on behalf of the Scottish seminary,[6] and again, at the intercession of Malvasia, obtained by the Scottish Jesuit Crichton, the Pope had recourse to the Archduke Albert in a brief of March 8th, 1597.[7]

A second Scots College had existed in Paris since the XIVth century.[8] At the suggestion of Cardinal Allen,[9] the repre-

---

[1] *Ibid.*, 464, 465.

[2] *Ibid.*, 464.

[3] *Ibid.*, 466.

[4] *Ibid,.* 464.

[5] *Ibid.*

[6] *Ibid.*, 222.

[7] Brevia, Arm. 44, t. 41, n. 80, Papal Secret Archives. *Cf.* BELLESHEIM, II., 223.

[8] BELLESHEIM, II., 190.

[9] *Ibid.*, 223, n. 3.

sentative of Scotland at the French court, Archbishop Beaton of Glasgow, together with the Bishop of Ross, resolved to restore this ancient foundation in order to meet the exigencies of the times, and to supply it with revenues for the training of Scottish priests. Clement VIII. supported this project by a brief of Henry IV.[1] The seminary at Braunsberg in East Prussia,[2] and the Scottish monasteries at Würzburg and Ratisbon also supplied several priests to the Church in Scotland.[3]

But the most important and most wealthy of these establishments was the Scots College in Rome ; this owed to Clement VIII. not only the support which he likewise gave to the above-mentioned seminaries in Flanders and Paris, but also its existence and its ample endowment. On December 5th, 1600, the bull of foundation was issued,[4] and two years later it was inaugurated with ten students, who attended the lectures at the Roman College, and were dependent upon the Jesuits for their spiritual direction.[5]

None of these institutions could be compared, even distantly, with the importance of the English seminaries. The Scottish Jesuit Crichton, who was doing all in his power to supply the lack of priests in his own country, was of opinion that once the seminaries were founded, many young men would flock thither from the three universities of Scotland, which were only lacking in the matter of theological instruction, so that within two or three years there would be a number of priests at his disposal.[6] But this forecast was not realized ; the enthusiasm with which the English youth flocked to the seminaries on the continent was not reproduced in the neigh-

---

[1] *Brief of September 1, 1601 ; Arm. 44, t. 45, n. 301, Papal Secret Archives.

[2] BELLESHEIM, II., 203, 456 seq.

[3] Ibid., 223 seq.

[4] Bull., X., 625 seqq., Synopsis, 214.

[5] BELLESHEIM, II., 221 ; HEIMBUCHER, II., 150. To a later date there belongs a second Scottish seminary in Paris, founded in 1627. FORBES-LEITH, 370 seq., BELLESHEIM, II., 282.

[6] To Cardinal Caetani, 1595, in MEYER, 459.

bouring kingdom, and the number of students in the Scottish seminaries remained relatively small, as it had been in the past.[1] Though rather later than Scotland or England, the sister island to the west also had its seminaries on the continent. About the middle of the XVIIth century there were to be found Irish Colleges for the study of philosophy and theology in Rome, Salamanca, Seville, Compostella, Madrid, Alcalà, Lisbon, Douai, Louvain, Antwerp, Paris, Bordeaux and Rouen ; to these must be added the educational establishments at Tournai and Lille, and numerous colleges of religious.[2] But very few of these went back to the time of the great founders of the colleges, Gregory XIII. and Clement VIII. In Spain and Flanders these institutions had their beginning when in 1588 the Irish Jesuit, Thomas White, at Valladolid, and the Irish secular priest Christopher Cusack in 1594 at Douai, gathered together the students of their race into communities.[3] Their subsequent development was due to Philip II. ; at the request of White, on August 2nd, 1592, he granted the students at Valladolid a college at Salamanca, while in 1596 he assigned an annual revenue of 5,000 florins for an Irish seminary at Douai, where in 1604 a site was acquired for a new and better building.[4] The beginnings of some other Irish colleges went back further still. In 1578 there came to Paris, an exile from his country, a priest named John Lee with several students, who, however, after thirty years had hardly succeeded in establishing a permanent abode.[5] Some Irish priests had established a school for missionaries in 1573 at Lisbon ; after this had been developed in 1593 under the direction of the Jesuit John Holing, it received a permanent abode in 1595, after which

---

[1] *Ibid.*, 98.

[2] BELLESHEIM, Irland, II., 217 *seqq.*, 314 *seqq.* 357 *seqq.*, 525, 613, 729. *Cf.* The Description of Ireland, in anno 1598, now for the first time published by E. HOGAN, Dublin, 1878.

[3] BELLESHEIM, II., 221, 223.

[4] *Ibid.*

[5] *Ibid.*, 217.

White assumed the direction of the establishment.[1]   When
the Archduke Albert supported a number of Irishmen in the
seminary at Antwerp, he was eulogized by the Pope in 1604,[2]
as was the King of Spain at the same time on account of his
generosity towards the Spanish and Flemish Irish seminaries.[3]
The Pope had already in 1597 strongly urged the Archduke
Albert to care for the Irish students in Flanders.[4]   The
seminaries on the continent were rendered doubly necessary
as a counterweight to Trinity College, which Elizabeth had
established in Dublin to act as a bulwark of Protestantism,
and which was endowed, both by her and by her successors,
with enormous revenues and extensive privileges.   All the
students and officials of Trinity College had to subscribe to
the Thirty Nine Articles, while a third part of the students
who were educated there were trained in Anglican theology,
which was taught in a spirit entirely hostile to Catholicism.[5]

According to medieval ideas, Ireland was a country that
had special ties and obligations towards the Holy See.   When
Paul IV. in 1555, at the request of Philip II. and Queen Mary,
raised Ireland to the dignity of a kingdom, he expressly
reserved the rights of the Apostolic See.[6]   This was probably
the reason why Clement VIII., in dealing with Irish affairs,
departed from his customary principles.   From 1590 onwards
the severity and cruelty of the viceroy had goaded the Irish
leaders into rebellion, and after certain successes on the part
of O'Neill, Bishop Cornelius O'Melrian addressed to the Pope
on November 4th, 1595, from Lisbon a request that, on the

[1] *Ibid.*, 222.

[2] *Brief of May 28, 1604, Brevia, Arm. 44, t. 50, p. 213, Papal
Secret Archives.

[3] *Brief of May 28, 1604, *ibid.*, p. 212.

[4] *Letter of September 20, 1597 : " Tibi igitur catholicos
Hybernos in universum et illos nominatim egreriae spei iuvenes
efficaciter commendamus." Négociations de Rome, I., 1582-
1597, State Archives, Brussels ; Brevia, Arm. 44, t. 41, n. 220,
Papal Secret Archives.

[5] BELLESHEIM, II., 215.

[6] *Ibid.*, 108.   *Cf.* Vol. XIV, of this work, p. 360.

strength of the bull of donation of Adrian IV., he would separate Ireland from England and nominate O'Neill as king.[1] Clement VIII. naturally refused this request, but when in 1598 O'Donnell and O'Neill had defeated the troops of Elizabeth at the battle of Blackwater, and O'Neill had applied to the Pope for assistance, Clement, by the agency of the Franciscan, Matteo d'Oviedo, who had recently been appointed Archbishop of Dublin, sent O'Neill a Papal brief, congratulating him on his victory and urging him to continue the war " so that the kingdom of Ireland may not henceforward be subject to the yoke of the heretics, nor the members of Christ any longer have the impious Elizabeth as their sovereign."[2] A brief to the commander of the army renewed the indulgences formerly granted for the crusades.[3] There then followed a series of Papal briefs. On January 20th, 1601, Clement VIII. again sent his eulogies, confirming the Irish in their struggle for religion, and promising to send a nuncio.[4] On June 5th in the same year there was a further series of briefs : to the King of Spain, to the Archduke Albert,[5] to O'Neill, to the clergy of Ireland, and to the notabilities of the kingdom.[6] The Jesuit Lodovico Mansoni, who had been chosen as nuncio, was recommended in these to the protection of the king and the archduke, but his mission was postponed in accordance with the representations of O'Neill.[7]

After the battle of Blackwater O'Neill attained to the summit of his power, and only the cities of the island still held out against him. O'Neill thought that he could easily overcome these as well if Spain would help him with troops,

[1] BELLESHEIM, II., 225.

[2] *Ibid.*, 226 *seq.*

[3] *Ibid.*, 227, 228.

[4] Brevia, Arm. 44, t. 45, n. 22, printed in P. F. MORAN, History of the Catholic Archbishops of Dublin since the Reformation, I., Dublin, 1864, 221. *Cf.* BELLESHEIM, II., 228.

[5] *Brevia, Arm. 44, t. 45, n. 221, 223. Papal Secret Archives.

[6] *Ibid.*, 212-222.

[7] BELLESHEIM, II., 229. Brief of May 19, 1601, with authorization for Mansoni, see Synopsis, I., 216.

and especially with artillery. In the years that followed, however, his position changed for the worse in an alarming way, and the Spanish help, which arrived at last on September 23rd, 1601, under the command of Juan de Aguila, and occupied Kinsale, came too late. Kinsale was invested by the English, an Irish army that marched to its relief was defeated, and the Spaniards were forced to surrender on January 12th, 1602.[1] With this the capitulation of Ireland was assured ; Munster and Ulster were devastated in such a way by the English that the viceroy, Mountjoy, wrote to James I. that nothing remained to his majesty in Ireland save to rule over corpses and heaps of ashes.[2]

After the King of Scots had ascended the English throne, with the name of James I., he still carried on for a time his undignified double-dealing towards the Pope. In the summer of 1603 he announced to Clement VIII. his desire to resume the negotiations.[3] At the same time he chose the zealous Catholic, Antony Standen, to be his representative in Venice and Florence, but when Standen incautiously assisted at mass in public, James had him thrown into the Tower, and sent back to Rome the sacred objects which Clement VIII. had given him for the queen ; but while everyone was expecting that Standen would have to expiate his excessive zeal by death, his imprisonment was quietly changed into confinement in his own house, and he was finally set at liberty.[4]

The hopes of Clement VIII. rose high at the beginning of 1605, when James Lindsay once more made his appearance in Rome, bringing replies to the briefs which he had taken with him to London in 1602. A year before this James I. had conveyed to the nuncio in Paris the royal instructions which were to guide Lindsay's actions in Rome. As to the

[1] BELLESHEIM, II., 230 ; KELSO, 55–94.

[2] BELLESHEIM, loc. cit. Clement VIII. once again raised his voice on behalf of Ireland in the *letters to the nuncio in Spain of June 18 and September 28, 1603, Aldobrandini Archives, Rome.

[3] MEYER, 292.

[4] Ibid., 292 seq.

principal matter, which meant most to the Pope, namely the
Catholic education of the heir to the throne, and to which
he had so often called the attention of the king, the latter
remained definitely hostile, saying that immediately after
he had received the Pope's request, James had ordered his
reply to be written, and that it was only due to Lindsay's
illness that it had come to the knowledge of the Pope so late.
In other respects the king did no more than make vague
promises, assuring the Pope of the pleasure which he felt in
his friendship, and promising to treat the English Catholics
who preserved the peace with justice and in accordance with
his duty.

Such expressions as these naturally contained very little
to cause the arrival of Lindsay to be awaited with any
particular impatience. In August, 1604, the Pope's sentiments towards the King of England were on the whole
unfavourable, while the great complaisance shown by Spain
in making peace with England displeased him as much as
her friendship with the heretics.[1] Nevertheless he still saw

---

[1] *" Hieri arrivò al Papa il corriero partito d' Inghilterra e
passato all' arciduca Alberto con la conclusione della pace conce-
duta da Inghilterra a supplicanti Spagnuoli ; hanno giocata di
gran somma di moneta verso li deputati e de' instantissime e
humili preghiere. Il Papa non l'approva così grande amistà con
eretici e disse all' ambasciatore di Francia le capitolationi vergog-
nose a Spagna, delle quali mi ricordo queste, che il Re d' Inghilterra sia per honore nominato nel primo luogo, che tenga le
fortezze che ha sotto nome per li danari che vi ha spesi, che non
si restituiranno mai, che Inglesi trafichino ne' paesi di Spagna
pagando solamente dieci per 100, che non sieno per questo nemici
a Olandesi, che il Re non mandi suoi' galioni in India, ma che
non può impedire che Inglesi non vadano alla busca, che è l' istessa
che prima." (Report of an anonymous agent to Mantua, August 14,
1604, Gonzaga Archives, Mantua). Disgust at the unfortunate
terms of the peace did not prevent the joy at the conclusion of
the peace itself which Clement VIII. expressed in a letter to the
nuncio in Spain, of August 24, 1604. *Cf.* Ph. HILTEBRANDT in
Quellen u. Forsch., XV. (1913), 308, n.

in these events reasons to hope for an improvement in the
religious position in England.   He therefore insistently urged
the Catholics there to give the king no grounds for suspicion.
The French nuncio, Maffeo Barberini, was instructed in
December, 1604, as his predecessor Bufalo had been, to
maintain friendly relations with the English ambassadors
in Paris, and thus prove to James I. that the Pope had no
care except the salvation of souls.[1]   In this way Clement VIII.
hoped in the end to win over James I., and this hope was
paramount in his mind when Lindsay actually made his
appearance in Rome, bearing a letter from Queen Anne,[2]
which contained, it would appear, brilliant promises.   According to Lindsay's report, the king was ripe for conversion, if
only the Pope would renounce his authority over the princes.[3]
Clement VIII. was overjoyed, and in January, 1605, replied
to the queen in a letter couched in the most friendly terms,
in which he praised her in the highest way,[4] while he appointed
a special commission of Cardinals to discuss the English
situation, which held two meetings on January 17th and
25th.[5]

The new King of England treated the English Catholics
in the same way as he did the Pope, for with them too he sought
to arouse constant hopes, without ever intending that they
should be realized.   The accession of James I. to the throne
had been hailed by the Catholics of England with the highest
hopes ; they trusted in the promises which he had repeatedly
made, since even on his way to London he had renewed his
assurance that he would not exact the fines for absence from

[1] See the *Instructions in Vol, XXIII, App. n. 45, Vatican
Library.

[2] So far not found.

[3] MEYER, 296.

[4] Printed copy in BELLESHEIM, II., 469.   For the date (January
23 or 28) see MEYER, 296.

[5] *Avvisi of January 19 and 26, 1605.   Urb. 1073, Vatican
Library.   The members of the commission, according to the
Avviso of January 19, were Galli (president), Medici, Baronius,
Pietro and Cinzio Aldobrandini, Avila, Bandini, A. Marzato, Du
Perron, Bufalo, Visconti and G. Agucchio.

Protestant worship.[1] The superior of the English Jesuits, Henry Garnet, wrote[2] " the death of the queen has brought about a great change ; our anxiety was very great, but it has now become changed into confidence, and we are rejoicing in a period of unhoped for liberty." Two Papal briefs concerning the succession to the throne, which had been entrusted to Garnet, and kept by him for use in case of need, were burned by him as useless ; in these the clergy and faithful of England were exhorted to support no claimant to the throne who had not sworn allegiance to the Apostolic See.[3]

These fair hopes, however, were nothing but beautiful dreams. James was playing a double game : on the one hand he hated the religion of his mother, while on the other he feared excommunication on account of its political consequences. He therefore kept Clement VIII. in suspense until 1605, deceiving him with fair words ;[4] things even reached the point when the Pope offered to inflict ecclesiastical penalties on turbulent Catholics,[5] and the king put forward the proposal, though to no purpose, that the power of inflicting

---

[1] GARDINER, I., 100.

[2] To Persons, April 16, 1603, in SPILLMANN, IV., 5. The Catholics united as a body in supporting the rights of James to the throne (LECHAT, 194 seq.). Cf. the *report of September 29, 1604 : " Progressi et augmenti de' cattolici in Inghilterra," Vallicella Library, Rome, n. 23, pp. 241-248. Ibid., 150–215, many matters concerning the English martyrs. *Reports of the nuncio in France, Maffeo Barberini (Urban VIII.) concerning England, in the Barberini Library, Rome, XXXI., 75.

[3] Confessions of Garnet of March 13 and 14, 1606, in FOLEY IV., 158–159. Particulars of these briefs, of July 5 and 12, 1600, by J. DE LA SERVIÈRE in Études, XCIV., (1903) 645.

[4] Cf. GARDINER, I., 225.

[5] GARDINER, I., 140 seq. " S.S^{tà} vole e comanda che li catholici siano obbedienti al re d' Inghilterra, come a loro signore e re naturale." The nuncio in France must take care " che conforme alla volontà di N.S. obedischino al suo re e non s' intrighino in congiure, tumulti ed altri cose, per le quali possino dispiacere quella Maestà." Alodbrandini to the nuncio in France, in RANKE, Engl. Gesch., I., 531.

such penalties should be conferred on an authorized agent,[1] who naturally would use his powers in accordance with the wishes of the government.   In a conversation with the French envoy-extraordinary, the future Duke of Sully, James pointed out[2] that he had not exacted the fines for failure to attend at church, and that he desired to remain on friendly terms with the Pope, if the latter would recognize him as the head of the Anglican Church.[3] After the conspiracy of Watson, the king again expressed himself unfavourably towards the Catholics to Beaumont, the French ambassador ; he seemed, however, to calm down when Beaumont pointed out that the conspirators were only exceptions among a body that was otherwise loyal to the king, and that conspiracies were difficult to avoid unless liberty of conscience was allowed.[4]

The practical attitude of James towards the Catholics showed even greater unreliability than his words. His promises were no more sincere, when he was striving to obtain the English crown,[5] for they always concealed a condition or limitation which escaped the notice of the too credulous adherents of the ancient faith. " As to the Catholics," he wrote,[6] " I do not intend to persecute any of them who maintain the peace and obey the laws at any rate externally, and protection will not be denied to anyone who is worthy of it

---

[1] " Quanto alla facoltà di chiamare sotto pena di scommunica i turbolenti, non ci par darla per sdesso, perchè trattiamo con heretici, e corriamo pericolo di perder i securi." Reply of Clement VIII. to the dispatch of Bufalo of December 14, 1604, in GARDINER, I., 143.

[2] *Ibid.*, 115

[3] *" Adulando il Pontifice in quello che si può, nei regni suoi rovina il Pontificato " is the judgment passed on the frequent expressions of James in favour of Rome in a " Comparatione tra i trè gran Re dell' Europa l' anno 1605," State Library, Berlin, Inform. polit., XII., 450.

[4] Beaumont to Henry IV., July 23, 1603, in GARDINER, I., 115.

[5] This is shown by his correspondence with Cecil, 1602 ; see ZIMMERMAN in the *Röm. Quartalschr.*, XVI. (1902), 392 *seq.*

[6] Degli Effetti to Bufalo, June 26, 1603, in GARDINER, I., 100.

on account of his good services." So long as " at least external
obedience " to the laws was demanded, the king, despite these
fair words, had a free hand to do as he pleased, and in fact,
in direct contradiction to the sense of the promises which he
had made since his arrival in England, James caused the fines
for non-attendance at divine worship to be collected ; if
the Catholics, he publicly declared at that time,[1] professed a
different religion from his own, they could not be good subjects.
When, however, on July 17th, 1603, a deputation of Catholics
made complaint before the Privy Council in the presence of
the king, James promised that the fines should be stopped,
and that the Catholics, provided they obeyed the laws, should
have access to the highest offices in the service of the state.[2]
For a time the wealthy adherents of the ancient Church
were no longer troubled with the fines, and those who had no
means, " to the enormous loss " of the revenues of state, were
excused from the confiscation of their lands.[3] Among the
Catholics of high estate, the king had admitted to his entourage
in a special way, Henry Howard, a man of unprincipled
character, who was later on Earl of Northampton, and was a
brother of the executed Duke of Norfolk ; he had to serve
" the royal huntsman " as a decoy, in order to cover the
king's immorality.[4]

The majority of the Catholics, however, proved themselves
more sound in their principles than Howard, and the apparent
favour of the king did not last very long. " We no longer
have any need of the Papists," the king replied, when Watson,
who had hitherto been his favourite, reminded him of his
promises.[5]

The fact that the number of the Catholics had considerably

[1] Degli Effetti, June 23, 1603, ibid., 101.

[2] GARDINER, I., 115.

[3] " The income accruing to the Crown from this source (the
two-thirds of the property of the recusants) was enormously
diminished." GARDINER, I., 116.

[4] Ibid., 115 seq. For Howard, ibid., 93.

[5] " Na, na, we'll not need the Papists now." LINGARD, IX.,
10 n. ; GARDINER, I., 100.

increased once the laws were no longer enforced, filled the
king with anxiety ; by May, 1604, the number of those who
had returned to the ancient religion had risen to 10,000 in
the diocese of Chester alone ; the number of those who did
not attend Anglican worship increased from 2,400 to 3,433.[1]
The fear of passing in the eyes of the public as the friend of
the Catholics then drove the unprincipled monarch openly
to declare himself against them.

On February 22nd, 1604, James, under pressure from the
Privy Council, ordered that on March 19th, the day of the
opening of Parliament, all Catholic priests must leave the
country.[2] On March 22nd, in a speech before Parliament,[3]
he excused himself for his leniency towards the Catholics,
by saying that he had allowed himself to be guided by the
hope that proposals would be laid before the Lords and
Commons for the removal of certain indefinite points in the
existing laws against the Catholics, in that these had led to
an excessive severity which was contrary to the intention of
the legislator, and to the condemnation of the innocent.
Catholic priests could not be tolerated in the kingdom so long
as they professed the doctrine that the Pope had temporal
authority over all kings and emperors,[4] or that excommunicated princes could be killed with impunity. The laity too
must be prohibited from drawing anyone to their own religion,
in order that the Catholics might not acquire a power which
contained within it danger to the liberties of the country
and to the independence of the crown.

[1] GARDINER, I., 202, 222, 231. James I. had caused lists of
the recusants to be drawn up in each county (ibid., 144). " In
principatu Walliae et in provinciis septentrionalibus . . . .
numerus eorum non ita pridem crevit in immensum " (Discursus
status religionis 1605, in RANKE, England, I., 531). Cf. GARDINER.
I., 242. For the disturbances at Hereford see FOLEY, IV., 452.

[2] GARDINER, I., 144. In less than nine months after the death
of Elizabeth it is said that 140 priests arrived in England. Ibid.,
143.

[3] Ibid., 166.

[4] " An imperial civil power over all Kings and Emperors '

In this way James revealed himself to the whole country as a good Protestant, but the cunning monarch at the same time did not wish to irritate the Catholics too much. After his edict against the priests he told the Spanish ambassador that he had not been able to act otherwise because of the Privy Council, but that the enforcement of the law would be wanting in any kind of rigour.[1] As a matter of fact, a month afterwards, not one of the persons conecrned had been banished, and a priest who had been arrested for saying mass was once again set at liberty.[2]

The Catholics, however, were under no illusion as to the continuance of such a state of affairs.[3] Good Protestants bitterly complained that Catholics enjoyed a liberty such as they had not had for years past.[4] James accordingly anticipated their wishes. On May 17th, 1604, he expressed in Parliament his disgust at the increase of the Catholics, and urged the passing of a law to set bounds to it. On June 4th a proposal to that effect was laid before the House of Lords, which was confirmed by the Commons in July.[5] In this the existing laws against the Catholics were renewed and made more severe ; all the alumni of the seminaries over-seas were declared incapable of possessing land or any other property on English soil, while all professors were forbidden to set up a school without the approval of an Anglican bishop.[6] James I. rejected a petition of the Catholic priests offering to take an oath of allegiance to the king, as well as another in which the laity pledged themselves for the good behaviour of the Catholic priests whom the law should allow them to have in their own houses ; he merely confirmed the law.[7]

[1] From Bufalo to Aldobrandini, March 22, 1604, in GARDINER, I., 144.

[2] *Ibid.*, 201.

[3] From Bufalo to Aldobrandini, May 31, 1604, supplement, *ibid.*, 202.

[4] *Ibid.*, 201 *seq.*

[5] *Ibid.*, 203.

[6] LINGARD., IX., 28.

[7] GARDINER, I., 203.

In spite of this the king did not wish even now altogether to cut his bridges behind him, and his negotiations with Rome still continued. In dealing with the representatives of the old Church, James I. spoke of a General Council, which should settle the question of reunion among the churches by a free discussion of their points of difference ;[1] he assured the French ambassador that for the moment he had no thought of enforcing the laws,[2] and had excused the sixteen nobles who refused to attend church the monthly fine of twenty pounds.[3] In a conversation with a representative of the Duke of Lorraine he declared his readiness to accept the Roman Church as his mother, and the Pope as universal bishop, with universal ecclesiastical jurisdiction. If the Roman Church would take one step towards the restoration of unity, he would take three. It was distasteful to him to have been forced against his will to give his assent to the new law, and he would not enforce its penalties on religious grounds.[4] In the same sense on September 24th, 1604, even the Privy Council had decided by seven votes to three that the persecuting laws should not be enforced in the case of the laity.[5]

Their enforcement, however, had already been entrusted to over-zealous officials. During the years 1604 and 1605 at least six Catholics died at the hands of the executioner on account of their faith.[6] But James I. naturally had no part in their condemnation,[7] and six other Catholics, five priests and one layman, who had been condemned to death by the courts during these same years, were pardoned by him.[8]

It was, however, easy to foresee that the leniency of the king would not last long, and that the first concessions made

[1] From Bufalo, June 12, 1604, in GARDINER, I., 202.
[2] Beaumont to Henry IV., July 18, 1604, *ibid.*, 203.
[3] *Ibid.*, 203 *seq.*
[4] From Bufalo, September 21, 1604, *ibid.*, 220 *seq.*
[5] *Ibid.*, 222, 223, n. 1.
[6] SPILLMANN, IV., 10–16.
[7] " Senza la partecipatione di quel Re " wrote Bufalo on August 24, 1604, in GARDINER, I., 222, n. 1.
[8] SPILLMAN, IV., 16.

to the Protestants must soon be followed by others. At the end of September, 1604, he caused all the Catholic priests who were incarcerated in the English prisons to be sent out of the kingdom over-seas.[1] From November 28th onwards absence from Anglican worship was again punished by heavy fines.[2] It is possible that this measure was solely due to the financial straits of the king,[3] and as the heavy fine of twenty pounds a month could only be paid by the most wealthy Catholics, it only affected thirteen gentlemen.[4] But when the action taken by James against the Puritans aroused a suspicion of his favouring the Catholics, and the public obtained some inkling of his negotiations with the Pope, the king preferred his reputation as a good Protestant to any sense of justice towards the Catholics. On February 10th, 1605, he declared at the Privy Council that he detested in the highest degree the superstitious religion of the Papists, and if he thought that his son and heir would show the slightest favour to them, he would rather see him buried before his eyes. The Lords of the Council and the other bishops must instruct the judges that the laws were to be enforced with all possible severity.[5]

The effects of this exhortation were not long in making themselves felt, for on the day after its proclamation by the Lord Mayor of London, forty-nine citations were issued in the capital and the county of Middlesex. 5,560 persons were condemned in the various districts of England for having failed to attend Protestant worship.[6] Enormous fines were once more levied upon the wealthy Catholics, while many had two-thirds of their property confiscated.[7] In October, 1605,

---

[1] GARDINER, I., 222.

[2] *Ibid.*, 224.

[3] Thus GARDINER (*ibid.*).

[4] *Ibid.*

[5] *Ibid.*, 227.

[6] *Ibid.*

[7] Exact details from the Receipt Books of the Exchequer, in GARDINER, 227–230, who brings out especially the relaxation

the superior of the Jesuits wrote[1] that the action taken by the
government was even more severe than in the days of
Elizabeth.[2]

Strict investigations in private houses were the order of the
day, and every six weeks a special court of justice sat, which
despoiled the Catholics of their possessions ; the enforcement
of the laws was entrusted to the most rigorous Puritans, who
in other respects were disliked by the king. If one of the
" recusants " offered to buy back his confiscated property,
he exposed himself to the risk of losing the sum thus offered
as well. If this process continued, said Garnet, they would
have at last to be content with buying back every six months
the bed in which they slept. The justices openly said that
the king wanted blood ; he no longer desired caresses for the
Papists as of yore, but blows.[3] In the county of Hereford 409
families were reduced to beggary at a single blow.[4] The
bishops were instructed to excommunicate the more wealthy
Catholics ; these could then be thrown into prison, and thereby
lost a number of their civil rights ; they could not even
recover their debts, buy or sell anything, nor dispose of their
property by will.[5]

Death spared Clement VIII. the sorrow of witnessing this
last development.

of the severity. We here join with Gardiner against Lingard
(IX., 30 *seqq.*) although it does not appear that Gardiner has
removed all the difficulties.

[1] LINGARD. IX., Note C., p. 387 ; FOLEY, IV., 63.

[2] " The courses taken are more severe than in Queen Elizabeth's
time." LINGARD, 388. In like manner an unnamed contemporary in SPILLMANN, IV., 17 : " They (the Catholics) pay their
two parts more roundly than ever they did in the time of the late
queen, not any as I think being left out before Michaelmas."
Northampton in July, 1605, in LINGARD, IX., 42 n.

[3] " That the King has hitherto stroaked the papist, but now
will strike." LINGARD, IX., 388.

[4] LINGARD, IX., 41.

[5] *Ibid.*, 42.

CHAPTER III.

ATTEMPTED CATHOLIC RESTORATION IN SWEDEN.

THE principal event during the life of Cardinal Ippolito Aldobrandini had been his legation to Poland in the year 1588, and the energy that he had then displayed had contributed not a little to his elevation to the See of Peter.[1] It is no wonder, then, that he should have taken a great interest in, and shown a sincere sympathy for, the whole of the North, and especially for the immense kingdom in the north-east and its king, Sigismund III., a man of strictly Catholic sentiments.[2] Clement fully realized the supreme importance for the future of the Church in Europe of the way in which events should develop there in that kingdom which extended from the Warta to the Dnieper, and from the Baltic to the Carpathians.

The fact that the King of Poland intended to marry the Archduchess Anna, of the Styrian branch of the Hapsburgs, who was a staunch Catholic, was certain to win the sympathy of the Pope. He therefore at once, at his first consistory on February 14th, 1592, appointed Cardinal Georg Radziwill as legate for the marriage,[3] and afterwards sent the new queen the Golden Rose.[4] At the beginning of June, 1592, the nunciature in Poland was entrusted to the Bishop of San

[1] Cf. Vol. XXIII. of this work, p. 23 seq.

[2] See PARUTA, Dispacci, I., 27, 105. PARUTA, Relazione, 431. See also BIAUDET in the periodical Histor. arkisto, XIX. (Helsingissä, 1905), 187.

[3] See *Acta consist. card. S. Severinae, February 14, 1592, Cod. Barb. XXXVI., 5, III., Vatican Library. In the suite of the legate was P. Alaleone ; for his *Diarium cf. Arch. Rom., XVI., 19 seq.

[4] See the brief of May 28, 1592, in THEINER, Mon. Pol., III., 209 seq.

Severo, Germanico Malaspina,[1] who had already distinguished himself in other diplomatic missions under the predecessors of Clement VIII.[2]

Malaspina found a very difficult state of affairs in Poland. King Sigismund was engaged in disputes with his nobles, and especially in a violent altercation with the chancellor of the crown, Zamoiski. The nuncio rightly looked upon a reconciliation between these two as his first duty, and this he soon succeeded in bringing about, after the celebrated Diet of Inquisition in the autumn of 1592.[3] The Pope was alike gratified at this first success of his nuncio and with his attitude at that celebrated diet.[4] When in the following year there arose another dispute between Sigismund and Zamoiski, it was once more Malaspina who, at the Diet of Warsaw in

[1] See the brief of June 6, 1592, in THEINER, *loc. cit.*, 209. The statement of Hansen (Nuntiaturberichte, I., 308 n.), that Malaspina only became nuncio in 1595, is incorrect. The reports of the nunciature of Malaspina from June 15, 1592, to April 20, 1598, in BORGHESE, III., 52 a, b; III., 66 c, d; III., 15 a; III., 91 a, b; III., 89 c; III., 89 d; III., 96 e, Papal Secret Archives, were already prepared for publication in 1892-93, by the Polish Academy of Science : cf. *Anz. der Krakauer Akad.*, 1894, February, p. 26. Recently a scholar of Finland has announced the publication of the acta which refer to Sweden ; see BIAUDET, Le St. Siège et la Suede, I., viii. *seq.* Some reports of Malaspina belonging to 1592 were published by SCHMURLO in his work, Russland u, Italien, t. II., fasc. 1, Petersburg, 1908, 172 *seq.* Free use was made of them recently by Sven Tumberg (Sigismund och Sverige, 1597-1598, Upsala, 1917). L. KARTUNNEN, Chiffres dipl. des Nonces en Pologne vers la fin du 16ᵉ siècle, Helsinki, 1911, treats both of the cypher letters of Malaspina in Cod. M. II., 56, of the Chigi Library, Rome, which Meister missed, as well as of the cypher letters of Caetani, Mandina and Rangoni. For the personality of Malaspina *cf.* HJÄRNE, Sigismundus svenska resor, 10 *seqq.*, and PÄRNÄNEN, 32 *seqq.*

[2] *Cf.* Vol. XXII. of this work, pp. 73, 88.

[3] F. v. WEZYK, Der Konflikt des Konigs Sigismund III. Wasa mit den poln. Ständen u. der Inquisitionsreichstag vom 7 September, 1592, Leipzig, 1869.

[4] *Cf.* PARUTA, Dispacci, I., 27-29.

1593, succeeded in reconciling them. The nuncio enjoyed the complete confidence of both the king and the chancellor, and during the course of both Diets all important questions that were to be brought forward for discussion were first examined in private by the nuncio, so that he was able to smooth over all difficulties with the tact of a skilled diplomatist,[1] and even settled the disputes between Cardinals Radziwill and Bàthory.[2]

The most important question with which the Diet of 1593 was concerned was the journey of Sigismund III. to Sweden, his native country, which he had already planned in the previous year. At that time, on account of the difficult position of affairs in Poland, the Pope had discouraged this.[3]

---

[1] *Cf.* the report in *Anz. der Krak. Akad.*, 1894, February, where it is stated : " Les dépêches de Malaspina, fort longues et fort nombreuses, nous dévoilent les dessous de toutes les intrigues qui se nouèrent pendant ces deux diètes ; elles entrent dans les détails les plus minutieux de la vie parlementaire de cette époque et nous permettent de faire au jour le jour pour ainsi dire son histoire secrète, de compendre la tactique qu'on y mettait en œuvre, en un mot jettent la plus vive lumière sur ces curieuses assemblées. On y trouve aussi quantité d'informations sur le roi et la cour, Zamoyski, le primat Karnkowski, le maréchal de la couronne Opalinski, et sur beaucoup d'autres personnes. La grande figure de Zamoyski ressort singulièrement imposante de ces correspondances. Cela est d'autant plus digne de remarque que Malaspina, loin d'être favorable au Chancelier, semble plutôt avoir une sorte d'antipathie pour lui ; il est, au moins au commencement, son adversaire déclaré et se porte avec chaleur dans le parti au roi qu'il sert de toute son influence et de tout son pouvoir. Ce n'est qu'avec le temps qu'il abandonnera ses préventions contre Zamoyski."

[2] See the *briefs to the two Cardinals of April 3 and May 1, 1593, Arm. 44, t. 38, p. 282, 310, Papal Secret Archives. *Cf.* the summary *Attioni seguite in Polonia et in Suetia dapoi l'assuntione al pontificato di N.S. Clemente VIII. in Cod. N. 34, p. 433, of the Vallicella Library, Rome.

[3] See the brief of August 28, 1592, in THEINER, II., Doc. p. 82 *seq.*

But when, on November 17th, 1592, Sigismund's father, John III., died, and the crown of Sweden fell to the King of Poland, the situation was entirely altered, but from the first the greatest difficulties stood in the way of his taking possession of his lawful inheritance. These difficulties came above all from his uncle, Charles, Duke of Södermanland, who was determined at all costs to possess himself of the Swedish crown. This unscrupulous politician. who was both far-seeing and a cold-blooded schemer, set himself to his task with unparalleled astuteness ; he had an advantage in the fact that he had already during the latter days of John III., practically controlled the government of Sweden, and Sigismund III. was unable for the time being to prevent his uncle from continuing to direct the affairs of state.

On January 8th, 1593, Duke Charles obtained from the councillors of the kingdom a statement that they looked upon him as the head of the government in the absence of the king. They further bound themselves to uphold all that should be decided with the consent of Charles without distinction, " all for one and one for all." Even though this agreement did not actually do any wrong to their loyalty towards the lawful king, Sigismund, it was not only contrary to the laws, but also the greatest imaginable usurpation of his liberty of action. He found himself obliged to give his assent to a form of government set up without his knowledge, and should he disapprove of any measure taken by Charles and his councillors, this would at once have been the signal for a schism.[1]

It was easy to make use of the pretext of religion for keeping out the lawful Catholic king,[2] and this in fact Duke Charles did as soon as possible. Its religion and its freedom, he said to the councillors, were the benefits which my father bestowed upon his country, and it was in recognition of this that the States declared the crown to be hereditary in the house of Gustavus ; therefore, only one who will maintain this in the

---

[1] Opinion of Rühs (Gesch. Schwedens, II., 258).
[2] See Biaudet, I., v.

kingdom, can be the true hereditary King of Sweden. As the new king was subject in conscience to the power and will of the Pope, it was all the more necessary to lay down, in the interests both of religion and liberty, the conditions which the Swedes of old had been accustomed to impose upon their kings from the earliest times.[1]

This was done at the ecclesiastical assembly held at Upsala on February 25th, 1593, at which many persons assisted, nobles, burgesses and peasants. This decided that the Holy Scriptures, understood in themselves, were to be one rule of faith ; all accepted the articles of the unreformed confession of Augsburg. It also prohibited in its entirety the exercise of Catholic worship, closed to Catholics access to any office, and banished all those who had studied abroad in the Jesuit Colleges. It is obvious that these radical decrees abolished the liturgy of John III., which had never been approved by the Holy See,[2] and the Catholic usages still retained in it, such as episcopal vestments, ciboriums, candles, banners, and the blessing of dead bodies and graves. Prayers for the dead were removed from the ritual. Duke Charles was highly pleased with all this, save that he further wished for the abolition of the elevation of the host, and of the exorcisms at baptism. The Lutheran pastors, however, were determined to retain the exorcisms at baptism, as a mark of distinction from the Calvinists. It was finally agreed to retain the exorcisms in a modified form, and as a non-essential ceremony. It was harder for Charles to assent to the decree which expressly declared as heretics, not only the Catholics and Sacramentarians, but also the Calvinists and Zwinglians. But he gave way on this point, though he scornfully remarked : " You had better join on to them all those

---

[1] See GEIJER, II., 271.

[2] In a cypher *instruction from Cardinal C. Aldobrandini to Malaspina of August 1, 1593, the liturgy is described as " mescuglio," and it is remarked that John III. " hebbe però pensiero, per quanto dicono, di introdurre per quella porta il catholicismo." Borghese, II., 68, p. 469, Papal Secret Archives.

that you know of that kind, even the devil in hell, since he too is my enemy."[1]

On the whole Duke Charles had every reason to be satisfied with the ecclesiastical assembly at Upsala, during the course of which he had carefully kept in the background. He had accomplished all that he could have hoped for in the matter of making it impossible for his nephew to exercise the royal power fully, for he had induced men to look upon him, not as their king, but rather as a foreign pretender to the crown, and as an apostate against whom they must be on their guard as a danger to religion.[2]

Duke Charles would very gladly have seen Sigismund remain permanently in Poland. The king himself hesitated. It was said that he had asked the advice of the Pope, but that the latter would not take the responsibility of answering either in the affirmative or the negative.[3] This is easy to understand, as after recent events the hope of recovering Sweden had become very doubtful, and there was no small danger of losing ground in Poland. There was much to be said for those who advised Sigismund first to consolidate his position in Poland, so that he might be able to face Duke Charles and his other enemies in full strength in his attempt to recover the crown of Sweden ; on the other hand Sigismund thought that he ought not to defer his journey to his hereditary kingdom, or his taking possession of the Swedish crown which belonged

---

[1] Cf. MÜNTER, Magazin, II.. 1, 69 seq. ; RÜHS, II., 259 seq. ; GEIJER, II., 272 seq. On the occasion of the third centenary of the Council of Upsala K. Hildebrand published the acta of the synod. Cf. K. HILDEBRAND, Upsala möte 1593, Stockholm, 1893, and Hist. Tidskrift, 1893, 89 seqq. ; A. N. SUNDBERG, Om den svenska Kyrkoreformationen och Upsala möte 1593, Sundberg, the Archbishop of Upsala, makes the confession, doubly interesting from his lips, that in the Swedish " reform " inaugurated by Gustavus Wasa, political motives were paramount.

[2] Opinion of RANKE (Päpste, II., 248).

[3] See PARUTA, Dispacci, I., 110.

to him by right. Thereupon Clement VIII. did all that he could to help him.

Immediately after the death of John III. the Pope had appointed a congregation composed of Cardinals d'Aragona, Galli, Bonelli, Salviati, Sforza and Montalto, in order to discuss what should be done in view of the new state of affairs.[1] In April, 1593, he reminded the nobles and bishops of Poland of their duty to Sigismund ;[2] at the beginning of August he sent thither, in the person of Bartholomew Powsinski, a special delegate, who was furnished with instructions and a subsidy of 20,000 scudi.[3]

Powsinski was ordered to act in close conformity with Malaspina.   After he had congratulated the king on the recent confinement of the queen and the successful issue of the Diet at Warsaw, he was to draw the attention of the king to the opportunity that now offered itself for the restoration of the Catholic religion in Sweden.   The sum sent by the Pope was above all intended for this purpose, and Clement VIII. would willingly have made it larger if his financial circumstances had permitted.   The king should avail himself of the circumstance that the archdiocese of Upsala and the bishopric of Strengnäs were vacant, in order to appoint Catholic bishops in both cases.

---

[1] See the reprot of Peranda, February 16, 1593, in LAEMMER, Melet., 237 n.

[2] See the brief to Zamoiski, April 10, 1593, in THEINER, II., Doc. p. 84 *seq.* ; *ibid.* 86, the brief to the episcopate, May 1, 1593. In Rome there was an idea of sending a legate to Poland for the period of Sigismund's absence ; see the letter of Peranda, February 16, 1593, in LAEMMER, *loc. cit.*

[3] *Cf.* PARUTA, Dispacci, I., 286, the *brief to the King of Poland concerning the mission of Powsinski is dated July 29, 1593 (Arm. 44, t. 38, p. 373, Papal Secret Archives) ; the Instruction of August 1 (according to BORGHESE, I., 758 *ibid.*) in PÄRNÄNEN, L'ambassade de Bartol. Powsinski à Danzig en 1593, Helsinki, 1911, 30 *seqq.*   To the manuscripts here mentioned must be added IV., 34, p. 288 *seq.* of the Vallicella Library, Rome. B. Powsinski restored a chapel in S. Maria degli Angeli ; see FORCELLA, IX., 160.

In case the king should find himself in a position to fill other dioceses Powsinski gave him a list of Catholic Swedes who seemed fitted for such positions. Sigismund was especially urged to give thought to the training of Catholic priests in Sweden, who could be educated, partly at his court or with the Polish bishops, and partly in the colleges at Riga, Dorpat and Braunsberg. Mention was also made of the possibility of establishing a Jesuit college at Stockholm, and of the importance of propagating good Catholic books in the Swedish language.[1]

It was fatal when Sigismund, in order to avoid any appearance of coming as an enemy, or with any hostile intentions towards his new subjects who had thus invited him, or perhaps from a mistaken idea of economy, decided to go without any armed force to his hereditary kingdom,[2] which had been thrown into confusion by the intrigues of Charles. Malaspina had vainly urged him to take some troops with him.[3]

After the Diet of Warsaw had been brought to a happy conclusion in June 1593, and Sigismund had been reconciled with Cardinal Báthory, the king went first of all to Dantzig, where he was awaited by the loyal governor of Finland, Admiral Klas Fleming, with the fleet and some ships that had

---

[1] See PÄRNÄNEN, loc. cit. In a *memorial (Urb. 860, p. 230 seq. Vatican Library) which was drawn up immediately after the news of the death of Sigismund, the hope is expressed of claiming for Catholicism that liberty of religion which was so openly used by the Protestants ; see LAEMMER, Analecta, 50.

[2] Cf. in App. No. 13 the *Relatione dello stato di Suetia (Vallicella Library, Rome) attention to which was first drawn by CIAMPI (I., 92). RANKE (Päpste, II., 250, 253 ; III., 90*-91*) acknowledges that in this " the first undertaking of Sigismund is described with every appearance of truth by a well-informed person " but he has made very little use of this rich source. Ranke, according to his wont, does not say where he found the report. It is to be found in Cod. H 155, of the Ambrosiana Library, Milan, and in Cod. N 33 of the Vallicella Library, Rome.

[3] Cf. the cypher *report of Malaspina to Cardinal C. Aldobrandini, dated Stockholm, January 10 (Gregor. Cal.) 1594 (decif. March 10) in Borghese, III., 91 a-b, Papal Secret Archives.

been sent by Duke Charles.[1]   Powsinski, who reached Dantzig
on August 28th,[2] not only discharged all the tasks that had
been laid upon him by the Pope, but also gave to the nuncio
Malaspina a cypher letter from the Cardinal Secretary of State,
dated July 27th, concerning the manner in which Sigismund
should act in Sweden.[3] This letter contained no definite
reply to Malaspina's question of January 28th, but only advice,
as the conferences in Rome had not as yet come to a definite
conclusion. It was only added that it would be well if the
king deferred receiving the royal unction until a more favourable moment, as the Protestants had no chrism nor holy oils ;
if he found himself obliged to undergo any other civil ceremonial, he should consent to this, without however giving any
interior assent to anything that was forbidden. As to his
coronation, which pertained to the Archbishop of Upsala,
it was the wish of Rome that Sigismund should appoint a
Catholic to perform this ceremony, and it was agreed that
should time be lacking to obtain the confirmation of the
Holy See, the nuncio should supply what was required.
During the celebrations of the obsequies of the dead king,
Sigismund must take care that no polemics against Catholic
doctrines found their way into the funeral oration. If the
king should be asked to recognize the religious constitution of
Sweden, on the lines of the Confession of Augsburg, he must
temporize. If this could not be done without danger of a
revolution, then he must avoid coming to any decision which
would render the exercise of Catholic worship more difficult
or impossible. If, however, the letter goes on to say, it should
happen that he found himself forced by necessity to take an

[1] See *Ragguaglio istorico di quanto segui in Polonia quando
il Re Sigismondo volle andare a prendere possesso del Regno di
Suetia, con il racconto del medesimo viaggio e delle cose occorse
tanto circa gli affari pratici quanto intorno agli interessi della
religione cattolica, in Cod. N. 34, p. 540 seq. of the Vallicella
Library, Rome. The author is some person closely connected
with Malaspina, probably his auditor, Ruggiero Salomoni.

[2] See PÄRNÄNEN, 10.

[3] See ibid., 12 seq., where the letter is given for the first time

oath in this matter, then the formula which had been adopted in these sad times by the German Emperor and the King of Poland would be less blameworthy than that other " to treat Catholics and Protestants with a like affection," a formula which was impossible for an honourable prince. The text of the oath should be furnished as far as possible with saving clauses, every care being taken to avoid a formula prohibiting the exercise of the Catholic religion. Malaspina must communicate these matters to the two Jesuits, Justus Rabe of Cracow and Sigismund Ernhoffer of Bavaria, who were accompanying the king and queen as their confessors.[1]

Neither Sigismund nor Malaspina were under any illusions as to the difficulties of the situation. The appointment of a Catholic to Upsala was out of the question. The king, as well as the nuncio, were agreed that Sigismund must in any case claim the free exercise of the Catholic religion for himself in Sweden.[2]

The king embarked on September 6th, 1593. He was accompanied by the queen, his sister, the nuncio Malaspina, the two Jesuits, the vice-chancellor, and a number of Polish nobles. The military escort of the king only consisted of 400 men.[3]

Sigismund intended first of all to go to Kalmar, but serious storms prevented this, and at the end of September, after a long voyage he safely arrived at Stockholm.[4] There he was received by Duke Charles and Abraham Angermann, the Archbishop of Upsala, who had been elected in the meantime, and who was the most violent opponent of the liturgy of John III. Charles feigned, it is true, reverence and submission,[5] but soon disclosed his true sentiments by forthwith demanding the dismissal of the Papal nuncio, a thing which

---

[1] See HJÄRNE, Sigismunds svenska resor, 42. For the interpreter, P. I. Rabe, see *Script. Rer. Pol.*, XIV., 63 *seqq.* For Ernhoffer see DUHR, I., 680 *seq.*, 706.

[2] See PÄRNÄNEN, 13 *seq.*

[3] See *Ragguaglio (supra,* p. 89, n. 1).

[4] See *ibid.* Cf. HURTER, III., 355.

[5] *Cf.* HURTER, III., 355 *seq.*

had already been demanded at Dantzig by the councillors who had been sent to meet Sigismund. The king refused this demand on the ground that Malaspina had not been sent to the kingdom of Sweden, but to himself ; he had done no wrong to Sweden, but had done good service in promoting the king's journey ; if the envoys of the Tartars and Muscovites were admitted, why not he as well ?[1] Sigismund also refused to confirm the decrees of the ecclesiastical assembly of Upsala, as well as to recognize Angermann as archbishop. The nuncio encouraged him in this, reminding him not only of his duty as a Catholic, but also pointing out to him how much opposed it was to his royal authority that he should submit to decisions which had been arbitrarily taken during his absence.[2] It was said, however, that Sigismund was already personally pledged, in that, as a youth, together with King John, at the request of the nobles and Duke Charles, he had signed an undertaking that he would change nothing in Sweden as far as religion was concerned, and would not admit Catholics to hold public office. This undertaking, however, had been expressly revoked by King John in 1591,[3] when he realized the danger it involved to his civil authority.

[1] See GEIJER, II., 278 n. 1 ; HURTER, III., 358.

[2] *Non mancava il Nuntio Apost. di rappresentarli che ne per coscienza ne per dignità dovea confirmare decreti risoluti nel suo regno senza l' autorità sua ne essi havean bisogno di cotal approvatione in cosa che senza lui haveano stabilita. Ragguaglio istor. etc., loc. cit., 541 b.

[3] *Ma accorgendosi Giovanni che da Carlo e da senatori in questa loro procurata esclusione de' cattolici si era mirato ad escludere anzi Sigismondo e i suoi figliuoli dal dominio e dagli ufficii del regno per tirarne tutta l' autorità in loro stessi che ad altro fine, havea nell' anno 1591 privati i senatori del grado e delle facoltà et tolto loro di mano lo scritto sudetto e lacerato fattolo riporre nella cancelleria del regno, in cui pur così squarciato tuttavia si serbava, ne da quell' hora in poi haveva permessa ne l' assoluta confessione Augustana ne l' esclusione de' cattolici (Ragguaglio ist. loc. cit., 542). It is surprising that Ranke (Päpste, II.[8], 245) who had the Ragguaglio at his disposal, paid no attention to this important source.

In the meantime the seeds of suspicion of Sigismund sown by Charles were bearing fruit, and the Protestant clergy eagerly encouraged it. It seemed intolerable to them that the king should have sent a Jesuit to the Castle of Drottningholm, where he could give the Catholics of the neighbourhood the comforts of their religion.[1] One of the preachers hurled from the pulpit anathemas against all who had any relations with the Papists ; when he was threatened with imprisonment, however, he declared that he did not intend to include the king in this.[2] When two Catholics of the retinue of Sigismund died, the king had to have recourse to force in order to obtain Catholic burial for them. The preachers then spread the rumour that Sigismund intended to restore all the churches of Sweden to Catholic worship by force ; some 4,000 armed men gathered together and threatened the nuncio, against whom quite absurd accusations were made, as for example that he had ordered stones to be thrown from his house at some boys who were singing in church. Malaspina defended himself against the accusations, but refused the guard offered to him by Sigismund.[3]

Duke Charles did all he could to fan the excitement, and for this purpose deliberately made use of foolish fables, which, however, had their effect upon the populace. Thus he spread the story that near Linköping two dragons had been seen fighting, one with a crown and the other without ; the latter had been victorious over the one that was crowned.[4] The

[1] See THEINER, II., 49.

[2] See HURTER, III., 357.

[3] See *Ragguaglio ist., loc. cit. Cf. also RÜHS, II., 269, and HURTER, III., 357 seq.

[4] *Carlo spargeva che in Nicopia sua città fossero aparsi in aere due dragoni, l'uno con la corona in capo et l'altro senza e che essendo venuti insieme a battaglia in fine dopo molto sangue l'incoronato perditore e squarciato havesse lasciato l'altro vittorioso volendo dimostrare a popoli facili a muoversi da vane superstitioni che i cieli e gli elementi per liberare il regno di travagli promettevano a lui la corona di Sigismondo. *Ragguaglio loc. cit.

preachers spread the calumny that on the way to Sweden, the nuncio had been guilty of profaning the consecrated hosts. However foolish these stories were, they did not fail to produce their effect, and stirred up the people against the Catholics. Some forty men and women who had intended to return to the ancient Church, thereupon drew back.[1]

Sigismund endeavoured to calm the excitement by declaring that he would do no injury to anyone on account of his religion. He also tried to sow dissensions between the aristocracy and Charles, counting on the fact that the duke was hated by many of them on account of his greed for money. In spite of this the king's position remained very difficult ; if he were to leave the government in the hands of the aristocracy, it was easy to foresee a return to an elective monarchy ; if he were to hand it over to Duke Charles, it was only to be expected that his desire to be king would lead to a like result. " Of what use is it to us," wrote Malaspina to Rome, " to fathom the evil intentions of our adversaries ? Our position is like to that of a ship without oars which finds itself tossed about in a storm, and unable to count upon any human help."[2] The fervour with which Sigismund fulfilled his religious duties aroused among the Protestant population partly hatred and partly contempt, while his great leniency was taken for weakness.[3] With all the greater insistence pressure was brought to bear upon him to confirm the decrees of the ecclesiastical assembly of Upsala. Duke Charles declared

[1] See the *report of Malaspina to Cardinal C. Aldobrandini, dated Stockholm, January 12 (Gregor. Cal.) 1594, Borghese, III. 91, Papal Secret Archives.

[2] *" Che giova a noi conoscere li fraudulenti arteficii di costoro poichè siamo a guisa di naviglio senza remi in mezzo di un tempestoso mare destituti da ogni humano auxilio, et non sapendo per cio quello che dobbiamo fare non ne resta altro rifugio se non rivoltare gli cchi al Signore." Cypher report to Cardinal C. Aldobrandini, dated Stockholm, 1594, January 25. Borghese, III., 91 a-b, Papal Secret Archives.

[3] See *Ragguaglio ist., loc. cit., 542b.

that if he would not do so he would not be present at the
ceremonies of the coronation.[1]   Against this both the nuncio
and the queen pointed out that he had no right to impose
laws upon the consciences of his subjects, for they too could
claim liberty of conscience.[2]   The nuncio also advised the
few Catholics who still remained in Sweden to address
complaints to the king on account of the violations of the law
which were imposed upon them, but they could not find the
necessary courage to take such a step.[3]

In the reply which he made to the Council in January,
1594, Sigismund expressed his surprise at their wishing to
impose conditions for his coronation upon him, and hinted
at the difference between an hereditary and an elective
monarchy.   He was the hereditary king of a kingdom which
professed a different religion from his own ; it was his intention
to leave the Protestants undisturbed as soon as they had told
him what liberty they intended to allow to his Catholic
co-religionists.[4]

A decision had to be come to by the beginning of February,
1594, when the king would go to Upsala, where the States
were assembled, in order to celebrate at the same time the
obsequies of John III. and the coronation of King Sigismund.
As this occasion might be made use of in order to extort the
desired concessions, Malaspina advised the king to defer the
latter ceremony, which was not absolutely necessary in the
case of an hereditary king, and as Sigismund's predecessors
had done on several occasions.   The king, however, pointed
out the difference in his own position, which obliged him to

---

[1] See the report of Malaspina to Card. C. Aldobrandini, dated
Stockholm, 1594, January 11th, loc. cit.

[2] *" Il Nuntio e la Reina moglie . . . facevano ogni opera della
sua riputatione a non lasciarsi da suoi sudditi mettere leggi nella
propria coscienza, la quale essi tuttavia volevano libera."
Ragguaglio, loc. cit.

[3] See the remarks from the *Ragguaglio, loc. cit. already given
by RANKE (II., 247, n. 2).

[4] See GEIJER, II., 279.

return to Poland.[1] Duke Charles also attended the coronation, not as Sigismund did, with a simple body-guard, but with
a retinue of 3,000 armed men, both infantry and cavalry.[2]
This fact increased the boldness of the Protestants. They
had demanded that Malaspina should not appear at Upsala,
but Sigismund remained firm on this point, despite violent
pressure that was put upon him, and in answer to the
threatening attitude of the Protestants, gave Malaspina an
armed escort.[3] During the obsequies of his father in the
cathedral of Upsala, Sigismund tried to maintain, as far as
was possible, his attitude as a Catholic. He was obliged,
however, to allow Archbishop Angermann to deliver a funeral
oration from the pulpit, which was not lacking in attacks
upon the ancient Church. After this a Catholic delivered
a Latin discourse, but not from the pulpit.[4] The nuncio was
satisfied with the ceremonial observed, in so far that there
was no ritual of a Protestant character.[5]

[1] *Non lasciò il Nuntio di raccordare al Re che se egli pur
temeva com'era da temersi che i suoi sudditi con coronarlo
volessero farlo servire a loro dishonesti voleri potrebbe per non
ricevere con questa corona questa servitù differirla ad altro tempo
non essendo la coronatione a principe hereditario e giurato come
lui fuorche un'atto di cerimonia che di sostanza e che Gustavo
istesso suo avo dopo l'elettione era stato quattro anni a coronarsi
et Arrigo suo zio e Giovanni suo padre l'havevano pur differita
molto tempo amministrando tuttavia ogni cosa con assoluta
autorità. Replicava il Re, che a quelli che doveano continuare
la stanza nel regno era stata facil cosa, ma che a lui che dovea
partirne sarebbe molto difficile a conservarsi Re senza la corona
Ragguaglio *loc. cit.*, 543.

[2] See GEIJER, II., 279.

[3] See the *report of Malaspina to Card. C. Aldobrandini, dated
Stockholm, 1594, February 8, Borghese, III., 91 a-b, Papal Secret
Archives.

[4] See the *report of Malaspina to Card. C. Aldobrandini, dated
Upsala, February 12, *ibid.*

[5] *" Quello che in questa attione si è ottenuto di buono è stato
che non si è fatto atto alcuno secondo il rito heretico." Report
of Malaspina of February 12, 1594, *ibid.*

Duke Charles once again declared that he would not allow the coronation unless Sigismund first gave his assent to the decrees of Upsala. Charles also declared himself opposed to the cession of a few churches to the Catholics, or even of one in Stockholm. Some of the royal councillors were in favour of this concession, but ultimately agreed with the duke. The latter declared to the States : " I will not separate myself from you ; if Sigismund desires to be your king, he must assent to your demands."[1]

Sigismund was attached with all his heart to the Catholic religion ; it is no wonder, then, that he resisted to the end giving his consent to demands which would not only seriously injure his royal authority, but which would also weigh heavily upon his conscience. He declared that he would rather lose his crown than condemn the Catholics to forfeit all their rights. They must at any rate be allowed the free exercise of their own religion. The Protestant States, led by Duke Charles and the Archbishop of Upsala, wished on the other hand only to allow the king to have the Catholic mass cele-brated in private, in his own chapel, during his sojourn in the kingdom. At his departure he was to be accompanied by all the priests, and the two Jesuits. Subsequently the States insisted absolutely on the prohibition of all public Catholic worship ; moreover, no Catholic must hold any public office in Sweden, and anyone who passed over to the Catholic religion, or caused his sons to be educated therein, was to lose his civil rights.[2] Lastly, the States declared to their king, in openly threatening terms, that if he would not agree to their demands, they would not pay him homage.[3]

One who was well informed as to the events of the time reports that Sigismund's sister, who was a zealous Protestant, and the Protestant Swedes of her household, urged their co-religionists not to desist from continuing to attack the king, to make him consent to their demands, saying that

[1] See RÜHS, II., 271 ; GEIJER. II., 279.
[2] See RÜHS, II., 272 ; GEIJER, II., 280.
[3] See RANKE, II., 249.

even though at first he showed himself resolute and firm, he would end, according to his wont, by giving way.[1] This policy of annoyance was adopted, and an attempt was further made to deprive the king of the support of the Papal nuncio. Six Swedish noblemen presented themselves before the latter and asked him to leave the country. Malaspina replied that he had come openly and had been received as the envoy of his sovereign ; he could not, and did not intend to go away, as he had done nothing to deserve that the rights of nations should be violated in his case.[2] Finally the Protestants openly told the king that they would have recourse to revolution if he did not consent to their demands ; they even went so far, Sigismund reported to the Pope, " as to threaten me with imprisonment, my Polish retinue with destruction, and the Swedish Catholics with death."[3] The nuncio was in obvious danger of death, as an assault by violence upon his house was in preparation.

Sigismund warned Malaspina that his life was in danger, and that there was no time to be lost, for the attack would be made within three hours. The Pope's representative calmly replied that the king must in that case wait quietly for those three hours, when it would be seen whether the threats of the Protestants were really serious. He, the nuncio, did not fear death, and would never consent to the king's giving way to the Protestant demands. The king's

[1] *Dall'infanta sua sorella ostinatissima heretica e da Suetesi ch'erano dimorati appresso l'Re in Polonia, heretici anch'essi, venivano confortati i senatori e gl'altri a non cessare di battagliare il Re, il quale benche di sua natura si mostrasse a primi assalti costante e intrepido si lasciava nondimeno doppo non lunga batteria facilmente espugnare. Ragguaglio, *loc. cit.*, 543.

[2] See in App. No. 13, the *Relatione dello stato di Suetia, Vallicella Library, Rome. Malaspina refers to this episode in his *Dialogo sopra li stati spirituale e politico dell' imperio et delle provincie infette d'eresie " in Cod. N. 17, p. 31, of the Vallicella Library, Rome.

[3] See the *letter of Sigismund of March 8, 1594 (Doria Archives, Rome) in App, No. 2.

Polish councillors were of the opinion that he should give way.[1] But Malaspina remained inflexible : the king must not yield to the demands of the Protestants.

As the threats became more and more alarming, the king turned in panic to Rabe and Ernhoffer, the two Jesuits who had come with him from Poland. Rabe was of the opinion that in the circumstances, and in view of the difficulties and dangers to which Sigismund was exposing himself by his refusal, he might yield to the Protestant demands ; Ernhoffer, who had hitherto been of the same opinion as Malaspina, did not dare to oppose this definite decision.[2] Sigismund made public this decision in writing, and then, without notifying Malaspina, gave the assent which the Protestants demanded as to their religion, reserving to himself, however, the right to grant later on, in accordance with the advice of the States, more favourable conditions to his own co-religionists.[3] It was only with great difficulty that Sigismund brought himself to recognize Angermann as Archbishop of Upsala, as the latter's appointment had undoubtedly been an unheard of usurpation of his royal prerogatives.[4] In the end, however, he gave way on this point as well ; he only insisted that not Angermann, but the Protestant bishop of Vesteras should place the crown upon his head.

The nuncio Malaspina had reported to Rome as early as the last days of January, 1593, concerning the question of the unction and coronation. At that time Sigismund as well was resolved not to allow this ceremony to be performed by a Protestant bishop, who, as he rightly thought, was only a layman. As the Swedes, on national grounds, refused a Polish bishop, the king for a time thought of Malaspina.[5]

---

[1] Cf. the *report of Malaspina of August 15, 1594, in App. No. 6, Papal Secret Archives.

[2] See in App. No. 2, the *report of Malaspina of March 8, 1594 (Papal Secret Archives) and No. 13 the *Relatione dello stato di Suetia, Vallicella Library, Rome.

[3] See GEIJER, II., 281 n. 1.

[4] Opinion of RÜHS (II., 273).

[5] See the *report of Malaspina to Card. C. Aldobrandini of January 15, 1593, Borghese, II., 68, p. 477, Papal Secret Archives.

The point of view of the Holy See had by the Pope's orders been sent to the nuncio in a long cypher letter from Cinzio Aldobrandini of August 1st, 1593.[1] They had reason to hope in Rome that Sigismund would take these observations into account, as Malaspina again reported in September concerning the firm intentions of the king, and his unwillingness to receive the crown from the hands of an heretical archbishop.[2] But the circumstances were stronger than his good will, for Duke Charles threatened to declare any other form of coronation than this invalid.[3] On February 19th, in the magnificent cathedral of Upsala, Sigismund had the crown placed upon his head by the Bishop of Vesteras.[4] His consort did not receive the unction, for this descendant of the Hapsburgs, in her strong faith, refused to make any compromise.[5]

Malaspina was quite in agreement with her. He had threatened to enter a protest, and it was for that reason that Sigismund had concealed from him the reply of the two

[1] See *ibid.*, pp. 469-471.

[2] *Report of Malaspina, September 23, 1593, *ibid.*

[3] See *report of Malaspina of March 8, 1594 (Papal Secret Archives) in App. No. .

[4] THEINER (II., 348 *seq.*) has published the report of Malaspina's auditor, Ruggiero Salomoni, whicu makes it clear how greatly Sigismund felt himself to be threatened by Charles. Sigismund described his position to the Pope by means of the nuncio : see his *letter dated Upsala, 1594, March 8, Doria Archives, Rome, In this it is stated : " Occurrebant nonnulla quae S.V. quam secretissime significanda duximus, quae quidem ill. legatus S^{tis} V. in notam S^{tis} V. forman redegit. Mittimus igitur hac ipsa S.V. hisce inclusa." The enclosed letter of the king, which was read in consistory, in App. No. 2. A second similar *letter from Sigismund to the Pope, dated Stockholm, 1594, March 17, is also in the Doria Archives, Rome. Even before these letters reached Rome, Clement VIII. had expressed himself very leniently as to the surrender of Sigismund, which had been forced upon him by the circumstances ; see in App. No. 4, the *Instruction to Malaspina of April 30, 1594, Papal Secret Archives.

[5] See *report of Malaspina of March 8, 1594 (Papal Secret Archives) in App. No. 3.

Jesuits.   When two days later the nuncio learned the truth,[1]
he wished to set out for Denmark, where the king had resolved
to prepare for him a courteous welcome, so as to show, as he
said, the barbarous Swedes, how the envoys of sovereigns
should be treated.   But Sigismund succeeded in holding the
nuncio back.   The latter sought to profit by the complaisance
which the king had shown before his coronation, persuading
him to put into writing a protest that the oath had been
extorted from him by force, for according to the universally
accepted doctrine an oath that is thus extorted is void.
Taking his stand upon this, Malaspina persuaded the king to
make adequate concessions to the Catholics, since, as had
been the case with himself in Poland, and with the Emperor
in Germany, he was bound by oath to favour the Catholic
party.[2]   In conformity with this, before his departure, the
king conferred offices and titles upon Catholics as well, and
obliged the four lieutenants, although they were Protestants,
to swear to protect the Catholics and their religion.   Sigismund
acquired two houses in Stockholm and Upsala, in which he
established chapels for the Catholics who still remained, and
installed a priest.   Two other Catholic priests were sent by
him to the ancient and celebrated convent of Vadstena, which
had almost miraculously survived all the storms.[3]

Even before this change of attitude, of which Sigismund
sent a report to the Pope,[4] had become generally known, the

[1] See *ibid.*

[2] See in App. No. 13, the *Relatione dello Stato di
Suetia, Vallicella Library, Rome.   The text of the passage
concerned was incorrectly given by RANKE, Päpste, II., 250 *seq.*,
and the passage is also wrongly interpreted.   It is wrong when
Ranke, *loc. cit.* says : " Sigismund, in order to free himself from
all the obligations which he had undertaken upon oath, took
a contrary oath to the opposing party."   In the opinion of
Malaspina, the oath which had been extorted by force implied no
obligations.

[3] See in App. No. 13 the *Relatione dello Stato di Suetia,
loc. cit.

[4] See his *letter in App. No. 2.   Doria Archives, Rome.

Lutheran preachers, exulting in the victory which they had
won over the king at Upsala, had become guilty of grave
excesses.   They openly deplored the fact that Sigismund had
allowed himself to be blinded by the tricks of Papistry, as
they called it.   When the king and queen, in accordance with
ancient usage, had washed the feet of twelve beggars, the
Lutheran pastor, Eric Schepjerus, delivered a discourse on
Easter Sunday against this work of charity, and forbade
anyone to give alms to those beggars, so that these
unfortunates almost died of hunger.[1]   Again, the circumstance
that Sigismund asked the Pope to act as sponsor to his
daughter,[2] who was born in May, gave rise to fresh attacks
upon the king.   Moreover, disgraceful disputes broke out
between Poland and Sweden.   We cannot wonder then that
Sigismund felt the ground giving way under his feet when he
saw everyone in a state of irritation against him in his Swedish
kingdom.[3]

The news from Poland was such as to make the return of
the king appear to be urgently necessary,[4] and when Sigismund
had provided, as far as he could, for the security of his sovereignty in Sweden, he embarked once more in the middle of
July, 1594.[5]   Malaspina took his place in the principal ship,
so that the standard of the Holy See once more floated over
the waters of the Baltic.   While on the high seas the nuncio
wrote a report to Rome, in which he drew a retrospective
picture of the events of which he had been a witness.   In
this the nuncio makes it appear that the complaisance shown
by Sigismund towards the religious problem at the advice

[1] See RÜHS, II., 275.

[2] See the brief of February 17, 1594, in THEINER, II., Doc.
p. 95. The *letter of thanks from Queen Anna to Clement VIII.
dated Stockholm, 1594, June 27, in which she informs him of the
death of her daughter, who had died soon after her baptism, in
Doria Archives, Rome.

[3] See THEINER, II., 276 seq.

[4] Cf. *Ragguaglio (supra, p. 89, n. 1) Vallicella Library,
Rome.

[5] Cf. HURTER, III., 363.

of the Polish " politicians " of his retinue had not silenced
the political aims of the Protestants, but had rather encouraged
them. Sigismund was opposed by his powerful uncle, who
was ambitious and unscrupulous, and by the undisciplined
aristocracy, while the people, instigated by the Protestant
preachers, only recognized the new king in word. The Polish
chancellor was of the opinion that Sigismund, by residing in
Poland, would be far more respected than if he remained
where he was. This may be the will of God, says Malaspina,
but many are of quite another opinion ; Sigismund is to be
counted among the optimists, but how, concludes the nuncio,
can one have confidence in men who have been found wanting
in their loyalty to God ?[1]

This fear was only too well founded. Sigismund had given
Duke Charles, who had solemnly sworn fealty to him at
Upsala, full powers to govern the kingdom in conjunction
with all the councillors, though he had expressly forbidden him
to hold Diets or to introduce new ordinances.[2] In open
defiance of this order, and in spite of the protest of the council
of the kingdom, with which the aristocracy associated themselves, Charles convoked a Diet at Söderköping in the autumn
of 1595, which ventured upon the greatest usurpations of the
rights of Sigismund, and issued decrees for the extermination
of the Catholics who still remained in Sweden. All
" sectaries," so the ordinance ran, who are opposed to the
Protestant religion, must leave the kingdom within six weeks.[3]

This ordinance was at once enforced with a rigour that
often was indistinguishable from cruelty.[4]

This time the death knell had struck for one of the most

---

[1] See in App. No. 6, the *report of Malaspina, August 15, 1594,
Papal Secret Archives.

[2] See RÜHS, II., 279 *seq.*, who defends Sigismund against the
accusation of having left his kingdom without having made the
necessary arrangements for its government.

[3] See BAAZ, Inventarium, IV., 567 ; RANKE, II., 151 *seq.*
Cf. also MESSENIUS, Secondia illustrata, VIII., Stockholm, 1702.
30.

[4] Opinion of G. DROYSEN, Gesch. der Gegenreformation, 221.

venerated places in Sweden.   After ten years of martyrdoms, there still remained at Vadstena eleven virgins consecrated to God, who with prayer and contemplation faithfully watched over the tomb of one of the greatest of Swedish women, Saint Bridget.   In the eyes of the Lutheran preachers this was an abuse that could no longer be tolerated, and the nuns were driven out, after they had been submitted to disgraceful tortures in the presence of Duke Charles, in order to make them apostatize from their religious convictions.   The church of the convent was despoiled and the library dispersed.   With the help of Sigismund eight of the exiled nuns found an asylum in Dantzig, while three remained in Sweden ; only one was faithless to her vows and religion.[1]

After the few Catholic priests who were still carrying on their work in Sweden had been banished from the kingdom,[2] Archbishop Angermann of Upsala undertook a great visitation of the churches, in the course of which all traces of the ancient faith were destroyed with violence.   " With un-relenting fury," says a Protestant historian, " all the sacred images were destroyed, and all the monuments of the past, which had for long been the objects of deep veneration, were broken down."[3]   The people were forcibly compelled to assist at Protestant worship, and those who failed to do so were scourged.   Angermann had this chastisement carried out under his own supervision.[4]   All Catholic ceremonial which had remained in use since 1593 onwards was abolished. It was then made manifest how little the Swedish people had understood Protestant doctrines in their true significance. Above all the country folk murmured against these proceed-ings, and attributed the bad harvests to the abolition of the remains of the ancient faith, which had always been dear to them.   How enduring was the attachment of the people to the ecclesiastical usages of their fathers was shown by the fact

---

[1] See MESSENIUS, VIII., 31 seq. ; RÜHS, II., 85.
[2] See MESSENIUS, VIII., 32.
[3] RÜHS, II., 285.
[4] See RANKE, II., 252.

that even in 1602 the peasants of Svintuna remonstrated with
their parish priest because he had refused to celebrate mass
on the feast of St. Lawrence.[1] Highly significant too was
the fact that the people would not hear above all of the
abolition of the elevation of the host. One who wrote from
Sweden was of the opinion that many of the country folk
would once again become Catholics, if they could be allowed
to have the mass in their native tongue.[2] The brutality
with which the destruction of Catholic memories was carried
out was bound to scandalize the minds of such people. It
sounds incredible, but is vouched for by credible witnesses,
that a Lutheran preacher, who had taught a crow to babble
a few words, made it express its sorrow at being excluded
from heaven, whereupon he baptized the bird according to
the Catholic rite.[3]

Just as had been the case at Vadstena, where the splendid
silver reliquaries of St. Eric, St. Bridget and St. Catherine
were destroyed, no consideration was shown for the precious
memorials of the early history of the country, so was it in
other places as well. The statue of the saintly king, Eric of
Sweden, was dragged from a parish church into the open air,
and a soldier was ordered to fire his musket at it : the ball
came back and killed the man, an occurrence which made a
profound impression on the people.[4]

Sigismund was not blind to the attachment of the common
people to the ancient faith, nor to the indignation which the
despotic rule of Charles aroused among the nobles. But
Sigismund could not bring himself to the point of making a
fresh attempt to recover his kingdom, which his perjured uncle

---

[1] See GEIJER, II., 299 n. 1. In Finland as well the people
wished to retain the old Catholic customs ; see SCHYBERGSON,
Gesch. Finnlands, Gotha, 1896, 154.

[2] See the *report of September 21, 1596, in THEINER, II., 68 ;
cf. ibid., 49.

[3] See in App. No. 13, the *Relatione dello Stato di Suetia,
Vallicella Library, Rome.

[4] See ibid.

had stolen from him[1] by revolutionary methods, for he was temperamentally averse to any resolute action.[2] He constantly thought of returning to Sweden, and felt remorse for the weakness which he had shown in order to bring about his coronation. He once confessed to the nuncio Malaspina that he saw the chastisements of God in the various calamities which had fallen upon him since then, above all the death of his wife. For the future, he told the nuncio, he would at all costs do nothing further to burden his conscience.[3]

This news revived in Rome the hope of the recovery of Sweden for the Catholic faith.[4] A memorial which was drawn

[1] " Very rarely were any more rebellious measures employed to save the national (sic) monarchy ! Sweden stood firm amid its glorious revolution," says DROYSEN, Gesch. der Gegensreformation, 222.

[2] See GEIJER, II., 287.

[3] See in App. No. 13, the *Relatione, etc.   Vallicella Library, Rome.

[4] The first tidings, which were too optimistic, had raised great hopes in Rome, see PARUTA, Dispacci, II., 131, 152.   To a letter from Sigismund to the Pope, of September 16, 1593, Clement VIII. replied on December 16 (see THEINER, II., Doc. p. 88 seq.) and caused it to be read to the Cardinals in consistory on December 20, 1593 ; see Acta consist. card. S. Severinae, Cod. Barb., XXVI., 5, III., Vatican Library, and the *Relatio gestorum et dictorum in consist. die 20 December, 1593, in the Rospigliosi Archives, Rome, t. 55. Sigismund's ambassador for Poland and Sweden made his obedientia to the Pope on January 17, 1594 (see THEINER, loc. cit., 90).   In spite of the bad news contained in Sigismund's letter of March 1594 (see supra, pp. 97 seq), Clement VIII. still hoped in the autumn of 1594 for a successful issue to Sigismund's efforts on behalf of the Swedish Catholics ; see the brief of October 29, 1594, in THEINER, loc. cit., 92 seq.   At the consistory on December 2, 1594, information as to Sweden, which must have been unsatisfactory, was given, but on the other hand, at the consistory of June 19, 1595, Clement VIII. reported an improvement in Sweden, saying that " *quod Carolus ille dux non est adeo infestus catholicis eo quod ecclesia illa in arce N. frequentatur etaim ab haereticis."   Acta consist. card. S. Severinae, loc. cit., Vatican Library.

up in the Eternal City at that time by one who was well acquainted with affairs in Sweden, brought out, among other things, the European importance of such an event.[1]   Finland, in the hands of a Catholic prince, would become of decisive importance in the relations of the Church with Russia. From thence the Muscovite kingdom could be successfully attacked, and that province could also furnish the infantry which was lacking in Poland.   Even if it should not come to war with Russia, the possession of Finland would always exercise a decisive pressure upon the Muscovites. The author of the memorial enlarges in detail upon the importance of the ports of Kalmar and Elfsborg in Westgothland. Anyone who held Kalmar was the master of the Baltic, and could also take possession of the Duchy of Prussia, as it might be taken for granted that the house of Brandenburg would never consent to the restoration of the ancient Church.[2] It would perhaps be of even greater importance if the beautiful harbour of Elfsborg, which had such a splendid situation, were in the hands of a Catholic.   If the King of Spain were to be given a base there for his fleet, he would be in a position to cause so much annoyance to the kingdom of Elizabeth, which was only three days distant, that she would have plenty to do without attacking the West Indies. An alliance between Sigismund and Spain, on the express condition that the latter should bear the expense of garrisoning Elfsborg, would greatly consolidate the power of the king, both in Poland and in Sweden.

All these projects were frustrated by the energetic if treacherous activity of Charles, for whom Sigismund was no match.[3] From the time of his departure from Sweden, said Malaspina in August, 1597, Sigismund, for the protection of

[1] See in App. No. 13 the *Relatio, etc., Vallicella Library, Rome, from which it is clear that the author knew of the *Ragguaglio (*supra*, p. 89, n. 1).

[2] The passage concerned, from the *Relatione di Polonia by Malaspina (Vallicella Library, Rome) was given in part, though without indication as to its source, by RANKE (II., 254).

[3] *Cf.* SVEN TUNBERG 83 *seqq.*, 142 *seqq.*

his rights, had confined himself to severe words, while Charles
in the meantime cleverly and astutely gathered all the power
into his own hands.[1]   As Sigismund's adherents had no one
to support them they could easily be driven out.   Charles
also succeeded in getting possession of Elfsborg and Kalmar,
and successfully began a war against Finland.[2]   One after
another the important positions fell into the hands of Charles,
and in proportion as the lawful king showed himself inert
did the duke seek to win popularity.   The preachers were
already on his side, and he knew well how to win over the
country folk.   Many were tricked by a report that he was
acting in union with Sigismund.   He cleverly described the
latter as not caring about the Swedes, saying that he would
never leave Poland to come to Sweden.[3]   Sigismund never
really fathomed his uncle, and it may be seen from the negotiations which he carried on with Charles, by means of his
ambassador, Samuel Lascý, how he still hoped to come to
terms with him.[4]

   The Diet which assembled at Arboga in February, 1597,
had resolved that Sigismund must be invited by means of an
embassy to visit his kingdom ; but this project remained on
paper.   Sigismund realized that he would have to act with
decision if he did not wish to lose Sweden.   He then made
known his resolve to go thither at once, and for that purpose
summoned the fleet to Dantzig.   Charles, in reply, obliged the
States to enact, at two further Diets, held in February and
June, 1598, at Upsala and Vadstena, that they pledged themselves, even at the cost of their lives and property to the
observation of the earlier decrees, saying that they were ready
to suffer anything rather than allow violence or persecution
to be inflicted on the duke or any of their number on that
account.[5]   After Sigismund had waited in vain for the Swedish
fleet, and had failed to obtain ships from the Hanseatic

---

[1] See report of Malaspina of August 17, 1597, *ibid.*, 146 *seqq.*
[2] See GEIJER, II., 302 *seq.*
[3] See report of Malaspina cited *supra*, n. 1.
[4] See SVEN TUNBERG, 49 *seqq.*, 67 *seqq.*
[5] See GEIJER, II., 303.

League,[1] he had recourse to the desperate step of forcing English merchant vessels to make the crossing, which was done from Dantzig in July, 1598. He took with him 5,000 Polish troops and a brilliant court, and on July 30th landed at Kalmar, which at once opened its gates to him.[2]

What were his prospects ? Not over favourable, according to the description of the Swedish exiles, but at the same time not altogether hopeless, since many Swedes, and among them the majority of the councillors of the kingdom, even though they were Protestant in their sympathies, did not approve of Charles governing the kingdom against the express wishes of the lawful king, and who, throwing aside the mask, would have raised the banner of revolt.[3] Sigismund's principal mistake was that he had begun his enterprise too late, and with an insufficient number of troops. An adversary so determined and cunning as Charles had to be opposed by an overwhelming force.

In spite of this, the undertaking, which was followed with the greatest attention in Rome, opened favourably. A great part of Finland remained loyal to the legitimate sovereign, while Stockholm, the capital, declared for Sigismund.[4] After having parleyed for a month without any result, the army took the field. At first the fortunes of war smiled upon Sigismund, but his generosity towards Charles after his first victory and his unwillingness to shed Swedish blood, led

[1] Cf. J. PAUL in Hist. Zeitschr., CXXXIII., 448.

[2] See GEIJER, 304. The question whether a Papal representative should accompany Sigismund, was decided in the negative by Malaspina, since, should affairs turn out favourably, one could be sent at once ; see SVEN TUNBERG, 154 seq.

[3] See BIAUDET, I., v.

[4] See GEIJER, II., 304 ; SCHÄFER, Gesch. Danemarks, V., 299. In Sigismund's retinue there was to be found his court preacher, the Jesuit Laterna, who had, however, to return to Poland for reasons of health. On his way back he fell into the hands of the soldiers of Duke Charles, who drowned him ; see MESSENIUS, Secondia illustr., VIII., 68 ; JUVENCIUS, V., 262 ; J. METZLER, Martyrergestalten aus der schwed. Missionsgesch., in Xaverius-Missionskalender, 1923.

to this initial advantage being quickly lost, and the disastrous battle near Stängebro, not far from Linköping, which was fought on September 25th, 1598, obliged Sigismund to return to Poland.[1] He continued thence to carry on his struggle with Charles, but once again his plans, which were supported by Spain, were shipwrecked owing to the passive resistance of the Hanseatic cities.[2] Charles, who was Sigismund's superior in energy and strength of will,[3] thus remained the victor. In July, 1599, he caused Sigismund to be deposed by the Diet, and then began a bloody persecution of all those who wished to remain loyal to their lawful sovereign and the ancient religion.[4] Clement VIII.[5] lived long enough to see Charles, overbearing all opposition, place on his own head the crown,[6] which he had thus taken by violence from his nephew.

[1] A still unpublished report by N. Sergardi, an Italian who accompanied Sigismund, on his second expedition to Sweden (*Breve compendio hist. del passaggio in Suetia di Sigismondo III., 1598) is preserved in the Library at Siena, Cod. K. III., 58.

[2] See J. PAUL, *loc. cit.*, 449 *seq.*

[3] See BIAUDET, II., 1 (1912) x. *seq.*

[4] See GEIJER, II., 306 *seq.* ; THEINER, II., 70 *seq.* BIAUDET (I., v.) describes the measures taken by Charles as " une série de répressions barbares." The cruelty of Charles is also brought out in the poem by Joh. Messenius " The Catholic martyrs of Sweden " in Vol. 9 of his *Secondia illustrata*, and also by ODHNER, Lärobok i Sveriges, Norges och Danmarks historia[6], Stockholm, 1886, 148 *seq.* ; LEINBERG, Om finske studerande i Jesuitcollegier, in the periodical *Histor. arkisto*, XI. (Helsingissä, 1891), 196 *seq.*, 203 *seq.* BIAUDET : Om finske studerande i Jesuitcollegier, *ibid.*, XIX. (1903), 178 *seqq.* gives further information concerning the Jesuit missionaries.

[5] *Cf.* the *letter addressed to Clement VIII. by Count Eric of Visinburg, March 20, 1602, Doria Archives, Rome.

[6] BIAUDET (I., v. *seq.*, 335 *seq.*) promises to give fuller information concerning an anti-Protestant league which was projected at that time in Rome, and which was to be especially directed against Sweden. STEINHUBER (I., 360 *seq.*) shows how Sigismund endeavoured to get young Catholic Swedes to enter the Germanicum.

CHAPTER IV.

PROGRESS OF CATHOLIC RESTORATION IN POLAND.—REUNION OF THE SCHISMATIC RUTHENIANS.—THE FALSE DEMETRIUS.

SOME compensation for the loss of Sweden was afforded by the consoling progress of the Catholic religion in the Kingdom of Poland. At first things had been by no means encouraging, for although Sigismund III. was genuinely attached to Catholicism, there were nevertheless serious restrictions upon freedom of worship in Poland in consequence of the right which the aristocracy had extorted from King Henry III. in 1572, and which had been confirmed by his successors, of deciding their own religion and that of their subjects.[1] To this was added the fact that Sigismund was in no sense a man of energy and resoluteness.[2] His weakness in the matter of distributing the offices of State degenerated into a favouring of the Protestants.[3] But little by little the Pope's representative, the nuncio Malaspina, as well as the higher Polish clergy, and especially the Archbishop of Gnesen, Karnkowski (died 1603), succeeded in leading Sigismund to a different course of action.[4] In course of time the change in the king became so complete that a well-informed correspondent was able to report to Rome in 1596 that in the whole world there was

[1] For the so-called Confederation of Warsaw see Vol. of this work. An opinion by the Jesuit Toledo " *De juramento Stephani regis Poloniae de impunitate haereticorum " (in Borghese III., 72b, pp. 460 *scqq.*, Papal Secret Archives) puts forward the view : " Juramentum tale multis ex partibus iniquam est. Male emissum multo tamen peius est adimplere."

[2] See PARUTA, Relazione, 431 ; DOLFIN, Relazione, 473.

[3] See E. BARWIŃSKI in : Reformacye w Polsce (ed. KOT) I. (1921).

[4] See *ibid.*

no such obedient son of the Church as Sigismund III.[1] Clement VIII. therefore always spoke of him in terms of the highest praise. In order to examine more fully the Polish question, the Pope, in the first year of his pontificate, had appointed a special congregation, composed of Cardinals Tagliavia, Galli, Caetani, Salviati, Sforza and Montalto, to whom was added Cinzio Aldobrandini. Minuccio Minucci acted as its secretary.[2]

It was a special joy to the Pope that he was able to satisfy a long-standing wish of the Poles by bringing to an end in the spring of 1594 the process of canonization of St. Hyacinth. On this occasion he recalled how greatly St. Hyacinth was venerated in Poland in 1588 when he had been there as legate.[3]

Besides the duty of watching over ecclesiastical interests, Germanico Malaspina, who was nuncio in Poland from 1592 to 1598, had been charged with the task of encouraging the war against the Turks. Clement VIII. hoped to win over Poland to the great league which he projected against the Turks, and when the king had returned from Sweden in 1594, Malaspina laboured in every possible way for this purpose ; it seemed, however, that he had not reckoned sufficiently on the difficulties.[4] When, therefore, the success which the Pope so ardently desired, and even expected on the strength

---

[1] *Si è fatto così ossequente il sereniss. Re alla Sede Apost. che in niuna parte del mondo è in maggior authorità essa sede ne li ministri di essa ne l'ordine et giurisdittione eccles. è più difesa et aiutata da Re alcuno di quello ch'è dalla M^{tà} del Re di Polonia, it is stated in an account written in 1598, with the title : *Attioni seguite in Polonia et in Suetia dopo l'assontione al pontificato di N.S^{re} Clemente VIII. a benefitio del Re, del regno et della religione, Cod. N. 34, p. 433 seq., of the Vallicella Library, Rome. Orig. in Borghese, III., 96b, p. 97 seq., Papal Secret Archives.

[2] See SIIEVE, IV., 126 n. 1.

[3] See *Acta consist. card. S. Severinae, March 31, 1594, loc. cit., Vatican Library. Cf. also infra, Chapter VI.

[4] See BENTIVOGLIO, Memorie, 133. Cf. Vita di Msgr. Ces. Speciani, 181 seqq.

of the reports of Malaspina,[1] was not attained, it was resolved in Rome to send a special embassy. Therefore, at the beginning of 1596, the Bishop of Caserta, Benedetto Mandina, who belonged to the Theatine Order, was appointed,[2] and in April of the same year, the Cardinal legate Caetani.[3] The latter left Rome on April 25th with a large retinue and reached Vienna about a month later. The master of ceremonies, Mucantius, who accompanied the legate, wrote a very interesting description of this journey from the point of view of history and culture.[4]

[1] *Cf.* *Acta consist. card. S. Severinae, December 2, 1594, and March 6, 1595, *loc. cit.*, Vatican Library.

[2] *Cf.* Vol. XXIII. of this work, p. 290.   See also B. MANDINAE, congreg. cleric. regul. episc. Casertini, nuntii ad regem senatumque Polonum Apost. Oratio de foedere cum christianis contra Turcam paciscendo habita in comitiis Varsaviae, 3 Cal. April, 1596, printed at Cracow, 1596, and also ROBERTI TURNERI ORATIONES, II., 80 *seqq.*   *Cf.* also *" Successo de comitii di Polonia circa la lega contra il Turco," dated Warsaw, 1596, May 14, in Cod. N. 35, p. 133 *seq.*, Vallicella Library, Rome.   *Ibid.* 108 *seq.* *" Motivi ne Polachi per difficoltare la conclusione della lega contro il Turco con le risposte alli detti motivi, 1596."   LÜNIG (Staatsconsilia, I., 487) makes the " reflection as to whether it is better for the Poles to break the peace with the Turks or to maintain it, and of the disputation concerning the reasons for and against held in 1597 before Pope Clement VIII."

[3] *Cf.* Vol. XXIII. of this work, p. 291.

[4] *" Itinerario o diario di tutte le cose occorse nel tempo di Clement VII.. nella legatione del card. Gaetano al Re di Polonia libro I e II scritto da Giov. Paolo Mucante, maestro di ceremonie," in Ottob. 2623, Barb. LVI., 103, and LVII., 26, Vatican Library, and in Arm. I., vol. 82, Papal Secret Archives, the dedicatory letter, dated Ferrara, 1598, May 15, to Cardinal C. Aldobrandini. Copy in Cod. 567 of the Palatine Library, Parma.   *Cf.* CIAMPI, I., 157, 349 *seq.*, II., 49 *seq.* ; ZÖCHBAUER, Ein röm. Reisebericht über Osterreich aus dem Jahre 1596, in *Archiv. f. Gesch. der Diöz. Linz*, V. (1909), 75 *seq.*   I have not succeeded in finding the article by O. F. TENCAJOLI : Un légat du Clement VIII. en Pologne, 1596, cited in *Quellen u. Forsch.*, IV., 407.   The

Cardinal Caetani received from Mandina more definite information as to the position of the league while he was at Vienna, where for eight days he enjoyed the hospitality of the Austrian court. They both expected to meet with less difficulties from Poland than from the Emperor, since the Archduke Maximilian, who was intended for the office of commander-in-chief against the Turks, still refused to renounce the title of King of Poland. What would happen, the Poles asked themselves, should the archduke, instead of marching against the Turks, turn his forces against Poland in order to vindicate his supposed claims? To this was added, as Caetani reported to Rome, the dilatoriness of the Emperor's policy, which was averse to applying the proper remedies to any evils. If Maximilian would not renounce his claims to the throne, the legate rightly pointed out, the Poles would offer such a resistance that all efforts would be in vain.[1]

---

*Registro di lettere scritte dal card. E. Caetano nella sua legazione di Polonia in Cod. X.-VI., 13 and 14 of the Casanatense Library, Rome. *Ibid.*, 15 other *documents pertaining to this legation.

[1] *Circa la lega Mons. di Caserta, che arrivò qui alli 27, me n'ha dato gran luce. Convenghiamo in questo, che i Polacchi siano per caminar bene, ma dubitiamo che dalla parte degli Imperiali non si zoppichi, poichè quanto al punto della renuntia del titolo, secondo che me ne scrive il vescovo di Cremona [C. Speciani], arciduca Massimiliano par che non ci venga bene attaccandosi a certe speranze che hanno più fiori che frutti e possono anzi deluderlo che aiutarlo oltre che il vederlo disegnato capo e generale di questa impresa fomenta la sospettione de Polacchi che habbiano almeno apparente ragione di dubitarne tanto più vedendolo armato e munito et atto a poter piegare l'armi e le forze communi a libito de'suoi proprii e privati interessi. S'aggionge a questo che l'espeditioni della corte Cesarea nel presente negotio vanno lente e fredde e par che si cammini a fine non di curare l'infermo, ma di sostenerlo co'fomenti e panni caldi più tosto che con remedii opportuni e gagliardi. Chiara cosa è, che senza questa cessione i Polacchi non solo staranno duri, ma ostinatissimi e sarà vana ogni fatica che s'impieghi in questa pratica se non si rimuove la pietra di quello scandalo. Casanatense Library, Rome, *loc. cit.*

Caetani decided to send Mandina to the Imperial court, after which he was to come to Poland to report.

On June 16th the Cardinal legate reached Cracow,[1] but it was not until August 8th that he was able to inaugurate the negotiations between the Polish delegates and those of the Emperor at the Radziwill palace. Rudolph II. had placed the distinguished Bishop of Breslau, Andreas von Jerin, at the head of his representatives.[2]

The inaugural address of Caetani to the envoys of the Emperor and the King of Poland, besides explaining the efforts which the Pope was making for a crusade, expressed a fervent hope that they would give effect to his plans by coming to an agreement as to the financial contributions and the preparations for the war. In the reply which he made in the name of the Imperialists the Bishop of Breslau praised the zeal of the Pope, and also brought out the efforts of the Hapsburgs for the protection of their hereditary territories and of the whole of Christendom against their sworn enemy, and appealed to the chivalrous sentiments and the ancient military glory of Poland, which in close alliance with the Imperialists, could destroy that dreaded foe for their own salvation and that of others. At the end the bishop called attention to an inveterate and serious defect of Polish assemblies : namely that owing to the vehemence of the speeches and the excessive character of the demands, the desired object was too often lost sight of and an alliance rendered impossible. The orator of the Polish representatives, Bishop Goslicki of Przemysl, thanked the Pope and the Emperor for their complaisance, but asked of the latter, deeds instead of words, as well as the fulfilment of the indispensable conditions.[3] These were at once put into writing. Caetani was unwearied in his efforts to reconcile the warring interests, and in turning the attention of the Poles from their just insistence upon Maximilian's oath of

---

[1] Detailed description in Mucantius, *Itinerario, loc. cit.

[2] See JERIN-GESESS, Biscof Andreas Jerin, Neisse, 1900, 84 seq., and NAEGELE in Katholik, 1911, I., 364 seq.

[3] See JERIN-GESESS, loc. cit.

renunciation to the principal point at issue, the war against
the Turks.   The Bishop of Breslau had great difficulty in
answering the attacks, which were to a great extent justified,
upon Austrian policy, and, in order to come to a discussion
of the league, in dealing with the just demand for a renunciation of all claims to the Polish throne.   At length the Polish
representatives gave way, on condition that the Archduke
Maximilian would take an oath of renunciation within a
determined period, a period which was extended until
November 11th, at the proposal of Caetani.   Thus, with great
difficulty, an agreement was arrived at concerning the league
on August 31st.[1]

The hopes expressed by the legate at the conclusion, that
the still outstanding difficulties would soon be overcome, were
not, however, realized, as neither the Emperor nor the King
of Poland would accept the terms agreed upon.[2]

Caetani's journey to see Sigismund III. at Warsaw, which
he entered on September 10th,[3] proved of no avail, and at
his first audience, which he received on the 24th, the difficulties which were finally to render his mission void were
brought forward.   The profound distrust of the King of
Poland was expressed in his opening words : that very morning
he had received news that peace negotiations were being carried
on between the Porte and the Emperor at Constantinople,
through the mediation of the English ambassador.[4]

At the end of October the legate followed the King of
Poland to Cracow, where the interment of his aunt, Queen
Anna,[5] who had died on August 9th, was to take place.
Caetani again laboured on behalf of the league at Cracow,

[1] See *Acta et gesta legationis Poloniae et tractionis Cracoviensis super negotio confoederationis faciendae inter Papam,
Imperatorem, regem et regnum Poloniae, 1596, in Ottob. 3184,
pp. 226-314, Vatican Library.

[2] See JERIN-GESESS, loc. cit., 97 seq., and NAEGELE, loc. cit., 369.

[3] Cf. the report of Mucantius, *Itinerario, Papal Secret Archives.

[4] Cf. the *report of Caetani, dated Warsaw, 1596, September 24,
Cod. X.-VI., 14, of the Casanatense Library, Rome.

[5] Described in detail by Mucantius, Itinerario, loc. cit.

while he also interested himself in getting Imperial representatives sent to the Diet at Warsaw. The Poles pointed
out that a league was very dangerous since Rudolph might
die and the succession of the House of Austria to the Empire
was very uncertain. In these circumstances a league against
the Turks would expose Poland, as the weaker party, to grave
danger.[1]

In spite of the unfavourable conditions, Caetani went in
February 1597 to the Diet at Warsaw.[2] There, in the presence
of the king and all the senators he delivered a discourse which
lasted for three quarters of an hour, in which he urged war
against the Turks, pointing out in the most emphatic way the
dangers which threatened Christendom.[3] But his words fell
on deaf ears. The Diet did nothing, and the laments which
Skarga made in his celebrated discourse that followed were
only too well justified.[4] Discouraged and unwell, the legate
resolved to return to Italy. He went by way of Lowicz,
Gnesen, Ostrava in Moravia, Olmütz, Nikolsburg, Vienna,
Graz, Villach, Pontebba, Treviso, Padua and Ferrara,[5] to

[1] *I Polacchi dicono l'Imperatore è mortale e la successione
dell'Imperio in casa d'Austria non è certa e l'esporre il regno a
queste incertezze con evidentissimo pericolo non è resolutione da
buon politico, atteso che le leghe possono sciogliersi et all'hora
chi può meno suol devenir preda da chi può più e rimaner solo
alle botte ; e questi dubii si aumentano per non si veder fatta
l'elettione del Re di Romani. Caetani in his *report addressed
to C. Aldobrandini, dated Cracow, 1597, January 13, Cod. X. VI.,
14, of the Casanatense Library, Rome.

[2] Cf. Diaria comitiorum Poloniae anni 1597, in Script. rer.
Pol., XX., Cracow, 1907.

[3] Cf. Mucanzio, *Itinierario, Papal Secret Archives.

[4] See BERGA, 247.

[5] See the detailed description of the return journey in the
*Itinerario of Mucantius, loc. cit. together with a report of the
impressions of the Cardinal legate of the religious conditions in
the places through which he passed, and of the honour paid to
the representative of the Pope. Mucantius also gives the whole
of the scholastic drama performed at Graz by the " scolari della
prima classe di grammatica " of the Jesuit School.

Rome, where he gave the Pope a full report. From this Clement VIII. learned with sincere satisfaction that in Poland, owing to the piety of the king, the zeal of the bishops, and the labours of the Jesuits, religion was visibly reviving.[1]

Malaspina was profoundly disturbed by this two-fold mission of special legates. Often made the subject of attacks and of severe judgments,[2] it must have seemed to him an emancipation when he was recalled from the Polish nunciature in 1598. At the beginning of 1599 Clement VIII. appointed Claudio Rangoni, Bishop of Reggio Emilia, to succeed him.[3]

In his final report Malaspina drew an interesting picture of the state of affairs in the kingdom where he had resided for eight years.[4] After he had described in the most lucid manner the peculiar constitution of Poland, where the powerful aristocracy did not permit of the development of a strong monarchical power, as well as the dangers to which the kingdom was exposed, threatened as it was on the north by

[1] In the *Relatio card. Caetani ad Papam de sua legatione (Ott. 3184, p. 143 seq., Vatican Library) it is stated : " Religio catholica in Polonia, ut apostoli verbis utar, fructificat ac crescit et novis quotidie haereticorum conversionibus et animarum lucris augetur." Then follows praise of the " eximia pietas imo sanctitas " of the king, and of the zealous labours of almost all the bishops, whose greatest helpers are the Jesuits.

[2] Cf. PARISI, Epistolografia, I., 196 ; CIAMPI, II., 51.

[3] His *Instructions, February 22, 1599, in Nunziat. div. 239, p. 238 seq., Papal Secret Archives, and in Cod. H. 155, n. 2 of the Ambrosian Library, Milan. The *briefs of January 11, 1599, concerning the legation, in Arm. 44, t. 43, n. 13-29 (cf. n. 113 : " Regi Poloniae," dated " Cal. Mart."), Papal Secret Archives. Cf. THEINER, III., 271 seq. For Claudio Rangoni see COTTAFAVI, Il seminario di Reggio nell'Emilia, Rome, 1907, 3 seqq.

[4] See *" Relatione di Polonia al vescovo di Caserta del 1600," Cod. N. 33, pp. 120-144, Vallicella Library, Rome ; ibid. Cod. N. 35, pp. 235-270, and in Urb. 837, pp. 480-512, of the Vatican Library, here with the name of Malaspina. RANKE (II., 254 ; III., 90*) made use of the report without knowing its author, and without giving the source. A Polish translation in Relacye Nuncyuszów Apost., II., 75 seq.

the Swedish Lutherans, on the east by the Orthodox Russians and the Cossacks, and on the south by the Turks, he could see no other hope of salvation than in an alliance with Austria and Transylvania, and in the re-establishment of unity of faith at home. As to the former, Malaspina, at the end of his mission, had witnessed the oath by which the Archduke Maximilian renounced the Polish crown (May 8th, 1598).[1] But this, as he fully realized, by no means removed all the obstacles that stood in the way of an alliance with Austria. Malaspina also formed a just estimate of the difficulties which the conditions in Poland put in the way of a Catholic revival, although he by no means despaired of the possibility of one day seeing unity of faith restored there. He gave his successor a number of valuable counsels for the realization of that purpose. Above all, the nuncio should encourage the king in his good intentions, and maintain unity among the Catholics, so that they might oppose a united front to their adversaries in the Diets. The nuncio, Malaspina pointed out, must prove himself the impartial and dispassionate servant of the Holy See, for thus he would be in a better position to maintain unity among the Catholics, clergy, laity and the sovereign. If disputes should break out, then he could more easily act as peacemaker, since the Poles would rather have a representative of the Holy See to act in that capacity than one of their own countrymen.[2]

A brief but weighty summary belonging to August 1598 shows how Malaspina had devoted all his powers to the restoration of the Church in Poland. Special credit is due to him for having induced the bishops to follow the good example set them by the Pope in visiting their dioceses and holding diocesan synods, a thing that had been neglected for a long time past.[3] Clement VIII. had encouraged these

---

[1] Cf. HIRN in *Mitteil. des österr. Instit.*, Erg. Bd., IV., 248 *seq.*

[2] Relatione di Polonia, *loc. cit.*

[3] *" Si è indotto li ecclesiastici che a imitatione di N.S. hanno visitate le diocesi, fatto li sinodi diocesani che da molte decine d'anni si era tralasciato et hora cercano di potere celebrare un concilio nazionale o provinciale " (Attioni seguite in Polonia, etc.,

efforts in every way, and had taken a special interest in the visitation of the Polish Dominicans[1] and Carmelites.[2] The Pope's representative, Alexander Komulovič, who was labouring in eastern Europe on behalf of the anti-Turkish war, undertook by Malaspina's direction, a visitation of the great diocese of Wilna,[3] which, after the translation of Cardinal Georg Radziwill to Cracow in 1591, had been left without a bishop. In 1596 Komulovič succeeded in persuading Sigsmund to appoint Bernard Maciejowski to Wilna, thus giving that diocese a new and virtuous bishop.[4]

As far as was possible, Malaspina endeavoured to enforce the decrees of the Council of Trent, which had been accepted in Poland.   In this respect too his labours were crowned with much success.[5]   The nuncio had also worked for the restoration of the Catholic Church in Poland in other ways as well ; in many of the cities the heretics and schismatics had taken away their churches from the adherents of the old faith, and

loc. cit., Vallicella Library, Rome).   For the visitation of 1596 *cf.* Script. rer. Pol., XV., 252.   The brief of praise to the Archbishop of Gnesen on account of the provincial synod of July 17, 1598, in THEINER, III., 273 *seq.*   Clement VIII. highly praised the Bishop of Ermland in a *brief to the King of Poland, April 26, 1603, Arm. 44, t. 57, n. 104, Papal Secret Archives.

[1] See the *brief to the " Cancell. Poloniae," August 7, 1593, Arm. 44, t. 34, n. 53, Papal Secret Archives.

[2] See *ibid.*, t. 46, n. 100, the *brief to Sigismund III., April 10, 1602.   Clement VIII. also intervened on behalf of the Orders, in favour of the right of investiture of the abbeys, but did not succeed in obtaining anything from Sigismund, all the more so as Malaspina had adopted the Polish point of view on this matter. See the details in the article by LÜDTKE in *Zeitschr. f. osteurop. Gesch.*, IV. (1914), 7 *seq.*

[3] See PIERLING, II., 359.

[4] See the *report of Cardinal Caetani, July 26, 1596, in Cod. X.-VI., 14, of the Casanatense Library, Rome.

[5] *" Se bene il Concilio era stato ricevuto non era tuttavia posto in essecutione onde restavano più tosto illaqueate le anime che assicurate.   Si è in buona parte posto in uso la essecutione di esse."   Attioni seguite in Polonia, *loc. cit.*

the number of sacred edifices which had been lost in this way was about 4,000. Malaspina encouraged the bishops to enforce their legal rights over the ecclesiastical buildings which had been erected by their labours, and often with the help of the Holy See. King Sigismund strongly supported these efforts, and when the Protestants had recourse to him, appealing to the confederation of Warsaw, which had ensured equal protection to both confessions, he remarked that this did not apply to the churches which had been usurped contrary to all rights.[1] In this way by 1598 at least half the churches had been recovered.[2]

Malaspina reported that the exemplary manner of life of the king had brought many Protestants back to the Church.[3] Great influence in this respect had been exercised by the fact that the King of Poland had in his hands the conferring of nearly all the civil offices as well as many ecclesiastical ones, in all some 20,000.[4] Before this time Hosius, Bolognetti and Clement VIII. himself, when he was Cardinal legate,[5] had advised the making use of this circumstance on behalf of the Catholic cause. This was first done in the time of Stephen Báthory,[6] and from 1592 onwards in an ever increasing degree by Sigismund III.; even to the senate, into which many Protestants had made their way, none but Catholics were now admitted. The change which was effected in this way was

---

[1] Cf. RANKE, II., 244.

[2] *" Havevano li heretici et scismatici usurpate dà quattro mila parocchie; se ne sono ricuperate intorno a due mila." Attioni seguite in Polonia, loc. cit.

[3] *Relatione di Polonia. Cod. N. 35, Vallicella Library, Rome.

[4] *[Il Re] ha il pane in mano et lo può distribuire a chi li piace et si non i Polacchi poveri di patrimonio et senza i beni regii cioè palatinati, capitanati, castellanie et altri ufficii et dignità, che sono al numero di circa 20,000 comprese le nominationi et dignità ecclesiastiche non potrebbono vivere con splendore. Relatione di Polonia, loc. cit.

[5] Cf. Vol. XXIII. of this work, App. no. 45, the instructions for M. Barberini, Vatican Library.

[6] Cf. Vol. XX. of this work, p. 393.

so great that in a letter belonging to the latter days of
Malaspina's nunciature it was stated : " If before the pontificate of Our Lord the Pope, it seemed as though heresy were
driving Catholicism into its grave, it is now manifest that
Catholicism is burying the said heresy."[1] There can be
wonder then that Clement VIII. was highly delighted.[2]

In the same way as he had laboured for its external development, so did Malaspina devote his attention to the interior
renewal and consolidation of the ancient Church. He advised
his successor Rangoni above all to see to it that the Papal
juridical authority suffered no usurpation in Poland, that
the bishops fulfilled their duty of residence, and that they
established good seminaries for the training of the secular
clergy, and paid much attention to the filling of the parochial
offices. He also drew the attention of Rangoni to the Catholics
of Livonia, the Duchy of Prussia, Dantzig, Elbing, and the
diocese of Wilna, who were oppressed by the Protestants.
Mixed marriages, which were on the increase in spite of
ecclesiastical prohibitions, called for special vigilance.[3]

[1] *Era il senato pieno di soggetti heretici ; si è purgato di
modo che appena tre sono infatti di heresia et si è indotta S. M[tà]
a non dare offitii ne dignità a persone aliene dalla nostra santa
religione di modo che sicome avanti l'assontione al pontificato di
N. S[re] pareva che la heresia conducesse il cattolicismo alla
sepultura, hora si vede manifestamente che il cattolicismo
seppellisce detta heresia. Attioni seguite in Polonia *loc. cit.*,
Vallicella Library, Rome.

[2] *" Noi restiamo sodisfatto del vostro servitio, stimiamo le
vostre fatiche et ci teniamo obligati di rimunerarle," he said to
Malaspina, according to the latter's report dated Ferrara, August
20, 1598, Borghese, III., 96b, p. 96, Papal Secret Archives.

[3] See *Attioni seguite in Polonia, *loc. cit.* In 1596 Cardinal
Caetani had, at the request of the Bishop of Kulm, addressed a
question to the Inquisition in Rome on a similar matter. Cardinal
Santori replied in a *letter of December 5, 1596, that the Congregation had discussed the matter under the presidency of the Pope :
Non è parso in modo alcuno che si possa permettere ne tollerare
senza peccato che li sacerdoti cattolici coniungano in matrimonio
persone heretiche e benedicano le loro nozze poichè se bene tra

A great misfortune for Poland, of which Queen Anna had complained in 1594 in a letter to Clement VIII., was the great lack of priests.[1] All the more important, then, was the assistance given by the Jesuits, who had proved themselves the loyal co-operators in the work of restoration carried out by Malaspina and the king.[2]

During the pontificate of Clement VIII. the Society of Jesus flourished in Poland to an extraordinary degree, both internally and externally. If hitherto their members had been to a great extent foreigners, namely Italians, Spaniards and Germans, the number of natives now increased, among whom were numbered many of the aristocracy. During the first years of the pontificate of Clement VIII. there were thirteen houses of the Order in Poland, while by 1596 there were already seventeen. There were colleges at Posen, Braunsberg, Wilna, Poltawa, Jaroslaw, Lublin, Nieswiecz, Riga, Dorpat and Polotzk ; professed houses at Cracow, Lemberg, Dantzig and Thorn, and noviciates at Cracow and Riga. To these must be added a special " station " at the royal court, which after-wards became a professed house, when Warsaw became the capital. As a single superior could not govern all these houses, about the end of the century Lithuania was formed

loro il matrimonio si tiene, non di meno i cattolici e i sacerdoti, che v'intervengono, peccano. Di più si desidera maggiore explicatione se quegli heretici tengano il matrimonio per sacra-mento come i primi heretici Luterani e non come i posteriori et i Calvinisti. Di più se nel dubbio [of the Bishop of Kulm] si parla quando tutti doi coniugi sono heretici o vero uno heretico et l'altro cattolico. Cod. X-VI., 14, of the Casanatense Library, Rome.

[1] *" Magna laboramus sacerdotum inopia." Letter of Queen Anna to Clement VIII., dated 1594, die XVII. (sic), copy in Doria Archives, Rome.

[2] Cf. for what follows Litt. ann. Soc. Iesu, 1592, 67 seq. ; 1593, 253 seq. ; 1594-95, 318 seq. ; 1596, 11 seq. ; 1597, 45 seq. ;: 1598, 403 seq. ; 1599, 445 seq. ; 1600, 535 seq. ; 1601, 747 seq. ; 1602, 716 seq. ; 1603, 647 seq. ; 1604, 763 seq. ; 1605, 880 seq. ; IUVENCIUS, III., 239, V., 399 seq. ; ZALESKI, Jesuici w Polsce, I., 2.

into a separate province, with nine houses and about two hundred members ; the Polish province proper contained about the same number of members.

As before, the principal care of the Jesuits in Poland, was devoted, besides their ministry, to instruction and education, because they clearly realized that another generation would have to arise before the work of Catholic restoration could be fully effected. The greater number of the four hundred and more members whom the Society had in Poland were occupied in the education of the young, and they succeeded in imparting a sound education to their pupils besides a sincere piety and a true loyalty to the Catholic faith. The attendance at the Jesuit schools, which soon surpassed all others, was very large. Their academy at Posen, for example, had no fewer than 650 pupils in 1592, of whom the greater number belonged to the aristocracy ; four years later there were 800. The Jesuit school at Wilna could boast of a similar number in 1597.[1] The effect of the Marian congregations which had been set up for the pupils was very beneficial. On festal occasions scholastic dramas in Latin were presented, a thing which was also done elsewhere.

The high reputation enjoyed by these Jesuit institutions led even those of another faith to entrust their children to them. The latter were only asked to be present at the sermons, but the fathers left everything else to their free choice, only taking care that the non-Catholic scholars were not in any way hurt in their feelings ; many of these returned to the Church.[2]

King Sigismund protected the Jesuits in every way he could. It was at his expense that the beautiful Renaissance church of St. Barbara at Cracow was erected, the architect of which was a Jesuit, Giovanni Maria Bernardoni of Milan. This religious, who was distinguished for his great humility, lived for forty-three years in the Society, until his death in 1605.[3]

---

[1] *Litt. ann.*, 1592, 89 ; 1596, 19 ; 1597, 46.

[2] See ZALESKI, I., 2, 377.

[3] *Litt. ann.*, 1605, 881.

The Jesuits did not limit themselves to their ministry in the cities, and missions in the neighbouring and more distant districts were undertaken by almost all their houses. As far as the Carpathians and Hungary, and even beyond the actual borders of Poland, they made their way into the neighbouring territories of Germany and Russia,[1] and brought to those neglected peoples the knowledge of the true Church. They spent themselves in a special way during the epidemics which frequently broke out in Poland, and the courage which they displayed in the service of the sick and dying won the admiration even of their enemies. They showed themselves equally intrepid in the way they attacked the many heresies by means of the public disputations which were then in vogue.[2] At first the fathers found themselves in a difficult position in Polotzk, and in the largely Lutheran cities of Riga, Dantzig and Thorn,[3] but they courageously held their ground. At Thorn where they preached in German, the situation improved so greatly that it was possible in 1598 once again to hold the procession of Corpus Domini.[4]   At Dantzig too they were able to point to considerable successes, but the war with the Swedes gave them great trouble at Riga.[5]

At Cracow and other places the Jesuits also visited the prisons and hospitals. In the ancient Polish city which was the coronation place of the kings, the Confraternity of the Misericordia, at whose mass the king on one occasion assisted incognito, became very wide-spread,[6] while the house of the Jesuits founded in 1598 at Warsaw attained to a special importance.[7] They preached in German, Polish and Lithuanian at Wilna, where, as at Dorpat, they established the Confraternity of the Blessed Sacrament for men and

---

[1] *Ibid.*, 1594-95, 345 ; 1599, 197, 453 ; 1601, 768.
[2] Werher, Gesch. der polem. Lit., IV., 871 *seq.*
[3] *Litt. ann.*, 1596, 60 *seq.* ; 1597, 65, 82 ; 1599, 479.
[4] *Ibid.*, 1598, 453.
[5] *Ibid.*, 1600, 563 ; 1601, 786 ; 1604, 729.
[6] *Ibid.*, 1594-95, 348 ; 1598, 423 *seq.* ; 1599, 451.
[7] *Ibid.*, 1598, 403, 439, 453.

women ;[1] Livonia too, where priests were greatly lacking, was evangelized with special zeal.[2]

The Polish bishops fully appreciated the valuable collaboration of the Jesuits. Above all the Bishops of Luzk, Lemberg, Posen, Riga, Dorpat, Kulm and Wenden encouraged them in a special way. The Bishops of Posen and Luzk asked for the fathers to make visitations of their dioceses. The Bishop of Jaroslaw got them to give the exercises to his clergy, and the Bishop of Pultowa entrusted to them his seminary.[3]

The Jesuits in Poland also showed a special activity as writers, and the fathers who above all distinguished themselves in this direction, besides Peter Skarga, whose reputation had spread far beyond Poland, were Benedict Herbest, Adrian Jung and Jakob Wujek, to whom Catholic Poland was indebted for an excellent translation of the Bible.[4]

The conversion of the Jews, who were so numerous in Poland, also attracted their zeal, and in this respect they met with as notable a success as in the conversion of the heretics, and the renewal of the clergy, who had in many ways become decadent. As missionaries, preachers, writers, controversialists and educators, they kept one purpose in view : the complete recovery of Poland for the Catholic Church.

It was not only to the moral and religious renewal of the people, and their liberation from heresy, that the Jesuits devoted their labours ; they also worked for the removal of the separation which since the beginning of the XVIth century had involved the Ruthenians (Little Russians) in Galicia, Podolia, Wolynia and Ukrainia as well as the natives

---

[1] *Ibid.*, 1594-95, 338 ; 1599, 437.

[2] *Ibid.*, 1597, 75.

[3] *Ibid.* 1594-95 325 *seq.* 334 ; 1596, 18, 25, 31, 41, 49, 57 ; 1597, 67, 78 ; 1604, 733. Light is thrown upon the state of the various dioceses by the *reports of the Bishops of Przemysl, Samogitia, Wilna, and Ermland of the end of the sixteenth century and the beginning of the seventeenth, in the Archives of the Congregation of the Council, Rome, already used by Prof. Boratyński in 1901, but not yet published.

[4] See WERNER, *loc. cit.*, 344 *seq.*

of White and Black Russia in the Grand Duchy of Lithuania.
The famous Peter Skarga was the first and the outstanding
champion of the project for the reunion of the Ruthenians
who were subject to the Polish crown with the Catholic Church.
After he and his fellow labourers had struggled for seventeen
years in the Grand Duchy of Lithuania and its capital Wilna,
both against the new errors of the Protestants, and the more
ancient ones of the Greeks, Skarga published in 1577 his
wonderful book " Of the government and unity of the Church
of God under one only pastor, and of the Greek schism."
The first volume of this celebrated work[1] was dedicated by
him to the voivode of Ukrainia (Kiew), Prince Constantine
Ostrogskyj, who, as the most important Ruthenian magnate
was patron of about a thousand Ruthenian churches, and
of the dioceses of Luzk and Pinsk.[2] Skarga proved to the
Ruthenians in the clearest way that their church differed from
the Roman Church, not only in external customs that were
of no great importance, but as to the truths of faith necessary
for salvation. He drew attention to the decadent state
of the Ruthenian Church which was the result of the schism,
to the contempt for the ecclesiastical state which prevailed
there, and to the rule exercised by the laity over the house of
God. No improvement could be looked for from the Greek
Patriarch, who was bound to submit himself to the will of
the Turks, but only from the lawful head, the Vicar of Christ.
He pointed out that reunion would not be difficult, and himself guaranteed that in the event of the metropolitan being
ordained by the Pope, and following the Apostolic See in
questions of faith, they would be allowed to retain their rite
and usages of worship, since the Church of God was clothed
with variety, like a queen with the glory of many hued
garments.

The idea of reunion, thus gloriously set forth by Skarga,
was vigorously supported by another Jesuit, Antonio Posse-

[1] *Cf.* BERGA, 195 *seq.*
[2] See LIKOWSKI, 52 *seq.*, 68.   *Cf.* SPILLMANN in *Stimmen aus
Maria-Laach*, XI., 89 ; BERGA, 195.

vino, who had been sent in 1581 as ambassador to the King of Poland, Stephen Báthory, and by the nuncio Bolognetti. It was Possevino who decided Gregory XIII. to establish a seminary at Wilna for the Ruthenian and Russian youth, and to provide free places for the Ruthenians and Russians at the Greek College in Rome, and in the Jesuit schools at Olmütz, Prague and Braunsberg.[1] At the same time as Possevino, the professor of the Polish University at Cracow, the court preacher Stanislaus Sokolowski, maintained the necessity of reunion in two works.[2]

Following the example of Skarga, the Jesuits, especially those at Wilna, which was the principal centre for attempts at reunion, laboured to prepare men's minds by sermons and other forms of instruction for the process of reunion. For this purpose they appealed to the internal renewal and revival of the Catholic Church which had been effected within a comparatively short time after the Council of Trent, to which they held up by way of contrast the uninterrupted decadence of the Greek Church. These attempts to bring about conviction by means of instruction and the return of the Ruthenians to the Catholic Church by a completely free decision, produced good results, but naturally met with opposition, which principally manifested itself in the academy founded by Prince Ostrogskyj.[3] In consequence of this resistance, King Stephen Báthory did not venture to support the movement for reunion. Sigismund III. acted in a like manner at first, until the Patriarch of Constantinople and the Ruthenian episcopate morally forced him to come to a decision.[4]

The most trustworthy sources of information leave us in no doubt as to the fact that in the case of the Ruthenian Church the words of St. Cyprian were verified : that a branch

---

[1] *Cf.* Vol. XX. of this work, pp. 398, 415.

[2] See LIKOWSKI, 76 *seq.*

[3] See LIKOWSKI, 77, who shows that no one can accuse the Jesuits of ever having urged the Polish government to employ rigorous measures, or to employ violence against anyone's conscience.

[4] See LIKOWSKI, 79.

that is cut off from the living tree must wither away.[1]   As the greater number of the episcopal sees were filled by unworthy men, and profaned by simony, both the secular and regular clergy were bound to fall into a state of great ignorance, and profound demoralization.   Owing to decadence of the pastors, the religious life of the Ruthenian people was for the most part limited to the maintenance of external forms and the strict observance of many rigorous fasts.   The educated classes, especially the aristocracy, had either embraced Protestantism or had entered the Roman and Catholic Church. Those among them who still adhered to the Ruthenian Church looked upon their depraved clergy with profound contempt. Only the religious confraternities, in which the inhabitants of the cities had banded themselves together, still showed anything of the vitality of the Ruthenian Church.   These steadily acquired greater importance and power, but interfered in an ever increasing degree in matters that concerned the clergy.   In the end they terrorized over the parish priests and even the bishops.   Even worse was the fact that into the schools that were maintained by the confraternities masters found their way who taught errors of religion to the young, as dogmas of the Ruthenian Church.   Thus no religious renewal could be looked for from that quarter.

Nor was the patriarchate of Constantinople, torn asunder by internal discord, and oppressed and humiliated by the Ottomans, in a position to render assistance to the Ruthenian Church.   It was only when they found themselves embarrassed by want of money that the Patriarchs of Constantinople began to interest themselves in the Ruthenians ; thus in 1586 an envoy from the Patriarch of Constantinople presented himself among them, and two years later the Patriarch himself. On his return from Moscow, where Jeremias II. had allowed himself to be induced to set up an independent Russian patriarchate, he sojourned among the Ruthenians for some

---

[1] *Cf.* for what follows SPILLMANN, *loc. cit.*, X., 435 *seq.*, and above all LIKOWSKI, 30-59, and 90 *seq.*, where many details are given.

time in 1589. Sigismund III. granted him full liberty for
his ecclesiastical work, but it was soon seen that it was of far
greater concern to the patriarch to confirm them in their
already threatened schism than to reform the morals of the
decadent clergy. Yet the measures which he took for this
purpose proved unfortunate for the end which Jeremias II.
had in view. The Ruthenian episcopate had already been
divided by the appointment of an exarch, while a further
misguided blow was struck by the elevation of the religious
confraternities of Lemberg and Wilna to the " stauropigiac "
rank ; by this these lay communities were withdrawn from
episcopal jurisdiction, and they were authorized to watch
over the orthodoxy, not only of the lower clergy, but also of
the bishops themselves ![1]

As a result of the general disappointment occasioned by
the action of the Patriarch Jeremias, it came about that soon
after his departure the Ruthenian bishops seriously discussed
the idea of separating themselves from Constantinople, and
of seeking for a renewal of ecclesiastical conditions by reunion
with Rome. At the same time a firm determination to detach
the Ruthenian Church from its union with the patriarchate
of Constantinople, and to unite it with the Holy See developed
in the minds of the Polish chancellor, Zamoiski and King
Sigismund. Sigismund was led to this determination principally by religious considerations, under the influence of Peter
Skarga, who in 1590 dedicated to him the second edition of
his book " On the Unity of the Church of God."[2] The
chancellor was principally actuated by political considerations.
His shrewd outlook was not blind to the danger of the
Ruthenians entering into a rapprochement with Russia, a

---

[1] See LIKOWSKI, 63 *seq.*, 81 *seq.*, 84 *seq.* The earlier opinion
that Jeremias II. had asked for large sums from the metropolitan
of Lithuania for his consecration has been refuted by the publication of MILKOWICZ : Monum. Confraternitatis Stauropigianae
Leopoliens. (I., Leopoli, 1895, n. cclviii.). But as this sum was
demanded by an intimate and companion of the patriarch,
indignation fell upon the latter as well.

[2] *Cf.* BERGA, 223 *seq.*

people closely akin to them, in the new patriarchate established
at Moscow in 1589, the titular of which called himself the
Patriarch of the whole of Ruthenia.   As for the Ruthenian
bishops, if Gedeon Balaban of Lemberg allowed himself to be
guided, in the matter of reunion, principally by private
motives, Cyril Terlecki of Luzk on the other hand, was
influenced by the consideration that the renewal of his Church
would only become possible by detaching it from the decadent
patriarchate of Constantinople, and uniting it to the Catholic
Church which was then vigorously springing into new life.[1]
A great influence in this matter was also exercised by the
Latin Bishop of Luzk, Bernhard Maciejowski, so that later on
Clement VIII. warmly thanked him for the part he had taken
in bringing about the reunion.[2]

Of the greatest importance for the reunion with Rome was
the fact that Terlecki found a most capable, enthusiastic and
energetic collaborator in 1593 in the person of the new Bishop
of Vladimir, Hypatius Pociej.   Far-seeing, prompt in his
decisions, energetic, outspoken without regard for persons,
and yet when necessary, very cautious, he was the very man
needed to attain to victory in this difficult task.[3]

On June 12th, 1595 (old style), the metropolitan of Kiev,
Michael Rahoza, called together the Bishops of Vladimir,
Luzk and Pinsk, together with the archimandrite of Kobryn,
at Brest.   There they drew up a joint letter to Clement VIII.,

---

[1] *Cf.* LIKOWSKI, 87 *seq.*, 92 *seq.*, who, especially against the
opinion maintained by the Ruthenian and Russian historians, that
the union of Brest (see further *infra*, p. 132 *seq*), was nothing but
a device of the Jesuits, proves that the chief and more important
part was the work of the Ruthenian bishops.   Criticism has
confirmed the thesis of Likowski ; see *Przeglad Polski*, 1898,
and *Kwartalnik Hist.*, XI., 162 *seq.*, as well as KAINDL in *Mitteil.
aus der hist. Lit.*, XXXIII., 499 *seq.*   *Cf.* also BERGA, 242.

[2] See THEINER, Mon. Pol., III., 256.

[3] For Pociej, besides the earliest biography, which L. Kiszka
added to the edition of the sermons of that prince of the Church
(Kazania i homiliye Hipacyusza Pocieja, Suprásl, 1714), see
especially LIKOWSKI, 93 *seq.*, 102 *seq.*, 110.

in which they declared that since the Patriarchs of Constantinople, as subjects of the Turks, were not in a position
to do anything to restore ecclesiastical unity, in the interests
of the salvation of their own souls, and those of their flocks,
they wished, with the consent of their king, Sigismund, to
adhere to the reunion entered into at Florence, in which their
fathers had already concurred, provided that the Pope would
consent to their preserving their oriental liturgy, and the whole
of their ecclesiastical ritual. For the carrying out of this
reunion they had resolved to send Bishops Pociej and Terlecki
to Rome to the Holy Father.[1] After the two above-mentioned
had persuaded the absent Ruthenian bishops to sign this
document, they entered into negotiations with the Papal
nuncio Malaspina and King Sigismund.[2] The latter, on
August 2nd, granted them all that they asked, and by the
privilege accorded to them on that date, the Ruthenian Church
was to have all the rights and privileges of the Latin Church,
and protection against possible reprisals on the part of the
Patriarch of Constantinople ; henceforward the bishoprics
were only to be governed by born Ruthenians, elected from
among four candidates chosen by the episcopate. The
bishops were to have restored to them the property that had
been taken from them, and the confraternities were once more
to be subjected to their jurisdiction. They were also given
seats and votes in the senate, though this matter had first
to be laid before the Diet.[3]

Once the negotiations had reached this point, it became
possible to reveal the secret which had hitherto been closely
kept. The Bishop of Luzk, Chelm, Prezemysl and Lemberg
informed their flocks, in a pastoral letter of August 27th, that
the whole of the episcopate, including the metropolitan, had
resolved, for the salvation of the souls entrusted to their care,

[1] See THEINER, loc. cit., 237 seq.

[2] See LIKOWSKI, 116 seq.

[3] See the acta relating to the history of Western Russia
published by the Archeological Commission, IV., Petersburg,
1851, N. 78-79, and LIKOWSKI, 116 seq.

to make their obedience to the Bishop of Rome.   On September 24th King Sigismund addressed an open letter to the Ruthenians, in which he made known his will and desire that all his subjects should praise God with an united voice and heart, and that the faithful should follow the example of their pastor, whose representatives would repair to Rome in order to give effect to the reunion of the Ruthenian Church with the Apostolic See, on the condition of the maintenance of their own rite.

These words on the part of the king were rendered necessary by the fact that the timorous metropolitan Rahoza, who was unwilling to disturb his relations with the Ruthenian magnates, who were opposed to the reunion, was still hesitating.[1]

Clement VIII., who had been informed by his nuncio of the important events that were taking place in Poland, was awaiting, with an anxiety that is easy to understand, the appearance of the Ruthenain bishops in Rome.   He, who had himself once been legate in Poland, fully realized the importance of that great kingdom as a bulwark of Christendom against the Turks on the east, as well as against the schismatics on the north.   The reunion of millions of orthodox Ruthenians with the Church would not only strengthen that kingdom politically, but would give the Catholics an absolute preponderance over Protestantism, which was divided into so many sects.[2]   It might also become a natural bridge to Russia. From the fact that the audience of the Bishop of Plock, when he came to Rome, lasted for three whole hours on November 12th, 1595,[3] it was possible to deduce that an important decision concerning Poland was imminent.   A few days later Bishops Terlecki and Pociej arrived in the Eternal City. Clement VIII. assigned them lodgings in a special palace, and on November 17th they had their first audience.[4]   The

---

[1] See LIKOWSKI, 118 seq., 138.

[2] See SPILLMANN in Stimmen aus Maria-Laach, XI., 97 seq.

[3] See *Avviso of November 15, 1595, Urb. 1603, Vatican Library.

[4] See *Avviso of November 15, 1595, ibid.

Pope, so the bishops reported, welcomed them as a father his sons, with indescribable affection and courtesy.[1] On account of its importance, the matter was first referred for examination by Clement to the Congregation of the Inquisition.[2] The Ruthenian bishops were prepared to renounce the schism and all doctrines rejected by the Roman and Cahtolic Church, but they begged that, in conformity with the Council of Florence, the administration of the holy sacraments and the whole of the Byzantine rite should remain unchanged, nor should they undergo any change in the future. In agreement with the above-mentioned Congregation Clement VIII. granted this request, which was in absolute conformity with the principle admitted by the Council of Florence : namely, unity of faith despite diversity of rite. In his anxiety to promote the reunion the Pope desisted from his demand for the immediate introduction of obligatory celibacy, and thus gave up the apparently well-founded hope that the renewal of the decadent Ruthenian Church, thus begun with the reunion, would proceed of its own accord as time went on. Clement VIII. also gave up the adoption of the Gregorian calendar, as Terlecki and Pociej declared that this would meet with determined opposition.[3] The Pope appointed December 23rd, 1595, for the definite accomplishment of the reunion. On that day he assembled the thirty-three Cardinals who were in Rome, the whole of the court and the diplomatic corps in the Hall of Constantine at the Vatican. The historian Cesare Baronius, who had a

---

[1] See the letter of the two bishops of December 29, 1595, in HARASIEWICZ, Annales ecclesiae Ruthenicae, Leopoli, 1862, 198.

[2] See Bull, X., 247. The notes referring to this question in the Archives of the Roman Inquisition are still unpublished. The other acta are given by G. HOFFMANN : Ruthenica I. ; Die Wiedervereinigung der Ruthenen, Sofia, 1923-24, in *Orientalia christiana*, III-2, Rome, 1924-25.

[3] SPILLMANN, *loc. cit.*, 98 ; LIKOWSKI, 139 ; see SMOLKA, Die reussische Welt, Vienna, 1916, 162.

short time before been raised to the purple, has described the accomplishment of the reunion as an eye-witness.[1]

After the two Ruthenian bishops had paid the customary homage, the canon of the cathedral of Wilna, Eustace Wollowicz, read first in Ruthenian and then in Latin the synodal letter of June 12th, 1595, addressed to the Pope, which had been signed by all the Ruthenian bishops. After this Silvio Antoniano, by the Pope's command, welcomed the Ruthenian bishops, who, for their own good and that of their country, and to the unspeakable joy of the Pope, had, after a separation of 150 years, once more returned to the rock on which Christ had founded His Church, the mother and mistress of all Churches, the holy Roman Church. " Oh how great and how well deserved," he exclaimed, " is the praise which you yourselves have given to the goodness and wisdom of God, which has enlightened you to see that members divided from the head cannot remain in life, and that he who has not the Church for his mother, cannot have God for his father."[2] Then Pociej, in his own name and that of all the Ruthenian bishops read in Latin the Catholic profession of faith, according to a formula based upon those of Nicaea, Florence and Trent, and then accepted it on oath.[3] Terlecki

[1] See BARONIUS, Annales, VII., Venice, 1739, 859 seq. Cf. *Diarium P. Aleleonis on December 23, 1595, Barb. 2815, Vatican Library.

[2] The *discourse of Antoniano in Ottob. 1088, p. 142, Vatican Library. Pichler, whose account of the union is both biassed and inaccurate, calls Antoniano (II., 95) a Cardinal, which he only became in 1599. False too is the statement of Pichler that the union took place at a consistory. P. Alaleone (*Diarium, loc. cit.) expressly calls the assembly congregatio generalis. The event is not entered in the *Acta consist card. S. Severinae (Cod. Barb., XXXVI., 5 III., Vatican Library). The publication of the Documenta de Ruthenorum unione (1595) has been prepared by G. Hofmann.

[3] The text, omitted in Bull., X., 243, of the " Professio fide praesulum Ruthenorum " is in THEINER, Mon. Pol., III., 238 seq.

then did the same in Ruthenian, and thereupon the Pope repaired to the church to receive the Ruthenian bishops ; his eyes were shining with tears of joy. " To-day," he said, " a joy fills our heart on account of your return to the Church, that cannot be expressed in words. We render special thanks to the immortal God, Who, by means of the Holy Spirit has guided your minds so as to lead you to seek a refuge in the Holy Roman Church, your mother, and the mother of all the faithful, who lovingly welcomes you once more among her sons." In significant words the Pope paternally exhorted these sons who had come back to him, to humility as the groundwork of the obedience they owed to the Church, " since, owing to her pride, Greece, which deserves our pity, and whose misfortunes we deeply deplore, has lost the light of truth, and now groans under the yoke of the most bitter slavery." With the assurance that his protection and help would never be lacking to them, and with the bestowal of the apostolic blessing, this memorable solemnity came to an end. On the vigil of Christmas the Ruthenian bishops appeared in their vestments in St. Peter's for vespers,[1] and on the following day they were appointed assistants at the pontifical throne.[2]

By a bull dated December 23rd Clement VIII. announced to the Catholic world the return of the Ruthenians to ecclesiastical unity ; in this document he confirmed their rite in all particulars, with the exception of anything which might eventually prove to be contrary to the truth and the doctrines of the Catholic faith.[3] A commemorative medal[4] immortalized the important event by which, a century and a half after the Council of Florence, the bond of union between the Ruthenian Church and the Roman Church was once again formed. A similar purpose was served by a constitution of February 23rd, 1596, which granted to the metropolitan

---

[1] See the letter of the bishops, December 29, 1595, cited *supra*, p. 133, n. 1.

[2] See *Diarium P. Alaleonis, Barb. 2815, Vatican Library.

[3] Bull., X., 239 *seq.*

[4] Reproduced in BARONIUS, *loc. cit,*

of Kiev the faculty to consecrate his bishops, but obliging him himself to obtain confirmation from the Pope.[1]

When Pociej and Terlecki made preparations, in February, 1596, for their return journey, Clement VIII. gave them letters for King Sigismund, the civil and ecclesiastical senators, the metropolitan Rahoza and the Ruthenian bishops. All were warmly urged to maintain the glorious work of reunion, the king in particular being urged to admit the Ruthenian bishops to the senate as he had promised to do, and to grant the same rights to the Ruthenian clergy as to the Latin. The Pope enjoined the metropolitan to convoke a council as soon as possible for the solemn proclamation of the union formed with the Holy See.[2]

While the feeble Rahoza delayed until the autumn in fulfilling this duty, the supporters of the schism, under the leadership of the aged Prince Ostrogskyj, in conjunction with declared heretics, raised a powerful agitation against the work of pacification.[3] Fortunately Sigismund stood firm, although every attempt was made to stir up the populace against Rome, Above all others, Cyril Lukaris, who was inclined to Calvinism. encouraged schismatical hatred, in which he was assisted by a Greek adventurer, named Nicephorus, who had been obliged to leave Constantinople on account of various thefts.

In spite of the prohibition of the king, Nicephorus repaired to Brest, while, in defiance of the royal commands, there also appeared there Prince Ostrogskyj with an armed following, together with Lukaris, who, by the command of the Patriarch of Alexandria, was working against the reunion. As the Bishops of Lemberg and Przemysl joined the party at Ostrogskyj, the hopes of the schismatics grew stronger. This party assembled in a Protestant house in Brest, and formed a kind of opposition synod, under the presidency of Nicephorus, who proclaimed himself, though quite untruly, the envoy of

---

[1] Bull., X., 250 seq.

[2] See the briefs, all dated February 7, 1596, in THEINER, Mon. Pol., III., 250 seqq. Cf. PELESZ, II., 11 seq.

[3] Cf. for what follows, the excellent description of LIKOWSKI (143 seq., 151 seq.).

the Patriarch of Constantinople, though that see was vacant at the moment. But neither he nor his companions were able to prevent the lawful synod from taking place. In this there took part, besides the metropolitan Rahoza, the Archbishop of Polotzk, the Bishops of Vladimir, Luzk, Pinsk, and Chelm, as delegates of the Pope, the Latin Bishops of Lemberg, Luzk, and Chelm, and as theological advisers, the Jesuits Peter Skarga, Justin Rabe, Martin Laterna and Gaspar Nahaj. On October 9th (old style) the metropolitan celebrated the sacred liturgy in the church of St. Nicholas, after which the Archbishop of Polotzk, Hermogenes, read in his own name and those of the other Ruthenian bishops a declaration of their reunion with Rome. " We know well," he said, " that the sovereignty of the Church of God, according to the gospel and the words of Christ, founded upon Peter alone as the rock, must be exercised and administered by one alone, that over one body there must be but one head, over a well-ordered house but one master and administrator of the treasures of divine grace for the guidance of the flock, who must provide for the well-being of all, and that this must endure in a like manner, from the time of the Apostles through all the ages." After the reading of this declaration the Latin and Ruthenian bishops embraced each other, and then proceeded, as a sign of their brotherhood, in a single procession to the Latin church of the Mother of God, where the *Te Deum* was sung. The synod then deprived the Bishops of Lemberg and Przemysl, who had apostatized from the union, and declared Nicephorus and all who had taken part in the opposition synod excluded from ecclesiastical communion. The latter for their part retaliated by depriving all those who accepted the reunion. But King Sigismund cited Nicephorus before the courts, which sentenced him to imprisonment for life as an impostor and a Turkish spy. In a message dated December 15th, 1596, addressed to the Ruthenian nation, the king called upon the people to recognize only the bishops who were in communion with Rome. In this document, however, nothing was said of a confirmation of the promises made to the Ruthenian bishops or to the Holy See. The opposition of the Polish bishops and senators did not make it seem an opportune moment for the king to summon the Ruthenian bishops to form part of the senate.[1]

The great dangers to which the reunion was subsequently exposed came above all from Prince Ostrogskyj, whose agents worked indefatigably against the union with Rome. Against the acceptance of the union it was principally urged that it was not legal, because it had been concluded without the consent of the Patriarch of Constantinople, and without the agreement of the whole of the clergy, nobles and people. Although these reasons were fallacious, and were in evident contradiction of the ancient principles of the Church with regard to the episcopal office, nevertheless the agitation which was skilfully directed by Ostrogskyj and his collaborators of the protestant party, was successful in stirring up the Ruthenian clergy, both secular and regular, and with them the majority of the people and the aristocracy against the uniat bishops. The constant reiteration of the same complaints and grievances led the people in the end to adopt them, to show their sympathy for the schismatics, and to withdraw their allegiance from the uniat bishops,[2] who were described as tyrannizing over men's consciences and as disturbers of the public peace.

The union continued to be more and more severely threatened, yet the powerful Prince Ostrogskyj did not attain his true purpose, namely its complete destruction ; on the contrary he was forced to witness two of his own sons become Catholics.[3] In Rome it was clearly understood how much depended upon this man, and therefore Clement VIII. sought to make the prince change his views.[4] For a long time the

---

[1] See LIKOWSKI, 152 *seq.*, 162 *seq.*, 170 *seq.*

[2] See *ibid.*, 180 *seq.*

[3] See *ibid.*, 194. A *letter of Janus Ostrogskyj, dated March 24, 1602, vouches for his zeal for the Catholic religion in spite of the calumnies ; his enemies are the heretics and the " frigidi catholici." Original in Doria Archives, Rome.

[4] See THEINER, Mon. Pol., III., 285.

reason why Ostrogskyj attacked the union with such fury and hatred was supposed to be his pride, but more recent research attributes it also to the heretical atmosphere which surrounded the prince, namely the learned Greek, Cyril Lukaris, the Arian Bronski and Motowila, and other religious innovators, who exercised an evil influence over him.[1]

The principal champion of the union was Hypatius Pociej, who became metropolitan of Kiev in 1599. Difficulties only increased his courage, and more descriptive of him than anything else is his own saying : " Even if I had to beg my bread, I would still continue to serve the Church of God."[2]

Clement VIII. too, continued to the end the loyal defender of the union. He repeatedly sent the Archbishops of Gnesen and Lemberg to take the part of the uniats against the machinations of the Greeks, as for example in July 1598 and March 1604.[3] The Pope had recourse to the king on April 3rd and July 10th, 1599, with the request that he would grant the Ruthenians the rights and privileges promised to them, and would protect them from the schismatics.[4] Again on March 31st, 1604, he urgently reminded Sigismund of his promise to receive the uniat bishops into the senate ; at any rate the metropolitan should have a place there, so that he might reply to the attacks of the schismatics and defend the rights of the uniat Church.[5] A further proof of the long-suffering of the Pope and his pastoral care was the fact that when, owing to the efforts of Maciejowski, there was a glimmer of hope that Ostrogskyj would give up his opposition in view of his approaching death, he addressed a letter to the prince on January 15th, 1605, in which he once again refuted all the

[1]See LIKOWSKI, 198 seq.
[2]See ibid., 244.
[3]See THEINER, loc. cit., 271, 282.
[4]See ibid., 272 seq. ; PELESZ, II., 33 seq.
[5]See THEINER, loc. cit., 283. Cf. also the briefs to Bishop Peter Tylicki of Ermland, of the years 1593 and 1604, in EHRENBERG, Ital. Beiträge zur Gesch. von Ostpreussen, Königsberg, 1895, 64 seq.

objections to the reunion, and exhorted him in paternal words
to accept it.[1]

While reunion with the Ruthenians was still in the balance,
there unexpectedly opened out a prospect of once again
uniting Russia to the Catholic Church.

With the death of Ivan IV., which took place in 1584, there
had begun in that kingdom the " period of the disturbances "
which lasted until the accession of the Romanoff dynasty.[2]
Under Ivan's successor, the imbecile Feodor I., the real power
passed more and more into the hands of his cousin, the Tartar
Boris Godunov.   As Feodor had no heirs, it seemed, according
to all human expectation, that the second son of Ivan, Dimitrij
(Demetrius), would ascend the throne of the Czars, but this
was not in accordance with the plans of the ambitious and
energetic Boris, who aimed at obtaining that supreme dignity
for himself.   With this was evidently connected the mysterious
disappearance of Demetrius in May 1591.   It was said that
the boy had, by pure accident, been mortally injured in a game,
but the suspicion was at once aroused that he had been
removed purposely.   In face of the suspicion which fell
upon himself, Boris caused an inquiry to be made, which,
as might have been foreseen, went to show that the last
male descendant of the house of Rurik had met with an
accidental death.   This official statement at once aroused
doubts, and later on the rumour was spread that the child
had been saved, and that his mother had substituted
another who resembled him in his place.[3]

---

[1] See THEINER, loc. cit., 286 seq.

[2] Cf. WALISZEWSKI, Les origines de la Russie moderne.   La
crise révolutionnaire, 1584–1614, Paris, 1906.

[3] Among the more recent works on the false Demetrius mention
must first be made of the profound researches, based on
new authorities by PIERLING : Rome et Démétrius, Paris, 1878 ;
Un manuscrit du Vatican sur le tzar Dimitri, in the Rev. des
quest. hist., 1894, II. ; Lettre de Dimitri dit le Faux à Clément
VIII., Paris, 1898, and La Russie et le St-Siège, III., Paris, 1901.
The problem has also frequently been dealt with by others ;

When in 1598 the Czar Feodor I. died, Boris Godunov attained the object of his ambitions, cleverly profiting by the state of affairs in the country and his friendship with the Hapsburgs.[1] With feigned reluctance he yielded to the urgent request of the Patriarch Job of Moscow, who was completely under his influence, and that of the aristocracy, and assumed the government as Czar. Far-reaching plans filled the mind of the new sovereign, who was a far-seeing and highly gifted statesman. Although he could not even read, he was nevertheless the friend of culture. At the opening of the century he tried to establish schools and a university in Moscow, and summoned thither German scholars ; he had his sons taught by foreigners, and even sent Russian youths to the west to be educated. Thus this Tartar on the throne of the Czars stood out as the first "western" in the line of Russian sovereigns. In his efforts to Europeanize Russia, and by his alliance with the Protestant north of Europe, he recalled Peter the Great. But as far as the people were concerned he lacked the blood of the Ruriks, while he was too autocratic for the powerful boyars.[2]

Diplomatic complications were added to domestic difficulties. This man, who had sprung from nothing, would gladly have seen the beautiful Xenia, his only daughter, married into one of the ancient European dynasties, but his proposals were courteously rejected everywhere, both at

cf. especially HIRSCHBERG, Dymitr Samozwaniec, Leopoli, 1898 ; BAUDOUIN DE COURTENAY in *Rozprawy . . . z posiedzen wydz, filologieznego*, 2nd Series, XIV. (1898), 183 *seq. ;* ŠČEPKIN, Wer war Pseudodemetrius ? in *Archiv. f. slaw. Philol.*, XX–XXIII. (1898–1900) ; CARO in *Hist. Zeitschr.*, LXXX., 264 *seq. ;* WALISZEWSKI, *loc. cit.* and also the critique of Pierling in the *Rev. des quest. hist.*, LXXXI. (1907), 213 *seq. ;* SKRIBANOWITZ, Pseudo-Demetrius I., Berlin, 1913. PANTENIUS (Der falsche Demetrius, Bielefeld, 1904), gives a number of interesting illustrations, but adds nothing new.

[1] *Cf.* KARAMSIN, X., 90 *seq.*, 97 *seq. ;* ÜBERSBERGER, Österreich u. Russland, I., 541 *seq.*, 564.

[2] *Cf.* WALISZEWSKI, *loc cit.*

Stockholm, London and Prague.[1] The little court of
Copenhagen at last showed itself more favourably disposed,
but Prince John, the brother of King Christian IV., met with
a premature death.   To this domestic disappointment there
was added a great national disaster ; the years 1601 and 1602
brought bad harvests, which resulted in terrible famine,
scarcity and disease.   Brigands made their appearance, who
levied contributions from the people, who credulously listened
to the prophecies of the monks, foretelling a great catastrophe.[2]

In the midst of this social and economic crisis, the throne
of Boris Godunov was seriously threatened when the alarming
news reached the Kremlin in 1603 that a youth, who gave
himself out as the son of Ivan IV., the Demetrius who had
died in 1591, had met with a great following in Poland.

The claimant to the throne had first made himself known
to the powerful Prince Adam Wisniowezki in Lithuania, and
had won the latter, who hated Boris Godunov, to his plan
for conquering the throne of the Czars which belonged to him
with the help of the Cossacks and Tartars.   The ambitious
George Mniszek, voivode of Sandomir, who was gravely in
debt, and the confidant of Sigismund III., who was an ardent
supporter of the Ruthenian reunion, also put his faith in the
story of Demetrius, and received him so cordially that the
claimant to the throne asked him for the hand of his daughter
Marina.   The reply was deferred until Demetrius had presented himself before the king at Cracow.   Accompanied by
Mniszek and his father-in-law, Prince Adam Wisniowezki,
Demetrius went at the beginning of March 1604 to the ancient
capital of Poland.   There the voivode of Sandomir prepared
a great banquet on March 13th, at which Demetrius was the
guest of honour, though, out of consideration for the still
dubious senators, the latter preserved his incognito as far as
possible.   Even the nuncio Rangoni took part in the festivity.
The mysterious pretender made a good impression upon him :
his white and slender hands pointed to high birth, he was

[1] See ÜBERSBERGER, I., 564 *seq.*, 568 *seq. ;* PIERLING, III., 89.
[2] See PIERLING, III., 89.

frank in his conversation, and his whole attitude and behaviour had something majestic about them.[1] Rangoni also makes mention of a large wart at the corner of his left eye, and the contraction of one of his arms,[2] which were said to be marks of the missing son of the Czar.

On March 15th Demetrius had a private audience of the King of Poland at Wawel, and this determined the attitude of Sigismund, who had at first refused to believe in the identity of the pretender. After this, however, the king made up his mind to support Demetrius, and showed this by loading him with gifts.[3] So far the nuncio Rangoni had remained completely neutral, but on March 19th he had a conversation for the first time with Demetrius, who was successful in winning over the Pope's representative.[4] Rangoni then put the claimant to the throne into touch with the Jesuit Gaspar Sawicki,[5] and in the presence of these two Demetrius expressed his desire to be received into the Catholic Church. When Sawicki had satisfied himself as to the genuineness of his intentions, he received from him, on Holy Saturday, April 17th, 1604, the Catholic profession of faith at the Jesuit college of St. Barbara.[6] All this, however, was done

---

[1] See *ibid*. 67 *seq*., where there is a reproduction of the portrait of Demetrius in the Historical Museum, Msocow.

[2] See PIERLING, III., 68 *seq*.

[3] See *ibid.*, 69.

[4] See *ibid.*, 73 *seq*.

[5] This fact, which is proved for the first time by PIERLING (Rome et Démétrius, 14 *seq*.) in the light of the documents, destroys the older view, which was especially propagated by RANKE (Päpste, II., 256) in a wider field, that the intrigue was engineered by the Jesuits and the nuncio, and that it was only later on that Sigismund was won over. The contention of Ranke that the conversion was precipitate, is also false. For this Ranke depends upon the Historia di Moscovia by ALESS. CILLI (Pistoia, 1627), whom he considers worthy of all credence. Pierling has proved the contrary opinion, and has refuted the many and grave errors of Cilli. SKRIBANOWITZ too (*loc. cit.* 19, 36, 38) shows how little worthy of belief Cilli is.

[6] See PIERLING, Rome et Démétrius, 27 *seq*., 183 *seq*.

in secret, on account of the Russian adherents of the pretender.

With the assistance of Sawicki, two days later the convert wrote a letter to the Pope in Polish, dated April 24th ; this was to the following effect : " Who I am who thus venture to write to your Holiness will have been explained to you by the Polish nuncio, to whom I have made known all my resolves and the motives therefor. Having been saved by the help of God while still a child from the hands of a bloody tyrant and from death, kindly Providence has brought me to the realm of the King of Poland, whose acquaintance I have set myself to make. In Poland I came to the knowledge of the flourishing state of the Roman Catholic religion, I became more and more drawn to it, and found in it a treasure far more precious and a kingdom far more noble than that which the injustice of a tyrant had robbed me of. While I was meditating concerning the salvation of my soul I clearly saw the grave danger in which Moscow stood by reason of the schism, and how unjustly the authors and propagators of that schism had attacked the pure and ancient doctrine of the Catholic, Roman and Apostolic Church. Therefore, by the help of divine grace I have returned without delay to the unity of the Catholic and Roman faith, and by means of the sacraments have become a little sheep of your Holiness, the supreme Shepherd of all Christendom. My position constrains me still to conceal this, and to await what God, Who has saved me from so many perils, wishes to do with me. I hope that God will soon be willing to assist me, the descendant of the ancient and renowned princes of Muscovy, to recover my inheritance. If this should not prove to be the case, there still remains to me the consolation of Catholic truth, and my union with the Church which will lead me to the kingdom of heaven. If God should see fit to assist me to win back my inheritance, then I urgently implore your Holiness not to deny me your support. The almighty God may be able to make use of me, however unworthy I may be, to spread His glory, by the conversion of so many lost souls, and by the reunion of so great a country to the Church. Who knows

whether it be not for that very purpose that He has led me
into the Church ? "

This letter, the author of which reveals himself as a native
of Greater Russia, and not very familiar with the Polish
language, ended with an assurance of his complete submission
to the supreme pastor of Christendom, and with the request
that he would keep silence as to its contents for a time.   The
document is signed : Demetrius, son of John, Czar of Greater
Russia and heir to the Muscovite monarchy.[1]

When Demetrius handed his letter to the nuncio Rangoni
on April 24th, he threw himself at his feet and assured him
of his submission to the Holy See ; at the same time he
promised, in the event of his accession to the throne of the
Czars, to use all his power for the spread of the Catholic
religion.[2]   Henceforward Rangoni was completely won over
to the cause of the pretender, whom Sigismund III. also
favoured in secret, although a very strong party in Poland
would not hear of any warlike undertaking against Russia.
In the meantime the Czar Boris had taken up a defensive
attitude ; supported by the Patriarch Job he spread the
report everywhere that Demetrius was an impostor, and an
apostate monk named Gregor Otrepjev,[3] who had escaped
from the Tschudow monastery at Moscow.

The pretender, who had become betrothed to Marina
Mniszek, was also very active.   He succeeded in raising a
small army of Poles and Cossacks, with which at the end of
October 1604, he crossed the Dnieper, which then marked the
boundary between Russia and Poland.   Counting on meeting

---

[1] The letter of Demetrius to Clement VIII. has been published
from the original in the Archives of the Roman Inquisition by
Pierling in a photographic reproduction, together with a French
translation, in a little work of which only 100 copies were printed
(Lettre de Dimitri dit le Faux à Clément VIII., Paris, 1898).
The Latin translation by Sawicki in PIERLING, Rome et Démétrius,
157 seq.   For the style and the authorship see SKRIBANOWITZ,
46 seq., and the literature cited there.

[2] See PIERLING, III., 83 seq.

[3] See ibid., 92 seq., 96 seq.

with support in Russia, he hoped, in spite of the small force at his disposal, to recover the throne of the Czars. Among his troops there were Jesuits who acted as military chaplains for the Catholics. Demetrius kept up a correspondence with Rangoni, who was very necessary for the attainment of his purpose, while the nuncio cherished the hope that within a short time there would be a Catholic ruler in the Kremlin, who would undertake the conversion of his great kingdom by means of Catholic missionaries.[1]

In contrast to the optimistic ideas of his representative, Clement VIII. displayed his customary prudence in the matter of Demetrius. He was perhaps confirmed in his attitude of reserve by the fact that he had by his side, as his confessor and friend, Baronius, the great historian. When the first news of the appearance of the pretender reached the Curia from Rangoni, the Pope's scepticism went so far as to attach to the letter of Rangoni a marginal note to the effect that this was probably a case of a person like the false Sebastian who had come forward in Portugal.[2] Only the conversion of Demetrius and his letter of April 24th, together with the reports of Rangoni, brought about a change of mind in the Pope. He handed over that important document to the Roman Inquisition for examination ; this tribunal had to decide whether the desire expressed by Demetrius to the nuncio could be granted, namely whether on the day of his coronation as Czar he could receive communion from the hands of the Patriarch of Moscow.

While this matter was still under discussion, on May 22nd a Papal brief was addressed to " our beloved son and noble lord Demetrius " in which he was exhorted with paternal kindness to persevere in the way of piety and virtue. If Clement VIII. in this abandoned his attitude of cold reserve which he had so far maintained, he nevertheless avoided all mention of politics, nor were the great interests of Christendom

[1] See *ibid.*, 85, 114 *seq.*, 220.
[2] " Sarà un altro Re di Portogallo resuscitato." PIERLING, III., 41.

even mentioned in the brief. Demetrius had looked for a great deal more. In a letter of July 30th he treated of spiritual matters as well as political, and expressed his thanks in anticipation for the help offered to him. Clement VIII. left this letter unanswered.[1] The later developments of this affair, which ended with the murder of Demetrius, do not belong to his pontificate.

---

[1] See *ibid.*, 86 *seq.*, 230 *seq.* The letter of July 30 in PIERLING, Rome et Démétrius, 160 *seq.*

CHAPTER V.

CLEMENT VIII. AND THE INTERIOR LIFE OF THE CHURCH.—
THE RELIGIOUS ORDERS.—THE EPISCOPATE.—THE SACRED
COLLEGE.

FILLED with a conviction that the clergy of the Eternal City
ought to stand out before all the world for their virtue and
piety, Clement VIII., immediately after the beginning of his
pontificate, proclaimed a general visitation of all the churches,
religious houses, and pious institutions of Rome. In the
document which was published on June 8th, 1592,[1] it was
declared that just as none but a well cultivated field can
produce an abundant harvest, so was it also in spiritual
matters, and for that reason the Council of Trent had so
strongly urged canonical visitations. To this end a commission composed of cardinals and bishops was appointed, which
was to begin its labours with a visitation of the Lateran
basilica. In order to obtain the divine assistance the Pope
ordered the Forty Hours to be celebrated in the principal
churches of Rome.

Mindful of the words of Our Divine Lord, that the good
shepherd must know his sheep,[2] Clement VIII., regardless
of his high dignity, took a personal share in the visitation of
the greater number of the Roman churches. In this he was
assisted by Cardinals Medici and Valiero, as well as by three
bishops, among them the distinguished Lodovico de Torres,
Archbishop of Monreale.[3] After the Pope had celebrated

[1] See Bull., IX., 562 seq.
[2] See ibid., 564.
[3] See *Commentarius visitationis Clementis VIII. a. 1592 ;
Urb. 837, p. 268 seq., Vatican Library ; BORGHESE, I., 869 and

148

high mass in the Lateran basilica on June 18th, 1592, and distributed holy communion to the clergy, he gathered them together in the sacristy, and delivered a discourse to them, in which he spoke of all the duties of their office, threatening grave punishments to those who had failed therein.   Then, assisted by four Cardinals, he made a visitation of the church, and especially of the tabernacle, ordering that a place of greater honour should be assigned to it.   He also demanded a more splendid reliquary for the heads of the Princes of the Apostles. The visitation was continued in the afternoon and on the following day.   When the Pope visited the Lateran Hospital, he found there a sick man at the point of death, and Clement VIII. rendered him all assistance with as much fervour as though he had been a simple parish priest.[1]   The Pope also carried out in person the visitation of the Lateran clergy, and of the house of the penitentiaries attached to the basilica, where he arrived quite unexpectedly.   One penitentiary, in whose room he found a copy of the love-songs of Petrarch, was deprived of his office ; the same fate befel another penitentiary who was found to be unfit. Clement VIII. declared that he would proceed in like manner everywhere, as he preferred to have a few well instructed priests to many who were ignorant.[2]

In the same way as the Lateran basilica, St. Mary Major's and St. Peter's[3] were subjected to a strict visitation, and after them one by one according to their rank, all the churches of the city.   It was at once realized that Clement VIII. knew in every case how to observe a just mean between excessive

Arm. 7 t. 4, Papal Secret Archives.   *Cf. ibid.* t. 3 *Decreta visit. sub Clemente VIII.   See also the *report of G. Niccolini, June 19, 1592, State Archives, Florence.   Med. 3303.

[1] See *Avvisi of June 17 and 20, 1592, Urb. 1060, I., Vatican Library, and the *letter of G. Niccolini of June 26, 1592, State Archives, Florence, *loc. cit.*

[2] See *Avviso of June 27, 1592, Urb. 1060, I., Vatican Library.

[3] See *Avvisi of July 4 and 8, 1592, Urb, II., Vatican Library. *Cf.* the *report of G. Niccolini, July 3, 1592, State Archives, Florence, *loc. cit.* and Collectio bull., etc.   Basil. Vatic., III., 186.

severity and too great leniency.[1]   However much he clung
to the splendour of divine worship, he energetically protested
against the exaggerated pomp displayed at processions by
the Spaniards in their national church.[2] Wherever it was
necessary he intervened with great severity.[3]   The exactitude
with which he proceeded could not have been greater, and he
paid attention to the smallest details.[4] He made a very
searching visitation of the Hospital of Santo Spirito,[5] and at
the Aracoeli he went into the cell of every one of the friars.[6]
The confessors were everywhere examined with special
vigilance.[7] The Pope preferred to make his appearance
without warning and quite unexpectedly,[8] and, as in the case
of all his reforms, he took steps on his own initiative.[9]

[1] See *Avviso of July 8, 1592.   Urb. 1060, II., Vatican Library.

[2] See *Avviso of April 30, 1596, Urb. 1064, I., Vatican Library.
The Pope would not make his appearance even in St. Peter's
with the tiara ; see *Studi e docum.*, VIII., 28.

[3] The *Avviso of November 25, 1592, reports : " Sabbato
N.S. visitò la chiesa di S. Maria in Trastevere, et vi fece il solito
sermone con maggiore vehementia del consueto, toccando certi
tasti et minutie, che non ha costumato nell' alter chiese " (Urb.
1060, II., Vatican Library).   The commandant of the Hospital
of S. Spirito was dismissed, according to the *Avviso of July 15,
1593 (Urb. 1061, *ibid.*).

[4] Examples are given by the *Avvisi of August 22, 1592, and
June 22, 1596, Urb., 1060, II., and 1064, Vatican Library.   *Cf.*
BAUMGARTEN, Neue Kunde, 25.

[5] See *Avviso of September 23, 1592, Urb. 1060, II., Vatican
Library.

[6] See *Avviso of February 22, 1595, Urb. 1063, *ibid.*

[7] See *Avvisi of September 9 and November 7, 1792, Urb.
1060, II., *ibid.*

[8] See besides BENTIVOGLIO, Memorie, 46, the *Avvisi of
September 23, 1593, February 22, 1595, and August 22, 1601,
Urb. 1061, 1063, 1069, Vatican Library.

[9] *" Il card. Rusticucci afferma, che quanti editti di riforme,
bandi di donne, restrittioni di camere locande et simili ha mandati
fuori in questo pontificato, sono stati tutti di ordine del S.P.
vivae vocis oraculo."   *Avviso of November 25, 1592, Urb. 1060,
II., *ibid.*

The visitation of the Roman churches in 1592 was continued by the Pope in person even after the commencement of the cold season,[1] and the Venetian ambassador reports that in this he displayed a zeal that could not have been greater if he had been a simple bishop.[2] The reforms which he prescribed were all entered in the Acta.[3]

In view of the minuteness with which the visitation was carried out, it is not surprising that it was prolonged from 1593 to 1596.[4] It proved very efficacious[5] so that it was again repeated later on.[6] In July 1603 Clement VIII. took part in the visitation of the church and convent of S. Salvatore in Lauro.[7] The Pope also insisted on taking part in the examinations, begun in 1597 onwards, of the parish-priests of Rome, which were entrusted to a commission of Cardinals, even though it was pointed out to him that in so doing he was fatiguing himself unduly.[8]

Convinced as he was of the importance of the religious

---

[1] See *Diarium P. Alaleonis, Cod. Barb. 2815 ibid.

[2] PARUTA, Dispacci, I., 21.

[3] See ibid. and *Avviso of November 28, 1592, Urb. 1060, II., Vatican Library. Cf. *Acta visitationis multarum ecclesiarum Urbis sub Clemente VIII. Cod. 7, 59, Vallicella Library, Rome. See also *Borghese, II., 51a and 52 Papal Secret Archives.

[4] See *Diarium P. Alaleonis, loc. cit. Cf. *Avvisi of 1596, June 22 (visitation of the convent of the Minims), June 26 (convent near S. Croce in Gerusalemme), July 10 (S. Prassede). Urb. 1064, I. and II., Vatican Library.

[5] Cf. the *brief to Archbishop Ernest of Cologne of November, 1592, Arm. 44, t. 34, n. 10, Papal Secret Archives (see Vol. XXIII., App. n. 5), and *Vita et gesta Clementis VIII. in Inform. polit., XXIX., State Library, Berlin.

[6] See *Avvisi of August 22, 1601, and July 2, 1603, Urb. 1069, 1071, Vatican Library.

[7] See *Avviso of July 2, 1603, according to which the Pope found in the cell of P. Massimiliano some jewels which he at once caused to be sold. Urb. 1071, ibid.

[8] See *Avvisi of January 18, February 12, 15 and 22, 1597, Urb. 1065, ibid.

Orders to the Church,[1] Clement VIII., in the course of his visitations, devoted special attention to the state of the religious houses of Rome. As early as March 1592 he had summoned before him the generals and procurators of all the Orders, and had exhorted them, with threats of grave penalties, to lead an exemplary life.[2] This warning was repeated in the severest terms in September, when it had transpired that the enactments ordered during the visitation had to a great extent not been carried out. The Pope asked for a list of all those who failed to obey, and said that in the place of so great a number of small houses which were difficult to supervise, he would like to see in every province three or four large houses in which the reform could be carried out exactly.[3] In October 1592 all the gratings and windows in the convents of women which gave upon the street were walled up.[4] At the visitation in 1593 the Capuchins in the convent on the Quirinal had to listen to words of severe reproof.[5] In 1596[6] there were fresh measures of reform for the religious houses of Rome. Later on too the Pope took advantage of his visits to the houses of the Orders to address serious observations to them,[7] though wherever he found a satisfactory state of affairs he did not spare his praises.[8]

In December 1592 a prohibition, addressed for the time

---

[1] The Pope called the Orders " ossa et medullas christianismi " ; see ZACHARIAE, Iter. litt., 302. The Cod. Vat. 3565 contains among the *discourses of Giov. Paolo Eustachio dedicated to Clement VIII., n. 1 : " Della necessità et utilità della visita che fa N.S. alle religioni. Vatican Library.

[2] See *Avviso of March 14, 1592, Urb. 1060, I., ibid.

[3] See *Avviso of September 19, 1592, Urb. 1060, II., ibid.

[4] See *Avviso of October 21, 1592, ibid.

[5] See *Avviso of July 7, 1593, Urb. 1061, ibid.

[6] See *Avvisi of May 4, and November 16, 1596, Urb. 1064, II., ibid.

[7] See *Avviso of February 24, 1599, Urb. 1067, ibid.

[8] See the *brief to the General of the Carthusians, in which the Pope speaks of his visitation of S. Maria degli Angeli, November 15, 1603, Arm. 44, t. 56, n. 24, Papal Secret Archives.

being to the religious houses of Rome, was issued against the making of gifts, which did not apply, however, to alms to the poor.[1]   On June 19th, 1594, this ordinance was extended to all the religious houses in the world.[2]   In the same way the constitutions concerning the erection of new houses,[3] and the punishment of exempt religious who had committed some fault outside their own houses,[4] were also made universal.

Clement VIII. rendered good service to the Orders by his constitution of March 12th, 1596, and four subsequent decrees of the years 1599, 1602 and 1603, concerning the exclusion of those who had no true vocation, and the training in deep piety of young religious.   These contained the most salutary prescriptions, limited for the time being to Italy, on the reception of novices.[5]

With what care Clement VIII. laboured everywhere for the re-establishment of religious discipline, where it had become relaxed, and for its maintenance, where it still existed, is shown by the visitors whom he sent,[6] by his many instructions to the nuncios,[7] and by a whole series of special enactments.   These applied to the Augustinian Hermits,[8] the

[1] See *Avviso of December 26, 1592, Urb. 1060, II., Vatican Library.

[2] Gifts to individual inhabitants of religious houses were also prohibited ; see Bull., X., 146 *seq.   Cf.* PARUTA, Dispacci, II., 365, 485.

[3] See Bull., XI., 21, and the *declaration of August 26, 1603, copy in the Cod. 55 of the Theodoriana Library, Paderborn.

[4] See Bull., X., 348 *seq.*

[5] See Bull., X., 769 *seq.* and *Archiv. für kath. Kirchenrecht,* CXI. (1911), 696 *seq.*

[6] See ZACHARIAE, Iter. litt., 302.

[7] Especially to the nuncio at Venice were instructions given to persevere in the work of reform ; see in App. n. 7 the *instructions to M. A. Graziani, March 30, 1596, Graziani Archives, Città di Castello.   Caetani devoted himself to the reform of the religious houses in Spain from the beginning of his nunciature ; see *Nunziat. di Spagna, 43, Papal Secret Archives.

[8] See " Clementis P. VIII. pro reformatione fratrum ord. Eremitarum s. Augustini decreta," Pisauri, 1599.

Basilians,[1] the Camaldolese,[2] the Cistercians,[3] the Cluniacs,[4] the Order of the Holy Ghost,[5] the Hermits of the Hieronymite observance,[6] the Knights of St. John,[7] the Carthusians,[8] the Servites[9] and the Dominicans.[10] Clement VIII. introduced more strict rules in the case of the Brothers of Charity and the Fathers of a Good Death.[11] He greatly encouraged among the Franciscan Order the new reforms of the Observants, the

[1] Bull., X., 623 seq.

[2] Ibid., 293 seq.

[3] See the *brief to " capit. general. ord. Cisterc.," dated March 14, 1601, Arm. 44, t. 45, n. 70, Papal Secret Archives.

[4] See the *brief of blame to " Abbas Cluniacensis," October 27, 1592, Arm. 44, t. 38, p. 78, ibid.

[5] Cf. BRUNE, L'ordre du Saint-Esprit, Paris, 1892, 263, and E. MICHAEL in Zeitschr. f. kath. Theol., XXIII., 210.

[6] Bull., X., 34 seq.

[7] See the severe *briefs to the Grand Master of Malta, May 14, 1592, June 15 and September 2, 1594, and April 30, 1602, Arm. 44, t. 37, n. 304 ; t. 39, n. 214 and 258 seq ; t. 46, n. 129, Papal Secret Archives. See also C. FEDELI, Carteggio dei Gran Maestri di Malta con i duchi d'Urbino, Pisa, 1912, 69 seq., 82 seq.

[8] See the *brief to the chapter general of the Carthusians, April 15, 1599, Arm. 44, t. 43, n. 217, Papal Secret Archives.

[9] See Bull., X., 658 seq., 662 seq., and Decreta Clementis P. VIII. pro reformatione fratr. ord. Serv. B. Mariae Virg., Rome, 1604.

[10] See Bull., IX., 561 seq. For the reform of the Dominicans at Naples, where there were bad relations between the secular clergy and these religious, see Arch. stor. ital., IX., 441 seq. ; MUTINELLI, II., 176 seq. Cf. the *brief to the Cardinal of the Dominicans, June 29, 1596, concerning the enclosure, Arm. 44, t. 40, n. 200, Papal Secret Archives. The *Avviso of June 13, 1601, states : When the Dominicans went on Saturday with their General to the Pope, " N.S. fece loro un breve ragionamento, esortando in particolare tutti alla concordia et esso Generale al giusto governo et a far osservar la lor regola, senza che sia bisogno venghino d'altronde chi la facci loro osservare." Urb, 1069, Vatican Library.

[11] See Bull., X., 295 seq., 635.

Riformati in Italy and the Recollects in France.[1] Francisco
Sousa of Toledo who in 1600 was elected General of the
Observants in Rome, presented to the Pope a memorial on
the state of his Order, in which he had lived for thirty-five
years, filling almost all the offices, and making visitations of
almost all the provinces.[2] He described in detail the condition, to some extent not very consoling, of the convents in
Germany, France, Spain and Italy, and makes suggestions
for their improvement. He lays it down as a maxim for
reform that it must not be universal, but adapted to the very
varied needs of the different districts.[3]

In the Benedictine Order, reform had been carried out,
in accordance with the decrees of the Council of Trent, both
in Italy and Spain, by means of the institution of congregations ; at the beginning of his pontificate Clement VIII.
gave some salutary ordinances to the Cassinese Congregation.[4]
In France, where the system of commendams had exercised
a harmful influence, they did not prove of any particular
importance, except in the case of the congregation of Saints
Vanne and Hydulphe, established in Lorraine at the
beginning of the seventeenth century, and in that of the
Feuillants. The former was confirmed by Clement VIII.,
from whom it received new and milder rules.[5] In Germany
the most important congregation was that established in 1564

[1] *Cf. ibid.*, 299 *seq.* ; GAUDENTIUS, Beiträge, 242 *seq.* ;
HOLZAPFEL, 312.

[2] *" Informazione copiosa del P. Sosa ministro generale de
Min. osserv. a P. Clemente VIII. sopra il modo di riformare la
religione " in a miscellaneous codex of the Communal Library,
Ancona, which was not yet catalogued when I made use of it in
1884.

[3] *" Che in una parte sarebbe riformatione, nell'altra causarebbe
scandali et nell'altra distruttione," says Fr. Sousa in his
*Informazione, *loc. cit.*

[4] See Bull., X., 28 *seq.* ; Bull. Casin., I., 266 *seq.*, 270 *seq.*

[5] *Cf.* Bull., XI., 64 *seq.* ; ASCHBACH, Kirchenlex, I., 653 *seq.* ;
SCHMIEDER in *Studien aus dem Bened. Orden*, XII., 60 *seq.* ;
HEIMBUCHER, I., 150 *seq.*, 242.

in Swabia, which was confirmed in 1603 with the title of the Congregation of St. Joseph.[1] The most important Benedictine monasteries in Switzerland, St. Gall, Einsiedeln, Muri and Fischingen, were united into one congregation in 1602. Clement VIII. confirmed this and also invited other Swiss monasteries to join it. Pfäfers and Rheinau did so at once, and all the others later on.[2]

In the matter of the reform of the regular and secular clergy, Clement VIII. addressed himself repeatedly to the bishops. If the latter were fulfilling their pastoral duties he expressed his satisfaction,[3] but if not, he addressed severe admonitions to the archbishops, and sometimes even to the princes.[4] Occasionally he also sent special visitors, as was the case with Sardinia in 1598.[5] His nuncios at Naples and Venice laboured incessantly for the reform, which was very much needed in many of the religious houses there.[6]

However cold Clement VIII. showed himself towards the

----

[1] See HEIMBUCHER, I., 149.

[2] See *Hist.-polit. Bl.*, CV., 729 *seq.*

[3] *Cf.* *briefs to the Bishop of Oria, June 20, 1598, and March 31, 1599, Arm. 44, t. 42, n. 176 ; t. 43, n. 203, Papal Secret Archives. *Ibid.*, t. 46, nn. 177-180 *briefs to " episc. Lausan. Constant, Curiens. Basiliens," June 15, 1602.

[4] *Cf.* Bull., IX., 541 *seq.* (to the Patriarch of Venice), X., 731 *seq.* (to the Bishops of Corsica) ; *brief to the Duke of Savoy, March 15, 1597 (orders the Bishop of Maurienne to reform a monastery of Cistercians) Arm. 44, t. 41, n. 83, Papal Secret Archives. *Ibid.*, t. 43, n. 45 and 208, *briefs to Rudolph II., January 30 and April 3, 1599, concerning the reform of the religious houses in Suabia. See also n. 111, *brief to the Archbishop of Crete, February 19, 1599.

[5] See Bull., X., 78 *seq.*

[6] For Venice see in App. n. 7 the *instructions to the nuncio there March 30, 1596, Graziani Archives, Città di Castello. On January 29, 1605, Clement VIII. recommended to the Doge the visitor sent for the Congreg. di S. Giorgio in Alga, which was in need of reform (*Brief in State Archives, Venice). For conventual reform at Naples see Cod. L. 23, p. 172b, Vallicella Library, Rome, and *Carte Strozz.*, I., 2, 237, 290.

Jesuits,[1] he was not blind to their success in popular missions,[2] for which work they were especially fitted. Therefore in 1598 he induced the Jesuits in Rome to preach such missions in the Campania, the Sabines, and the Roman Campagna. The self-denial of the fathers in this work among the poor country folk, in the full heat of summer, was indeed admirable, and their success was in the highest degree consoling. The Bishops of Città Castellana and Montepulciano asked that these missions might also be extended to their dioceses.[3]

In Rome, where the Jesuits were doing very useful work,[4] above all encouraging in their churches the devotion to the sufferings of Christ,[5] they were rivalled by the Theatines and the Oratorians. Clement VIII. confirmed for the Theatines their emended rule,[6] and granted them many favours.[7] The Capuchins[8] and the Barnabites[9] who were spreading through-

[1] Cf. supra, p.   .

[2] Cf. Litt. ann. 1592, 13 seq.

[3] See ibid., 1598, 14 seq.

[4] Cf. " Domus ac pietatis opera quae B.P. Ignatius facienda Romae curavit quaeque societas suae curae commissa habet " (rare engraving of 1600).

[5] See *Avviso of January 1, 1603, Urb. 1071, Vatican Library The *Avviso of April 17, 1604 (Urb. 1072, ibid.) states : The Jesuits have made in their church a beautiful sepulchre, like that at Jerusalem ; " è ben vero, ch'era ogni cosa di bianco et dentro et fuori, cosa non approbata cosi generalmente da tutti in questi tempi che la S. Chiesa va certando con le candele le cose meste et di malencolia."

[6] Bull of July 28, 1604, Theatine Archives, Rome. Ibid. a *brief dated " sexto Idus Augusti : " Clement VIII. grants to the Theatines the church of S. Stefano at Vicenza ; also a *document concerning the grant of the church of S. Bartolomeo in Porta at Bologna (1599) and a bull of Clement VIII. " per la fundazione de Teatini nella chiesa di S. Giorgio in Rimini." The Theatines were also brought to Florence in 1592 by Clement VIII.

[7] See Carte Strozz., I., 2, 323 seq.

[8] See Bull. Capuc., II., 113, 172 seqq., 223, 318, 407 ; III., 19 seqq., 62 seqq., 78 seqq., 100 seqq., 116 seqq.

[9] Cf. PREMOLI, 335 seq., 355 seq., 357 seq., 370 seq., 374 seq., 379 seq., 381 seq., 388 seq.

out Italy, received many proofs of the good-will of the Pope. The same was the case with the Oratorians, who were very dear to the Pope, who had Baronius as his confessor. In the matter of the absolution of Henry IV. it was seen what influence that distinguished man, as well as Philip Neri, had over him. The relations between Clement VIII. and the holy founder of the Oratorians, who died on May 26th, 1595, were both cordial and intimate, as between father and son. Clement VIII., who, like all the Aldobrandini, loved cheerfulness, was well able to adapt himself to the joking and humourous methods which Philip Neri loved to adopt, and we have evidence of this in certain letters which were exchanged between them.[1] But though the Pope willingly yielded to the wishes of Philip Neri, he nevertheless preserved his independence even with him. Thus he remained immovable when the saint presented a plea on behalf of a bandit who had been condemned to death, for Clement judged it necessary that in this case the law should take its course in all its rigour.[2] Nor would he suffer himself to be moved from his intention of making the most beloved of the disciples of Philip Neri, Tarugi, Archbishop of Avignon, and though the saint did all he could to induce the Pope to change his mind, he adhered to his purpose, saying that he could not give way, because it was incumbent upon him to care for the well-being and the betterment of the whole Church.[3]

[1] See CAPECELATRO, Der hl. Philipp Neri, revised by Lager, Freiburg, 1886, 324 *seq.*, where we find corrected the interpretation which a thinker like Goethe, who otherwise so well understood the life of men, gave to these letters.

[2] Others on the other hand, who had been condemned to prison for lesser crimes, were released in 1593 at the instance of St. Philip ; see *Avviso of June 30, 1593, Urb. 1061, Vatican Library. For the favour which the Oratorians enjoyed with the Cardinals, see *Avviso of December 25, 1596, Urb. 1064, II., *ibid.* A Relatione of that period tells us that the number of the Oratorians, who in turn delivered two or three sermons every day, was 40 ; see *Carie Strozz.*, I., 1, 393.

[3] See CAPECELATRO, *loc. cit.*, 335.

The Minorite, Angelo del Pas, was held in high esteem by Clement VIII. He had also been esteemed by his predecessors on account of his theological works and the purity of his life ; he died in 1596 in the odour of sanctity.[1] The same was true of Camillus of Lellis, the founder of the Fathers of a Good Death.[2]

Two other saints also found a fervent protector in the Aldobrandini Pope : Giovanni Leonardi and Joseph Calasanctius.

Giovanni Leonardi,[3] who was born in 1543 in a village near Lucca, and who first, by the wish of his parents, became a chemist, only attained to the goal of his desires, the priesthood, later on. Although he was already twenty-six Giovanni took his place once more on the benches of a school in order to learn Latin. Ordained at the end of 1572, he devoted himself with ardent zeal in Lucca to the catechizing of poor children and the instruction of the young in their religion. The first fellow-labourers that he met with there were a hat-maker named Giorgio Arrighini and Giambattista Cioni, the scion of a noble family. Together with these he established himself in 1574 in a room near the church of the Madonna della Rosa. Among the companions who joined them there were above all two brothers, Cesare and Giulio, of the Franciotti family, and related to the della Rovere. Being asked by his companions for a written rule, Leonardi took a sheet of paper and wrote the single word : " Obedience." Although the members of this new company lived for nothing but their own sanctification and the good of their fellow-citizens, they did not lack persecution, but the Bishop of Lucca, Alessandro Guidiccioni, supported the work of these pious men.

---

[1] *Avviso of August 28, 1596, Urb. 1064, Vatican Library. For A. del Pas cf. HURTER, I., 89 seq., 397.

[2] Cf. Vol. XXII,, p, 398, of this work, and M. AMICI, Mem. stor. intorno S. Camillo de Lellis, Rome, 1913 ; ibid., p. 219, the protection given to him by Clement VIII.

[3] Cf. the biographies by L. MARRACCI (Venice, 1617 ; Rome, 1673) and CARLANTONIO ERRA (Rome, 1758). Cf. also BARELLI, Memorie de chierici regol. di S. Paolo, L. Bologna, 1703, 26 seqq.

Giovanni Leonardi drew up a catechism, and did such useful work in Lucca and the neighbourhood, that the Bishop of Lucca called him the apostle of his diocese.   With unwearied activity he introduced into the cities, on the last Thursday of the Carnival, a general communion, and, following the example of Charles Borromeo, the pious exercise of the Forty Hours during the last three days of the carnival.   When he was once again subjected to persecution, the holy man was not discouraged, not even when he and his companions came to lack all means, and their house was taken away from them.   His firm trust in God was not in vain ; in 1580, the rector of the church of S. Maria Cortelandini, made over to him, with the consent of the bishop, his presbytery, and in 1583 Leonardi and his zealous companions established there a religious congregation, under the name and patronage of the Madonna, for their own perfection and the preaching of the word of God.[1]

While on a pilgrimage to Rome Leonardi formed a friendship with Philip Neri.   This proved very valuable to him when a fresh persecution at Lucca forced him to have recourse to the Holy See.   On his return the inhabitants of Lucca closed the gates of the city against him.   Although Sixtus V. had declared Leonardi innocent, the latter was unwilling to stir up his adversaries against him any further, and he therefore remained in Rome, in close relationship with Philip Neri, and furthering the work in the hospitals and schools. Clement VIII. esteemed his labours in the highest degree ; it did not seem fitting to him that the work of a religious society, which sought for nothing but the welfare of the inhabitants of Lucca and its own members, should be any longer hampered, and accordingly, on October 13th, 1595, at Leonardi's request, he approved his congregation.[2]

In 1596 the Pope arranged that this zealous priest should be able once more to return to Lucca.   Since men's minds there were not yet quite calmed, Clement VIII. for the time

---

[1] See Bull., IX., 227 seq.
[2] See ibid.

being made use of Leonardi as apostolic commissary for the
introduction of reforms into the Order of Montevergine in
the province of Naples. After this Leonardi also reformed
certain monasteries of the Vallombrosans, and visited Monte
Sennaro, the cradle of the Servite Order. Cardinal Tarugi
asked for him in 1597 for the reform of his diocese,[1] and in
the same year he visited his house at Lucca. In 1601
Leonardi was successful in founding a second house in Rome
near the church of S. Maria in Portico.[2]

Two years later the Pope entrusted to Cardinal Baronius
the protectorate of the Clerks Regular of the Mother of God,
whose first General Leonardi became. A brief of June 24th,
1604, allowed the new congregation to establish houses everywhere, provided the diocesan bishops gave their permission.
" Take care of the young," said the Pope to the founder,
when he presented himself before him with Baronius.[3]

There was another saint who was likewise predestined to
the priesthood, who was filled with enthusiasm for the good
of his neighbour, and whose efforts were encouraged by
Clement VIII. : this was Joseph Calasanctius,[4] so called
from the mountainous hamlet in Aragon, near Petralta de
la Sal, where he was born in 1556. After the young nobleman
had studied philosophy and jurisprudence at the university
of Lerida, and theology at Valencia and Alcalá de Henares,
he was urged to contract matrimony after the death of his
brother without issue, so that his ancient family might not

---

[1] See ERRA, loc. cit., 63 seqq.

[2] Cf. Storia di S. Maria in Portico, Rome, 1750.

[3] See ERRA, 81 seq., Bull., X., 229 seq.

[4] See the biographies by ALESSIO DELLA CONCETTIONE (Rome,
1693), TOSETTI (Rome, 1767 ; Florence, 1917), LIPOWSKY
(Munich, 1820), KELLNER (Skizzen u. Bilder aus der Erzichungs-
gesch., I., Essen, 1862), TIMON-DAVID (2 vols., Marseilles, 1883),
HUBART (Mayence, 1862), TOMMASEO (Rome, 1898), CASANOVAS
Y SANZ (Saragossa, 1904), HEIDENREICH (Vienna, 1907). Cf.
also HEIMBUCHER, II., 272 seq. ; Hist. pol. Bl., VII., 599, XXXIII.
746, CXX., 901 seq. ; FALOCI PULIGNANI, Notizie del ven. G.B.
Vitelli da Foligno, Foligno, 1894, 49 seq.

die out. The young man would not hear of this, but it was only after he had been miraculously cured of a grave illness, that his father abandoned the project.

Having been ordained priest at the end of 1583 Joseph Calasanctius devoted himself for nine years to the care of souls in various parts of his native Spain. It seemed that he might confidently look forward to some great ecclesiastical office, but a secret desire drew him to Rome. He arrived there in a state of poverty in the spring of 1592, for after his father's death he had distributed the whole of his inheritance. The inhabitants of the Eternal City were still suffering at that time from the effects of the plague and famine, which had scourged them from 1590 onwards ;[1] thus there were many orphan children wandering about the streets, without clothing, food or instruction. A friend of Philip Neri, the noble and pious Giovanni Leonardo Ceruso, known as " Il Letterato," had already in the time of Gregory XIII. founded an institute for abandoned children,[2] of which, after his death on February 13th, 1595,[3] Baronius, by the order of Clement VIII. under-

[1] *Cf.* Vol. XXII. of this work, p. 345.

[2] See *Avvisi of September 9, 1592, and February 18, 1595, Urb. 1060, II., and 1063. According to the *Avviso of April 28, 1601, the number of the " poverelli dell'hospitale di Letterati " was at that time about 200 (Urb. 1069, Vatican Library).   These children were called " i poveri letterati." See MORONI, XIV., 45. Fra Marcello Fossataro of Nicotera, a hermit of St. Francis *asked Clement VIII. for permission to found at Naples an asylum " come fece il Literato in Roma," State Archives, Florence ; see *Carte Strozz.*, I., 2, 250).   About 1600 Carlo Carafa founded a congregation " dei pii operaii " at Naples, and converted many Turkish servants there ; see *Freiburger Kirchenlex.*, I[2]., 1231 *seq.* Art. *Arbeiter*, and F. CEVA-GRIMALDI, Della città di Napoli, Naples, 1857.

[3] *Cf.* MANSIO, Vita di Giov. Leonardo Ceruso detto Letterato, Rome, 1834 ; CALENZIO, Baronio, 103 *seqq.* ; ORBAAN, Documenti, 151 n. and Rome under Clement VIII., 62 *seqq.*   In the *Memoirs relating to the Congregation of the Oratory by Pompeo Pateri, a description of the influence of the " opera di Litterato " as follows : In questo tempo s'era cominciata già l'opera di Litterato

took the care.[1] But this alone could not overcome the evil.
Joseph Calasanctius, who immediately after his arrival in
Rome had become a member of the confraternity for teaching
Christian Doctrine, saw with profound grief how many
abandoned children were growing up without instruction or
supervision. When he applied to the masters of the schools
to be allowed to instruct the little ones gratuitously, he was
referred by them to the magistracy. But he failed to obtain
a hearing there as well. Then it seemed to him that he heard
the words of Holy Scripture : " To thee is reserved the care
of the poor, and to the orphans thou shalt be a helper." Thus
there sprang up in his mind the idea of founding a special
school for the poor, and of becoming its director. To this
end he met with his first helper in the parish priest of the
church of S. Dorotea in Trastevere, Antonio Brendani, who
put a few rooms at his disposal, and promised to help him
with the instruction. It was in that church that the Oratory
of Divine Love had once sprung into existence, from which
the work of Catholic reform and restoration had begun.[2]

(che così era chiamato il fondatore d'essa quale cominciò a
radunare li poveri figliuoli di poc'età ch'andavano spersi, et li
menava per le strade cantando laudi spirituali et scopando le
strade dove era bisogno ; poi dimandava d'elemosina per quei
poveri figliuoli, quali la sera conduceva al coperto sotto le grotte
del monasterio di S. Lorenzo in Panisperna, che all'hora ci poteva
entrare chi voleva dalla parte di S. Maria Maggiore ; et così cosa
nuova il card. Rusticucci m'ordinò ch'iò m'informassi dell'huomo
et come governava quei figliuoli. Andai una sera all'improviso
alle dette grotte et trovai che teneva quei figliuoli con quell'ordine
bono che poteva in quel luogo et li governava con tanta carità
ch'io ne restai con grande edificazione, vedendo che li dava tutti
quelli soldi ch'haveva, senza pensare punto a se stesso : et con
questa relatione si lassò seguitare. Carpegna 62 p. 58[b], Papal
Secret Archives.

[1] See MORONI, L., 4. Cf. ibid., IX., 203, and XIX., 247, for
the asylum of S. Eufemia founded at that time. The " Letterato "
was buried in S. Maria dell'Orazione e Morte ; see LANCIANI, IV.,
68 ; FORCELLA, VIII., 475.

[2] Cf. Vol. X. of this work, p. 390 seq.

It was a strange coincidence that now, at the moment of the highest development of that movement, a new and important institution was to spring up in the same place. As soon as some of the members of the Society of Divine Love had promised their co-operation, the first popular free school in Europe was able to come into existence.

Clement VIII. extended his protection to a work on which the blessing of God visibly rested. The number of children, of whom from the first there were about a hundred, grew from year to year. They were given the necessary books and writing materials gratuitously ; they were also given clothing, since, following the example of the open-handed Pontiff, other benefactors as well provided ample alms.

In 1601 it was possible to hire a larger house near S. Andrea in Valle, in which Joseph Calasanctius began to lead a community life with his companions, who had by 1604 reached the number of twelve. Thus were laid the foundations of the Piaristi or Clerks Regular of the Pious Schools, afterwards called the Poor Clerks of the Madonna, the " Scolopi " (Scuole pie) or the Poalini. Since noble and wealthy families also sent their children to the excellent school of Calasanctius, jealousies and envy were aroused, but the Pope convinced himself that the accusations made against the school of the poor children were unfounded, and he continued as before to be their protector.

Clement VIII. founded in Rome, for the Roman nobles and foreigners, the " Collegium Clementinum " the direction of which he entrusted to the Somaschi.[1] This institution, the Protector of which was Cardinal Pietro Aldobrandini, soon attained great celebrity.[2]

---

[1] See Bull. XI., 90 *seq.*

[2] *Cf.* Elogio del nobile e pontificio Collegio Clementino di Roma, Rome, 1795 ; PALANTRINI, Notizie dei convittori illustri del Clementino di Roma, 1595-1795, Rome, 1795 ; DONNINO, I convittori del nobile Collegio Clementino di Roma, Rome, 1898. The inscription affixed to the building, which is situated in the

The Society of Christian Doctrine, founded in 1560 by the noble Milanese Marco de Sadis Cusani, found an ardent protector in Clement VIII.   From this sprang in 1596 the Congregation of Clerks Secular of Christian Doctrine and a confraternity in connexion with it.   After the death of Cusani (September 17th, 1595) the connexion between the two bodies was severed ;   the confraternity was given a director of its own, and the Congregation was given a provost and the church of S. Martina near the Forum.   In order to confirm both young and old in Christian doctrine, the Society of Christian Doctrine established disputations in the churches, which are still in use to-day in the Eternal City.[1]

It was of importance too that the Pope confirmed[2] the French teachers of Christian Doctrine founded by César de Bus, and in 1598 charged Bellarmine himself with the composition of a catechism, which by its perfection very quickly superseded all other works of a similar nature.[3]

The attempts of certain Spanish Jesuits to modify the Constitutions, drawn up by Ignatius of Loyola, met with no success in the time of Clement VIII., although the struggle took another aspect after the confirmation of the Constitutions by Gregory XIV.   In the time of Sixtus V. the two or three dozen malcontents had stormed the Inquisition and the king

---

Piazza Nicosia, was destroyed after the college was confiscated. For the bull for the college founded in 1596 at Aosta, see FRUTAZ in the periodical *Société acad. du duché d'Aoste*, XIX. (1905).

[1] See MORONI, XX., 246 *seq.* ; *Freiburger Kirchenlex.*, III., 1871 ; HEIMBUCHER, II., 339 *seq.*   The exemption of the " Congreg. clericorum doctrinae christ.," dated 1596, December 29, confirmed by Clement VIII., in Bandi, V., 15, p. 95, Papal Secret Archives.   The " Confirmatio (Clementis VIII.) erectionis congreg. doctrinae christ in civitate Avenion," of December 23, 1597, in Bull., X., 411 *seq.*

[2] See HEIMBUCHER, II., 338 *seq.*

[3] See SOMMERVOGEL, I., 1182 ; TACCHI VENTURI, I., 295, 301. A second edition of the rare Catechismo di Don Giovan Paolo da Como, sacerd. dei chierici regol., Cremona, 1595, mentioned *ibid.*, 300, in the City Library, Frankfort a M., Ital., 24 V.

with an array of memorials, in order that with their help their own schemes might be carried into effect.[1] But in the time of Clement VIII. such memorials were but few,[2] so that it seemed that the grave penalties which Gregory XIV had threatened against all attacks on the Constitutions of the Order seemed not to have been without their effect. But the bull of Gregory had not been able to close the last resource to the malcontents ; it had of necessity to leave open the way of appeal to the Pope himself, and to the general congregation of the Order.[3]

It was a strange thing that no less a man than José de Acosta adopted this course, for it was he whom Aquaviva had sent a short time before to Rome as his confidant, in order to set matters straight and who had dissuaded the King of Spain from his plan of causing a visitation of the Orders to be made by externs, and had himself carried out the visitation in two provinces.[4] Yet Acosta was no more pleasing to some of his brethren on account of his having made the visitation. It was seen that he was overcome with ambition, and was waiting until the General should confer upon him the office of provincial. The appointment did not come, and a deep despondency and hatred of Aquaviva took possession of him, though he was otherwise very capable and resolute. It seemed to him that the powers of the General ought to be limited by the General Congregation of the Order, and he persuaded King Philip to entrust his task to him, obtaining, should it prove necessary, a command from the Pope for such a restriction. He arrived in Rome on December 2nd, 1592, and through the Spanish ambassador, though without the knowledge of the General of the Order, had an audience with the Pope. He explained to Clement VIII. that the disputes among the Jesuits did not arise so much from the subordinate members, who were acting from simplicity, obedience and the love of God, as from the ambition

---

[1] *Cf.* Vol. XXI. of this work, p. 154 *seq.*

[2] ASTRÁIN, III., 417.

[3] Bull of June 28, 1591, §21, Bull., IX., 441.

[4] *Cf.* Vol. XXI. of this work, p. 165 *seq.*

and worldly outlook of the superiors.   The underlying cause
of everything lay in the unrestricted power of the General,
as that office had come to be in the hands of Aquaviva, and
the only means of repairing the trouble was the General
Congregation.[1]

At first Clement VIII. was not ill-disposed towards the
Jesuits, and recognized their services to the Church, especially
in the matter of missions,[2] while he had striven for their
re-admission to France.[3]   He was the first Pope to raise two
Jesuits, Toledo and Bellarmine, to the purple.   Both of these
had great influence with him, and he made use from time to
time of the services of Bellarmine as his spiritual father.[4]
But Clement VIII. allowed himself to be influenced by the
general trend of the moment.[5]   Under Gregory XIII. the
Jesuits counted for everything, and would have all been
looked upon as saints, if certain defects, which are generally
inseparable from success, had not manifested themselves
among them.   They certainly stood in the first rank where
it was a question of the welfare of the Church, but there were
those who thought that they went too far in their zeal, so as
to wish to be first in everything, give their opinion on all
subjects, and intrude themselves into matters which did
not concern them.

Thus there sprang up in the time of Sixtus V. and
Clement VIII. and still more during the first years of Paul V.,
a reaction against the high esteem which they had formerly
enjoyed.   One after another occurrences took place, which
were bound to affect their good name.   It was certainly an
act of too great severity when Sixtus V., publicly and in the
full light of day, caused a Jesuit to be carried off to prison,

[1] ASTRÁIN, III., 516-525.

[2] Cf. supra, p. 157.

[3] Cf. Vol. XXIII. of this work, p. 174 seq.

[4] A warning from Bellarmine to the Pope, and the latter's
replies in FULIGATTI, I., 3, c. 5, HH 2 seqq. ; LE BACHELET,
Auctarium, 513-518.

[5] What follows is based on POLLEN in The Month, XCIV. (1899),
233-248.

and ordered another to be brought from Spain to be executed
at the Bridge of St. Angelo, but there could be no doubt as
to the fact that at any rate one of them had allowed himself
to make use of unlawful expressions.   It was unjust when
the Spanish Inquisition, in the time of Sixtus V., imprisoned
four Jesuits on vexatious accusations, and entered upon a
bitter warfare against them and their privileges,[1] though it
is highly probable that the Jesuits had not been prudent in
the use of these privileges, and in the way in which they spoke
of them.   When, after the attempt of Chastel on Henry IV.,
a Jesuit had been put to death in Paris as an accomplice,
and the Jesuits were banished from Paris and other cities,
this too was a crying injustice ; but after all it was the
consequence of the fact that some of them, during the struggle
of the League, had meddled in politics.   If during the struggle
with the English appellants and the secular clergy, there
had been such strong feeling against Persons and the Jesuits,
part of the blame for this was due to the political writings of
Persons.   Clement VIII. had once clearly expressed the view
that he personally blamed the Jesuits, and on the occasion
of an appeal which a Jesuit, the confessor of the Queen of
Spain, had made against the attacks being made from all
quarters upon his Order, the Pope had drily written in the
margin of this document the words : God resists the proud.[2]
While on the journey which Aldobrandini had made to Poland
as legate, the Cardinal was of the opinion that he had
convinced himself with his own eyes that the Jesuits were
too intimately mixed up with the court and the aristocracy.[3]
In a word, dislike of the Jesuits had made itself felt in Rome,
Spain, France and England ; to this fact were added the
internal disturbances of the Order itself, the rebellions in
the seminaries in Rome and Valladolid, which injured their
reputation as educators, and the accusations made by the
Dominicans against their teaching as to grace, which damaged

[1] *Cf.* Vol. XXI. of this work, p. 155.
[2] POLLEN, *loc. cit.*, 240.
[3] IUVENCIUS, I., II, n. 5, p. 12.

their good name as men of learning. There can be no wonder then if even well-disposed men asked themselves whether all was well with the Order. Charles Borromeo had long before seen the storm approaching, and had sought to avert it, especially by recommending the election of his confessor, the Jesuit Adorno, as General of the Order.[1] That Clement VIII. would have something to say concerning the Order was placed beyond doubt by the remarks which he wrote with his own hand on the reports of his envoys ;[2] he was also personally annoyed with Aquaviva, because the latter had refused him the services of the skilled Possevino as his companion on his journey to Poland.[3] Nor was the learned and very influential Cardinal Toledo a friend of the General of the Order. Even in the time of Pius V., when he was preacher to the Apostolic palace, Toledo had taken up his abode there, leading almost a prelate's life,[4] and thus losing in a distressing way all contact with his Order.

Clement VIII. listened attentively to the remonstrances of Acosta ; if the General did not desire the Congregation, said the Pope, then he himself would order it. Aquaviva, with whom Acosta had recently spoken in great detail, was in fact opposed to a General Congregation. In view of the divisions in the Order, he said to Acosta, it might be that even the Congregation might not come to an agreement, and the foreigners would certainly bring pressure to bear to obtain, not what was for the good of the Order, but what would add to their own aggrandizement ; moreover deputies could not be sent either from Flanders or France.[5] But the attempts of Aquaviva to induce the Pope to change his mind were without effect. In his second audience with Acosta

---

[1] ASTRÁIN, III., 215 n. 1 ; VAN ORTROY in *Anal. Boll.*, 1912, 514 ; Carlo Borromeo, Lettere per la prima volta date in luce, Venice, 1762 (a work of anti-Jesuit sentiments).

[2] POLLEN, *loc. cit.*, 237.

[3] IUVENCIUS, *loc. cit.*, p. 5.

[4] See ASTRÁIN, III., 573 ; *cf.* 652.

[5] *Ibid.*, 527, 528.

Clement VIII. expressed his firm determination that the Congregation should be held, and on December 15th Toledo had to take orders to this effect to his General.[1] Aquaviva had not been consulted throughout the affair. Alonso Sanchez, a Jesuit visitor of the Spanish provinces, who had gone to Spain four months before Acosta left that country, might perhaps have prevented the carrying out of Acosta's plans, but he was hindered by illness from speaking to the king until February.   He was able during the course of his visitation to remove various abuses, and he changed the provincials, but when he had succeeded in making the king better disposed towards Aquaviva,[2] it was already too late ; the General Congregation had already been promulgated.

Thus there was begun a fresh struggle against the Constitutions of the Order, that is to say against one of its fundamental points : the power of the General. When Ignatius of Loyola laid down with such exactitude the choice of the General, placing in the hands of one man the whole of the power to appoint the superiors, he was probably influenced by the wish to keep far from his institute the alarming decadence of the religious Orders of his time with which he found himself faced.   His idea was that a capable General would appoint capable superiors, and that everything else would follow of itself.   The very disputes in Spain had proved how important it was for the Order to be firmly governed by a single hand. The Spanish superiors were under the dominion of Philip II. and his Inquisition ; they were in his power and did not dare to take energetic action.   Salvation could only therefore come from Rome, and certainly was not to be found by giving the Spaniards a special superior on Spanish soil, nor in entrusting the appointment of the provincials and rectors to men who were bound to be influenced by a thousand other considerations. If Acosta's plans were to be acted upon, then the great work of Loyola was ruined, and was bound to be broken up into as many parties as there were nations ; in place of an

[1] *Ibid.*, 531.
[2] *Ibid.*, 533-553.

impressive unity of action there would be division and discord. But the danger of Acosta proving victorious was by no means small ; if Clement VIII. and Philip II. seriously wished to do so, they could bring pressure to bear, to which the General Congregation, whether it liked it or not, was bound to yield.

Fortunately for the work of Loyola, it found a highly intelligent and resolute defender, in the very man against whom the principal attack was directed, the General of the Order, Claudio Aquaviva. Alonso Sanchez was of the opinion that if there could be fused into one man the eight or ten most able Jesuits, both as regarded their natural and their supernatural qualities, this would not produce another Aquaviva. This was his own conviction, and all those with whom he had spoken on the subject admitted that he was right.[1] The young Duke of Bavaria, Maximilian I., later on Prince-Elector, was enthusiastic on his behalf. " I cannot praise him enough " he wrote from Rome to his father,[2] " one is forced, so to speak, to fall in love with him, and to look to him alone."

Deeply penetrated with the ideas of Loyola, Aquaviva stood like a sentinel for some thirty-four years, as his champion. No attack could move him. A man of prayer, who sought his recreation in the Fathers of the Church, and who looked at everything from a supernatural point of view, he gave his decisions clearly and firmly, and without any trace of passion as though they were law incarnate. In the countless writings that came from his pen, he never even once abandoned his dignity or unalterable calm, and it is impossible to tell from these pages whether he was well or ill, or whether they were written by him in youth or old age.[3] The esteem which he thus won was added to by the nobility of his family which held a ducal title, as well as by his relations with his nephews, one of whom was a Cardinal, another Archbishop of Naples,

---

[1] *Ibid.*, 541 *seq.*

[2] On April 24, 1593, in ARETIN, Maximilian I., Passau, 1842, 389.

[3] Opinion of ASTRÁIN, IV., 738.

a third Bishop of Cajazzo, while a fourth, also a Jesuit, had
won the martyr's palm in the Indies.[1]   Of great advantage
to Aquaviva was the fact that before he entered the Society
of Jesus, he had been a Papal chamberlain, and thus knew
exactly the conditions of the Roman Curia.[2]   If, however,
Philip II., by the advice of the Inquisition, and Clement VIII.,
by the advice of Toledo, were to impose their will upon the
General Congregation, then the hand of its most skilful pilot
would be rendered powerless.

In spite of the efforts of Acosta the malcontents were not
successful in obtaining the election of one of their number
to the General Congregation.   Only in the province of the
Society at Toledo was there any probability of the election
of a man who, although he was a celebrated scholar, had never
been able to overcome the harshness and bitterness of his
haughty temperament, and who through all his life remained
a burden upon his brethren.   This man, who for several years
had identified himself with the malcontents, was the celebrated
historian Juan de Mariana.[3]

Philip II. had not interfered with the freedom of the
elections, but he informed those who were elected that he
had submitted certain proposals to the General Congregation.[4]
By means of a letter addressed to Clement VIII.,[5] he arranged
for Acosta to participate in the Congregation with the right
to vote, but on the other hand the Pope would not consent
to his wish that Acosta should present his suggestions to the
Congregation in the king's name.[6]   More troublesome to

[1] *Cf.* Vol. XVII. of this work, p. 168.

[2] *Cf.* as to him IUVENCIUS, I., 25, par. 19, n. 33 *seqq.* ; p. 888
seqq. ; ASTRÁIN, III., 211 *seqq.*, IV., 734 *seqq.*

[3] ASTRÁIN, III., 554-562.   The work of Mariana against the
institute of the Society of Jesus is authentic.   When the papers
of Mariana were confiscated in 1609 on account of his writings
against the debasement of the coinage, his manuscript fell into
the hands of the enemies of the Order, and was printed by them
after the death of Mariana (1624) ; *ibid.*, 559 *seq.*

[4] ASTRÁIN, III., 565 *seq.*

[5] *Ibid.*, 567.

[6] *Ibid.* 570.

Aquaviva than the presence of Acosta at the Congregation was the fact that a short time before its commencement Toledo was appointed Cardinal,[1] since Acosta had suggested to Philip II. that he should ask for the elevation of Toledo so that he might as Cardinal preside at the Congregation, and thus act as a counterweight to the influence of Aquaviva.[2] The General of the Order succeeded, however, in inducing the Pope to abandon the much debated proposal that a Cardinal should act as president.[3]

At the beginning of the Congregation, on November 3rd 1593, Aquaviva and seven other Jesuits presented themselves before the Pope, who received them graciously. " From the beginning of my pontificate," he said, "I have heard from men of judgment that your Society has relaxed its first zeal, and I have therefore assembled the Congregation in order that you may provide a remedy. You can do so better than anyone else ; you have in your hands seven-eights of the Christian people, and thanks to your care they remain firm in the Christian faith. I am an eye-witness to this, and I know how well you are working in Poland and Germany for the Christian religion. If then your Order has anywhere weakened, you must remedy this. Inquire whether the final vows of the professed are not delayed overlong, and whether it is wise that any should hold the office of superior so long. As to learning it is my wish that you should follow Thomas Aquinas, that great master whose writings were confirmed and accepted by the Council of Trent."[4]

In this discourse Clement VIII. had clearly shown his own point of view as regards the Jesuits ; he was not guided by any antipathy for them, but by anxiety on their behalf. He had not formed any definite opinion as to the complaints and accusations brought against them, and he seemed to leave it absolutely to the Congregation to arrive at a decision as to the truth of these.

[1] *Ibid.* 575.
[2] *Ibid.* 570.
[3] *Ibid.* 575 *seq.*
[4] *Ibid.* 580 *seq.*

Thus the first task of the assembly[1] would have to be to discuss abuses and the accusations against Aquaviva. Some of the fathers wished to abstain from any judgment upon the General, but Aquaviva insisted upon a full examination. For this purpose Clement VIII. granted all the necessary powers, and sent to the Congregation all the memorials against the Jesuits which had reached him. The examination of the charges against the General, which was carried out by a deputation of five delegates, lasted for a whole month. No blame of any impotrance was found to rest upon the person or life of Aquaviva. As to his method of government the criticism was made that he clung with too great tenacity to his own opinions, and that he had favoured some more than was fitting. Aquaviva begged to be allowed to present this document to the Pope, who was favourably impressed by it.[2]

Besides the inquiries into the matter of the General, certain points of minor importance were first dealt with. Then began the intervention of Philip II. On November 15th he presented five demands, which were principally concerned with the relations of the Order with the Inquisition ; none of these touched the really burning questions, and the assembly accepted them all without difficulty.[3] But this was far from exhausting the wishes of the Spaniards, and soon afterwards the ambassador of Philip, the Duke of Sessa, presented a memorial in the sense desired by Acosta, concerning certain changes in the Constitutions ; he said that the assembly must consider this in all freedom, but at the same time he sought to obtain from the Pope a suggestion to the Jesuits favourable to his wishes ; to this request Clement VIII. would not consent at first. From November 24th to December 3rd there were no general meetings, though discussions were held in private as to the proposals made, but between

---

[1] Their deliberations in the *Institutum Soc. Jesu*, II., 262-283.

[2] ASTRÁIN, III., 583.

[3] Decr. 18, 19 in *Instit. Soc. Jesu*, II., 266 ; ASTRÁIN, III., 584.

December 3rd and 8th, these were unanimously rejected by vote. Acosta, seeing himself powerless and completely isolated, voted with the rest.[1] In accordance with the renewed pressure brought to bear by Sessa, the Pope had laid down the subject of discussion for the meeting on December 8th ; it must be decided whether the final vows were to be made after a fixed period of time, so that once that period had elapsed, there was a right to make them. The Congregation declared that if it considered this essential point, it was purely out of obedience to the Pope. There then followed once more a unanimous resolve to adhere in this as well to the prescriptions of Loyola.[2]

During the weeks that followed there was a discussion as to the attitude to be adopted towards the theology of Thomas Aquinas, and as to diversity of theological opinions,[3] the members of the Order were forbidden to meddle in politics,[4] and the descendants of Jews and Moors were refused admission to the Order.[5] A decisive factor in this last provision was the discovery that out of the twenty-seven writers of memorials against the Constitutions, at least twenty-five were so-called

---

[1] ASTRÁIN, III., 585-587. Iuvencius on several occasions puts matters erroneously, as though the malcontents had a party in the Congregation. As to this see ASTRÁIN, III., 603 n.

[2] ASTRÁIN, III., 587 seq.

[3] Ibid. 589.

[4] Cf. Vol. XIX. of this work, p. 389.

[5] ASTRÁIN, III., 588-593 ; cf. 338, 369, 493, 498. In the case of the Dominicans there was the same difficulty at anyrate in the case of Spain (Bull. ord. Praed., IV., 125 ; Monumenta ord. Praed. hist., X., 231), as well as in the Portuguese province of the Carmelites (ANTONIUS A SPIRITU SANCTO, Consulta varia, Lyons, 1675, 360). For the Franciscans cf. Bull. Rom., VII., 918 ; VIII., 59. The doubt felt as to the neo-Christians in general is treated of by AG. BARBOSA, Votorum decisivorum, t. II., Lyons, 1723, I., 3, vot. 93, pp. 102-128. Cf. Clement VIII. on January 14, 1603, Bull., X., 889 : In Portugal they may not receive canonries with a care of souls, and in Coimbra itself only those of the third and fourth rank.

neo-Christians.[1] On December 31st the Order addressed itself in severe words to its disloyal sons, the disturbers of its peace and the stirrers up of rebellion, as well as against the " false calumnies " which they had " without any justification " brought against the Order. It was true that their memorials bore these words : " So demands the whole of the Society of Jesus," but actually they were but few in number, and reprobate sons ; they ought as soon as possible to be cut off from the Order as a " plague," and where this was not possible they should under pain of expulsion, take an oath to the institute of the Society of Jesus, and to the Papal bulls of confirmation. Anyone who should come to learn of their schemes must denounce them ; the Pope should be asked for a fresh confirmation of the institute.[2]

These last words show that the assembly felt full confidence in the Pope, but it was soon to be undeceived. Clement VIII., as well as his adviser Toledo and the Duke of Sessa, could not but marvel that in spite of the many memorials on the subject of the dissension in the Order, its representatives turned as one man against the handful of innovators, and declared unreservedly for the Constitutions of Loyola.[3] To Clement VIII. this looked like a kind of defiance, which was unwilling to make any change at all. The Spanish ambassador could not feel satisfied at seeing that the exhortations of his king had had no other effect than to cause the decree against the innovators to be followed by a second, which was aimed at further enlightening the king as to the state of affairs.[4]

---

[1] ASTRÁIN, III., 593. Cardinal Henry of Portugal had already on the occasion of the General Congregation of 1573 asked for the intervention of the Pope in order that no neo-Christian should be received by the Order, for otherwise there was reason to fear " ne Societas ista periclitetur et destruatur " (ib id., 695). Ignatius had only desired that care should be taken in the admission of neo-Christians (Mon. Ignat., I., 336, V. 335, Zeitschr. für kath. Theol., 1923, 589).

[2] Decr. 54, in Instit. Soc. Jesu, II., 279.

[3] ASTRÁIN, III., 595.

[4] Decr. 55, ibid., 281.

Toledo too had expected the assembly to have recourse to himself, the great scholar, in frequent consultations, and he was annoyed when he found himself simply ignored. When, on January 3rd, 1594, a fresh decree had laid down the essential points of the Constitutions of the Order, the Duke of Sessa sent a confidant of his to Toledo. The Cardinal complained that the Congregation could not be in worse plight ; he said that the Spanish demands were just, that a proof of the bad disposition of the assembly was the fact that, despite the Pope's orders, they had not asked for any advice, and that they had spoken of the sovereign of Spain as though he were a mere esquire. The Pope, however, would remedy all this on the very next day.

On January 4th, early in the morning, Clement VIII. went with six Cardinals to the professed house of the Jesuits, celebrated mass there with great recollection, and then delivered an allocution to the assembled fathers.[1] He began by bringing out the great merits of the Order, but this very thing should be an incentive to humility. After speaking of humility and pride, he blamed the meddling of the Order in politics and in matters that did not concern it, its preference for peculiar doctrines, and its censure of the doctrines of others, and further blamed them in that they had no regard for princes, king or Emperor, that they discussed whether the Pope had or had not the right to do this or that, that they despised monachism and looked upon their own constitutions as being so perfect and inalterable that there was nothing in them that could be improved ; they were of the opinion that they stood in no need of visitations or reform. All this he said with great gravity, but at the same time with a manner that was altogether friendly, and he ended with a warning that they must consider a remedy, for otherwise he would himself intervene.[2]

This allocution, with its enumeration of defects, threw the

---

[1] Printed copy in J. WIELEWICKI S.J., Diarium domus professae Cracoviensis. *Script. rer. Pol.*, VII., Cracow, 1881, 180-183.

[2] ASTRÁIN, III., 597 *seq.*

Congregation into confusion. Decrees had already been issued concerning divergence of doctrines and adherence to St. Thomas Aquinas ; but what point in the constitutions could be changed in order to impose upon the Jesuits a greater respect for the King of Spain and the monastic Orders ? As far as humility was concerned, Loyola gave place to none as an apostle of that virtue, especially in the case of his own Order, the " lowliest " Society of Jesus, as he often called it, thereby going a step lower even than the friars " minor." It was decided to have recourse to the Pope himself, so that he might point out the matters that required to be changed. Cardinal Toledo, who was asked to further this request, refused in his ill-temper to present it ; as he told the Spanish ambassador, he had presented to Clement. VIII., the day before his visit to the Jesuits, a document naming nine points in the constitutions which called for emendation.[1]

But to the Pope it seemed dangerous to change the constitutions of the Order by force, and on January 8th he pointed to the Congregation four matters for their consideration, as to which they were to come to a free decision.[2] The acceptance of the first two points met with no difficulty ; these concerned the tenure of their office for only three years by the superiors, and the account which the provincial must render at the termination of his period of office. The third point, the acceptance of the Papal reservation of certain sins, was obvious.[3] It was only the fourth suggestion, that in certain cases the assistant of the General should be given the right of decision, which met with difficulties. By a unanimous vote, with five exceptions, the assembly decided that this restriction of the supreme power was inopportune.

But very soon further demands were put forward, which had their origin in conversations between Toledo, Acosta and

---

[1] *Ibid.*, 599.

[2] Decr. 64, *Instit. Soc. Jesu*, II., 284 ; ASTRÁIN, III., 600.

[3] On May 26, 1593, Clement VIII. himself had verbally dispensed the Jesuits from his decree concerning reserved cases. Thus the dispensation was now annulled. *Synopsis*, 155.

the Duke of Sessa.[1] On January 12th Toledo informed
Aquaviva that the Congregation must come to a decision
as to two questions, namely whether another General Congregation should be held after six years, and whether
Aquaviva's assistants ought not to be changed, with the
exception of a German who had only recently been appointed.
The Congregation resolved to declare to the Pope its readiness
to obey, but to beg him not to press the second demand, and
to be allowed to express their reasons against the recurrence
of General Congregations at fixed intervals, as well as against
the change of the assistants.[2] This explanation was never
made, and on January 14th Toledo conveyed to the Congregation an order to accept them without more ado. In
accordance with this order three new assistants were elected
on January 18th, 1594.[3]

This ended the Congregation, which had brought to the
malcontents the opposite of what they desired. All their
aims, though not yet dead, had received a mortal blow.
Aquaviva had been splendidly justified, and nothing essential
had been changed in the constitutions. The order concerning
the limitation of the office of superior to three years, was
afterwards mitigated by Clement VIII. himself, and was later
on altogether abrogated.[4] The fixed period for General
Congregations also seemed to the Pope, after the six years
had elapsed, to be useless, and none was held.[5] The
Inquisition in Spain became reconciled with the Jesuits, while
the king as well declared himself satisfied with the course of
events.[6] Even Acosta realized that his procedure had been

[1] ASTRÁIN, III., 600-602.

[2] Decr. 73, *loc. cit.* 286. ASTRÁIN (III., 602) interprets the
demand as meaning that " cada seis años " another General
Congregation was to be held, but Decr. 73 only says : " ut post
sequens sexennium congregetur denuo generalis congregatio."
Cf. Decr. 75.

[3] Decr. 74, *loc. cit.*

[4] Alexander VII. on January 1, 1663, *Instit. Soc. Jesu,* I., 109.

[5] ASTRÁIN, III., 605.

[6] *Ibid.* 607 *seqq.*

a mistake, and he was reconciled with Aquaviva.[1] After the next General Congregation of the Order in 1608, no more was heard of the party of the malcontents,[2] and with Loyola's beatification in 1609,[3] his constitutions received a new importance.

One of the principal points which had been desired by the king at the Congregation, namely the question whether there should not be appointed a special superior for Spain and the Indies, and whether the life-long duration of the office of General should not be limited, had not even been discussed at the meetings. We learn the reason for this from Acosta, who had been charged, in a special brief to Philip II., to report to him concerning the Congregation. Acosta told the king that not only the Congregation itself, but the Pope himself had been opposed to the discussion of these matters, and that therefore neither the Duke of Sessa nor himself had made any mention of them.[4]

In spite of this Clement VIII. was still thinking in 1595 of abolishing the life-duration of the office of General of the Jesuits. According to what was written to the king at that time by the Spanish ambassador, whom the Pope had informed of his proposal, his motives were " the same as those presented at the last General Congregation by Your Majesty " Aquaviva must therefore be removed from his office and sent to Naples as archbishop. Naturally the Jesuits laid their remonstrances before the Pope, but in vain. They then turned to Cardinal Toledo, who had boasted that he held the Pope in his hand ; but in his case too all petitions were at first of no avail ; it was even bitterly said that Toledo, by getting Aquaviva removed, intended to have a free hand to interfere in the Order. But the Portuguese assistant devised

---

[1] *Ibid.* 611.

[2] *Ibid.* 667 *seq.*

[3] *Ibid.* 676 *seq.*

[4] *Ibid.* 610, *cf.* 608. The brief of Paul V. of September 4, 1606, mentions in the first place the desire of the disturbers of the peace that the duration of the office of General should be shortened. *Instit. Soc. Jesu,* I., 131.

a remedy. He said to Toledo : if Aquaviva has to be an archbishop, then the Jesuits would be very glad to see him a Cardinal ; this could easily be managed by the intercession of the princes, and after that it would remain to be seen which of the two Jesuit Cardinals would have the upper hand in the Order. Aquaviva would not have been a pleasing colleague to Toledo, so he took steps to get the Pope to abandon his plan.[1]

But this did not bring the intrigues against Aquaviva to an end, Ferdinand Mendoza, one of the party of the malcontents, had already in 1592 been on the point of being expelled from the Order on account of his unseemly behaviour, but he had been treated indulgently and had been sent to the lonely college of Monforte. But this step led to a fresh dispute, in which the Pope intervened several times against Aquaviva. Mendoza, who was well versed in the ways of the world, was able by his *savoir faire* to win the high esteem of the Count of Lemos, who possessed vast properties in the neighbourhood of Monforte, and still more that of the countess, a sister of the future Duke of Lerma, who was the true king of Spain in the time of Philip III. When Lemos went to Naples as the new viceroy, Aquaviva vainly tried to prevent the rebellious Jesuit from accompanying him as his confessor. Once he was in Italy, Mendoza was very soon able to stir up against his General even the Pope, who was unwilling to annoy the viceroy. Mendoza had addressed to Aquaviva several arrogant letters, which he afterwards wished to have sent back to him. By the Pope's orders the General was forced to send them. Aquaviva had sent to Naples a man whom he could trust to obtain information as to the conduct of the viceroy's confessor. Owing to the insistence of the latter, this confidant had to be recalled, and when Mendoza spread the rumour that this had been done by the Pope's orders, Clement VIII. did not dare to deny it. The inquiries that had been begun had brought to light many

---

[1] ASTRÁIN, III., 629-632. Sessa to Philip II., February 18, 1596, *ibid.* 717 *seq.*

unseemly things, but Clement VIII. forbade all interference,
and when further accusations had reached him, " on account
of more important considerations " he refused permission
even for an inquiry to be begun.   After the death of the Count
of Lemos in 1601, Mendoza wished to return home with the
countess.   The Spanish Jesuits made every effort, but in
vain, to be freed of his presence ; Aquaviva could only reply
that if he retained Mendoza, the Pope would give orders to
let him go.[1]   Armed with a secret brief forbidding all superiors
to make any inquiries about him, Mendoza accompanied the
countess to the court at Valladolid.   There he soon began to
make his influence felt, for the all-powerful Duke of Lerma
suddenly showed himself opposed to the Jesuits.

Aquaviva took every means to remove this dangerous man
from the court. Of the two attempts he made, the first failed
to attain its purpose, while the second, even before it had been
begun, was rendered impossible by an intrigue.[2]   The General
then sought to obtain the consent of the Pope to a third
attempt.   Clement received the remonstrances of the Jesuits
graciously, and assured them that he did not wish to hamper
the   steps   they   were   taking   against   Mendoza.   But
Clement VIII. was above all anxious not to offend the Countess
of Lemos, as is clear from a letter of Aldobrandini to the
Spanish nuncio.[3]   Aldobrandini wrote that the Pope had
refused to give the Jesuits a brief against Mendoza, as he did
not wish to mix himself up with the affair, and that the nunco
must not pay any attention to it.

The Pope was not ill-advised in acting thus ; he probably
foresaw that in face of the power of Lerma, Aquaviva would
not have any more success with his third attempt, and so it
proved.   Counting upon the Pope, Aquaviva had charged
the superior of the professed house at Toledo to take steps
against his presumptuous subject.   When the superior
threatened him with excommunication and other penalties,

[1] ASTRÁIN, III., 634-638.

[2] *Ibid.* 641-644.

[3] Of August 23, 1604, *ibid.* 645.

Mendoza promptly declared himself ready to leave the court. But while the two were still in negotiation, a visit from the nuncio Ginnasio was announced ; Lerma and the Countess of Lemos had learned from him what had occurred, and both of them " spat fire." Two days later Hojeda was able indeed to repeat to Mendoza in the presence of the provincial and other Jesuits his commands, but on the same day the nuncio summoned the provincial and Mendoza to his presence, forbade Mendoza under grave ecclesiastical penalties to leave Valladolid, and ordered the provincial not to give his consent to his departure. Ginnasio wrote to Aldobrandini that this step had been taken in the interests of the Order itself, and that Aquaviva had not perhaps realized the consequences of his interference. Clement VIII. approved the action of his nuncio, and soon afterwards issued a brief to Mendoza withdrawing his correspondence and his relations with the countess from the supervision of his superiors, and permitting him to have a lay-brother and two secretaries in his service, as well as other privileges.[1]

Mendoza had thus won a brilliant victory. In order to humiliate the General yet more, and as it were display his power, there occurred to this arrogant man the strange idea of bringing Aquaviva to Spain and thus tying his hands completely. Philip III. was therefore obliged to invite the General to Spain, and a sheet attached to the king's letter gave a number of reasons for his making the journey. On November 10th, 1604, Aquaviva thanked the king for his kindness and sent to Spain by means of his assistants a refutation of the king's reasons. But Mendoza found a way out of the difficulty, and a second letter from the king asked the Pope to order the General to set out. Clement VIII. issued this order and adhered to it. Aquaviva pointed out that the summons to Spain was nothing else but an act of vengenace, but to no purpose ; the assistants set forth their reasons verbally and in writing, but this too was useless. The Jesuits then succeeded in obtaining some fifty letters

[1] *Ibid.* 644-649.

on behalf of the General, from the most distinguished persons, among them the Kings of France and Poland. But Clement VIII. was unwilling to deprive the sovereign of the two worlds of the modest pleasure of a visit from the General of the Jesuits.

Thus the head of the Society of Jesus found himself faced with the danger of finding himself handed over with tied hands to his rebellious subject, and this proved too much even for the iron constitution of Aquaviva, and he fell dangerously ill. The Pope sent his private physician to ascertain if the illness was really serious, but the latter as well as seven other doctors certified that there could be no question of his thinking of the journey. When Aquaviva recovered, Clement VIII. was dead, and there was no longer any talk of the journey to Spain.[1]

Of great importance was the impulse given by Clement VIII. to the reform of the Carmelite Order,[2] inaugurated by

[1] ASTRÁIN, III., 649 *seqq.* The difficulty was not ended, even after the death of Clement VIII. The premature death of Leo XI. made his help against the Jesuits of the court inefficacious (*ibid.* 653 *seq.*) ; Paul V. seemed at first to wish to leave the Jesuit superiors a free hand towards their subjects, but he probably wished to make use of the work of Mendoza for a family marriage, and made him (brief of June 1, 1606, *ibid.* 655) a concession that was perhaps even greater than that of Clement VIII., namely that in the houses of his Order he must naturally be subject to his superiors, but outside of them he was allowed to live in his own way and in opposition to the will of his superiors, being subject only to the Pope, and freed moreover from his obligation to poverty and obedience. But this very excess of privilege brought its own remedy. Aquaviva succeeded in getting hold of a copy of the brief, and thus he and his assistants had the means of persuading the Pope that Mendoza would lead a better life outside the Order. Paul V. resolved to make him Bishop of Cuzco in Peru, and Mendoza was at last, whether he liked it or not, compelled to accept this unsought-for dignity. He was preconized on January 12, 1609, and Aquaviva was able once more to breathe freely (*ibid.* 654-659).

[2] *Cf.* Vol. XIX. of this work, p. 148.

St. Teresa. This had spread further and further, and in 1593 had reached Rome. In that year Clement VIII. allowed the reformed Carmelites to elect a General of their own, and in 1600 approved of their forming congregations independent of each other, a Spanish one with the Indies, and an Italian one called that of St. Elias, which later on included France, Germany and Poland.[1] A Spaniard, Andrea Diaz, introduced, at the beginning of the pontificate of Clement VIII., the discalced Augustinian Hermits into Rome, where they were treated with favour by the Pope.[2]

There were few Orders to which Clement VIII. did not extend his favour.[3] The Barnabites, whom he had once described as the best collaborators of the bishops,[4] were in several cases encouraged by him. He confirmed the privileges of the Somaschi,[5] the separation of the reformed Basilians from the unreformed,[6] the Order of Capuchin nuns,[7] the statutes of the Italian Annunziate,[8] and the reform, inaugurated in Spain, of the Orders of the Trinitarians and Mercedari,[9] whose work was the liberation of the slaves.[10]

But however much the interests of the religious Orders occupied the attention of Clement VIII., he did not neglect his care for the secular clergy. Cardinal Rusticucci, who had already been made Cardinal Vicar by Sixtus V., continued to discharge that important office.[11] To him was attached a special commission of reform, which was to carry out the

---

[1] See *Freiburger Kirchenlex.*, III.[2], 971.

[2] See Bull., X., 548 *seq.*

[3] See *Dict. de théol. cath.*, III., 85. For the Capuchins see Bull., X., 763 *seq.*

[4] See PREMOLI, 337, 358, 366, 378, 381, 388, 393 *seq.*

[5] See Bull., X., 42 *seq.*

[6] See *Archiv f. kath. Kirchenrecht*, VIII., 82.

[7] See HEIMBUCHER, I., 362.

[8] See *ibid.* 621. *Cf. Aschbachs Kirchenlex.*[2], I., 224 *seq.*

[9] Bull. X., 184 *seq.*, 580 *seq.*, XI., 128 *seq.*

[10] Bull. X., 529 *seq.*

[11] See DOLFIN, Relazione, 463.

ordinances made during the visitation.[1] As he had already done in the case of the Auditors of the Rota,[2] so did Clement VIII. at the beginning of his pontificate address to the directors and students of all the pontifical colleges paternal exhortations to live and make progress in virtue.[3] In order to put an end to all abuses he issued salutary ordinances concerning indulgences.[4] Nor did the inscriptions, nor the tomb of the inamorata of Alexander VI. in S. Maria del Popolo escape his attention, and these were removed in April 1594.[5] In the same way he caused to be removed from the cathedral of Siena the image of the so-called Pope Joan which was there.[6]

From the beginning of his pontificate the Pope above all insisted, both in the case of the parish-priests[7] and of the bishops, upon their observance of the duty of residence.[8] In so doing he met with the same difficulties from the bishops as his predecessors had done. Still, as in the past, many bishops remained without necessity at the Curia in Rome. The verbal exhortations of the Pope that they should return to their dioceses only had a partial effect. One made one excuse, another another, and the requests for dispensations grew in number.[9] A new and more severe ordinance became

[1] *Cf.* BENTIVOGLIO, Memorie 46.

[2] See *Avviso of March 21, 1592, Urb. 1060, I., Vatican Library.

[3] See Bull., IX., 573 *seq.*

[4] REUSCH, Bellarmins Selbstbiographie, 134 *seq.*

[5] See *Avviso of April 19, 1594, Urb. 1062, p. 193, Vatican Library.

[6] See DÖLLINGER, Papstfabeln des Mittelalters[2], Munich, 1863, 18.

[7] See *Avvisi of February 5, 1592, and November 12, 1594, Urb. 1060, I., 1062, Vatican Library.

[8] See *letter of G. Niccolini of February 6, 1592, State Archives, Florence ; *Avviso of February 12, 1592, Urb. 1060, I., Vatican Library, and PARUTA, Dispacci, I., 93, 220.

[9] *S.D.N. proposuit constitutionem contra praelatos non residentes, ut non possint esse cardinales, faciendam, an per bullam an vero per decretum consistoriale. . . . Dixit canones et

inevitable ;[1] this was to include even the Cardinals, and the only diversity of opinion was whether the enactment should be made by bull or by consistorial decree.[2] After a discussion by the Congregation of the Council and Bishops,[3] on July 5th, 1595, Clement VIII. laid down a decree, which renewed all the previous enactments concerning the duty of residence, and laid it down that no one could receive the purple who had failed in this respect.[4]

There was then a sensible improvement, but rigorists like Cardinal Bellarmine were not yet satisfied. To the remonstrances made to the Pope by the Cardinal in an out-spoken memorial,[5] Clement VIII. frankly admitted that he had been

constitutiones Patrum nostrorum satis superque testari, quantum semper optatum fuerit ut episcopi in suis ecclesiis resideant et ad munia pastoralia incumbant. Hoc ipsum tam concilio Tridentino quam aliis postmodum S.P. constitutionibus sancitum esse. Verum adhuc non satis provisum, cum se plerique variis excusationibus ab ipsa residentia eximere conentur, et non levi S[tem] S. molestia afficiant, importune instantes, ut eis ab ecclesiis suis abesse permittatur, non sine magno crediti sibi gregis compendio. He ordered them to ponder well the constitution. Acta consist. June 2, 1595, Cod. Barb. lat. 2171, III., Vatican Library.

[1] *Cf.* PARUTA, Dispacci, III., 157.

[2] See *acta consist, June 5, 1595, *loc. cit.* *Cf. supra*, p. 186, n. 9.

[3] See PARUTA, *loc. cit.* 171,

[4] *S.D.N. laudavit residentiam et eius necessitatem et utilitatem, et e sinu decretum proferens, illud legit, innovans omnia decreta et constitutiones de residentia, et constituens, ne quis episcopus vel superior non residens actu in sua ecclesia vel non solitus residere possit in cardinalem assumi. Acta consist, July 5, 1595, *loc. cit.*

[5] This document, together with the " Responsiones S. Pontificis " which show how humble the Pope was, and at the same time how profoundly convinced he was of the great and difficult task of his pontificate, were immediately spread abroad by means of manuscript copies. Urb. 538, p. 1 *seqq.*, and 859, p. 504 *seqq.*, Barb. lat. 2620, p. 58 *seqq.*, Vatican Library ; Cod. X.-IV., 43, Casanatense Library, Rome ; Cod. 38 B. 1, p. 61 *seq.*,

wrong in allowing the bishops to come to Rome so easily, so that it was only with difficulty that they could be sent away again. With regard to the eleven non-resident Cardinals whom Bellarmine had named, the Pope was able to point out that in their case there were legitimate excuses, as well as for the employment of bishops as nuncios, because persons suited for that office were only to be found in limited numbers, and because the nature of their business prevented frequent changes. That the state of affairs was very much better than it had been, is clear from the fact, that in the whole of the States of the Church there was only one bishop who held a political office ; another, the Bishop of Camerino, who was vice-legate of the Marches, did not count, because there he was able to go every day to his diocese.

But even Clement VIII. was obliged to realize how difficult it was to eradicate the abuse, by which bishops were absent from their dioceses, and remained without excuse in Rome. In spite of his warnings,[1] towards the end of his pontificate,

Corsini Library ; Cod. 75 of the Library of S. Pietro in Vincoli (see LÄMMER, Zur Kirchengesch. 47) ; Cod. C. IV., 21, p. 21 *seqq*, Library at Siena ; Inform. polit., II., 1 *seqq*., State Library, Berlin ; also elsewhere, *e.g.* among the Italian manuscripts of the Library at Stockholm. This document was also repeatedly reprinted, *e.g.* in ALBERICIUS, Baronii epist., III., 3 *seqq*., HOFFMANN (Collectio, I.), BARTOLI (Opere 24, IV., 42 *seqq*.). DÖLLINGER (Beiträge, III., 83 *seqq*.), LÄMMER (Melet., 367 *seqq*), and LE BACHELET (Auct., 513 *seqq*.) from a copy revised by Bellarmine himself. From a letter of Clement VIII. of October 14, 1600 (in LE BACHELET in *Rech. de science relig.*, XIII., 444 *seq*.) it is clear that Bellarmine had presented his memorial a short time before, and that the replies are those of Clement VIII. himself and not of Baronius. A. RATTI (Opuscolo inedito e sconosciuto del card. Baronio, Perugia, 1910) has published a memorial presented by Baronius in the spring of 1595 to the Pope, concerning the government of the Church in accordance with the prescriptions of Gregory the Great.

[1] *Cf.* the *briefs of exhortation to the Bishop of Oristano (Sardinia) Ant. Canopolo, July 5, 1600, and " Episc. S. Jacobi insulae Capitis Viridi," March 22, 1602, Arm. 44, t. 44, n. 198,

in 1603, there were so many bishops present in the Curia that he was obliged to take fresh steps.[1] Even then it was only with reluctance that some obeyed ; but the Pope insisted upon his order being carried out.   In April 1604 almost all the bishops had left Rome, and only a few who had not found the opportunity for going still remained.[2] When the Pope informed the nuncio at Madrid of this success, he urged him to do all he could to see that this example was followed in the Spanish capital as well.[3]

Gregory XIV., who had taken part in the Council of Trent as Bishop of Cremona, in order to comply with the feeling of that Council, which in its twenty-second session had required in the case of the bishops a special training in theology and canon law, had resolved to submit the candidates for the episcopate to a two-fold examination before they were confirmed.   In the first place, by means of an informative process, the previous manner of life of the nominee was to be inquired into, and then they were to be examined in their knowledge of the above-mentioned sciences.   His premature death had prevented Pope Gregory from carrying out this project.   Clement VIII., at the very beginning of his pontificate, gave effect to this by prescribing such an examination in the case of all the bishoprics of free collation in Italy and the neighbouring islands, as well as for those of royal nomination.   For this purpose he set up a Congregation, and to the Cardinals appointed to it there were added certain prelates as examiners.[4] The Congregation began its work as early

and t. 46, n. 75, Papal Secret Archives. *Cf.* also the *report of G. C. Foresto, October 14, 1600, Gonzaga Archives, Mantua.

[1] See *Avviso of November 12, 1603, Urb. 1071, Vatican Library.

[2] See *Avvisi of March 30, April 3 and 7, 1604, Urb. 1072, Vatican Library.

[3] *Warning to D. Ginnasio, April 6, 1604, Barb. 3852, Vatican Library.

[4] *Cf.* *report of G. Niccolini, July 3, 1592, State Archives, Florence ; DE LUCA, Rel. Cur. Rom. for. disc., 21 ; MORONI, XVI., 195 *seq.* ; BANGEN, 89 *seq.*

as July, 1592. The Pope himself assisted at the examinations. These were held with great detail and no dispensations were allowed.[1] The greater the success obtained by this method of procedure, the more firmly did the Pope adhere to it.[2] Clement VIII. also gave proofs of extraordinary rigour in the matter of granting resignations of ecclesiastical revenues.[3] He would not allow any accumulation of benefices ; the only exception he made was in the case of the cardinalitial dioceses, because his predecessors since the Council of Trent had not changed the conditions of those dioceses.[4]

This careful selection of bishops, as well as the example set by the Pope, as supreme pastor of Rome, had an important effect in the improvement of the Italian episcopate,[5] and Clement VIII. had the joy of seeing how many bishops in Italy were labouring in the spirit of Catholic reform by establishing seminaries, and holding synods and visitations.[6] Thus the following acquired great merit as conscientious pastors and as reforming bishops in the fullest sense of the word : at Adria, the Carmelite Lorenzo Laureti ; at Aquileia, Francesco Barbaro ;[7] at Venice, Lorenzo

---

[1] Cf. *Urb. 839, p. 298 seq., and *Avvisi of July 4 and 18, 1592, Urb. 1060, II., Vatican Library, and PARUTA, Dispacci, I., 35, II., 73.

[2] Cf. *brief to the Archduke Ferdinand, October 25, 1597, Arm. 44, t. 41, n. 232, Papal Secret Archives.

[3] See *report of G. del Carretto, November 31, 1593, Gonzaga Archives, Mantua.

[4] See LÄMMER, Melet., 377 seq.

[5] See ZACHARIAE Iter litt., 303.

[6] For the following list, which does not claim to be complete, cf. UGHELLI, Italia sacra, and MORONI, Dizionario, above all for those bishops in whose case no special works or dissertations are given.

[7] For the synod held at Udine in 1596, and the pleasure it gave to Clement VIII., see IUVENCIUS, V., 430. For the synodal activity of Barbaro see MARCUZZI, Sinodi Aquileiesi, Udine, 1910, and for his activity in visitations see, besides SCHMIDLIN, 6 seq., JOPPI, Relazione d. visita apost. in Carniola Stiria e

Priuli;[1] at Belluno the learned Luigi Lollini;[2] at
Ceneda, Marcantonio Mocenigo ; at Treviso, Francesco
Cornaro ; at Verona, Cardinal Agostino Valiero,[3] well
known as a Christian humanist ; at Pavia and Mantua,
the Franciscan Francesco Gonzaga ;[4] at Cremona, Cesare
Speciani ;[5] at Modena, Gaspare Silingardi ;[6] at Milan,
the great and learned Frederick Borromeo, who was a
patron of the arts ;[7] at Reggio-Emilia Claudio Rangoni ;[8]
at Como, Feliciano Ninguarda ;[9] at Pavia and Novara, the
Barnabites Alessandro Sauli[10] and Carlo Bascapè,[11] imitators

Carinzia, Udine, 1862. There too the report to Clement VIII.
concerning the highly necessary visitation which he had suggested.
The manuscript is preserved in the parochial archives at Cremona,

[1] L. Priuli founded the seminary and held a synod in 1592 ;
cf. P. PASCHINI, La riforma del seppelire nelle chiese nel sec.
XVI., Monza, 1922, 20 seqq.

[2] See A. RATTI, Opuscolo ined. del card. Baronio, 15.

[3] See C. LIBARDI, *De vita et rebus gestis episc. Veronens.,
Cod. DCC.-LXXXIII., pp. 253, 286 seq., Capitular Library,
Verona. For the magnificent Dialogue by VALIERO " Philippus
sive de christiana laetitia " see KNELLER in Zeitschr. f. kath.
Theol., XLII., 186 seqq. Cf. MAI, Spicil., VIII., viii. seq., 89 seq.
118 seq.

[4] See the monograph by FR. M. PAOLINI, Rome, 1906. Cf.
MAIOCCHI in Riv. di scienze stor. (Rome), 1907 ; Arch. Veneto,
N.S. XXI. (1911), 295 seqq.

[5] See Vita di Mons. C. Speciani, Bergamo, 1786, 320 seqq.,
355 seqq, 366 seqq., 497.

[6] See RICCI, II., 92 seq. 255 seq., where the special literature is
given.

[7] Cf. MAI, Spicil., VIII., 473, and more fully infra.

[8] Cf. G. SACCANI, I vescovi di Reggio, R. 1902, 130 seq. ;
COTTAFAVI, Il Seminario di Reggio-Emilia, R-E, 1907, 3 seq.

[9] See MONTI, Atti d. visita past. d. F. Ninguarda, 1589-1592,
Part I., in Racc. Comense, II., Como, 1882, 94. Cf. Röm.
Quartalschr., 1891, 62 seq., 124 seq.

[10] Cf. Vol. XIX., of this work, p. 210.

[11] See J. CHIESA, Vita del ven. C. Bascapè, 2 vols., Milan, 1858.
Cf. C. BASCAPÈ, Scritti publ. nel governo del suo vescovato

of Charles Borromeo ; at Asti the Franciscan Francesco Panigarola ;[1] at Saluzzo, Giovanni Giovenale Ancina ;[2] at Genoa the Benedictine Matteo Rovarola ;[3] at Pisa, Carlo Antonio Pocci ;[4] at Colle, Usimbardo de' Usimbardi ;[5] at Volterra, Guido Servidio ; at Fiesole the disciple of Philip Neri, Francesco Maria Tarugi ;[6] at Bologna, Cardinal Gabriele Paleotto ;[7] at Imola, Alessandro Musotti ; at Fossombrone, Ottavio Accoramboni ;[8] at Camerino, Gentile Dolfino ; at

dall'a. 1593 al 1609, Novara, 1609.   The correspondence between Bascapè and Alessandro Sauli, 1591, was published by PREMOLI in *Riv. di scienze stor.* (Rome), 1907-8.   See also PREMOLI, Una gloria di Novara. C. Bascapè, 1593-1615, in the single number, *L'Azione*, Novara, 1908 ; RATTI, *loc. cit.*, 17 *seq.*   PREMOLI, 303 *seq.*, 326 *seq.*, 342 *seq.*, 360 *seq.*

[1] *Cf.* Vol. XIX. of this work, p. 210.

[2] For this disciple of Philip Neri, who was beatified by Leo XIII. in 1890, and his fruitful labours in his diocese, *cf.* the monographs by RICHARD (Mayence, 1892) and DUVER (Rennes, 1905) and also SAVIO, Marchesato e diocesi di Saluzzo nel sec. XVII., Saluzzo, 1915.

[3] In the *brief addressed to the Duke of Mantua, July 26, 1596, the Archbishop of Genoa is described as " vir insigni vitae integritate et zelo Dei quem multis nominibus valde amamus." Gonzaga Archives, Mantua.

[4] For the foundation of the seminary at Pisa (1604) see *Mem. d. accad. di Torino, Sc. mor. stor. e fil.*, 2nd series, I., 53.

[5] See Constitutiones synodales et decreta condita a rev. D. Usimbardo Usimbardio episc. Collensi primo in dioces. synodo habita A. 1594, Florence, 1595.   There also the decrees published by Usimbardo in 1595 at the diocesan synod of Arezzo.

[6] *Cf.* Vol. XIX. of this work, p. 169.

[7] For the synod of Bologna, 1594, see LOZZI, Bibl. ital., II., 49. *Cf.* Archiepiscopale Bonon. auctore card. GABR. PALEOTO, Rome, 1594, and UGHELLI, II.   *Cf.* also Gabr. Paleotti *Sermones in visitat. Alb. et Salin. dioc. 1590 to 1595, Cod. 630 (1166), University Library, Bologna.

[8] *Cf.* *Memoria e rito dell'orazione della sera instituita da Msgr. vescovo Accoramboni l'anno 1591 in Fossombrone e sua diocesi.   Urb. 1509 A. Vatican Library.

Urbino, Antonio Gianotti and Giuseppe Ferreri ;[1] at Gubbio, Mariano Sabelli ;[2] at Assisi, Marcello Crescenzi ; at Amelia, Antonio Maria Graziani ;[3] at Spoleto, Alfonso Visconti ;[4] at Rossano, Lucio Sanseverino ; at Sarno, Antonio de Aquino ; at Siponto, Domenico Ginnasio ;[5] at Teramo, Vincenzo de Monte Santo ; at Capua from 1602 onwards, Cardinal Bellarmine ;[6] at Matera, Giovanni de Mira ;[7] at Reggio Calabria, Annibale d' Afflitto ;[8] at Messina, Antonio Lombardi ;[9] at Monreale, Lodovico de Torres ; at Cefalù, Francesco Gonzaga, who there and later on at Pavia and Mantua rendered good service and established the first Tridentine seminary in Sicily.

Clement VIII. also displayed a salutary activity in filling the gaps which death had occasioned in the College of Cardinals. These were very considerable, for Clement VIII. witnessed the disappearance of altogether forty-five Cardinals, among them men so distinguished as Scipione Gonzaga, William Allen, Francisco Toledo, Gabriele Paleotto, Errico Caetani, Georg Radziwill, Iñigo de Avalos de Aragonia, Lodovico Madruzzo, Giulio Santori, Alfonso Gesualdo, Silvio Antoniano, Lucio Sassi, Arnauld d' Ossat and Antonio Maria Salviati.[10]

[1] *Acta of the canonical visitation of 1578, 1587, and 1597, in the Archiepiscopal Archives, Urbino.

[2] M. SARTI, De Episcopis Eugubinis, Pisauri, 1755, 225 seqq.

[3] See Synodus Amerina ab A. M. Gratiano episc. habita, 1595, edit. sec. cui accessit vita eiusdem, Rome, 1792. For Graziani cf. Vol. XXI. of this work, pp. 62, 65, and MAI, Spicil., VIII., 469 seq. A diocesan report by Graziani in Bull. stor. per l'Umbria, XIII. (1907), 138 seq.

[4] Made a Cardinal in 1599.

[5] See C. MEZAMICI, Notizie d. operat. del card. Dom. Ginnasio, Rome, 1682.

[6] See COUDERC, I., 367 seq.

[7] For the synod held at Matera in 1597 see Arch. Napol., IX., 366.

[8] See the biography of D'Afflitto by MINASI (Naples, 1898) and Roma e l'Oriente, VII. (1914), 111 seq.

[9] See *Constitutiones synodales Messanen, 1591, Cod. 20, of the Library, Girgenti.

[10] See the list of all the Cardinals who died under Clement VIII.

The number of new Cardinals appointed at the seven cardinalitial creations of Clement VIII. was as great as fifty-three.[1]
In these the Pope accorded hardly any influence to the
Cardinals, and far less to the civil governments.[2] " Cardinals
who are appointed at the request of the princes," he said,
" almost always follow private interests, as I have myself
experienced at the conclaves."[3]

The Cardinalitial appointments of Clement VIII. are almost

in ALBÈRI, II., 4, 354, where, however, Báthory, who was killed
in 1599, is omitted. For this prince of the Church, who at the
end, forgetful of the duties of his ecclesiastical state, came to a
miserable end, see KOLBERG, Zur Gesch. des Kard. Andreas
Báthory, and Aus dem Haushalt des Kard. A. Báthory, both
Braunsberg, 1910. For the death of Cardinal S. Gonzaga see
the *brief to Giulio Cesare Gonzaga, February 5, 1593, Arm. 44,
t. 38, n. 203, Papal Secret Archives. For the death of Allen see
BELLESHEIM, 201 seq. The sorrow of the court at the death of
Caetani is *reported by G. C. Foresto, December 18, 1599,
Gonzaga Archives, Mantua. For Santori see *Avviso of June 13,
1602, where it is stated : " the Cardinal did many good works,
and after thirty-five years of the cardinalate left 14,000 scudi of
debts " (Urb. 1070, Vatican Library). Cf. also DOLFIN, Relazione,
485. The tomb of Santori, with a fine bust, in his chapel in
St. John Lateran, see FORCELLA, VIII., 51. At the consistory
of February 19, 1603, Clement VIII. pronounced the funeral
discourse for Gesualdo. See *Acta consist. card. S. Severinae,
Cod. Barb. lat. 2871, III., Vatican Library.

[1] Cf. Vol. XXIII. of this work, p. 248 ; cf. PHILLIPS, VI., 231.

[2] See Carte Strozz., I., 2, 269, and in App. n. 15 the *report
of G. C. Foresto of February 27, 1599, Gonzaga Archives, Mantua.
Cf. the *brief to the Duke of Lorraine, June 20, 1592, Brevia,
Arm. 44, t. 37, n. 413, Papal Secret Archives, and the autograph
*letter of Charles Emanuel of Savoy, August 4, 1596, State
Archives, Turin. For the most part the requests of other princes
as well were not considered, especially those of Philip II. : e.g. at
the very beginning of the pontificate the request of the King of
Spain that the Pope should confer the purple on the Archbishop
of Saragossa, Andrea Bobadilla ; see *letter of Philip II. to
Clement VIII., April 25, 1592, Doria Archives, Rome.

[3] Report of the Este envoy, June 8, 1596 ; see RICCI, II., 245.

without exception deserving of praise. Setting aside the too young Giovanni Battista Deti, the Cardinals appointed by Clement VIII. proved themselves men of worth ; such were the learned Jesuit Toledo, the venerable Sassi, the Oratorian Francesco Maria Tarugi, whose life may be called truly apostolic, Camillo Borghese who was afterwards Paul V., the Auditors of the Rota, Lorenzo Bianchetti, Francesco Mantica and Pompeo Arigoni, the great Bonifacio Bevilacqua, the versatile Alfonso Visconti, Domenico Toschi who had sprung from the lowest ranks purely by his own merits, the disinterested d'Ossat, and lastly like three brilliant stars outshining the rest : Baronius, Silvio Antoniano and Bellarmine, who in their humility had refused to accept so great an honour, so that Clement VIII. was forced to constrain them under obedience, threatening them with excommunication.[1] These three Cardinals were assigned apartments at the Vatican,[2] since Baronius was the Pope's confessor, Silvio Antoniano his secretary of briefs, and Bellarmine, after the death of Toledo his theologian, an office which he exercised with great freedom.[3] The lofty sentiments which animated Cardinals Baronius and Tarugi is clear from a letter of the last-named belonging to the year 1598, only recently discovered, in which he unites himself to Baronius in his desire to renounce the purple, so as to return once more to the peace of the Oratory.[4]

These new Cardinals vied with the older ones, such as Valiero, Frederick Borromeo, Tagliavia, Sfondrato, Aquaviva and Alessandro de' Medici, who was to succeed Clement VIII. If among these many Cardinals there were to be found two of

---

[1] See COUDERC, I., 260 *seq.* For Baronius see ALBERICI, III., 391 *seq.* ; CALENZIO, 419 *seq.*, 459 *seq.* *Cf.* also the *Avvisi of November 29, 1595, and June 1, 1596, Urb. 1063, 1064, Vatican Library. See also the *letter of L. Arrigoni, June 8, 1596, Gonzaga Archives, Mantua.

[2] BENTIVOGLIO, Memorie, 151.

[3] *Cf.* COUDERC, I., 234 *seq.*, 295 *seq.*

[4] See the text of the letter in the opusculum L'Oratorio Filippino di Firenze, al ven. Card. Cesare Baronio, Florence, 1908, 71 *seq*

worldly sentiments, like Sforza[1] and Deti, these only served, as Bentivoglio remarks, to bring out all the more brilliantly the virtues of the rest. Clement VIII. for his part, left nothing undone to bring back Deti to a better manner of life.[2] He also made use of every opportunity that offered to remind the Cardinals of their duties.[3]

However many eminent men the College of Cardinals contained under Clement VIII., its influence as a college visibly diminished. This was due in great measure to the

[1] Sforza only became a priest in the autumn of 1614 ; see *Studi e docum.*, XV., 282.

[2] See BENTIVOGLIO, Memorie, 85 *seq.*, 126 *seq.* The description of the Sacred College of Clement VIII. by Bentivoglio (59 *seq.*, 92 *seq.*) is completed by DOLFIN, Relazione, 479 *seq.*, 493 *seq.*, who principally discusses the political position of the Cardinals, and their hopes at a conclave. The same is the case in the *Informazione for the Marchese Vigliena spoken of in Vol. XXIII. of this work, p. 254, and in the *Discorso* which is preserved in the Boncompagni Archives, Rome, which was composed in view of a conclave, and contains many Roman *dicerie*, and is identical with the report published by RATTI (Opuscolo ined. di Baronio, 38 *seqq.*). The Bolognese FABIO ALBERGATI published Libri tre del cardinale, Rome, 1598. GIOV. BOTERO wrote Dell'uffitio del cardinale libri, II., Rome, 1599, where the duties of the Cardinals as against heresy are also discussed. Botero was not fairly judged by MEINECKE (Die Idee der Staatsraison in der neueren Geschichte, Munich, 1924) ; see *Giorn. d. lett. ital.*, LXXXVI., 176.

[3] See *Acta consist. card. S. Severinae, March 10, 1593, March 28, 1594, and December 4, 1600, *loc. cit.*, Vatican Library ; *Avviso of December 29, 1593, Urb. 1061, *ibid.* Clement VIII. also tried to reintroduce the ancient custom by which the Cardinals went to the Consistory on horseback ; see *Avviso of March 28, 1594, Urb. 1062, *ibid.*, and for the Holy Year (1600) BAUMGARTEN, Neue Kunde, 17 *seq.* According to the *Avviso of August 29, 1601 (Urb. 1069), special sermons were ordered for the Cardinals. Cardinal Este, who gave scandal by his behaviour (see MEYER, Nuntiaturberichte, 218, 220, 223), received on June 19, 1604, a *Monitorium in which the Pope disapproved of his intention " longe lateque peregrinari " ; Arm. 44, t. 56, p. 250, Papal Secret Archives.

independence of Clement VIII.[1], which was much felt by the Cardinals, and to the predominant position held by his nephew, Cardinal Pietro Aldobrandini ; it may also be attributed to the increase of the Papal authority, and to the establishment of the Congregations, by which the power of the Consistory had been considerably lessened. Although certain Cardinals, as for example Paleotto, complained of this and sought to restore the ancient order, the advantages of the new method of transacting business were nevertheless evident. The transaction of affairs by way of process, and the cumbrousness of a conciliar assembly, in which there were always to be found a diversity of opinions, had rendered the treatment of important matters by the Consistory almost impossible.[2] Once the change had been inaugurated, it was no longer possible to stop it, all the more so as it was based upon the strictly monarchical character of the ecclesiastical constitution. From this time onwards the Consistories served more and more to give to more important ecclesiastical matters a fitting conclusion.[3]

[1] Cf. the Este report for June, 1594, in RICCI, II., 207.

[2] Cf. RANKE, II.[8], 204.

[3] Cf. PARUTA, Relazione, 412 seq. The work by Cardinal Paleotto there mentioned bears the title : De sacri consistorii consultationibus, Rome, 1592. Cf. as to this PHILLIPS, VI., 293, 577. The opinion of DOLFIN (Relazione, 460) that the Congregations, except for the Inquisition, only functioned in appearance, is wrong. The union of the " Congregatio episcoporum " with the " Congregatio regularium," did not take place, as PHILLIPS (VI., 642) supposes, in the time of Sixtus V., but only under Clement VIII. ; see PARUTA, Relazione, 374.

CHAPTER VI.

The Roman Inquisition.—Giordano Bruno.— The Index.—The Vulgate.

Of the Congregations, that of the Roman Inquisition preserved the greatest degree of independence, having entrusted to it the safeguarding and surveillance of Catholic doctrine. At the beginning of the pontificate of Clement VIII. it was composed of Cardinals Santori, Deza, Pinelli, Bernerio, Boccafuoco and Sfondrato,[1] with whom the Pope himself was associated as president. Toledo too, and later on Bellarmine, were placed on the Congregation after their elevation to the cardinalate ;[2] it met twice in the week, once at the palace of Cardinal Santori, who was the senior in rank, and at the same time Grand Penitentiary,[3] and on the other occasion at the Vatican.

[1] See Antonius Diana, Coordinatus seu omnes resolutiones morales, V., Lyons, 1667. The " Constantius S. Petri in Monte Aureo Servanus" mentioned there is Boccafuoco ; see Christofori, 193 " Quintilianus Adrianus " was at that time notary of the Inquisition ; see Diana, V., 580. Clement VIII. appointed " Aug. Galaninus commissarius generalis S. Inquisitionis de Urbe," see Catalanus, De magistro s. Palatii, 144. A manuscript of Clement VIII. of 1592, which assigns the Acta of the Inquisition then kept in the Papal " guardarobba " to the Congregation, in Gori, Archivio, VI., 4 (Spoleto, 1880), 14 seq.

[2] See the *Notes of Santori, January 6, 1594, Papal Secret Archives, I., 28 ; Couderc, I., 269. In a decree of the Inquisition of February 5, 1598 (in Stieve, IV., 524 seq.) there are mentioned as members : L. Madruzzo, Santori, Deza, Pinelli, Bernerio, Sfrondato, Borghese and Arigoni. Cf. also Vol. XIX. of this work, p. 626.

[3] Cf. the *letter of Giulio del Carretto, February 22, 1592, Gonzaga Archives, Mantua, and Dolfin, Relazione, 462 seq.

The Inquisition, in addition to its principal duty of taking action against heresy, was also occupied with many other matters.[1] Thus it issued an ordinance against litanies which had not been approved by the Congregation of Rites ;[2] it was also concerned with the false Demetrius,[3] and was also consulted as to whether it was lawful to form an alliance with heretics and the heterodox.[4] Of very frequent occurrence too were questions concerning relations with the heterodox, and especially about disputes with Protestants, and mixed marriages, that is between Catholics and those of another religion. There also came within its competence questions concerning Christians of Jewish origin, especially in relation to the procedure of the Inquisition in Portugal.[5] Besides

After the death of Santori, June 14, 1602) P. Aldobrandini became Grand Penitentiary ; see *Avviso of July 21, 1604, Urb. 1072, Vatican Library.

[1] Cf. besides the following cases mentioned the reports based on the acta in the *Anal. iuris pontif.*, XXVI. (1886), 576 *seq.* 676 *seq.*, and PASTOR, Dekrete, *passim*.

[2] See Bull., X., 732 *seq.*

[3] See PIERLING, La Russie, III., 214 *seq.*

[4] See PARUTA, Dispacci, I., 232.

[5] A collection of *" Decreta s. Inquisitionis fere omnia sub Clemente VIII." drawn up in accordance with the subjects, in Barb. 1369 (copy 1370) Vatican Library. A *Monitorium of Clement VIII. to the Inquisitor of Portugal, September 19, 1596, to act juridically, in the Papal Secret Archives, App. n. 9. In Barb. 1369, p. 326 *seq.* (Vatican Library) are contained *Responsiones ad obiecta contra Inquisitores regni Portugalliae, of March 28, 1598, which were presented, when translated by Fr. Peña to the Pope. A *brief of Clement VIII. to Philip III., December 30, 1601, concerning the absolution of " christianos nuevos de Portugal " which the Pope only granted with difficulty, in the National Archives, Paris, Simancas. *Ibid. K.* 1631, a *Memorial concerning the Portuguese neo-Christians, March 24, 1602. *Cf.* also the *Tractatus de statu S. Inquisitionis in regno Portugalliae, addressed to Clement VIII. (especially concerning the neo-Christians and Jews) in Barb. XXXII., 213, Vatican Library.

grave cases of fornication, falsifiers of Papal briefs were also
brought before the Inquisition.[1] With regard to those who
were accused of magic, the Inquisition acted with great
caution.[2]

The special tribunals of the Inquisition in the various cities
were dependent upon the Roman Inquisition, by which they
were directed.[3] Clement VIII. devoted the greatest attention
to the Inquisition ;[4] he confirmed a number of decrees
concerning the preservation of secrecy in its discussions, and
the improvement of its procedure.[5] The decree by which
every month the names of those imprisoned were to be
presented to the Congregation was directed against the often
unduly prolonged imprisonment of the accused.[6] A decree
of November 29th, 1594, laid it down that the jailors must
not receive presents from the prisoners, even after their
release ;[7] another of March 14th, 1595, ordered a more
humane treatment of the prisoners.[8] The decree of Sixtus V.,
that all briefs, bulls and other documents relating to the
Inquisition must be issued gratuitously, was renewed by
Clement VIII.,[9] and it was further ordered in 1601 that the

[1] *Cf.* in App. n. 16, the *List of those imprisoned in the Holy
Office from 1599, Borghese Archives, Rome.

[2] Opinion of SANDONNINI in *Giorn. stor. d. lett. ital.*, IX., 347 *seq.*

[3] See AMABILE, Il S. Officio d. Inquisitione in Napoli, II., 19.
Cf. ibid. I., 337 *seqq.*, 343 *seqq.* For the development of the
Inquisition at Naples, and its activity in that city, see a *Report
concerning an " Auto da fe celebrado en Palermo, 1596 " in the
Archives of the Spanish embassy, Rome, P. III. In 1595
Clement VIII. asked the Archduke Ferdinand to hand over an
ex-Dominican to the Roman Inquisition ; see *Steiermärk.
Gesch.-Bl.*, I., 81.

[4] *Cf.* PARUTA, Relazione, 374 ; CIBRARIO, Lettere di Santi,
Papi, etc., Turin, 1861, 243 *seq.*

[5] See PASTOR, Dekrete 51 *seq.*

[6] See *ibid.* 52.

[7] See *ibid.* 55.

[8] See *ibid.* 55 *seq. Cf.* BATTISTELLA, 85.

[9] See PASTOR, Dekrete, 57. *Cf. Zeitschr. f. schweiz. Kirchengesch.*, VII. (1914), 70.

bishops and their officials were not to receive the smallest emolument.[1] A decree of the same year laid it down that the consultors of the Inquisition were not to act as advocates of the accused.[2]

The strict bull of Paul IV., against those who, without being priests, dared to say mass and hear confessions, was confirmed, together with another constitution of the Carafa Pope against those who denied the Most Holy Trinity.[3] Also the bull which forbade Italians to live in countries where they were not able to fulfil their religious duties,[4] was aimed at the defence of the faith.

The first execution of heretics under Clement VIII. took place in 1595. On May 16th in that year twelve persons abjured their errors in the church of the Minerva ; a relapsed Fleming, who obstinately persisted in his error, by denying the immortality of the soul, as well as an absent Spaniard, were condemned to the stake.[5] In the following month a terrible crime was committed, which deeply grieved the Pope. An Englishman attacked with a dagger the priest who was

[1] See Bull., X., 648. *Cf. Carte Strozz.*, I., 2, 314.

[2] " Die 4 aprilis 1601 lectis litteris vicarii Januensis, ill[mi] [et rev.[mi] domini cardinales generales inquisitores] decreverunt ut consultores s. Officii non possent esse advocati reorum " (Decreta s. Officii, 1524-1668, p. 321, State Archives, Rome, with the further remark : " Romae tamen practicatur contrarium "). Cardinal Bernerio was entrusted in 1593 with the arrangement of the Archives of the Inquisition ; see PASTOR, Dekrete, 52.

[3] These constitutions in DIANA, V., 546 *seq.*, 574, and in Bull., X., 750 *seq.*, XI., 1 *seq.*

[4] See Bull., X., 279 *seq. Cf.* STIEVE, V., 310 ; BATTISTELLA, Il S. Offizio in Bologna, B. 1905, 138. The *opinion of an Augustinian concerning this bull of Clement VIII., which was renewed and amplified by Gregory XV., in Cod. Capponi, III., 19, National Library, Florence.

[5] Besides the Lettres d'Ossat, I., 153, *cf.* the *Avvisi of May 17 and 20, 1595, Urb. 1063, Vatican Library, and *Diarium P. Alaleonis, May 16, 1595 : " In Minerva abiuratio 12 in s. Officio detentorum, unus relapsus obstinatus et imago Jo[is] Lopez, qui curiae saeculari traditi." Barb. 2815, Vatican Library.

carrying the Blessed Sacrament in a procession leaving the church of S. Agata a Monte Magnanapoli, so that the Most Holy fell to the ground. He expiated his crime at the stake. It was thought that this was a case of a spy of Queen Elizabeth.[1] There were also other executions, thus five more in 1595, seven in 1596 and one in 1597.[2] A heretic who maintained his erroneous doctrines dressed as a Capuchin, was executed in September 1599.[3] There were several imprisonments of heretics in the following years,[4] and six condemnations to death.[5] One of the latter was the case of a Neapolitan, who was also a treasure-seeker.[6] Another native of southern Italy was the philosopher, Giordano Bruno.

The life of this unhappy man seems like that of a restless adventurer.[7] Born at Nola near Naples in 1548 of poor

---

[1] See Lettres d'Ossat, I., 153 seq., the report in N. Antologia, XXXIV., (1877), 298, and the *Avvisi of June 17 and 21, 1595, Urb. 1063, Vatican Library.

[2] See RODOCANACHI, Réforme, II., 433 seqq. For G. F. Barro, arrested by the Inquisition in 1595, cf. TIRABOSCHI, VIII., 134 seq.; MAZZUCHELLI, II., 3, 1790 seq.

[3] See *Avviso of September 14, 1599, Urb. 1067, Vatican Library. According to RODOCANACHI (loc. cit., 433) there were two other heretics executed in November, 1599.

[4] Cf. *Avvisi of February 23, 1600 (yesterday a heretic was arrested at S. Marcello); July 21, 1601 (on Sunday at the Inquisition, the abjuration of a German Jesuit, who denies the Trinity; condemned to imprisonment for life; Bosso da Bassi, to five years in the galleys, because he invokes the devil, and practises treasure-seeking); November 6, 1604 (abjuration of an Apulian priest, who had preached errors at S. Eustachio), Urb. 1069, 1070, 1072, Vatican Library. Cf. in App. n. 16, the *List of the prisoners of the Holy Office on April 5, 1599, Borghese Archives, Rome.

[5] Cf. in App. n. 16, extract from the *Diario, from the Papal Secret Archives.

[6] See *Avviso of July 9, 1603, Urb. 1071, Vatican Library.

[7] Cf. the special works by CHR. BARTHOLOMÈS (2 vols., Paris, 1846-47), M. CARRIÈRE (Philos. Weltanschauung der Reforma-

parents, but a man of extraordinary intellect, he resolved as a youth to enter a religious Order. He changed the name of Philip, which he had received at baptism, to that of Giordano when at the age of seventeen he entered the celebrated Dominican convent at Naples.[1] This convent, in which at one time Thomas Aquinas had lived, was at that time in a very decadent state.[2] The young religious, who had a lively imagination and a restless spirit, studied indis-

tionszeit, Leipzig, 1847[2], 1887), F. J. CLEMENS (G. Bruno e Nic. di Cusa, Bonn, 1847), D. BERTI (Florence, 1868, Turin, 1889), CHR. SIGWART (Tübingen, 1880), H. BRUNNHOFER (Leipzig, 1882), L. PREVITI (Prato, 1887), J. FRITH (London, 1887), RIEHL (Leipzig, 1889[2], 1900), L. KUHLENBECK (Leipzig, 1890), TOCCO (in Atti dei Lincei, 1892), V. SPAMPANATO (G. B. e Nola, Castrovillari, 1899 ; concerning his country and family), TOCCO (Nuovi docum. Rome, 1902), LEWIS MacINTYRE (London, 1903), G. GENTILE (Milan, 1907), BOULTING (London, 1916). The writings of G. Bruno are edited by PAUL DE LAGARDE, 2 vols., 1888-89 ; Opera latine conscripta ed. Fiorentino, Imbriani, Tallarigo, Tocco et Vitelli, Naples and Florence, 1879, 1891 ; Opere ital. p.p. G. GENTILE, I. and II., Bari, 1907-1908 ; Opera ined. ed. Tocco, Florence, 1891. German translation by LASSON in Kirchmanns Philos. Bibl.[2], Berlin, 1889, and by L. KUHLENBECK, 6 vols., Jena, 1904 seq. ; of the different phases in the development of the philosophy of Bruno, we have the best account in Tocco : Le opere lat. di G. B. esposte e confrontate con le ital., Florence, 1889. Cf. also R. CHARBONNEL, La pensée ital. et le courant libertin, and L'éthique de G.B. et le deuxième dialogue du Spaccio, both Paris, 1919. A full biography of Bruno, based on the plentiful archival materials was written by V. SPAMPANATO : Vita di G.B., con docum. editi ed inediti (Messina, 1921) which also at last throws light upon Bruno's youth. Cf. also OLSCHI in Deutsche Vierteljahrschr. f. Literaturwissensch. u. Geistegesch., II. (Halle, 1924), 1-79. For G. Bruno see also ZABUGHIN, Storia del Rinascimento cristiano in Italia, Milan, 1924, 350 seq. ; S. CARAMELLA, G. Bruno a Genova e in Liguria, in Giorn. stor. d. Liguria, I., 1 (1925).

[1] On June 15, 1565 ; profession on June 16, 1566 ; see SPAMPANATO, Vita, 606, 608.

[2] See ibid. 136 seqq.

criminately the philosophers of antiquity, the Middle Ages and the Renaissance. In so doing he formed a profound aversion for Aristotle and scholasticism, and drifted away from God and the Christian religion. He began to feel doubts about the doctrine of the Holy Trinity, as well as about the divinity of Christ. In spite of this in 1572 he was ordained priest and exercised the priestly office in various places. But his attitude of mind endured, and as he did not conceal his heretical opinions, he was threatened with a trial before the Inquisition, which he avoided by taking to flight in February 1576.[1]

Giordano Bruno then completely burned his bridges behind him, and began a life of wandering, which in three lustrums took him half over Europe. After having travelled through north Italy, he went to Geneva, where he passed over to Calvinism,[2] so as to be able to enter the university. Punished by imprisonment in 1579 for having published a defamatory libel against a professor of Geneva, Bruno, whose nature was as impulsive as it was presumptuous, left the head-quarters of Calvinism, against which he thenceforward displayed an even greater hatred than that which he had shown for the Catholic Church. He went by way of Lyons to Toulouse, where he succeeded in obtaining a chair at the university. In his lectures on philosophy he especially attacked Aristotle, whom he later on called the most stupid of all the philosophers, whose soul after his death had passed into the body of an ass ! After two years teaching, in 1581 the restless professor turned his steps towards Paris, where he devoted himself principally to the art of mnemonics. In this way he attracted the attention of Henry III., who conferred a special chair upon him. Bruno thanked him by the dedication, filled with adulation, of his work concerning the " shadows of ideas,"

[1] See *ibid*. 255 *seq*.

[2] Later on before the Inquisition at Venice G. Bruno denied his apostasy ; but the documents published by Dufour (G. Bruno à Genève, 1579, Docum. inédits, Genoa, 1884) show that he lied. *Cf*. Fiorentino, G. Bruno, in Napoli lett., I. (1884), n. 32.

in which could already be seen the fundamental signs of his pantheistic philosophy. As well as shorter dissertations, Bruno also published at that time (1582) a comedy " Il Candelaio " which proves how the loss of faith had also brought about his moral shipwreck. The work is full of indecencies ; according to competent judges, it surpasses in its obscenities the most infamous productions of the cinquecento.[1]

As early as 1583 Bruno left France, which was in a state of ferment, and went to live in London, where he passed, according to his own statement, the happiest hours of his life in the house of the French ambassador, Michel Castelnau de Mauvissiére. Mauvissiére brought him into contact with many illustrious persons,[2] and he was even presented to Queen Elizabeth, of whom he sang as " a goddess upon earth." He bestowed similar adulation upon her courtiers and counsellors. This however did not prevent him later on from reviling the English as uncouth, savage and rustic. He wrote thus : " If an Englishman sees a stranger he becomes like a wolf or a bear, and stares at him as furiously as a hog who sees someone taking away his trough from him."

During his sojourn in England there appeared Bruno's most important works in Italian : " La cena delle ceneri " ; " Lo spaccio della bestia trionfante " ; and " Dell'infinito, universo e mondi." " La cena delle ceneri " contains in the form of a dialogue a popular instruction concerning the new system of the universe according to Copernicus, of which Bruno was an enthusiastic supporter, and together with this

[1] *Cf.* A. BACELLI, Il candelaio di G. Bruno, Rome, 1901, and the preface by SPAMPANATO to the Opere ital., III., Bari, 1909.

[2] It is very uncertain whether Bruno knew Shakespeare personally. The influence of Bruno on the great dramatist, which is maintained by TSCHISCHWITZ (Shakespeare-Forschungen, Halle, 1868) and by W. KÖNIG (in Shakespeare-Jahrbuch, XI., 79 *seq.*) is convincingly denied by R. BEYERSDORFF (G. Bruno u. Shakespeare, Oldenburg, 1889). For the harmful influence of Bruno on the English at that time, as against positive religion, see the article by STONE in *The Month*, L. 81.

there are rabid invectives against his adversaries, whom he
describes as " Mad, demented, beasts and sows," and especially
against the University of Oxford, which is called a " con-
stellation of the ignorant, pedantic and obstinate, and a mass
of donkey and swine."   In his work, " Lo spaccio della bestia
trionfante " astronomy is only quite a secondary matter ;
polemics and satire hold the first place.   Even worse than the
obscenities in which Bruno takes delight here as well, are the
scandalous blasphemies which he permits himself to utter.
This incendiary work, disgraceful in its title, was regarded by
contemporaries as being directed against the Pope, but
anyone who studies it more attentively will see that Bruno's
attacks are not only directed against the doctrines of the
Catholic Church, but also against those taught by Luther
and Calvin.   Logically enough, the pantheistic philosopher
of Nola did not break only with the Catholic Church, but also
with positive Christianity in general, pouring out against its
doctrines such a mass of hatred that it would be difficult
to go further.[1]   Moreover, Bruno entertained so deep an

---

[1] Bruno, in the opinion of one of his admirers, Arthur Drews,
broke at first with the Church and Christianity with full knowledge, and opposed both of them with marked hostility. Especially
in the " Spaccio della bestia trionfante," he has poured forth
such venomous scorn upon Christian dogmas, that it would be
impossible to go further.   Bruno did not believe in the divinity
of Christ.   He only looked upon Him as the noblest of men, and
classes Him with Pythagoras, Socrates, Plato and other wise men.
But since the essence of Christianity lies in faith in the God-Man,
he could not call himself a Christian, and was sincere enough to
say so openly, seeing more clearly in this matter than many do
to-day.   As well as Catholicism, he also condemns Protestantism,
and looks upon the doctrine of justification by faith as absurd.
(*Beilage zur Alg. Zeitung*, 1900, n. 40).   Erdmann had already in
his *Gesch. der Philosophie* given the opinion : That the original
part of Bruno's action was that he had " broken with the Catholic
Church and with all Christianity.   He professes to do so, and is
the first to put himself entirely outside Christianity. . . . He
himself knows that his doctrine is pagan."   In accordance with
this is Bruno's defence of prostitution, and his demand for

aversion for the Jews that he showed it in almost all his works by biting expressions.[1] Thus in his blasphemous satire on Christianity and its Divine Founder, who figures under the title " Ass of Cyllene," he says that the Jews have always been " a despicable, slavish, self-interested and misanthropic people, repulsive to all other races, and very properly spurned by them."[2]

When Mauvissiére was recalled from his post in London in 1585, Giordano accompanied him to Paris, where he again

polygamy ; see SIGWART in *Gott. Gel. Anz.*, 1883, II., 836 *seq.* This same scholar says that the collection of sneers against Christian dogmas made by Brunnhofer (226 *seq.*) is the best proof of the truth of the accusations brought against Bruno by the Venetian Inquisition.

[1] The German translator L. Kuhlenbeck, who on this point is of the same opinion as Bruno, brings this out in his comments with special delight (v., 289). *Cf.* also BRUNNHOFER, 219 *seq.* The freemasons and free-thinkers, to a great extent Jews, who exulted at the erection of the monument to Giordano Bruno in Rome in 1889, and hailed Bruno as the representative of liberty, equality and fraternity, knew nothing of the dislike and hatred which their hero felt for the whole of their race. The leader of political radicalism in Italy, the Jew Barzilai, seems to have been better informed when, on February 17, 1910, at the inauguration of the site of the club for Roman free-thinkers facing the Vatican (pulled down in 1925), which bore the name of Giordano Bruno, confessed that for anti-clerical democracy the name of Giordano Bruno was only a battle-cry, and that his other views had not been taken into consideration. In like manner the Protestant professor Van der Wyck, in the periodical *De Gids*, 1890, 342, was of the opinion that the monument in Rome to Giordano Bruno had not been erected on account of his learning, but because the philosopher despised Christianity : " Het monument will een kaakslag aan het pausdom zijn." *Cf.* also ZABUGHIN, who says (*loc. cit.*) : " Nessuno al mondo su meno ' libero pensatore ' di quest'uomo [G. Bruno] che l'infinita beozia dei politicanti innalzò a simbolo sovrano del così detto libero pensiero."

[2] See WYCK, *loc. cit.*

indulged in attacks upon Aristotle.[1] The restless man then went to Germany, and tried his fortune in no fewer than eight German cities, without, however, finding rest in any of them. At Marburg he was refused permission to deliver public lectures, which annoyed the philosopher so much that he openly insulted the rector of the university in his own house. At Halberstadt he aroused such scandal by his attitude of opposition to all positive religion, that the superintendent-general Mebes warned people from the pulpit to avoid all contact with " this wolf and assassin of souls."[2] From Wittemberg, where he extolled Luther as the new Hercules, and where his attacks upon the Roman " wolf," gave much pleasure, he was driven out by the Calvinists in 1588. At Frankfort on Maine Bruno supervised in 1591 the printing of three didactic Latin poems, which are of importance for his philosophical opinions ; in the same year he accepted the invitation to go to Venice extended to him by Giovanni Mocenigo, who was on terms of close friendship with his publisher. Mocenigo wished to learn from Bruno the mnemonic art, and how to read thoughts, which had already been put forward by Raimondo Lulli in the thirteenth century, and to the perfecting of which Bruno had devoted himself all through his life. But now, whether because the Venetian gentleman thought himself deceived in this matter by Bruno, or because he felt remorse for having given hospitality to a heretic, or because the too great interest taken in his beautiful wife by the philosopher aroused his jealousy,[3] it is certainly

[1] See the new information given by AUVRAY, G. Bruno à Paris, Paris, 1901. Cf. TOCCO in N. Antologia, XXXVII. (1902), September.

[2] See what is said by FR. KOLDEWEY (Braunschw. Magazin, Wolfenbüttel, 1897) concerning the earlier biographies.

[3] FR. ALBANESE (L'Inquisizione religiosa nella repubblica di Venezia, con docum. orig., Venice, 1875) endeavours to make this last view credible ; he connects with it the circumstance that the document of accusation against Bruno contained among other charges " that he had taken great pleasure in women, as he did not consider it a sin to follow the impulses of nature."

the fact that in May 1592 the disciple made over his master into the hands of the Venetian Inquisition.

The view that Giordano Bruno presented himself before the Venetian Inquisition as the bold champion of his doctrines, and that the tribunal listened quietly to his philosophical explanations, became obviously untenable once the acta of his trial became known.[1] From these it is clear beyond all possibility of doubt that the philosopher of Nola cut but a sorry figure. In open contradiction to his own writings, and his previous discourses, he showed himself ready to abjure anything that was asked of him. " I reject," so he declared, " I detest and deplore all errors and all heresies, as well as every doubt of the doctrines of the Catholic Church." He begged that he might be " pardoned for his weakness, and be received into the bosom of the holy Church, and that he might be treated with leniency." When he was brought before the tribunal a second time, after a longer interval, he made the same declaration, adding that he had already sought for reconciliation with the Church from the nuncio in Paris, and from a Jesuit ; he begged to be readmitted to her bosom, but to be allowed to live a life of study outside his convent ; he condemned and deplored all the harm that he had done, and all the errors that he had thought and taught, and promised henceforward to lead a life " which would repair the scandal which he had hitherto given, and serve as an example and edification to everyone."

A report of the process at Venice was sent to the Roman

---

[1] Published for the first time by BERTI in 1868 in his Vita di G. Bruno ; later emended copies printed in BERTI, Docum. intorno a G.B., Rome, 1880, and in PREVITI, 305 seqq. ; German translation in KUHLENBECK, VI., 145 seqq. The best text is now to be found in SPAMPANATO, 687 seqq. BROSCH too, in Hist. Zeitschr., LX., 187 seq. pronounced against the attempt of Tocco to justify the attitude of Bruno before the Venetian Inquisition. How damning the Acta were for the philosopher is above all clear from the fact that Fiorentino thought of falsifying them. SIGWART (loc. cit.) shows how erroneous are the statements of Brunnhofer concerning the trial by the Venetian Inquisition.

Inquisition, which, by means of Cardinal Santori, asked on September 12th, 1592, that Bruno might be handed over to it. At first the government in Venice was unwilling to grant this request, but the nuncio in Venice, Lodovico Taverna, pointed out that Bruno was not a subject of the Republic, but a Neapolitan, that he had already in the past been summoned to appear in Rome, that he was an escaped monk and an arch-heretic ; in such cases it had often happened that guilty persons were handed over to the supreme tribunal in Rome. · The Great Council then sought the legal advice of its procurator Contarini. The latter replied that Bruno certainly possessed rare intellectual gifts, but that he was also accused of the most atrocious heresies ; since he was a foreigner, and as processes against him had already been commenced in Naples and Rome, it was possible to yield to the Pope's request and hand Bruno over.

Thus in 1593 Bruno was taken to Rome. In the absence of the acta of the process, we have but very insufficient information as to his conduct there during the six years of his imprisonment.[1] On February 27th, 1593, the case of Bruno

---

[1] A desire has been expressed in many quarters that the Roman Inquisition would make up its mind to render the acta of the Roman process accessible for historical research. Recently even Kuhlenbeck, who is otherwise an enthusiastic supporter of Bruno, has expressed himself in this sense when he says (VI., 295 *seq.*) that : " by so doing the only ones who would suffer would be the demonstrators at the monument of Bruno, who make this man of Nola their saint, without in any way having felt the breath of his spirit." It has escaped the notice of Kuhlenbeck that G. Güttler relates in 1893 in *Archiv. f. Gesch. der Philos.*, VI., 344 *seq.* that Pope Leo XIII., that enthusiast for historical truth, was prepared as early as 1882 to throw open the documents relating to Bruno, if they could be found in the archives of the Roman Inquisition. " The result, however, of the most careful research was that in those archives nothing could be found on the subject ; since, owing to upsets and revolutions, these archives have undergone many vicissitudes, it is not even now possible to say whether these acta are still preserved,

was discussed by the Inquisition.[1]   But it is only for the end
of 1599 and the beginning of 1600 that we have a few short
protocols,[2] from which in each case it only appears that Bruno
asserted again and again that he " had never set forth heretical
opinions, and that the doctrines which were held by the
members of the Inquisition to be heretical, had only been
misinterpreted."   If these attempts of the philosopher to
escape the terrible penalties which threatened him are
humanly speaking easy to understand, they do not show the
smallest shadow of *the courage of his opinions.*   Even his
bold and haughty words at the last, when all hope of pardon
had vanished : " You are perhaps pronouncing sentence upon
me with a greater sense of fear than I have in hearing it,"
do not prove much in the light of his earlier conduct, and all
the more so as they are only confirmed by a single witness
who is not over worthy of belief, Gaspar Schopp.[3]

or whither they may have gone in the end."   Encouraged by this
information, dated October 7, 1882, Güttler went to Rome,
where the archivist and commissary of the Inquisition very
courteously made repeated new search, which however, like the
researches of Güttler in the Papal Secret Archives and other
libraries of Rome, were without result.   Cardinal Rampolla too,
at that time Secretary of the Inquisition, has assured me that in
the Archives of the Roman Inquisition nothing was found which
had not already been published by Berti in 1868 and by Martinori
in 1880.

[1] *Cf.* in App. n. 16, the *list of the prisoners of the Holy
Office, Borghese Archives, Rome.

[2] These extracts from the Archives of the Roman Inquisition,
made by an Italian scholar during the revolution of 1849, were
first printed in *Documenti* by Berti ;   more recently in
SPAMPANATO, 771 *seqq.   Ibid.* 780 *seqq.* the " Sentence " of the
Inquisition on Bruno.   For Bellarmine and the process against
Bruno see the periodical *Gregorianum,* IV. (1923), 193 *seqq.   Cf.*
CARUSI, Nuovi documenti sul processo di G. Bruno in the *Giorn.
crit. d. filosofia ital.,* VI. (1925), 121-130, where there is also the
text of the final judgment of the Inquisition on Bruno of February
8, 1600.

[3] Isabella Oppenheim has given in her English biography of

After Bruno had been handed over on February 9th, 1600, to the secular arm for punishment, as an obstinate heretic and apostate, he was still given another eight days to recant his heresies,[1] which were directed against the fundamental dogmas of Christianity. But the theologians who were sent to him, as well as the members of the Confraternity of S. Giovanni Decollato, who gave the condemned man spiritual assistance in his last hours, laboured in vain. On February 17th, Giordano Bruno, impenitent to the last, suffered death at the stake in the Campo di Fiori.[2]

Bruno, under the pseudonym J. Frith, a printed and revised copy of the letter of G. Schopp (Scioppius) to Rittershaus, based on the manuscript at Breslau.

[1] BROSCH too (*Hist. Zeitschr.*, LX., 189) who is so great an admirer of Bruno, judges that the philosopher of Nola was no longer a Christian. *Cf.* also RENIER in *Giorn. stor. d. lett. ital.*, L., 427.

[2] See besides the letter of G. Schopp, cited *supra*, above all the contemporary *Avvisi of February 12, 16 and 19, 1600, contanedi in Urb. 1068 (Vatican Library). (RODOCANACHI, Réforme, II., 434 *seq.*; SPAMPANATO, 784). In spite of these absolutely trustworthy witnesses, the Frenchman DESDOUITS (La légende tragique de J. Bruno, Paris, 1885) tries to prove that the death of Bruno at the stake did not take place ; that the sentence was not carried out, but that Bruno was kept in prison for the remainder of his life. This strange attempt was rightly refuted by E. NARDUCCI (G. Bruno e la legenda tragica del Sig. Desdouits, Rome, 1886) and by the Jesuit PREVITI (*loc. cit.*). Kl. Bäumker too has declared against Desdouits in his valuable dissertation on Bruno, published in *Wissenschaftl. Beilage zur Germania,* 1900, Nr. 7. In this he brings out the importance of Bruno as a naturalist (he is not a naturalist who analyses, but one who uses his imagination), while as a philosopher he estimates him fairly. Bäumker however missed the important work, also directed against Desdouits, by A. POGNISI : G. Bruno e l'Archivio di S. Giovanni Decollato, Turin, 1891. There, p. 62 *seq.*, we find all the information concerning the last hours of Bruno, in the " confrateria di ponte S. Angelo," which were in those archives, but now removed to the State Archives, Rome, and which remove

Although the Venetian government had handed over Giordano Bruno to the Roman Inquisition, it refused to do so when in July 1593 the latter asked the same thing in the case of the Greek Bishop of Cerigo, Massimo Marguni, saying that the many Greeks who lived in Venice and the possessions of the Republic in the Levant had never been the subjects of that authority. The Venetian government, however, offered to order the rector of Padua to demand the writings

all doubt concerning the carrying out of the sentence (16-17 February, 1600). If Kuhlenbeck calls the death of Bruno at the stake a judicial murder, a critic has remarked in the *Lit. Beilage zur Köln. Volkszeitung*, 1904 n. 15, that " from the legal point of view this act was no more a judicial murder than that of having hanged, disembowelled and quartered 142 Catholic priests in the course of twenty years, in the freest country in the world, and under the auspices of an enlightened sovereign. We make this comparison because the author does not fail to offer incense to the era of Elizabeth, and to British society which courteously welcomed this unbalanced guest, and showed that they understood the trend of his ideas. If the philosopher of Nola, who, according to what the author himself says, had every reason to be on his guard against the Calvinists, had crossed the seas, not as an apostate, but as a friar who had remained true to his vows, his tonsured head would have been insulted in Ireland, or he would have had to lay down his life at Tyburn amid tortures such as are unheard of to-day except in China. Probably in Rome, just as a generation later Galileo did, he irritated his judges exceedingly by his obstinate and contradictory behaviour, men who probably were not anxious to increase the difficulties of the time by condemning a heretic to the stake ; they believed—and perhaps equally firmly as the English judges under the Virgin Queen— that they had to perform a painful duty, without heeding the consequences. In this sense we may interpret the words of the condemned man : " You are pronouncing sentence with greater fear than I feel in hearing it." KUHLENBECK says (Vol. I., p. 176) in a like sense : " Moreover the behaviour of the Roman Inquisition, which would gladly have seen Bruno saved by a recantation, does not approach the diabolical cruelty of Calvin, who delighted in assisting in person as a spectator at the death of Servetus at the stake."

of this man, and to inform him that should he cause scandal by his life and doctrines, he could no longer be allowed to remain in Padua.[1]

In the same year Clement VIII. called the attention of the Venetian ambassador to the fact that the English were carrying on Calvinist propaganda in the city of the lagoons. Paruta maintained that at that moment there were very few Englishmen living in Venice, and that the government was zealously watching over the Catholic character of the inhabitants. Clement VIII. replied that he was quite ready to believe this, but that vigilance against the Calvinists could never be sufficient.[2]   Later on it was realized only too clearly how fully justified the Pope's exhortation had been. As a matter of fact numerous heretics were already establishing themselves there on various pretexts. Some were living in the palaces of the ambassadors of England and Holland, others were employed in commerce, and not a few were studying at Padua.[3] The meetings of noble Venetians at the house of the Dutch merchant Gerard Nis, who possessed many heretical books, filled Clement VIII. with anxiety.

[1] See PARUTA, Dispacci, I., 256 seq., 281 seq., 291 seq.

[2] See ibid. 265 ; cf. III., 63 seq., concerning the dispute with Venice about the Inquisitor of Bergamo. With regard to the Inquisition in Venice and the position of the nuncio see in App. n. 7, the *Instruction for A. M. Graziani, March 30, 1596, Graziani Archives, Città di Castello. Here belong the *acta in Barb. 5195 and 5205, Vatican Library. Cf. also Anal. iuris pontif., XXVI. (1886), 576 seq.

[3] *" In Venetia et altre città del suo dominio dimorano heretici sotto diverse cause e pretesti. Alcuni vi stanno come familiari e servitori degli ambasciatori d'Inghilterra e di Olanda ivi residenti. Altri vi allogiano come soldati, molti vi tengono domicilio con- tinuo. Altri vi capitano alla giornata per ragione di traffico e di mercantia. Alcuni ve ne sono di passagio e non pochi per occasione dello studio di Padova " (Barb. 5195, p. 83, Vatican Library).   *Decrees of the Roman Inquisition " de ultramontanis haereticis praecique Paduae commorantibus " in 1595, in Barb. 1369, p. 159 seq., loc. cit. Cf. Barb. 5195, p. 56 seq.

There the Servite friar, Paolo Sarpi, whose father was also a merchant, formed an acquaintance for the first time with anti-Catholic literature. Clement VIII. was already well aware how dangerous this man was, and when Sarpi was suggested for a diocese in Dalmatia, he replied that friar was deserving of punishment rather than reward. Sarpi swore to be revenged.[1] In 1604 a Calvinist preacher had the effrontery to preach a sermon which caused great scandal in the house of the English ambassador.[2]

With the exception of Venice and the Waldenses in Piedmont,[3] Clement VIII. had no reason to fear any serious danger to the preservation of unity of faith in any part of Italy.[4] This happy state of affairs, which was also of value

[1] Nicoletti, who is very well informed, writes in his *Vita d'Urbano VIII. : " Questo [Sarpi] fu già un tempo accusato a Clemente ottavo di esser direttore e capo di un'accademia, che si faceva in Venetia in casa di Gherardo Nis mercatante Olandese, di setta Calvinista, e che teneva una numerosa libreria di libri proibiti. Frequentavano questa congrega molti nobili Veneziani, che si credevano poco ben'affetti alla Santa Sede apostolica ; e correva voce che non havessero sensi buoni e sinceri intorno all'immortalità dell'anima ragionevole. Mentre Clemente andava pensando di trovar qualche modo circospetto per disgregar quella pratica, fu pregato a voler promuovere Fra Paolo ad un vescovado in Dalmatia ; rispose quel saggio Pontefice, ch'egli conosceva molto bene il frate, e che meritava più tosto gastigo che premio. Alterato da questa ripulsa Fra Paolo pensò sempre di vendicarsene. Barb. LII., 7 p. 626 *seq.*, Vatican Library.

[2] See the *report in Cod. Barb. 5195, pp. 83-86, Vatican Library.

[3] See JALLA, La riforma in Piemonte, 1595-1596, in *Bull. de la Soc. d'hist. Vaudoise,* 1924. In the *Decreta s. Inquisitionis in Barb. 1369 (Vatican Library) mention is made of other heretics in Calabria ; p. 21 *seq.* : ' De haereticis in terris dioc. Cusent. (1592, 1599, 1600).

[4] *Cf.* TACCHI VENTURI, I., 85. At Vicenza, where there had formerly been many heretics, in 1598 there was only one ; see SECEGNI, Le lettere a Vicenza a tempo della reazione cattolica, Vicenza, 1903, 17. Clement VIII. asked for the handing over of Giov. Batt. Angelotto, a native of Vicenza, who had escaped to

for the preservation of national unity, was due not only to the spread of the Catholic reform, and the zealous action of the Roman Inquisition, which was for the most part supported by the various governments,[1] but also to the vigilance of the Congregation of the Index of prohibited books, which was closely connected with it.[2] Sixtus V. had died before the new edition of the Index which he had ordered had been completely finished.[3] At the meetings of the Congregation of the Index which were resumed under Clement VIII. it was decided to suspend that work, and make a new list of prohibited books. When this was finished in 1593, it was found that Clement VIII. was not satisfied with the work, against which objections had also been raised by others, especially by Baronius. The Venetian ambassador Paruta profited by this circumstance, as the Index of 1593 contained in an appendix a prohibition of many books in Italian, from which he feared grave loss to the booksellers' trade in his native city. By his remonstrances Paruta succeeded in persuading Clement VIII. to withdraw the Index of 1593, and to order the Congregation to prepare a new list.[4]

Laibach, and was there stirring up trouble against the Church, in *briefs of August 21, 1593, to the Archduke Matthias, and of September 19, 1593, to the Archduke Maximilian ; see Arm. 44, t. 34, p. 96 ; t. 38, p. 387, Papal Secret Archives.

[1] Cf. the *briefs of praise to Genoa, March 16, 1596, for the punishment of two heretics (Arm. 44, t. 40, n. 95, loc. cit.). By a *brief of October 20, 1601, Clement VIII. exhorted the Duke of Savoy to take action against the heretics in the valleys of the marquisate of Saluzzo, the governor there being well disposed (ibid. t. 45, n. 365). Cf. ibid. t. 46, n. 24 and 198, the *briefs of thanks to the duke of January 12 and June 28, 1602, for having heeded this request. See also Vier Dokumente aus rom. Archiven, Leipzig, 1843, 93 seq. For the mission of 1602 to the heretics of Saluzzo see PELISSIER in Piccolo Arch. stor. del marchesato di Saluzzo, II. (1903-1905).

[2] Cf. PASTOR, Dekrete, 46, 47, 48, 49, 50, 55.

[3] See HILGERS, 12 seq., 529, where the view of Reusch is refuted.

[4] Cf. PARUTA, Dispacci, I., 296 seq., 323, 332 seq. ; II., 180, 245 seq., 488 ; HILGERS, 13, 529 seq., 531 seq. See also

This Index obtained the approbation of Clement VIII. ; it was published on March 27th, 1596, in accordance with the instructions, and was enforced for the Curia on May 17th by an edict of the Master of the Sacred Palace.[1]   On the same day is dated the brief printed in the preface to the Index, which after a short account of the origin of the new list, confirms it under threat of the penalties laid down in the past by Pius IV., and grants to the Congregation of the Index the power to pass judgment concerning any doubts and controversies that might arise.[2]

The Index of Clement VIII. differs from that of Sixtus V., especially by the absence of the appendix of Italian books. The list of prohibited books agrees in its contents almost

BAUMGARTEN, Neue Kunde, 211 seq. Neither Reusch nor Ottino-Fumagalli knew of the Index of the year 1593, although copies are to be found in the Vatican and Angelica Libraries. Hilgers was the first to draw attention to these. The description in Brosch is misleading (I., 305) ; he wrongly transfers to 1595 the Index that was definitively approved.

[1] See HILGERS, 536 seq. The statement of REUSCH (I., 533) that the Index was only finished in the latter part of the summer of 1596 is irreconcilable with the *Avviso of May 4, 1596, which speaks of the Index as already published (Urb. 1064, I., Vatican Library) and with the *report of L. Arrigoni of June 29, 1596 (Gonzaga Archives, Mantua) in App. n. 8. Cf. also VERESS, Mon. Vatic. Hung., 228, and BAUMGARTEN, Neue Kunde, 222 seq. For its carrying into effect in Rome see PASTOR in Hist. Jahrb., XXXIII., 537. The strange prohibition of the book by the Capuchin Girolamo a Politio, mentioned by Hilgers (535 seq.) and by Baumgarten (223) is also noted in the *acta consist. card S. Severinae, December 27, 1595 (Cod. Barb. lat. 2871, III., Vatican Library). Clement VIII. issued a brief against the writings of Charles Dumoulin on August 21, 1602 ; see DU PLESSIS D'ARGENTRÉ, Collectio iudiciorum, Paris, 1724 seq., I., App. xl., III., 2, 171.

[2] See Bull., X., 53 seq. Ibid. 230 seq. a bull of October 17, 1596, which again confirms the Index and once more confers on the Congregation of the Index the power of passing judgment upon doubts arising therefrom.

exactly with that prepared by Sixtus V. ; only Bellarmine and Francesco a Victoria are omitted ; otherwise it contains almost all the writings of Catholic authors, which Sixtus V. had already declared worthy of censure. With regard to its form and division, Clement VIII. adhered to the so-called Tridentine Index issued under Pius IV. with its three classes, though Clement VIII. added to each class, and even to each letter, a considerable number by way of appendix. The Index of the Aldobrandini Pope also includes unchanged the ten Tridentine rules, to which there is added by way of appendix, an instruction to bishops, inquisitors, printers and booksellers.[1] As this instruction, compared with that drawn up under Sixtus V., was made more severe in certain points, Venice again raised opposition. Clement took into account the energetic remonstrances of the Signoria by mitigating the instructions for Venetian territory.[2] The Index of Clement VIII. was accepted without any objection by the other Catholic states, and later on its observance was made more strict by means of synods, not only in Italy, but also in France, Belgium and Germany.[3]

In the Index of Clement VIII. there are also added to the ten Tridentine rules, certain modifying decrees concerning translations of the Bible, astrological writings, the Talmud

---

[1] See REUSCH, I., 533 seq., 560 seq.

[2] See PARISI, II., 183 seq. ; CECCHETTI, II., 257 seq. ; REUSCH, I., 546 seq.

[3] See REUSCH, I., 543-546. L. Arrigoni wrote on October 5, 1596, that the new Index had been accepted by all the Italian states, even Venice, and begged the Duke of Mantua to do the same (Gonzaga Archives, Mantua). For the prohibition of books after 1596 see REUSCH, I., 552, Carte Strozz., I., 2, 318. Cf. CAVAZZUTI, Castelvetro, 35 seq., BAUMGARTEN, Neue Kunde, 230 seq. For the prohibition of all the books of the Gallican, Charles Dumoulin see Bull., X., 858 ; REUSCH, I., 442, 605 ; HILGERS, 252. Four letters from Cardinal Santori to the Inquisitor at Florence, which show that these prohibitions of the Roman Inquisition were notified to the booksellers, who had to acknowledge their receipt, in Bibliofilo, XI. (1890), 49 seq.

and other Jewish books.[1] There is also printed in it an extract
from the bull of February 28th, 1593, which prohibited not
only the Talmudic, cabalistic and irreligious books already
condemned in its predecessors, but also all books in Hebrew
or any other language, already written or printed, or to be
written or printed in future, which contain heresies or errors
against the Holy Scriptures, insults to Catholic doctrine, to
ecclesiastical usages, to priests or neophytes, or indecent tales.
All such books, it was enacted, must not be kept or propagated
by the Jews, not even under the pretext that they were
expurgated (nor even provisionally until they were expurgated) ; moreover the pretext must not be put forward that
these works under a different title, had been reprinted with
the permission of some member of the Council of Trent, or
on the strength of a decree of the Index of Pius IV., or of a
Papal indult, or by the permission of Cardinals, legates,
nuncios, bishops, inquisitors. At the same time the Pope
revoked all concessions made by his predecessors and others,
authorizing the retention of such books for a fixed or an
indeterminate period ; he forbade the making of such concessions, and ordered the books to be handed over in Rome
within ten days, and elsewhere within two months, and that
they should be burned immediately, under the threat of
confiscation of goods, and under even more severe temporal
penalties, including, in the case of Christians, " excommuni-
catio latae sententiae."[2] The Roman Inquisition also made
other decrees in the same sense on August 6th, 1592, and
May 10th, 1593, and ordered their carrying out by the
inquisitors and nuncios.[3]

The action taken by Clement VIII. against the books of

[1] See REUSCH, I., 50, 333, 339, 534.

[2] See Bull., X., 25 seq., and DIANA, V., 572 seq. (with wrong
date 1599 ; cf. *Avviso of April 7, 1593, Urb. 1061, Vatican
Library). REUSCH (I., 49 seq.) gives the bull the wrong date of
1592, as does A. BERLINER, Zensur u. Konfiskation hebr. Bücher
im Kirchenstaate, Frankfort on Maine, 1891, 7 seq.

[3] See PASTOR, Dekrete, 50, 52. Cf. ALBITIUS, 296, 298, and
REUSCH, I., 51.

the Jews, which they strongly resented,[1] was not an isolated
administrative act. The lenient treatment of the Jews by
Gregory XIII. and Sixtus V.[2] had led to grave abuses ; above
all the usury which they practised had become unbearable.[3]
Clement VIII. therefore resolved to revert to the severe
measures of Paul IV. and Pius V. On February 25th, 1592,
he renewed the ordinances of those Popes which had limited
Jewish commerce at Avignon.[4] In the summer of 1592 the
sermons for the conversion of the Jews were reintroduced,[5]
and the inscriptions which might offend the Christians were
removed from the Jewish cemetery near Porta Portese.[6]
Moreover a census of the Jews in the city was ordered, and
their commerce with Christians restricted by an edict.[7] As
the census showed that there were 3,500 Jews in Rome, it was
supposed that strict steps would be taken against them.[8]
Indeed, on February 25th, 1593, the strict ordinances of
Paul IV. and Pius V. were renewed, and they were forbidden
to live in Papal territory, except in Rome, Ancona and
Avignon.[9] On May 25th, 1593, their usurious dealings were

[1] See *Avvisi of April 7, 10 and 14, 1593, Urb. 1061, Vatican
Library. Cf. BAUMGARTEN, Neue Kunde, 342.

[2] Cf. Vol. XIX. of this work, p. 311 ; Vol. XXI., pp. 116, 197.

[3] Santori wrote a special dissertation concerning this ; see
Barb. lat. 4592, p. 64b, Vatican Library.

[4] See Bull., IX., 523 seq.

[5] The sermons took place in S. Lorenzo in Damaso ; see *Avviso
of July 29, 1592, Urb. 1060, II., Vatican Library. Cf. Hist.-polit.
Bl., LVII., 515 seq.

[6] See the two *Avvisi of August 1, 1592, Urb. 1060, II., Vatican
Library. Cf. *Avviso of May 4, 1596, Urb. 1064, I., ibid.

[7] See *Avvisi of August 1 and 19, 1592, Urb. 1060, II., ibid.
Cf. the *report of L. Arrigoni of June 29, 1596, Gonzaga Archives,
Mantua. A prohibition of entering the synagogue, March 13,
1603, in Editti, V., 10, p. 53, Papal Secret Archives. Descendants
of Jews were excluded from the priesthood in Spain and Portugal ;
see Bull., X., 414 ; LÄMMER, Analecta, 56.

[8] See *Avviso of August 1, 1592, loc. cit.

[9] Bull., X., 22 seq. Certain facilities, however, were granted
to the Levantine Jews domiciled at Ancona ; cf. PARUTA, Dispacci,

repressed.[1] This great strictness, however, did not prevent the Pope from repeatedly checking by means of decrees any unjust persecution of the Jews.[2]

Throughout his pontificate Clement VIII. showed himself the ardent champion of ecclesiastical jurisdiction. The strict ideas on this matter which he held as a jurist,[3] frequently brought him into conflict with the cesaropapalism of the Kings of Spain,[4] while conflicts with Florence and Venice became inevitable,[5] on account of the views of the governments in those places. Clement VIII. loved Venice, and valued her as a counterweight to Spain,[6] but the way in which the Republic of St. Mark put before everything else a cold calculation of her own advantage, and her national selfishness, were bound again and again to renew his annoyance. His complaints of the usurpations of episcopal jurisdiction by the

I., 204 ; (BROSCH, I., 306, gives this report the wrong date of May 25 instead of 15), II., 362. See also RODOCANACHI, Le St. Siège et les Juifs, 189 ; BERLINER, II., 24 seq. ; BLUSTEIN, Storia degli Ebrei di Roma, Rome, 1921, 142 seqq. Cf. *Bandi, V., 10, p. 50 seqq., Papal Secret Archives. For the Jews at Ferrara see FRIZZI, V., 90, and CAPILUPI, ed. Prinzivalli, 148, n. 2. Cf. Regesti di bandi (see title infra, Cap. X, 367, n. 1), I., 109 seq.

[1] Bull. X., 269.

[2] The first *" Bando che non si debbano molestare ne dare fastidio alli Hebraei " bears the date January 28, 1595. Similar *bandi were again issued in 1596, 1599, 1603 and 1605 ; see Bandi V., 10, p. 128 seqq., Papal Secret Archives. Cf. Rev. juive, II., 289 ; RODOCANACHI, loc. cit., 189 seq.

[3] *" El Papa Clemente fue de los mas zelosos de la jurisdicion ecclesiastica de quantos se an conocido muchos annos," say the *Instructions for the Spanish ambassador " duque de Aytona " in 1605, Archives of the Spanish Embassy, Rome, III., 9.

[4] Cf. Vol. XXIII. of this work, p. 195 seqq.

[5] For the disputes with Florence in 1599 concerning the usurpations of ecclesiastical rights by the government there, cf. MUTINELLI, II., 66 seq.

[6] Cf. PARUTA, Relazione, 435. See also DOLFIN, Relazione, 495.

Senate sometimes became very bitter ;[1] it was these that made the situation of the nuncios in the city of the lagoons so difficult.[2] To these were also added many disputes of a secular character, but however strained relations may have become, a breach was always avoided ;[3] this was not to be attributed only to such prudent diplomatists as Paruta and Dolfin, but also to the Pope, who was as prudent as he was peace-loving in character.[4]

A year and a half had elapsed since the death of Sixtus V. and the strange and complicated position into which the Sixtine Bible had fallen had not yet been cleared up. The Louvain and Paris editions of the book of books could be freely republished, and in the time of Gregory XIV. care had been taken not to interfere with their further diffusion by any express prohibition, even after the definitive Roman version had been issued. The latter edition of the Vulgate, on the other hand, to which more care had been devoted than to any other, and in which the Pope had personally taken part, was left lying in the vaults of the Vatican Press like a dangerous book, in the expectation of its being destroyed

---

[1] *Cf. e.g.* PARUTA, Dispacci, II., 118 *seq.*, 127 *seq.*

[2] See *Arch. Veneto*, XXXVII., 2 (1889), 273. *Cf.* *instructions of the nuncio Graziani in 1598 to the new nuncio, Cod. 1621, Corsini Library, Rome. Some passages in LÄMMER, Zur Kirchen-gesch, 123. See also in App. n. 7, the *instructions to A. M. Graziani in 1596, Graziani Archives, Citta di Castello.

[3] In July 1595 he threatened the withdrawal of the nuncio on account of a violation of the jurisdiction of the Bishop of Ceneda ; see *Arch. stor. ital.*, XII., xxix. Many *letters concerning this in Nunziat. di Venezia, XVII., Papal Secret Archives. In one *letter preserved there (p. 182) from Pietro Levade to Cardinal Cinzio Aldobrandini, dated Ceneda, October 27, 1601, it is stated : " Delle cose di questa giurisditione credo V.S. sia avisata da Msgr. Nuntio di Venezia andando ella ogni giorno di mal in peggio." The other side of these disputes, naturally from the Venetian point of view, was given by Paruta and Dolfin in their reports cited *supra*, p. 221, n. 6. *Cf.* also ROMANIN, VII., 14 *seqq.*

[4] *Cf.* DOLFIN, Relazione, 500.

and forbidden by the Pope's orders from being presented to the public.

For the new Pope it became one of his most pressing tasks to interest himself in this delicate question. Clement VIII. placed the matter in the hands of Cardinals Frederick Borromeo and Valiero, to whom was added Toledo as a collaborator. These re-examined the proposals for emendation made by the Gregorian commission, and decided upon the definitive text, which they enriched with learned notes.[1] On August 28th, 1592, they were able to present their completed work.

Cardinal Carafa had died on January 14th, 1591 ; the text which had been drawn up under his direction, and which had been emended in many points by Sixtus V., was no longer accepted either by the Gregorian commission nor by that of Toledo. Whereas Carafa and his collaborators had been guided in their edition of the text only by scientific motives and by consideration of the best manuscripts, other points of view now became of decisive importance, and above all, following the example of Sixtus V., both under Gregory XIV. and Clement VIII. care was taken not to depart too widely from the wording hitherto in use. Certain things, which from the purely scientific point of view called for change, were for this reason left exactly as they were, in order to avoid scandal or surprise.[2]

Not all of those who were allowed to take part in the discussions could be said to be satisfied by this method of procedure. The learned Valverde addressed an impassioned appeal to the Pope to have the text of Toledo examined once more before it was handed over to the printers. At first Clement VIII. seemed inclined to agree to this course, but

---

[1] HÖPFL, 169. " These notes, a fine example of the learning of Toledo, are still of value to-day " (*ibid.*) According to Ghislieri, Toledo relied especially upon Agellio (*ibid.* n. 2).

[2] HÖPFL, 166 *seq. Cf.* the preface to the Vulgate : " In hac tamen pervulgata lectione sicut nonnulla consulto mutata, ita etiam alia, quae mutanda videbantur, consulto immutata relicta sunt, etc."

was then led to an opposite decision when it was pointed out to him that the Church had already been waiting for the Roman Vulgate for some fifty years, and that it was time finally to put an end to erudite labours, and to begin with the printing.[1]

Before, however, the completed work was handed over to the printers, another ordinance against the Sixtine Vulgate was issed. In order to avoid as far as possible the scandal which was feared from this, Clement VIII., following the suggestion of Bellarmine, gave orders for the acquisition of all the copies already issued, in Venice to the Inquisitor and the nuncio, and in Germany and the countries across the Alps to the Jesuits ; the Pope promised to bear all the expense. On December 22nd, 1592, the ambassador of Spain was also asked to address to Philip II. a request that he would hand over to the nuncio the copies that were still in his possession. The search went on until 1595 ; all the copies that were found were sent to Rome and burned, in accordance with the wishes of the Pope.[2] In spite of this more than forty Sixtine Bibles have been preserved until our own day.[3] But with this all the difficulties had not been overcome. Already, in the time of Clement VIII. the doubt had been raised as to how the errors of the Sixtine Bible could be reconciled with the doctrine of Papal infallibility in questions of faith and morals.[4] The question assumed an even greater importance in the time of Paul V. ;[5] as early as 1600 the Protestants

---

[1] HÖPFL, 173.

[2] LE BACHELET, 54 seqq. ; SANTORI, Diario, ibid. 150 seq. ; PRAT, Recherches, V., 10 seq. ; BAUMGARIEN, Neue Kunde, 274 seqq., AMANN, 79-101.

[3] Enumerated in BAUMGARTEN, Vulgata, 65-91 ; Neue Kunde, 150 seq. If it was hoped that it would be possible to withdraw the printed copies already sold, then their number cannot have been very great.

[4] LE BACHELET, 56 seq.

[5] The difficulty was discussed at the University of Ingolstadt as early as 1608 (ibid. 58 seqq.). Cf. the letter of Gretser to Bellarmine, June 23, 1608, ibid. 155-158.

brought forward against that doctrine the differences between the Clementine and Sixtine Vulgates,[1] although none of the divergent texts contained any difference as to faith or morals.

The printing was begun at the beginning of September 1592, and was completed in about four months, so that the ambassador of Spain was able to send the new Bible on December 22nd.[2] As early as November 8th, 1592, a privilege was granted to the Vatican Press, which only allowed other presses to reprint it after an interval of ten years, and on condition of exact conformity with the Vatican copy.[3] Externally the Clementine Bible is altogether similar to the Sixtine ; its format, and even the engravings on the frontispiece are the same,[4] the number of pages corresponds almost exactly.[5] Clement VIII. was not named on the title-page, but all the honour was left to Sixtus V. alone.[6] Indeed, to him was due the credit for the fact that the Latin Church had now at length been given its ancient Bible with an officially authorized text, and in spite of many differences[7] on various points, it was his text that had been followed. It is obvious that it did not occur to anyone, in spite of the dissatisfaction aroused by the errors in his edition, to compromise in any way the great dead Pope by the new Vulgate ; the ill-luck of the

[1] THOMAS JAMES, Bellum papale, London, 1600.

[2] HÖPFL, 179 seq. On January 16, 1593, G. del Carretto *reports that the Pope had given him a Bible for the duke, and that the duke must send back the Bible of Sixtus V. Gonzaga Archives, Mantua.

[3] Bull., IX., 636 seq.

[4] The title page of the Sistina in AMANN, 135, that of the Clementina in HETZENAUER's edition of the Vulgate, Innsbruck, 1906 ; both title-pages in KAULEN-HOBERG, Einleitung in die Heilige Schrift, I.[2], Freiburg, 1911, 218.

[5] VERCELLONE, Variae lectiones, I., lxxiii.

[6] Clement VIII. was mentioned for the first time in the edition of Bonaventura Nugo, published by the heirs of Guglielmus Rovillius, Lyons, 1604 ; also in that published at Mayence and Cologne in 1609 ; cf. FALK in Katholik, 1899, I., 448 seqq.

[7] List principally in HETZENAUER, loc. cit., 108*-148*. Hetzenauer estimates the number of variants at about 4900.

Sixtine Bible is mentioned and excused in the preface of
Clement VIII., almost exactly in the indulgent way suggested
by Bellarmine.[1]

The haste with which the Vulgate of 1592 had been printed
resulted in a number of typograpical errors. In 1593 there
appeared a new edition in quarto, and in 1598 another in
octavo, which differ from each other and from the first in
many points, but for the most part only of minor importance.[2]
Many therefore cherished the hope that the work of perfecting
it would be continued in Rome,[3] but it was only after the lapse
of three centuries that this expectation was realized in the
time of Pius X. The Clementine text is thus sufficient " for
the theological use of the Vulgate, while from the critical point
of view, even though it is not perfect and free from errors, is
nevertheless on the whole good ; in a word a text of which
the Church has no need to feel ashamed."[4]

---

[1] In the autobiography of Bellarmine it is said of the Sistina :
" Irrepsisse aliqua errata vel typographorum *vel aliorum*," in his
opinion drawn up for Gregory XIV. : " Multa emendatione digna
variis de causis in iis bibliis irrepsisse." In the preface to the
Vulgate it is only stated that Sixtus V. had understood that
" non pauca in sacra Bibbia *preli vitio* irrepsisse." *Cf.* LE
BACHELET, 90. It does not appear therefore that either in this
or in other respects was the advice of Bellarmine entirely followed.
For the rest the preface sets forth the matter, as it had been
conceived by Sixtus V. ; it was not possible to put into the
Pope's mouth what had only been the opinion of Bellarmine.
" Preli vitio " does not mean a printer's error as it does to-day
(*Zeitschr. f. kath. Theol.*, 1924, 150 *seqq.*).

[2] A critical comparison of the three texts in HETZENAUER,
loc. cit., 72*-102*, according to his estimate the second edition
differs from the first in 230 points, the third from the second
and the first in 930 points ; in an index at the end of the edition
of 1598, 94 are pointed out (*ibid.* 104*). For the editions of the
Clementine Vulgate *cf.* GRAMATICA in *La Scula catt.*, 1912, I.,
186 *seqq.*, 465 *seqq.* ; KNELLER in *Zeitschr. f. kath. Theol.*, XLIII.
(1919), 391 *seq.*

[3] HÖPFL, 225 *seqq.*

[4] REUSCH in HÖPFL, 186.

Clement VIII. won enduring merit by his correction of the liturgical books.   Pius V. had carried out the revision of the Breviary and the Missal demanded by the Council of Trent, and had published in 1568 the new Breviary, and two years later the new Missal.   Sixtus V. ordered the Congregation of Rites which he established to revise the Pontificale, the Rituale and the Caerimoniale episcoporum.[1]   These labours were energetically pushed forward under Clement VIII., and to some extent completed.   The first to appear, in 1596, was a new edition of the Pontificale, that is to say, the episcopal functions, exclusive of the formularies and rubrics of the Mass. The introductory bull, dated February 10th, 1596,[2] points out what vast labours had been involved in this first edition of the Pontificale.   Four years later the Pope published the Caerimoniale episcoporum, which also eliminated certain abuses which had been introduced into the churches with the use of the organ, and laid down detailed rules concerning them.   Whereas the Pope, in publishing the Roman Pontificale, forbade the use of all pontificals hitherto in use, in favour of the new one issued by him, in the case of the Caerimoniale episcoporum he declared that he did not intend to abolish ancient ceremonial in so far as it corresponded with the reformed edition.[3]   This was probably the result of the outspoken remonstrances of Giovan Battista Bandini against the ecclesiastical monopoly, epsecially of liturgical books, and

---

[1] *Cf.* Vol. XVII. of the work, p. 224 ; Vol. XXI., p. 254.

[2] See Bull., X., 246 *seq.*   Baumgarten, Neue Kunde, 342. With regard to the ideas of a reform of the chant under Clement VIII. see the exhaustive work of Molitor, Die nachtrident. Choralreform, II. and also Th. Schmid in *Stimmen aus Maria-Laach*, LXV., 33 *seq.*   Clement VIII. made all steps in this matter dependent on the opinion of the Congregation of Rites. Four Roman musicians in 1595, by command of this Congregation, undertook a revision of the melodies of the chant.   For the Pontificale see Molitor, II., 47 *seq.*

[3] Bull., X., 597 *seq.*   *Cf. Freiburg. Kirchenlex.,* III[2]., 16 *seq* , VIII., 53 *seq.*, IX., 1049.

which were very graciously listened to by the Pope, who was as humble as he was prudent.[1]

In the year 1602 there appeared by the order of Clement VIII. a new, and emended and enlarged edition of the Breviary, together with a bull dated May 10th, which ordered, under pain of excommunication, that henceforward the Roman Breviary should only be printed with the permission of the bishop, and in exact conformity with the Vatican edition, without any additions or omissions.[2]

The reform of the Breviary had already been begun by Sixtus V., and energetically carried on by Gregory XIV., in spite of his short pontificate ;[3] Clement VIII. brought it to completion.[4] The commission appointed by him for this purpose could not have been better composed. It consisted of Cardinals Baronius, Bellarmine and Silvio Antoniano, the Archbishop of Monreale, Lodovico de Torres, the Barnabite Bartolomeo Gavanti, the Theatine monk Michele Ghislieri, and Giovan Battista Bandini, canon of St. Peter's, who acted as secretary. The commission had partly to draw up new critical reports, which was done by Cardinals Baronius and Bellarmine in the case of the historical lections drawn from

[1] See G. MERCATI in *Rass. Greg.*, V. (1906), 12 *seq.*

[2] See Bull., X., 788 *seq.* By a *brief of October 26, 1596, Clement VIII. had granted the use of the *Proprium Salisburg.* which had been reformed by the Archbishop of Salzburg, Wolf Dietrich von Raitenau (Orig. in Consistorial Archives, Salzburg).

[3] *Cf.* Vol. XXII. of this work, p. 390.

[4] *Cf.* for what follows BERGEL in *Zeitschr. f. kath. Theol.*, VIII., 293 *seqq.*, and BÄUMER, 492 *seq.* See also BATTIFOL, 256 *seq.* ; P. A. KIRSCH, Die hist. Brevierlektionen, Würzburg, 1902 ; A. GUITTARD in *La Croix*, 1908, July 1 ; G. BAUDOT, Il Breviario Rom. Origini e storia, Rome, 1909. The *Avviso of November 17, 1593, Urb. 1061, Vatican Library, mentions the labours of the reform commission. A *" Dissertatio de differentiis inter Breviarium Pii V. iussu editum et Clementis VIII. auctoritate recognitum 1604 " composed by the Servite Petrus Martyr Felinus is dedicated to the Duke of Urbino, in Urb. 606, *ibid.*

the legends and lives of the saints,[1] and partly to examine the opinions previously obtained from various sources, the universities, the bishops and scholars. The report as to these was entrusted to Baronius and his assistant, Marcello Francolini. These discharged their task with the greatest exactitude. If they did not in some matters succeed in arriving at the truth, and left certain things to be corrected later on, this was due to the state of historical research at that time.

Some of the corrections suggested by Baronius and, Bellarmine did not meet with the approval of the Congregation and therefore not of the Pope. The latter had laid it down as a rule for the work of reform that only those things were to be corrected which contained a manifest error.[2] The Congregation was of the same opinion.[3] In the hymns very little was changed, but two were added, of which that for the feast of St. Mary Magdalen was composed by Bellarmine.[4] The principal changes were in the lections, by the removal of points that were historically untenable, and of expressions which seemed unfitting. Certain things in the general rubrics were altered and improved, the rank of certain feasts was raised, and with the introduction of greater doubles, a new grade of feasts was established,[5] while new feasts were extended to the whole of the western Church.

In the case of the revision of the Missal introduced by Pius V., in which the printers were not allowed to make any

---

[1] *Cf.* BELLARMINE, Dubia quaedam de historiis in Breviario Romano positis (LE BACHELET, Auct. Bellarm., 461 *seq.*) ; " quae non sunt mutata, quamvis nonullis viderentur esse mutanda " (*ibid.* 467 *seqq.*).

[2] *" S. Pontifex declaravit, ut ea tantum mutentur, quae manifestum errorem continent." Vat. 6242, p. 54, Vatican Library.

[3] See BÄUMER, 494.

[4] Pater superni luminis. *Cf.* the autobiography of Bellarmine in LE BACHELET, 443.

[5] See BÄUMER, 495 *seq.*

changes arbitrarily, the principal work fell upon Baronius, Bellarmine and Gavanti. The new edition of the Missal was published together with the bull of July 7th, 1604.[1]

The labours begun under Gregory XIII., and continued under Sixtus V., to form an authoritative collection of the pontifical constitutions,[2] which had increased by another thousand since the appearance of the Clementina, seemed likely to be brought to a happy ending under Clement VIII., all the more so as the Pope himself had been a member of the commission engaged upon this work. This work was already well advanced. The collection of the material that was to be included, its division into five books, and its arrangement according to titles was so far advanced that the first book could be printed in 1592, and in 1593 the second to the fifth, according to the Roman usage, in forty special copies for the use of the Congregation.[3] But the whole thing had still to be submitted once more to a general discussion. This revision was completed on December 17th, 1593, and when all had agreed as to the matter to be included, Cardinal Pinelli undertook its final preparation for the press.[4] This still required some time, and it was only on July 25th, 1598, that the complete work was ready under the title S.D.N.D. Clementis Papae VIII. Decretales.[5]

---

[1] Bull., XI., 88 seqq.

[2] Cf. Vol. XIX., of this work, p. 279, and BAUMGARTEN, Neue Kunde, 242, 248 (list of the collaborators and the sessions, from the 4th to the 25th, between August 3, 1589, and April 6, 1590).

[3] See SENTIS, Clementis VIII. Decretales, vi. seq.; SINGER in Zeitschr. f. Rechtsgesch., Kan. Abt. VI., 113 seq.; BAUMGARTEN, loc. cit. 249 seq.

[4] See SENTIS, loc. cit., xxvii.; LÄMMER, Kodifikation, 9 seq.; SINGER, loc. cit.

[5] S.D.N.D. Clementis Papae VIII. Decretales, Romae ex typographia Cam. Apost. 1598, only three copies of which are preserved (Casanatense Library, Vatican Library, and Theiner's copy in the Library of the University, Leipzig; see SINGER, loc. cit. 116; BAUMGARTEN, 249 seq., 255 seq., 257 seq.

This plan for the codification of the decretals and constitutions of the Councils which were not included in the
Corpus Iuris Canonici, was presented to the Pope for his
approval on August 1st.   But it was not carried into effect,
even though Clement VIII., on account of his personal
participation in the work, was interested in the work in a
special way.   Fagnani, who was secretary of the Congregation
of the Council from 1614 onwards, gives as the only reason
the prohibition of Pius IV. to write commentaries on the
decrees of Trent, a prohibition which was violated by including
them in the collection.   But this reason was not actually
the principal nor the only one which determined Clement VIII.
as well as his successor, Paul V., not to publish the work.[1]
As a matter of fact other doubts had arisen ; the work did
not altogether answer all requirements, dogmatic material
was predominant, while many Papal decrees and rescripts
had been passed over.   To this there had to be added another
circumstances in view of the attitude of many governments
towards questions of state, which had been manifested with
great violence, especially in Spain, France and Venice, care
had to be taken to avoid serious disagreements.   The Pope
in his prudence did not wish to push things so far, and in the
end decided to abstain from the publication of the book,
which had cost so much time, money and labour.[2]

In the collection undertaken by Cardinal Pinelli there had
been included a decree of Innocent IV. concerning the Papal
election, which, however, had never been promulgated as law,
and which had certainly never become of constitutional force.
In this decree it was laid down that the vote of the person
elected could never be decisive in giving the two-thirds
majority.[3]   This principle, however, is recalled in the draft

[1] Cf. SENTIS, xv. ; SCHULTE, Quellen, III., I., 73 ; SCHERER,
Kirchenrecht, I., 275 ; LÄMMER, Kodifikation, 21.

[2] The whole was submitted to yet another revision by a Congregation which continued its labours even under Paul V.   (See
proofs of 1607-1608 in SENTIS, xiv.) ; in the end the whole thing
was abandoned.

[3] Cf. SINGER, loc. cit. 11 seq., 114 seq.

of a new bull concerning the election of the Pope, drawn up
under Clement VIII.[1] It has not yet been found possible
to ascertain who drew up this draft, nor do we know the
circumstances which prevented its publication ; it is beyond
question that the projected reform was substantially aimed
at abolishing election by adoration, a form of election which
had become very common in the conclaves since the time
of Julius III., and at introducing the secret ballot as of
obligation.[2]

Innocent IX. had already set up a Congregation for the
reform of Papal elections,[3] and Clement VIII., who had been
present at the confusion of the three conclaves which had
succeeded one another in a short space of time, at once ordered
the work to be resumed. It was already fully in hand in
March, 1592,[4] and it was confidently stated that the plan of
reform would be ready in August,[5] but in October an opinion
of a Jesuit on the abuses in the Papal elections was submitted.[6]
At length in February, 1595, the bull on the reform of the
conclave had reached the point of being able to be sent to
all the Cardinals for their opinion.[7] In the end, however,
the opponents of a reform of the conclave obtained the victory:
the party leaders in the Sacred College were unwilling to

---

[1] Cf. WAHRMUND in Archiv für kath. Kirchenrecht, XLII.,
225 seq.

[2] See ibid. 204, 207.

[3] See ibid. 203 n. 3, the opinion of Maretti.

[4] See *Avvisi of March 14 and 18, and May 13, 1592, Urb. 1060,
Vatican Library. Cf. *report of G. Niccolini, March 9, 1592,
State Archives, Florence.

[5] See *Avviso of August 22, 1592, Urb. 1060, II., Vatican
Library. G. del Carretto in his *report dated Rome, 1593,
February 13, a prohibition of all " le pratiche del pontificato "
(Gonzaga Archives.. Mantua).

[6] I have found the *Parere con una lettera dell'autore, Diego
Ximenes S.I., dated Della casa, 1592, October 19, in the Doria
Archives, Rome.

[7] See PARUTA (February 18, 1595), Dispacci, III., 60. The
draft itself in WAHRMUND, loc. cit. 223 seq.

renounce their predominant and decisive position in the election of the Pope.[1]

Very remarkable was the reluctance of Clement VIII. to proceed to canonizations. Together with Philip Neri the Roman people venerated, and had done for some time, Ignatius Loyola, Charles Borromeo, and other representatives of Catholic reform, as though they were already canonized. Clement VIII. did not approve of this, and he expressly forbade pictures which represented the miracles which were attributed to these great men. Very often too ex votos were offered at the tombs of Philip Neri and Ignatius Loyola. At first Clement had made an exception in the case of Philip Neri, the founder of the Oratorians, whom he venerated in a special way, but in the end he extended the prohibition which had been made in the case of the founder of the Jesuits to Philip as well.[2] The Pope took as his rule of action the order issued in 1170 by Pope Alexander III., that without the permission of the Church no one, even when many miracles had been worked by his intercession, might be publicly venerated as a saint.[3] The special Congregation which was consulted by Clement VIII. concerning the veneration of recent saints decided in conformity with this.[4]

The cause for the beatification of Philip Neri had been introduced a few months after his death, but as it was conducted with great minuteness, it was not brought to a

---

[1] See SINGER, loc. cit. 120. An attempt by Clement VIII. to put an end to the influence of Spain in the Papal elections, had already been frustrated a year before by the Spanish ambassador, Sessa.

[2] Cf. *Avvisi of September 9, 1595, June 16, 1601, and November 27, 1602, Urb. 1063, 1069, 1070, Vatican Library.

[3] See Freib. Kirchenlex., II²., 145.

[4] See *Avvisi of December 14 and 28, 1602, Urb. 1070, Vatican Library. According to the latter the Pope said that it was not a case of those who by a cultus " ab immemorabili " or in virtue of a Papal brief had been numbered among the saints, but of the moderns " Philippo, Ignacio, Philippo de Conventuali che andava gridando lodato sempre sia il nome di Jesu e Maria, cappuccino Felice, P. Marcellino, P. Angelo de Paz (scalzo) e card. Borromeo."

conclusion in the time of Clement VIII.   The first steps for
the canonization of the founder of the Jesuits were taken by
Cardinal Farnese.[1]   For the beatification of Charles Borromeo
the senate of Milan,[2] as well as Cardinal Frederick Borromeo,
Philip III. and the Swiss Catholics, had interested themselves.
The Pope praised this,[3] but he caused the necessary inquiries
to be made with all exactitude and without haste[4] by the
Congregation of Rites, as well as in the case of Philip Neri.
He acted in the same way with regard to the canonization of
Francesca Romana, the foundress of the Oblates of Tor di
Specchi,[5] which was promoted by the Romans.

In view of the extreme care of the inquiries,[6] we cannot be
surprised that Clement VIII., in spite of his long pontificate,
only celebrated two canonizations.   On April 17th, 1594,
he raised to the altars the Dominican Hyacinth,[7] the celebrated

[1] See *Avviso of July 10, 1599, Urb. 1067, Vatican Library.

[2] See *Acta consist. February 4, 1604 : " Lectae litterae
senatus Mediolan. pro canonizatione Caroli card. Borromaei."
Barb. XXXVI., 5, III., Vatican Library.

[3] See the *briefs to those mentioned, February 15, 1604, Arm.
44, t. 56, Papal Secret Archives. In that to Philip III. it is
stated : *" Carolum card. Borr. fecimus semper plurimi dum
viveret, mortuum praecipue habuimus in honore, quod in sita
nobis et quasi in animo insculpta esset magna de eius viventi
integritate opinio, de mortui sanctitate maxima " (ibid. p. 143b).

[4] Letters concerning the veneration of Philip Neri, 1596-1597
are in Carte Strozz., I., 489.

[5] See the *report of G. B. Thesis, August 26, 1604, Gonzaga
Archives, Mantua.

[6] For Raymond of Peñafort cf. *Avviso of May 15, 1599,
Urb. 1067, Vatican Library.

[7] See LUBOMLIUS, De vita, miraculis et actis canonizationis
S. Hyacinthi Poloni, Rome, 1594, and Bull., X., 123 seq. Cf.
PARUTA, Dispacci, II., 188 seq., 263 seq., the consistorial *acta
of March 14, 24 and 31, 1594, Papal Secret Archives, the *Avvisi
of March 5, April 20 and 27, 1594, Urb. 1062, Vatican Library,
and " *Vita et gesta Clementis VIII." in Inform. polit., XXIX.,
380b seq., State Library, Berlin. For Hyacinth see also B.
ALTANER, Die Dominikanermissionen des 13 Jahr., Habelschwerdt,
1924, 196 seqq.

apostle of the North, and on April 29th, 1604, he did so in
the case of Raymond of Pennafort,[1] well known everywhere
as a jurist, who also belonged to the Dominican Order.   In
the case of Hyacinth the Queen and King of Poland had
especially interested themselves,[2] and for Raymund
above all Philip III. of Spain.[3]   But the Pope rightly
resisted the efforts that were made for the canonization of
Savonarola.[4]

Clement VIII. was very slow to grant indulgences.[5]   In
accordance with the spirit of the prescriptions of the Council
of Trent and of the constitution of Pius V. of 1567, in 1593
he set up a special Congregation of Indulgences, whose duty

[1] See *Avviso of May 3, 1601, Urb. 1069, Vatican Library.
The " Carmen " by Mutius Ricarius " De beato Raymundo a
Clemente VIII. P.M. in divorum numerum relato " in Barb. lat.
XXIX., 142, and Urb. 1205, p. 31 *seq.*

[2] Sigismund III. bore the expense of the canonization ; see
*Diarium P. Alaleonis, Barb. 2815, Vatican Library.   Queen
Anna had already asked Clement VIII. for the canonization of
Hyacinth in a *letter of March 20, 1594, Doria Archives, Rome.
Ibid. a *letter from Sigismund III. to the Pope, dated Wilna,
September 6, 1601, asking him to promote the cultus of St.
Casimir, to insert his feast in the Missal and the Roman Breviary
and to make his feast a " duplex."

[3] See *acta consist, December 16, 1600 :   " Advocatus petit
nomine Philippi III." the canonization of Raymund ; on December 22 :   " S.S. habuit orationem de Raymundo " (Cod. Barb,
XXXVI., 5, III. Vatican Library).   *Cf.* the *brief to the
" deputati principatus Cataloniae " of September 26, 1602.
Arm. 44, t. 46, n. 297, Papal Secret Archives.

[4] He therefore did not even wish the Vita di Savonarola by
S. Razzi to be printed ; see *Arch. stor. ital.*, 5th ser. XXVIII.,
291.   The " Epistola Clementis VIII. de stigmatibus S. Catherinae
de Senis," dated 1599, November 27, was published in Rome in
1599.   St. Thomas Aquinas was declared patron of Naples by
Clement VIII. ; see *briefs to the viceroy of Naples and to that
city, dated 1603, November 22, Arm. 44, t. 56, n. 35 and 36,
Papal Secret Archives.

[5] See PARUTA, Relazione, 368.   *Cf. Carte Strozz.*, I., 2, 215.

it was to do away with long-standing abuses in this matter, as well as to prevent them in the future.[1]

With regard to the internal government of the Church as carried out by Clement VIII., mention must also be made of his ordinances against duelling,[2] and his condemnation of the opinion which allowed people to confess by letter or messenger, or to receive absolution from a confessor who was absent, as being erroneous, temerarious and scandalous.[3]

---

[1] See PARUTA, Dispacci, I., 256, which removes the doubts of Bangen (248).

[2] Bull., IX., 604 *seq.*

[3] See Bull., X., 855. The decree as to this, which was issued by the Inquisition on June 20, 1602, under the presidency of the Pope, was published on July 19, 1602. Original printed copy in Decreta s. Inquisitionis in Barb. 1370, Vatican Library. For the controversy connected with this decree see WILDT in *Freib, Kirchenlex.*, II., 231 *seq.* ; SCORRAILLE, Suarez II., 55-116.

CHAPTER VII.

FOREIGN MISSIONS.—THE BEGINNINGS OF PROPAGANDA.

AN important part in the ecclesiastical activities of Clement VIII. was taken by his propagation of the missions in the countries outside Europe. During his pontificate important progress was made in this respect, even in Japan, where a persecution of the Christians had begun in 1587.[1] In March, 1591, the intrepid Jesuit Alessandro Valignani penetrated into the presence of Taikosama, as envoy of the viceroy of the Indies, and obtained permission for the Christian missionaries to remain there ; only public religious functions were prohibited. The number of conversions to Christianity continued to increase. Many Christians were to be found in the army with which Taikosama attacked Corea ; two religious of the Society of Jesus acted as military chaplains, who spread the first seeds of Christianity in Corea.[2]

In 1585 Gregory XIII. had forbidden all missionaries, except the Jesuits, to set foot in China and Japan,[3] but as Sixtus V., himself a Franciscan, had granted to that Order the mission " to all parts of the Indies," some Franciscans also went to Japan.[4] Others soon followed them. Into the disputes which then broke out between the two Orders, there also entered the question of nationality, as the Franciscans were Spaniards, and the Jesuits Portuguese.[5]

---

[1] Cf. Vol. XXI. of this work, p. 180.

[2] See JUVENCIUS, V., 180 seq. ; BARTOLI, Del Giappone, Turin, 1829, I., 2.

[3] See Synopsis, 139 seq. Cf. Vol. XX. of this work, p. 511.

[4] See H. BÖHLEN, Die Franziskaner in Japan, Treves, 1912, 14.

[5] Cf. DELPLACE, II., 23 seq. ; SCHMIDLIN, Missions geschichte 283.

Taikosama allowed both the Franciscans and the Jesuits to do as they liked. In 1596 he very courteously received the Jesuit Pedro Martinez, who had been appointed bishop, and who presented letters from the governor of the Indies. But in that same year a change took place which put the Christians of Japan, who had now reached the number of 300,000, in a very difficult position. The cause of this change is said to have been the conduct of the pilot of a stranded Spanish ship, who, in order to save his cargo from confiscation, allowed himself to be led into making the most rash statements about the power of his king. Among other things he said that Philip II. was sending his priests among the foreign nations, so as first to convert the people and thus facilitate their conquest! These words were reported to Taikosama.[1] They were enough for that monarch, who in the spread of a strange religion was every day seeing more and more danger to the national unity which he aimed at,[2] to lead him to take bloody measures. Six Franciscans, the Jesuit Paul Miki, a pupil of the seminary at Ankusiama, two Japanese catechists, and fifteen other Japanese Christians, among them three children, were arrested and condemned to be crucified. On February 5th, 1597, this sentence was carried out at Nagasaki.[3]

In the persecution which then broke out, the Jesuits acted with great prudence ; being exiled they only apparently went away. When Taikosama died in September 1598,

[1] Cf. JUVENCIUS, V., 595 ; DELPLACE, II., 29 seq.

[2] The Japanese Mitsukuri saw in this the true cause of the persecution ; see Hist. Zeitschr., LXXXVII., 196.

[3] See the detailed report sent by P. Froes to the General Aquaviva, printed in Acta Sanct., February 1, 742 seq. The acta of the beatification (1616-1627) are used by BOUIX, Hist. des vingt six martyrs de Japon, Paris, 1862. The canonization took place at Pentecost, 1862, and gave rise to a number of works on the martyrs of Japan, of which I here mention those of PAGÉS (Paris, 1862) and BOERO (Rome, 1862). A contemporary picture of the martyrs is to be found in the church of St. Michael at Munich.

and his successor Daifusama, whose succession was opposed, showed himself favourable to the missions, better days began for the Christians. The Franciscans as well as the Jesuits were able to resume their work, and the number of Christians increased considerably, even though the persecution still continued in certain provinces. In 1599 40,000 received baptism, and 50,000 in the following year. At the beginning of the seventeenth century it was estimated that there were 750,000 Christians.[1] At Nagasaki in 1605 it was possible to hold the procession of Corpus Domini publicly.[2] The Jesuits, whose college was effectively subsidized by Clement VIII.,[3] developed great literary activity : they printed religious books, a Japanese-Portuguese dictionary, and a Japanese grammar with Portuguese explanations.[4] But they neglected to avail themselves of the co-operation of the native secular clergy, and it proved fatal to try and follow European methods in teaching.[5] The number of the Jesuit missionaries was by no means sufficient for their requirements, and therefore Clement VIII., suspending the privilege granted by Gregory XIII, to the Society of Jesus, on December 12th, 1600, granted faculties[6] to all the

---

[1] See DELPLACE, II., 129 seqq. ; PAGÉS, Hist. de la religion chret. au Japon depuis 1598 jusqu'a 1681, I., Paris, 1869, 110.

[2] Cf. JUVENCIUS, V., 606 seq. ; SPILLMANN in Freib. Kirchenlex., VI., 1246 seq. ; PAGÉS, loc. cit., I.

[3] Cf. the *instructions to D. Ginnasio, August 31, 1601 : " Assegnamento fatto da Gregorin XIII. di 4000 scudi annui sopra cotesta collectoria di Spagna da pagarli alli seminarii et chiese del Giappone et da Sisto V. accresciuti a 6000 et per le guerre d'Ungheria tralasciati di pagare S.S. ordina si seguiti di pagare e anchi li decorsi." Barb. 5852, Vatican Library.

[4] Cf. E. SATOW, The Jesuit Mission Press in Japan, 1591-1610, London, 1888, and STRASSMEIER in Stimmen aus Maria-Laach, XXXVII., 219 seq.

[5] See HUONDER, Der einheimische Klerus in den Heidenlandern, 101 seq.

[6] See Bull., X., 631 seq. Cf. JANN, 182 seq., who well shows how in this as well the Pope had to take into account the political claims of the Portuguese.

Mendicant Orders to work as missionaries, both in Japan and China.

The entry of the Christian missions into the Chinese Empire is closely connected with the labours of the talented Jesuit Matteo Ricci, who together with his faithful companion Michele Ruggieri, had reached Tschaoking, in the province of Kwangtung, in the autumn of 1583, and was there held in high esteem, without, however, being able to make more than a few conversions.[1] At the suggestion of the far-seeing Valignani, in 1593 Ricci began to study the Chinese language. At first this was not easy for a man who was already forty, but, as he says in a touching letter, he willingly once more became a schoolboy for the love of Him who became man for the love of us.[2] In an incredibly short time, Ricci, by his determined assiduity, obtained such a mastery of Chinese that in 1595 he was able to publish in that exceedinly difficult and subtle language his book "The true doctrine of God," which later on was included in the collection of classics undertaken by Khian-lung.[3] After this Ricci continued to labour indefatigably in the field of literature. His works were not confined to religious subjects alone, but extended to all manner of subjects[4] : arithmetic, geometry, astronomy,

[1] *Cf.* Vol. XX. of this work, p. 469. To the literature there mentioned may be added the article by J. ALENI in the *Rev. de l'hist. des missions*, I., 52 *seqq.*

[2] Letter to Aquaviva, December 10, 1593, in TACCHI VENTURI, II., 118.

[3] See DAHLMANN, Sprachkunde, 27 ; BAUMGARTNER, Welt-literatur, II., 511.

[4] Ricci worked out among other things a translation of the Gregorian Calendar into Chinese. *Cf.* SOMMERVOGEL, XVI., 1792 *seq.*, and CORDIER, Bibl. Sinica, III. (1905), 1090 *seq.*, the information in which has been considerably added to by the edition of the *Commentarii* (Macerata, 1911) of Ricci made by Tacchi Venturi. For the importance of Ricci to geographical studies see G. CARACI in *Bollet. d. Geogr. Ital.*, V. (1918), 845 *seqq.*, *Riv. Geogr. ital.*, XXVIII. and XXIX. (1921-1922) and H. BOSMANS in the Rev. des quest. scientif., 1921 ; for his map of China see *Études*, CXXXI., 217 *seq.*, 220 *seqq.*

geography, music and philosophy. Even though it was only an exaggeration when a Chinese viceroy said that Ricci knew all Chinese books, it is beyond question that he was the first profound sinologist. The Chinese called him the " great man of Europe."[1] But he remained as humble as a child. Witness to this is borne by his own commentaries, in which he has described so attractively the nascent Christianization of China. An additional testimony is to be found in his letters, in which he continually repeats that the easiest way to convert his beloved Chinese was by books.[2]

Ricci was not only an academic scientist, but an eminently practical man. His keen insight did not fail to grasp that the work of the missions would always be in jeopardy owing to the caprice of the officials, unless the Imperial court at Pekin could be won over. The first attempt to penetrate there, made in 1595, came to nothing, as also did the second, in 1598. In spite of this, certain important consequences ensued. Ricci succeeded, at Nantschang and Nanking, in entering into important relations with Chinese scientists, and other persons of authority, which rendered possible the establishment of mission stations in those two cities. If greater results than before were now obtained, this was above all the result of the fact that Ricci, in accordance with the prudent advice of his companion Lazzaro Cattaneo, adopted the costume of the Chinese scholars, thus putting an end to his being continually confused with the despised bonzes. The silken attire which the missionaries now adopted in place of their poor habit had also to be accompanied by a more distinguished appearance. Valignani, who was very far-seeing, gave his consent to all this, and also obtained that of the General of the Jesuits and of the Pope.[3]

It was characteristic of this new method of procedure that

---

[1] See CORDIER, Bibliographie des ouvrages publ. en Chine par les Européens au xviie et xviiie siècles, Paris, 1883, 33.

[2] See TACCHI VENTURI in *Civ. Catt.*, 1910, III., 47.

[3] See TACCHI VENTURI, Commentarii, I., 3, cap. 9, cap. 53. *Cf. Civ. Catt.*, 1910, II., 558 *seq.*

Ricci, in the house which he built at Nantschang avoided in every way the appearance of a building devoted to divine worship. "The house in which we preach" was the simple inscription which he chose for it. He expressly insisted upon his character of scholar, and it was in accordance with this that he resumed his earlier catechism. Though he was indefatigably devoted to the work of explaining to the Chinese scholars and grandees, hitherto unthought of ideas of mathematics and astronomy, Ricci was very cautious in dealing with religious questions. While keeping silence therefore as to the mysteries of Christianity he sought first to convince his hearers of the fundamental truths of the creation of heaven and earth by God, of the immortality of the soul, of the punishment of the wicked and the reward of the good. He openly combated the doctrines of the Buddhists, but the more cultured philosophy of Confucius were treated by him with all due respect.[1]

In the midst of these labours, which produced surprising results, Ricci did not lose sight of his project of reaching the presence of the Emperor at Pekin. In May 1599 he undertook for the third time his journey to that distant capital, accompanied by the Spanish Jesuit, Diego Pantoja, and two brothers of Chinese origin. In spite of the manifold dangers and obstacles of every kind, which would have discouraged anyone else, he at last, in 1601, thanks to his indomitable energy, reached his goal. Ricci excited the interest of the Emperor Wanglié, who was enthusiastic over the gifts which he had brought, striking clocks, a universal geographical map, engravings on copper, and two paintings representing the Redeemer and the Madonna. Although the learning of this stranger, which was superior to that of the mandarins, won the admiration of the Emperor, there nevertheless arose difficulties : the tribunal set up for the surveillance of

---

[1] So too G. NATALI (Di M. Ricci, Macerata, 1905) though anything but well-disposed towards the Jesuits, praises Ricci highly. Other opinions have been given by us in Vol. XX. of this work, p. 469 *seq.*

foreigners demanded that he should be sent away. The Emperor would not consent to this, but for the time being left unanswered the written request which Ricci had made to be allowed to remain permanently. It was only after some time had passed that he caused the learned Jesuit, who had become indispensable to him, to be informed that His Majesty would be very unwilling for him to leave the capital, where he had thought of taking up his abode. Thus Ricci saw himself rewarded in a marvellous way for his perseverance and his unshaken confidence in God.

At last the great plan for the conversion of China, which, as Francis Xavier had already realized, would be of decisive importance for the future of eastern Asia, in view of the supreme influence which that land of ancient culture exercised over Japan and the other neighbouring countries, could be begun with the hope of permanent success. Nobody seemed to be so well suited for this work as Ricci, since the funda-mental traits of his character were, as his biographer tells us, courageous and unwearied zeal that was at the same time wise and patient ; caution and slowness, followed by action that was equally energetic ; fear of being too daring.[1]

Valignani did all he could to support Ricci. In 1604 he sent him three more fellow-workers, and in 1605 as many more. He also made him entirely independent of the rector of the college at Macao. His successes gradually increased sensibly ; eminent scholars and officials were converted to Christianity with full conviction. At Nanking Father Rocca won over the great statesman and scholar Paul Siu, who became the principal support of the infant Church. In 1605 the first Chinese presented themselves for admission to the Society of Jesus. Their chapel at Pekin was found to be too small, and after a short time there was erected in the Chinese capital a public church, in which the sacred mysteries were

---

[1] See TACCHI VENTURI in *Civ. Catt.*, 1910, II., 39 *seq.*, who there summarizes in a beautiful article the results of his profound studies collected in the new edition of the *Commentarii. Cf.* also BRUCKER, in *Études*, CXXIV., 751 *seq.*

celebrated as in Rome and other parts of the Christian world. To this worship of the " Lord of Heaven " there came an ever-increasing number of converts and catechumens, and also of pagans, whose hearts had been touched by divine grace.

The work of the missions in the Philippine Islands developed[1] in a very consoling way owing to the labours of the Franciscans, Dominicans and Jesuits, all of whom were able to adapt their unwearied labours to the neds of the native population with wisdom and prudence. Clement VIII. especially supported the Jesuits and the Dominicans.[2] On August 14th, 1595, there took place the division of the diocese of Manila, established by Gregory XIII.,[3] and which had so far included the whole mission, into four bishoprics, while it was at the same time made into an archbishopric. It retained the central part of the island of Luzon while the northern part was assigned to the new diocese of Neuva Segovia, the southern part to the diocese of Nueva Cáceres, and the remaining islands of the archipelago to the diocese of Cebú. This new arrangement proved very advantageous ; it consolidated Christianity in the districts already converted, and gave a vigorous unity to missionary activity in those that were still pagan. The missions prospered so well under the Dominican Michele Benavides, who was appointed Bishop of Nueva Segovia in 1595, that of the three pagan provinces in his diocese in the course of a few years two were almost entirely converted and the third to a great extent. When Domenico de Salazar died in 1602, Benavides succeeded him in the archiepiscopal see of Manila. In this important position the good metropolitan[4] continued to promote the work of the missions with

---

[1] See *Cath. Encyclopedia*, XII., 17, and *Schmidlin*, 261 *seqq.*, where the copious literature is given.

[2] See Bull., IX., 526 *seq.*, 529 *seq.* *Cf.* *brief to Philip II., March 11, 1592, Arm. 44, t. 36, n. 277, Papal Secret Archives.

[3] See Vol. XX. of this work, p. 479.

[4] See *acta consist. Cod. Barb. lat. 2871, III., Vatican Library ; Gams, 113-115 and the literature there indicated ; Neher in *Freib. Kirchenlex.*, VI[2]., 692 ; *American Cath. Hist Soc.*, XI. 1900), 455.

indefatigable zeal. At his death, which occurred on June 25th, 1607, he was lamented as a father by Spaniards and converts alike, and venerated as a saint.

Under Clement VIII, there revived the hope of the conversion of Akbar, the Great Mogul of the Indies.[1] In May 1595 there appeared at Lahore, Fathers Girolamo Xavier, a relative of the Apostle of Japan, and Emanuel Pinhero, where they were courteously received by the Great Mogul. Akbar gave them permission to establish missions at Lahore, Cambaia and Agra, which flourished exceedingly, in spite of the hostility of the Mahometans. At Lahore at Christmas 1599 many catechumens, with palms in their hands, went through the flower-decked streets of the city to the church of the Jesuits to receive baptism.[2] There were among the converts men of exalted station. In 1600 Akbar confirmed in writing his permission for the free preaching of the Gospel, which he had at first only granted orally, and then subsidized the building of the Jesuit church which was erected at Agra in 1602 ; he also caused a copy to be made of the picture of the Madonna in S. Maria del Popolo which was there, and placed it in his palace. He read with the greatest interest the life of Jesus Christ, which had been translated into Persian by Father Xavier, but could not bring himself to the point of conversion ; like a real sceptic he remained until his death in 1605 in a state of hesitation.[3]

The efforts to unite the Nestorian Church (Christians of

[1] *Cf.* besides the account of DU JARRIC (see vol. IX., 737, n. 3), G. B. PERUSCHI, Informatione del regno et stato del Gran Re di Mogor, della sua persona, etc., et congietture della sua conversione alla nostra s. fede, Rome, 1597 (lat. Mayence, 1598).

[2] This occurred for the first time in 1589, but the envoys had returned despairing of any success. This was not approved of in Rome ; see JUVENCIUS, 451 ; MÜLLBAUER, 145 *seq.* On December 17, 1592, Clement VIII. addressed a letter to Akbar to recommend the Jesuits to him ; see Bull., IX., 646 *seq*

[3] *Cf.* JUVENCIUS, 451 *seq.* ; *Litt. ann.*, 1597, 576 *seq.* ; MÜLLBAUER, 146 *seq.* ; GRUBER, Aquaviva, 181 *seq.* ; VÄTH in *Kath. Missionen*, XLIX., 201 *seq.*

St. Thomas) to the Catholic Church, which were promoted by the Archbishop of Goa, Alessio de Menezes, with the assistance of the Jesuits, met with a happy result. This prince of the Church, who was compared to Charles Borromeo, won undying fame by his services to the Church in the Indies.[1] He at once held a visitation of the whole of the territory subject to him, so that Clement VIII. sent him well-merited praise.[2] In 1599 Alessio held a synod at Diamper, in the kingdom of Cochim, at which the reunion of the Nestorians was effected. At the same time as he confirmed the synodal decrees, Clement VIII. sent by the Jesuit Alberto Laerzio a Syriac printing press, by means of which the Roman Ritual, and some missals and breviaries were printed.[3] The Pope appointed the Jesuit Francisco Roz Bishop of Angamala, which became a suffragan diocese of Goa ; the bishop by his knowledge of the Syriac and Malabar languages had laboured for many years for the reunion of the Nestorians. Roz at once made a visitation of his diocese, and held a diocesan synod, at which the errors of Nestorius were once again condemned. In spite of this the danger of a relapse into schism was not altogether destroyed, and therefore Paul V. transferred the see to Cranganor and made it into an arch-diocese. Roz remained metropolitan, and was assisted by several Jesuits.[4]

Clement VIII. further showed his zeal and care for souls by making use, in the interests of the missions, of the rapproche-

---

[1] Opinion of DÖLLINGER (Handbuch der Kirchengesch., II., 2, 369).

[2] See *brief of praise to the Archbishop of Goa, April 1, 1599, Arm. 44, t. 43, n. 206, Papal Secret Archives.

[3] See RAULINUS, Hist. ecclesiae malabaricae, Rome, 1745 ; MÜLLBAUER, 166 ; *Zeitschr. f. kath. Theol.*, XX., 728 *seq.* ; JANN, 167 *seq.* By the *brief to " clerus e populus christianus S. Thomae prov. Serrae " of May 19, 1601, he sends congratulations on the synod, and gives deserved praise to the Jesuits. Arm. 44, t. 45, n. 147, Papal Secret Archives.

[4] See MÜLLBAUER, 167 *seq.* ; JANN, 169 *seq.*

ment with the European powers which had been brought about,
in the interests of the war against the Turks, by the Shah of
Persia, Abbas I. the Great.   The Portuguese Jesuit, Francisco
da Costa, informed the Pope in the autumn of 1600 that the
Shah was very well disposed towards the Christians, that he
wished for the presence of Catholic priests, and had sent
envoys to Rome.   After mature reflection Clement VIII.
resolved to profit by this favourable opportunity himself to
send an embassy to Persia.   For this purpose he entered
into communication with the King of Spain, Philip III.[1]
When the latter had given his account, in February 1601,
two Portuguese, the above-mentioned Francisco da Costa
and Diego de Miranda, who had previously been to Persia,
were sent, bearing pontifical letters to the Shah.[2]   The
instructions they were given naturally referred to the common
war against the Turks, but above all dealt with religious
questions.   Costa was instructed to explain to the Shah the
truths of Catholic doctrine and to urge him to enter the Church,
in which matter it was thought that it would be possible to
count upon the assistance of the queen.   If the Shah should
be unwilling to be converted to the Christian faith, then the
envoys must at least obtain from him permission to preach
freely, and for the free exercise of the Christian religion, which
even the Sultan of Turkey permitted in his kingdom.[3]

While Costa and Miranda were on their way, there arrived
in Rome, on April 5th, 1601, the two envoys of the Shah.[4]
They brought good news both with regard to the participation
of their sovereign in the war against the Turks, and the
permission for the Christian mission in Persia.   Clement VIII.

---

[1] Brief of September 4, 1600 (Papal Secret Archives) in App.
n. 17.   A letter from Persia to the General of the Augustinians,
May 24, 1599 (in LÄMMER, Zur Kirchengesch., 94) also refers to the
favourable dispositions of the Shah.

[2] See the *letter to the Shah, February 24, 1601 (Papal Secret
Archives) in App. n. 20.

[3] LÄMMER, Melet., 452 seq.

[4] See ORBAAN, Documenti, 8.

thanked the Shah on May 2nd, 1601, alluding to his own action and that of the Shah against the Turks, and announcing the sending of missionaries to Persia.[1]

When in 1602 Philip III. sent three Augustinian friars to Persia to promote the war against the Turks,[2] Clement VIII. devoted much attention to the missions there.[3] The Augustinians sent by the King of Spain, in addition to arousing interest in the war against the Turks, also laboured for the propagation of Christianity. In the summer of 1604 the Pope sent six members of the Italian Congregation of reformed Carmelites, which had been founded a few years before, to assist them. Among these there were three of the most distinguished members of the Order : Paolo di Gesù Maria, Giovanni di S. Eliseo, and Vincenzo di S. Francesco.[4] The letters to the Shah with which they were furnished indicated as the primary purpose of their missions congratulations on the victories won against the Turks ; the request for permission to preach the Gospel was reserved for oral negotiation.[5] Instead of the long and dangerous sea voyage, the Carmelites chose the land route across Russia. Clement VIII. followed their journey with the greatest

---

[1] See more fully in Vol. XXIII. of this work, p. 299. (*Brief to the Shah, May 2, 1601, Papal Secret Archives, in App. n. 21).

[2] See PHILIPPSON, Heinrich, IV., Vol. I., 276 seq., and MEYER, Nuntiaturberichte, 186.

[3] See the *original letter of Card. C. Aldobrandini to the Archbishop of Siponto, nuncio in Spain, August 28, 1603, and November 7 and 14, 1603, Aldobrandini Archives, Rome, t. 287.

[4] See Dict. de théol., II., 1783. Cf. *Avviso of July 24, 1604, Urb. 1072, Vatican Library, and the *report of G. B. Thesis, August 26, 1604, Gonzaga Archives, Mantua. See also JOH. A JESU MARIA, Hist. Missionum (Opera omnia, IV., Cologne, 1650), I., 328 seq. ; PETRUS A S. ANDREA, Hist. generalis fratr. Carmelit. discalc. congreg. S. Eliae, I., Rome, 1668 ; BERTHOLD-IGNACE DE ST. ANNE, Hist. de l'établissement de la Mission de Perse par les Pères Carmes déchaussés (1604-1612), Brussels, 1885.

[5] See the briefs of June 30, 1604, in MEYER, Nuntiaturberichte, 177 seq. (cf. 201). See also CHARDIN, Voyages (1829), XV., 36.

interest,[1] but their great successes in the Persian kingdom came after his death.

Much more difficult than the journey to Persia, in the then existing conditions, was that to Abyssinia (Ethiopia), as the Turks were masters of the Red Sea, and were fighting the Portuguese wherever they could. In order to provide for the Portuguese Christians and the natives scattered throughout Abyssinia, who were entrusted to the sole care of Francisco Lopez, the last companion of the Patriarch Oviedo, who died in 1577, in February 1589 two Spanish Jesuits were sent, the great linguist Antonio de Monserrato and Pedro Paez, who was burning with youthful enthusiasm. They disguised themselves as Armenian merchants, but were discovered, and taken first to Terim and then to Sana'a in Arabia, where they were kept for five and a half years, two of which they passed in prison, because it was supposed that they were spies. At the end of 1595 they were taken to Mocha, where they were made to serve in the galleys, until a subject of the Indies, representing the rector of the Jesuits at Goa, rescued them. Thus, seven years after their departure, in December 1595, they returned once more to Goa, the place from which they had set out. Both the fathers were ill; Monserrato, the elder, died as a result of the sufferings he had undergone, but Paez recovered. His wonderful spirit of self-sacrifice had not grown less, and he impatiently awaited another opportunity of bringing religious help to his beloved Ethiopians.[2]

---

[1] See MEYER, 201, 211, 217 seq., 220, 259. In a *brief to "Cancellarius Lithuaniae," on January 8, Clement VIII. thanked him for the help given to the Carmelites who were passing that way (Arm. 44, t. 56, p. 390, Papal Secret Archives). Cf. the *brief to the viceroy of Naples, January 22, 1605 (ibid. p. 405b). Ibid. p. 430b, a *brief to the Augustinian Hermits in Persia, February 4, 1605, in which Clement VIII. expresses his joy at the good results of their labours; he thought of them at the Holy Sacrifice, "lattissimum habetis campum"; he intended to send them companions in the Carmelites, and they must work in harmony with them.

[2] Cf. the reports of P. Paez in BECCARI, II., x. seq., and X.,

During the imprisonment of the two fathers, in the summer of 1594, an Abyssinian priest, Tekla Maryam, who had joined the Catholic Church, had brought more detailed information concerning Abyssinia to Rome.[1] In the following year the Maronite, Abram de Guerguis, who had joined the Society of Jesus in Rome, was charged to go to the assistance of Lopez ; he was disguised as a Mahometan, but his companion, a merchant from the Indies, betrayed him, and as he refused to adjure his faith, he was put to death.[2] More fortunate was the Jesuit Melchior da Sylva, an ex-Brahmin priest, who in 1598 reached Ma'assaua, and thence Fremona, the house of the Jesuits on the north Tigre, near Adua.[3] Lopez had died in the previous year after an apostolate of forty years, and Sylva now took his place.[4]

After a Jesuit college had been established at Diu at the beginning of the XVIIth century, at length in 1603 the hour so longed for by Paez had come. Through great perils and privations he penetrated by way of Ma'assaua to the interior of the country ; at Fremona he encouraged the Catholics in their faith, and finally reached the court of the Emperor Za-Denghel, whose confidence he was all the more easily able to win, as the Portuguese had recently rendered valuable services to that monarch against his enemies. At a private audience Paez learned from the Emprtor's own lips of his intention of accepting the Roman faith, and of entering into a treaty of alliance with the King of Spain. Therefore on June 26th, 1604, Za-Denghel wrote letters to Clement VIII.

2-30, Hist. Aethiopiae by ALMEIDA. See also BECCARI, XI., 1 seq. For Paez see also Civ. Catt., 1905, III., 562 seqq.

[1] See *Avvisi of June 2, 1594 (cf. *that of June 5, according to which a special commission was discussing the question of Abyssinia, Urb. 1062, Vatican Library, as well as THOMAS A JESU in Thesaurus theol., VII., 1261 seq.

[2] See ALMEIDA, loc. cit., 35 seq.

[3] The ruins of the Jesuit church there are still preserved ; see the Veröffentlichungen der deutschen Aksum-Expedition, III., 64 seq.

[4] See ALMEIDA, loc. cit., 45 seq. Cf. Litt. ann., 1597, 553.

and Philip III., asking for some Jesuits to be sent. In these letters, which were written in the Abyssinian language, nothing however was said for the moment of his willingness to accept the Catholic faith ; Paez had to add this in Portuguese. In spite of this, in Abyssinia, where four other Jesuits had arrived in the meantime, knowledge of the Emperor's intention had got abroad. Accordingly a rebellion broke out and Za-Denghel was killed.[1] But Paez had also acquired such great influence over the new Emperor Jacob that hopes could be entertained of his conversion.[2]

Of great importance for the missions in west Africa was the establishment by Clement VIII. in 1596 of a diocese for that kingdom (San Salvador) at the request of the King of the Congo, this diocese being detached from that of São Thomé. The Franciscan Rangel was given charge of the new district.[3] This distinguished man, who was consumed with zeal for souls, succumbed prematurely in 1602 to the fatigues to which he had been exposed.

In the case of Angola, which joined the Congo on the south, fair prospects were aroused when in 1599 the king joined himself to the tribal chiefs who had already been converted. The same thing was true of Guinea where the Jesuits effected many conversions, even among the notabilities.[4]

In Mexico, in addition to the Franciscans and Augustinians, the Dominicans and Jesuits were especially active. Both these Orders directed their efforts above all to the Indians. Towards the end of the century the Dominicans had more

[1] See the report of P. Paez of July 24, 1603, in BECCARI, XI., 47 seq., and VI., 49-94 ; ALMEIDA, Hist. Aethiopiae, where on p. 80 seq. is printed the letter to Clement VIII.

[2] See ALMEIDA, loc. cit., 107 seq.

[3] See the *brief to Alvares II., King of the Congo, May 20, 1596, Papal Secret Archives. Cf. *Acta consist., May 20, 1596, Barb. XXXVI., 5, III., Vatican Library ; GAMS, 473 ; JANN, 79 ; ALYS DE CARAMAY-CHIMAY BORGHESE, Belges et Africains, Rome, 1916, 15 seqq.

[4] See SCHMIDLIN, Missionsgeschichte, 228.

than sixty houses there.[1] In 1594 the Jesuits penetrated into the north of Mexico, and in 1596 established a mission at Tepuhuanca, and later on another at Topia.[2] Of great assistance to the work of the missions was the support which Clement VIII. gave to the university established in the capital.[3] At Puebla de los Angeles he granted to the Dominican school the rights of a university.[4] Towards the end of the century some intrepid Franciscans began the missions in Lower California, New Mexico and Florida, but did not meet with any success, except in New Mexico.[5]

In the great kingdom of Peru, besides the Dominicans, Franciscans and Jesuits, the Augustinians were labouring with fervent zeal.[6] In concert with such excellent bishops as Turibio of Lima, and Francisco de Vittoria of Cordoba (Tucumán), they sensibly raised the tone of ecclesiastical life, supported as far as possible by Clement VIII., who had expressed himself in favour of the liberty of the Indians of Peru.[7] The Peruvian province of the Jesuits, the members of which increased under Clement VIII. from 240 to 340, was repeatedly favoured by the Pope.[8] On account of its immense

[1] See *ibid.* 341.

[2] See ASTRÁIN, IV., 437 *seqq.*, 442 *seqq.* *Cf.* M. CUEVAS, Hist de la Iglesia en Mexico, II., TLÁLPAM, 1922, 371 *seq.*

[3] See Bull., X., 225 *seq.* *Cf.* CUEVAS, *loc. cit.* 284 *seqq.*

[4] See Bull., X., 415 *seq.*

[5] See SCHMIDLIN, *loc. cit.*, 347 *seq.*

[6] See *ibid.* 367 *seq.*

[7] *Cf.* MARGRAF, 147. Besides the literature concerning Turibio, cited in Vol. XX. of this work, p. 503, see also CARLOS GARCIA IRIGOYEN, Santo Toribio, 4 vols., Lima, 1906 ; LEVILLIER, Organización de la Iglesia y órdenes relig. en el virreinato del Peru en el siglo xvi., 2 parts, Madrid, 1919 ; *Hist. Jahrb.*, XLVI., 42 *seq.*

[8] See, besides the *Synopsis*, 198, 200, 213, the *brief of July 31, 1592, addressed to the Archbishop of Lima, Turibio (*cf.* JUVENCIUS V., 723), on the occasion of a disagreement between him and the Jesuits, in which it is stated : " Nos certe in eo ordine diligendo nullius unquam caritati concessimus." Arm. 44, t. 37, n. 454, Papal Secret Archives.

extent it was then divided into three parts : the central part
under the equator remained the true province, to which were
added two sub-provinces, one in the north and one in the south.
The fact that the Jesuits educated the blind and the deaf
and dumb in the city of Cuzco, shows how thorough they were
in their mission work. At Quito, where a rebellion against
Spain had broken out, the fathers restored peace. Besides
this they were indefatigable in preserving the Spanish
colonists from complete demoralization.[1]

In 1593 the Jesuits, under the leadership of Father Luis di
Valdivia, also reached Chili, where they founded an establishment which soon became very flourishing. They displayed
a most beneficial activity among the savage people of the
Araucani, who were devoted to hunting and pastoral life,
among whom the Franciscans had already laboured from 1541
onwards.[2] The Jesuit Gabriel de Vega, in the midst of his
many occupations, found time to compose a grammar and
dictionary in the Araucani tongue ; in 1602 Luis di Valdivia
published a catechism in the dialect of the Alentinos.[3] He
and his companion of the same Order, Diego de Torres, who
was justly highly praised by Clement VIII.,[4] won undying
merit by their efforts for the preservation and more humane
treatment of the red races ; they saved the Araucani from
complete extermination.[5]

[1] See *Litt. ann.*, 1594-1595, 674 *seq.* ; 1596, 871 *seq.* ; 1603,
199 *seq.* ; 1604, 240 *seq.* ; 1605, 315 *seq.* *Cf.* JUVENCIUS, V., 727 ;
ASTRÁIN, IV., 532 *seqq.*, 560 *seqq.* ; SCHMIDLIN, 312.

[2] *Cf.* M. DE OLIVARES, Hist. de la Comp. de Jesus en Chile,
escrita 1736, publ. p. D. B. Ararna, Santiago, 1874 ; F. ENRICH,
Hist. de la Comp. de Jesús en Chile, I., Barcelona, 1891 ; ASTRÁIN,
IV., 668 *seqq.*

[3] See DAHLMANN, Sprachkunde, 79.

[4] See the *brief to the Bishop of Cuzco, Ant. de la Roya,
March 7, 1603, Arm. 44, t. 47, n. 27, Papal Secret Archives.

[5] *Cf.* the monograph by ENRICH, cited *supra* n. 2. J. T.
Medina, on the basis of the Acta tells us of two valuable monographs concerning the Inquisition in South America : Historia
del tribunal del S. Oficio de la Inquisición de Lima (from 1569

The Dominicans and Franciscans vied with the Jesuits in
the kingdom of the Incas. Among the Franciscans there
stood out Francisco Solano, whose figure was soon made the
centre of many legends. A man of prayer and mortification,
burning with the love of God and his neighbour, this son of
St. Francis exercised an extraordinary influence over those
round him. Very soon after his death, which took place at
Lima on July 14th, 1610, the people venerated him as a saint,
and many cities chose him as their patron.[1]

Francisco Solano laboured as an apostle, not only in Peru
among the degenerate Spanish colonists, but also among the
Indians in the province of Tucumán. During many years
(1589-1602) he unweariedly travelled about that plateau, as

onwards), 2 vols. Santiago di Chile, 1887, and Historia del
tribunal del S. Oficio de la Inquisicion en Chile (from 1570 onwards)
2 vols., *ibid.* 1890. In a review in the *Hist. Zeitschr.* (LXVII.,
371) it is stated : " A careful study of both these works makes us
realize that the tribunal of the Inquisition, for all its terrors, and
its power to supply for the insufficient civil legislation, did great
service in the matter of customs and morals. Thus there were
cited before the court of the Holy Office bigamists and priests
who were leading immoral lives, and who abused the confessional
for this purpose. The punishments in these cases were certainly
not cruel, especially if we remember the " law " of the XVIth
and XVIIth centuries which was in force everywhere, and the
customary punishments for all manner of faults and crimes. For
the same reason we can explain why blasphemies and outrages
against the Catholic Church were more severely punished than
they are to-day. Thus we only have the trials for heresy and
those of baptized Jews and Mahometans who had relapsed into
their former errors, and the study of which may well excite
terror. It was in these cases that torture was most frequently
applied, and death sentences passed."

[1] *Cf. Acta Sanct.*, Iulii V., 859 *seq.* ; MARCELLINO DA CIVEZZA,
Storia d. Miss. Francesc., VII., 2, Prato, 1891, 99 *seq.* ; *Freib.
Kirchenlex.*, IV[2]., 1836 ; HIRAL, Vie de St. François Solano,
Lille, 1906 ; HELLINGHAUS, Der hl. Franziskus Solanus, Trèves,
1912, and with these the critique by SCHMIDLIN in the *Zeitschr. f.
Missionswiss.*, III., 250.

well as the immense plain of the Gran Chaco. His companion
Luis Bolaños was the author of the earliest catechism in the
dialect of the Guarani, and the founder of the mission in
Paraguay, properly so called.[1] The Jesuits went to Tucumán
at the invitation of the Dominican bishop, Francisco de
Vittoria. Another Dominican bishop, Alfonso Guerra di
Asunción, had summoned them to Paraguay proper. From
their house, established in 1588 in the above-mentioned city,
they undertook " mobile missions " among the savage tribes
of the immense surrounding territory. As these mobile
missions did not prove effective, in 1602 the General of the
Order Aquaviva and the visitor Paez ordered the establishment of fixed missions, avoiding as far as possible men of
alien blood, a step which was approved by the Spanish
government.[2]

The Jesuits too in the province of Brazil, where the celebrated Father Anchieta laboured until 1597,[3] took part in
the missions in Paraguay. A law made by the King of Spain,
in the year in which Anchieta died, prohibited slavery in
Brazil. Thus a great hindrance to the progress of
Christianity was removed, and the messengers of the
faith now penetrated into the depths of the virgin forests
with renewed zeal.[4]

Clement VIII. followed with the closest attention the
progress of the missions in America, and furthered them by
many proofs of his favour. If he heard of the discovery of

[1] For the Catechism of Bolaño see SOUTHEY, Between the
Amazon and Andes, by Mulhall, London, 1881, 248 seq.

[2] See JUVENCIUS, V., 732 seq. ; HUONDER in Freib. Kirchenlex.,
IX[2]., 1464 ; ASTRÁIN, IV., 614 seqq. ; 625 seqq. ; PFOTENHAUER,
I., 87 seq. ; SCHMIDLIN, Missionsgeschichte, 317 seq.

[3] For Anchieta cf. Vol. XX. of this work, p. 510.

[4] For the Jesuits in Brazil see Litt. ann. 1594-1595, 789 seq.,
1597, 492 seq. ; JUVENCIUS, V., 731 seq. ; F. GUERREIRO,
Relaçam annal das cousas que fezeram os padres da Companhia
de Jesus nas partes da India oriental e no Brasil, Angola,
Caboverde, Guine nos annos de 1602 e 1603, Lisbon, 1605,
III., 125.

new peoples, he hastened to exhort the bishop concerned to
spread Christian doctrine among them ; if he learned of abuses,
he at once intervened.[1] His care also extended to civil
matters ; thus he urged Philip III. not to oppress the natives
by taxes.[2]

From a description of Spanish America, published in Madrid
in 1601, we learn that at the beginning of the XVIIth century
the success of the missions presented externally an impressive
appearance ;   there   were   five   archdioceses,   twenty-seven
dioceses, two universities, more than four hundred convents
of Dominicans, Franciscans, Augustinians, Mercedari and
Jesuits, innumerable confraternities and hospitals, parishes
and mission stations for the million pagans who had been
converted to Christianity.[3]   In Mexico and other places the
building of magnificent cathedrals had been begun.[4] Naturally
there were also abuses and dark places which reacted upon
these external signs of progress, a thing which continues down
to our own times.[5]

While in the colonies of Spain and Portugal the Church
could rejoice in the fullest support and protection of the civil
authorities, in all the countries subject to the Turks it had
to suffer severely from the Mohamedans and schismatics.
In spite of all the efforts of the Latin missionaries of the various
Orders there was a perceptible diminution of the Christian
population.   Clement VIII. did all in his power to remedy
this.   One of his first cares was to resume the question of
the reunion of the Copts which had been begun by Sixtus V.,[6]
but which had been interrupted during the brief pontificates
of Urban VII., Gregory XIV. and Innocent IX.   In March
1592 Clement VIII. sent an envoy to the Patriarch Gabriel of

[1] Cf. Bull., X., 767 ; XI., 60 seq.

[2] See the *instructions to D. Ginnasio, September 18, 1600,
Barb. 5852, Vatican Library.

[3] See A. DE HERRERA, Descripcion de las Indias ocidentales,
Madrid, 1601, 80.

[4] Cf. BRIGGS, Barock-Architektur, 186 seq.

[5] See SCHMIDLIN, Missionsgeschichte, 314 seq.

[6] Cf. Vol. XXI. of this work, p. 185.

Alexandria[1] in the person of Girolamo Vechietti. As a result of this the Patriarch sent representatives to Rome, with a letter of November 22nd, 1593, addressed to the Pope, in which he recognized the primacy. The same was done by the archpriest John of Alexandria, who in a letter dated December 18th, 1593, said that the pitiful state of the Egyptian Church and its harassing by the Turks, was in his opinion a punishment for its schism.[2]

The Coptic envoys reached Rome in June 1594. After the difficulties connected with the differences of rite had been adjusted with the help of the Jesuits,[3] on January 15th, 1595, in the presence of Clement VIII. and twenty-four Cardinals they made the Catholic act of faith, and paid homage to the Pope,[4] in the name of those who had sent them. The completion of the reunion was, however, delayed by unfortunate circumstances, and it was only on October 7th, 1602, that Clement VIII. could express to the Patriarch of Alexandria his joy at his return to Catholic unity. At the same time he informed him that he had established a Coptic college in Rome, and asked that suitable students should be sent thither ; for his part he offered to further the printing of ecclesiastical books in the Coptic language.[5] The archdeacon of the Alexandrian Church, Barsum, was to take this letter with him. In the meantime, unfortunately, the Patriarch Gabriel died, and his successor Mark, to whom

[1] See *brief of March 27, 1592, Arm. 44, t. 36, Papal Secret Archives.

[2] See BARONIUS, Annales, VIII., Lucca, 1741, ad an. 452, n. 23, and Append. p. 636 *seq.*

[3] See *Avviso of June 9, 1594, Urb. 1062, Vatican Library.

[4] See *Diarium P. Alaleonis, Barb. 2815, p. 390, Vatican Library ; *Avviso of January 18, 1595, Urb. 1063, *ibid.* ; BARONIUS, *loc. cit.*

[5] See *letter of October 7, 1602, Arm. 44, t. 46, Papal Secret Archives. This and the following documents were unknown to RENAUDOT (Hist. Patriarch. Alexandr. Jacobit., 612), and to PICHLER (II., 516).

Clement VIII. addressed himself in 1604,[1] held different views from those of his predecessor.

Clement VIII. showed great affection for the Maronites, whose college in Rome he did his best to help.[2] In June 1596 he sent the Jesuit Girolamo Dandini to Lebanon,[3] where he found certain evils and abuses. In September he held a national council at the monastery of Kanobin, at which the Maronites protested at dogmatic errors being attributed to them. At this assembly certain canons were laid down concerning external worship and the administration of the sacraments ; in future they were all to make use of the reformed missal[4] published in Rome by pontifical authority. In 1599 Clement VIII. granted to the new Patriarch of the Maronites the confirmation he asked for, and sent him the pallium.[5]

---

[1] See *brief of May 26, 1604, Arm 44, t. 56, Papal Secret Archives.

[2] See ANAISSI, Bull. Maronit., 104 seq. The Pope supplied the college with Spanish wine ; see *instructions to D. Ginnasio in Barb. 5852, Vatican Library.

[3] See ANAISSI, loc, cit., 106 seq. The instructions of the General Aquaviva for Dandini and his companion Fabio Bruno in RABBATH, Documents, I., 170 seq.

[4] Cf. DANDINI, Voyage du mont Liban par R.S.P. (Richard Simon), Paris, 1685, 109 seq., 158 seq., PICHLER, II., 458 seq., Coll. Lacens., II., 413 seq. A " Missale chaldaic. iuxta ritum Maronit," dedicated to Clement VIII. and printed in 1594 at the " Tipografia Medicea," in Vat. lat. 5477, Vatican Library.

[5] See ANAISSI, Bull. Maronit., 107 seq. Cod. M. 8, p. 77 seq. of the Vallicella Library, Rome, contains an " *Epistola Simeonis patriarchae totius Iberiae et Orientis ad S.P. Clementem VIII. a. 1596, de statu religionis christianae in illis partibus," especially concerning Georgia, where some Capuchins were working at the beginning of the XVIIth century. Cf. Beilage zur Allg. Zeitung, 1896, n. 101, May 1. See also *briefs of April 1, 1598, to the King and Patriarch of Iberia (Georgia) in Arm. 44, t. 42, n. 75 seq., 106, Papal Secret Archives. In a *brief to Philip III. of September 13, 1602, the Pope recommends " archiep. Dersinensis in Armenia " who had been sent to him by the Armenian Patriarch

In the Balkan peninsula Clement VIII. sought to bring
about the reunion of the Serbs with Rome, by means of the
Franciscans who were labouring there in a self-sacrificing
spirit, but national jealousies prevented the success of his
efforts.[1] In the principality of Moldavia, which had been
reduced to a state of vassalage by the Turks, the efforts of
the voivode Peter the Lame, which had been begun under
Gregory XIII. and Sixtus V. to reunite his subjects to the
Catholic Church proved vain, since that prince, fearing that
the Sultan would forcibly make his son John Stefan embrace
Mohamedanism, had taken to flight.[2] Clement VIII.

Melchisedech for recognition by the Holy See ; in the brief it is
stated that the archbishop had told him of the oppression and
persecution of the Armenians by the Turks. He complains that
the Armenian Catholic uniats are treated as pagans by your
representatives in the east ; at Ormuz, the port in the Persian
Gulf, where a tenth is paid as customs duty, they have to pay
double like the pagans, whereas at Ancona they are treated by
us, as by other princes, as Christians ; they are excluded from
trading in the East Indies. The archbishop asks you to make
restitution. We recommend to you the Armenian Catholics, and
the Armenian merchants, who greatly help the bishops (Arm. 44,
t. 46, n. 281, Papal Secret Archives). A *brief to Philip III.,
October 21, 1604, recommends the Armenians, so that they may
be able to return by an indirect route, as the Turks bar their way
(*ibid*. t. 56, p. 326). According to the *Avviso of November 20,
1604, Stefano Sirleto, nephew of the Cardinal, of the new Order
" della continua oratione," or of S. Agnese who, being very
learned and pious, had preached to the Jews, was sent by the
Pope to Armenia as archbishop. Urb. 1072, Vatican Library.

[1] *Cf.* FABIANICH, Storia dei Frati minori in Dalmazia et Bossina,
I., Zara, 1863, 315 *seq.* BALAN, La chiesa e gli Slavi, 207 *seq.* ;
HUDAL, Die serbisch-orthodoxe Nationalkirche, Graz, 1922, 13.
For Clement VIII. and the Bulgarians *cf. Archiv. f. österr. Gesch.*,
LIX., 344 *seq.*

[2] *Cf.* NILLES, Symbolae ad ill. hist. eccl. orient., II., Lisbon,
1885, 978 *seq.*, and HIRN in *Hist. Jahrb.*, VII., 434 *seq.* Documents relating to the Catholics in Moldavia, 1600 *seqq.*, in the
Roumanian periodical *Columna lui Traian*, 1876, 299 *seqq.* See

repeatedly implored the help of foreign princes for the Christians of Moldavia, Wallachia[1] and the Epirus,[2] who were gravely threatened by the Turks. At the very beginning of his pontificate he had assigned an annual subsidy to the bishop of the Latin Catholics in Moldavia, which was to be paid by the Apostolic Camera.[3]

With a like generosity the Pope made provision for the Latin bishops in the islands of Chios, Andros and Naxos, who found in their poverty an obstacle to their fulfilling their duty of residence.[4] To give spiritual assistance to the Christian inhabitants of the archipelago was all the more near to the heart of Clement VIII., in that the Greeks living there had not as yet formally detached themselves from the Roman Church.[5] For this purpose he made use by preference of the Jesuits. Bishops such as the bishop of Crete, which island still belonged at that time to the Venetians, put difficulties in the way of the fathers, on which account they received

also ABRAHAM in *Kwartalnik Hist.*, XVI. (1902), 206. JORGA in Gesch. der europ. Staaten, XXXIV., 36; KOROLEVSKIJ in *Rev. catolica*, 1915.

[1] See the *brief to the King of Poland, September 6, 1602, Arm. 44, t. 46, n. 272, Papal Secret Archives, and *ibid*. the *brief of the same date to the " episc. Argensis." The report drawn up a short time after the death of Clement VIII., cited by GOTTLOB in *Hist. Jahrb.*, VI., 54 *seq.*, shows how Protestantism, by penetrating into Transylvania, had hastened the decline of the Catholic Church in Moldavia.

[2] See the *brief to Philip III., February 14, 1603, Arm. 44, t. 47, n. 10, Papal Secret Archives. The brief to the Christians of the " Cimarra " in Epirus in 1594, in *Bessarione*, XVII. (1913), 195.

[3] Bull., IX., 549 *seq.* For Bishop Vincenzo Quirini, who in 1599 sent to Clement VIII. a report that was often quite incorrect (printed in HURMUZAKI, III., 1, 545 *seq.*) *cf.* NILLES, *loc. cit.*, 1008, 1026 *seq.*

[4] See Bull., IX., 549 *seq.*

[5] The definite breach only took place at the beginning of the XVIIIth century ; see PIOLET, I., 133.

severe admonitions.[1] In 1592 Clement VIII. sent to Chios
the Jesuits Benedetto Muleto and Vincenzo Castanola. When
three years later the latter sent to Rome a report of the sad
conditions in Chios, it was decided to establish a house for
the Jesuits there, for which the Pope gave the necessary funds.
Their work in Chios was so beneficial that the inhabitants
of the island sent a letter of thanks to Rome.[2] The inhabitants
of Naxos also asked that a Jesuit might be sent to them, and
Clement VIII. entrusted that mission to the learned Vincenzo
Cicada, who was a relative of the owner of the island, the
Count of Cicada.[3]

In a yet more comprehensive way Clement VIII. occupied
himself with the condition of the Greeks, a hundred thousand
in all, who lived in different parts of Italy, especially in
Calabria and the island of Sicily. These consisted in part of
old inhabitants, and in part of exiles, who had left their own
country on account of the Turkish rule. To these were added
a number of Albanians, who had sought a refuge in Italy after
the death of their national hero Skanderbeg, but who had
nothing in common with the Greeks but their liturgical rite.[4]

In common with all the Italian bishops, those of southern

---

[1] See the *brief to the Archbishop of Crete " Laurentius
Victurius," February 4, 1595, Arm. 44, t. 40, p. 41, Papal Secret
Archives. Cf. as to this Synopsis, 196 seq.

[2] See Juvencius V., 436 seq. ; Synopsis, 183 seq., 194, 219.

[3] See the *briefs to V. Cicada and the Count C. Cicada, of
May 5 and 8, 1600, Arm. 44, t. 44, nn. 127-129, Papal Secret
Archives. Ibid. t. 43, n. 336, a *brief to C. Cicada, in which
Clement VIII. recommends to him the faithful in the island.
The direction of the Greek College in Rome, which Clement VIII.
had entrusted to the Jesuits (Synopsis, 158) was taken from them
in 1604. It is false to say that this was done on account of bad
administration, as was said (see *Avviso of September 25, 1604,
Urb. 1072, Vatican Library) ; cf. KOROLEVSKIJ in Stoudion, 1929,
in course of publication. Cf. Bull., IX., 518 seq.

[4] Cf. J. GAY, Étude sur la décadence du rite grec dans l'Italie
méridionale à la fin du XVI. siècle, in Compte-rendu du IVe.
Congrès Scientif. internat. des Catholiques, Sect. I., 163 seqq.

Italy, encouraged by the Holy See, had again commenced
to hold regular visitations of their dioceses during the period
of Catholic reform.   In doing this they had come to know
more fully the religious conditions of the Greeks, which
frequently called for improvement.   Like the magistrates
and some of the barons, not a few of the bishops were guilty
of grave mistakes in dealing with the Greeks and Albanians ;
often almost force was used to compel them to adopt the
Roman rite.[1]   Faced with this fact, the Holy See held firmly
to its ancient principle of energetically protecting the discipline and liturgy of the Greek Catholics, so long as these
were not opposed to dogma.   Just as Leo X. and Clement VII.
had strongly admonished[2] those Latins who attacked the
Greeks on account of their different discipline, so had Paul III.
forbidden under grave penalties the Bishops of Cassano,
Bisignano, Rossano and Anglona-Tursi to disturb the
Albanians in the exercise of their liturgy.   But as many
abuses which affected doctrine had become introduced,
especially among the Greeks of Sicily, on February 16th,
1564, Pius IV. had expressly recalled the duty of vigilance
over their doctrines and worship which was incumbent on the
Latin bishops.[3]   But both he and Pius V. had insisted on the
inviolability of the Byzantine rite.   In the Greek college
as in all the oriental colleges which he established, he had
the students strictly educated in their own rite.[4]

---

[1] *Cf. ibid.*

[2] See HERGENRÖTHER in *Arch. f. kath. Kirchenrecht*, VII., 179.

[3] See RODOTA, Dell'origine e stato presente del rito greco in
Italia, III., Rome, 1758, 138.

[4] See HERGENRÖTHER, *loc. cit.* 179, 355.   Professor H. Gelzer,
who died in 1906, was occupied in 1903 with the manuscript
material for a history of the Greeks and Albanians in southern
Italy.   For this purpose he obtained documents from the archives
of the Congregation of the Council and Propaganda, and even
some from that of the Holy Office in Rome, which is so jealously
guarded.   I have already frequently stated, and once again in
1912 in *Hist. Jahrb.*, XXXIII., 481 *seq.*, that not only in the
interest of historical studies, but also in that of the Catholic

Clement VIII. too was guided by the principle that the Byzantine liturgy had its full rights, within the limits assigned by dogma. On August 31st, 1595, he issued a special instruction which dealt exhaustively with the controversy which had arisen concerning the rites and usages of the Greeks.[1] The publication of this document had been preceded by a detailed inquiry by a Congregation expressly intended for the reform of the Greeks.[2] Of decisive importance in this matter were the views of Cardinal Santori, who was very expert in these questions, and had collected detailed information.[3] The instruction aimed above all things at the removal of undoubted abuses, especially in the administration of the sacraments. With regard to sacerdotal ordination, it laid down that the Greeks could only receive this from a bishop of their own rite. It was expressly ordered that one of their bishops should reside in Rome. Clement VIII. at the same time renewed the edicts of Innocent IV. in 1254, and of Pius IV. in 1564, as well as the prohibition issued by Pius V.

Church, it is ardently to be desired that these may at last be made accessible. The researches of Professor Gelzer, which have not as yet been published, have confirmed this. Gelzer wrote to me from Naples on March 10, 1903, that his work would be " an honourable page for the Roman Curia and for the Holy Office itself. They did all they could on behalf of these exiles, and for the safeguarding of their liturgy and privileges. The pressure to make them accept the Latin rite always came from the local authorities, the bishops, barons and magistrates." Cf. KOROLEVSKIJ, in Stoudion, IV., 82-91.

[1] Bull., X., 2, 11 seq.

[2] Part of the protocols to be found in Barb. 2607, Vatican Library, was published from this in the periodical Bessarione, XVII. (1913), 345 seq.

[3] Cf. the *Miscellanea de riti specialmente greci, from the Santori bequest, in Cod. I-B 6 of the Brancacciana Library, Naples (now at Propaganda) from which GAY, loc. cit., 164 seq. gives information. Cf. also " Ant. Lombardi archiepisc. *Consultatio super abusibus Graecorum degentium Messanae ad Ioh. Ant. Santori card. s. Severinae," in Vat. 5544, Vatican Library. Cf. also Bessarione, XVII. (1913), 466 seq.

in 1566, of any fusion of the Roman and Byzantine rites.[1]
The indefatigable Cardinal Santori remained the advocate
of the Greeks in Rome.[2]

Several memorials presented to the Pope show how great
was the interest taken at that time in the world-wide mission
of the Church. One of these documents treats with great
learning and knowledge of the political and religious conditions of the East, and of the principles which must be firmly
adhered to in the negotiations of the Holy See with the oriental
princes in the interests of a reunion of the Patriarchs of
Alexandria and Constantinople.[3] A second memorial makes
proposals for missions to be undertaken in Denmark and
Norway.[4] A third, whose author through modesty does
not make himself known, urges, probably in connexion with a
petition[5] from the Bishop of Tournai, Jean Vendeville,
presented to Sixtus V. in 1589, the establishment of a special
Congregation, which may be called the forerunner of " Propaganda fide," since its suggests to the Pope the erection of
a similar institution as the best means of propagating the
Catholic faith.[6] The author is of opinion that it would be

---

[1] See HERGENRÖTHER, loc. cit. 355.   The edict of Innocent IV.
in RAYNALDUS, 1254, n. 7.

[2] The reply of Santori to the Archbishop of Reggio, Annibale
d'Afflito, concerning the Byzantine rite in his diocese : Roma e
Oriente, VII. (1914), 106 seq., 339 seq.

[3] *Discorso in Urb. 854, p. 1 seq., Vatican Library, used for the
first time by LÄMMER, Analecta, 52.

[4] This *memorial addressed to the Pope and to the Cardinals
of the Congregation of Propaganda Fide in Barb. 1992, Vatican
Library.

[5] See RENSENS, La première idée du collège de la Propagande
ou mémoire presenté en 1589 par J. Vendville, etc., in Mém. de la
Soc. hist. et litt. de Tournai, X. (1870). Cf. also GOYAU, Les
initiatives Belges dans la Fondation de la Propagande, in Revue
Générale of Brussels, July 15, 1924, p. 1 seq.

[6] *" Modus propagandi fidem Catholicam," an unsigned
manuscript from the collection of Magliabecchi ; I made use of
this in 1879 in Florence in the Marucelliana Library ; the manu-

necessary to employ four or five secretaries, distinguished for their knowledge of languages, their learning and their piety, who should lay proposals before the Congregation and supervise their carrying out. The first of these secretaries, who were also to draw up a list of all persons of importance for the work of the missions, was to be concerned with the spiritual needs of England, Scotland, Ireland, France, Germany, Denmark and Sweden ; the second with the Poles, Lithuanians, Russians, Ruthenians, Hungarians and Transylvanians ; the third was to be assigned Dalmatia, Bosnia, and in a special way the whole of the Balkan peninsula ; the fourth Cyprus, Asia Minor, Syria, Jerusalem, Alexandria and Algeria ; the fifth all the missions in the Spanish-Portuguese colonies in America and Asia.

The memorial also treats in detail of the training to be given to the missionaries in Rome. This work was to be divided between the Franciscans, Dominicans and Jesuits. The author attaches great importance to the spread of Catholic books translated into the languages of the various peoples. He suggests that there should be interested in this work, besides the Generals of the above-mentioned Orders, the Latin Bishops of Cattaro, Ragusa, Crete and Corfù, the nobles who had remained loyal to the Church in Andros and Chios the many merchants who traded with the east, and their consuls at Pera, Alexandria and Aleppo. At the end the author remarks that if the city of Geneva alone had been able

script was at that time to be included in the National Library, then closed. The author of the manuscript was probably the distinguished Provincial of the Carmelites, Tommaso a Jesu, a friend of Santori, who in his work, " De procuranda salute omnium gentium," Antwerp, 1613 (cf. SCHMIDLIN, in Zeitschr. f. Missionswiss., III., 112) repeats almost word for word a part of the things set forth in the memorial (1. 3, c. 1, p. 103 seq.). Tommaso a Jesu, who relates in his introduction that he had made use of the library of Santori, probably saw the memorial there. For Tommaso a Jesu (1568-1626) cf. also SALAVILLE, Un théoricien de l'apostolat catholique au XVII. siècle, in Echos d'Orient, XX., 129-152.

in a short space of time, by means of books and writings, to win over so great a number of souls to Calvinism, how much more reason there was to hope for the winning, by the help of God, of so many immortal souls, for which Christ had shed His blood ; it was only essential for attention to be drawn to this argument, while the necessary power was not wanting in Rome.

This memorial contains the germ of the great idea of Propaganda, and it is the undeniable merit of Clement VIII. that he sought to realize it.   The Pope had already in 1594 established a similar Congregation for the missions in Abyssinia,[1] and in 1595 for the Italo-Greeks.[2]   In continuance of the efforts of Pius V.,[3] in 1599 he established a Congregation composed of nine Cardinals, which was to concern itself principally with the propagation of the faith.   The president was Cardinal Santori, together with Baronius and Bellarmine, who also formed part of the new Congregation, but he was undoubtedly the most important and zealous Cardinal of his time.   Besides this indefatigable supporter and proved expert in the work of the missions, there were also added[4] Medici, Borromeo, Visconti, Antoniano, and Pietro and Cinzio Aldobrandini.   The constitution of the Congregation took place on August 11th, 1599, in the presence of the Pope ; on August 16th the members held their first meeting at the palace of the president, Santori.   Unfortunately only the notes of the first ten meetings have been preserved ; the last took place

[1] According to the *Avviso of June 9, 1594, there belonged to this Congregation Cardinals Galli, Paleotto, Santori, Toledo and the Camerario.   Urb. 1062, Vatican Library.

[2] Cf. supra, p. 263.

[3] Cf. Vol. XVIII. of this work, p. 350.

[4] Cf. his *Audientiae in Arm. 52, t. 17 seqq., Papal Secret Archives.   See also Castellucci in the publication (p. 162 seq., 178 seq., 248 seq.) mentioned in the following note.   The "Catechismo generale" drawn up by Santori concerning the treatment of catechumens and neophytes is published in the appendix of the work on the missions by Tommaso a Jesu ; see Zeitschr. f. Missionswiss., III., 112.

on August 14th, 1600.[1] The acta were written by a secretary, and in the margin Cardinal Santori wrote with his own hand the Pope's replies to the decisions of the Congregation. The procedure was the same as that followed by the German Congregation of Gregory XIII., and later on by Propaganda.

At its first three sessions the Congregation was called " Congregatio super negotiis sanctae fidei et religionis catholicae " and later on " De propagatione fidei " or " De propaganda fide." In this latter title its scope was concisely expressed. In accordance with a decision arrived at at the first congregation, the meetings were to be held twice a month. The questions proposed were discussed and decided. After each meeting Cardinal Santori went to the Pope to tell him of the decisions come to. The Pope's replies were communicated to the Congregation at the next meeting, and carried out in accordance with his wishes.

The matters discussed by the Congregation were very varied and related to every country ; the faculties of the Archbishop of Goa, the Philippines, New Mexico, Scandinavia, Africa, the Greeks in south Italy, the Nestorian Christians in the Indies, Transylvania, Moldavia and Wallachia, and Persia. Above all a fresh impulse had to be given to the missions in the East, in which Sixtus V. had placed little

[1] For the " Acta Congreg. super negotiis s. fidei et relig. cath." contained in Cod. Misc. com. 17 of the archives of Propaganda, see SCHMIDLIN in *Zeitschr. f. Missionswiss.*, XI. (1921), 232 *seq.*, where, however, the statement that I found further Acta in the Papal Secret Archives is based upon a misunderstanding. Lemmens found some Acta in a Cod. Ottob. in the Vatican Library ; see LEMMENS, Acta S. Congr. de propag. fide pro terra sancta, I., 1, concerning the first session in the presence of the Pope. A. Castellucci has recently published all the Acta preserved, in *Le Conferenze al Laterano*, marzo-aprile, 1923, p. 223 *seq.* The Congregation is mentioned in the *Avvisi, hitherto unknown, of August 14 and 18, 1599, and June 10, 1600, Urb. 1067, Vatican Library. Clement VIII. distinctly said in the *brief of September 4th, 1600 (Papal Secret Archives) that the Congregation was consulted because of the mission to Persia ; see App. n. 17.

hopes. The colleges founded by Gregory XIII. were also placed under the Congregation, which was in all ways similar to Propaganda. There was no possibility of the Congregation being dissolved, in view of the zeal of Clement VIII. for the missions ; the death of Santori, which occurred in 1602, brought about an interruption,[1] but this was of short duration, as Clement VIII. ordered the Congregation to resume its labours in 1604.[2] Thus the Aldobrandini Pope must be given the credit for having for the first time created in Rome a central control for the missions, the ends and objects of which corresponded with those of Propaganda, founded by his second successor.

[1] As the presidency, and therefore the Acta now passed into the hands of another Cardinal, this explains their disappearance. But perhaps it will still be possible to find them.

[2] See in App. n. 23, the *report of Fr. M. Vialardo of December 11, 1604, Papal Secret Archives.

CHAPTER VIII.

THE GREAT JUBILEE OF 1600.

A POPE so pious as Clement VIII. was certain to have much at heart the worthy celebration of the universal Jubilee, which fell in the year 1600. The first preparations were made as early as the beginning of 1599.[1] On March 3rd the Pope appointed two Congregations, each composed of twelve Cardinals ; the first, of which Santori was president, was to devote itself to the spiritual preparations ; the second, presided over by Galli, to the material ones.[2] Orders were issued to all the authorities in the Papal States to provide for the maintenance and security of the roads ; the hospices fn Rome received ample subsidies, so that they might get ready to receive the pilgrims.[3] Clement VIII. addressed himself to Philip III.[4] for a supply of grain from Sicily. The governor of Milan was exhorted to repair the roads and assist the pilgrims.[5] All the Cardinals were to take part in the solemnity.[6] The bulls of May 19th and 21st, 1599, announced the celebration of the Holy Year, its duration and the suspen-

---

[1] Cf. *Avvisi of January 30 and February 3, 1599, Urb. 1067, Vatican Library.

[2] See *Acta consist. card. S. Severinae, Cod. Barb. lat. 2871, Vatican Library.

[3] See BENTIVOGLIO, Memorie, 188 seqq.

[4] See *brief to " Vicerex Siciliae," asking him to carry out the promise of Philip III., September 1, 1599, Arm. 44, t. 43, n. 352, Papal Secret Archives. Cf. the *instructions to the nuncio in Spain, D. Ginnasio in Barb. 5852, I., Vatican Library.

[5] *Brief of April 28, 1599, Arm. 44, t. 43, n. 288, Papal Secret Archives.

[6] See *Avviso of March 13, 1599, Urb. 1067, Vatican Library.

sion of all other indulgences.[1] On May 22nd letters of
invitation were sent to the Emperor, and the kings and
Catholic princes,[2] and on October 30th was published the
invitation to the whole of Christendom.[3] The princes were
urgently exhorted to show themselves kind and generous to
the pilgrims from their own countries, and to those who should
pass through them, and to provide for their safety.   In
November the Pope prepared a special house in the Borgo
to receive the bishops and poor priests from beyond the Alps ;
he also provided refuges for needy layfolk, especially from
the countries where Protestantism was predominant.[4] The
prelates of the reform Congregation were ordered to visit the
national hospices in Rome, and to assist in every way the
strangers who came for the jubilee.   The prelate Mona was
charged with the pilgrims who came from Spain, Sorbolongo
with those from France, Seneca with those from Germany,
Benaglia with those from Venice, Tarugi with those of the
Papal States and Urbino, and Gessi with those from Poland.[5]
The Pope and the Cardinals assisted in a special way the
celebrated Confraternity of the SS. Trinità de' Pellegrini.[6]
Other congregations, such as that of the Stigmata of
St. Francis, founded in 1594, received money for the entertain-
ment of needy pilgrims.[7] The Pope also gave orders that
the pilgrims should not be exploited by the inn-keepers in

[1] Bull., X., 504 seq., 509 seq.

[2] See *Arm. 44, t. 43, nn. 241-255, Papal Secret Archives.
The letter to Rudolph II. in Archiv f. österr. Gesch., XV., 228.
Originals of the briefs to Mantua and Venice in the respective
archives.

[3] Bull., X., 548 seq.   Cf. Bull. indict. s. Iubilaei cum C. Schoppi
annotat.   Monachii, 1601.

[4] See BENTIVOGLIO, Memorie, 188.

[5] " Inventione molto buona et santa " says of this ordinance
the *Avviso of December 8, 1599, Urb. 1067, Vatican Library.
Cf. BAUMGARTEN, Neue Kunde, 22.

[6] See *Avvisi of November 20 and 25, December 4 and 15,
1599, Urb. 1067, Vatican Library.

[7] See *Avviso of December 18, 1599, ibid.

their greed for gain,[1] and that throughout the Holy
Year Rome should display the manifestation of the
greatest religious seriousness. The Carnival amusements
were prohibited, and distinguished preachers and good
confessors were sent to all the churches.[2] The Cardinals

[1] See ORBAAN, Documenti, 91 n. For the inns of that time see
ibid. 426 *seq*. For the punishment of certain inn-keepers in
May, 1600, for being greedy of gain see BAUMGARTEN, *loc. cit.* 23.

[2] See MANNI, Anni santi, 159. Besides this fundamental work,
which also treats in detail of the coins of the jubilee, *cf.* the *Liber
de anno iubilaei* 1600 dedicated to Clement VIII. by Cardinal A.
Valiero (often in manuscript, *e.g.* Vat. 3792 and 5479, Vatican
Library ; Cod. Sess. 236, Vittorio Emanuele Library, Rome),
printed at Verona, 1601 (a copy of this rare edition in the Vatican).
Besides other works cited by MANNI (173 *seq*.) it is to be noticed
that RUTIL. BENZONII de anno s. iubilaei libri VI. was printed at
Venice in 1599. In Manni there are lacking : 1. GIROL.GRATIANO
(Carmelite), Trattato del Giubileo dell'Anno Santo, trad. d. Spag.
in Ital. da JAC. BOSIO, Rome, 1599 ; 2. FR. FORNER, Von Ablass
und Jubeljahr, Ingolstadt, 1599 ; 3. " Tractatus de quibusdam
observationibus circa annum iubilaei a Io. PAULO MUCANTIO "
(dedicated to Cardinal Pietro Aldobrandini, 1599, Cal. Maii),
Barb. XX., 6, Vatican Library ; 4. *Diarium anni iubilaei 1600
JACOBO GRIMALDO Bonon. basil. Vatic. sacrista auctore, Barb.
lat. 2210, Vatican Library, and Cod. B, 111, Capitular Archives
of St. Peter's. For the treatise by Bellarmine " De indulgentiis
et iubilaeo " see COUDERC, I., 243 *seqq*. For C. Scioppius, who had
become a Catholic by studying the Annals of Baronius, and who
published on the occasion of the jubilee a " Commentarius de
indulgentiis " (edition of 1601 in British Museum, London) see
Forschungen z. deutschen Gesch., XI., 408 *seq*. ; RÄSS, Konvertiten,
III., 396 *seq*. As a souvenir for the pilgrims was intended the
" Deliciae Urbis Romae divinae et humanae anni sacri iubilaei 1600
Dom. Custode Aug. Vindel. 1600," 29 plates with an illustrated
frontispiece and a picture of Clement VIII. by Sadeler (Venice,
1600). Another portrait of Clement VIII. engraved at that time, and
adorned with medallions, representing the absolution of Henry IV.,
the reconciliation between Spain and France, the canonization of
St. Hyacinth, the entry into Ferrara, the marriage of Philip III.,
the reunion of the Ruthenians, etc. See P. PERALI, Prontuario

were ordered not to wear their purple during this time of penance.[1]

According to tradition the Holy Year should have begun on the vigil of Christmas, with the opening of the Holy Door at St. Peter's, but as Clement VIII. was ill with gout, this ceremony had perforce to be postponed until the last day of December. Even then the Pope had to do violence to himself to leave his bed of suffering, and perform the function, at which eighty thousand persons were present. On the following day, after the High Mass celebrated by Cardinal Sfondrato in St. Peter's, he gave the solemn benediction *urbi et orbi*.[2]

Although after this the Pope was still very often unwell,[3] Clement VIII. displayed the greatest zeal in gaining the jubilee indulgence. Thirty visits to the churches had been

bibliografico per la storia degli Anni Santi, published in the appendix to the *Cronistoria dell'Anno Santo* MCMXXV., Rome, 1928.

[1] See Alaleone in Thurston, 269.

[2] See the *report of G. C. Foresto, January 1, 1600, Gonzaga Archives, Mantua, and the *letters of G. Moceni̧o of January 1 and 8, 1600, State Archives, Venice. *Cf.* *Diarium P. Alaleonis, Barb. 2816, Vatican Library; *Avviso of January 1, 1600, Urb. 1068, *ibid.*; *Relazione intorno alle ceremonie, in Vat. 9314, p. 889 *seq.*, *ibid.* K. Löw, Gründl. Bericht, was bei Klemens VIII. mit Eröffnung und Zuthun der goldenen Porten sich verlaufen hat, Cologne, 1601; Lettres d'Ossat, II., 282, 298; report of the architect Heinrich Schickhardt, who accompanied the Protestant Duke Frederick of Würtemberg; during the ceremony Frederick was given a place near the Pope (see the new edition of the description of the journey of H. Schickhardt published from the first in 1602, by W. Heyd, Handschriften u. Handzeichn. des Baumeisters H. Sch., Stutgardt, 1902; Prinzivalli, Gli anni santi 1300-1925, Rome, 1925, 92 *seq.*). The medal reproduced in Manni, 151, represents two shepherds sounding a trumpet or horn before the throne of the Pope, evidently in reference to the " Jubilee " of the ancient Jews.

[3] See the *reports of G. C. Foresto, March 4 and 11, May 20 and December 29, 1600, and January 6, 1601, Gonzaga Archives, Mantua.

laid down for the Romans, and fifteen for strangers, but the Pope made sixty. He began on January 2nd, and declared that he intended every Sunday to visit the four great basilicas of St. Peter's, St. Paul's, St. John Lateran and St. Mary Major's. He also frequently made the visit to the Seven Churches. His deep piety edified everyone. It was exceedingly touching to see him ascend the Scala Santa, although his gout caused him great pain in his hands and feet.[1] He assisted in person[2] at the celebration of the Forty Hours in the church of the Gesù, during which Baronius preached. In spite of his sufferings he could not be restrained from repeatedly washing the feet of poor pilgrims, and waiting upon them at table, together with some of the Cardinals.[3] In Lent he was especially careful to provide good preachers,[4] and himself set a good example in this by having, in addition to the customary sermon by the Capuchin Anselmo da Monopoli, special discourses delivered in his private chapel. It gave him special pleasure to hear the word of God there from the lips of Cardinals Silvio Antoniano, Bellarmine and Baronius.[5]

[1] See BENTIVOGLIO, Memorie, 191, whose information is confirmed by the *Avvisi (Urb. 1068, Vatican Library) and the *Diarium P. Alaleonis (Barb. 2816, ibid.). For the beginning of the pilgrimages see Mucantius, *Diarium, Papal Secret Archives.

[2] See DE SANTI, Quarant'ore, 286 seq. Cf. Mon. hist. Soc. Iesu., Mon. Ignat., II. (1918), 473.

[3] See *Avvisi of February 12 and 26, and May 3, 1600, Urb. 1068, Vatican Library. Cf. BAUMGARTEN, Neue Kunde, 19.

[4] The *Avviso of February 16, 1600, mentions as the most celebrated preachers : the Spaniards P. Scalzo at St. Peter's, Acquapendente at S. Luigi, the Franciscan P. Rocca of Genoa at the Vallicella, P. Paolo da Cesena (Capuchin) at S. Lorenzo in Damaso, Mazarino at the Gesù, Tolosa at S. Andrea. In 1601 (*Avviso of March 7) the best preachers were supposed to be P. Scalzo, the Franciscan Castelfidardo and the Theatine Cieco. Urb. 1068, 1069, Vatican Library.

[5] See BENTIVOGLIO, Memorie, 194. The above mentioned Cardinals, as well as Piatti, also preached at the Gesù during the Forty Hours. See *Avviso of February 19, 1600, Urb. 1068, Vatican Library.

In Holy Week, to the general surprise, the Pope took his place
in the seat of the Grand Penitentiary in St. Peter's and
confessed for hours together all who came.[1] He was unwearied in helping poor pilgrims with abundant alms.[2] He
also ordered that the feasts of the Church, especially Easter,
Pentecost and that of the Princes of the Apostles, should be
celebrated with the greatest solemnity.[3]

As had happened before,[4] on this occasion as well the
Italian pilgrims came organized in confraternities, and made
their entry in solemn procession. Almost every week fresh
bodies arrived on pilgrimage to the holy places, the greatest
crowds coming during the months of May and June.[5] Up
to July 408 confraternities were counted.[6] The entry of

[1] See *Avviso of April 8, 1600, Urb. 1068, *ibid*.   This happened
on May 3, 1600 ; see *Diarium of J. Grimaldi, Barb. lat. 2210,
Vatican Library.

[2] See MANNI, 166.   *Cf.* *Avvisi of January 1 (the Pope enter-
tains many pilgrims in the Belvedere) and April 8, 1600 (the
Pope daily sends extraordinary alms to the Trinità), Urb. 1068,
Vatican Library.

[3] *Cf.* *Avvisi of May 25 (Easter Day ; the Pope suffering, but
forces himself to give the blessing), June 28 (feast of St. Peter
and St. Paul), and October 11, 1600 (great procession to the
Minerva), Urb. 1068, Vatican Library.

[4] *Cf.* Vol. XIX. of this work, p. 209.

[5] See the *Diarium of J. Grimaldi, according to which the
number of the pilgrims belonging to the confraternities during
these months was 12324 and 11695.   Ba.b. 2210, Vatican Library.

[6] *Cf.* BENTIVOGLIO, Memorie, 194 ; MORONI, II., 124 ; ORBAAN,
Rome, 85 *seqq.*   See also the *Avviso of May 10, 1600, for the
arrival of the Confraternity " dell'Aquila " and " della
Misericordia " from Foligno, and that of November 29 for the
Company of the Stigmata of St. Francis of Assisi, who all appeared
in the Franciscan habit with black crosses in their hands (Urb.
1068, Vatican Library).   The *Preces d. compagnia della morte
e della misericordia di Foligno fatte in Roma nel giubileo 1600,
in Cod. B. II. of the seminary Library, Foligno.   Interesting
notes concerning the payment of travelling expenses of foreign
communes in the commentary of Giac. Cohelli on the Bull. " Del

these companies, with their crosses and banners, and figurative representations of saints, made an imposing spectacle. An extraordinary impression was made on May 9th by the entry of the Confraternity della Misericordia from Foligno, which was met by the Confraternity of the Trinità. Evening had already fallen, and by the light of many torches there were to be seen, first, boys dressed as angels, with the instruments of the Passion, followed by a number of cars upon which were shown the whole of the Passion of the Redeemer.[1]

For the most part the Pope received the pilgrims in the cortile of the Belvedere.[2] The confraternities from his native city, Florence, were received with special honour, Clement himself giving communion to the members in St. Peter's, after which they were given a sumptuous repast in the Galleria Gregoriana.[3] Suitable honour was shown to the many important personages who had come for the jubilee. Among these the first place must be given to Cardinal Andrew of Austria,[4] to whom in his mortal illness the Pope himself administered the sacraments, making for him in the early hours of a cold November morning the pilgrimage to the

buon governo " (see *infra*, p. 367, n. 2) ; *cf.* P. PERALI, I pellegrinaggi giubilari nell'antico diritto pubblico, in *Corriere d'Italia*, October 1, 1924, reproduced in *Prontuario Bibliografico*, 1199.

[1] See CLEMENTI, 307.

[2] See *Avvisi of May 10 and November 29, 1600, Urb. 1068, Vatican Library. *Cf.* MANNI, 165.

[3] See the two *Avvisi of April 29, 1600, Urb. 1068, Vatican Library. *Cf.* MANNI, 161 *seq.* ; BAUMGARTEN, Neue Kunde, 17.

[4] See *Avviso of November 15, 1600, Urb. 1068, Vatican Library. *Cf.* Lettres d'Ossat, II., 244 ; *Freiburger Diözesan-Archiv*, XVIII., 441 *seq.* ; ORBAAN, Documenti, 91 n. ; SCHMIDLIN, Anima, 445 *seq.*, where there is a reproduction of the tomb ; *Bulletin de l'Institut Belge à Rome*, I. (1919), 299. Only the Cardinal's heart was buried in the Campo Santo de' Tedeschi, and not, as is often said, his body. Cardinal Andrew had never received major orders, and had not observed celibacy ; see HIRN, Maximilian, 262.

Seven Churches.[1] Cardinal Count Dietrichstein and the Duke of Bavaria presented themselves as simple pilgrims.[2] There also came the Duke of Lorraine,[3] many German prelates and nobles,[4] the viceroy of Naples, Lemos,[5] Archbishop Sourdis of Bordeaux, accompanied by the historian Spondanus,[6] two Hungarian bishops, and one from Mexico. The noble Venetian lady, Caterina Zeno, made the pilgrimage to Rome on foot.[7] Among scholars mention must be made of Claude de Peiresc, who on that occasion formed a friendship with Bosio.[8]

It was a great consolation to the Pope to see the coming of many priests, not only from Germany,[9] but even more from France.[10] The greater part of the pilgrims had been attracted by true devotion and sincere piety, but some only by curiosity. Great was the amazement of the Protestants who came to Rome, whose preachers had again described the solemnity as a mere financial speculation,[11] when they saw with their own eyes the Pope assiduously visiting the churches, and imitating, as the true servant of God, the humble actions of the Saviour, and washing and kissing the feet of the pilgrims ;

[1] See DE WAAL, Das hl. Jahr in Rom, Münster, 1900, 51.

[2] See *Avviso of January 15, 1600, Urb. 1068, Vatican Library.

[3] See *Avvisi of June 3 and July 15, 1600, ibid.

[4] See DE WAAL, loc. cit., 50 seq.

[5] See *Avviso of March 22, 1600, Urb. 1068, Vatican Library Cf. ORBAAN, Rome, 13 ; BAUMGARTEN, Neue Kunde, 17.

[6] See RÄSS, Konvertiten, III., 292.

[7] See MANNI, 159.

[8] See VALERI, Bosio, 34.

[9] Cf. BROWERUS, Annales Trevir., II., 136 ; EYZINGER, Relat. Hist., 1600, II., 49 ; STIEVE, V., 587.

[10] We have some information concerning the number of foreign priests in the *Diarium of J. Grimaldi, who gives exactly the number received in the pontifical Hospice ; there were 2545 from France and Brittany, 109 from Poland, 32 from Belgium, 83 from Germany, 2 from Spain, 2 from Portugal, 1 from England, 126 Greeks and Dalmatians, 3 Serbians, 2 from Muscovy, in all 2905.   Barb. lat. 2210, Vatican Library.

[11] Cf. STIEVE, V., 587.

how he furnished the needy with money, waited upon the sick, consoled everyone, and heard the confessions of penitents like a simple priest. Such a man could not be the Antichrist, as the preachers had described the supreme head of the Catholic Church. It is not surprising then that a number of Protestants, and even some Mahometans were converted to the Catholic faith.[1] Clement VIII. showed a special interest in the conversion of the son of a German preacher, at the end of 1600, who bore the same name as the founder of Calvinism. Justus Calvin came by his invitation to Rome, and received the sacrament of confirmation on September 1st, 1602, from the hands of the Pope, while Cardinal Baronius himself was his sponsor in confirmation ; the latter allowed Justus to take his name instead of that other of ill omen.[2]

As the Holy Year had begun on December 31st, 1599, its completeness demanded that its closure should take place on the same date in 1600. But a fresh attack of gout on the part of the Pope caused a further delay, and it was only on

[1] According to the *Avviso of June 17, 1600, two heretics made their abjuration on Sunday, who had first been confessed by the Pope. (Urb. 1068, Vatican Library). According to the *Avviso of August 5 (ibid.) the company of the SS. Trinità de' Pellegrini on that day brought 40 Protestants who had returned to the Church to the Pope, who entertained them. The number of 400 converts (MANNI, 169) must be an exaggeration, as according to the *Diarium of J. Grimaldi " 122 haeretici hospitati " at the expense of the Pope, which conversions were for the most part the work of the Jesuits ; " 73 erano Germani, 23 Galli, et Genevenses, 12 Angli, 9 Scoti, 1 Hibernus, 1 Transilvanus, 1 Hungarus, 1 Suevus, 1 Saxo " (Barb. 2210, Vatican Library). The Calvinist preacher, Arnulph Martin, gave the reasons for his conversion in a special work ; see RÄSS, III., 473 seq.

[2] Cf. BUSCHBELL, Zur Biographie des Iustus Calvinus (Baronius) Veterocastrensis in Hist. Jahrb., XXII., 298 seqq., which information I have been able to complete by the *brief of December 12, 1601 (Papal Secret Archives) printed in App. n. 22. A *brief to Philip III. of May 2, 1602, recommends to him the Genevese convert " Petrus Boverus." Arm. 44, t. 46, n, 131, Papal Secret Archives.

January 13th, 1601, that he was able to carry out the solemn function.[1]

According to the testimony of all contemporaries, the number of pilgrims who went to Rome during the Holy Year was very large, especially at Easter.[2] The charitable institutions with which Rome was filled, for it possessed more than the whole of England, stood the test.[3] As before, the hospice of the Trinità de' Pellegrini, founded by Philip Neri,[4] was

[1] Cf. *Avvisi of January 3 and 18, 1601, Urb. 1069, Vatican Library. For the extension of the jubilee to foreign countries see MANNI, 172 seq., and NÖTHEN, Jubeljahre, 126.

[2] See BENTIVOGLIO, Memorie, 128. Cf. *Avvisi of 1600 : March 22 (so many pilgrims that the Trinità de' Pellegrini is not sufficient), April 1 (the Trinita provided for more than 6000 pilgrims), April 19, 22, 29 (" è miraculoso il concorso de' forastieri in Roma tutto il giorno "), May 13 (the number of pilgrims present here to-day is estimated at about 50,000), May 25 (15,000 pilgrims have gone, but there are still many here), May 31 (yesterday at the Trinità about 2,500 women ; arrival of 13 companies ; very many foreigners), June 7 (the crowds continue ; every evening at the Trinità more than 13,000 persons ; so far the confraternity has expended 30,000 scudi), September 16 (the arrival of companies of pilgrims is beginning anew), September 27 (2,500 persons at the Trinità), November 11 (very many pilgrims), December 12 (satisfaction of the Pope at the great number and the piety of the pilgrims), December 27 (the number of foreigners is extraordinary). Urb. 1068, Vatican Library. See also the *brief of May 12, 1600, to the " Vicerex Siciliae " (request for more grain on account of the number of the pilgrims) and the *brief of August 2 to Philip III. (" ingens peregrinorum multitudo"; request for corn) Arm. 44, t. 44, n. 137, 221, Papal Secret Archives. At St. Peter's alone 41,239 masses were celebrated during the Holy Year, and 318,900 communions given (*Diarium of J. Grimaldi, see supra, p. 271, n, 2. For the German pilgrims see LANG, Bruderschaftsbuch der Anima (1900), 144 ; SCHMIDLIN, 445 seq. ; DE WAAL, loc. cit.

[3] See THURSTON, 290.

[4] Cf. the *Avvisi of April 1, May 31, and September 27, 1600, Urb. 1068, Vatican Library.

pre-eminent ; the Pope, the Cardinals, the aristocracy, and above all Flaminia Aldobrandini, gave such abundant alms[1] that this institution, which hired many houses, had been able to give hospitality to 8,000 pilgrims by the end of January 1600. According to careful estimates the hospice gave lodging and food to half a million pilgrims. As many more found a welcome in the other hospices, while there were others who were received in the many convents and private houses.[2] Thus the estimate of 1,200,000 pilgrims in all is not excessive.[3] In this way the Church and her head could hail the dawn of the XVIIth century with high hopes. The past century which, by reason of the great apostacies in the

[1] In the Diario of Presutti cited in the following note, the alms are given exactly.

[2] See the work by AG. VALIERO, De iubilaei (*supra*, p. 271, n. 2) ; MANNI, 157 ; PRESUTTI, Diario e memoria delle cose avvenute et governo dell'archiconfraternita dei Pellegrini della Sant[ma] Trinità a Ponte Sisto l'anno del Giubileo 1600, published from Cod. ottob. 737 in the periodical *Cosmos cath.*, Rome, 1900. The charitable work of the confraternities was all the more necessary, in that in Rome the inns were insufficient ; in 1587 there were only 687 and only 350 " camere locande," see *Arch. Rom.*, VII., 523 n. 2.

[3] See THEOD. A SPIRITU SANCTO (Ord. Carm.), Tractatus de iubilaeo, Rome, 1701, 61, and STROCHI, Anni Santi, Faenza, 1824. The statement in KRAUS, Kirchengesch., Treves, 1896, 576, that there were three million pilgrims, is an exaggeration. But it is quite wrong when in Herzogs Realenzyklop. it is stated that the crowds at the jubilee were only moderate. Also the statement of BROSCH (I., 322) that the number of pilgrims was only moderate, is more niggardly than the former, and quite false. In the Diario of Presutti (previous note) such exact figures are given that there is no possibility of doubting them. It is there established by figures how much larger the number of pilgrims was in 1600 than it had been in 1575. The *Diarium of J. Grimaldi (supra*, p. 271, n. 2) shows that whereas in 1575 the number of confraternities from without was about 400, this had increased in 1600 to more than 600.

north and centre of Europe had perhaps been one of the most disastrous in the long history of the Church, had also been one of the most consoling, because during its second half there had come the great change brought about by Catholic reform and restoration.

CHAPTER IX.

THE CONTROVERSY ON GRACE.

THE dispute concerning the doctrine of grace, which had arisen between the Dominican Order and the Society of Jesus, and had become steadily embittered, led in the time of Clement VIII. to very serious strife. After the celebrated book concerning freedom and grace by the Jesuit Luis Molina (died 1600) had stated the point at issue in the most exact possible form, it seemed to have become necessary to transfer the discussion to Rome, under the eye of the Pope himself, in order to arrive at an agreement. Nevertheless, the discussions lasting through many years, and conducted by the most learned doctors in the presence of the Pope himself, were unable to attain the desired end or any immediate result ; the keen expectation with which Catholics and Protestants throughout Europe, and later on the princes and diplomatists awaited the issue, had to remain satisfied with seeing both opinions tolerated by the Church for the time being.[1]

[1] The manuscript material for the history of the controversy is superabundant, but consists for the most part of letters and reports which relate mere hearsay, or bear the evident impress of passion and uncertainty. The library which is richest in valuable documents on the controversy is the Angelica Library, Rome (H. NARDUCCI, Catalogus codd. mss. praeter graecos et orientales in bibl. Angelica, Rome, 1893 ; cf. SOMMERVOGEL, Bibliothèque, V., 1170 seq.). The so-called Acta of the Congregations de auxiliis, which bear the name of Peña or of Thomas de Lemos, were declared unworthy of credence by a decree of the Inquisition of April 23, 1654 (published in ASTRÁIN, IV., x-xii) when the Jansenists sought to make use of them (cf. Analecta iuris pontif., I., 1226). A description of the controversy from the Jansenist

Delight in a learned scholastic dispute was not the only reason why the Jesuits turned all their skill and energy to so thorny and obscure a problem. Grace and free will, pre-destination and eternal punishment, had become burning questions during the period of the Protestant schism. According to Calvin, God has predestined everyone *a priori*, even before foreseeing his good or evil works, either to eternal happiness or eternal flames. The views of Luther as to this matter were almost the same, since, as man in his opinion was not possessed of free will, it followed that not even his eternal destiny could depend upon his own will. Accordingly this, whether it were happy or unhappy, was allotted to him purely by divine predestination, without his being able to change it in the slightest degree.

To-day it will perhaps seem strange that any such doctrine can have met with so much support in the XVIth century. By way of explanation it may be remarked that the numerous priests and monks who became preachers and teachers of the people among the innovators, found some comfort in being able to attribute their own fault to an inevitable destiny. Moreover the immutable divine predestination was made use of, as a proof of the fundamental principles of the innovators concerning the denial of free will, and the uselessness of good works. But whatever may have been the reason, the fact

point of view was first given by the Dominican GIACOMO GIACINTO SERRY, under the pseudonym Augustin Le Blanc, Historiae Congregationum de auxiliis divinae gratiae sub summis Pontifi-cibus Clemente VIII. et Paulo V., libri quattuor, Mayence, 1699, and later from the reply of LIVINUS DE MEYERE under his real name (Antwerp, 1709). The documents from the Angelica Library printed there are of value. De Meyere also first wrote under a pseudonym : Historiae controversiae de divinae gratiae auxiliis sub summis Pontificibus Sixto V, Clemente VIII. et Paulo V., libri sex, auctore Theodoro Eleutherio. A second edition, Venice, 1742, is a fresh defence against Serry (Historiae controversiae . . . ab obiectionibus R. P. Hyacinthi Serry vindicatae, libri tres, Brussels, 1715) under his real name. *Cf.* ASTRÁIN, IV., x-xvi ; SCHNEEMANN, 339 *seqq.*

remains that under the influence of the Protestant preachers this terrible doctrine penetrated among every class of the people. " Who can resist the will of God ? " was to be heard from the lips of quite ordinary folk. " If He wishes to save us for all eternity, then we shall be saved, but if He does not so wish, then we shall be lost. God knows our destiny from all eternity ; from all eternity it has been irrevocably decreed. Why then should we take trouble and wear ourselves out, why should we do good works ? "[1] Naturally the moral consequences of such opinions could not fail to be deplorable.

In the Book of the Exercises, Ignatius of Loyola points out that certain people were arriving at the above conclusion from the doctrine of predestination, and were for that reason neglecting good works. Nevertheless he urges caution in speaking of such matters ; he says that ordinarily, pre-destination should not be dealt with, but that if, as an exception, this should be done, care must be taken to ensure that the common folk do not arrive at erroneous conclusions. In like manner the power of divine grace must not be exaggerated in such a way as to impair human freedom.[2] The disciples of Loyola had followed this warning of their master, and from the first, and long before Molina, had treated the mysteries of predestination and grace in such a way as not to infringe in the least degree on the freedom of man ; they had from the first been opposed to those learned

[1] FRANC. ROMAEUS (General of the Dominicans), De libertate operum a necessitate, Lyons, 1638, 142, in SCHNEEMANN, 173 *seq.*

[2] No debemos hablar mucho de la predestinacion por via de costumbre, mas si en alguna manera y algunas vezes se hablare, asi se hable, que le pueblo menudo no venga en eror alguno, *como algunas vezes suele,* diciendo, si tengo de ser salvo o condemnado, ya está determinado, y por my bien hazer o mal no puede ser ya otra cosa, y con esto entorpeciendo se descuydan en las obras que conducen a la salud y provecho spiritual de sus animas. . . . Assimismo no debemos hablar tan largo instando tanto en la graçia que se engendre veneno para quitar la libertad etc. Ejercicios espirituales de S. Ignacio de Loyola. Reproducción fototípica del original, Rome, 1908, 63 *seq.*

systems in which human freedom seemed to them to be threatened.[1] This explains how it was that, when the book and doctrine of Molina was in question, the whole Society of Jesus rallied to his side.

Before Molina had come forward as a writer, he had long taken counsel with himself and others as to the subject to which he could best devote the fruits of his scientific studies for the greater advantage of the Church. In the end he resolved upon an exhaustive treatise as to the best way to reconcile grace and liberty.[2] The main thesis and the end of his book is therefore an examination of that conclusion which was at that time so often propounded : if the divine decree which assigns to me heaven or hell is fixed and sealed from all eternity, then my free will has no influence upon my destiny. He aimed at scientifically examining this sophism which denied free will, and at refuting it.

The solution of this difficulty which Molina puts forward is fundamentally very simple. All men whom He has created or will create, or could create are present in the mind of God from all eternity. He also foresees the countless situations and different circumstances in which it is possible for each of these to find himself ; he also foresees how each one will act in each of these circumstances, especially under the interior influence of grace. He foresaw, for example, that the Apostle Peter would deny the Saviour when the servant maid accosted him in the courtyard of the high priest, and that he would rise again after his fall, when, together with the interior action of grace, the look of Christ met his own. If then God wished to permit the fall of the Apostle or bring about his conversion, it would be sufficient that he should allow Peter to go to the courtyard of the high priest and that the servant maid should attack him with her provocative words ; it would be sufficient that he should allow the grave and gentle look of Christ to meet that of the Apostle ; if he falls the fault is his own, since according to the will of God he could

---

[1] SCORRAILLE, I., 357 *seqq.* ; SCHNEEMANN, 161 *seqq.*
[2] SCORRAILLE, I., 425 n.

and should have resisted the temptation ; if he rises again
after his fall, the merit is his ; neither the look of the God-Man,
nor the interior action of grace have destroyed the freedom
of his conversion.

According to Molina then, so-called efficacious grace is, it is
true, infallibly united to the consent of the will, for otherwise
it would no longer be efficacious grace, but this infallible
efficacy comes from the foreknowledge of God, so that the will
really co-operates with this determinate grace in these
determinate circumstances, even though *in se* and *per se* it
could resist it.[1]   " God has compassion," says St. Augustine,
" upon him who is called by Him in the manner which He
knows will be suitable to him, so long as he does not reject
His invitation."[2]

Molina's bitter adversary, Domenico Bañes (died 1604)
held quite a different view of the question.[3]   Whereas the

[1] This knowledge which God has of the free acts which a creature
would do, if it finds itself in certain circumstances, was called
" scientia media," because it stands half way between the
knowledge which God has of the purely possible and of the actual.

[2] " Sic eum vocat quomodo scit ei *congruere*, ut vocantem non
respuat " (Ad Simplicianum, 1. 1, q. 2, in MIGNE, Patr. lat., XL.,
119).   From this passage is derived the name of " congruism "
in the Jesuit system.   As to this *cf.* H. QUILLIET in Dict. de
théologie cath., III., Paris, 1908, 1120-1138 ; concerning the
doctrine of St. Augustine E. PORTALIÉ, *ibid.* I. (1903), 2386-2392 ;
HERGENRÖTHER-KIRSCH, Handbuch der allg. Kirchengesch., 1.[4],
Freiburg, 1902, 549.

[3] The original principles of the system of Bañes were already
to be found in Francisco de Vittoria and Peter Soto (*cf.* FRINS,
470 *seqq.*) but they were not fully developed before Bañes, so that
he passes for the real founder.   " As the principle representative,
and also probably as the champion of the Thomist system, we
must name Dom. Bañes." (ATZBERGER in SCHEEBEN, Handbuch der kath. Dogmatik, IV., 1, Freiburg, 1898, 221 ; *cf.*
GUTBERLET-HEINRICH, Dogmatische Theologie, VIII., Mayence,
1897, 446).   While Bañes was still living not all the Dominicans
were followers of his doctrine on grace (SCORRAILLE, I., 359 *seqq.* ;
FRINS, 344 *seqq.*).   For the earlier theologians from the time of

Jesuit theologian started with the free will of man, the Dominican fixed his attention before all else upon the power and operation of God, which embraces everything and penetrates everything, and without which the creature is absolutely helpless. And since the existence of the creature is inconceivable without the creative and conservative power of God, the same thing, according to Catholic doctrine, applies to the acts of the creature ; God must co-operate in every human act, and these must also receive from Him their origin and their impetus ; for every act of the creature springs from the desire for something which contains a certain good for him who aspires to it. But this tendency of the will towards its own good is implanted in it by God, and all man's actions have their origin in it ; the Creator makes use of it in order to spur men on to act. Thus even the free acts of men have their origin in God, and it is God who causes the free will to embrace the object of its desires.

So far there are no differences of opinion between the Catholic schools, but in what follows they diverge. According to some, such as Molina, this divine impulse may be affected by the free action of the will, in so far as that, in contrast to the original will of God, it may receive a tendency towards illusory good. But this kind of auto-dominion on the part of the creature was emphatically attacked by Bañes. In his view, the majesty of God, his unlimited sovereignty over all created things, and the idea of divine omnipotence, demanded that every manifestation of the human will, both in its essence and its extension, down to the smallest detail, must be completely dependent upon the influx and predisposition of God. Free will makes its own decision, but is always and exclusively determined to that decision to which the influx of God has predestined and predisposed it, and it is infallibly certain from the first that it will not decide in favour of any other. But the influx of God into the will is not manifested by inspirations, warnings or attractions, that is to say by

Anselm of Canterbury *cf.* LUD. DE SAN, Tractatus de Deo Uno, I., Louvain, 1894, 426 *seqq.*, 527 *seqq.*

moral means, but by direct influx, which consists, as it is
called in controversial terminology in the schools, by " physical
predetermination." Despite all this, according to Bañes,
free will remains, because in all things God works in conformity with the nature of things ; necessary causes he makes
to operate of necessity, free causes he makes to operate with
freedom ; thus even freedom of action is produced by Him.

What has been said holds good in the case of the purely
natural actions of man, and also holds good in the case of
those acts which call for a supernatural influence, that is to
say the grace of God. According to Bañes, efficacious grace
in the supernatural order corresponds to the physical predetermination and predisposition in the supernatural order.
Lacking this efficacious grace, the will cannot bring itself to
act ; but where it is present, then it infallibly produces
precisely that determination of the will, which is pre-ordained.
In the case of inefficacious graces, Bañes naturally adheres
to the term already in use among theologians, of " sufficient "
grace, but these " sufficient " graces only give the will the
power to act, which, however, can never be transformed
into act.[1]

As we can see, the scholastic dispute here touches
upon the most profound depths of the inmost life of
the soul : the mysterious mingling of divine and human
action in the heart of man, the infinite variety of the
devices which the divine love employs for the conquest of
the soul of man, the thrice incomprehensible decrees of
election and reprobation, the depths of which a Paul[2] thought
that he could not better honour than by a reverent silence.

[1] More fully in J. POHLE, Lehrbuch der Dogmatik, II[4].,
Paderborn, 1909, 458 *seqq.*, 474 *seqq.* ; HEINRICH-GUTBERLET,
Dogmatische Theologie, VIII., Mayence, 1897, 446 *seqq.* ;
MORGOTT in *Freib. Kirchenlexikon,*[2] I., 1952 *seqq.* ; VIII., 1737
seqq. The historian cannot escape a more detailed explanation
of the controverted matter, and even Ranke found himself
obliged to attempt it (Päpste, II.[8], 194). This is not the place to
dwell upon the many errors of Ranke.

[2] Epist. ad Rom., II., 33.

The necessary presupposition and foundation for understanding and appreciating the dispute is that doctrine of Christianity which, intimately united to the dogmas of the Most Holy Trinity and the Incarnation, offers the strongest possible contrast to every kind of rationalism and superficial naturalism, namely the doctrine of the natural and the supernatural.

According to the Catholic doctrine man is destined to a supernatural end, that is to an end to which he would have no right by his nature, and to which he is incapable of attaining, or even of imagining by his natural powers alone. This means that he is to be admitted in eternity to the direct contemplation of God, a thing to which *per se* none would have a right but the only-begotten Son of God, who by His Incarnation became the brother of man, raised him to the sonship of God, and made him his co-heir. To this sublime end there corresponds on earth a mysterious raising of the justified man in the order of grace. He is no longer only the servant of God, but by means of justifying grace he becomes His son ; his soul is ennobled, as a wild tree by a noble grafting, his spiritual nature is as it were transfigured by sanctifying grace, his intellect by the infused virtue of faith, his will by the infused virtue of charity. Eternal glory therefore is not cast to the thus ennobled soul as a pure alms, but it is enabled on the contrary to gain it for itself. But since the natural powers of man are not sufficient for this purpose, God comes to his assistance with that kind of grace, concerning which the dispute between the Jesuits and the Dominicans arose : prevenient and co-operating grace, which consists in the illumination of the intelligent and the incitement of the will. This assistance of grace is an absolutely gratuitous gift of God, and all that man can do by means of his natural powers is insufficient to merit it ; but once furnished with it he is in a position, not only to merit an increase of justifying grace, but also the crown of eternal glory.

These remarks show that the efficacy of this assistance of grace offers further enigmas to the keen intellect. The manifestations of the will which are developed under its influence cannot of their nature be operated by any but God, for otherwise they would no longer be supernatural. But at the same time, according to the whole of their interior essence they must come from the free will, since the question at issue is precisely the activity of freedom. The operation of God and that of man must therefore be united, just as in red-hot iron the metal is united with the fire. but the manner in which this takes place still remains obscure. To this is added the difficulty of reconciling the rights of freedom with the supreme authority of God, which shines forth yet more in the supernatural order than in the merely natural order. God cannot be deprived of his supreme sovereignty over his creature, yet if He creates free beings, it seems that he is renouncing a part of his rights over His creature. A third and a vast difficulty is presented by the mystery of the choice of grace. As grace cannot be merited, the beginning of the supernatural life as well as the distribution of graces to individual men can only come from God. Now God in distributing His graces sincerely wills that all men should co-operate with them, and thus attain to eternal glory. But in the case of many he foresees that they will not actually attain to this by means of the graces given to them, although they could do so. Why then does He not give them other graces ? In every case it is for reasons dictated by His wisdom ; and who can say or imagine what those reasons may be ? When it was a case of the scientific discussion of the true issue of the dispute, yet another difficulty had to be taken into consideration : the taking into account of the opinions of the Fathers of the Church and of the scholastics. This was above all the case with St. Augustine, the master of grace, and St. Thomas Aquinas. Thus both one and the other were claimed as their own by the representatives of the two opinions.

It is no matter for surprise then that differences of opinion should have arisen even among Catholic theologians over a question of such difficulty, and that neither view was able to throw light upon all its obscurities. In the view of Molina it remained an impenetrable mystery how God could foresee

the free acts of the will which were never to be realized ;
for this knowledge no satisfactory explanation is to be found.
It would not seem at first sight that the school of Bañes felt
any difficulty on this point ; according to this God had *ab
aeterno* predestined the free decisions of his creatures, and
therefore knows them just as He knows His own will.   But
at once the question arises : to what purpose should God
make milliards of decrees of predestination concerning milliards
of possible acts ?   Such decrees do not seem to have been
invented for any other purpose than to give the theologian
a way of explaining the prescience of God on the strength of
them.   Other difficulties as well result from the theories
of the Dominican theologian.   He was naturally bound to
hold firmly that man possesses free will, and that God is
not the author of sin ; he must admit with the Council of
Trent that it is also possible to reject grace if one wills.   But
the explanations of this point given by the followers of Bañes
seem to other theologians to be forced and artificial.[1]   It
was brought against them that they were teaching a sufficient
grace which was not enough for anything in practice, a liberty
which was tied hand and foot, a power to resist grace which
could never amount to a real resistance, and therefore did
not deserve the name of power.   To this was added that,
according to the point of view of the Dominicans, it is difficult
to explain how God does not become the author of sin.

From these brief remarks it will in any case be understood
that the historian cannot pass over the dispute which arose,
by describing it as a mere monks' quarrel.   The question
concerns one of the most sublime and profound doctrines
of Christianity, a question to which a man of intelligence
and heart might very well devote all his powers.

The dispute between the two schools had already made
itself felt in the discussions between Lessius and the theo-

---

[1] According to some of the followers of Bañes the infallible
efficacy of grace together with liberty is " a mystery as impenetrable by human knowledge " as that of the Most Holy Trinity.
Morgott in *Freib. Kirchenlexikon*, I.², 1957.

logical faculty of Louvain. A greater uproar first arose on the occasion of a disputation at Salamanca, on January 20th, 1582, at which the Jesuit Prudencio di Montemayor had to defend a series of propositions, in the course of which he was attacked by Bañes.[1] These propositions contained nothing that could have provoked the Dominicans. This is clear from the fact that a friend and disciple of Bañes, the Trinitarian Francisco Zumel, had accepted the presidency at this ecclesiastical tourney. But while the difficult question of the liberty of Christ was under discussion,[2] the matter passed at length from objection to objection, and from reply to reply on the burning question of the doctrine of grace, and went so far that Bañes and the Dominican Guzman described the replies of the Jesuit as heretical. There then intervened in the discussion the celebrated theologian and poet Luis de León of the Order of St. Augustine. Under the impression that such strong expressions were only being employed out of hatred for the Jesuits, he chivalrously took up their defence. Montemayor retired into the background and all eyes were turned on the celebrated Augustinian. Even after the closure of the theological disputation the discussion was carried on with vehemence. Names such as " Pelagian " for Luis de León, and " Lutheran " for the Dominicans, filled the air, and when several days later it was rumoured that the discussion was to be resumed in a further disputation, the hall was crowded with the curious. Once more Bañes and Luis de León battled vehemently with each other. This time the Jesuits were silent, but in justification of their theory they arranged for January 27th a disputation at their own college, at which the question was discussed why, of two men who find themselves under the influence of the same grace, one may be converted and the other remain impenitent.

[1] ASTRÁIN, 129-146. (When in future we cite Astráin without giving the volume, we are always referring to Vol. IV.). The second trial of Luis de León in Ciudad de Dios, XLI. (1896), 32 *seqq.*, 102 *seqq.*, 182 *seqq.*, 273 *seqq.*

[2] See POHLE, Lerbuch der Dogmatik, II.[4], 109, for the matter at issue.

The Hieronymite Juan de Santa Cruz then laid before the Inquisition[1] sixteen propositions as having been defended by Luis de León and Montemayor, and the licenciate Juan de Arrese at once appeared at Salamanca to open the process against four principal offenders. The Dominicans had in meantime collected signatures against the accused, and issued a warning that no one must declare himself on the side of the Jesuits as the cause was pending before the Holy Office. In spite of this, at Valladolid all the doctors of repute, with the exception of the Dominicans, took the side of the Jesuits ; in Andalusia even some members of the Order of Preachers pronounced in their favour, so that it is evident from this as well as from other attestations, that at that time, at the beginning of the dispute, not all the colleagues of Bañes shared his views concerning the doctrine of grace.[2]

Arrese, who was to conduct the process, at once found himself in an impasse. The accuser, Juan de Santa Cruz, had not been present at the first disputation, and it was quite clear from the statements of Luis de León that his theses had been very incorrectly formulated. The opinions of the Spanish universities, to which Arrese had appealed, were not in agreement. At Alcalà it was held that both views, that of the Jesuits, as well as that of Bañes, were probable ; one of Bañes' was, however, found fault with, but this had no bearing upon the doctrine of grace.[3] It would seem that the doctors of Salamanca were of the opposite opinion.[4] Then the Jesuits asked, in the name of justice, that their reasons should be heard before a judgment was formed ; they had gone into this question much more thoroughly than the others, and their view was safe, or at least worthy

---

[1] Reprinted from Ciudad de Dios, XXXVI. in ASTRÁIN, 133 *seq.*, and MANDONNET, O.P. in Dict. de théologie cath., II., 143.

[2] ASTRÁIN, 133.

[3] *Ibid.* 143.

[4] Arrese at anyrate wrote on April 24, 1582 : " Les calificaciones de Alcalá son muy diferentes de lo que en esta Universidad (Salamanca) se tratta " (Astráin, 143). Further particulars are not known.

of preference.[1] Luis de León even spread the report that the propositions of the Jesuits would shortly be declared safe in Rome.[2]

Almost two years elapsed before a judgment was pronounced. At last, on February 3rd, 1584, Luis de León, the principal culprit, was cited to appear before the Grand Inquisitor, Cardinal Quiroga, and was reprimanded for his faults, which had been confirmed in the light of the acta. He was warned to refrain from maintaining, either in public or in any other way, the propositions which, it would appear, he had defended. Montemayor too received an admonition from the Grand Inquisitor and from his Provincial ; he was no longer to be employed in lecturing. Montemayor complained to his General, and among other things pointed out that he had only defended what he had been taught by his professors, among whom he named Suarez and Toledo.[3] Some years later, with the consent of Quiroga, Montemayor was again teaching theology at Toledo.[4]

The questions raised at Salamanca were only a prelude to the great struggle that was soon to follow. It was shown that the burning question of the efficacy of grace had for a long time past been eagerly discussed among the Jesuits, and that on the whole the question had been harmoniously settled, but that there still remained certain obscure matters

[1] " Porque ellos han estudiado ests materia de proposito con más cuidado que otros y darán a entender que es lo cierto, e lo menos lo que conviene lo que ellos dicen." ARRESE, loc. cit., 193 seq.

[2] Ibid. 144.

[3] Lo tercero, y lo que principalmente hace en mi descargo, es que la doctrina que yo defendí no fué inventada de mi cabeza, sino leída, dictada y enseñada por mis maestros. . . . Así la leyó el P. Miguel Marcos, más largamente el P. Francisco Suárez y el P. Bartolomé Pérez [de Nueros] que son los maestros que yo he tenido en mis estudios. El P. Toledo también la leyó en su primera parte. To Aquaviva, Medina del Campo, July 27, 1585, in ASTRÁIN, 145.

[4] Ibid. 146.

of detail, which showed that a thorough scientific examination of the difficult question was indispensable. The ground was therefore prepared for that work which for ten years held the whole of Europe in a state of suspense, the work of Molina upon the relations between grace and liberty. This was published at Lisbon at the end of 1588.[1] As far as its outward appearance was concerned it was one of the least imposing of that author's works, yet that modest quarto volume has a history such as few books in the world can boast. A few years before Bañes too had set forth his views on the same subject, not in a work specially devoted to grace, but in various parts of his commentaries on the *Summa* of St. Thomas.[2]

Three Jesuits had been charged by their Portuguese province to examine the work of Molina, among them Jorge Serrano, who was held in high esteem by the Inquisition. Molina wished that, on the strength of the favourable opinion of Serrano, a *nihil obstat* might be asked for the publication without any further censorship, because he was afraid of the Dominicans, upon whose judgement depended the permission to print the book. The other Jesuits, on the other hand, thought that the usual course should be followed, and that not the least distrust of the Dominicans ought to be shown. Molina had hardly handed over his manuscript to the censor, Bartolomeo Ferreira, when there began disputes about his book, which seemed destined to be the apple of discord between the parties.[3] Ferreira was bombarded with accusations against Molina ; it was naturally supposed that the Jesuit propositions which had been found fault with at Salamanca would be found in the book ; the confessor of the Grand Inquisitor, the Dominican De las Cuevas, brought

[1] Concordia liberi arbitrii cum gratiae donis, divina praescientia, providentia, praedestinatione et reprobatione (4°, 512 pp.).

[2] Scholastica commentaria in primam partem Angelici D. Thomae usque ad sexagesimam quartam quaestionem complectentia, Salamanca, 1584.

[3] ASTRÁIN, 147-175.

forward the judgment in which those propositions had been
found fault with, while other Dominicans thought that the
honour of St. Dominic demanded a refusal of the permission
to print. Ferreira, who was not opposed to the Jesuits,
informed Molina of these accusations. The latter was not
the man to stand and watch these attacks with folded hands,
and he pointed out that Ferreira had not been appointed
censor of the Inquisition in order to protect the interests of
the Dominican Order ; he had in no case taught the propositions found fault with at Salamanca, and Ferreira could
satisfy himself as to this. If there were anything in his book
which called for blame, in that case he himself would ask for
its prohibition.[1]

The unexpected end of all this was that Ferreira was
persuaded, and gave the book that was the subject of so many
attacks a glowing *imprimatur*. In this he states that the work
contained nothing that was not in accordance with our religion,
and that many passages taken from the Councils and the
Holy Scriptures were explained and elucidated therein very
happily. He therefore considered the work worthy of
publication, and of advantage to the whole Church. In
accordance with this, in the middle of July the printing was
begun, and on January 6th, 1589, Molina went to the
governor, Cardinal Albert, in order to present him with the
first copy.

While the book was being printed its adversaries did not
remain with folded hands, and Molina was soon made to
realize that their efforts had not been ineffectual. Cardinal
Albert received the first copy coldly and forbade the sale of
the edition until further orders. Molina then asked for a strict
examination of his work, adding the request that the objections
should be made only in writing, and signed with the name of
the critic. He pointed out that a favourable judgment had
been passed upon his book by three of his brethren in religion
and by Ferreira, that he had sent it to the royal council, both

---

[1] On the strength of some letters from Molina to Aquaviva,
January 28, 1589, in ASTRÁIN, 152 *seq*.

of Castille and Aragon, so that it might be examined there,
and that the objections only sprang from the jealousy of the
Dominicans.[1]   At a second audience Molina was able to point
out that not only Ferreira, but some of the latter's colleagues
as well, who had formerly been his adversaries, had described
the work as a good book, after Ferreira had enabled them to
read it, comparing the printed edition with the manuscript.[2]
This proved what Molina had confidently said to Ferreira,
namely, that if only his book were read, there would no longer
be any question of suppressing it.[3]   Naturally not all the
Dominicans passed a favourable judgment on Molina's
volume, and some thought that they could detect in the book
the theses which had been found fault with at Salamanca.
The pressure they brought to bear upon De las Cuevas, the
spiritual director of the governor, led to Cardinal Albert's
causing Molina's book to be once more examined by the
Dominican Cano.   Cano thought that he discovered in it the
very theses which had been found fault with in Castille, and
thus it came about that Molina's work, which had already
been so often examined, could not be sold for three months.[4]

But in the meantime Molina, about the end of February
1589, had been informed of the state of the affair ; he therefore
hastened to come to the rescue of his child of sorrow, by an
apologetic work.   He confessed that he was indeed the author
of some of the disputed theses, but that there was no reason
at all to suspect them of being erroneous or heretical.   In
the majority of cases, however, he proved that opinions were
being attributed to him which he would never have dreamed
of defending.[5]   In the meantime in Spain Molina's book had
been judged by the royal council of Castille, as well as by

[1] Molina, *loc. cit.* in Astráin, 154 *seq.*

[2] " Ellos la vieron y respondieron que estaba muy buena y que
habia declarado mucho." Molina, *loc. cit.* 156.

[3] Astráin, 154.

[4] De las Cuevas to Quiroga, in Norbert del Prado, O.P.,
De gratia et libero arbitrio, III., Freiburg, i. Ü., 1907, 579 ;
Astráin, 157 *seq.*

[5] Astráin, 158.

that of Aragon, in a manner highly honourable to the author, nor were any of his theses called in question there.[1] The Archduke Albert then gave permission for the sale of the book.

So far, then, the attacks on Molina had had no other result than that his book had appeared under the protection of the Portuguese Inquisition, and with the arms and protection of the royal council of Castille and Aragon. Later on to these was added the approbation of the Castilian Inquisition.[2] Molina might be said to have been recompensed for his past troubles by the applause which he gained in far wider circles. Even during his life-time his book ran into new editions at Cuenca, Venice, Lyons and Antwerp.[3] The professor of theology at Valladolid, Garcia Coronel, said that though it was true that the fundamental idea of the book contained nothing new, and was to be found, in his opinion, clearly stated in Augustine and Thomas Aquinas, Molina was nevertheless the first who had treated of the matter in detail, by solving the difficulties and building up the proofs ; theologians who had to fight against the heretics were grateful for the weapon which he placed in their hands.[4] Leonhard Lessius, who was in conflict with the doctrines of Baius at Louvain, pronounced enthusiastically in favour of Molina,[5] who defended the same opinion as to efficacious grace as himself. The opinion of Lessius is also of importance for the reason that

[1] *Ibid.* 156.

[2] See *infra*, p. 300.

[3] SOMMERVOGEL, IX., 683. The Antwerp edition of 1595, apart from some minor unessential differences, is distinguished by the addition of an appendix in which Molina defends himself against misunderstandings and attacks. In the editions of Cuenca, Venice and Lyons some paragraphs are replaced by new ones in which Molina again uses the arguments which he had previously employed (SOMMERVOGEL, I.re partie, V., 1169). Between 1602 and 1876 five further editions appeared.

[4] Letter of October 17, 1600, in ASTRÁIN, 225.

[5] Letter to Bellarmine, in LE BACHELET, Bellarmin avant son cardinalat, 272.

Francis of Sales, who was later on declared a doctor of the Church, declared that he shared his views on the doctrine of predestination.[1]

New ideas, however, even though they are only such from this or that point of view, are hardly ever introduced in science without serious disputes, and certainly Molina's book offered many points of attack. His opinions excited opposition both from Bellarmine[2] and from many Jesuits in Spain.[3] These differences of opinion, however, do not in any way concern the question as to how efficacious grace may be reconciled with human freedom. Besides the principal object of his book, Molina also treats of many other matters, and it seemed to some that in these secondary questions he devoted too much space to the natural powers of man in regard to supernatural things. Others again found matter for blame in the expressions he used, but not in the substance of what he said.[4]

The principal part in the struggle against Molina was undertaken in about 1590 by a scholar who has attached his name to the theory of the Dominicans on grace as inseparably as Molina has done in the case of the corresponding theory of the Jesuits : Domenico Bañes. Bañes was a distinguished theologian.[5] Among the Dominicans who, together with Francisco de Vittoria, founded the so-called neo-scholasticism, he holds an outstanding place as a shrewd dialectician, and a profound student of metaphysics. As the influential

---

[1] Francis of Sales to Lessius, August 26, 1613 ; SCHNEEMANN, 4 ; facsimile of the letter in CRÉTINEAU-JOLY, III., 22. The doctrine of predestination of Lessius completely excludes the physical predetermination of Bañes ; see SCHNEEMANN, 325-327.

[2] LE BACHELET, Bellarmin, 292 ; ASTRÁIN, 163. For the attitude of Bellarmine towards Molina cf. LE BACHELET, Auctarium, 1-31.

[3] ASTRÁIN, 164.

[4] SCHNEEMANN, 220 seqq.

[5] Cf. MORGOTT in Freib. Kirchenlex., 1[2]., 1951 seqq. ; MANDONNET, in Dict. de théologie cath., II., 145 ; F. EHRLE in Katholik, 1885, I., 415-424 ; BELTRAN DE HEREDIA in La Ciencia Tomista, XIV. (1922), 64-68.

adviser of St. Teresa of Jesus, he became even more widely celebrated. By the concise and determined form which gives an impress to his intellectual originality, and by the positively fascinating influence which he exercised over those around him, he seemed destined to become the leader of a school ; he became so, in spite of his assertion that he did not intend to depart by even a finger's breadth from Thomas Aquinas. In the world of learning he displayed the independence of his intellect by various paradoxical opinions.[1] When confronted with the Jesuits his determination degenerated into bitterness and rancour ; when they were not of his way of thinking he described them as ignorant men, or men who, against their consciences, refused to recognize better doctrines;[2] in some respects he seems the spiritual heir of his master and fellow Dominican Melchior Cano.

During the years 1590–1594 the Spanish Inquisition was preparing a supplement to its Index of prohibited books for Spain. Bañes and his friend Zumel were among the scholars whose opinion was asked concerning more recent publications. They attempted to aim a first blow at Molina by proposing that his writings, that is his book on grace, and his commentaries on St. Thomas, should be included among the prohibited books.[3] The attempt failed, and brought down upon its authors a denunciation that was not altogether harmless. Molina had learned of the plan, and addressed a letter[4] to the Inquisition in which from the defence of his book he passed on to the attack. He said that he had turned against Bañes and Zumel because their teaching on grace and free will was not reconcilable with the Council of Trent. Starting from the principles upon which Bañes based his proofs, the Lutherans had gone on to the absolute denial of free will. In proof of this he brought forward a list of texts from Luther,

---

[1] Morgott, *loc. cit.* 1951.

[2] *Cf.* the passages from his " Relectio de merito et augmento charitatis " (1590) in Astráin, 164 *seq.*

[3] Astráin, 165 *seqq.*

[4] January, 1594, *ibid.* 166 *seq.*

Calvin and Chemnitz, together with others from Bañes and Zumel. The title of this collection is remarkable, for in it Bañes is spoken of as the first to have introduced such doctrines into Spain.[1] It was perhaps on this occasion that the Spanish Inquisition itself examined the book of Molina and expressly gave it its approval.[2]

At the same time the Dominicans Mondragón and Avendaño sought to stir up a storm against the great Jesuit theologian Suarez, who in 1590 and 1592 had published, as the first fruits of his labours, two volumes on the Incarnation which had been received with great applause.[3] When in October 1593, on the occasion of his being transferred from Alcalà to Salamanca, Suarez paid a visit to the Grand Inquisitor Quiroga, the latter spoke to him on the subject, and thus gave him an opportunity of showing the falsity of the accusations.[4] About a year later it was rumoured that the Dominicans were trying to get almost all the theological books written by Jesuits included in the list of prohibited books.[5]

In the apologetic works of the Jesuits there occurs again and again a complaint at the manifest injustice of such attacks. The reason why they were being thus persecuted could not be found in the doctrines which they had taught, since others had taught the same things without their having provoked any attack. The historian certainly cannot describe this complaint as unfounded ; the passion displayed by some of the Dominicans against the new Order is too manifest to allow of any such thing. On the other hand the bitterness is easy to explain. The young and rising Society of Jesus had in several cases entered the lists against the older Order, which was already covered with renown, and had

[1] Summa de las herejias de Lutero, Calbino y Chemnitio, que hacen a este proposito, y de lo que con ellos el Maestro Bañes tiene impresa y introducido en España. ASTRÁIN, 168 n.

[2] *Ibid.* 168 ; *cf.* 159.

[3] SCORRAILLE, I., 251 *seqq.*

[4] In a letter to Quiroga, January 15, 1594, in ASTRÁIN, 169-173.

[5] Letter of H. de la Cerda, rector of the Jesuit college at Medina, *ibid.* 173 *seq.*

won brilliant successes, especially in the field of pastoral work
and teaching. How then could it have failed to seem unjust
to certain Dominicans, who for centuries had borne the heat
and burden of the day, that they should be left behind by
these new-comers at the eleventh hour ? The Order of
Preachers had jealously looked upon theological science as its
privileged field. But now that the work of Molina, which
had made its appearance as the first book by a Jesuit on
scholastic theology, had been followed by other important
works by Molina himself and by Suarez, it seemed as though
the younger Order was preparing to storm the last fortress
of the older. The Dominicans would not have been a body
of men, if there had not been among them some of choleric
temperament, who from the first looked with suspicion and
jealousy upon the works of their special rivals, and who in
their mistrust did not fail to find in their writings things
which in reality were not there. In order to increase the
tension yet further, it was only necessary for the ecclesiastical
courts to pronounce in certain other juridical questions in
favour of the Jesuits against the Dominicans.[1] Bañes in
particular, the senior professor at Salamanca, had been
obliged, in the sight of the whole university, to submit to the

[1] The visitor Gil Gonzales Davila, in the exhortations which he
sent in writing to the Jesuit province in Castille, says that the
doctrine and the supposed differences from St. Thomas are only
a pretext for the attacks of the Dominicans, and that the true
reason was to be found in the fact that at Salamanca the Jesuits
had associated themselves with the Augustinians, and that at
Toledo, Soria and Salamanca the Dominicans had been surpassed
by the Jesuits. The fact that Miguel Marcos had attacked
Bañes by name, and that some spoke in disparaging terms of the
Dominicans, had served to pour oil on the flames. " Hemos de
procurar " concludes Davila, " que si es posible, tengamos paz
con todod " (ASTRÁIN, 174 seq.). Aquaviva had already written
to Castille on August 12, 1585, that they must avoid disputes
with the Dominicans, and should try on the contrary to treat
them with great humility and keep very much on their guard.
(SCORRAILLE, I., 250).

humiliation of the sentence of the Spanish nuncio on the
occasion of the dispute concerning the simple vows of the
Jesuits.   But in spite of all this, it was not the whole of the
Order of Preachers, nor even perhaps a majority of its
members, as became more and more clear, who allowed themselves to be governed by hostility towards the Jesuits, although
actually the over-zealous excesses of a single member attracted
more attention than the moderate behaviour of a hundred
others.

The ever increasing tension reached its climax at
Valladolid.[1]   There, at the Gregorian College of the
Dominicans, the declared adversary of the Jesuits was
Diego Nuño ; he set the doctrine of Molina before the students
as being contrary to faith, and Molina himself as an ignorant,
presumptuous and blaspheming man, and often attributed
to his adversary opinions which the latter had expressly
rejected and refuted.   The horror aroused against the
supposed heretic was manifested in the lecture halls by a
general stamping of feet every time the name of Molina was
mentioned.[2]   A colleague of Nuño prayed for the conversion
of Molina, since he might become a dragon like the one in the
Apocalypse, who swept away a third part of the stars of
heaven.[3]   To complete the confusion, the most bitter anti-
Jesuit among the Dominicans Alonzo de Avendaño, went to
Valladolid to preach the Lent, and inveighed from the pulpit
against the new Order, though he did not mention it by name.
Gradually even the best friends of the Jesuits began to be
afraid lest not all these accusations which were hurled from
the pulpit and the lecturer's chair, should prove to be purely
imaginary.[4]

The Jesuits then, to justify themselves, formed the idea
of defending the doctrines of Molina at a public disputation,

[1] ASTRÁIN, 176-200.
[2] Gonzalo Perogila, the advocate of the Jesuits, sent it in
their name to the Inquisition (ASTRÁIN, 195 seq.).
[3] Ibid. 197.
[4] Ibid. 177.

above all showing that he did not maintain the theses which were being attributed to him. This disputation took place on March 5th, 1594, but Nuño took care that it should not serve its purpose. Since all those who were present were allowed to bring forward objections to the theses advanced for the defence, Nuño availed himself of this right and declared certain theses which he attributed to the Jesuits to be heretical and erroneous. The Jesuit appointed to conduct the defence, and the president at the disputation, the Jesuit Antonio de Padilla, declared that the theses attacked were neither heretical nor to be found in Molina. The latter wished to prove this by reading certain passages from Molina's book, but Nuño would not allow this ; he began to cry out in a loud voice that he had already adduced proofs that the passage which had been read was heretical, and continued thus to cry out when Padilla began to read another of the passages. Some of the bystanders tried to calm the angry man. " Let me be," he replied, " I am fighting for the faith." Then the Jesuit who was charged with replying to the objections lost patience, and addressed to him the contemptuous question : " Perhaps you have the keys of wisdom on your side ? " To which Nuño rejoined that to speak like that was a sign of great pride.[1]

Then Diego Alvarez began to speak, and he later on gave the best explanation of grace from the Dominican point of view. The Jesuits bear witness that his attitude was modest, and that he presented his case very well.[2] But Nuño would not even now be silenced, and frequently interrupted the discussion, until at length Padilla permitted himself to remark that in scientific discussions it was not a question of strength of voice, but of strength of arguments. Nuño then rose with a clatter and said that Padilla's remark was an insult, and that he did not intend to submit to it ; he was going away and would not return any more, but would hold his own disputation concerning Molina at the Dominican

[1] *Ibid.* 179 *seq.*
[2] *Ibid.* 183.

college. Not much better than the behaviour of Nuño was that of his colleague, Jerónimo de Vallejo, the man who said that Molina reminded him of the dragon in the Apocalypse.[1] He read some passages from Molina, adding the remark that all that he had read was erroneous. He would not suffer anyone to reply to him, and went on reading and condemning.[2]

Two days after the disputation occurred the feast of St. Thomas Aquinas. Avendaño was to preach the panegyric of the saint, and if he had already on other occasions made use of the pulpit to speak against the Jesuits during those days of commotion, he now surpassed himself. He applied to them the words of the prophet : " Their face is now made blacker than coals."[3] He said that certain people had begun well, but that now they were sinners like others ; then followed allusions to the disputation just held. " If God made anyone the master of the sun in the firmament, that man might say ; the light is mine." Therefore, if St. Thomas, the sun of the Church, is one of our number, then too the light which he radiates is ours, just as the keys of wisdom are ours and not yours ; our key is the true one, yours is but a pick-lock. You do not enter by the door, but enter as a thief, unlike us who hold firmly to clear and sound doctrine without turning aside to innovations.[4]

After his sermon Avendaño could justifiably boast of the severe blow that he had delivered against his adversaries ; the Jesuits might expect another and perhaps deeper injury from the disputation which Nuño had announced before he went away. They therefore addressed themselves to the Inquisition and asked that at least a book which had received the approbation of the Portuguese Inquisition should not be described by the Dominicans as an heretical book. Once more in this petition was expressed the complaint which the Jesuits had already put forward, namely that the reason

[1] See *supra*, p. 302.
[2] ASTRÁIN, 183.
[3] Lamentations, iv., 8.
[4] ASTRÁIN, 183 *seqq.*

why they were being attacked was not to be found in questions of doctrine. The same theses had been defended at the chapter-general of the Franciscans as at their college, without the Dominicans who had been present raising any objection.[1] In a report of the disputation on March 5th, and of the attitude taken up thereat by Nuño, this complaint was set forth in even greater detail. In this it is stated that at the chapter-general of the Benedictines these theses had been defended in the presence of Dominicans without causing any scandal. Even before the time of Molina this doctrine had been taught by Mancio at Salamanca, and at Alcalá by Juan Alonso, afterwards Bishop of León. The same doctrine had been defended at Alcalá by Deza, though it had been contested by Bañes, who held a chair at that university, but he had been unable to effect anything against the prestige which Deza enjoyed there.[2]

At first the Inquisition had intended to forbid the proposed disputation altogether, but when it was approached by the Dominicans it only asked of them what had been suggested in the petition of the Jesuits, namely that the doctrine of Molina should not be called heretical. Nuño therefore restricted himself in the theses which he brought forward for the disputation to stating that some of the propositions which he was combatting were " worse than false " ; thus

[1] Petition of March 28, 1594, in ASTRÁIN, 186.

[2] ASTRÁIN, 180. According to Bañes himself (see QUÉTIF-ECHARD, II., 243) the Dominican Mancio (died 1576) enjoyed so great a reputation in Salamanca " ut vel unus omnes opprimeret, tanta erat eius auctoritas." His writings have not been published (cf. as to this F. EHRLE in Katholik, 1885, I., 172-174). For Juan Alonso de Moscoso, Bishop of León, 1593-1603, cf. ELEUTHERIUS, 173 seq.; MEYER, 208. The Dominican Diego de Deza (died 1523) was indeed " a Molinist before Molina " (cf. CR. PESCH in Zeitschr. f. kath. Theol., IX., 1885, 171-177 ; FRINS, 465 seqq.), but according to Quétif-Echard this Deza was a professor at Salamanca ; there is no mention of Alcalá. Perhaps another Deza is meant, who was a professor at Alcalá, where Bañes taught theology from 1567 to about 1572.

the word heresy was evaded, but the accusation remained substantially the same. At the disputation itself the Jesuit Padilla admitted that the propositions as now enunciated were erroneous, but he denied that they had been taught by Molina. Even this concession was turned to good purpose by Nuño and his followers, for when Padilla wished to prove from Molina's book that the latter had taught the opposite of these theses, they prevented him from reading them by making an uproar, and when the disputation was over they spread the rumour that Padilla had recanted at San Gregorio what he had upheld at the previous disputation at the Jesuit college. Naturally the Jesuits at once drew up and issued a report contradicting this,[1] and thus it seemed that the matter would drag on indefinitely.

It was time for the ecclesiastical superiors to intervene and put an end to this scandal. Alonso de Mendoza, who was administrator of the church at Valladolid as Abad Mayor, wrote on April 2nd, 1594, to the nuncio Gaetano at Madrid and complained of Avendaño, who on the previous day had again preached against the new Order, which he hated so much, as well as of the passionate behaviour of Nuño at the disputation on March 5th.[2] The Jesuits had already drawn up a letter to the Grand Inquisitor ; in this they stated that they were commonly looked upon as the defenders of doctrines contrary to the faith, and that the students in the lecture halls began to stamp their feet as soon as the very name of Molina was mentioned. The rector of the college at Medina, Hernando de Lacerda, was charged to take this letter to Madrid, and to defend the cause of the accused before the Grand Inquisitor and the nuncio.[3] The nuncio referred the matter of Avendaño and Nuño to Rome, whereupon the whole affair assumed an unlooked for aspect. On June 7th,

[1] Report of the Jesuits in ASTRÁIN, 190-194.

[2] ASTRÁIN, III., 312. The letter was written on a Saturday ; from the various dates (ibid. 312, 314 n.) we can only suppose it was on April 2, 1594.

[3] ASTRÁIN, IV., 195.

1594, Gaetano was ordered to open a process in full from against Avendaño, which ended on January 5th, 1595, with the condemnation of this infatuated man.[1] In the meantime Cardinal Aldobrandini wrote on June 28th, 1594, in the name of Clement VIII. to the nuncio, on the subject of the quarrel between the Dominicans and Jesuits. Since a question of faith was at issue, and a matter of no small importance, the decision pertained to the Roman See, and no one else must interfere. The Grand Inquisitor therefore must no longer concern himself with it ; the nuncio was to summon the superiors of the two Orders to his presence, order them to lay the matter of controversy before him in writing with full proofs, and then send the two statements to Rome. The nuncio was to order both superiors, under the gravest penalties, to forbid their subjects to discuss the matter any further pending the decision of the Pope.[2] Gaetano communicated the Papal letter to the provincial of the two Orders on August 15th, 1594 ; anyone who dared to discuss the question of efficacious grace either in public or in private was to be excommunicated.[3]

The superiors of both Orders set themselves to calm the excited feelings of their subjects. The General of the Jesuits, Aquaviva, on February 13th, 1595, urged the provincials by circular, in emphatic words, to maintain peace with the Dominicans, and to show them all charity in word and deed.[4] The Spanish provincials at once acted upon these exhortations ; their replies to Aquaviva[5] constitute a justification of the Order of Preachers, in so far as they prove that it was by no means the majority of the Dominicans who were allowing themselves to be actuated by antipathy for the Jesuits.

---

[1] *Ibid.* 199, 201. *Cf.* Vol. XXI. of this work, p. 150.

[2] Published in ASTRÁIN, 811 *seq.* (*cf.* 199 *seq.*). A corresponding brief to the Grand Inquisitor in COUDERC, I., 358.

[3] ASTRÁIN, 200.

[4] *Ibid.* 202.

[5] *Ibid.* 202-204.

Not long before the great quarrel between the two Orders
had once again been manifested. Just as the Dominicans
had previously tried to induce the Inquisition to prohibit
almost all the books of the Jesuits, so once more was this the
case with the programme of studies issued by the Jesuits
in 1591, and with the writings of Cardinal Toledo. They
were of opinion that both Aquaviva and Toledo were innovators, and that if the latter were allowed to have his own
way he would destroy the Church.[1] Only the week before
the condemnation of Avendaño had caused great excitement
among his fellow Dominicans,[2] but the storm thus aroused
had been quickly calmed, a thing to which an appeal to the
truce made by the king may have not a little contributed.[3]
The provincial of the Jesuits wrote from Aragon to Aquaviva
that in his province they had always lived in peace and
harmony with the Dominicans.[4] The provincial of Andalusia
bore witness that at that time they were showing great
friendship towards the new Order, everywhere inviting Jesuits
to preach on the feasts of their Order, so that it seemed that
they took pleasure in being on good terms with them. A
Dominican Visitor at Valladolid had shown himself a great
friend of the Society of Jesus.[5] In the very pulpit at Valladolid, from which in the previous year Avendaño had launched
his attacks, in 1595 there stood a Jesuit on the feast of St.
Thomas, who made a good impression on the Dominicans
when he said that the Soicety of Jesus held to the doctrine
of St. Thomas, and that it was bound to do so by the Statutes
of the Order. A similar report came from Toledo, although
a long altercation between the two Orders there had embittered men's minds.[6]

At Alcalá a Dominican and a Jesuit provincial had a

---

[1] Cristobal de los Cobos to Aquaviva, June 14, 1594, *ibid.* 197.

[2] *Cf. supra*, p. 307.

[3] February 4, 1595, ASTRÁIN, III., 345.

[4] Pedro de Villar, April 15, 1595, in ASTRÁIN, IV., 202.

[5] Cristobal Méndez to Aquaviva, April 12, 1595, *ibid.*

[6] The Jesuit provincials Avellaneda and Acosta to Aquaviva,
Toledo, March 20, and Valladolid, March 20, 1595, *ibid.* 202 *seq.*

conference in order to consolidate the peace, and to consider
the best means to attain that end. They decided that the
members of both Orders should speak well of the other, and
that if anyone forgot this duty he should be admonished
by his superior in order that he might repair his fault. If
doubts concerning doctrine should arise, appeal should be
made to the Inquisition, if the matter pertained to that
tribunal ; otherwise, as became good brethren, the question
should be settled amicably.[1]

If the Papal command not to discuss efficacious grace
helped the maintenance of peace, in course of time the obligation of silence was resented by both parties as a heavy burden,
which in the end would become unbearable. Among the
Jesuits, Molina was planning an apologetic work concerning
his doctrine, which had so often been attacked and falsified.
Gabriel Vasquez had just completed a volume of his theological
works, in which the question of grace was dealt with. To
both of these it seemed hard not to be able to express their
views. Vasquez therefore had recourse to the nuncio, but
on April 1st and Nov. 29th, 1597, received a reply from Rome
that he must not print his book. Vasquez obeyed,[2] nor
on the part of the Jesuits do we know of any offence against
the Papal order of silence.

The Dominicans were less submissive. Some of them who
were of ardent temperament could not even now restrain
their tongues ; in pulpits and lecture halls and at disputations
fresh attacks on the Jesuits and their doctrine occurred, as
at Burgos, Palencia, Valladolid, Salamanca, Valencia,
Saragossa and Calatayud.[3] Philip II. therefore decided to
intervene once again. By his command, at the beginning of

[1] *Ibid.* 204.
[2] *Ibid.* 204 *seq.*
[3] Porres in ASTRÁIN, 205. We do not know the details.
" Hanlos obedecido puntualmente los de la Compañia ; pero in
Calatayud, después del dicho mandato se tuvieron por los Padres
Dominicos públicas conclusiones de esta materia, y lo mismo en
Salamanca, en los actos públicos mayor y menor de los dichos
Padres." Report of the Jesuits, in ASTRÁIN, 193.

1596, the visitor of the Jesuit province of Toledo and Castille, Garcia de Alarcón, together with the king's confessor, Diego de Yepes, and the provincial of the Dominicans, were ordered to confer as to the best means to prevent these abuses. At the suggestion of Alarcón the best means to maintain peace would be to remove the disturbers of the peace from the work of teaching.[1] Alarcón and the Dominican provincial, Juan de Villafranca, were to present themselves before the king's confessor in March, 1596, and he was to communicate their decision to Philip II. The king gave orders that only such men should occupy professorial chairs as had the doctrine of St. Thomas deeply at heart; that for the present the members of one Order should not be present at the disputations of the other; that they were not to be allowed to declare the doctrine of their adversaries heretical or erroneous, and that they should even be exhorted to speak well of the others; those who contravened these orders were to be punished. Alarcón and Villafranca added a further order to burn within eight days all writings against members of the other Order.[2] In consequence of this there were removed from the work of teaching, Nuño, Padilla, and another Jesuit, who had often disputed with Bañes; Bañes himself received a severe reprimand and admonition. The Dominicans did all they could to have the deprivation of Nuño revoked, in which they saw an insult to their Order, but the king adhered to his decision, and peace was restored for a whole year.[3]

If the Dominicans showed themselves less submissive than the Jesuits, this may perhaps be explained by the fact that they looked upon it as an injustice that they should be treated on equal terms with a younger Order. This impression was clearly expressed in a memorial which Bañes addressed to Clement VIII. on October 28th, 1597, in the name of the General of the Dominicans and the whole Order, in order to obtain the removal of the prohibition in the case of the

[1] *Ibid.* 206 *seq.*
[2] *Ibid.* 208 *seq.*
[3] *Ibid.* 210.

members of the Order of Preachers, and of them alone.[1] In this petition it was taken for granted, as quite certain, that the doctrine of grace taught by Bañes, including the controverted question, was the ancient Catholic doctrine taught by Augustine and Thomas Aquinas, just as that it was most obvious that the Jesuits were introducing innovations. Following the example of the Apostle Paul, who even resisted Peter, the Thomists had always shrunk from innovations, and now prayed the Apostolic See not to condemn the true doctrine to silence, on account of the strange theory[2] that had been set up against it. Before a decision on the part of the Pope was made years might elapse, while the authors of these innovations would do all they could to make the question drag on. In the meantime the new doctrine would strike deep roots. So long as the obligation of silence held good, it would be impossible to teach the doctrine of grace and predestination, a thing that would be all the more troublesome in that that doctrine reacted upon so many other theological questions. Moreover this prohibition placed the Dominicans in the universities in various practical difficulties.

By the command of Clement VIII., Bellarmine, at that time the Pope's theological adviser, wrote an opinion on this memorial of the Dominicans.[3] He examined all the reasons set forth by Bañes, and above all pointed out that the Dominican scholar took for granted those very things which had still to be proved, namely that the Dominican doctrine could be taken as expressing ecclesiastical tradition. According to Bellarmine what was above all at issue was the question whether physical predetermination was in accordance with the Holy Scriptures, the councils and the Fathers of the Church or no. The theologians of the Society of Jesus denied this conformity, and maintained that such predetermination was especially contrary to the Council of Trent, and was

---

[1] Printed, together with the counter-observations of Bellarmine (see *infra*) in L. DE MEYERE, 231 *seqq.*

[2] " Curiosedad."

[3] In LE BACHELET, Auctarium 114 *seqq.* ; ASTRÁIN, 214 *seq.*

therefore an innovation. If then the matter was still awaiting a decision it would be very rash to condemn the Jesuits as innovators as the memorial desired ; to do this would be to anticipate the judgment of the Apostolic See, and to cry triumph before the victory was won.

On one point, however, Bellarmine was in agreement with the Dominican theologian ; he too thought that it would not be wise to allow the prohibition to treat of efficacious grace to go on for years.[1] The Holy See should therefore intervene as soon as possible. Both parties could be exhorted by brief to mutual charity, and forbidden to describe the view of the opposing party as temerarious, erroneous or heretical, but that a discussion which brought forward real proofs might be allowed.[2]

Accordingly Cardinal Santori, Prefect of the Roman Inquisition, in a letter to the nuncio in Spain[3] of February 26th, 1598, allowed a learned discussion of the question, not only by the Dominicans, but also by the Jesuits. The Spanish Inquisition informed both Orders of this Papal decision,[4] without, however, giving the text of Santori's letter. The Dominicans complained of this to the Holy Office in Rome,[5] because in the extract that had been published no mention had been made of two important facts : first, that the Papal permission, and thus the equal treatment of the two Orders, was only to continue until the final definition of the question, and second, that the expressions used in Santori's letter were favourable to themselves. As to this they were indeed telling the truth ; the permission given to the Dominicans stated " that they might freely read and dispute as they had done in the past concerning the ' Auxiliis divinae gratiae et eorum efficacia,' in conformity with the teaching of St. Thomas." The Jesuits were given a like permission with

[1] LE BACHELET, 119 ; ASTRÁIN, 217.

[2] LE BACHELET, 121 seq.

[3] In SERRY, 138.

[4] In ASTRÁIN, 219 ; Latin translation in SERRY, 141.

[5] SERRY, 143.

the addition " that they might continue to read and dispute concerning this question, always however teaching sound and Catholic doctrine."[1] In the case of both parties was added an exhortation to abstain from litigation, from innovations, and from any censure of the opposing opinion. It had to be admitted, as was clear from the letter of Santori, that the Dominicans held a predominating influence in government circles in Rome. As a matter of fact a first Roman opinion, though it was precipitate, was imminent at that time, even though the documents which would have to form the basis of the Papal decision had not as yet reached Rome.

Actually, in June and August, 1594, an invitation had been issued by Cardinal Aldobrandini and the nuncio in Spain to the opposing parties to send to Rome an exposition and defence of their doctrine of grace,[2] while the Spanish Inquisition for its part had, in a circular of July 21st of the same year, asked for the opinions of twelve bishops and of a number of scholars as to the controverted point.[3] But it took almost three years before the Spanish Inquisition sent (October 23rd, 1597) in a large chest an enormous number of papers in three great packets.[4] The Dominicans sent a folio volume of 135 pages, entitled : Apologia of the Friars Preachers in the Spanish province. The first part, dated August 28th, 1596, is signed by seven professors, among them Bañes and Nuño, and sets forth the doctrine of Molina ; the second part, which was already completed on September 29th, 1595, and is therefore earlier than the other, bears the same seven signatures, together with an eighth. At the end of the whole volume sixteen other Dominicans have attached their names, among

---

[1] ASTRÁIN, 812 " che possino [the Dominicans] liberamente circa la materia de Auxiliis divinae gratiae et eorum efficacia conforme alle dottrina di S. Thomaso leggere e disputare, como hanno fatto per il passato . . . che possino [the Jesuits] ancor essi leggere et disputare della medesima materia, insegnando però sempre sana e cattolica dottrina."

[2] Cf. supra, p. 307.

[3] ASTRÁIN, 227.

[4] Ibid. 228. Cf. ELEUTHERIUS, 180 seqq.

whom are to be found the confessors of the king and Cardinal Albert.[1]

The Spanish Jesuits naturally could not produce the signatures of the confessors of princes. The four Spanish provinces of the Order gave their opinion separately ; for the province of Castille and Toledo, the speakers were Francisco Suarez and Gabriel Vasquez, who still to-day rank as the greatest dogmatic masters of the Order. Both of them in the first place combat physical predetermination, and then explain the view of the Jesuits. From certain words at the end of the exposition of Suarez, just before the signatures, it is clear that the disapproval of physical predetermination was quite general among the Jesuits, and that among them there was no doubt upon this point.[2]

Not all the bishops and scholars whose views had been asked for by the Inquisition could bring themselves to express their views. Besides the three universities of Salamanca, Alcalá and Siguenza, only five bishops and four scholars had given their views on this difficult question. Of the three universities, Salamanca could not be taken into consideration, since it limited itself to stating what all Catholics held as to the controverted matter.[3] Alcalá did not pronounce any judgment ; the professors there described both opinions as probable but inclined rather towards that of the Jesuits, and did not accept that of the Dominicans except with a proviso in favour of free will.[4] Siguenza declared openly and in all things for Molina, and defended him against a censure which had been sent by the Inquisition together with its circular. According to the judgment of the University of Siguenza the three propositions which were put forward in the censure as being altogether blameworthy were not to be found in the work of the Jesuit theologian.[5]

---

[1] ASTRÁIN, 228 seqq.

[2] Ibid. 231 seqq. Cf. LÄMMER, Zur Kirchengeschichte, 111.

[3] ASTRÁIN, 234 seq. The signature of the censure bears the date June 22, 1595.

[4] Ibid. 235 seq.

[5] Ibid. 236.

Of the five bishops who sent their opinion, the Bishop of
Cartagena had not even read Molina's book ; he relied upon
the censure that had been sent to him, and took the side of
Bañes.   The Bishop of Mondonedo was also altogether for
Bañes against Molina.   Pedro Gonzales de Arevedo on the
other hand was all for Molina.   Pacheco of Segovia blamed
Bañes as much as Molina ; both of them should be corrected
in the case of a new edition of their works.   The Bishop of
Coria emphatically defended indeed the doctrine of Molina
against the suspicion of heresy, but otherwise blames it
severely ; his views were false and an innovation.[1]

Just as the views of the five bishops differed entirely from
each other, so was it with the four scholars who sent their
opinion.   Two were opposed to Molina.   A third, the
Augustinian Miguel Salon, rejected out of hand about forty
propositions of the Jesuit theologian, only to agree with him
entirely on the principal point of his teaching.   Then he turns
against Bañes and condemns even more strongly the principles
from which physical predetermination is drawn.   The opinion
of another Augustinian, Luis Coloma of Valladolid, is confined
for the sake of brevity to the principal point, and absolutely
rejects physical predetermination.[2]

All these documents reached Rome on March 28th, 1598,[3]
and thus the final preparations for the great duel between
the two Orders were complete ; the battle could now begin.

The General of the Jesuits, Paolo Oliva, later on was of
opinion, looking at the matter in retrospect, that the issue
had been very beneficial, but that as long as the controversy
lasted the Order had been in great danger.[4]

[1] *Ibid.* 237 *seqq.*

[2] *Ibid.* 240 *seqq.*

[3] The signature of the notary in ELEUTHERIUS, 180.

[4] " Magnos motus excitavit in Ecclesia Dei P. Molina, quando
produxit novam, ut tunc videbatur, gratiae et liberi arbitrii
concordiam, et quamvis tendem feliciter ii sedati fuerint
cesserintque in magnam Ecclesiae utilitatem, tamen gravissimum
tunc Societas adducta est in discrimen." Oliva, January 12,
1664, in PRAT-GRUBER, Ribadeneira, 414.

The young Society of Jesus indeed found itself face to face with an adversary of overwhelming power.   No other body in the Church could match the scientific laurels of the Dominicans ; they had in their ranks a number of scholars of the first rank, some of whom had been adorned with the aureole of sanctity by the judgment of the Church.

The forms of learning and the defence of dogma had become to a great extent based upon their labours.   Even in recent times, the restoration of scholasticism[1] had come from the Dominican convent at Salamanca, the very place where Bañes had launched his attack upon the Jesuits.   The Jesuits themselves, thanks to the organizer of their studies, Toledo, had become the pupils of the Dominicans at Salamanca. At Trent, under Pius IV., about twenty-five bishops, and thirty theologians of the Dominican Order, had taken a leading part in the discussions and definition of the decrees on faith.[2]   For all these reasons the Order of Preachers enjoyed throughout the Catholic world the reputation of being the custodian of true Catholic doctrine.   To this had to be added the influence of the Dominicans at the Inquisition, with many secular and ecclesiastical princes, and with notabilities, whose confessors belonged to a great extent to their Order.

In all these matters the Society of Jesus, which was still young, was far from approaching the Order of Preachers. It was true that Salmeron and above all Lainez, had held a brilliant place at the Council of Trent ; Toledo enjoyed an uncontested reputation as a scholar in Rome ;[3] in the matter of polemics the Dominicans could produce nothing equal

[1] MANDONNET in Dict. de théol. cath., VI., 914. For the founder of neo-scholasticism, Francisco de Vittoria, cf. the articles in La Ciencia Tomista, I.-III. (1910-1913) ; F. EHRLE in Katholik, 1884, II., 497, 505-522 ; for the importance of the school of Salamanca, ibid. 497.

[2] MANDONNET, loc. cit., 908.

[3] Cf. the extracts from the briefs of Gregory XIII., Sixtus V. and Clement VIII. in FRANCISCI TOLETI in Summam Theologiae

to the learned works of Bellarmine. But in the matter of the
doctrine of grace it was a question of scholastic theology, and
it was only now that the younger Order was preparing to
make a triumphant entry into that vast realm ; the first
work by any Jesuit on such matters was the book of Molina
on grace and liberty. The Jesuits could not rival the Dominicans in their influence in high places in Rome, nor in their
knowledge of the conduct of affairs in the Curia, for the very
reason that among them it was only by way of exception
that men were to be found who had embarked upon a
prelatical career, or even the first steps towards it. It was
true that the General of their Order was one of these exceptions.
Bishops filled with the spirit of asceticism and men of importance might indeed choose Jesuits as their confessors, but
these were exceptional cases. When it was rumoured that
Philip II. had entrusted the direction of his conscience to
a Jesuit, the king wrote with his own hand : " If he intended
to change his confessor, there were too many approved Orders,
much older and well supplied with able men, to make it
necessary to seek one in the new Order."[1] At the time of
the dispute concerning grace in Rome, besides the two
Dominican Cardinals, Bonelli (died 1598) and Bernerio, the
influential Dean of the Rota, Francisco Peña (died 1612)
was above all their declared adversary ; he even laid it down
in his will that the revenues of a legacy which he had made
for poor students must never be given to a pupil of the
Jesuits.[2]

All this explains how it was that, in the intellectual contest
that was beginning, it was the Dominicans whose influence
decided the place and conditions of the battle, chose the

S. Thomae Aquinatis enarration, ed. Ios. Maria Paria e S.I., I.,
Rome, 1869, ix. seq., xii. Cf. Synopsis, I., 77, 160, 156 ; II.,
526, 531.

[1] " There are many old approved religious Orders which have
men fit for this, without seeking in this new one." Castagna to
Bonelli, December 19, 1560, in SERRANO, Corresp. dipl., I., 422.

[2] SCORRAILLE, I., 405 seq.

judges of the contest, and "supplied the sun and the wind."

The standpoint of the Jesuits from the first had been that it was not of importance to defend at all costs all the theses of Molina ; some of their number did not altogether agree with Molina.[1] In their opinion it was not persons or books that were primarily at stake, but a dogmatic controversy, and the critical point of the question consisted, to their way of thinking, in physical predetermination. They wished for an ecclesiastical definition as to this, and as to how it was reconcilable with the maxims of the faith and with the Council of Trent ; once this was cleared up, all the rest, so they believed, would not present any further difficulties.

But the Dominicans, as far as they were concerned, wished expressly to avoid the examination of this vital point, as to which there was not full agreement even in their own Order. They looked upon physical predetermination as a dogma, which simply could not be called in question ; therefore the whole discussion, according to them, must turn upon Molina's book, not restricting itself to the doctrine of the reconcilability of grace and freedom, but extending to all the theses which he had maintained. The contrary position taken up by the two Orders with regard to physical predetermination entirely governed the course of the struggle and all its vicissitudes.

Once Clement VIII. had transferred the dispute on grace to Rome in 1594, it was natural that both the Dominicans and Jesuits should send a representative to the Eternal City, to speak on behalf of his Order as occasion should arise. The General of the Jesuits thought of summoning Molina himself to Rome, but the latter replied to an invitation of February 16th, 1595, by excuses which Aquaviva had to admit were justified. Bañes too excused himself on the score of age, but in the place of the old master there came to Rome in November 1596 his disciple Diego Alvarez, a young man of great talent, who certainly did not remain idle.[2] After

---

[1] Cf. supra, p. 298.

[2] ASTRÁIN, 245 seq.

he had for many days examined the matter together with Cardinal Bonelli, the Protector of the Order, and other friends, in June 1597 he presented a memorial to the Pope,[1] which was intended not only to hasten the beginning of the discussions, but also to set the whole question upon the lines desired by the Dominicans.[2]

When in 1594 Aldobrandini transferred the discussion to Rome,[3] no mention of Molina was made in his letter ; it was rather a matter of a dogmatic question, the decision of which was withdrawn from the Inquisition and reserved to the Pope, namely the question in what the efficacy of grace consists. Alvarez, on the contrary, came forward in his memorial as the accuser of Molina ; the books of Molina must form the central point of the discussion ; they must be examined and condemned, and the examination must not be restricted to the principal question, as to which there were differences of opinion between the Jesuits and the Dominicans, but must extend to the whole contents of Molina's book on grace and liberty. And whereas so far it had been intended only to begin the discussions when the opinions that had been asked for had arrived from Spain, Alvarez wanted the examination to begin as soon as possible, as all delay was full of danger ; the work of Molina was meeting with much applause, and the younger theologians were adopting his ideas with the enthusiasm of youth ; once this opinion had taken deep root among them, it would be too difficult to bring them back to the true doctrine of grace and liberty.[4] To put it in another way : the Dominicans and Jesuits were not to meet as two parties with equal rights, but the Dominicans were to be the accusers, and the Jesuits were to sit, like poor sinners, on the bench of the accused. The attack on Molina thus had a vast field open to it, for not only would an error concerning

---

[1] Printed in SERRY, 149.
[2] ASTRÁIN, 245 *seq.*
[3] See *supra*, p. 313.
[4] For the historical inexactitudes of what Alvarez wrote *cf.* ASTRÁIN, 248 *seq.*

the principal question of the efficacy of grace be fatal to him,
but every mistaken or equivocal thesis in his book.   Moreover
the Dominicans enjoyed all the advantages of the attack ;
the weak point of their own doctrine was for the time being
outside discussion.

In addition to his own petition to the Pope, Alvarez had
drawn up another document for Cardinal Bonelli, in which
the scandalous propositions of Molina were pointed out and
refuted.[1] Bellarmine, as Papal theologian, had to draw up
an opinion which is distinguished by its calmness and its
absolute objectivity,[2] as compared with the other writings
which owe their existence to the violent struggle that had
begun. Bellarmine rejects physical predetermination, but
does not dare to condemn it absolutely,[3] as it is supported
by men of eminence.   He also defends the " scientia media "
of Molina ; the name indeed is a new one, but the thing itself
is very ancient.[4] On the other hand it seemed to him that
several of Molina's propositions were false, or at any rate
inexactly expressed, but he will not admit that they are
deserving of any real ecclesiastical censure.[5] In Bellarmine's
opinion no bitter expression against the Dominicans is used ;
the authors of the attacks on Molina are, on the contrary,
called " very pious and learned men."[6]

At that juncture the Pope was exceedingly pleased with
this little production of his theologian, which he afterwards
caused to be examined[7] by others as well,[8] but from the whole
of its tenor he was confirmed in his intention of having the

---

[1] The title in Le Bachelet, Auctarium, 102.

[2] Ibid. 101-113.

[3] Ibid. 106 seq.

[4] Ibid. 105 seq. Cf. supra, p. 285, n. 1.

[5] Ibid. loc. cit., 102 seqq.   For the attitude of Bellarmine
towards Molina, ibid., 1-31.

[6] Ibid. 109.

[7] Ibid. 113 n. 6.

[8] " Quod opusculum Pontifici mire probatum est initio."
Autobiography of Bellarmine, c. 45, in Le Bachelet, Bellarmin
avant son cardinalat, 465.

serious accusations against Molina examined. For this purpose a special commission was appointed.

The Dominicans had thus obtained what they wanted : the inquiry was confined to Molina's book. This was for the Jesuits a first defeat. The composition of the commission was a second. Not a single friend of Molina was included, although the course of affairs up to that point has shown that there were many such.

A third defeat was soon to follow. The commission held its first session on January 2nd, 1598 ; at its eleventh, which took place on March 13th, it was decided that the book and doctrine of Molina must be prohibited, as well as his commentaries on St. Thomas, at any rate until they were emended.[1] In the final judgment it was stated that Molina had repudiated in a haughty manner the doctrine of St. Augustine, which had been handed down by the Fathers, and more than once confirmed by the Church, and that the principles on which he based his doctrine were entirely opposed to St. Thomas. St. Augustine and the other Fathers ; that they contained many things which openly conflicted with the Holy Scriptures and the Councils, but were on the contrary in agreement with Cassian and Faustus of Riez, who had been combatted by Augustine.[2]

The Roman commission could not have dreamed at that time that the discussions concerning Molina would drag on for years to come, and then end without coming to any definite conclusion. Even before the materials contained in the Spanish acta had come, they had arrived at a definite judgment, as it were in the twinkling of an eye ! This was eventually explained by the fact that among the members of the commission there was not to be found a single man of any scientific weight.[3] Even Clement VIII. was surprised

---

[1] ASTRÁIN, 249 seqq.

[2] SERRY, 161.

[3] The members were the Franciscan Properzio Resta de Capelli, Bishop of Cariati and Cerenza ; the Franciscan Giulio Santucci, Bishop of S. Agata dei Goti ; Lelio Lando, Bishop of Nardo ;

at this unexpectedly rapid solution of the question, for soon afterwards, on March 28th, 1598, when the opinions sent from Spain had at last arrived, he ordered the commission to study them, and then reconsider their judgment.[1]

Thus the members of the commission found themselves face to face with a troublesome task. In October 1597 Bañes had written to Rome that the mere reading of these Spanish opinions would take two years, and that before the whole of the material had been carefully examined more than one pontificate might elapse, and that it was for this very reason that he had asked that the prohibition of any discussion of the controverted point of the doctrine of grace might be suspended.[2]

The commission, however, once more made quick work of the task. In the eight months between April and November, in which were included the protracted vacations, all was completed, and the former judgment, namely the condemnation of Molina, was substantially confirmed. That all the Spanish opinions had actually been read by all the members seems unlikely, especially as there were not as many copies as there were members of the commission. The

Enrico Silvio, vicar-apostolic of the Carmelites ; the Franciscan Francesco Brusca, later Bishop of Lettera ; Giov. Battista Piombino, procurator-general of the Augustinians ; the Augustinian Gregorio Nuñez Coronel, doctor of theology ; Louis de Creil, doctor of the Sorbonne. Coronel had written several books on the Church, on Tradition and on the State (NIC. ANTONIO, Bibl. Hisp. nova, I., Madrid, 1783, 546). RESTA had written De vera et falsa sapientia, Rome, 1599 (JOA. A S. ANTONIO, Bibl. universa Francisc., II., Madrid, 1732, 492). Lelio Landi had been employed under Gregory XIV. on the revision of the Vulgate. Nothing else is known of the literary activities of the members of the commission. Cardinals Lodovico Madruzzi and Arigoni were the nominal presidents of the commission, but it would seem that they took no part in the sessions. The real president was Resta, and the secretary Coronel.

[1] ASTRÁIN, 252.

[2] *Ibid.* 212 ; DE MEYERE, 231 *seq.*

Jesuit Fernando de la Bastida was able later on in the presence of the Pope to point out a single person, who was in any case quite incapable of any such work,[1] as the author of the censure. On March 12th, 1599, the secretary of the commission, the Augustinian Coronel, presented a document which purported to be the acta of the sessions, but which was in reality a violent attack upon Molina. Whereas the universities of Alcalá and Siguenza had found nothing to censure in Molina's book, Coronel condemns more than 60 theses.[2] Inevitably, as the result of these events, the most unfavourable reports against the Jesuits at once became common. It was even said that the Papal condemnation of their doctrine had already taken place, or that at any rate it would not be long delayed.[3]

Before, however, things could reach that point, the Jesuits had to be allowed to speak. After having thus far been kept entirely in the background, and only with difficulty obtaining any information of what was being done by the commission, they now prepared themselves for their defence. In December 1598, after the second censure had been pronounced in the previous month, skilful theologians of their Order came to Rome : Cristobal de los Cobos and Ferdinando de la Bastida, followed soon afterwards by Pedro de Arrubal and Gregorio de Valencia, hitherto professors at Dillingen and Ingolstadt.[4] Molina himself addressed a letter to the Pope and asked for a hearing.[5] He said that he had been urged to write his book by the same zeal as had led others to take up their pen against the heretics ; he intended to confute the errors of Luther and Calvin, and had done so by relying in all things upon the Holy Scriptures and the Councils, especially the Council of Trent, on the Fathers of the Church, and among them above all on St. Augustine. The attacks

---

[1] ASTRÁIN, 254.
[2] *Ibid.* 253.
[3] *Ibid.* 262.
[4] *Ibid.* 256.
[5] From Cuenca, September 22, 1598, *ibid.* 257-262.

upon him were due to the fact that he had himself attacked
Bañes, whose doctrines on the controverted point he had
always thought to be more than dangerous, and irreconcileable
with the Council of Trent. Bañes indeed accused him of
Pelagianism, but according to Luther the whole Church had
fallen into that error, since it defended free will. His book,
on the other hand, had met with much approval, but now,
when he had thought that the dispute about the book had
come to an end, it had reached his ears that he had been
accused before the Pope himself. This caused him much
anxiety, because he knew from experience how often things
had been attributed to him by his accusers which had never
entered his mind, and he therefore feared lest the same thing
should have happened in Rome. He therefore asked to be
allowed to speak, as was the right of the accused ; let the
Pope either summon him himself to Rome, or listen to the
defence which he had laid before the Inquisition in Spain.

Molina had previously connected his defence of his doctrine
with an attack upon his adversaries. He now did the same
thing. Some of his theses, he said, had been declared to be
suspect, but he too could enumerate many opinions in the
works of his accusers, which seemed to him to be manifest
errors of faith, Calvinistic in doctrine, and contrary to the
Council of Trent. He knew that the Dominicans had great
influence, being the confessors of powerful princes, and
occupying posts of importance, so that their help even in
worldly matters was often asked by highly-placed personages.
But even though they were superior in power and influence
in other matters, they must not be given a preference where
a question of faith and soundness of doctrine was at issue,
nor could they alone be listened to, and he himself rejected.
He therefore asked His Holiness to have the theses which he
had noted in their works to be examined. When these were
compared with the heresies of Calvin and Luther, it would
be clearly seen that they were errors of faith. Moreover,
according to Molina, the discussions about grace had
attracted the attention of the Protestants, and they were
waiting in expectation of a decision contrary to the Council

of Trent.[1] If, finally, the Pope was unwilling to listen to any of his requests, would he at least examine the concise exposition of his doctrine which he enclosed.

Perhaps a greater impression was made upon Clement VIII. by the letters of King Philip III., the wife of the Archduke Maximilian, and the Archduke Albert, whom the Jesuits had won over to their side, than by the petition of Molina.[2] The Pope decided that the Jesuits as well must be given a hearing. On January 1st, 1599, he cited Beccaria and Aquaviva, Generals of both Orders before him, and ordered them to discuss, together with some of the theologians among their subjects, the chief points of divergent doctrine in the presence of Cardinal Madruzzo.[3]

The first meeting took place on February 22nd, 1599. The General of the Dominicans appeared accompanied by the procurator of the Order, and two theologians, Diego Alvarez and Raffaele de Ripa ; Aquaviva's theologians were Pedro de Arrubal, Michele Vasquez and Cristóbal de los Cobos. In his opening discourse, Madruzzo explained the object of the discussions, namely to put an end to the struggle between the two Orders, in accordance with the wish of the Pope as well as of the King of Spain ; both Beccaria and Aquaviva gave their opinion as to the way in which, to their thinking, that purpose could be attained. The General of the Dominicans declared that his Order had nothing against the Society of Jesus, and that it was only the theses of Molina which were the rock of offence ; it his book were condemned and St. Thomas followed, then everything would be smoothed

---

[1] *Ibid.* 261.

[2] *Ibid.* 263. The Spanish nuncio also wrote on November 14, 1598, to Cardinal Aldobrandini concerning the efforts of the Dominicans and Cardinal Davila, who wished to obtain the condemnation of the book of Molina from the Spanish Inquisition. The nuncio suggested, either that such attacks should be suppressed in view of the earlier approbations of Molina's book, or that Molina and Bañes should be summoned to Rome and the writings of *both* examined (SCORRAILLE, I., 411).

[3] ELEUTHERIUS, 210 ; SERRY, 169 ; ASTRÁIN, 265.

over. Aquaviva took up quite a different position. He declared that Molina indeed was not the Society of Jesus, and that therefore his cause was not necessarily their own. The Pope might do what he liked with the works of a Spanish theologian or with the writings of any individual Jesuit, without the order offering any resistance. But there was a dispute between the two Orders, arising from their different explanation of "sufficient" and "efficacious" grace; as far as could be seen, the intention of the Pope was not to give a judgment on Molina's book, but rather to inquire into the differences of the doctrines in question, to establish the true doctrine, and to settle the questions at issue between the two great bodies.[1] The conference ended with an injunction from Madruzzo to the two Generals to prepare for the next meeting three expositions concerning the controverted point in the doctrine of grace; the first was to summarize in a few words the idea of his own Order, the second was to give the objections to the opposing theory, and the third the principal proofs in support of their own opinion.[2]

The second discussion took place on February 28th. Aquaviva presented himself with the three expositions in writing which had been asked for,[3] but Beccaria on the other hand only presented one; a further accusation of Molina divided into six points. He said that he had not thought it opportune to prepare any others, because the only point at issue was the book of Molina, and the Spanish Dominicans had not taken up arms against the Society of Jesus, but against Molina. Moreover, the Dominicans were there as the accusers, and he could not allow them, by defending their doctrine, to confess themselves as accused. To this Aquaviva replied in the sense in which he had spoken at the previous meeting, but Beccaria adhered to his opinion. Aquaviva then placed on the table the second document he

[1] ASTRÁIN, 266.

[2] *Ibid.* 267.

[3] Reprinted in ELEUTHERIUS, 214-217.

had brought with him, the objections of the Jesuits to the Dominican doctrine of grace, handing over the other two at the end of the meeting to Cardinal Madruzzo as a proof that he had obeyed him.   The conference was over ; it now remained to be seen what the Pope would do.

On March 5th, 1599, Clement VIII. appointed the Jesuit Bellarmine a Cardinal, and assigned him, together with the Dominican Cardinal Bernerio to act as assessors to Cardinal Madruzzo in the conduct of the conferences.

At the third meeting, which was held on March 29th, it was seen that the situation had become considerably changed in favour of the Jesuits.   Bellarmine brought forward six questions, in which he asked for an explanation as to whether physical predetermination was necessary for the good acts of the will, and for its evil decisions, whether the infallible efficacy of grace was based upon physical predetermination, or upon the contact of grace with the soul in the sense of St. Augustine.[1] These questions therefore, without any evasions, were directed to the point which formed the kernel of the dispute on grace, and on the solution of which everything depended.   But now the Dominicans refused to give an answer.   They said that these six questions had evidently been thought out and brought forward by the Jesuits, thus arrogating to themselves a right which belonged only to the Cardinals.[2]

The Dominicans, however, were no longer able to adhere to their own standpoint, of entering into no discussion save on the book of Molina.   It would seem that, soon after the questions of Bellarmine, they in their turn asked for an answer to eight points on the doctrine of grace and freewill.[3] But now it was the Jesuits who refused to give an explanation, until Clement VIII. obliged them to reply.   To five of these

[1] ELEUTHERIUS, 217 ; SERRY, 174.

[2] ELEUTHERIUS, 218 ; ASTRÁIN, 270 *seqq.*

[3] In ELEUTHERIUS, 218 ; SERRY, 174.   Whether the Dominicans were the first to present their eight questions, or whether on the other hand, which is more probable, Bellarmine first proposed his six, is variously reported.   *Cf.* ASTRÁIN, 272.

questions an affirmative reply could be given without more ado,[1] but these five questions did not touch the controverted point of the matter, and the others only uncertainly.

Later on they declared that this had been the real reason why they had at first refused to reply,[2] In other respects the Jesuits took all possible pains clearly to explain their view. When the Dominicans complained of a gap in the replies of their adversaries, they hastened to remedy it, though in doing so they took the opportunity thus offered them of once again alluding to physical predetermination, which, according to them, was opposed to the Holy Scriptures, the Councils, the Fathers of the Church, the scholastics and philosophers, and above all to St. Augustine and St. Thomas.[3]

The whole of April passed in these exchanges, and it would seem that a kind of impatience at these fruitless negotiations seized upon the Jesuits. They suggested to Cardinal Madruzzo, in order to make some progress, that they should briefly summarize the points as to which they had come to an agreement or a disagreement at the meetings which had been held so far.[4] Madruzzo then took three theses from among the expositions of the Dominicans, on which the Jesuits were to pronounce at the next session ;[5] actually, at that meeting both parties agreed upon seven points ;[6] this at anyrate made it clear that the Jesuits did not deny efficacious grace. But they at once transferred the discussion to the most critical point of the whole question by bringing forward

[1] ELEUTHERIUS, 218.

[2] ASTRÁIN, 273.

[3] *Ibid.* 274.

[4] *Cf.* the memorial of the Jesuits in ELEUTHERIUS, 221 *seq.* ; " Hactenus compertum est, mutuis hisce responsionibus . . . non solum quaestionis statum non attingi, sed rem ipsam fieri propemodum infinitam," etc.

[5] In SERRY, 178 ; ELEUTHERIUS, 222.

[6] *Ibid.* 222 *seq.* Concerning an eighth thesis, as to which, according to a manuscript in the Angelica Library, there was no agreement (and directed against Eleutherius [223]), see ASTRÁIN, 276.

the question whether, according to the Dominican view, the infallible efficacy of grace was based upon physical pre-determination.[1] It might have been supposed that the answer would have been a plain Yes, and that thus the question would have been solved. But, strangely enough, the discussion of the pros and cons went on for so long that, although the Jesuits would not allow their adversaries to escape for a good three hours, they were unable in the end to get a definite reply.[2]

But a clear reply was absolutely necessary if the discussion was to go on. On May 20th, 1599, therefore, the Jesuits sent a document to Cardinal Madruzzo, divided into five points, in which they explained, from their point of view, what they meant by physical predetermination in the sense of the Dominicans,[3] and asked him to induce their adversaries to reply. The latter, on May 22nd, sent a document to the Cardinal in which they explained their view sufficiently clearly.[4] But the expression " physical predetermination " was avoided in this. The Jesuits therefore again insisted that they must pronounce as to this expression, and received as a reply that the Jesuits must express themselves clearly as to what, in their opinion, the efficacy of grace consisted, for that so far they had only said in what it did not consist.

---

[1] ELEUTHERIUS, 223.

[2] So say the Jesuits in their memorial of June 24, 1599 : Deinde ulterius progressa est disputatio, quae eo spectabat, ut eliceretur, quid tandem illud esset, quo auxilium efficax differret a sufficiente. Et quoniam Patres Dominicani nihil interrogabant, illud pro-posuimus, utrum ratio auxilii efficacis consisteret in physica praedeterminatione voluntatis, ut hactenus docuerunt. Dum huic propositioni respondent, tres fere horae elabuntur, nec tamen ex eorum dictis quidquam certi colligi potuit, in quo vel a nobis differrent, vel inter so convenirent. Non enim omnes videbantur velle admittere hanc physicam praedeterminationem, et eorum, qui eam admittebant, unus affirmabat, ea tolli aliquam indifferentiam, alius negabat. SERRY, 189 A.

[3] ELEUTHERIUS, 224.

[4] *Ibid.* 224 *seq.*

The Jesuits complied with this demand without any difficulty, in an explanation of May 28th, 1599.[1]

The continued insistence of the Jesuits, and the way in which they kept on returning to the weak point in their adversaries' doctrine of grace, irritated the Dominicans all the more in that in their opinion it was not they but the Jesuits who, in the whole affair, should be subjected to examination concerning their doctrine.

Their annoyance so long suppressed, found vent in a written protest of June 8th, 1599, in which they gave a resumé of the discussions, and described the behaviour of the Jesuits as intriguing and deceitful.[2] The Jesuits replied to this on June 28th.[3]

These two documents are among the most important relating to the negotiations before Cardinal Madruzzo ; they complete and confirm our knowledge of what had happened on various points, while the intellectual outlook of both parties is set forth more clearly than usual. The Dominicans who took part in the discussions declared that they were not the representatives of the whole Dominican Order, and that in order to be so they would first have had to consult their universities and their most eminent theologians ;[4] they only presented themselves as a deputation of Dominican theologians in Rome. They further maintained absolutely that at the discussions nothing was at issue but Molina and his book, and if they also pronounced upon the doctrine of grace, they only did so as the theological advisers of the Pope, in order to give him the benefit of their scientific opinions. But the Jesuits maintained the opposite view with equal tenacity. They asserted that the Pope had not transferred the controversy

---

[1] ELEUTHERIUS, 225. Cf. ASTRÁIN, 279 seq.

[2] SERRY, 182 seqq. ; ELEUTHERIUS, 226.

[3] SERRY, 185 seqq. ; ELEUTHERIUS, 226.

[4] " In prima Congregatione . . . nobis prius semel et iterum professis, non totius Predicatoriae fam:liae nomine (cuius genrealia studia et theologi alii praecipui temporis opportunitate concessa fuissent consulendi), sed tantum professorum qui in Urbe essemus, congressibus illis interesse." ELEUTHERIUS, 226.

to Rome in order to pronounce judgment on Molina, as was clear from the briefs to the nuncio in Spain and to the Spanish Inquisition, and, as had been several times declared to the Dominicans by Cardinal Madruzzo, the General of the Jesuits had expressly stated that he had no interest in defending all the theses of Molina.

It is also clear from the complaints and accusations of both parties that both the Dominicans and the Jesuits refused to reply to certain definite questions. The Dominicans tried to avoid an explanation of physical predetermination ; this is definitely stated several times in the memorial of the Jesuits. " The most eminent Cardinal knows " so states the document, " how we have openly said that it is our desire that the Dominicans should explain their view just as we ourselves have done and will do, but they have attempted to evade doing so on various pleas.   The first time they said that they could not speak for the whole Order, and would first have to consult the theologians of the various provinces ; another time they were not ready, and could not carry on the disputation without preparation ; again, it did not affect the object of the discussion ; lastly they openly declared that they did not intend to give their opinion, because as the accusers they did not wish to become the accused, or to admit that they should be subjected to an interrogatory.   All who were present, and the most eminent President are witnesses as to this."[1]   On a copy of this accusatory document, there is to be found attached to these assertions of the Jesuits a marginal note in the hand of a Dominican : " This is the simple truth, as the General of the Dominicans cannot at his pleasure prescribe a doctrine for his whole Order, nor had he time or opportunity to consult the universities of the Order on this matter."[2] This passage is of great value to the disinterested historian ; what the Jesuits had several times

[1] Serry, 186, D ; Eleutherius, 227.

[2] " Verissime neque enim Magister generalis Praedicatorum doctrinam arbitratu suo toti suae religioni praescribit, neque eiusdem Ordinis universitates super his consulendi occasio et tempus ei oblata fuere." Astráin, 282 seq.

asserted is thus confirmed, namely that physical predetermination was not yet at that time the doctrine of the
Dominican Order.

On the other hand the Jesuits refused to give an answer
to the question whether the infallible efficacy of grace came
only from God, or whether it derived to some extent from
the free will. If a proper order was to be followed in the
discussions, they remarked, first it must be established in
what the efficacy of grace consists, for only then would it be
possible to discuss whence it came.[1]

But on July 17th, 1599, Madruzzo proposed to both parties
this question, together with others : can the free will refuse
its consent to efficacious grace ? Both were required to reply.
Each party dealt with the question from their own point of
view.[2] Further discussion at length led the theologians of
the Society of Jesus in November, 1599, to summarize in
eight propositions the points on which they could not agree
with the Dominicans, and concerning which they desired a
disputation.[3] On January 28th, 1600, they also presented
to the Cardinal a number of theses which had been defended
by the Benedictines, the Augustinians, the Franciscans, the
Carmelites and the Minims, and which were in favour of
Molina.[4] The last thing we know of the discussions in the
presence of Madruzzo are certain observations of the Dominicans concerning these eight theses of the Jesuits.[5] They
were presented on February 12th, and on April 20th 1600, the
old Cardinal of eighty-eight breathed his last.[6] This ended
the conferences in which both the Generals personally took
part.

The only result which the conferences had had was that

[1] Memorial of June 28, 1599, in SERRY, 189.

[2] ELEUTHERIUS, 232.

[3] Ibid. 239.

[4] ASTRÁIN, 286.

[5] ELEUTHERIUS, 239.

[6] Cf. the *reports of Fabio Maretti and G. B. Laderchi, dated
Rome, April 22, 1600, who point out what a great loss the death
of the Cardinal had been. State Archives, Modena.

the views of the two rival parties had been more clearly
defined, and had become better understood by their adversaries.   For the moment it seemed as though a rapprochement
had been brought about.   On one occasion the General of the
Dominicans, as the Jesuits report, had said that if Molina
had admitted all that the Jesuits had conceded in the presence
of Madruzzo, there would have been no reason to take action
against him.   But the Jesuits thought that they could prove
without any difficulty that all the theses in question had been
expressly taught by Molina.[1]

But a book by the Spanish Dominican Francisco Davila,
which was printed in Rome in 1599, and immediately suppressed by the Pope's orders in consequence of the
remonstrances of the Jesuits,[2] showed on the contrary how
bitter the dispute really was, and how serious were the
misunderstandings and prejudices.   This book made the
Jesuits appear as semi-Pelagians, and put together, without
mentioning them, the most plausible accusations against their
doctrine.   In spite of this Davila had dared to dedicate his
book to the Pope, and the imprimatur, given by a fellow
Dominican, and full of encomiums, bore the signature of the
General of the Order.[3]

On April 24th, 1600, the General of the Dominican Order
went to the Pope, and in the name of the whole Order
expressed his gratitude for a decision which gave the whole
dispute, now so long drawn out, a new turn, and which, at
any rate according to the statement of the adversaries of the
Jesuits, "filled all good men with incredible joy."[4]   This
was because, after the death of Cardinal Madruzzo,
Clement VIII. had thought it better not to continue the

----

[1] Memorial of June 28, 1599, in SERRY, 188 seq.

[2] De auxiliis divinae gratiae ac eorum efficatia, Rome, 1599.

[3] ELEUTHERIUS, 240 seqq. ASTRÁIN, 287 seqq. A writing in
which 16 of the errors attributed by Davila to Molina are refuted
as calumnies and compared with the true doctrines of the Jesuit
theologian does not belong to Bellarmine, as Astráin (289) supposes. LE BACHELET, Auctarium, xxi.

[4] SERRY, 195 (according to Peña).

discussions between the Generals of the Orders, but to revert
to that method by which the solution of the difficult question
had first been sought, namely, that the book of Molina should
once again become the central point of the discussions. A
letter from Philip III., in which he expressed his desire for
a speedy solution of the question,[1] perhaps contributed to
giving a fresh direction to the controversy. Therefore the
commission which had first pronounced judgment on Molina's
book, was completed by the addition of Bishop Ippolito
Masseri of Montepeloso, and the procurators of the Franciscan
Observants and Conventuals, Giovanni de Rada[2] and Girolamo
Palantieri. Their task was to examine the voluminous
censure of Coronel, and to point out, after a careful examination, which of the objectionable theses were to be found in
Molina. This work was completed on August 31st, 1600,
and was presented to the Pope in the middle of October.
Of the eleven consultors two had refused their signature,
Piombino and Bovio, while all the others were in agreement
in condemning twenty theses taken from Molina. There still
exist a number of writings of that time from the individual
members of the commission, all of whom pronounce against
Molina,[3] with the exception of Bovio.

While the commission was still engaged upon this work,

[1] Among the "negotios que dexò pendentes el Duque de Sessa"
it is noted : *El dicho 29. de Hebrero de 1600 scrivió Su M. al
dicho Duque pidiese a S. S. mandar que los cardinales y otros
ministros [who were treating of the controversy on grace] tomasen
en este negocio con brevedad la resolucion que mas conveniese a
servicio de Dios y bien universal de la cristiandad. . . . El 29.
de Hebrero 1600 scrivió Su M. al dicho Duque pidiese a Su S.
proveyese lo que mas conveniese sobre un libro de Molina S.J. que
diz que esta censido por los cardenales a quien Su B. mando le
biesen. The king wrote on the matter to the Pope on September
3, 1603. Archives of the Spanish embassy in Rome, I., 9.

[2] Rada (died 1608) was really the most capable theologian on
the commission ; cf. HURTER, Nomenclator, II., Innsbruck,
1907, 396.

[3] ASTRÁIN, 291 seqq.

the Jesuits succeeded in getting a sight of the censure of Coronel, and at once saw that it was defective in many points. In this Molina was blamed for several theses which were in common use among other theologians, or else things were attributed to the Jesuit theologian which he had never taught. The Jesuits reported these discoveries to the Pope in various expositions.[1] A special impression seems to have been made upon Clement VIII. by a writing of Aquaviva,[2] in which, so as to show the censure to be unjust, Molina's own words are compared with a number of the accusations of Coronel. To these were added the remonstrances of Bellarmine and others, so that Clement VIII. gave orders that the commission must also hear the defence of the Jesuits.[3]

Nevertheless, in spite of this concession, the position of the Jesuits still remained very unfavourable, and even apparently desperate. They had asked to be allowed to present their defence before other judges than the commission, for otherwise the censors would have been bound to pass judgment upon complaints which were directed against themselves and their judgments. But they obtained nothing by their request.[4] By the Pope's orders the commission was to hear the Jesuits, but the judgment was left to them, and the Dominicans were their advisers. The discussions were now conducted in the following way : first the censure was read, and was then defended by the Dominicans Diego Alvarez and Tommaso de Lemos, being then attacked by the Jesuits Cobos and Arrubal ; at the end both Dominicans and Jesuits briefly summarized in writing what they had said orally.[5] Thus it seemed as though the last word lay with the Jesuits, but the Dominicans, in addition to the writings which were communicated to the theologians of the other party, secretly drew up others which were intended only for the

[1] ELEUTHERIUS, 248 *seq.*
[2] In ELEUTHERIUS, 249 *seq.*
[3] ASTRÁIN, 293 *seq.*
[4] *Ibid.* 295.
[5] *Ibid.* 295. Some specimens of the negotiations, *ibid.* 296 *seq.*

members of the commission, and in which they sought to refute anything that told in favour of Molina. The Jesuits learned of these intrigues, probably from their friend Bovio, and Gregorio de Valencia, who was present at the sessions together with Cobos and Arrubal, thereupon addressed his remonstrances to the Pope. Clement VIII. then gave orders that these observations of the Dominicans were also to be handed over to the defenders of Molina. This time the theologians of the Society of Jesus made use of very emphatic language in their reply. At the outset it is stated : " In this document the Dominican Fathers advance so many things which are not in accordance with the facts, that they could never have supposed that these observations which they have addressed to the censors unknown to us, would one day fall into our hands."[1]

The discussions before the commission lasted until May 7th, 1601. On August 31st of the same year the censors came to their final judgment, and, as was to be expected, this declared that the commission adhered to the censures already pronounced against Molina. Only Piombino and Bovio once again refused their signatures. On December 5th, 1601, the commission presented itself before the Pope to deliver the result of its labours.[2]

Clement VIII. was aghast at the quantity of documents and opinions that was laid before him. " A year may have been sufficient for you to write all this," he said, " but a year is not sufficient for me to read it." The commission laid the responsibility for such prolixity upon the objections and artifices of the Jesuits ; the Pope, however, with his great intelligence and learning had no need to read it all. Santucci, who after the death of Resta had acted as president, then made the strange suggestion that it would be well not to inform the Jesuits of their judgments, so that the matter might not be prolonged indefinitely.[3]

[1] *Ibid.* 302 *seqq.*
[2] *Ibid.* 301.
[3] *Ibid.* 301 *seq.*

Clement VIII. at once saw that this new censure, the fourth in four years, was of no great use to him.   If he was to settle the controversy personally by his supreme authority, then he must inform himself personally of all the details, and examine all these voluminous opinions.   The observations of the Jesuits too could not be left unexamined ; they would know how to lay their remonstrances before the Pope, even without being informed of the verdict of the commission.   The suspicions which had been spread throughout the world on account of what had happened in Rome gave an opportunity for so doing. Molina, who died on October 12th, 1600, certainly knew nothing of the rumour which was spread throughout Spain that he had been condemned in Rome by a Papal sentence, and burned in effigy.   On March 9th, 1601, Bellarmine had to reassure the Spanish Jesuits on this score ;[1] an edict of the Spanish nuncio of September 21st, 1601, reminded men[2] of the Papal prohibition of mutual censures, and removed the grounds for such rumours.[3]   But in Italy, Germany, France and Poland similar rumours did no little harm to the work of the Jesuits in the exercise of their ministry.[4]

In the meantime the Jesuits sought protection from the Pope, and on February 12th, 1602, they presented a memorial in which all the accusations which had been brought against them during the discussions in Rome were summarized under seven heads, together with a brief defence.[5]

In answer to the charge that they were exigent and would not be satisfied in their claims, they summarized the points in which their desires really consisted : 1. Since the origin of these discussions lies in the question : In what does the efficacy of grace consist, may it please Your Holiness to define what must be firmly held as to this, so that, following that infallible rule, everything that is not in accordance with that definition may be expunged from the books.   2. A judgment

---

[1] Letter to Padilla, in ELEUTHERIUS, 246.

[2] *Ibid.* 247.

[3] ASTRÁIN, 294.

[4] *Ibid.* 304.

[5] *Ibid.* 306-314, ELEUTHERIUS, 334-341.

should not be pronounced on the question of Molina, without his being heard. 3. That what we put forward on his behalf may be submitted, in accordance with the judgment of Your Holiness, to persons so well versed in dogma, and in such a degree specialists in scholastic theology, as such difficult questions demand ; men, moreover, who have not taken sides on the question, so as to give their signature against Molina before making a careful examination, and thus staining their reputation in this respect. 4. If questions and replies are not to be carried on indefinitely, let us be allowed to reply in the last instance, as we are defending the cause of the accused, to whom that right belongs. In forming a judgment as to these questions, attention should be paid to the documents which were presented at the session ; if anything has been brought forward against Molina in secret, of which we were not given a copy so that we might reply to it, such matter must not be taken into consideration until it has been communicated to us, and we have made our reply. 5. When our replies are examined, the judgment must not be restricted to generic observations as to Molina, but should state in detail which of his theses are blameworthy, so that we may know what to be on our guard against, as well as for other reasons. 6. Anything that is found deserving of censure in Molina, must also be deleted in those other theologians who hold the same doctrines.[1]

To the further reproach, that they were not satisfied with the judgment of the Roman censors, the Jesuits replied : 1. There are six on the commission who condemn the book, and two who approve it, and to each of those six we can oppose a tribunal, a university or a corporation that approves it. The Portuguese Inquisition has approved the book twice over, once by a majority of the votes of all the Qualificators, among whom were two Dominicans. The same was done by the supreme council of state of Castille and that of Aragon, who based their opinions upon those of the most eminent theologians. Moreover, the University of Alcalá, which

---

[1] Point 2, in ASTRÁIN, 307 seq.

examined the book with great care for a whole year, approved it when, by the orders of the Spanish Inquisition, the matter was discussed before that tribunal. On the same occasion the book was sent to the University of Siguenza, which is one of the four principal universities of Spain, and always has at its command persons of distinction, since canonries are attached to the professorial chairs ; this university approved the book, and replied point by point to the objections. In like manner approval came from Italy, France and the Low Countries when the work was re-examined there for reprinting, and an imprimatur given. Moreover it received many approbations from prelates and doctors, to enumerate whom would take too long, besides which it is already abundantly clear from what we have said that the number of those who approve is greater than that of those who condemn. 2. Admitting that the judgment of the members of the commission was completely just, yet they had not heard us when they pronounced judgment the first time, and from that time onwards we have been compelled in our replies to make perpetual contradictions. As their reputation, it would seem, was already compromised, we cannot deny that for that very reason and from other circumstances as well,[1] we must look upon them as partizans in the question, and, in a certain sense, in an even greater degree than the Dominicans themselves. 3. The book of Molina is concerned with doctrines of faith of great importance, which are connected with the most difficult questions of scholastic theology ; they demand on the one hand a most complete knowledge of the controversies with the heretics, and on the other a great familiarity with the most delicate subtleties of scholasticism. And although

---

[1] The " other circumstances " here alluded to, are more clearly expressed in the draft of a petition to Clement VIII. " The majority of the censors were for various reasons biassed in the matter, and had been selected by Cardinal Bonelli : two of them were his dependants and belonged to his famiglia : another belonged to the famiglia of Cardinal Ascoli (a Dominican), while there were other ties of dependence between them and the Dominicans." ASTRÁIN, 304.

we look upon the censors as very capable in their profession, and eminent for their learning, we take it for granted that they themselves would not deny that they have never before been forced to studies of this kind, either for the purpose of printing a book, or for disputations with heretics, or for teaching, outside their own Order, theses of this kind at any university. They themselves say that in their day nothing was known of such questions, and that they were not treated of; although, therefore, we look upon them as pious and learned, it is not going too far if we express our doubts as to the value of their opinions in such matters. 4. We know by experience that they have looked upon certain theses as being Molina's, which he himself looked upon quite otherwise, and that they have censured others to which they could not have attached any importance if they had sent a copy of them to us. 5. We cannot feel satisfied with their judgment because we see, for example, that they declare a thesis of Molina's to be Pelagian, which the universities of Alcalá, Bologna and Siguenza hold to be true, and which has been defended as such by the most learned men of almost all the Orders of Spain, and the contrary theses to which Bellarmine, Stapleton and Gregorio de Valencia, who have read so many of the books of the heretics, and have held disputations against them, and confuted and written against them, declare to be a Calvinist error. In like manner, nine universities in the countries bordering upon those of the heretics have passed a similar judgment on that thesis.[1]

When the Jesuits presented this memorial, Clement VIII. had already resolved to leave on one side the mass of judgments and opinions upon the dispute. He thought that the purpose would be more quickly attained if he were to allow himself to be informed verbally of the reasons in support of the two controverted opinions by those who themselves represented them. Thus began the last and most celebrated phase of the negotiations in Rome : the disputations in the presence of the Pope.

---

[1] Point 4, in ASTRÁIN, 309 seq.

The fatality which had hitherto pursued the Jesuits throughout the whole controversy, seemed destined to follow them
from the opening of the new congregations.　An imprudent
act of theirs irritated the Pope against them exceedingly at
the very moment when more than ever his good-will was so
important to them.　The occasion for this fresh storm was
afforded by a subtle question of scholastic theology which
had been defended at their college at Alcalá on March 7th,
1602.[1]

If, for example, a Pope has been canonically elected and
recognized by the Church, then according to Catholic principles
it must infallibly be held that he is truly Pope and successor
of St. Peter ; but it is possible to go further and ask : is it
only infallibly certain that such and such a Pope, for example
Clement VIII., is the successor of St. Peter, or is this a truth
of faith revealed by God ?　If God has revealed that all men
are descended from Adam, then He has also revealed that
such and such a man is descended from Adam.　Thus, in the
phrase, which is certainly revealed : all legitimate Popes are
the successors of the Prince of the Apostles, is there in like
manner contained the other : in Clement VIII. is continued
the true succession of Peter ?　On this point theologians are
of different opinions ; some reply in the affirmative, and others
in the negative.　The question is of no practical importance ;
no theologians questioned that Clement VIII. was the true
Pope, not even those who could not see in this a revealed
truth in the full sense of the words.[2]　Such a question was

---

[1] ELEUTHERIUS, 333-337 ; ASTRÁIN, 315-331.

[2] This is in accordance with the expression of RANKE (Päpste,
II.[8], 200 n.) ; " The doctrine which they (the Jesuits) threatened
before Contarini, is that the Pope is indeed infallible, but that it
is not an article of faith to hold this or that man to be the true
Pope."　It is not a question of the Jesuits in general but only of
those of Alcalá, and there is certainly no threat to be found in
their doctrine.　Perhaps the passage of A. Harnack also refers to
the thesis of Alcalá (or to the " threat " of a council ?　Cf. infra,
p. 353, n. 1) : " Not only did they threaten the Pope and seek
to intimidate him, when it seemed that he was too favourable to

treated of in the lecture halls as an example by the help of
which certain theses of the doctrine of faith could be explained.[1]

The Augustinians, for example, had, on May 7th, 1601,
at Saragossa, maintained the negative view[2] without anyone
being disturbed.   When in the following July the same theses
had been presented before the University of Alcalá by a
professor, Peña called attention to this in Rome, and asked
for the intervention of the Roman tribunals, without any
steps being taken.[3]   It was only when the Jesuits at Alcalá
followed the example of the university on March 7th, 1602,
at a public disputation,[4] that a veritable tempest broke out.
A Dominican stated at a public disputation at Valladolid
that the Jesuits had denied that Clement VIII. was truly
Pope, and that if a Papal sentence was pronounced against
them on the question of grace, they would maintain that they
had not been condemned by a lawful Pope.   It was in
this sense that the matter was brought before the Pope
himself.

Clement VIII. was not a theologian, and did not understand
very much about the subtleties of scholasticism.   Moreover,
in the Eternal City suspicions were held of the Spaniards,
for which their cesaropapalism and other pretensions against
Rome had afforded abundant reason.[5]   Clement VIII.
therefore felt violent anger against the Jesuits of Alcalá.
Aldobrandini was told to write at once to Ginnasio, to upbraid
him for not having reported this unpleasant incident at
Alcalá.   If the Inquisition had not already interfered it must
do so at once.   The nuncio must then take the matter in hand
with all speed, and he was therefore sent the censure which

the Dominicans, but even the most zealous Papalists shook the
whole system to its foundations." (Lehrbuch der Dogmengesch.
III., Freiburg, 1910, 739).

[1] Fuller details e.g. in Christ. Pesch, Praelectiones dogmaticae,
VIII., Freiburg, 1910, n. 272 *seqq.*

[2] Astráin, 321 *seq.*

[3] *Ibid.* 315.

[4] In general the Jesuits maintained the opposite thesis

[5] *Cf.* Vol. XXIII. of this work, p. 195 *seq.*

Rome had launched " against this bestiality, not to call it a thesis."[1]

The Inquisition feared that unless it interfered at once, the process would be transferred to Rome with the loss of its own prestige ; it therefore at once caused four Jesuits to be thrown into prison, namely the student who maintained the thesis at the disputation, his professor, the rector of the college, and the celebrated theologian Gabriel Vasquez.[2] The nuncio would have liked first of all to have sent to Rome, as being responsible, the three doctors of Alcalá, who were the predecessors of the Jesuits in their defence of the thesis, but on May 8th, 1602, the king intervened on their behalf.[3] Clement VIII. decided that the cause of the four Jesuits, as well as that of the three doctors, must be judged in Spain. But the form in which he wrote this order in his own hand, on the last page of the letter to Ginnasio, shows once more the anger with which the events at Alcalá had filled him. " The pride and presumption of these Spaniards in this matter —for there is no question of inculpating the Italians—is so great that they dare to write and print new and most perilous doctrines ; it is therefore necessary that the Inquisition there should keep its eyes open . . . How true this is, is shown by this last act of misconduct, while another proof is to be found in the obstinacy with which they defend Molina, since in this matter as well it is not a case of more than four Spaniards, who spring from God knows what race.[4] Write to him (the nuncio) that we are satisfied, on account of the pressure brought to bear by the king, that the Inquisition there should examine, not only the cause of the Jesuits, but also that of those who have been summoned to Rome, but on condition that We are kept informed of what takes place.[5]

[1] Letter of March 30, 1602, in ASTRÁIN, 318.

[2] Ibid. 319.

[3] Ibid. 319 seq.

[4] De la Bastida was of Jewish origin ; the same is asserted of Molina in the *Annales, composed by Paolo Emilio Santori, Vallicella Library, Rome, K. 7 seq., 615.

[5] ASTRÁIN, 320.

It was not difficult for the accused Jesuits to make clear before the Spanish Inquisition the mistake of which they had been the victims. They were able to produce a number of skilled theologians who taught exactly the same thing.[1] After a month and a half Vasquez and the rector of the Jesuits were set at full liberty as being innocent ; in the case of the two others the professed house of the Jesuits at Toledo was to serve as their prison.[2]

However serious the situation might be for the Jesuits there was not wanting a humorous side to the question.[3] Among the theologians whom the Jesuits had cited in their defence was no other than their old adversary Bañes, and thus the seventy-five year old scholar, after his long struggle with the Jesuits, found himself entangled in the same net as themselves. The old scholar had for a long time retired from his chair and from disputations, but on this occasion the old lion felt himself moved once more to enter the lists. On July 2nd, 1602, at Valladolid, where the court then was, he organized a public disputation, which was to be as brilliant as possible, in the Church of the Dominicans. The nuncio and many illustrious gentlemen were present. A thesis was discussed, which, though it did not recede from his previous theses, left nothing to be desired in the matter of devotion to the Roman See.[4] He would have liked Spanish to have been chosen as the language for the discussion, so that the greatest possible number of persons might be convinced of his true opinions, but the Constable of Castille to whom he expressed this wish, drily replied that he preferred Greek, because in that way even less of the question would be understood. But Bañes was able to repair the loss by delivering a panegyric on Clement VIII. after the disputation. "Before God I am speaking the truth," he began, "when I say that I have read of and seen many holy and good lives of Roman

---

[1] *Ibid.*

[2] *Ibid.* 322.

[3] *Ibid.* 323 *seqq.*

[4] Text of the thesis, *ibid.* 323.

pontiffs, from the time of the Apostles to our own day, but I
have never read of greater holiness and goodness than that
of this Pope, by which I mean to say that Clement VIII.
always has been, and always will be a true representative
of Christ, and successor of the Prince of the Apostles." He
said that this to him was a dogma, that he had always taught
it and looked upon the contrary view as heresy and a shame-
less act of effrontery.[1] Then the Constable spoke, and pointed
out that such assertions were superfluous, for no one of those
present had called the authority of the Pope in question.
Bañes replied that this was true, but that it was necessary
to consolidate those sound sentiments, and that if anyone
should maintain the contrary it ought to be made plain to
all that for such persons there were always judges in Spain to
brand them as heretics. Bañes then wrote to the Pope that
by his disputation he had stamped out a dangerous error,
which on account of the reputation of its supporters might
have spread throughout the world, and begged him at the
same time to decide the dispute on grace by a pontifical
sentence.[2] The Trinitarian Zumel also held a similar disputation with his old friend Bañes, and wrote an account of it to
Rome, receiving, in accordance with the usage of the Curia,
a eulogistic reply, as did Bañes himself.[3] Naturally the
Jesuits could not now be left behind. On July 10th, 1602,
they also prepared a disputation at Valladolid, in which they
endeavoured to give satisfaction to the offended Pope; this
they could do all the more easily in that probably the greater
number of them did not share the opinions of their brethren
at Alcalá. They allowed themselves to say, however, without

---

[1] " Disse di N.S. molte lodi, tra le quali la prima fu, que delante
de Dios que yo diga la verdad, disse egli, che dagli Apostoli in
qua ha letto e visto molte vite di Pontifici Romani sante e buone,
ma maggiore santità, ne bontà di quella di questo Papa non l'ha
giammai letta, ne vista, ne intesa dire." Ginnasio in ASTRÁIN,
loc. cit.

[2] *Ibid.* 325 ; SCORRAILLE, I., 440.

[3] ASTRÁIN, 325 *seq.* The brief of March 10, 1603, in SERRY,
287.

naming Bañes, that the thesis recently maintained by a Dominican theologian was not altogether satisfactory.[1]

The nuncio, who was not a theologian, and had not a sufficient knowledge of the state of the question, made a report to Rome concerning the Jesuit disputation, but in rather frigid terms. On the other hand he zealously supported at the Inquisition the condemnation of the culprits of Alcalá.

The tribunal of the faith thus found itself in a position of much embarrassment; it understood perfectly well that there were no grounds for a condemnation, but on the other hand had to take into account the irritation of the Pope and the pressure of the nuncio. At length, in September, 1602, the sentenced was pronounced, which, however, was not published until the summer of 1603.[2] This was an acquittal, though an exhortation and admonition were to be addressed to the accused,[3] that is to say an exhortation to greater prudence, and an admonition for the imprudence already committed.

In the meantime the indignation of Clement VIII. had evaporated. Cardinal Aldobrandini wrote on April 12th, 1603, to the nuncio in Spain that the great accumulation of papers and opinions on the theses of Alcalá had been laid aside, together with the question itself. Clement VIII. had thus discovered that, notwithstanding the thesis of Alcalá, no one thought of calling his authority and dignity as Pope in question.

Nevertheless, all this presaged ill for the subsequent development of the controversies on grace.

The misapprehensions of the Pope had shown, clearly enough, that he had no profound dogmatic knowledge. Indeed, it is not even certain that he had ever studied dogmatics. In his youth he had attended the University of Bologna, but the students who intended to devote themselves to the service

---

[1] ASTRÁIN, 326.

[2] Ibid. 327 seqq.

[3] " Liberatoria, facta prius illis monitione seu correctione." Ibid. 331.

of the Curia studied canon law, nor is there anything to show that young Aldobrandini was an exception.[1] Yet now Clement VIII. intended to preside in person at the congregations at which the most thorny questions of dogmatic theology were to be treated of. In spite of his age he plunged eagerly into the study of theology, read far into the night, laboured and attended disputations, so that Cardinal Pierbenedetti laughingly remarked that in his old age he had changed from a jurist into a theologian.[2] He thought that in this way, and by listening to the discussions, he would attain to that clearness of view which was necessary in order to formulate a dogmatic judgment ; in this matter he acted rather as a private individual who wanted thoroughly to understand a scientific question, than as a Pope who was preparing to make a dogmatic definition.

The new series of disputations began on March 20th, 1602. There were assembled in the Pope's apartments his closest advisers, Cardinals Pompeo Arigoni and Camillo Borghese, besides the members of the commission who had already four times spoken in condemnation of Molina, and who were now reinforced by four more consultors. Lastly there were the two Generals of the Orders and the theologians chosen by them ; the General of the Dominicans, Girolamo Javieres, was again accompanied by Diego Alvarez ; the General of the Jesuits brought with him as his theologian Gregory of Valencia.

The discussions which now began followed exactly the same course as that which had previously had so little result. This time again the first place was not given to the dogmatic thesis —in what does efficacious grace consist—but to Molina's book. This time, in examining the book, they did not even

---

[1] *Ibid.* 332.

[2] *Ipse (Clement VIII.) efferventissime vigiliis, laboribus et libris incubare, disputationibus adesse, quaestiones invehere, disputare, sibi non parcere, atque, ut Perbenedictus ioco dicere solebat, ex iurisperito repente in senecta theologus evaserat !Annales of P. E. Santori, Vallicella Library, Rome, K 7 *seq.*, 615b). *Cf.* COUDERC, I., 346, 352.

confine themselves to the principal question, whether Molina was right in rejecting physical predetermination, and introducing in its stead the " scientia media " of God, but it was once more asked whether there were to be found in the disputed book theses which would justify its condemnation. Moreover, in the examination of the theses of Molina, the most difficult course was followed, namely their comparison with the doctrine of St. Augustine. Undoubtedly St. Augustine is looked upon by the Catholic Church as being par excellence the master of the doctrine of grace. But he often speaks with certain presuppositions, and refers to conditions which were well known and familiar to his first readers, but which cannot be understood by posterity, except by painful scientific study. Therefore he is not easy to understand in all particulars, and in the course of the history of the Church has given rise to many misunderstandings.

It was therefore easy to see that the disputations would be very long protracted, when, a few weeks after the opening congregation the Pope proposed as the subject of the next discussions the two questions: did Augustine or Molina attribute greater force for good to the free will, and was the thesis of Molina that God gives man His grace while he is doing what is within the reach of his natural powers,[1] to be found in Augustine, or was it at anyrate in accordance with his spirit, and recognized by him as a universal law of the order of grace. The first of these theses proposed by the Pope was treated of in eight congregations. The question was discussed whether man is capable of performing by his purely natural powers, without the help of grace, things that are naturally good, and whether he can do so even in difficult circumstances, for example, if he had to choose between death and sin; also whether man is capable of assenting by his natural powers to the truths of faith, and whether he is capable by his purely natural powers of aspiring to faith and to supernatural help, of asking both from God, and of disposing himself to receive them. Then came the

[1] ELEUTHERIUS, 341 ; ASTRÁIN, 337.

question : what is the part taken by the free will in receiving grace and in increasing it, and whether the free will is sufficient to arouse repentance for the love of God, or in general any act of the love of God which is purely natural, or to resist temptations.   At the ninth congregation, on September 30th, 1602, the second of the questions originally proposed was arrived at.   So far what had been always done was to first establish the doctrine of Augustine as to all these points, then that of Molina, and then to compare the two opinions. At the tenth congregation Augustine was abandoned, and until January 1603, that is to say for seven whole months, the doctrine of Molina was compared with that of Cassian,[1] who is suspect of semi-Pelagianism without scholars having come to an agreement on the question down to the present day.   Then the doctrine of Molina as to contrition and attrition, in accordance with the decrees of the Council of Trent, was examined,[2] after which a return was made to Augustine, in order to discover a contradiction between him and Molina.   In this way question succeeded question, and month after month went by, without any decision being come to.   It seemed as though the principal question was being almost purposely evaded.   The physical predetermination of the Dominicans almost disappeared from the scene during the discussions ; only three congregations concerned themselves with the " scientia media " of Molina, and these were the only ones during the whole of the year 1604 which were of any importance for the true point of the controversy. Then the matter was again allowed to lapse, and on January 4th, 1605, the question of eternal predestination was dealt with. Another congregation was fixed for February 12th, but by then Clement VIII. had already been seized by the malady from which he never recovered.

Each of these congregations lasted for several hours.   At the very first Alvarez and Valencia disputed for a full four hours ; the Avvisi of July 27th, 1602, relate that the dis-

[1] ASTRÁIN, 347 *seq.*
[2] *Ibid.* 348.

putation lasted uninterruptedly for seven hours on end.[1]
After the discussion by the theologians, as at first arranged,
the Cardinals and consultors were at once to pronounce their
judgment upon what had been said. From the eighth
congregation onwards the discussions by the Cardinals and
consultors were separated from the disputation by the
theologians, and transferred to one of the following days.
This explains how it is that the number of the congregations
is differently stated. Of the meetings, 68 took place under
Clement VIII. ; at 37 of these the theologians disputed, while
the Cardinals and consultors deliberated at the others. The
total number of congregations under Clement VIII. and
Paul V. was no less than 85.[2] If the method so far adopted
had been continued, such congregations could have carried
on for years to come without arriving at any conclusion.

That this method was a mistake was pointed out to the Pope
with great frankness by Cardinal Bellarmine. He frequently
told the Pope not to deceive himself, and said that, as he was
not a theologian, he must not suppose that he would be able
by his own studies to penetrate so obscure a question.[3] At
the end of 1601 or at the beginning of 1602, Bellarmine
addressed a letter to Clement VIII.[4] in which he gives him
information about Pelagius, and then implores the Pope to
free the Church from the scandal of the dispute about grace
as soon as possible, to restore unity, and to deprive the

---

[1] *Urb. 1070, Vatican Library.

[2] ASTRÁIN, 344. SCORRAILLE (I., 438) counts 70 congregations
under Clement VIII., 39 for disputations, and 31 for the corresponding deliberations ; under Paul V. he counts 11 disputations
of the theologians and 8 deliberations of the consultors, in all
therefore 89 congregations.

[3] " Ipse tamen N. saepe admonuit Pontificem, ut caveret
fraudem, et non putaret, se studio proprio, cum theologus non
esset, posse ad intelligentiam rei obscurissimae pervenire."
Autobiografia, 465.

[4] Original text in LE BACHELET, Auctarium, 143-147, and
DÖLLINGER, Beiträge, III., 83-87 ; extract in SERRY, 271-273 ;
LÄMMER, Melet., 382.

heretics of the opportunity of rejoicing at the discord among the Catholics. "And if it be lawful for me on a matter of such importance to say what I think as a Cardinal appointed by Your Holiness, and as your faithful servant, then I pray you to consider that the way which had been adopted had been shown to be very long and very fatiguing for Your Holiness." The direct way is not that of secret discussions with a few persons, but that of public discussions, and there would be scandal if a decision were to be made without public discussion. If a public discussion by a synod of bishops, or at any rate by an assembly of the doctors of the various universities, cannot be avoided, it should be summoned before the Pope has read all that he has set himself to read. Previous Popes, in matters of dogmatic decisions, have not relied principally upon their own study of dogmatics, but upon the general conviction of the Church, and especially of the bishops and doctors ; in this way, without personal fatigue, Luther, for example, was condemned by Leo X., and many errors by Paul III., Julius III., and Pius IV. with the assistance of the Council of Trent. The other method, that of personal scientific study, was attempted, for example, by John XXII., but without result, and " Your Holiness is faced by the danger to which Sixtus V. exposed himself and the whole Church when he set himself to correct the Holy Scriptures in accordance with his own views ; I do not know that it ever passed through a greater danger." There were two ways to put an end to the dispute on grace ; either to impose silence on both parties, or to convoke a synod of bishops or of chosen scholars from all the Catholic universities. But above all Bellarmine asked that, until a definite judgment was given, the mouths of those should be closed who went about spreading the rumour that the Pope had already formed his own convictions, that he leaned towards one of the parties, and was ill-disposed towards the other, for otherwise no one would any longer dare to express his own opinion.

For a long time Bellarmine had been held in high esteem by Clement VIII., and when he was made a Cardinal[1] the

[1] ASTRÁIN, 270.

Pope said that the Church had no one to equal him in learning.
As long as the influence of the Jesuit Cardinal lasted, the Pope
was favourable to the doctrine of grace of the Society of Jesus,
which he openly called, when talking with him " Our
opinion "[1]; but not later than April, 1600, when he ordered
the examination of Molina's book, Clement VIII. had become
subject to other influences, and altogether took the side of
the Dominicans. The whole course and result of the congregations on the doctrine of grace show this. The choice
of the subject to be discussed was entirely in accordance
with the wishes of the Dominicans ; the Jesuits, on the
other hand, were forced against their will to defend Molina's
book in all its theses, and never were able to obtain their
desire to see physical predetermination brought under
discussion.

Clement VIII., against the advice of Bellarmine, never made
a secret of his own leanings. The Roman weekly news-sheet
of March 23rd, 1602, says that he declared openly against the
Jesuits ;[2] a few months later it reported that he had openly

----

[1] Autobiografia, 465 : " Sententiam Societatis Papa vocabat
sententiam Nostram."

[2] *Avviso of March 23, 1602 (Urb. 1070, Vatican Library) :
This week the Pope held a congregation of Cardinals and theologians about the controversy on grace " et ci fù gran disbattere et
portare de libri hinc inde, in modo che S.S. risolve tener anco due
altre congregationi, ove vuole che intervenghino anco li cardenali
et prelati del Concilio, e poì sapirla, et già si vede l'inclinatione,
anzi S.S. si lascia intendere apertamente, che và contra Jesuitas,
ma ci è dubbio, che questi veglino et dimandino un Concilio, et
che ci sarà di fare, ma in tanto il P. Monopoli la predica publicamente contro di loro." Bellarmine had actually suggested to
the Pope that the convocation of a council would be the proper
way to decide the controversy (Vol. XXIII., p. 358). There are,
however no proofs of what certain people assert (SERRY, 270 seq.,
and following him, RANKE, Päpste, II.[9], 200), namely that the
Jesuits wished to obtain a council against the will of the Pope,
and that they asked this in order to deny the infallibility of the
Pope. Cf. L. DE. MEYERE, 289.

declared himself against them.[1] The Papal preacher of the Apostolic Palace, Anselmo Marzato of the Capuchin Order, who was one of the consultors at the congregations on the doctrine of grace, openly took the part of the Dominicans against the Jesuits in his conferences ;[2] in January 1603, in the Pope's presence he expressed himself in such a way that the coming condemnation of the Jesuits seemed to be heralded.[3] In July 1602 Clement VIII. distributed large alms to obtain the assistance of God in an important matter, and the decision as to the doctrine of grace seemed to be imminent.[4] When the Pope paid a visit to the Jesuits on February 10th, 1603, he was given a present of some oil from the Indies. He asked whether Extreme Unction should be given with this to the Dominicans or the Jesuits. He then paid a visit to the Friars Preachers, and sent them some food from his own table, in order to show that the Jesuits had not affected him by their Indian oil.[5]

Clement VIII. undoubtedly had the intention of putting an end to the controversy between the two Orders by means of a dogmatic decision, but he was too conscientious to do anything hastily in the matter, and a condemnation of Molina seemed to become more and more impossible. It was reported again and again that the Papal decision was imminent, but those who looked more deeply into the question

[1] *Avviso of July 27, 1602 (Urb. 1070, Vatican Library) : At the congregation of this week seven hours of uninterrupted disputation about Molina " et finalmente S.B. disse che unusquisque abundet in sensu (Rom. xiv. 5), seben per Roma si dice pubblicamente, che habbia dichiarata contra Jesuitas." The *Avviso of August 3 (ibid.) reports : " Si crede secundo dicono tutti che andrà contra li Jesuiti, li quali però si aiutano quanto possono, ma pur si quieteranno, come si sono quietati del decreto fatto, che non si possa confessare per epistolam, come essi tenevano."

[2] *Avvisi of March 9 and 23, 1602, Urb. 1070, Vatican Library.

[3] *Avviso of January 8, 1603, Urb. 1071, ibid.

[4] *Avviso of July 31, 1602, Urb. 1070, ibid.

[5] *Avviso of February 15, 1603, Urb. 1071, ibid.

did not allow themselves to be deceived by such rumours. At the beginning of 1602 Bellarmine had gone so far as to tell the Pope that His Holiness would never give a dogmatic decision on the question, and he had remained fixed in his opinion, in spite of the assurances of the Pope to the contrary.[1] Clement VIII. was not a little disturbed by the apparent obstinacy of the Cardinal, and gave him a severe admonition.[2] But Bellarmine knew well enough what he was saying. Molina in his book had always connected his theses with the traditions of the past ; it was impossible to condemn any of his assertions without at the same time involving a number of other illustrious theologians ; the Dominicans would have to allow their own theologians to be involved if they wished to obtain the condemnation of Molina. Bellarmine had written in this sense to the Spanish Jesuits,[3] and the celebrated Jesuit theologian, Gabriel Vasquez, had spoken to the same effect.[4] The remonstrances of Bellarmine had no other effect than to cause the Pope to appoint him Archbishop of Capua, and thus remove him from Rome.[5]

[1] Autobiografia, 465 : " aperte ille praedixit, a Sanctitate sua quaestionem illam non esse definiendam ; et cum ille replicaret se definiturum, respondit N. : Sanctitas vestra non eam definiet."

[2] Peña, Diarium, in ASTRÁIN, 340.

[3] Bellarmine to Padilla, March 9, 1601, in SCORRAILLE, I., 421.

[4] Vasquez to De Hojeda, Alcalá, June 20, 1601, *ibid*. 421 n.

[5] *Cf.* COUDERC, 341 *seq.* We may also make mention of other motives for the tension between the Pope and the Cardinal. *Ceterum Pontifex suique in arcano infensi Bellarmino censebantur, quod cum Parmensi nuptias, quod amplissiman dotem et pauperum patrimonium inter nuptialia instrumenta distributum improbasset. . . . Aperte ambitionem atque in maritanda tam praeclare pronepte elationem animi improbavit, et crebris principem schedulis exaratis de animae salute commonuerat, Baronii misertus, quod principi a sacris confessionibus, multa reticeret,—nam ita iussum sibi fuisse mihi affirmabat—, quae ad publicam utilitatem deferri oportebat. Horum princeps haud inscius . . . dissimulata in Bellarminum iracundia, Iesuitas acriter agitare, tanto violentior Sixto, quanto honestior premendi species videbatur [in the controversy on grace]. . . . Bellar-*

The view of Bellarmine and of a few others, who were especially well versed in the matter, was not, however, that of the great majority. All Europe was impatiently awaiting the issue of the controversy. Even the Protestants eagerly gave ear to the rumours that were constantly being spread that Molina had already been condemned. Scribani, the rector of the Jesuits, wrote from Antwerp,[1] " I can find no words to describe the expressions of joy with which this news has been received by the heretics of our city. Some of them have gone so far as to congratulate themselves that the view of Calvin as to free will has at last been recognized as true, and that the Papists who were formerly so proud of their unity, now find themselves at issue as to the principal dogmas of faith." Scribani does not hesitate to say that such a condemnation would be a graver blow to the Catholic religion in Flanders than the long and bloody years of the civil wars. The Catholics were living in a state of fear, and were miserably depressed by the rumours which were being spread in Holland, and which would provide an opportunity for a flood of libels against the Catholics at the coming fair.

These rumours, which continued to be spread, were a sore trial to the whole Society of Jesus ; the reputation of their teaching and their schools were bound to suffer grievous injury on their account. The very fact that the Order had had to sacrifice some of its most distinguished scholars for the absolutely sterile work of the congregations on the doctrine of grace, was in itself no small loss. Gregory of Valencia,

minum Capuano archiepiscopatu demulsum specie honoris Urbe amolitus, donec in vivis egit, regredi non est passus. [the dispute on grace], totius Europae academiis in factiones distractis Apostolico Dominicanis aequiore et Iesuitarum opiniones pre- mente. . . . Et cum in arcano odisset, illorum disciplinas atque instituta palam laudare. [In view of the attitude of John XXII. the Jesuits had no doubt as to the issue] nec aliter permissurum Deum credere, ieiuniis et precibus dediti ad averruncandam in se, quamquam occultaretur, in se principis iram. Santorii Annales, Vallicella Library, Rome, K 7 seq., 615 seq.

[1] March 16, 1602, in SCORRAILLE, I., 441.

who was first appointed to defend their cause there, fell
seriously ill after the first eight congregations. His recovery
was awaited for a month, and then he was replaced by
Pedro di Arrubal. Valencia died soon afterwards, on
March 26th, 1603, the victim, it was supposed, of the excessive
work which he had had to undergo during the hottest months
of the summer, with the oppressive feeling that the whole
honour of the Order depended upon him.[1] His successor,
too, Arrubal, was taken ill in June 1603[2] ; after four months
respite in the disputations, his place was taken by Ferdinando
de la Bastida. After the latter had had to carry on the
disputations at three congregations in the fourteen days
between November 10th and 25th, 1603, it was only on
December 1st that he received information of the subject
that he was to defend on December 8th, and poured out his
grievance to the Pope in a letter[3] that was somewhat excited.
In this he said that even if he were able to study uninterruptedly day and night he would not have time to prepare
so difficult a subject, in view of this hasty procedure. Nor
was the hint lacking that the Dominicans wished to wear out
their adversaries and prevent them from preparing themselves
as they should. The Pope should not permit him to lose his
health and his life by such excessive labour.

The Dominicans too replaced the defender of their cause,
immediately after the first congregation, by Tommaso de
Lemos. The reasons for this change are not known ; it is
only known that at the end of the session silence was imposed
under pain of excommunication, and that according to
De Lemos the Jesuits were satisfied with the reuslt of the
disputation. De Lemos, who is described as a man of great
physical robustness, lasted until the end of the congregations,[4]
although, in spite of all remonstrances, these were very long
drawn out.

[1] ASTRÁIN, 345.
[2] Ibid. 348.
[3] Ibid. 351 seq.
[4] Ibid. 337.

The pressure which was brought to bear on the Pope by the Spanish government to hasten the discussions was especially importunate. Philip II. had already addressed himself to Rome for this purpose ; his son, although he knew nothing about the controverted matter, signed, under the pressure of those interested, a whole series of similar letters, both to the Pope and the ambassador in Rome,[1] even before the congregations in the presence of the Pope had been begun. De la Bastida hinted, in the letter already mentioned, that the king was acting under the influence of the Dominicans, but there are also to be found edicts of the king to his ambassador which can only have been inspired by the Jesuits. Thus a royal order to the Duke of Sessa, of June 2nd, 1600, contains a command to present to the Pope, in the king's name, a request that he will first direct the examination to the question of doctrine, and only then examine in the same way, *both* the suspected books, that of Bañes equally with that of Molina.[2] The Duke of Sessa wrote on July 12th, 1601, that so far there had been no talk of the principal point, and that all that had been dealt with was the work of Molina, its correction and its condemnation. According to the assertion of the Dominicans, the whole discussion would come to an end if certain theses of Molina's were condemned ; the Jesuits were defending these theses, but asserted that the controversy which the Pope should decide was not principally concerned with these.[3] Such expressions obviously revealed the point of view of the Jesuits. Duke William of Bavaria and the widow of the Emperor Maximilian II. also intervened on behalf of the Jesuits, but the Pope rather angrily replied : " We are convinced," he wrote to the Duke of Bavaria, " that your intercession can be traced to certain people who would comply better with their office and their duty if they

[1] ASTRÁIN (349 *seq.*) mentions the letters of Philip III. of the year 1600 : Viso February 29, Cercedilla, June 2, Medina del Campo, July 21 ; in the year 1601 the letters of the Duke of Sessa of July 12 and December 3, etc. *Cf.* COUDERC, I., 360 *seq.*

[2] ASTRÁIN, 349.

[3] *Ibid.*

paid attention with humility and submission to the judgment
of the Holy See, instead of seeking for such intercession."[1]
He wrote in the same sense to the Archduchess Maria.[2]

Throughout the whole of this matter Clement VIII.
preserved a holy gravity.   When at the opening of the first
congregation he recited on his knees aloud a prayer to the
Holy Ghost, it was to be seen that he was deeply moved, and
the tears flowed from his eyes.   He celebrated mass before
each congregation, or at any rate received Holy Communion
if his gout did not permit of his doing so.[3]   During the summer
months of 1602, which were oppressively hot, he took part
like the others at the wearisome sessions which lasted for
hours, and not even in the October of that year would he
leave Rome, so as not to be absent from the heated controversy.[4]   He assured the Spanish ambassador, when the
latter urged him to take more care of himself, that he was
working and toiling to the best of his ability, in order to get
to the bottom of the matter.[5]   Some marginal notes and
underlined words in a printed copy of the book of Molina,
preserved at Tortosa, prove that he had at any rate attempted
to make a profound study of the not easily to be understood
work.[6]

[1] In SCORRAILLE, I., 422 seq.

[2] August 20, 1601, in Archiv. f. österr. Gesch., XV. (1856), 233.
The University of Würzburg in a letter of July 7, 1601, to the
Pope regretted the report that certain Catholic theologians were
teaching that physical predetermination to which the will cannot
refuse its consent, and it feared that on account of this assertion
the heretics would become more obstinate in their errors.
(RULAND, Series professorum theologiae Wirceburgensium (1835),
258 seq.   The Duke of Sessa also said on February 28, 1603 (in
COUDERC, I., 362) that the Protestants were exploiting the
controversy against the Jesuits.

[3] SCORRAILLE, I., 431 seq.

[4] *Avviso of October 9, 1602, Urb. 1070, Vatican Library.

[5] Sessa, December 3, 1602, in ASTRÁIN, 350.

[6] Ibid. 354 seq.   For the small copy of Molina, belonging to
Clement VIII., with autograph notes by the Pope, see Razon y Fe,
XXIV. (1909), 183-194.

If in spite of all this he did not succeed in settling the controversy between the two Orders, the fault must be attributed to those about him. Not being himself a theologian, he had to trust to the advice of others, and he was badly advised. Above all, the way which he chose for the solution of the controversy was quite unusual, and never before attempted. Previous Popes had left the judgment on literary works either to the Inquisition or to the Congregation of the Index, and then considered their judgment with full confidence. But now an unheard of thing happened ; a special congregation was appointed of which the Pope held the presidency in person. The disputations were indefinitely protracted, and all to ascertain whether a book contained heretical theses or not. For a thousand years no such unheard of honour had been accorded to any author. Peace between the Dominicans and Jesuits could be restored by the condemnation of Molina, yet the learned and careful theologian could not be convicted of heretical thesis. Certain Jesuits, for example Bellarmine, were not in agreement with Molina as to all his theses, but it is one thing to hold a thesis to be mistaken or inexact, and quite another to hold it to be heretical and deserving of theological censure, and the congregations held in the presence of Clement VIII. finally justified Molina in this respect. Moreover, it was certainly a mistake to suppose that peace would be restored between the two Orders by the condemnation of certain theses of Molina. If this end was to be attained by means of a dogmatic decision, the principal question which was dividing the Order of Preachers and the Society of Jesus would have to be directly dealt with. But this was entirely set aside. The " scientia media " of Molina was only briefly dealt with in comparison with other questions of minor importance ; " physical predetermination " was hardly discussed at all. The dispute turned always on secondary questions, while the burning principal question was entirely neglected. Lastly, it may be asked whether it was fair morally to force the Jesuits to defend Molina and his book ; they always clung firmly to the point of view that the whole Society of Jesus as such could not be held responsible for every thesis of Molina. Nevertheless circumstances had worked together to embitter the quarrel in such a way that a condemnation of Molina would have been looked upon as a defeat of the whole Jesuit Order, and as a proof of its scientific incapacity. The Jesuits therefore, whether they willed or not, had to resolve upon the defence of Molina if only to prevent a mortal blow against themselves. From the beginning the two Orders were not treated on equal terms. The Dominicans were allowed to come forward as the "defenders of the doctrine of grace," and as the accusers, while the Jesuits had to take their place on the bench of the accused; thus the Pope put himself into a position which, after the end of the matter, proved a false one.

"Pope Clement" so judged his successor Paul V., "regretted that he had allowed himself to be engulfed in this business, and that after many years of disputations he could find no way of coming out of it well."[1] It could not have been otherwise, once he had allowed himself to be led into the mistake of making Molina's book the centre of the discussions. It would seem, however, that towards the end of his days, Clement VIII. regarded the opinion of the Jesuits more kindly when there came to Rome Cardinal du Perron, after Bellarmine and Stapleton the greatest controversial theologian against Protestantism, who said to him that all the Calvinists and Lutherans in France and Germany would hold jubilee over the condemnation of the opinion of the Jesuits, and would see in it an acceptance of their own doctrine of free will.[2]

---

[1] "Che Papa Clemente era pentito d'esseri ingolfato in questo negozio, et che dopo molti et molti anni di dispute non trovava il verso d'uscirne bene." SCHNEEMANN, 296; SCORRAILLE, I., 445.

[2] SCORRAILLE, I., 443. Bellarmine says in a reply to a letter of Du Perron of February 10, 1605: Rendo ancora a Dio Benedetto molte grazie, che abbia fatto venire a Roma in tempore della controversia de auxiliis la persona di V. S. Illma perche se bene io più volte ho fatto sapere a N. S. quanto sia vicina al Calvinismo l'opinione della fiscia predeterminatione, e come è

Thus the failure of the Pope in this difficult matter seemed to be inevitable and beyond doubt. In spite of this, from another point of view, Clement is deserving of every admiration. It is impossible not to realize his zeal to free the Church from a troublesome disunion, nor the conscientiousness and perseverance with which he took upon his own shoulders the crushing burden of personal attendance at the congregations, nor the self-control which never suffered him to take any mistaken action of importance against the Jesuits, in spite of his distrust of them, nor his sincere desire to arrive at the truth. If with all this it was not granted him to gather the harvest of his labours, he at anyrate has the credit of having smoothed the way for his successor to a happy solution of the question.

Both the scholars whose controversy had laid such a heavy burden on the head of the Church preceded Clement VIII. to the grave. Bañes died on October 21st, 1604, at Medina del Campo. It is said that a short time before he breathed his last he protested that he believed all that he had written concerning the question of grace as firmly as he believed in the unity and trinity of God, but that he submitted everything to the judgment of the Pope and the Church.[1] If Bañes really said this he has in so doing given a further proof that his undoubtedly great intellect often allowed itself to be guided more by his strong will than by the conviction of proof,

abborita dalla maggior parte delle Università cattoliche, massime da quelle, che stanno a fronte degli eretici : nondimeno la parte contraria ha procurato, che non mi sia data piena fede per essere Gesuita, e per conseguenza interessato. Ma in V. S. Ill. non si può trovare eccezione alcuna essendo noto a tutti, como Lei può giudicare meglio di qualsivoglia altro di questa controversia e non ci ha altro interesse che della verità e fede cattolica : siche Iddio l'ha mandata, acciò le passioni de molti altri e l'emulazione, che hanno colle Gesuiti, non faccia intorbidare la verità in cosa di tanto momento (Laemmer, Meletemata, 382). Du Perron was a " buona lancia " for the Jesuits, wrote later on, on September 7, Canon Gualdo to Peiresc (Prat, Coton V., 243).

[1] SCORRAILLE, I., 445 seq.

since neither Dominican nor Jesuit could place his view on the controversy about grace on the same level as the great truths of faith.

Four years earlier, on October 12th, 1600, there preceded him to the grave the man against whom Bañes had in life carried on a struggle so long, and as the event proved, so unjust. Molina was without doubt one of the most acute minds of his time, a time so rich in great theologians. But with all this he was not one of those who immerse themselves in the world of their own ideas without heeding the course of events around them ; the star which had guided him in his scientific labours was always, in his eyes, the welfare of the Church. Just as his work on grace and liberty aimed at finding a foundation for a solid solution of a difficulty that was then very popular,[1] so the voluminous book to which he devoted the labours of his latter years aimed at providing a solid scientific basis for the decisions of the confessor and the parish priest, dealing in six volumes with the questions of canon law and justice. As they did in learning, so did Bañes and Molina stand at opposite poles in character ; Bañes the head of a school, as it were predestined to gather others round him, to imbue them with his ideas, and fill them with enthusiasm for difficult undertakings ; Molina, working in silence, as a man a picture of non-resistance, as a religious as submissive as a child to his superiors in spite of his great learning, yet a man according to the spirit of Thomas a Kempis, whose Imitation of Christ he read every day. In his last illness he no longer interested himself in scientific questions ; when his superior asked him concerning his still unpublished books he replied that the Society of Jesus might do as it liked with them. His life was filled with disputes and attacks, but he always maintained peace of soul, in the firm conviction that he had truth on his side. A kindly star seemed to shine over his life, for however desperate his cause might have seemed, in the end it turned steadily in his favour.[2]

[1] See *supra*, p. 284.
[2] SCORRAILLE, I., 433 *seqq*.

The controversy between the two Orders did not end with
the death of the two leaders, and the Roman discussions
had on the contrary embittered and indefinitely prolonged
the struggle ; but we must be careful not to attribute this
unhappy result only to the imprudent impetuosity of Bañes.
The struggle between the older and the younger Order took
its origin in the circumstances of the time and was difficult
to avoid.

Throughout their course of action the Jesuits were inspired
by the conviction that a new age had begun, and had brought
with it new requirements, and that it was not enough merely
to follow in all things the ways that had been trodden a
thousand times. Always in contact with tradition, and no
less than the others, mindful of the spirit of the Church,
wherever they saw their opportunity they sought for new
methods, both at home in the exercise of the ministry, and
in the foreign missions, as well as in science. Even though at
times this aim led to misunderstandings, yet their efforts
proved of great advantage to the Church. The result of their
labours in the field of learning was the development of ascetic
and moral theology, of apologetics against Protestantism, a
new manner of treating of the whole field of dogmatics, and
of Christian philosophy in accordance with the exigencies of
the times, together with vast labours on the Holy Scriptures.
But it was inevitable that their whole tendency, and their
attention to the needs of the times, which had been manifested
during the first ten years of their Order, should arouse
suspicion among those who, by the whole of their glorious
past, found themselves bound to the maintenance of those
forms in which they had hitherto moved, and by
means of which they had acquired their reputation in
the Church.

Some of this party watched with anxiety the actions of the
young Order which was springing up so lustily ; its proceedings
seemed to them not to be free from an innovating and anti-
ecclesiastical spirit, and they felt themselves called upon to
apply a barrier. With his incomparable perspicacity Ignatius
of Loyola had foreseen the future development of events in

this respect, exhorting his sons at every opportunity[1] carefully to try and avoid as far as possible all conflict with the friars and monks ; but it was not possible to do so altogether. Not to do so might even be of use to the Church, in that the two tendencies, that which aimed at going forward and that which sought to hold it back, it might be saved by the very struggle from remaining one-sided.

Molina did nothing more than to let loose the storm of indignation which had been gathering for a long time past. It must be admitted that in his new setting forth of the most ancient ideas he did some extraordinary things, and in subsidiary matters went a little too far, even in the opinion of Bellarmine. In his overpowering zeal and in perfect faith, such a man as Bañes might well suppose that the precious inheritance of traditional theology was threatened by him. After the question had been transferred to Rome, probably contrary to the intention or expectation of Bañes, the opposition to Molina—precisely because of the long duration of a struggle which was fought out in the highest places and in sight of all the world—became more and more a point of honour for the whole Order, and the final result was that what had never been so hitherto, as far as can be discovered, was raised to the dignity of a doctrine of the Order.

From what was said at the chapter-general, where the whole Order was officially represented, it is quite clear that not all Dominicans as a whole were animated by sentiments of hostility towards their younger colleague and rival. Immediately after the first flashes of the dispute about grace, when the incitements of an Avendaño were fresh in men's minds, such an assembly was held at Valencia in 1596. The conciliatory attempts which, at the suggestion of Aquaviva, were then undertaken by the Dominicans and Jesuits, were so to say crowned by an express order from the chapter-

---

[1] Ribadeneira in *Monumenta Ignatiana*, Ser. 4, Vol. I., 434. Out of consideration for the Dominicans he would not even have the Immaculate Conception included among the theses to be defended in public. *Ibid.*

general in favour of the Jesuits. This states[1] " We exhort in the Lord all the brethren of our Order to embrace in sincere and fraternal affection all those religious with whom we ought to be striving for the same end, and in particular those who are labouring without ceasing in the midst of others for the defence of the faith and salvation of souls, namely the Fathers of the Society of Jesus, whom with the others we warmly recommend to you. We desire that they should have evidence in your deeds of the affection and charity of your hearts, that you should be at their disposal wherever you can, and that you should not give offence to them in any way, either in word or deed." Those who act in any other way will be punished.

This exhortation was repeated by the chapters-general in Rome in the years 1644 and 1656. In 1644 it was laid down that the Dominicans must show to individual Jesuits and to the whole Society of Jesus " service and devotion, with the greatest kindness and conscientiousness, so that they may find in us the expression of an exquisite charity and a cordial affection. Even though we may not always be in agreement with them in their opinions and ideas, we must nevertheless always be in will of one soul and one heart." The chapter of 1656 asked " that the Jesuits and all others should realize from our hospitality, confidence, cordiality and union that we are disciples of Christ." The General of the Order, Giovanni Battista de Marinis warmly recommended his subjects in a circular of March 25th, 1661, to live in harmony with the Society of Jesus : " We ought on both sides to be one heart and one soul in Our Lord ; we ought both of us to prove this by our rivalry in fervent charity, while our undivided union must proclaim it."[2]

---

[1] Admonitiones n. 4, in Monumenta ordinis fratrum Praedicatorum historica, tom. X. (Acta capitulorum generalium, tom. V.), Rome, 1901, 371.

[2] List of these texts in MAXIMI MANGOLD, Reflexiones in R. P. Alexandri a. s. Ioanne de Cruce Carm. excalc. continuationem historiae ecclesiasticae Claudii Fleurii Abbatis, I., Augsburg, 1783, 449. Cardinal Zigliara, one of the most illustrious

These decrees were responded to, on the part of the Jesuit by decrees of the General of the Order, Vitelleschi, and were repeated by the eight general congregation of the whole Order in 1645. The exhortation of the congregation says :[1] " All our subjects must aim everywhere at speaking, both in private conversations and in public, in favourable terms of the venerable Order of Dominicans in general as well as of its institutions, its eminent learning and its distinguished works ; they must treat its members with such respect and courtesy as to rival one another in mutual hospitality and other manifestations of affection, as is becoming to our humble Society, and as is due to an Order which is greater than ours in antiquity and dignity." The same general congregation later on in 1661, following upon the letter of the General of the Dominicans, De Marinis, renewed and confirmed this exhortation.[2]

modern theologians of the Dominican Order, writes : " Ex sententiis autem, quae libere in contrariam partem agitantur inter catholicos, tene quae magis conformis tibi rationi videtur, sed contra eos, qui a te dissentiunt, cave ab iniuriis, quas sapientia reprobat, caritas detestatur. Sequere thomistas, sequere molinistas, utrimque habes magistros doctissimos et piisssmos et noli amplecti veritatem extra caritatem, nam et ipsa caritas veritas est (Summa philosophica, II.[15], Paris, 1912, 524).

[1] Congr. VIII. decr. 12 (Institutum Societatis Iesu, II., Florence, 1892, 346).

[2] Cong. XI. decr. 19 (*loc. cit.* 381) : " ut illustrissimum natuque maiorem in Ecclesia Ordinem, sanctitate, doctrina rebusque praeclare gestis de illa optime meritum, peculiari benevolentia completantur, de illo magnifice sentiant et loquantur, aliisque venerationis significationibus et charitatis officiis prosequantur."

CHAPTER X.

THE PAPAL STATES.—THE RE-ACQUISITION OF FERRARA.— DEATH OF THE POPE.

THE many anxieties which the Turkish peril and the religious conditions of all the countries of Europe caused Clement VIII. were yet further added to by the conditions in the States of the Church. These were administered by the cardinalitial Congregation of the Consulta, although the Pope also took a direct part in their affairs.[1] Carrying out a project of Sixtus V., Clement VIII., by a bull of October 30th, 1592, set up a special Congregation for the Administration of the States of the Church, composed of three Cardinals.[2] His

---

[1] Cf. PARUTA, Dispacci, I., 288. An Urbino *Avviso of July 24, 1593 (Urb. 1061, Vatican Library) says of the Consulta " La Consulta a Roma è a punto l'Udientia nel nostro Stato." Cf. PARUTA, Relazione, 415 seq. ; DOLFIN, Relazione, 461. Many instances of the care of Clement VIII. for Rome and for the States of the Church are now printed in the valuable publication compiled by the communal administration of Rome : Regesti di bandi, editti, notificazioni e provvedimenti diversi alla città di Roma e dello Stato Pontificio, 2 vols. (beginning with the XIIIth century and going as far as 1605), Rome, 1920-1925.

[2] See Bull., IX., 603 seq. The " Congregazione del Buon governo " was as it were a daughter of the Consulta. Cf. JAC. COHELLI, Comment. in bullam X. Clementis VIII. de bono regimine, Cologne, 1699 ; A. DE VECCHIS, Collectio constitut., chirographum et brevium Rom. Pontif. pro bono regimine universit. ac communit. status ecclesiae., 3 vols., Rome, 1732 seq. ; LE BRET, Statistik, 224 seq., 298 ; MORONI, XVI., 158 seq. ; RICHARD in Rev. d'hist. ecclés., XI., 728 seq. For the benefit of the future historian of the Papal States, I would point out that the Archives of the Congregazione del Buon governo, which have

ordinance for the visitation of each of the provinces, so as to suppress the abuses in the administration of the communes, may also be traced back to Sixtus V.[1]

Like the rest of Italy, the territories of the Holy See had since 1590 repeatedly suffered from bad or quite insufficient harvests. The scarcity of bread brought in its train a crushing increase in the cost of all other necessities. Even though this calamity was not so great in the Papal States, and above all in Rome, as in the other cities of the peninsula, it was nevertheless felt there all the more severely in that much better conditions had prevailed there before.[2]

All the reports agree in saying that Clement VIII. did all he could in the first years of his pontificate to overcome this scarcity, especially in Rome.[3] The superintendence of the trade in food left nothing to be desired, but the scarcity was universal, bad methods of provisioning were deep-rooted, while very often the officials were untrustworthy and un-businesslike.[4] The Pope was unable, as Paruta points out,

not as yet been used by anyone, were in the Vatican, and occupied no less than 16 rooms. The acta, however, only begin about the year 1630 ; the earlier ones are to be found in the Papal Secret Archives. This state of affairs was changed in 1918 ; Cardinal Gasquet, with the consent of Pope Benedict XV., who interested himself greatly in what concerned the archives, agreed to an exchange with the Italian government, as a result of which a small part of the acta of the Camera in the State Archives of Rome passed into the Papal Secret Archives, to which they obviously belonged, while the archives of the Buon governo were handed over to the State Archives, Rome. There they were re-arranged. *Cf.* the fully explanatory articles by A. LODOLINI, L'amministrazione pontificia del Buon governo, in the periodical *Gli archivi Ital.*, VI. (Rome, 1919), 181 *seqq.*, VII. (1920), 3 *seq.*, 88.

[1] *Cf.* LODOLINI, *loc. cit.*, VI., 214.

[2] See PARUTA, Relazione, 388 *seq.*

[3] See *ibid.* 389, the Avvisi in BAUMGARTEN, Neue Kunde, 23, and the *Avvisi of July 8 and 15, 1592 (Urb. 1060, II.) and of March 20, 1593 (Urb. 1061) Vatican Library.

[4] See PARUTA, Dispacci, II., 388, and Relazione, 389. *Cf.* *Avviso of July 28, 1593, Urb. 1061, *loc. cit.*

to keep in touch with all the details,[1] but he sought in this respect to do all he could, and even, in April, 1593, had a report made to him by his nephew whether the city was sufficiently supplied with bread.[2]   He laboured indefatigably to secure the importation of grain from outside,[3] although he met with great difficulties in this, as some of the provinces, as for example the fertile Romagna, were suffering from bad harvests.[4]

That the scarcity was general is shown by the fact that even the city of Bologna, which on account of its richness was named *la grassa*, was, from 1590 to 1592, the victim of serious scarcity,[5] and the number of the inhabitants fell from 90,000 to 70,000.[6]   Clement VIII. lent the city 80,000 scudi.[7]   The legation of Bologna, from October 16th, 1592, onwards, was in the hands of Cardinal Montalto.[8]   This office brought him a fixed revenue of 6000 scudi,[9] but he resided in Rome.[10]   The vice-legate or governor acted as his representative.   The latter had but little influence in the administration because

[1] See PARUTA, Relazione, 389 ; the *Avvisi frequently refer to the steps taken by Clement VIII. against bad officials : e.g. June 28 and August 4, 1593, Urb. 1061, *loc. cit.*

[2] *" Ogni sera viene dato al Papa dalli suoi nepoti minuto ragguaglio del pane che si fa per tutta Roma, della quale se ne trova hora abbondate per ciascuno." Avviso of April 10, 1593, Urb. 1061, Vatican Library.

[3] *Cf.* *Avvisi of July 8 and 15, 1592, Urb. 1060, II., *loc. cit.* ; PARUTA, Dispacci, I., 28, 49, 192, 243.   For the importation of grain from the Low Countries to Civitavecchia, 1593-1594, see MAERE in *An. de l'Acad. Archéol. de la Belgique*, 5th ser. VIII.

[4] See PARUTA, Dispacci, II., 81.

[5] *Cf.* Bull. IX., 553.

[6] See the Informazioni di Bologna in RANKE, III.[8], 107.*

[7] See Bull. IX., 553.

[8] See *Acta consist. card. S. Severinae, Cod. Barb. lat. 2871, Vatican Library.

[9] See the Informazioni di Bologna of 1595 by Guglielmo di Montolon, Cod. D. 181 n. 8, Ambrosinian Library, Milan.

[10] See DOLFIN, Relazione, 460.

the city was very independent.[1] In an instruction of the
year 1595 it is stated that the Bolognesi must be inspired
with respect, and at the same time with loyalty ; the
first will be attained if the representative of the Papal
authority devotes himself seriously to the administration
of justice and the importation of food ; devotion will best
be inspired by impartiality and the protection of good
citizens.[2]

In the Marches and the Romagna as well there had been a
decrease in the population in consequence of the epidemics
of 1590. A crushing state of misery was on the increase
among the survivors, because the officials exacted the taxes
with the utmost rigour. In these provinces, which in the
past had seemed to be veritable granaries, there was now an
alarming decrease in production.[3] In Umbria too there was
a scarcity of food, so that there as well as in the Marches
special ordinances had to be issued in order to meet the
emergency.[4]

The scarcity in Rome continued even in those years when
the harvest was good. The Pope was rightly incensed that
when the situation had improved, the people did not reap
the advantage.[5] The fault was partly due to the officials
of the Camera, and partly to the speculators, whose greed it
was sought to curb by special legislation.[6]

The Pope's intentions were always good, as is pointed out

[1] See RANKE, III.[8], 107.*

[2] *Instructions for a new legate at Bologna, Cod. G. 63 n. 9,
Vallicella Library, Rome.

[3] See PARUTA, Relazione, 389 ; BROSCH, I., 307.

[4] Cf. *Bando per l'Abbondanza dell'Umbria e della Marca of
September, 1596, Editti, V.. 49, p. 195, Papal Secret Archives.
Le Istruzioni segrete pel governo di Perugia ed Umbria in the
Bollet. per l'Umbria, XXI. (1915), 375 seq., shows how the Papal
government endeavoured to do away with abuses, and what care
it had for its subjects.

[5] See *Avvisi of July 14, 28 and 31, 1593, Urb. 1061, Vatican
Library ; PARUTA, Dispacci, II., 372, and Relazione, 389.

[6] See BENIGNI, Getreidpolitik, 44.

in a report from Rome of October 3rd, 1594 :[1] if in spite of
this he met with but little success, the reason was to be found
in the extraordinary state of affairs prevailing in the Papal
States. The independence of the barons and of the communes
created such an opposition to the central government that
not even so energetic a Pope as Sixtus V. had been able to
subdue it except for a short time.[2] The conditions in the
Roman Campagna, from which very little grain reached the
Eternal City, were especially unfortunate for Rome. Agriculture there had not entirely disappeared, but the greed for
gain on the part of the farmers, together with a type of
cultivation that was without a permanent body of tenants,
caused the arable land to pass more and more to pasturage.[3]

Clement VIII., like his predecessors, sought to provide for
the provisioning of Rome by strict vigilance, and by a rigorous
prohibition of exportation. A constitution of September 13th,
1597, forbade exportation of any kind, without special
permission from the Camera or the Annonaria[4] ; it also forbade
the hoarding of grain in private stores, and preventing its
free passage to Rome. In this document the Pope bitterly
censures the tricks of the speculators who, with abominable
usury, forced up the price of grain. He threatened the
barons and other landlords who hoarded grain, and forbade
them to keep more than a sufficient quantity for their own
domestic use for a year.[5]

[1] See *Avviso of October 5, 1594, which adds that the Pope
" quasi vorrebbe potersi transformare in forma del grano istesso
per fare abondanza," Urb. 1062, Vatican Library.

[2] Opinion of H. Sieveking in J. WOLFS, Zeitschrift f. Sozial-
wissenschaft, II., Berlin, 1899, 470.

[3] See PARUTA, Relazione, 389 seq. A more favourable picture
of the conditions in the Campagna is given in *Nota della entrata
di molti signori e duchi Romani, from which RANKE (III.[8], 109)
cites certain passages, without, however, saying where he found
this report. I have searched in vain for it in the Roman libraries.

[4] For the annona see also REUMONT, III., 2, 648 seq.

[5] See Bull. X., 373 seq. ; BENIGNI, Getreidpolitik, 45 ; CUPIS,
211 seq.

The Pope showed himself the sworn enemy of speculators in grain in his constitution of December 4th, 1604, which confirmed the celebrated bull of Sixtus IV. of March 1st, 1476, and the similar ordinances of Julius II., Clement VII. and Pius V.[1] for the development of agriculture in the Campagna. In this constitution he allowed the free exportation of a quarter of the harvest, provided that the price of grain in the Roman market was not more than 60 giulii a rubbio ; he allowed the vassals of the barons to cultivate other land than that belonging to their feudal lords, and also decided that priests might devote themselves to agriculture without its being considered a profane trade. He also made provision to supply the lack of tillage oxen.[2] The subsidy for carrying on the work of draining the Pontine Marshes was also aimed at increasing the cultivation of grain.[3]

Measures of this kind could only effect an improvement in course of time, so that in the meanwhile the conditions remained as little satisfactory as before.[4] The opposition

---

[1] Cf. Vol. IV., of this work, p. 426 ; Vol. VI., p. 227 ; Vol. X., p. 14 ; Vol. XVII., p. 109.

[2] See Bull. X., 622 seq. ; BENIGNI, 46 ; CUPIS, 215 seq. *Privilegia pro agricultoribus Corneti, Civitatis Vetulae, Tulphae et Bledae, dated February 9, 1601, in Editti, V., 49, p. 31, Papal Secret Archives. Cf. TOMASSETTI, I., 170.

[3] See NICOLAI, De' bonificamenti delle Terre Pontine, Rome, 1800, 140 seq. ; BENIGNI, 46.

[4] When the Pope set out with many Cardinals for Ferrara, the price of bread rose in Rome ; see the *report of Fr. Maria Vialardo, Rome, April 25, 1598, Gonzaga Archives, Mantua. The inundation of the Tiber at the end of 1598 had destroyed many stores of grain, so that there was a considerable scarcity ; see POSSEVINO, Gonzaga, 824 seq. In 1598 there was also a failure in the importation of wine ; see BAUMGARTEN, Neue Kunde, 24. The year of jubilee in 1600 naturally involved special requirements. Clement VIII. had to apply on January 16, 1600, to the viceroy of Naples, with a request for immediate permission to export grain to Rome ; " *Roma annonae inopia laborat, Roma petit " (Brevia Arm. 44, t. 45, n. 10, Papal Secret Archives) ; on December 15, 1600, a similar request was again sent (ibid. n. 428).

which the well intentioned zeal of the Pope had to cope with proved too strong. How difficult the task was has been shown by the fact that in modern times not even the state of United Italy, armed with far greater powers and means, has been able to overcome the opposition of the farmers to the cultivation of the Campagna, or meet with any better success in carrying on the efforts of the Popes.[1]

The discontent of the people at these economic disadvantages found vent towards the end of the pontificate of Clement VIII. in biting pasquinades.[2] The authors of such libels overlooked the fact that it was not the government alone that was to blame ; nor did they bear in mind that the imposts in the Papal States were on the whole very moderate, compared, not only with those parts of Italy which were subject to Spanish rule, but also with the majority of the small independent states.[3] Clement VIII. fought as much as he could against any increase in the burden of taxes,[4] and it was absolutely against his will if the subordinate officials in the Marches and the Romagna confiscated the

Cf. supra, p. 269. The Cardinals charged with the task of provisioning fulfilled their task so badly that there was a great scarcity in the summer, so that Clement VIII. intended to return once more with his court to Ferrara, in order to relieve Rome, but this did not take place as the Pope was deceived as to the real state of affairs ; see the information in BAUMGARTEN, *loc. cit.*, 21 *seq.* In 1599 Baronius called the attention of the Pope to the true state of affairs, after which Clement VIII. did not fail to express his displeasure to P. Aldobrandini. The nephew then complained to Baronius, but received from him a dignified reply which is given in CALENZIO, Baronio, 352. The scarcity of grain was very great again in 1603 ; see *briefs to the viceroy of Naples, February 12 and May 22, 1603, Arm. 44, t. 47, n. 9 and 137, Papal Secret Archives. *Cf.* the *letters of Cardinal Aldobrandini to the nuncio in Spain, January 13, April 8, June 18, September 28, November 7, 1603, Aldobrandini Archives, Rome, t. 287.

[1] Opinion of SIEVEKING, *loc. cit.*

[2] See *Avviso of January 19, 1602, Urb. 1070, Vatican Library.

[3] See PARUTA, Relazione, 389 ; REUMONT, III., 2, 597.

[4] See *Avviso of March 10, 1599, Urb. 1067, *loc. cit.*

agricultural implements and cattle of the peasants who could not pay. As a result of such tyranny some emigrated, while others gave themselves over to brigandage.[1] The crimes of such delinquents embittered for Clement VIII. the first lustrum of his pontificate.

Brigandage had already raised its head once more at the end of the reign of Sixtus V.[2] During the pontificates of Urban VII., Gregory XIV. and Innocent IX., which had followed each other at short intervals, this plague had been able to continue and spread.[3] Clement VIII., who in Rome was the rigorous champion of peace and order,[4] determined that it must be faced energetically. As early as February, 1592, he sent troops under the supreme command of Flaminio Delfino to the Marches, where Marco Sciarra, one of the most terrible brigand chiefs, was carrying on his crimes.[5] In March bands of brigands pillaged the nearer and more distant environs of Rome, and in April they burned the castle of Subiaco.[6] Terrible stories were told of the cruelty of these

---

[1] See PARUTA, Relazione, 389 seq. ; BROSCH, I., 307 seq.

[2] Cf. Vol. XXI. of this work, p. 88.

[3] Cf. ibid. pp. 359, 366.

[4] Cf. besides the report in Arch. stor, Ital., XII., xxi., and the report of Niccolini in NAVENNE, Rome et le Palais Farnèse, I., 7, the *letter of Giulio del Carretto, February 8, 1592 : N. S. si dimostra rigoroso nella giustizia et non ha voluto far gratia ad un gentilhomo Romano, che fu trovato con l'archibuggietto da rota in sede vacante, ancorche ne sii stato pregato da molti cardinali, dall' ambasciatore di Savoia suo parente et dal popolo Romano, al quale ultimamente disse che l'iscuse che proponevano a lui le proponessero alli giudici della causa che l'havrebbero in quella consideratione che si dovrebbe per giustizia. Gonzaga Archives, Mantua.

[5] See *Avviso of February 12, 1592, Urb. 1060, I., Vatican Library. For the plans for fighting the bandits see Arch. della Soc. Rom., XXXVI., 125, n. 1.

[6] See *Avvisi of March 11 and April 18, 1592, Urb. 1060, I., Vatican Library. Cf. KARTTUNEN, Grégoire XIII., Helsinki, 1911 92.

hordes,[1] and the Pope, who was deeply distressed, insisted upon energetic intervention.[2] He sent against them his nephew Aldobrandini with about 2000 men, and had previously enrolled 600 Corsican soldiers in his service,[3] who, however, pillaged almost more than the bandits.[4]

Marco Sciarra had entrenched himself with 500 bandits in a convent near Ascoli, but as soon as Papal troops under the command of Flaminio Delfino were sent to the rescue, he succeeded, through the intervention of Count Pietro Gabuzio, who was enlisting soldiers for the Venetian Republic against the rapacious Uscocchi, in getting himself taken, together with the flower of his band, into the service of the republic. Clement VIII. asked for the ruffians to be handed over, but in vain. In this refusal he saw a contempt for his authority, and was all the more offended at the action of the Republic in that Gabuzio had been born a Papal subject, and that the Venetians had already on other occasions permitted themselves innumerable usurpations of ecclesiastical authority.[5] In order to pacify the Pope, in June, 1592, there

[1] See the report of the Urbino envoy, April 11, 1592, Urb. 1060, I., 196, Vatican Library. Monsignor Schiaffinato at Perugia, replied with like cruelties to the cruelties of the bandits ; see *Arch. stor. ital.*, 3rd ser., VIII., 35.

[2] " Si consuma et afflige per provedervi," says an *Avviso of March 14, 1592 (Urb. 1060, I., *loc. cit.*). Another of *April 8, 1592 (*ibid.*) says : " Gran travaglio prende N. S. de banditi di questo Stato, et lo mostra a più segni et nel viso, vedendosi spesso immerso in profondissimo pensiero et ansieta, che l'occupi talvolta l'animo e con ragione."

[3] See the *report of G. del Carretto, March 28, 1592, Gonzaga Archives, Mantua. According to the *Avviso of April 22, 1592, Gian Francesco Aldobrandini set out against the bandits with 1500 soldiers and 300 horsemen, as well as some Albanians and Corsicans. The delay was because the Pope wished first to ascertain that all the neighbouring princes were keeping a good watch on their frontiers (Urb. 1060, I., *loc. cit.*). *Cf.* also the Relazione dell'inviato di Lucca in *Studi et docum.*, XXII., 201.

[4] See the dispatch of Donato in BROSCH, I., 309 n. 1.

[5] *Cf.* A. ROSSI in *Arch. Veneto*, XXXVII., 2 (1889), 259 *seq.*

was once more sent to Rome Leonardo Donato, who had just returned from the embassy which had been sent to congratulate the new head of the Church.[1] We learn from the account of his journey that organized bands of assassins were rendering the country round Spoleto, Terni and Ostia insecure.[2] The diplomatic skill of Donato was unable at the time to allay the Pope's displeasure, and the incident was only closed when, on April 3rd, 1593, Marco Sciarra was killed, and his companions sent to Candia, where some died of the plague, and the others were dispersed.[3] Gian Francesco Aldobrandini then moved against the remainder of the bandits, who had taken refuge in the mountains near Ascoli.[4]

It was only then that a certain degree of peace was restored in the States of the Church, but it is impossible to speak of a disappearance of the bandits. Just as during the spring of 1593 they appeared in the Romagna[5] and the Abruzzi, so did they in the neighbourhood of Rome in July,[6] and in October near Viterbo.[7] In the summer of 1594 they again appeared in large numbers, especially near Velletri.[8] The Venetian ambassador, Poalo Paruta, wrote in 1595 that no one was safe from the bandits. According to trustworthy information the number of outlaws inscribed in the public lists was 15,000 which meant a considerable diminution in the population of the state. The rigour of justice, Paruta con-

---

[1] See Viaggio da Venezia a Roma di L. Donato ambasc. straord. d. Repub. Veneta al papa Clemente VIII. l'a 1592, Venice, 1866.

[2] See *ibid.*

[3] See PARUTA, Dispacci, I., xlv. *seq.*

[4] See *ibid.* 184. The action of Clement VIII. against the bandits is also treated of in the letter of November 1592, in *Veress, Matric. et Acta Hung. in univ. Ital. student.*, I., Budapest, 1915, 246.

[5] See *Avviso of March 10, 1593, Urb. 1061, *loc. cit.*

[6] See PARUTA, Dispacci, I., 101, 106, 110 *seq.*, 133.

[7] See *ibid.* II., 62.

[8] See *Avviso of July 6, 1594, Urb. 1062, *loc. cit.* For the plans of that time for combatting the scourge of the bandits see ORBAAN, Documenti, 462 n.

tinues, is very great, and accomplices and abettors are being put to death. Those days are rare when there are not to be seen at the Bridge of St. Angelo the bodies and heads of those who have been executed, sometimes, four, six, ten, twenty, or even thirty. The number of those executed, from the time of Sixtus V. until now, is estimated at about 5000. But this extreme severity has been of no use, and has rather made things worse. If one is captured, others immediately take to the woods, because they recognize their accomplices. The mountainous districts on the Neapolitan frontier were especially affected, and the opinion was commonly held in Rome, as Paruta reports on July 29th, 1595, that the Spanish government was encouraging this disorder so as to bring pressure to bear on the Pope.[1]

An improvement in the situation depended above all upon a change in this state of affairs, and on the fulfilment of the duties of neighbourliness, a thing which applied also to the Florentine government. This was brought about later on, but by no means completely.[2]

---

[1] See PARUTA, Relazione, 392 *seq.*, and Dispacci, III., 235 (*cf.* 323). See also *Arch. stor. Ital.*, IX., 460. Many dangerous elements were removed from the States of the Church from 1595 onwards, with the departure of the soldiers for the Turkish war. In the army that was enrolled at the end of 1597 against Cesare d'Este there served " banditi ed altri contumaci " who were therefore pardoned. See the *Editto of June 8, 1598, in *Editti*, V., 57, p. 68, Papal Secret Archives. *Ibid.* 152 *seq.* some *" Bandi contra banditi " of 1597-1604.

[2] *Cf.* ADEMOLLO, Il brigantaggio e la corte di Roma, in *Nuova Antologia*, 2nd. ser., XXIV. (1880), 455 *seq.*, where there are further particulars of the harmful influence of the ecclesiastical right of sanctuary, which was rightly restricted by Sixtus V., and again extended by Gregory XIV., of which the bandits took advantage. *Cf.* also *Arch. stor. ital.*, IX., 460 *seq.* An *Avviso of May 11, 1596, testifies to the good effect of the edicts against the bandits, whose heads were exposed before the Castle of St. Angelo (Urb. 1064, Vatican Library). *Cf.* *Avviso of September 17, 1597 (Urb. 1065, *ibid.*) and Lettres D'OSSAT, I., 452. An

The principal reason why it was not possible to come to grips with this terrible scourge, besides the equivocal behaviour of the Pope's neighbours, lay in the military weakness of the Papal States.[1] There the army had always been neglected. The only exception had been that warlike Pope, Julius II. This was the natural consequence of the office and position of the head of the Church, while Clement VIII. lacked all knowledge of or inclination for military matters. In the whole of the States of the Church there was not a single fortress of importance, and only the citadels of Civitavecchia and Ancona were to a certain extent sufficiently armed. At Perugia there was a small garrison, and at Bologna a hundred Swiss and fifty cavalry. Places which, by their natural position, were well suited for fortresses, such as Orvieto, Civita Castellana and Spoleto, were so neglected that the Venetian ambassador could never sufficiently express his surprise. Not even Rome could be said to be adequately defended ; the fortifications had never been completed, and even the Castle of St. Angelo, the one safe refuge in case of danger, had not got the necessary armament. When in the autumn of 1592 the Huguenot Lesdiguières crossed the Alps to avenge himself on the Duke of Savoy with 4000 men, Rome trembled. Later on, after the reconciliation with Henry IV., it was felt that the Spaniards were even more to be feared, since the bandits were most numerous in the mountains on the Neapolitan frontier.[2]

The States of the Church were entirely without a paid and organized army. The soldiery on paper consisted of 30,000

*Avviso of April 1, 1598 (Urb. 1066 *loc. cit.*) also speaks of the executions of bandits. After this there is little mention of the bandits ; in September 1604 more troops were enlisted ; see *Avviso of September 29, 1604 (Urb. 1072, *loc. cit.*), and the *report of Giov. Batt. Thesis, October 23, 1604, Gonzaga Archives, Mantua.

[1] In this way large sums were spent on small engagements " instead of combatting the evil by means of a well thought out and vigorous procedure." BAUMGARTEN, Neue Kunde, 14.

[2] See PARUTA, Relazione, 384 *seq.*

men ; each province had a colonel, and under him captains and lower officers. But as only the colonels had a fixed pay, it is easy to imagine the condition of the troops. A paid army was only called into existence from time to time, when it was a case of facing the bandits or fighting the Turks ; in 1595 the whole of the cavalry of the Papal States was employed for this purpose, so that there only remained the Swiss Guard, 200 strong, and 1000 Corsican soldiers, afterwards reduced to 800. But these were only intended to fight against the bandits, so that it was impossible to speak of any real armed force. Even the captains of any experience were only enlisted for a period, according to necessity. The office of General of the Church, which was well paid, and held by Gian Francesco Aldobrandini, had become a mere post of honour. The fleet, too, of which Pius V. and later on Sixtus V. had taken such care, was in a state of decadence. Except the arsenal at Civitavecchia, there was no other in the Papal states. From a false economy Clement VIII. would gladly have suspended the payments for the six galleys, which had remained in that harbour since the time of Sixtus V., and it was only the necessity of protecting the coasts against the Turkish pirates which determined him to maintain them.[1]

Although the States of the Church were spared the regular cost of paid troops, such as burdened the finances of other states, the Papal finances were nevertheless in a deplorable condition, because of the enormous burden of debt, of twelve million scudi, which Clement VIII. found at the beginning of his pontificate. Of the total annual revenue, amounting to about a million and a half, more than a million scudi, that is two-thirds of the income, went to pay the interest on the debts in the offices and "luoghi di Monte."[2] With a net

---

[1] *Ibid.* 403 *seq.* *Cf.* DOLFIN, 466.

[2] See the summary of the Papal finances for 1592 which RANKE (III.[8], 98) has made use of from the manuscript in the Barberini Library. Bart. Cesi was still treasurer (see *Carte Strozz.*, II., 212) ; when he became a Cardinal he was succeeded by Tiberio Cerasa (*cf.* MORONI, LXXIV., 298), who died in 1601 (for this benefactor of the Hospital of S. Maria della Consolazione see the monograph

income of half a million, the expenses had to be met, which
were estimated at 400,000 scudi, so that there remained over
only a very small sum.[1] In these circumstances the very
greatest economy was necessary, but this was absolutely
wanting. Clement VIII. was one of those men who have
no idea of the value of money, and the expenses of the administration of the palace,[2] the pageants, the building works and
the endowment of his nephews,[3] devoured great sums of
money. To these were added the exorbitant and manifold
demands of the Christian princes.

Clement VIII. was not the man to provide the money for
such extraordinary necessities. It was proposed to meet
the difficulty by encroaching upon the treasure deposited
in the Castle of St. Angelo by Sixtus V., which still amounted
to two and a half millions, but the Pope was adverse to any
such step.[4] In order to comply with the enormous demands,
which were especially in connexion with the support of the
war against the Turks, there remained no other course, besides
the imposition of tenths upon the Italian clergy, than that
taken by previous Popes, namely the raising of new state loans
upon the revenues, or the so-called " luoghi di Monte."
Clement VIII. found himself compelled, in order to meet the
extraordinary needs, caused especially by the war against the
Turks, to undertake, in seven new " luoghi di Monte " a debt
to the amount of 2,893,200 scudi.[5] From an estimate of the

on that institution by PERICOLI, p. 102, 120 *seq.*). The successor
of Cerasa was Laudovisio Zacchia ; see MORONI, *loc. cit.*,
MARTINORI, 6.

[1] *Cf.* PARUTA, Relazione, 408 *seq.*

[2] *Cf.* BAUMGARTEN, Neue Kunde, 14, 30 *seq.* *Ibid.* 32, concerning the new and costly tiara. An *Avviso of November 1,
1601, Urb. 1069, Vatican Library, tells of a reduction of some
expenditure on the Pope's table.

[3] *Cf.* Vol. XXIII. of this work, pp. 48, 53.

[4] See PARUTA, Relazione, 410. *Cf.* RICCI, II., 164. The
confirmation of the bull of the treasure of Sixtus V., dated
February 14, 1592, in Bull., X., 523 *seq.*

[5] *Cf.* MORONI, XL., 155, LXXIV., 299, and MARTINORI, 5.
For the acquisition of Nettuno, for which Marcantonio Colonna

year 1598 it would appear that the interest on the debt then amounted to three-quarters of the total revenue.[1] The net revenue, towards the end of the pontificate, fell from 500,000 scudi to 343,473. As the annual expenditure was 450,126 scudi, there was an annual deficit of 106,653 scudi.[2]

The expenditure of the Pope, besides the war against the Turks, had been increased in a special degree in 1598 by the acquisition of Ferrara, and by the visit paid to this new territory of the States of the Church, for which, however, 150,000 scudi were taken from the treasure in the Castle of St. Angelo.[3]

The Venetian ambassador, Paolo Paruta, in giving his opinion in 1595 as to the strength and weakness of the States of the Church, says that they were not preserved either by a good constitution, or by the conditions which usually confer permanence and security on other states, but rather by the fact that no one wished or dared to do anything to their injury. " Above all " Paruta explains, " this is helped by the majesty of the person of the Pope, and by respect for religion : motives which have saved this State when in great danger. There is another circumstance which contributes, namely that there are many petty princes in Italy, who, since they cannot aggrandize themselves, are desirous that the neighbouring states should as far as possible maintain a balance between each other. And since to be a protector of the Church confers a certain dignity, each one refrains from attacking the Papal State, fearing to find all the others against

received 400,000 scudi, and of Monte S. Giovanni, for which the Marchese del Vasto had 350,000 scudi, *cf.* COPPI, Sulle finanze della stato pontificio, Rome, 1855, 14 *seq*. Clement VIII, justified the acquisition of S. Giovanni by the danger of the bandits ; see *Acta consist. June 12, 1595, Cod. Barb. 2871, Vatican Library. *Cf.* PARUTA, Dispacci, III., 171 *seq*.

[1] See DOLFIN, Relazione, 464 ; RANKE, *loc. cit.* The complaints of the scarcity of money (*e.g.* in the instructions to D. Ginnasio, August 22, 1601, Barb. 5852, Vatican Library) were therefore justified.

[2] See RANKE, *loc. cit.*

[3] See DOLFIN, Relazione, 465.

him. If, however, any great change should take place in
Italy, then the States of the Church, with all their elements of
disorder, would run no little danger. May it not be that
any advance made by the French in Savoy and Piedmont
has had its echo in Rome, and aroused and encouraged
thoughts of rebellion, which might be of even greater importance to the Holy See than to the other states ? "[1]

In his report, Paruta also mentions the question of the
succession to the fiefs of Urbino and Ferrara, which was
imminent owing to the likelihood of the extinction of the two
reigning families. " Urbino " Paruta thought, " will certainly once again come under the direct government of the
Church, but in the case of Ferrara this will be very difficult,
and certainly will not be done without a great struggle."[2]
In spite of this, to the amazement of everybody, this question
was solved by the skill and energy of the Aldobrandini Pope
with a " surprising facility."[3]

After the election of Clement VIII., all hopes entertained
by Duke Alfonso II. of Ferrara of obtaining from the new
Pope, whose father had once been cordially welcomed at the
court of the Este, what he had once tried to obtain from
Gregory XIV., were bound to vanish : this was to obtain
for his cousin Cesare the fief of Ferrara,[4] but even while he
was still a Cardinal, Clement VIII. had come to the conclusion
that such a step was illegal.[5]   Immediately at the beginning
of his pontificate he confirmed the bull of Pius V.,[6] which
excluded illegitimate branches from succession to Papal fiefs.[7]
The cardinalitial congregation[8] which was appointed for

---

[1] PARUTA, Relazione, 397.

[2] *Ibid.* 401.

[3] BROSCH, I., 314.

[4] *Cf.* Vol. XXII. of this work, p. 380 *seq.*

[5] *Cf.* RICCI, II., 183.

[6] See the Este report in RICCI, II., 84, 231.

[7] Bull. IX., 520 *seq.*

[8] See *Acta consist. April 22, 1592, Cod. Barb. lat. 2871,
Vatican Library. *Cf.* *Avviso of April 25, 1592, Urb. 1060, I.,
ibid. RICCI, II., 85 *seqq.*

further deliberation, was for the most part opposed to the declaration of Gregory XIV., which had still left Alfonso with some hopes.[1]

In spite of this Alfonso and Cesare, who made the *obedientia* to the Pope in the duke's name on May 18th, 1592,[2] hoped to attain their end all the more easily as the Emperor Rudolph II., who was in need of money for the Turkish war, granted in return for a repayment of 300,000 scudi, a renewal of the fiefs of Modena and Reggio, and the right of the duke to nominate his successor within a certain period (August 8th, 1594). While Alfonso's envoy was employing every means in his power in Rome to induce the Pope to change his mind, on July 17th, 1595, the old duke wrote his will, appointing Cesare d'Este as his successor.[3] But this information was conveyed to Rudolph II. so secretly that not even Cesare knew of the honour that had been done him.[4] It is evident that Alfonso did not wish the court to turn to the star that was rising on the horizon, and it was only in October, 1597, when the duke fell mortally ill, that Cesare was informed that he was the heir. The dying man said that he was leaving him a most beautiful state, and one that was strong, both by its military power,

---

[1] See *Acta consist, June 26, 1592, *loc. cit.* Cf. CAPILUPI, ed. Prinzivalli, 65 ; RICCI, II., 150.

[2] See FRIZZI, IV., 440 *seq.* ; RICCI, II., 87 *seq.*, 147 *seq.* Cf. Jo. Franc. Terzanius, Ad S.D.N. Clementem VIII. P. oratio habita cum eidem nomine Alphonsi II. Est. ducis, obedientiam praestaret ill. et ex. Caesar Estensis Marchio Monticuli et eiusdem ducis patruelis, Rome, 1592 (copy in the Aldobrandini Archives, Rome).

[3] See FRIZZI, IV., 44. Cf. RICCI, II., 96 *seq.*

[4] See the " Relatione di quello che è successo in Ferrara dopo la morte del duca Alfonso fino al possesso preso dal signor cardinal Aldobrandini con alcuni altri particolari spettanti a tale stato e ducato," Barb. lat. 5259, p. 80 *seq.*, Vatican Library (the relative passage in RANKE, II.[8], 177). The author of the report is " Domenico Rainaldi, mandato da Clemente VIII. a Ferrara al cardinale Aldobrandini," see Vat. 6196, p. 289, Vatican Library.

and by reason of the allies, both within and without Italy, upon whom he could count with certainty.[1]

Duke Alfonso, down to the year 1597, had made use of every expedient to obtain from the Pope the investiture of Cesare, but Clement VIII., convinced in his conscience that he could not grant it, had remained immovable.[2] In spite of this, after the death of the duke, which took place on October 27th, 1597, Cesare assumed the government, not only of the Imperial fiefs of Modena and Reggio, but also, contrary to all right, of the fiefs of Ferrara and Comacchio. The Bishop of Ferrara, Giovanni Fontana, was forcibly compelled to take part in the homage of the city.[3] Being resolved to defend his supposed right of inheritance against the Pope by force of arms, Cesare put Ferrara into a state of defence and enlisted troops.[4] At the same time envoys were sent to the Emperor, the German princes, Henry IV., Philip II. and the Italian states.[5] As both Spain and the Italian powers, especially Venice and Florence,[6] did not in any way wish for an aggrandizement of the Papal States, Cesare indulged in the most sanguine hopes. He thought that he could count with certainty upon

[1] See the *Relatione cited in previous note.

[2] Cf. RICCI, II., 226 seq., 233 seq., 246 seq, 258 seq.

[3] See CAPILUPI, ed. Prinzivalli, 76. For the festivities see fully in *Relatione.

[4] " Il pensier di Don Cesare fu da principio di voler ritenere tutto lo Stato che possedeva Alfonso suo cugino e nel ducato di Ferrara opporsi al Papa et alla Sede Apostolica e dimostrarsi con armi alla scoperta " *Relatione, supra.

[5] See *" Expeditioni fatte dopo la morte del duca Alfonso a diversi principi dal sig. duca Cesare : Il conte Girardo Rangoni a Spagna. Il marchese Scandiano in Alemagna. Il conte Giulio Tassone alla sig^{ria} di Genova. Il Sig. Renato Cotti alla sig^{ria} di Venezia. Il dott. Sasso a Fiorenza. Il conte Ettore Galeazzo Tassone a Savoia. Il marchese Rangoni a Parma. Il sig. Grilenzone a Mantova." Barb. lat. 5259, p. 89, Vatican Library. Cf. ibid. 81, the *Relatione, where Count Alvise Montecuccolo is mentioned as the envoy to France.

[6] Cf. PELLEGRINI, Relazione ined. di ambasciatori Lucchesi alle corti di Firenze, Genova, etc., Lucca, 1901, 130.

his cousin, the Grand Duke of Tuscany, and upon the powerful Republic of Venice, and he sent Count Girolamo Giglioli to Rome to inform the Pope that he had taken possession of Ferrara, which belonged to him by right.[1]

When the news of the death of the last Duke of Ferrara reached Rome on November 1st, 1597, the Pope at once summoned a general congregation of the Cardinals for the following day, at which he informed them that the legitimate line being now extinct by the death of Duke Alfonso, Ferrara, as a vacant fief, reverted to the Holy See in accordance with the bull of Pius V., and that he now expressly reconfirmed this.[2] With the exception of Sfondrato and Lancellotti, who wished for longer time for consideration,[3] all the Cardinals were in agreement with the attitude adopted by the Pope, because the laws of feudal right were clearly in his favour.[4]

[1] See the *Relatione cited *supra*. According to this Cesare counted on the help of the Elector of Saxony and other German princes.

[2] *" Qui è venuta nuova certa della morte del sig. duca di Ferrara et per questo domattina si farà congregazione di cardinali inanzi S.Stà " (Report of Lodovico Cremaschi, Rome, November 1, 1597, Gonzaga Archives, Mantua). *Cf*. *Acta consist, November 2, 1597, Barb. lat. 2871, Vatican Library, and the Avviso in CAPILUPI, ed. Prinzivalli, 79 n. 1.

[3] See Avviso of November 5, 1597, Urb. 1065, Vatican Library.

[4] As the bull of Pius V. expressly excluded all illegitimate branches, the advocates of Este have always tried to prove Cesare's legitimacy. Fontanini (Il dominio temporale della S. Sede sopra Comacchio, Rome, 1709, 305 *seq*.) has refuted these attempts. Against Muratori (Antiq. Est., II., 429) and other advocates of the Este, *cf*. LITTA in *Arch. stor. ital*. App. XII., 67; SUGENHEIM, 437 n. 119; BALAN, VI., 642 *seq*. In the light of more recent researches Reumont (Toscana, I., 343) admits that the feudal right was clearly with Clement VIII. ; see BALDUZZI in *Atti d. Romagna*, 3rd. ser., IX., 80, 83. The last scholar to deal with this question, G. Ballardini, considers the illegitimacy of Cesare to be certain, and remarks (*Arch. stor. ital*., 5th ser. XXXVIII., 341) that it was not only the bull of Pius V. that stood in the way of his succession, but also the contract which

Cardinal Pietro Aldobrandini especially defended this point of view.[1] There can be no doubt that the determined and bold stand of the Pope was also influenced by the recollection of the partly uncertain and partly openly hostile attitude which the House of Este had repeatedly taken up against the Pope, its overlord.[2]

In order to give force to his declaration Clement VIII. immediately gave orders for large armaments.[3] A congregation of nineteen Cardinals had been appointed to deal with the question of Ferrara, and this decided that a monitorium must be issued to Cesare, and that Cardinal Pietro Aldobrandini, who was chosen to take the supreme command of the troops, should go to Bologna for the fitting out of the force. The nephew set out on November 12th. On the same day the monitorium was affixed at the cathedral of Ferrara : this gave Cesare fifteen days in which to justify himself in Rome, and to present his pretended claims.[4] As this was not done the canonical process was begun. The attempts of Cesare to turn aside the Pope from his lawful attitude by means of a letter and promises of a quit-rent, as well as of considerable advantages for his nephew Gian Francesco

Paul III. had made with Ercole II. The very efforts which Alfonso II. made, show that a new enfeoffment was wanted, " il che " Cardinal Cinzio properly says in his letter to the nuncios, " non havrebbe fatto senza bisogno et con ingiuria di D. Cesare " (*Carte Strozz.*, I., 2, 257).

[1] See the *report in Miscell. XV., 37, Papal Secret Archives.

[2] FEDERICI in *Arch. Rom.*, XXI., 615, rightly points this out.

[3] See CAPILUPI, ed. Prinzivalli, 79 *seq. Cf. Atti per la storia Ferrarese*, XXII., 45 *seq.* The *Procura of Cardinal P. Aldobrandini to Duke Pietro Caetani to enroll 3000 infantry soldiers and 300 cavalry, is dated November 4, 1597 ; original in Gaetani Archives, Rome, I., 12.

[4] See the *Relatione in Cod. Barb. *supra* ; *Avvisi of November 5, 8 and 12, 1597, Urb. 1065, Vatican Library ; Cod. ital. 109 (*Ragioni d. chiesa sopra Ferrara, with the text of the monitorum), State Library, Munich ; CAPILUPI, ed. Prinzivalli 79 *seq.* ; FRIZZI, V., 3 *seq.* The posting of the monitorium in Rome is *reported by Fr. M. Vialardo, November 7, 1597, Gonzaga Archives, Mantua.

tated to accept the proposal of the governor of Milan, who offered him Spanish garrisons for his fortresses. Philip II., in his old age, feared the outbreak of war in Italy, and only expressed himself with great caution, in spite of the ill-will which he entertained towards Clement VIII. on account of the absolution of Henry IV. Nor could Cesare look for help from Rudolph II., as the Emperor himself was dependent upon the help of the Pope in his war against the Turks.[1]

While Cesare could only find lukewarm friends, Clement VIII. found a supporter in the King of France, who openly and decidedly took his part. As he had done in the case of the Italian States and the Emperor,[2] on November 6th, 1597, Clement VIII. had sent a special envoy to Henry IV. on the matter of Ferrara.[3] Even before the envoy reached France, Henry IV. had made his decision. He realized, with the same clearness as his representative in Rome, d'Ossat, what a great advantage he could gain for France by adopting a correct attitude in this matter. Any war that broke out in Italy could not fail to be useful to the King of France, without his mixing

[1] *Cf.* CAPILUPI, ed. Prinzivalli, 104 *seq.*

[2] The mission of Carlo Conti, Bishop of Ancona, is referred to in the *briefs to Rudolph II., the Doge of Venice and the Duke of Urbino, November 26, 1597, Arm. 44, t. 41, n. 243 *seq.*, 251-252, Papal Secret Archives. The original of the brief to the Doge in the State Archives, Venice, *Bolle.* The instructions to Conti, in CAPILUPI, ed. Prinzivalli, 98 n. 1.

[3] Besides Lettres D'OSSAT, I., 480 *seq.*, the *brief to Henry IV., November 6, 1597, concerning the mission of " Petrus Ursinus episc. Aversanus " in which it is stated " Agitur enim Dei honor, agitur ius et dignitas nostra et huius s. Apostoli Sedis." Arm. 44, t. 41, n. 253, Papal Secret Archives. *Ibid.* 254 *seq.* to the nobles of France ; 256 " duci Parmae " ; 257 " duci Sabaudiae " ; 258 " duci Memorantii " ; 260 " Lucensibus." It was only much later that Paolo Emilio Zacchia was sent to Philip II. ; *cf.* besides HINOJOSA, 392 *seq.*, the *brief to Philip II., November 23, 1597, in which it is stated that the king will perhaps already know " quae proxime apud nos Ferrariae acciderunt et quam certa et manifesta sint iura huius S. Sedis in ea civitate et ditione optime etiam nosti." Arm. 44, t. 41, n. 265, Papal Secret Archives.

himself up in it, because it would involve the Spaniards, Florence and Savoy. If the Pope should then turn to the King of France for support, he would reap even greater advantages. In this way Henry could easily lead men to forget how, on many occasions, he had thought it his duty to act against the wishes of the Holy See. If he alone came to the assistance of the Pope, he would bind him and his successors to eternal gratitude.[1] In the clear conviction that to support Clement VIII. in the matter of Ferrara would be the best course to adopt, as he expressed himself to d'Ossat, in order to give new splendour to the fleur-de-lys in Rome, and permanently to assure to France its former position at the Curia,[2] Henry IV. forgot the former friendly relations of France with the Este, and ordered his ambassador in Rome, Piney, to offer the Pope the assistance of the kingdom of France. He was not only prepared to send an army across the Alps, but even in case of need to appear in person with the whole of his army and give his assistance.[3]

This declaration made the greatest impression in Rome, and nothing else was spoken of. D'Ossat, overcome with joy, hoped that his sovereign would once again take up the position of Pepin and Charlemagne towards the Church. He reported that if the project was carried out, the enemies of France, and above all the Spaniards, would be eaten up with envy and jealousy ; there could be no better opportunity than this to give the lie to the Spanish calumnies that after his absolution Henry would show himself the greatest enemy of the Church.[4]

But Clement VIII., no matter how valuable the offer of assistance from France was, was unwilling, for the sake of universal peace, to have French troops appearing in Italy. In the case of his not being able to defend his rights by his own power, he would have preferred the assistance of the

---

[1] *Cf.* Lettres d'Ossat, I., 489.

[2] *Ibid.* I., 490.

[3] See Callegari in *Riv. stor.*, XII., 26.

[4] See Lettres d'Ossat, I., 490 *seq.*

Swiss.[1] He therefore breathed more freely when he saw that
the mere offer of French assistance had been enough to deprive
Cesare of all help. The Spaniards themselves showed themselves more accommodating to the wishes of the Pope, when
even in Venice, which at first had been opposed to the acquisition of Ferrara by the Holy See, and had forbidden Gian
Francisco Aldobrandini to pass with his troops or the
publication of the excommunication, a change had taken
place.[2]

At Ferrara the reaction showed itself in a way that no one
could have dared to hope for.[3] Not only was there a display
of the discontent which had been aroused by the frequently
oppressive government of Alfonso II., but Cesare himself
began to hesitate. He had hardly assumed the reigns of
government when he showed himself unfit to cope with the
complicated situation, owing to the fact that the dead duke
had deliberately excluded him from all share in the government. In consequence of this, he only had a superficial
knowledge of many of the members of the supreme council,[4]
while to those he knew best he had, almost without exception,
entrusted missions abroad.[5] Undecided by nature, without
the necessary money, and quite inexperienced in military
matters, Cesare saw his adherents vanish, both among the
upper and the lower classes. The people openly expressed
the hope that under the milder government of the Church
they would be less oppressed by taxes than heretofore.[6] To

[1] See the letter of P. Aldobrandini of November 29, 1597, in
CAPILUPI, ed. Prinzivalli, 102 n. 1.

[2] See *ibid.* 104, 113. A *brief to " Orator regis cath. apud.
Caesarem," January 10, 1598, thanks him for his support in the
question of Ferrara (Arm. 44, t. 42, n. 2, Papal Secret Archives).
For the opposition of Venice *cf.* HORVAT, 132.

[3] See Lettres D'OSSAT, I., 494.

[4] See Nicc. Contarini in RANKE, II.[8], 180.

[5] *Cf. supra*, p. 385, n. 5.

[6] See the *Relatione in Cod. Barb. cited *supra*, p. 383, n. 4,
Vatican Library. CALLEGARI in *Riv. stor.*, XII., 34 ; Lettres
D'OSSAT, I., 495 ; BALLARDINI in *Arch. stor. ital.*, 5th ser.,

all this had to be added the profound impression made by the Papal excommunication. Of the friendly governments in Italy, not one dreamed of giving any effective assistance. They restricted themselves to giving good advice, because none of the states wished to risk a serious conflict with the Holy See.

Cesare had taken all possible precautions that the bull of excommunication, which had been sent to all the bishops of Italy,[1] should not be known at Ferrara. In spite of this the Archbishop of Bologna succeeded in finding a courageous man who successfully conveyed the document to Ferrara sewn in his clothes, who handed it to the bishop there.[2] On the following day, December 31st, the obsequies of one of the canons took place ; the church was draped in black and filled with a large crowd of the faithful. After the function the bishop mounted the pulpit. He spoke of death, but much worse than the death of the body, he suddenly said, is the destruction of the soul. By excommunication both are lost, and Cesare d'Este has incurred this penalty. He then had the Papal sentence read. The impression made was tremendous, and the fear of the interdict was so great that many of those present broke out into sobs, and among them the bishop.[3]

XXXVIII., 341 seq. For the burden of the taxes under Alfonso II. see BROSCH, I., 314.

[1] See CAPILUPI, ed. Prinzivalli, 117. Cf. Carte Strozz., I., 2, 257 seq. Venice had tried to prevent the promulgation of the bull ; see Arch. stor., XII., xxxi.

[2] The name is given differently ; see FRIZZI, V., 9 seq., and the *Relatione in Cod. Barb. supra, p. 383, n. 4, Vatican Library. Cf. RANKE, II.[8], 181, and Riv. stor., XII., 49.

[3] *La mattina sequente, che fu l'ultimo di Decembre, giornata anco della partenza della sig. duchessa d'Urbino con l'occasione delle esequie d'un canonico, donde la chiesa era di negro manto parata, fece un sermone discorrendo sopra la morte e quanto fosse grave la perdita del corpo e maggiore dell'anima, soggiunse poi che con la scomunica il corpo e l'anima si perdeva e manifestò come dalla S.Stà di Sre era stato dichiarato escomunicato Don

The news of the excommunication and interdict at once spread through the city, and it was obvious that the majority of the citizens had no intention of running the risk of incurring material and spiritual destruction in order to adhere to Cesare. Count Francesco Villa was sent to the Pope as the envoy of the city.[1] The inhabitants hastened to approach the sacraments in the fear lest, should their envoy accomplish nothing in Rome, they might be deprived for some time of this spiritual consolation.[2]

Clement VIII., to the great surprise of everyone, had in a very short time raised a considerable army for those times, of more than 20,000 infantry and 3000 horsemen.[3] This was already encamped near Faenza, under the supreme command of Cardinal Pietro Aldobrandini. The city of Ferrara, although it was well defended by its low position in marshy territory, was in need of the munitions of war, and even more of money. No power took any serious steps to help Cesare, while the attitude of Spain was such as to cause Cesare to fear the loss of the Imperial fiefs of Reggio and Modena.[4] The consequences that this would entail for the Venetians were so dangerous that they preferred to see Ferrara occupied by the Pope.[5]

Cesare was bound to realize that in these circumstances

Cesare e subito ordinando che si leggesse ad alta voce tutta la bolla e letta si affigesse alla porta del duomo. Restò il popolo tanto attonito che vedendosi fra poco tempo come secchi tronchi dover restare tagliati dall'arbore della spiritual vita e repudiati dal grembo di s. chiesa mandava fuori lacrime, gemiti e sospiri così gravi che il prelato piangendo anco con loro dirottamente empivano la chiesa di singulti e pianti. *Relatione in Cod. Barb. *supra*, p. 383, n, 4, Vatican Library.

[1] See the *Relatione in Cod. Barb. *loc. cit.* ; FRIZZI, V., 10 ; CAPILUPI, ed. Prinzivalli, 123.

[2] See *Relatione in Cod. Barb. *loc. cit.*

[3] See CAPILUPI, ed. Prinzivalli, 79 *seq.*, 87 n. 1 ; *cf.* Corresp. de Frangipani, I., 125.

[4] See Lettres D'OSSAT, I., 495 *seq.*

[5] See CAPILUPI, ed. Prinzivalli, 140 *seq.*

it would be madness to attempt the fortunes of war, while
his confessor, the Jesuit Bartolomeo Palmio, advised him
not to push things to that point.[1]   In order to bring about
an agreement with the Pope, Cesare had recourse to the sister
of Alfonso II. ; the old Duchess Lucrezia of Urbino had
always been his enemy, but she was on excellent terms with
Cardinal Aldobrandini.[2]   Armed with full powers, Lucrezia
went on December 31st to Faenza, and on January 12th,
1598, she there, in Cesare's name, came to an agreement with
the legate Aldobrandini.[3]   By this Cesare restored the Duchy
of Ferrara to the Church, together with Cento and Pieve di
Cento, and the fiefs in Romagna.   He was accordingly
absolved from the excommunication, together with his
adherents.   He retained the allodial estates, the archives,
the art collections, the library, and half the artillery.[4]
Clement VIII. was on a visit to Palo on the sea[5] when he
received the news of the agreement come to at Faenza, and
his joy was as great as it was justified.   Without his army

---

[1] See *ibid.* 128.   For Palmio *cf.* RICCI, II., 117 ; BALDUZZI
(*Atti d. Romagna,* 3rd *seq.,* IX., 83) thinks that Cesare even began
at last to doubt the legitimacy of his claims.

[2] For this princess see CAMPORI, Luigi e Lucrezia d'Este,
Turin, 1888.   *Cf.* CAPILUPI, ed. Prinzivalli, 123 *seq.,* 127 *seq.*
An *Elogio to Lucrezia, dated 1598, " prid. Cal. Febr." in Arm. 44,
t. 42, n. 23, Papal Secret Archives.   Lucrezia died on February
12, 1598, before the conferring of the title of Duchess of Bertinoro,
which had been promised to her, had taken place.   She made
Cardinal Aldobrandini her general heir ; see CAMPORI, *loc. cit.*

[3] By a *brief of January 10, 1598, Cardinal Aldobrandini was
expressly authorized to make the negotiations.   Arm. 44, t, 42,
n. 1, Papal Secret Archives.

[4] *Cf.* THEINER, Cod. dipl., III., 554 *seq.* ; BALDUZZI in *Atti e
Mem. p. la prov. di Romagna,* 3rd ser., IX. (1891), 94 *seq.*   G.
BALLARDINI in *Arch. stor. ital.,* 5th ser., XXXVIII., 339 *seq.* ;
ibid. 355 *seq.,* 409 *seq.*   For the commemorative inscriptions at
Faenza, *cf.* also MONTANARI, Guida stor. di Faenza, F. 1882,
59 *seq.*

[5] *Cf.* *Avvisi of January 14, 21 and 24, 1598, Urb. 1066, Vatican
Library.

having fired a single shot, or lost a single man, he had succeeded in enforcing his rights, and in recovering for the Church a duchy, the holders of which had hitherto often opposed the interests of their overlord. This was a matter of substantial importance[1] for the political position and the liberty of action of the Holy See.

When he had returned to Rome, Clement VIII. had a mass of thanksgiving celebrated in St. Peter's, and reported the matter to the Cardinals appointed for the affairs of Ferrara.[2] On the following day the treaty was read in consistory and approved. Cardinal Aldobrandini was given the legation of Ferrara.[3] On January 29th the nephew made his entry into Ferrara, whence Cesare had departed on the previous day.[4] The first official act of Aldobrandini was to reduce the taxes, and make other concessions. In this way he won over the

[1] See DOLFIN, Relazione, 454 ; *Atti p. la storia di Ferrara*, XXII., 68 ; BROSCH, I., 320 *seq.* *Cf.* the Orazione della signora Isabella Cervoni da Colle a P. Clemente VIII. sopra l'impresa di Ferrara con una canzona della medesima a principi christiani, Bologna, 1598. This rare work (copy in Aldobrandini Archives, Rome) treats in detail of the advantages of the undertaking against Ferrara. This " Orazione " is also in manuscript in Vat. 5566, Vatican Library.

[2] See letter of C. Aldobrandini, February 4, 1598, in CAPILUPI, ed. Prinzivalli, 145 n.

[3] See *Acta consist. Cod. Barb. lat. 2871, Vatican Library ; CAPILUPI, ed. Prinzivalli, 137 *seq.* The ratification of the treaty concluded by Cardinal Aldobrandini, dated January 19, 1598, in Bull. X., 417 *seq.* Many *letters from Card. Aldobrandini to Clement VIII., to Cardinals, princes and nuncios concerning the recuperatione di Ferrara, in Barb. 5859-64, Vatican Library. *Cf.* also Barb. 5365, *ibid.*

[4] See CAPILUPI, ed. Prinzivalli, 144 *seq.* ; BALLARDINI, *loc. cit.*, 343 *seq.* A *Sonnet on the handing over of Ferrara by Cesare, beginning with the words " Cesare quel che venne e vide e vinse " in *Carte Strozz.*, CXCVIII., p. ˙502, State Archives, Florence. Many satires from the manuscripts in the Library of St. Mark's, Venice, in PILOT, Cesare d'Este e la satira, in the *Ateneo Veneto*, XXX., 2 (1907).

populace, only the aristocracy still showing themselves to a great extent attached to the House of Este,[1] which was connected with the duchy by such ancient ties. Just as Aldobrandini took possession of Ferrara in the name of the Holy See, so did Cardinal Bandini of Comacchio, and the vice-legate of Bologna of Cento and Pieve di Cento. The Pope informed all the ambassadors of this on February 17th, 1598, and the foreign powers through the nuncios.[2] Almost all the princes hastened to send their congratulations.[3] In March the Pope received in the Hall of Constantine the oath of fealty of the four envoys from Ferrara.[4] He was then occupied with his preparations for his journey to the newly acquired province.[5]

Not only the Romans, but also the ambassadors and Cardinals, Gian Francesco Aldobrandini and his physicians, advised him, especially on the grounds of the enormous cost, to give up this journey and remain in Rome.[6] But neither for this reason, nor on account of his gout, could the Pope be induced to abandon his plan, which he thought necessary[7] in the interests of the States of the Church. Cardinal Pietro

[1] See CAPILUPI, ed. Prinzivalli, 148 *seq.*, 152 *seq.* ; FRIZZI, V., 19 *seq.*

[2] See the *report of Lod. Cremaschi, February 7, 1598, Gonzaga Archives, Mantua, and the letter of Cinzio Aldobrandini in *Carte Strozz.*, I., 2, 264.

[3] See *Brevia, Arm. 44, t. 42, p. 6, 13, 21-38, 45, 48, 50, 52, 56, 71, 83, 84, 100, 104, 122, 129, 140, 150, Papal Secret Archives. The originals of the briefs of February 7, 1598, to the Duke of Mantua in Gonzaga Archives, Mantua, and to Venice in State Archives, Venice.

[4] THEINER, Cod. dipl., III., 571 *seq.* Renato Cato delivered the Latin discourse before the Pope ; *cf.* *report of L. Cremaschi, March 21, 1598, Gonzaga Archives, Mantua.

[5] See Lettres D'OSSAT, I., 498 ; FRIZZI, V., 22.

[6] *Cf.* *Avviso of April 8, 1598, Urb. 1066, Vatican Library ; CAPILUPI, ed. Prinzivalli, 153. According to the *report of L. Cremaschi, Rome, March 7, 1598, Venice tried in every possible way to prevent the journey. Gonzaga Archives, Mantua.

[7] See *Avviso of March 14, 1598, Urb. 1066, *loc. cit.*

Aldobrandini, too, was in favour of the journey; it would be good for the Pope's health and for the city of Ferrara, which had suffered so much from the burdens imposed on it by the prodigal Duke Alfonso.[1] The Cardinals at length agreed to 150,000 scudi being taken from the treasure in the Castle of St. Angelo for the journey.[2] On April 3rd Cardinal d'Aragona was appointed legate for the city of Rome during the absence of the Pope from the City, while other important provisions were made, especially for the eventuality of a conclave.[3]

After Clement VIII. had celebrated mass at the tomb of the Princes of the Apostles on April 13th, he set out on his journey.[4] In his retinue were Cardinals Baronius, Monte, Arigoni and Cinzio Aldobrandini; others joined him afterwards. The officials of the Rota, and all the court, made the journey at the same time. It is no wonder that the treasurer was in despair.[5] Clement VIII. spent the first night at Castelnuovo, the second at Civita Castellana, and then at Narni, where he urged the completion of the building of the

[1] See letter of Aldobrandini, February 5, 1598, in *Atti p. la storia di Ferrara*, XXII., 76.

[2] *Cf. supra*, p. 381.

[3] Bull. X., 436 *seq.*, 440 *seq.*, 445 *seq.*

[4] *Cf.* besides the summarized information given by BENTIVOGLIO (Memorie, 18 *seq.*) the exhaustive description of CAPILUPI, ed. Prinzivalli, 160 *seq.*, and the following still unpublished reports : 1. Matteo Argenti, *Giornale del viaggio di Clemente VIII. per Ferrara, Barb. lat. 4829, and *Diario de luoghi che passa Clemente VIII. per andare a Ferrara, Barb. lat. 4834, Vatican Library. 2. I. P. Mucantii *" Iter Clementis VIII. Ferrariense," Barb. lat. 2847, also in the Corsini Library, Rome, and State Archives, Modena, printed in part in the work of Gatticus (not published) Acta caerem., II., 193 *seq.* (copy in Vatican Library). *Cf.* also *Diarium Adami Klicishii militis s. Petri ab introitu suo in Italiam " for the years 1594-1598, Barb. 2259, Vatican Library. See also *Avvisi in Urb. 1066, which are used in part both by PRINZIVALLI, 160 *seq.*, and ARGENTI. The *register of the expenses of the journey in the State Archives, Rome.

[5] See BAUMGARTEN, Neue Kunde, 33.

cathedral.[1] His reception at Spoleto was very magnificent. Thence he went by way of Foligno,[2] Camerino,[3] Macerata and Loreto, where he made costly gifts to the Holy House, and, surrounded by fifteen Cardinals, gave the blessing to the people.[4] At Loreto he was joined by Cardinal Pietro Aldobrandini, who went with the Pope to Ancona, where the feast of the Ascension was kept. Here too his welcome was very magnificent.[5] The Pope took up his abode in the bishop's palace, high above the city, and adjoining the cathedral, where Pius II. had died on his crusade. At Pesaro the Duke of Urbino paid homage to the Pope.[6] On May 2nd Clement VIII. visited Fano, his native city,[7] and then at Rimini received Cesare de'Este, Duke of Modena and Reggio. He conversed with him for an hour, and entertained him at his table.[8] After a visit to Ravenna,[9] he continued his journey by Bagnacavallo[10] and Lugo[11] to Ferrara. May 8th[12] had been appointed for the solemn entry, at which an immense throng had assembled, including many strangers from Lombardy, Venice and Bologna. Clement VIII. was received at the Porta S. Giorgio by the bishop and clergy, and the magistrates delivered the keys of the city. The Pope then put on the

---

[1] See *Avviso of April 24, 1598, Urb. 1066, *loc. cit.*

[2] *Cf.* Faloci Pulignani, I priori d. cattedrale di Foligno, F. 1914, 276 *seq.*

[3] See *Cod. A. E. XI., 74, p. 144 of the Library of S. Pietro in Vincoli, Rome. *Cf.* Lämmer, Zur Kirchengeschichte, 45 *seq.*

[4] See Argenti in Prinzivalli, 166, n. 1.

[5] See Cascioli, Mem. stor. di Poli, Rome, 1896, 162 *seqq.*

[6] *Avviso of May 9, 1598, Urb. 1066, *loc. cit.*

[7] *Cf.* L. Masetti, Accoglienze fatte in Fano a P. Clemente VIII., Pesaro, 1881.

[8] See Argenti in Prinzivalli, 171.

[9] See Bentivoglio., Memorie, 19.

[10] See Balduzzi, *loc. cit.*, 91 *seq.*

[11] *Cf.* Vinc. Milani Lugensis In adventu S.D.N.D. Clementis VIII. P.M. oratio Lugi habita 1598 Cal. Maii, Bononiae, 1598.

[12] Not on the 9th, as Balduzzi states (*loc. cit.*, 92). The *Avviso of May 13, 1598 (Urb. 1066, *loc. cit.*) expressly says that the Pope made his entry on the Friday, and the Friday fell on the 8th.

pontifical vestments and mounted the sedia gestatoria, above which a baldacchino was carried.   In his retinue there were eighteen Cardinals, fifteen prelates, many dignitaries of the court, the Swiss Guard, and the ambassadors of France, Venice and Savoy.[1] The Blessed Sacrament, at the entry and throughout the journey, was carried in a precious portable tabernacle, on a white mule.[2]   The streets through which the cortège passed were adorned with tapestries, inscriptions and triumphal arches.   Clement VIII. went first to the cathedral, and then to the Castello, the former palace of the Este dukes, where he took up his abode.

The first and the most pressing care of Clement VIII., was to reorganize the government.   For this purpose he set

[1] For the entry, the day of which is often wrongly given, even in CAPILUPI, 174, cf. the *Avvisi of May 9, 13 and 16, 1598, Urb. 1066, loc. cit. ; Pregildo Piazza, *letter from Ferrara, May 11, 1598, to sig. N. Fozza, Coll. Antonelli, n. 669, Library, Ferrara ; Rocca (next note) ; GATTICUS, II., 193 ; Descrittione de gli apparati fatti in Bologna per la venuta di N.S.P. Clemente VIII. . . . co' disegni degli archi, statue et pitture, Bologna, V. Benacci, 1598 and 1599. The first edition, unknown to Brunet and Cicognara, is very rare. The text which describes the plates, includes, with the title, eight pages. See also Vero disegno dell'ordine tenuto da Clemente VIII. nel fel. ingresso di S.S^{tà} nella città di Ferrara, 1598, Antonio Tempesta sculp.   A fresco in the Palazzo Antici-Mattei in Rome, also shows the entry of the Pope into Ferrara ; it is of special interest for the costumes. The inscription is only partly preserved in CAPILUPI, ed. Prinzi-valli, 173 n.   The Cod. germ. 3993 of the State Library, Munich, contains *" Pompa " and entry of Pope Clement VIII., 1598, into Ferrara, German translation by A. Rocca, with an anti-papal introduction by Girolao Parco.

[2] See ANG. ROCCA (ord. S. Agost.), De ss. Christi corpore rom. pontificibus iter conficientibus praeferendo commentarius anti-quiss. ritus causam et originem, variasque ss. pontificum ss. secum hostiam in itinere deferentium profectiones itinerarium societatis ss. sacramenti Clemente VIII.   Ferrariam, proficiscente, Rome, 1599. Cf. Lettres D'OSSAT, II., 111 ; BAUMGARTEN, Neue Kunde, 33.

up a communal council, which was cleverly divided into three
sections, nobles, burghers and artisans.   Without restricting
the supreme authority of the Cardinal, he gave this new
council, which was to be elected every three years, certain
rights and powers, such as the provision of food, the regulation
of the rivers, the appointment of the judges and the podestà,
and even of the professors of the university, powers which the
Este had reserved to themselves.   The Pope condoned many
purely fiscal debts, and won over citizens of importance by
conferring on them ecclesiastical dignities.[1]   The inhabitants
of Ferrara were delighted by the confirmation of all their
ancient privileges and by the labours of the legate, Aldobrandini, to restore the finances, which had been seriously
damaged by the Este.[2]   On the other hand great discontent
was aroused by the construction of a fortress, to make space
for which many houses, and some churches and palaces had
to be destroyed, among them the celebrated Belvedere, so
much sung by the poets.[3]   Later on Ferrara, like Bologna,
was given the right to have its own ambassador in Rome,[4]
as well as a tribunal of its own for the settlement of causes.[5]
   During the stay of Clement VIII. at Ferarra, which lasted

---

[1] See Bull. X., 449 *seq.* ;   FRIZZI, V., 25 *seq.* ;   Contarini in
RANKE, II.[8], 183, n. 1.

[2] See FRIZZI, V., 27 *seq.*

[3] See besides FRIZZI, V., 37 *seq.*, CAPILUPI, ed. Prinzivalli, 184,
and the *Avvisi of July 25 and 28, and August 1, 1598, Urb. 1066,
loc. cit.   FRIZZI (*loc. cit.*) rejects on the strength of the Acta in
the Communal Archives, Ferrara, the suggestion that the pro-
prietors of the demolished houses were not indemnified, as
BROSCH (I., 321) claims.   The number of 4000 houses mentioned
by Brosch is a huge exaggeration ; see PARDI in *Atti d. Deput.
per Ferrara*, XX. (1911), 8.

[4] Brief of March 1, 1599, Bull. X., 481 *seq.*   *Cf.* CANCELLIERI,
Possessi, 209 *seq.*, 281 ;   MORONI, V., 302, XXIV., 152.   The
*reports of the Ferrara envoys in Rome, preserved to 1796, are
in the Communal Archives, Ferrara ;   *ibid.* the greater part of
the correspondence of the Cardinal legate.

[5] See Bull. X., 511 *seq.*   *Cf.* MORONI, XXIV., 152 *seq.*

for more than six months, the saying " ubi pontifex ibi Roma "
was fully confirmed. Envoys came from all parts, and
princes and princesses, some to express their devotion to the
vicar of Christ, and offer him their congratulations, and
some on private business. The first to come, on May 8th,
was the ambassador of the Emperor, and on the following
day the Archduke Ferdinand, on pilgrimage to Loreto, who
was received by the Pope as a son by his father.[1] There
followed the envoys of Lucca,[2] and at the beginning of June
the four representatives of the Republic of St. Mark, who were
received with special courtesy. At their farewell audience
the Pope jokingly said to them that he still hoped to celebrate
holy mass in Santa Sofia at Constantinople.[3] At the same
time there came from Mantua Duke Vincenzo, his consort
Eleanora and his sister Margherita, the mother of Alfonso II.
They were engaged in a dispute with Cesare d'Este over a
matter of inheritance. On May 29th there also appeared in
Ferrara[4] Ferrante Gonzaga, Prince of Guastalla. On June
19th the Pope received Federigo Pico, Prince of Mirandola.[5]
At the end of June there came the Duke of Parma, Ranuccio

---

[1] See *Avviso of May 20, 1598, Urb. 1066, *loc. cit.*   *Cf.* *reports
of L. Cremaschi, Ferrara, May 11 and 15, 1598, Gonzaga Archives,
Mantua. See also HURTER, III., 411 *seqq.* ; STIEVE, IV., 307 ;
Archiv. f. österr. Gesch., LXXXVI., 325 *seq.* For the envoy
sent by the Archduke Maximilian to Ferrara see HIRN,
Maximilian, I., 69.

[2] See *Avviso of May 27, 1598, Urb. 1066, *loc. cit.*

[3] See Al. P. Clemente VIII. Ambasceria Veneta straordinaria
in Ferrara nell'a. 1598, ed. R. FULIN, Venice, 1865. *Cf.* also
*Avvisi of June 3 and 6, 1598, Urb. 1066, *loc. cit.* For Cesare
Cremonino, who came as the envoy of Cento, and his successful
negotiations see SIGHINOLFI in *Atti d. Romagna*, 3rd ser., XXV.
(1907), 423 *seq.*

[4] See the *Avvisi of May 30, and June 6, 1598, Urb. 1066,
loc. cit. *Cf.* Narrazione della solenne entrata fatta in Ferrara
del ser. duca di Mantova e degli ill. ambasc. di Venezia, Rome,
1598.

[5] *Avviso of June 20, 1598, *loc. cit.*

Farnese, to pay his homage.[1]   He rivalled in pomp the Duke
of Mantua, who appeared with a retinue of 1200 persons.
Lastly there came the governor of Milan, who was treated
by the Pope with a like honour as the afore-mentioned
princes.[2]

At the end of September Clement VIII. undertook an
expedition to Comacchio.[3]   Everyone attempted to dissuade
him from this, partly on the ground of the expense, and partly
not to offend Venice, but he would not be moved from his
purpose.[4]   A month later there began the preparations for
the marriage of the Archduchess Margaret of Styria to
Philip III., who was represented by the Duke of Sessa.[5]   The
marriage of the Archduke Albert to the Infante Isabella
was to take place at the same time ;[6] the Pope wished to bless
both these marriages in person.   The future Queen of Spain
made her solemn entry on November 13th, mounted on a
white palfrey, and accompanied by nineteen Cardinals, and
numerous archbishops, prelates and ambassadors.[7]   After

[1] See Descrizione del viaggio fatto dal duca Ranuccio Farnese
a Ferrara per visitare P. Clemente VIII., Ferrara, 1598.   *Cf.*
*report of L. Cremaschi, June 30, 1598, Gonzaga Archives,
Mantua.   *Avviso of July 15, 1598, *loc. cit.*

[2] See, besides *Avviso of August 29, 1598, *loc. cit.* BENTIVOGLIO,
Memorie, 23-26.   *Cf.* also POSSEVINO, Gonzaga, 824.

[3] See *Avvisi of September 26 and 30, 1598, *loc. cit.*

[4] *Cf.* BAUMGARTEN, Neue Kunde, 30.

[5] See *Avvisi of October 7, 10, 24 and 31, and November 4,
7 and 11, 1598, *loc. cit.*   The principal hall of the palace was
decorated like the Sala Regia.   The expenses of the reception
of the queen given by ORBAAN in *Arch. Rom.*, XXXVI., 119 *seq.*

[6] The Archduke Albert put aside his sacerdotal dress on July 13,
1598 ; he had never received major orders ; see *Archiv. f. österr.
Gesch.*, LXXXVI., 328, 333.   For his laying aside of the
cardinalitial dignity see the *brief addressed to him, July 31,
1598, Arm. 44, t. 42, n. 212, Papal Secret Archives.

[7] See *Diarium P. Alaleonis, Barb. 2815, Vatican Library ;
*Avviso of November 14, 1598, Urb. 1066, *ibid.* ; *report of
L. Cremaschi, November 14, 1598, Gonzaga Archives, Mantua ;
La fel. entrata della ser. Regina di Spagna D. Margarita d'Austria

she had assisted at the Pope's mass on the following day, together with the Archduke Albert, who had previously renounced his cardinalate,[1] on the 15th both marriages were blessed by Clement VIII., after which the Golden Rose was conferred on Margaret.[2] The festivities which took place on the occasion recalled the most splendid days which Ferrara had witnessed in the time of the Este.[3] Margaret left the city on November 18th, accompanied by Cardinal Aldobrandini as far as the frontier of the States of the Church. After this the Pope began to prepare for his return journey, and on November 20th Cardinal Giovanni Francesco di S. Giorgio di Blandrata assumed the office of pro-legate. Giglioli was appointed ambassador of Ferrara at the Curia, and it was resolved to set up a bronze statue of Clement VIII.

nella città di Ferrara, Ferrara, 1598 ; BENTIVOGLIO, Memorie, 29 *seq.*

[1] The laying aside of the purple took place at a secret consistory : " Ferrariae in Castello die ult. Iulii " : *Dixit S^{tas} Sua ipsum cardinalem ac Philippum Hisp. regem summopere urgere pro admissione huius modi resignationis causamque ab ipso rege adduci optimam, nempe quia iudicat expedire conservationi relig. cath." Cod. 75, p. 254 *seq.* of the Library of S. Pietro in Vincoli, Rome.

[2] See *Diarium P. Alaleonis, Barb. 2815, Vatican Library ; *Avviso of November 18, 1598, Urb. 1066, *ibid.* ; Relazione di Paolo Mucante dell'entrata solenne fatta in Ferrara per la ser. D. Margherita d'Austria Regina di Spagna e del consistorio publico . . . con minuto ragguaglio della messa pontificale da S.B. e delle ceremonie delli sposalizii etc., Rome, 1598. *Cf.* also CAPILUPI, ed. Prinzivalli, 184 *seq.* ; BENTIVOGLIO, Memorie, 31 *seq.*

[3] *Cf.* *Avviso of November 18, 1598, according to which *maschere* were also allowed " havendo nome questi Ferraresi di fare cosa vaga in questa materia, massime che queste dame in maschera fanno molto bella mostra." The ladies of Comacchio performed dances in the moats around the castello, which greatly diverted the queen. On November 17 the " tragedia di Holoferne " was performed before the queen (Urb. 1066, *loc. cit.*). *Cf.* also the *Diarium P. Alaleonis, *loc. cit.*

The Pope granted further favours to the Ferrarese, and
promised them to make the Po navigable ; he showed himself
so magnanimous that the representatives of the city left
his audience chamber with tears of joy in their eyes.[1] On
November 26th Clement VIII., kneeling before the Blessed
Sacrament in the cathedral, recommended the new possession
to the protection of God in a touching prayer, and then set out
upon his return journey.[2]

He went first from Ferrara to Bologna, where he was
received with great honour. Guido Reni has preserved in
an etching the decorations of the festivities. Clement VIII.
remained in Bologna for three days ; he said mass at
S. Petronio, and visited the university, where he had once
made his studies.[3] The return to Rome, where the Pope
was anxiously awaited, was hastened as much as possible,
and to that end the retinue was reduced.[4] On December 1st
Clement VIII. reached Imola, and on the 2nd honoured
Faenza and Forlimpopoli[5] with his presence ; on the 3rd he
met Cardinal Aldobrandini at Meldola ; on the 4th Cesena
we reached, and on the 5th Rimini, where, on the following
day, the Second Sunday in Advent, he said mass in the
cathedral. From Rimini he went to Cattolica, on the 7th
by Pesaro to Fano, on the 8th to Sinigaglia, on the 9th to
Ancona, and on the 10th to Loreto. After having stayed

[1] See *Avvisi of November 21 and December 5, 1598, Urb.
1066, loc. cit.

[2] The *Diarium P. Alaleonis, loc. cit. gives this beautiful prayer.

[3] See *Diarium P. Alaleonis, loc. cit. ; *Avvisi of December 5
and 12, 1598, Urb. 1066, loc. cit. ; BELLENTANI, I papi a Bologna,
B., 1857, 27 seq. For the festival decorations see BÖHN, G. Reni,
3 seq., 30, and Jahrb. d. Kunstsamml. d. österr. Kaiserhauses,
XXVI., 137. Cf. also FRATI, Opere di bibliografia Bolognese, I.
(1888), 419.

[4] See *Avviso of December 12, 1598, Urb. 1066, loc. cit. We
have details of the return journey in the *Diarium P. Alaleonis,
Barb. 2815, ibid. Cf. also Lettres D'OSSAT, I., 610, 612 seq., 614.

[5] Cf. BALLARDINI in Arch. stor. ital., 5th ser., XXXVIII.,
362 seq., 366 seq.

there for several days, and having ordained Cardinals Pietro
Aldobrandini and Bartolomeo Cesi priests, on December 14th
the journey was continued by way of Foligno, Spoleto, Narni
and Civita Castellana. On the 19th the Pope reached Rome,
where the whole of the clergy went to meet him at the Porta
del Popolo. Accompanied by them he went in procession,
through richly decorated streets, to St. Peter's. The people
were filled with exultation ; the Pope looked very well, and
had falsified the prophecies of the astrologers that he would
die on the journey.[1] On the following days the audiences
at the Vatican were very numerous, and all flocked to congratulate him on the acquisition of Ferrara, which was celebrated by many poets and orators.[2] It was resolved to set

[1] See *Avvisi of December 23 and 26, 1598, Urb. 1066, *loc. cit.* ;
ODOARDO MAGLIANO, L'ordine tenuto nel ricevere il SS.
Sacramento nell'entrare in Roma con la processione et apparati
delle strade da S. Maria del Popolo a S. Pietro, Rome, 1598 ;
*report of L. Cremaschi, December 25, 1598, Gonzaga Archives,
Mantua. Commemorative inscription see CAPILUPI, ed. Prinzivalli, 215 *seq.* Clement VIII. had expressed the wish that there
should be no expense to celebrate his return (see the *brief to
Cardinal d'Aragona, December 9, 1598) as he already knew the
devotion of the city : " Romae enim aetatem egimus." Arm.
44, t. 42, n. 370, Papal Secret Archives.

[2] Ios. CASTALIONIS, Expeditio Ferrariensis et Ferraria recepta,
Rome, 1598 ; G. B. GENARI, Rime nella venuta di Clemente VIII.
a Ferrara, Ferrara, 1598 ; Ios. COMARINI, In S.D.N. Clementis
VIII. P.O.M. Ferrariam Bononiam, Romamque adventu.
Carmina, Ferrara, 1599 ; GIOV. PAOLO BRACCINO (of Ferrara),
Rime a diversi nella venuta di Clemente VIII. (Aldobrandini)
col sacro collegio et Romana Corte alla nobiliss. città di Ferrara,
etc., Ferrara, 1601 ; D. NIZZOLI, Viaggio di S.S. Clemente VIII.
a Ferrara in ottava rima, *s. l. et a.* ; Ottavio Micheli da Lucca,
*Ferrara recuperata in ottava rima (six canti), Vat. 5529, Vatican
Library ; FAB. PATRITIUS, Oratione a N.S. Clemente VIII.
nell'allegrezza dell'acquisto di Ferrara, Venice, 1598. Other
commemorative discourses in CAPILUPI, ed. Prinzivalli, 214 *seq.*
For commemorative coins see BONANNI, I., and AGNELLI, Ferrara,
Bergamo, 1906, 99.

up a commemorative inscription in honour of Clement VIII. at the Capitol.[1]

In the midst of these days of jubilation, there occurred a terrible disaster, owing to which the most fortunate year of the pontificate of the Aldobrandini Pope ended in sorrow.[2] The Eternal City was afflicted by an inundation, which far surpassed all previous ones. On December 21st torrential rains had fallen, owing to which the yellow and muddy waters of the Tiber were swollen in the most alarming way. On

[1] See NOVAES, IX., 38. The event was also celebrated in inscriptions, *e.g.* at the Villa Aldobrandini (see *infra*, pp. 496 *seqq.*), the castello at Spoleto, and the Palazzo del Podestà at Faenza. The banner with the device : " Ferrara ricuperata " is preserved at the Villa Aldobrandini at Anzio.

[2] In a *note in Cod. Barb. lat. 5259, p. 132, Vatican Library, it is stated of the year 1598 : Anno celebre e memorabile per la christianità, ma particolarmente per la riputatione e felicità della Sede Apost. e ni Clemente VIII. poichè in esso non solo ricuperò e ridusse sotto il dominio ecclesiastico Ferrara, et uno stato così grande suo, ma nell'istesso anno si rihebbe dalle mani de'turchi Giaverino pochi anni avanti da loro per forza occupato. Stabilissi la pace con l'autorità del medesimo Pontefice per mezzo del suo legato tra la corona di Francia e quella di Spagna dopo dieci anni di guerra, anzi si potrebbe dire cento. Quietossi con l'istessa pace il regno di Francia lacerato altretanto tempo dalle guerre civili, et essendo morto Filippo 2° Re di Spagna si congiunsero in matrimonio Filippo 3. suo figliuolo a Margherita d'Austria, facendosi solennità delle nozze in Ferrara con grandissima pompa degna di tanti principi per mano dell'istesso Pontefice ; ne questo sponsalitio fu solo ; poichè seco anche si celebrò quello dell' arciduca Alberto con l'infanta Donna Isabella di Spagna. Ne fu cosa di poca consideratione il muoversi il Papa con tutta la corte di Roma et andare a Ferrara con decoro ecclesiastico e pontificio, entrandovi solennissimamente, attioni, che bastarebbono ad illustrare un secolo, e far memorabili quattro pontificati. Ne poteva quest'anno esser più felice per quel Pontefice, se questa felicità non fosse stata alquanto temperata dall'innondatione, che fece il Tevere, nel suo ritorno a Roma, che non solo li recò non poco disturbo, benchè in esso anche havesse occasione di mostrare la sua pietà, et il card. Aldobrandini la sua diligenza,

December 23rd the river began to overflow at certain points.
At first no great fears were entertained, but the waters rose
from hour to hour with alarming persistence ; they passed
the floodmarks of 1557, and at last even those of 1530 by
two palms. It was estimated that the level of the water
had risen by ten metres.[1] Almost the whole city suffered
in a terrible degree from the stench, which in the poetry of
Horace was attributed to the vengeance of the Tiber god.[2]
Only the hills and some of the higher parts of the city were
spared.[3] With bewildering force the waters destroyed many
houses, especially in the Borgo, on the island of S. Bartolomeo,
and in the Ripetta. In many other cases the foundations
were so undermined that later on they had to be supported

[1] *Cf.* v. MOLTKE, Wanderbuch[5], Berlin, 1890, 61.

[2] Already on February 2nd, 1598, there had been an inundation
which had caused damage of 200,000 scudi (see *Avviso of
February 4, 1598, Urb. 1066, *loc. cit.*) and another on March 1
(*Avviso of March 7, 1598, *ibid.*).

[3] *Cf.* Lettres D'OSSAT, V., 5 *seq.* ; report of the procurator of
the Anima in SCHMIDLIN, Anima, 442 *seq.* ; *Avviso of December
30, 1598, Urb. 1066, *loc. cit.* ; *letter of Carpino Carpini, Rome,
December 30, 1598, in Vat. 8259, p. 342 *seq.* Vatican Library ;
Lettera di Maurizio Cataneo in Idea del Segretario, Venice, 1606,
37 *seq.* ; *letter of L. Cremaschi, December 26, 1598, Gonzaga
Archives, Mantua ; *report of M. Vialardo to the Archduke
Ferdinand, January 2, 1599, State Archives, Vienna. Two
*reports in Inform. polit., XVI., n. 15-16, State Library, Berlin.
See also JUVENCIUS, V., 291 *seq.* ; POSSEVINO, Gonzaga, 824 *seq.* ;
GROTTANELLI, Ducato di Castro, 21 *seq.* ; LANCIANI, Scavi, II.,
27 ; A. PILOT in *Riv. di Roma*, 1909. Contemporary accounts in
Archivio, V., 3 (1879), 300 *seq.* of GORI ; BERTOLOTTI, Art.
Subalp., 144 *seq.* Of other reports mention may be made of :
the Relatione de la spaventevole inondatione fatta dal Tevere
nella città di Roma e suoi contorni alli 23 decembre 1598, Milan,
1599 (copy in the Library of J. v. Görres, afterwards in the
possession of Fraulein Sofia Görres at Vienna). J. CASTIGLIONE,
Trattato dell'inondatione del Tevere, Rome, 1599, 5 *seq.*, 44 *seq.*,
73 *seq.* ; M. COGNATUS, De Tiberis inundatione, Rome, 1599.
For the inundation *cf.* also *Miscell. d. stor. ital.*, IV., 687.

by girders and beams, and new sub-structures ; older buildings, such as the professed house of the Jesuits, had to be rebuilt owing to the damage they had sustained.[1] The two outer arches of the Ponte Palatino, restored by Gregory XIII., fell before the raging waters, so that the medieval name of Ponte S. Maria was changed to that of Ponte Rotto.[2] The Ponte S. Angelo and the Ponte Molle were also damaged, and all the little shops of objects of devotion near the Ponte S. Angelo were destroyed ; three salt stores belonging to the Apostolic Camera, and nine out of the twenty corn mills on the Tiber—according to other accounts as many as twelve—were carried away with all their inhabitants. Two broke into pieces at the Ponte Sisto.

In a state of indescribable confusion there floated through the streets of Rome bales of merchandize, bundles of hay, doors, books, furniture and domestic utensils. The waters, which flowed with bewildering speed, frequently changed their course, and a terrible state of panic prevailed. At the terrified cry of " the floods " the people rushed out of their houses, and in the lack of sufficient boats, sought safety, amid terrible scenes, in the higher ground, at the Castle of St. Angelo, and in the larger houses. Others took refuge on the roofs. If the city had been carried by assault by an enemy, the terror and confusion could not have been greater. The terrible height to which the water reached may be seen with alarming clearness by the marks which are still to be seen to-day on the façade of the Minerva and in other places.[3] The inundation broke with such lightning speed that the greater number of the inhabitants were unable to provide themselves with

[1] See JUVENCIUS, V., 292, where there are particulars of the new building erected by Card. O. Farnese.

[2] As the last trace of the bridge there is still preserved a single arch in the middle of the river.

[3] See the illustrations in PASTOR, Rom zu Ende der Renaissance, 29. List of the marks showing the height of the water in *Inventario*, I., 86, 99, 165, 237, 305, 467. Inscription relating to the inundation of the Tiber at S. Giovanni de' Fiorentini, in TOTTI, 244.

food or the barest necessaries, and the Imperial ambassador reported that even Cardinals Madruzzo and Sforza nearly died of starvation.[1]

The damage done in the churches was terrible. " After the fatal floods—thus the procurator of the Anima describes the state of the German national church—had beaten strongly and for a long time against the walls of our church, throwing against them roofs, timbers from mills and ships and all manner of things that they had carried away with them from all parts, but in vain, because the architectural strength had defied their efforts, they began to rage in the interior of the church ; they overthrew all the tombs, scattered bodies, ashes, filth, mingling them with the water in the wells, the drinking water, earth and air, as they would ; they ruined the stalls in the choir, and in the sacristy, as well as the images of Our Lady which were near the altars ; as the doors could not be torn from their hinges, they were broken, crushed and to a great extent demolished ; the hangings which had been attached to the pillars and other places as decoration for the feast of the Nativity (for the water began to rise on the vigil of the Nativity) were discoloured and spoiled to half their height by filthy water ; almost all the marble monuments and inscriptions were damaged, among them those of the Duke of Cleves and of Pope Adrian VI. of holy memory."[2]

The Romans passed a terrible vigil of the Nativity ; no one slept, lights were burning in all the windows, and the rising of the water was anxiously watched. At last a slight subsidence of the flood could be detected. In spite of this on the following day the churches were still so immersed in water

[1] See the *report of Vialardo, January 2, 1599, State Archives, Vienna.

[2] SCHMIDLIN, Anima, 443. The report, as far as the churches are concerned, is confirmed by the *letter of Carpino Carpini in Vat. 8259, p. 342 *seq.* (Vatican Library), who says : " Non vi si può troppo dimorare per il gran fettore e puzza che rendono li cadaveri delle sepulture sfondate dal acqua." *Cf.* also PANCIROLI, Tesori nascosti (1600), 429, 538 ; CAVAZZI, S. Maria in Via Lata, Rome, 1908, 128.

that mass could hardly be said anywhere. Even the solemn Papal mass had to be omitted.[1] During the night before St. Stephen's day the waters began to disappear, leaving everywhere a deep layer of mire, which could only be removed with great difficulty. For a long time the basements remained filled with water, and the lower floors were uninhabitable on account of the water which had penetrated into them.[2] It is difficult to estimate exactly the number of persons in the city and the environs who were taken by surprise and drowned by the floods. The estimates vary from 4,000 to 1,400.[3] Immense loss was caused by the destruction of cattle, grain, wine, oil, hay, merchandize and objects of every kind, which were stored for the most part in the basements. It was estimated that there was a loss of two million gold ducats.[4]

The Pope, who was afflicted with the deepest grief at the misfortunes of the inhabitants of the capital, and prayed almost without interruption, did all he could from the first to give every help that lay in his power. He had those who were in danger rescued by boats, and distributed food and money in all the parishes. By his orders Cardinal Aldobrandini supervised the salvage works, in which Cardinals Santori, Rusticucci, Sauli, Sfondrato and Sforza also took part, and among the aristocracy above all the Marchese Peretti. At the hospital of Santo Spirito, Camillus of Lellis, the founder of the " Fathers of a good death," laboured all the night with six companions in moving the sick to an upper floor.

It greatly afflicted the Pope when wicked men spread the report among the people that the opening of a canal for the

---

[1] *December 24, 1598, " non fuit Capella propter inundationem Tyberis." Diarium P. Alaleonis, Barb. 2815, Vatican Library.

[2] See *report of Carpino Carpini, loc. cit.

[3] See SCHMIDLIN, Anima, 442 n. 2. The statement of Reumont here given, of 1500 drowned, is probably based on the Relatione della spaventevole inondatione, Milan, 1599, which mentions the number of 1400. The same number is to be found on the back cover of the manuscript n. 43 of the Stiftes Hohenfurth Library in Bohemia.

[4] *Avviso of December 30, 1598, Urb. 1066, loc. cit,

draining of the water from the Velino, which he had permitted, had been the cause of the inundation.[1] An examination carried out on the spot later on proved the groundlessness of these rumours.[2] In another quarter the blame for the inundation was attributed to the works of the Florentine government, for the draining of the valley of the Chiana. When for this reason the Romans began to construct dykes, which led to the flooding of some of the neighbouring districts of Tuscany, there followed a bitter quarrel with Florence, which threatened to develop into a war.[3]

On January 8th, 1599, Clement VIII. had made a report to the Cardinals on the catastrophe,[4] and on the 23rd a circular was issued to the clergy and people of Rome, exhorting them to look upon the inundation as a chastisement for their sins, and to appease the anger of God[5] by leading a better life and by doing penance. To this end processions were ordered at St. Mary Major's and St. Peter's.[6] But in order to avert the recurrence of such a disaster by human means as well, a congregation of six Cardinals was ordered to discuss with experts on the subject[7] plans for the regulation of the Tiber.

[1] See *ibid.* For the works on the Velino, hardly finished in 1601 cf. *Avviso of July 24, 1596, Urb. 1064, I., *loc. cit* CARRARA, La caduta del Velino nella Nera, Rome, 1799; NOVAES, IX., 39.

[2] *Cf.* *Avvisi of February 3 and 10, March 3 and 20, and April 3, 1599, Urb. 1067, Vatican Library.

[3] See REUMONT, Toskana, I., 365. " Disegni piante relazioni e visite con le transazioni fatte per le Chiane 1600 " down to 1658, preserved in Cod. Chigi, P. VI., 6, Vatican Library, are by the engineer Carlo Rainaldi.

[4] See *Acta consist. Cod. Barb. lat. 2871, Vatican Library.

[5] See Bull. X., 467 *seq.* *Cf.* the letter to the Romans (Papal Secret Archives) in App. n. 14.

[6] See *Avvisi of January 27 and 30, 1599, Urb. 1067, *loc. cit.*; *Diarium P. Alaleonis, Barb. 2816, *ibid.*

[7] Among them was Giov. Fontana; see BERTOLOTTI, Art. Subalp., Mantua, 1884; Art. Lomb., I., 98 *seq.*, II., 5 *seq.* The Pope had already in 1596 appointed this architect, together with Giacomo della Porta and three Venetian architects to regulate

The congregation ordered that the mire should be cleared out of the streets, as if it remained there was reason to fear the outbreak of epidemics.[1] A very prudent step was the prohibition to inhabit the lower floors of the houses for a month, for these had suffered especially from the moisture. There was also a prohibition of any increase in the price of food.[2] The rebuilding works had to be hurried forward, all the more so as the jubilee would occur in the following year.

In the meantime the plans for the regulation of the Tiber were so far advanced that in June it was possible to begin

the bed of the Tiber ; see BERTOLOTTI, Art. Svizz., Bellinzona, 1886, 11. At that time, as well as now, all manner of plans were suggested ; see Paolo Berti, *Ragionamento sul rimedio per impedire le inondazioni del Tevere (dated Padua, February 9, 1601), in Vat. 6557, p. 1 seq., Vatican Library. Cf. the rare work : P. BENI, Discorsi sopra l'inondazione del Tevere, Rome, 1599. See also Tarquinio Pinaoro, Discorso dell'inondatione del Tevere seguita, 1598, in Urb. 861, p. 85 seqq., Vatican Library ; EHRLE, Pianta di Maggi-Maupin-Losi del 1625, Rome, 1915, 8 seqq. ; ORBAAN, Documenti, 121 n. The architect Carlo Lombardi was appointed in 1599 as deputy for the clearance of the damage caused by the inundation of the Tiber ; see BERTOLOTTI, Artisti Svizz., 16. In 1593 he had already been appointed " exstimator et mensurator generalis omnium aquarum " ; see BERTOLOTTI, Art. Subalp., 43 seq. ; cf. Art. Lomb., I., 96, 218.

[1] Cf. *Avvisi of January 3 and 6, 1599, Urb. 1067, loc. cit. In other ways as well steps were taken in order to provide for hygienic conditions in Rome as far as possible. Thus steps were taken in the heat of the summer to prevent pestilence being introduced into the city. As to this see the *report of G. C. Foresto, July 3, 1599, Gonzaga Archives, Mantua, and the *Avvisi of July 7 and 28, and August 24, 1599, Urb. 1067, loc. cit. The first states that it had been decided at the Capitol to close that part of the city which lay open (from the Porta Cavalleggieri to the Porta Settimana) so as to be able to place guards everywhere, on account of the plague. For an epidemic in the Celimontana district in 1601, see TOMASSETTI, I., 166.

[2] See *Avviso of January 13, 1599, Urb. 1067, loc. cit.

the digging of a new channel across the Prati near Ponte Molle. It was feared, however, that this would not provide a really radical remedy, and that the enormous cost of 200,000 scudi would be money thrown away.[1] This plan was therefore abandoned, and it was decided to effect another deviation of the Tiber near Orte, the cost of which was estimated at 150,000 scudi.[2] In December 1600 and January 1601 there were fresh inundations, though less serious ones ;[3] but the plans so far adopted were proved to be impracticable.[4] Even though it had been possible to provide the money, there were at that time no technical means equal to so difficult a task, and one on which the efforts of the Roman Emperors had already failed.[5]

The question of the regulation of floods also caused Clement VIII. anxiety in the case of Ferrara. The Pope intended to make one arm of the Po navigable, namely the Po di Primaro, and to make its right bank cultivateable ; also to regulate the Reno and drain the marshes of the Romagna. The discussions[6] on this subject begun at Ferrara were continued in the following years. To the intrinsic difficulties of the matter itself were added serious disagreements with

[1] See *Avvisi of May 29, June 5 and 26, 1599, ibid. The two first in ORBAAN, Documenti, 121 n.

[2] See *Avviso of November 27, 1599, Urb. 1067, loc. cit.

[3] See *Avvisi of December 23, 1600, and January 3, 1601, Urb. 1068 and 1069, loc. cit.

[4] See *Avvisi of January 3, 19 and 23, 1602, Urb. 1070, loc. cit. Cf. also BERTOLOTTI, Giornalisti, astrologi e negromanti in Roma, Florence, 1878, 14 seq.

[5] J. CASTIGLIONE (Trattato dell'inondatione del Tevere, Rome, 1599, 71) foretold this.

[6] See *Avvisi of August 15 and 29, and December 5, 1599, Urb. 1067, loc. cit. Cf. *" Nota delle misure prese a Ferrara e suo territorio insieme con il livello per servizio della dissecatione di paludi et navigatione del Po di Ferrara—quali sono prese per ordine di Clemente VIII. 1598," Barb. lat. 4379, p. 115 seq., Vatican Library.

Venice,[1] but Clement VIII. would not abandon his plan for
that reason ; but it had not even begun to be carried out when
he died.[2] Among the engineers to whom the problem was
entrusted was Giovanni Fontana.[3]

[1] See the *briefs to the Doge, December 4, 1599, January 29,
May 27 and July 15, 1600, Arm. 44, t. 43, n. 418, and t. 44, n. 59,
143, 193, Papal Secret Archives (originals partly in State Archives,
Venice) ; DOLFIN, Relazione, 501 ; VENIER, Relazione, 23 seq.
Cf. *report of G. C. Foresto, March 25, 1600, Gonzaga Archives,
Mantua. See also *" Relazione della visita degli rev. Monsignore
Barberini, chierico di camera e di Msg. Agucchia, maggiordomo
del ill. e rev. card. Aldobrandini sul Polesine d'Ariano d'ordine
del Papa per vedere, informarli e considerare il taglio del Po, che
intendevano i sig[ri] Venetiani, 1599." Barb. lat. 4351, pp. 1-17,
Vatican Library. Ibid. 4343, pp. 154-273, *Negoziato del taglio
del Po tra la S. Sede e Venezia sotto Clemente VIII. 1599, with
original letter of Maffeo Barberini, Barb. lat. 5853 (ibid.) contains
*43 letters of Cardinals (especially Blandrata) and prelates
concerning the " negotio del taglio del Po disegnato da Venetiani
1598 sq. e ridotto a perfettura."

[2] Cf. FRIZZI, V., 28 seq., 43 seq., 50. Many *documents pertaining to this in Barb. lat. 4351, 4356, 4377, 4383, Vatican
Library. An anonymous *letter to the Duke of Mantua, Rome,
August 14, 1604, says : " Il Papa ha sborsato 20,000 ducati per
far prova se l'ingegno del venuto di Fiandra è a proposito per lo
negotio del Po, del Rone e delle lagune di Romagna." Gonzaga
Archives, Mantua.

[3] Barb. lat. 4351 contains, p. 48 seq. : *Discorso e giudizio
sopra il taglio del Po, signed by Giov. Rossi, Giov. Fontana and
Bartol. Crescenzio ; p. 64 seq. : *Discorso di Giov. Fontana sopra
il ritornare la navigatione a Ferrara, far la disseccatione di tanti
terreni, che sono impaludati et di ritornarli nel stato che erano
40 anni sono, scritto a Roma 28 luglio 1600 e presentato al Cardinal
Marcello ; p. 74 seq. : *Opinion of Giov. Fontana for Clement VIII.
concerning the " disseccatione et navigatione di Ferrara, Bologna
et Romagna 1601 " (Vatican Library). *Documents concerning
the measures taken against the overflowing of Lake Trasimeno,
on which occasion Maffeo Barberini acted as the Pope's commissary, in Barb. lat. 4353. There too an original *brief of
Clement VIII. to M. Barberini, June 13, 1602, Vatican Library.

In spite of the constant proofs of his favour which Clement VIII. continued to show Ferrara to the end of his pontificate,[1] the city greatly resented being deprived of its former brilliant court. Thousands of those who belonged there emigrated to Modena, while many of those who remained brooded regretfully over bye-gone days. " Thus passes the glory of the world "—wrote an aged retainer of the ducal house—" now there is no longer any duke in Ferrara, nor princesses, nor music nor singers."[2] Even though the city could not lose the stamp of a princely capital, it fell more and more into that silence which to-day still powerfully affects the wayfarer through its broad streets and its deserted piazzas. The diminution in the population of the city, however, has been enormously exaggerated by local chroniclers ; according to careful research it did not amount to more than 1800 persons.[3] Moreover a decrease of population was to be seen everywhere, not excepting Rome itself.[4]

This was all the more painful to Clement VIII. in that he did all he could to promote the welfare of his people. The greater part of what he did, however, in this matter has been forgotten and left unrecorded.[5] But in spite of this it is

[1] See FRIZZI, V., 40 seq. Cf. THEINER, Cod. dipl., III., 573 ; MORONI, XXIV., 153 ; Bull. X., 591 seq., 592 seq., 761 seq., 873.

[2] *Cronaca di Ferrara, MS. in the Albani Library, in RANKE, Päpste, II.[8], 184 seq. The manuscripts of the Albani Library were destroyed in 1857.

[3] See G. PARDI, Sulla Popolazione del Ferrarese dopo la devoluzione, Ferrara, 1911. How much this is exaggerated is clear from the fact that according to Agnelli (Ode Carducciane alla città di Ferrara, Bologna, 1899, 34), 20,000 Ferraresi emigrated with the duke.

[4] Cf. G. BELOCH, La popolazione d'Italia nei sec. XVI., XVII. a XVIII., Rome, 1888, 38. Rome had in 1600 : 109,729 inhabitants ; in 1601 : 101,546 ; in 1602 : 99,312 ; in 1603 : 104,878 ; in 1604 : '99,293 ; in 1605 : 99,647 ; see CASTIGLIONE, Della popolazione di Roma, Rome, 1878, 167 ; Studi e docum., XII., 170.

[5] Donato in 1592 reports a plan for establishing a single coinage for the whole of Italy, in BASCHET, 208. The constitution of

known that from the first years of his reign he interested
himself, as Sixtus V. had already done, in the revival of the
silk industry.[1] He devoted his attention to improving the
harbours of Terracina and Civitavecchia.[2] If in spite of
these and other praiseworthy efforts he was unable to prevent
the decadence of the Papal States, this was not only the
result of repeated bad harvests, scarcity, the scourge of the
bandits and the burden of taxes,[3] but other factors as well
must be taken into account, which are clearly pointed out
by the Venetian ambassador, Paruta. The provinces of the
States of the Church were governed in part by legates, and
in part by presidents ; the larger cities had governors and
the smaller ones a podestà. Once the offices of president
and governor had been attainable by laymen ; thus the father
of Clement VIII. had held the office of governor of Fano.
But gradually, especially in the time of Sixtus V., laymen
disappeared from the administration in such a way that they
only held the office of podestà ; all other offices were only
granted to ecclesiastics, into whose hands the whole juridical,
financial and political administration fell.[4] But how difficult
it was bound to be, even with the best will, for those who
had been educated for ecclesiastical purposes, to adapt them-

July 11, 1595 : " Officinae omnes monetariae status ecclesiastici,
Romana excepta, supprimantur," in Bull. X., 202 *seq.* For the
coinage of Clement VIII. see BAUMGARTEN, Neue Kunde, 34 ;
SERAFINI, I., 106 *seq.* ; MARTINORI, 7 *seqq. Ibid.* 35 *seqq.*,
concerning the medals of Clement VIII. For measures for
keeping away the plague from the Papal States see *Editti, V., 61,
Papal Secret Archives.

[1] See the Bando of October 30, 1592, in CUPIS, 211, and the
*Avviso of November 14, 1592 : " N.S. per introduttione dell'arte
della seta in Roma a beneficio della povertà vuole, che in ogni
rubbio di terra di questo stato si sementi un arbore Celso o Moro
sotto pena 10 sc. a transgressori, et che non si possino estrahere
sete da questo." Urb. 1066, II., Vatican Library.

[2] *Cf. infra,* p.   .

[3] *Cf.* PARUTA, Relazione, 394.

[4] See *ibid.* 419 *seq. Cf.* REUMONT, III., 2, 587 *seq.*

selves to matters that were entirely foreign to their vocation.
The very mixed duties of administration also occasioned the
disadvantage that it opened out a profound gulf between
laity and clergy, and that the laity were filled with a jealousy
of the ecclesiastics that often degenerated into definite aversion. Paruta says that he had often remarked, not without
amazement and disgust, how even prelates who were leading
lives that were very far from priestly, were held in high
esteem and rewarded, so long as they defended the privileges
of the clergy against the laity, and how sometimes a prelate
was blamed because he favoured the laity. He had often
heard people of eminence say, that it seemed as though the
clergy and laity did not belong to the same flock, and were
not to be found in the same Church.[1] Another disadvantage
arose from the fact that a new Pope hardly ever carried on
in the civil government the system of his predecessor.[2] This
was connected with the disastrous custom by which, at every
change in the pontificate, all the more important offices were
filled by new individuals. Thus men of proved experience,
who might have been of the greatest use, lost their office.
Too often they were replaced by others who, though in themselves they were good and learned, had no experience of the
matters they were called upon to administer.[3] This system
of change among the officials was all the more felt in that the
pontificates of the Popes, compared with the reigns of secular
princes, were for the most part very short ; the pontificate
of a Pope was on an average nine years in duration. Of the
sixteen Popes of the XVIth century, only two, Paul III. and
Gregory XIII. had been granted a longer reign (15 years in
one case and 12 in the other) ; six had reigned for less than a
year.[4] Compared with the sixteen Popes whom the Church
had had during the XVIth century, Germany had had five

[1] PARUTA, Relazione, 375.
[2] Cf. DÖLLINGER, Kirche u. Kirchen, 537.
[3] See PARUTA, Relazione, 420 seq.
[4] Cf. DÖLLINGER, loc. cit. 539, and PRINCE Z. V. LOBKOWITZ,
Statistik der Päpste, Freiburg, 1905.

Emperors, France seven kings, Spain four, and England five kings or queens.

Unsatisfactory conditions prevailed among the aristocracy of the States of the Church, for they sought to maintain themselves in their abnormal position, even after the aristocracy of other European states had become entirely subject to the power of the sovereign. They looked upon any serious enforcement of the laws as an infringement of their own rights, and therefore complained bitterly of the government of the Popes.[1] In reality the great days of the aristocracy had passed away even in the Papal States, and if in the treaty of peace concluded at Vervins in 1598 between Spain and France, the Colonna and Orsini had participated, although neither of these two houses had taken part in the war, this was only an echo of bye-gone days, and an act of courtesy towards the ancient representatives of the Guelph and Ghibelline princes.[2]

The number of the nobility in the States of the Church who devoted themselves to a military career had declined, together with the wealth and importance of the aristocratic families in general.[3] In spite of this the new families of the nephews of the Popes looked upon it as desirable to enter into matrimonial alliances with the ancient aristocracy, as had recently been seen in the time of Sixtus V., whose grand-nephews had formed such alliances with the houses of Colonna and Orsini.[4] The nearest approach to these celebrated families were the Conti and Savelli ; the rest of the Roman aristocracy were for the most part of quite recent date, and were composed to a great extent of those who had made their fortunes in the Eternal City.[5] Clement VIII. too was very free in conferring titles, so that in the course of a few years the dignity of duke had been granted four times.

---

[1] See PARUTA, Relazione, 396.

[2] See REUMONT, Beiträge, V., 96.

[3] See PARUTA, Relazione, 396 *seq.* ; REUMONT, III., 2, 596.

[4] *Cf.* Vol. XXI. of this work, p. 70.

[5] See PARUTA, Relazione, 395.

While men strove after high-sounding titles and a greater degree of magnificence, and disputes over rank often gave rise to grave scandals, financial conditions were going from bad to worse. Like everywhere else, so in Rome pomp and luxury had increased. Since the barons wished to live like princes, very often their large revenues proved insufficient ; in 1595 they were all more or less in a state of debt. The nephew of the victor of Lepanto was obliged, in order to pay his debts, to found a Monte of 150,000 scudi in 1587, the " loughi " of which had to pay six per cent. ; 9000 scudi had to be set aside for the payment of interest, and after three years another 9000 for the extinction of the capital, and since the revenues of Nettuno and Paliano were not sufficient for this, Nettuno was sold for 400,000 scudi to the Apostolic Camera.[1] Other nobles too were forced to sell castles, lands and jurisdictions. Thus Virginio Orsini sold the territory of Matrice to the brother of Cardinal Montalto for 130,000 scudi.[2]

The barons who had established Monti very often did not pay the interest, and this fact determined Clement VIII. to publish in 1596 the so-called " bull of the barons," which ordered, to satisfy the creditors of the Monti, the sale of allodial properties and jurisdictions without consideration for entail or for primogeniture.[3] The sale was secured by this measure, which at first seemed very hard.[4] It was in virtue of this bull that the Apostolic Camera acquired Castel Gandolfo from the Savelli.[5]

[1] See COPPI, Memorie Colonnesi, passim. Cf. PARUTA, Dispacci, II., 435.

[2] See PARUTA, Relazione, 396.

[3] The text of the bull, dated June 25, 1596, in Bull, X., 270 seq. Cf. B. CAPOGROSSI GUARNA, I titoli delle provincie pontificie nella seconda meta del sec. XVII., Rome, 1893, 5 ; FATINELLI DE FATINELLIS, Observationes ad constitutionem XLI. Clementis P. VIII. nuncupatam Bullam Baronum, Rome, 1714.

[4] See the *report of L. Arrigoni, July 13, 1596, Gonzaga Archives, Mantua. Cf. DOLFIN, Relazione, 454.

[5] The cost of acquiring this was, according to the *Avviso of December 7, 1596, the sum of 150,000 scudi. Urb. 1064, II., Vatican Library.

But the contracting of debts by the barons did not cease because of this. In 1600 the Sermoneta had 24,000 scudi of revenue as against 300,000 of debts. The heaviest burden of debt at that time lay upon the family of the Montalto.[1]

Many of the nobles gave great scandal, not only by their exaggerated prodigality, but also by their ill-regulated and immoral lives. A terrible example of this state of affairs, which was made worse by the abuse prevalent in Florence and other places, of punishing deeds of blood by pecuniary penalties, was given by the notorious story of the Cenci.[2]

[1] See the " Nota della entrata di molti signori e duchi Romani " of the time of Clement VIII. in RANKE, Päpste, III.[8], 109,* who however here as in many other cases, does not say where he found the manuscript. I have sought for it vainly in the Roman libraries. In 1605 Clement had to grant the Farnese permission to establish a Monte of 750,000 scudi, which was to pay $5\frac{1}{2}\%$ interest ; see GROTTANELLI, ll ducato di Castro, 32.

[2] *Of decisive importance for throwing light upon the legend of the Cenci, by which even Muratori allowed himself to be deceived, have been the diligent archival researches of A. BERTOLOTTI (Fr. Cenci e la sua famiglia, Florence, 1877 ; 2nd ed. enlarged, *ibid.* 1879). On this is based the spirited article by A. GEFFROY in *Études Ital.*, Paris, 1898. Bertolotti, however, goes too far when in his final conclusions he presents Francesco Cenci as a father of a family jealous of the honour of his house. This weak part of his account is attacked by LABRUZZI DI NEXIMA in *Nuova Antologia*, 2, Ser. XIV. (1879), 418 *seqq.*, against whom BERTOLOTTI wrote in the *Riv. Europea*, XIII. (1879), 51 *seq.* Bertolotti there skilfully defends the authenticity of his documents but his conclusions nevertheless remain rather hazardous. With regard to the attacks of Labruzzi on Clement VIII., even a writer as anti-Papal as Brosch says that it would be wrong to speak of the " excessive benignity " of Clement VIII., but that the charge that the Pope and the Aldobrandini drew advantage from the confiscation of the property of the Cenci " is unfounded." " We must also admit," BROSCH goes on to say (*Hist. Zeitschr.*, XLV., 177 *seq.*), " that the confiscation was legitimate, and was almost always done in such cases. We may also look upon it as an act of extraordinary kindness when Clement assigned to the widow of one of the condemned, Giacomo the brother of Beatrice, a sum

This noble family, whose dark palace stood not far from the
Tiber, close to the Ghetto, and near the church of S. Tommaso
dei Cenci,[1] had become degenerate in the second half of the
XVIth century. Christofero Cenci, a cleric of the Camera,
and holding a canonry at St. Peter's, but not a priest, for he
had only the four minor orders, abused his office of general
treasurer of the Apostolic Camera under Pius IV. in order to
enrich himself unduly. Being near to death, and tortured
by remorse of conscience, in 1562 he reisgned his offices and
married his mistress Beatrice Arias.[2] We can hardly feel

of 100 scudi a month for her support, or when he handed over to
the sons of the said Giacomo a capital sum of 80,000 scudi out of
the confiscated property." Recently RINIERI (B. Cenci secondo
i costituti del suo processo, Siena, 1909) has gone profoundly into
the matter. Sometimes he rightly finds fault with the faulty
editing of the documents by Bertolotti (p. 26 seq.) though he
rightly looks upon the work of that scholar as very valuable.
Rinieri has found in MAIOCCHI (La pretesa illibatezza di B. Cenci :
Riv. d. scienze stor., VII., 4 (1910) a defender against the attacks
of VECCHINI in La Letterattura, X., 1 (1910). CHELDOWSKI (Rom.
Die Menschen des Barock, II., Munich, 1912) although he is not
altogether in agreement with Rinieri, calls the latter's book
" the best account of the trial of the Cenci " (p. 80). At the end
he remarks : " Thanks to criticism European literature has lost
a tragic story. Beatrice Cenci was a common criminal, and not
a tragic heroine." The large work by CORRARDO RICCI, enriched
with many illustrations (Beatrice Cenci ; I. Il parricidio, II.
Il supplizio, Milan, 1923) says little that is substantially new,
but gives the whole material as completely as possible. RINIERI
in Civ. Catt., 1924, I., 33 seqq. has rightly protested against some
of the conclusions of Ricci. Other critical observations have
been made by BARON V. BILDT in the Swedish periodical Dagens
Nyhetten of March 30 and April 6, 1924.

[1] Cf. Studi e docum., 1881, 155 seqq. The tower of the Cenci
was destroyed in regulating the Tiber ; see SABATINI, La torre
dei Cenci e la leggenda di Beatrice, Rome, 1906. Civilta Catt.,
1925, September 19, 500 seq.

[2] That Cristoforo Cenci, though late, reformed and came to a
better state of mind, is proved by his restoration of the church of
S. Tommaso dei Cenci ; cf. for this ARMELLINI, 573.

surprised that the son of this couple, Francesco, who was born in 1549, soon developed the worst qualities, great immorality and a brutal disposition. As a young man he was twice imprisoned for deeds of blood, but recovered his liberty, as was common enough in the justice of that time, in return for the payment of a large sum. In 1572 he was exiled for six months from the Papal States, for ill-treating his servants.[1]

The many sons whom Francesco Cenci had by his marriage, contracted while he was still very young, with Ersilia Santa Croce, inherited almost all the vices of their father, who was as brutal as he was sensual, and whose depravity increased as the years went by. Although Francesco, after the death of his first wife, contracted a second marriage in 1593 with Lucrezia Petroni, he had not the least idea of changing his dissolute manner of life. A criminal process brought against him in the following year for sodomy united to acts of violence, ended with the payment of a sum of 100,000 scudi, and his confinement to his own house.[2]

Owing to the payment of such enormous fines, Francesco found himself in such financial straights that he could no longer maintain himself in Rome. He therefore retired in 1597 to Rocca Petrella,[3] a castle belonging to the Colonna on the road from Rieti to Avezzano, but situated in Neapolitan territory. He took with him his two sons Paolo and Bernardo; his wife and daughter Beatrice had already been sent by him to Petrella in 1595. The other sons remained in Rome; the eldest, Giacomo, had married against his father's wishes, and so had been disinherited by him. As thoroughly degenerate as Giacomo, who had forged his father's signature to a document for 13,000 scudi, were the two other sons :

[1] See BERTOLOTTI, 16 *seq.*, 20 *seq.*

[2] See *ibid.* 53 *seq.*, 414 *seq.*

[3] Francesco Cenci intended to go to Florence as early as 1594; see the periodical *Roma*, 1926, 241 *seq.* The castle, now a ruin, is not far from the river Salto and may be reached by carriage from Rieti in three hours. *Cf.* GORI, *Archivio*, 1877.

Christoforo, who fell in a duel in 1595,[1] and Rocco, who was
assassinated in Trastevere in 1598 in some amorous adventure.

Even in the solitude of Rocca Petrella terrible domestic
conditions prevailed ; quarrels and altercations were the
order of the day. In the autumn of 1598, the two sons of
Francesco made their escape ; the castellan of the castle
Olimpio Calvetti had facilitated their flight. Francesco's
rage increased when he then discovered that his twenty-one
year old daughter, Beatrice, was in love with Calvetti, a
married man. The castellan was ejected, and Beatrice was
punished with brutal cruelty and kept under strict surveillance, as was also her step-mother. But in spite of this
Beatrice found opportunities for continuing her relations with
her lover, and of planning with him and her brother Giacomo,
who was also burning with the desire for revenge, the murder
of her father. The horrible deed, to which Lucrezia also
consented, was carried out on September 9th, 1598, by
Calvetti and another assassin.

The authors of the murder were unsuccessful in concealing
the traces of their deed, which was discovered. Beatrice,
Lucrezia, Giacomo and Bernardo Cenci were arrested.[2] The
imprisonment of the accused was not unduly rigorous, as
was asserted later on ; they were able to provide themselves
with food and to take counsel with their defenders.[3] The
trial commenced on January 14th, 1599, in the course of which,
as it was a case of homicide, torture was employed in accordance with the law of the time.[4] It is clear from the minutes,
that Beatrice and Giacomo were the principal culprits ;
Lucrezia had at first vainly tried to dissuade them, and had
at last given her consent.[5] The death sentence which was

---

[1] Cf. BRUZZONE in *Fanfulla della Domenica*, V. (1883), n. 23.

[2] Cf. RINIERI, 143 *seq.*, 171 *seq.*, 209 *seq.*

[3] See BERTOLOTTI, 113 *seq.*, 147 *seq.*, 165, 280, 283, 289.

[4] Cf. G. SABATINI, La teoria delle prove nel diritto giudiziario,
Catanzaro, 1909 ; PRINZIVALLI in *Giorn. Arcadico*, I. (1910), 84.

[5] RINIERI (341 *seq.*, 401 *seq.*) publishes the authentic summaries
of the trial, of which one was the deposition of the prosecution,
the other of the defence. For the fate of the minutes of the
trial used by Giuseppe Spezzi see RINIERI, 59 *seq.*

pronounced on September 11th, 1599, at the conclusion of
the trial, was deserved by all three.[1] Bernardo, who was
still a minor, was only guilty in that he had not denounced
the crime, and his punishment was commuted to that of the
galleys, though he had to assist at the execution of his relatives.
This took place on September 11th on the gibbet near the
Ponte S. Angelo, now the Piazza S. Angelo. Lucrezia and
Beatrice were beheaded ; Giacomo was brained and quartered.[2]

Baldassare Paolucci, the agent of the Duke of Mantua,
attests that the tragic fate of the young Beatrice Cenci aroused
general compassion in Rome. She died with great courage,
and left a number of pious bequests. The public had no real
idea of the terrible facts which the trial had brought to light.
If the publicity of judicial trials which we have to-day had
then existed, the populace would have stoned the members
of this degenerate family even before the execution, instead of
paying honour to the corpse[3] of the parricide, when it was
taken to S. Pietro in Montorio. As no one had any knowledge
of the facts of the trial, it came about that in course of time
Beatrice was transformed from a criminal into a martyr.
It was stated that she had been driven into committing her
crime in order to defend her honour against the infamous
assault of her father. This view easily gained credence
owing to the notorious depravity of Francesco, and gradually
Beatrice came to be venerated as a second Roman Lucrezia.
This idea was borne out by the delightful portrait of a girl,
attributed to Guido Reni, with her yellow hair, and her head
covered by a white veil like a turban, which is preserved in
the Borghese Gallery. The tender and profound melancholy
which fills the eyes of the person represented in the picture,
has contributed not a little to the popularity of the legend

---

[1] See BERTOLOTTI, 150, 431 *seq.* *Cf.* RINIERI, 311 *seq.*

[2] See BERTOLOTTI, 135 *seq.* ; RINIERI, 316 *seq.* *Cf.* CESNOLA,
I manoscritti ital. di Londra (1890), 172 *seqq.*

[3] See the review of the works of Bertolotti by FERD. v.
HELLWALD under the title " The truth of the fable of the Cenci "
in the supplement attached to *Allg. Zeitung,* 1899, n. 297.

of the Cenci. In reality the painting can hardly be the work
of Guido Reni, who only came to Rome in 1602, while the
tradition that the person represented is Beatrice is very
uncertain.[1] From the trial it is clear, beyond all possibility
of doubt, that the unhappy girl has been made into a symbol
of outraged innocence without any reasonable grounds.
The defender of Beatrice, the celebrated Prospero Farinaccio,[2]
put forward in defence of his client a crime on the part of
her father, who tried to lead his daughter into incest, but he
gave no proofs. Nor did Beatrice herself nor her brothers
appeal to any such crime on the part of Francesco ; on the
contrary it is clear from the minutes of the trial that not only
was there immoral intercourse between the girl and the
castellan of Petrella, the murderer of Cenci, but also that
Beatrice co-operated in the killing of her father.[3]

Recent research has also destroyed that other part of the
legend of the Cenci, which made the execution an act of
judicial homicide, which had no other purpose than to secure

[1] BERTOLOTTI (143 seq.) rejects it as quite false, pointing out
that Guido Reni did not come to Rome until 1602, and that in
1623 the picture was not yet in the possession of the Barberini,
nor above all in that of the Colonna, from whom a great part of
the pictures of the Barberini came, though this does not afford
definite proof ; see REUMONT in Gött. Gel. Anz., 1880, n. 9. Cf.
also M. CRAWFORD in The Century Magazine, 1908 ; RODANI,
65 seq. ; KRAUSS-SAUER, III., 790 ; BÖHN, G. Reni, 35 seq., 40 ;
Jahrb. der Kunstsamml. des österr. Kaiserhauses, XXVI., 174.

[2] For the portrait of Farinaccio painted by the Cavaliere
d'Arpino, see ARTIOLI in Italia moderna, III. (Rome, 1905),
233 seq. ; PRINZIVALLI in Giorn. Arcadico, I. (1910), 88 seq.
For Farinaccio see the periodical Roma, 1926, 243 seq.

[3] Rinieri maintains that the idea of Francesco having made an
attack upon his daughter's honour must be entirely rejected ;
Vecchini defends the opposite view, and denies that Beatrice had
a son by Calvetti. The decision of this question is not of any
importance for the principal issue ; see PRINZIVALLI, loc. cit. 90.
BROSCH (Kirchenstaat, I., 311) says that even if the attempt of
Francesco had really taken place this would not justify the
parricide.

the enrichment of the Aldobrandini by the confiscation of
the family inheritance.   The confiscation of property which
followed upon condemnation to death, and the effects of which
Clement VIII. and his successors sought to narrow down by
successive acts of grace, was no exceptional case, but was in
complete accordance with the penal laws of those days.   The
State Archives of Rome contain hundreds of examples.[1]
Fundamentally, this law, in the case of homicide among
relatives—in which very often the desire to obtain property
was the principal motive of the crime—was very reasonable.[2]   It is therefore absurd to say that Clement VIII.
condemned the Cenci to the gibbet in order to give their
possessions to the Aldobrandini.[3]   Thus in this respect
as well the legend of the Cenci, which was afterwards often
made use of against the government of the Popes, falls to
the ground.[4]

If Clement VIII. allowed free course to the full rigour of
justice in the case of the Cenci, he was led to do so by the
frequent repetition of such crimes, especially among the
aristocracy.   Thus, about that time, a member of another

---

[1] See BERTOLOTTI, 324.   Against Ricci cf. RINIERI in Civ. catt.,
1924, I., 38 seq.

[2] So HELLWALD (loc. cit.) and RODANI (44) are unanimous in
saying.

[3] See besides RODANI, 45 seq., above all RINIERI, 329 seq., and
CHLEDOWSKI, II., 90.   For the much discussed property of the
Cenci, Terranuova, on the Via Labicana, which was for a long
time offered for sale, and was at last bought by Gian Francesco
Aldobrandini for a comparatively high price, see TOMASSETTI, I.,
276, and ORBAAN, Documenti, 58 n.

[4] For Baronius and the condemnation of B. Cenci see A. LAURI,
Il cardinal Baronio e il processo di B. Cenci, in Arte e storia,
XXXII. (1913).   HELLWALD (loc. cit.) says : " There can hardly
be any other episode which has so unfairly filled so great a place
in history, literature and art, and of which Guerazzi has made
use to undermine the prestige of the civil power of the Popes,
or therefore in politics, than what we may call the fable of the
Cenci."

family belonging to the Roman aristocracy, Paolo Santa Croce, through greed of money, killed his own mother. The assassin escaped punishment by flight, but his brother Onofrio was later on (January, 1604)[1] beheaded at the Ponte S. Angelo for having incited him to the crime. The same penalty had been inflicted in 1592 upon a certain Troilo Savelli, who had become a criminal in his early youth.[2] There was also a horrible tragedy in the house of the Massimi during the pontificate of Clement VIII. Lelio de' Massimi, Marchese di Prassedi, had in his old age become betrothed to a Sicilian lady of doubtful fame. His four sons killed their step-mother by shooting her. They took to flight, but all perished within a short time ; the second, Marcantonio, who wished to become the head of the house, got rid of his brother Luca by poison ; he was condemned to death, and died repentant on January 16th, 1599 ; the third lost his life in the Turkish wars, while the fourth was murdered by a jealous rival.[3]

In spite of the rigour of justice, crimes continued in the

---

[1] Cf. FR. ISOLDI in Studi stor., XIX. (1910), 227 seq., who puts full faith in the absolutely uncritical statements of Ameyden ; Isoldi could not even be sure of the date of the execution ; this is clear from the *report of L. Arrigoni, January 31, 1604, Gonzaga Archives, Mantua. The Relazione which GORI (Archivio, I., 358 seq.) published, gives 1601 !

[2] Cf. CANCELLIERI, Mercato, 286, and Possessi, 214. For the large number of executions in the year 1591 see Arch. d. Soc. Rom., XXXIX., 443 seq.

[3] The cases cited are related and to a great extent embroidered at will in the Italian manuscripts of the XVIIth century. LE BRET (Magazin, IV., 58 seq., 63 seq., 93 seq.), has translated them from the latter with all their original errors. More trustworthy data in GROTTANELLI, Il ducato di Castro, 28-29. Cf. Arch. d. Soc. Rom., XXXIX., 444 seq. An Italian broadsheet appeared concerning the execution of Savelli, which was translated : Discours sur la mort de Troile Savelli, Paris, 1598. An authentic description of the trials should now be given from the acta of the Archivio Criminale, now in the State Archives, Rome. Cf. also F. CRISPOLTI, Un giuri d'onore a Roma nel sec. XVI., in the periodical Roma, 1922, 221 seq.

city, as we are told in a report from Rome of January, 1604.[1]
Clement VIII. also had bitter experiences in his struggle
against public immorality in Rome.[2]   He also fought against

---

[1] *Avviso of January 7, 1604, Urb. 1072, Vatican Library.
In other cities the state of affairs was no better ; cf. e.g. for
Bologna the Atti e Mem. d. Romagna, 3rd ser., VIII. (1890),
112 seq.   See also the *instructions for a legate in Bologna in
Cod. G. 63, n. 9, Vallicella Library, Rome.

[2] See the *Edict concerning prostitutes and women of ill-fame,
March 26, 1592, in Editti, V., 60, p. 274, Papal Secret Archives.
Cf. PRINZIVALLI, Tasso, 82.   Detailed information concerning
the first measures as to the censorship of morals taken by
Clement VIII. in the *Avvisi of February 8, 15, 19, 22, 26 and 29,
March 4 and 28, 1592, Urb. 1060, I., Vatican Library.   According
to the *Avviso of March 28 it was enacted that : " Poichè
l'isperienza ha mostrato, che i luoghi già assegnati in Roma per
tollerarvi le meretrici non sono capaci per tanto numero, se li
assegna tutto il Rione di Piazza Padello, Ortaccio della Trinità
de Monti, cioè dal Arco di Portogallo fino alla Piazza del Popolo,
riservato 4 strade principali di essa contrada della Trinita " ;
this must be done within ten days, otherwise the meretrici must
leave Rome under pain of frusta and confiscation of goods.
According to an *Avviso of August 19, 1592 (loc. cit.) the Pope's
vicar prohibits everywhere the letting of camere locande to women.
An *Avviso of December 2, 1592, speaks of the introduction of
special sermons for meretrici, at S. Rocco and S. Ambrogio (Urb.
1060, II., loc. cit.).   Further measures followed in 1599 in connexion with the Holy Year ; all women of doubtful reputation
must leave the Borgo in July ; cf. *Avvisi of June 26, July 24,
and September 14, 1599 (Urb. 1067, loc. cit.) and the *report of
F. M. Vialardo, July 24, 1599, in BERTOLOTTI, Repressioni
straordinarie alla prostituzione in Roma nel socolo XVI., Rome,
1887, 15.   In the report *Cose occorse sotto il Pontificato di
Clemente VIII. it is stated : " Dato principio alla riforma de
costumi, et particolarmente contro alle cortegiane, come haveva
fatto con poco frutto Pio V. ; fra le cacciate di Roma fu Frances-
chiglia Spagnola, che doveva esser frustrata, ma fuggi " with the
help of the governor, who wished to render service to Cardinal
Sforza.   " Il marito con la sua moglie per dar concenso che alle
fusse meretrice fu messo sopra un asino, andando avanti uno che

the scourge of mendicity[1] and against extravagance in women's dress, but without any substantial success. He severely punished the spreading of false news.[2] He would have liked to have entirely forbidden the amusements of the carnival, but as this was not possible, he tried at least to restrain them.[3] and praised the efforts of the Jesuits who sought to distract the people from such dangerous amusements by means of the Forty Hours.[4] The increased severity of ecclesiastical penalties against duelling,[5] ordered by Clement VIII., and already laid down by Pius IV. and Gregory XIII., concerned not only the Papal States, but the whole of Christendom.

partava corne di bufalo, fu frustato et tagliatoli il naso e gl'occhi. (Barb. lat. 4592, p. 64, Vatican Library).   In spite of this severity the evil could not be eradicated.   Cf. the statistics in Studi e docum., XII., 174, according to which the number of prostitutes in Rome, even though it was not so great as is stated in the Avvisi themselves, was nevertheless increased.   Out of a population of 100,000 inhabitants, the number of unfortunates who lived by vice was 604 in 1600, and had increased to 900 in 1605. In the Archivio Criminale of Rome there are to be found many denunciations of crimes against nature ; see Giorn. stor. d. lett. ital., II., 148, where however it is erroneously asserted that immorality was only punished with difficulty under Clement VIII.

[1] See *Avviso of February 5, 1592, Urb. 1060, I., Vatican Library.

[2] See *Avvisi of February 25, 1595, and January 22, 1597, Urb. 1063 and 1065, loc. cit.   Cf. PRINZIVALLI, Tasso, 283 seq. ; Studi stor., XIX. (1910), 238.

[3] See CLEMENTI, 289 seq.   Many *Bandi relating to the carnival, for the years 1592, 1599, 1601, 1603, 1605, in Editti, V., 60, p. 10 seqq., Papal Secret Archives.   Ibid. 124.   *" Ordine circa le comedie delle gelosi " of January 21, 1593.   A description of the carnival in the *report of G. B. Thesis, February 28, 1604, Gonzaga Archives, Mantua.   La festa di Testaccio I. Orlandii formis, a rare folio of about 1600, belongs here.

[4] See *Avviso of February 24, 1599, Urb. 1067, loc. cit.

[5] Bull. IX., 604 seq.   Cf. BONAVENTURA COLONNESI, Tractatus de prohibitione Duelli, in quo quidquid a Clemente VIII.   P. M. de Duello sancitum est, Florence, 1625.

The relations between the aristocracy of the Papal States and the sovereigns of other states were an anomaly. The coats-of-arms of foreign powers on the Roman palaces, whose owners were in their service or belonged to their party, bore witness to this for a long time to come. A list of the Spanish ambassador Sessa, who left Rome in 1603, shows how many nobles were in receipt of or aspired to receive Spanish pensions. In this, besides the Colonna, we find the Orsini, Conti, Sermoneta, Frangipani, Caetani and Caffarelli.[1] The rebellion of the Farnese in August, 1604[2] showed how dangerous the relations of the Italian aristocracy with Spain might become. The events of that time caused Clement VIII. the greatest sorrow, and had a disastrous effect upon his health.

From the beginning of his pontificate Clement VIII. had frequently suffered from gout.[3] Stone developed for the first time in 1595,[4] and again in November, 1596, causing for a time serious anxiety for his life, especially as Clement would not hear of not discharging all business in person as usual.[5] During a long relapse in the summer and autumn of 1597,

---

[1] See *Memorie of the " Duque de Sessa sobre algunos cavalleros Romanos," Archives of the Spanish Embassy, Rome. *Cf. ibid.* the " Lista (drawn up a little later) de los barones y gentiles hombres Romanos que se muestran affecionados a el servicio de su M^d."

[2] *Cf.* Vol. XXIII. of this work, p. 259 *seq.*

[3] See *Avvisi of February 8 and 26, 1592, Urb. 1060, I., *loc. cit.* *Cf.* BAUMGARTEN, Neue Kunde, 26. See also the *report of Giulio del Carretto, March 28, 1592, Gonzaga Archives, Mantua. *Avvisi of May 6, 1592 (*loc. cit.*) and January 6, 1593 (Urb. 1061). *Report of A. Chieppio, May 14, 1594, Gonzaga Archives, Mantua ; *Avvisi of May 11 and July 6, 1594, Urb. 1062. Report of Paruta, January 7, 1595, in Dispacci, III., 1 ; *Avvisi of December 6, 1595 (Urb. 1063), January 24 and May 29, 1596 (Urb. 1064).

[4] See BAUMGARTEN, *loc. cit.*

[5] See the *reports of L. Arrigoni, November 9, 18 and 23, and December 7, 1596, Gonzaga Archives, Mantua. *Cf.* *Avviso of November 9, 1596, Urb. 1064, *loc. cit.* Lettres D'OSSAT, I., 358 ; BAUMGARTEN, *loc. cit.*, 28.

which confined the Pope to his bed for a long time, this was out of the question. During this year his state of health caused so much anxiety that contrary to his custom he was not able to go to Frascati.[1] When he fell ill again in January, 1598, the doctors attributed this to his having resumed work too soon.[2] The wearisome journey to Ferrara and his sojourn there benefited the Pope a good deal, but naturally his attacks of gout did not spare him even there.[3]

The Pope's health improved still more during the following years, although he was at times tortured by arthritis and nephritis.[4] In 1599 the astrologers predicted an early change in the pontificate, and their assertions sounded so convincing that they commanded a wide hearing ;[5] only Clement VIII. himself paid no attention to them.[6] During the Holy Year he underwent all the fatigue like a young man,[7] although he was repeatedly obliged to keep his bed by gout. He learned with great annoyance that during his illness men had

[1] See *Avvisi of July 23, August 16, October 22 and 29, December 6, 1597, Urb. 1065. Cf. *report of L. Cremaschi, November 1, 1597, Gonzaga Archives, Mantua. See also the *briefs to Cardinal Montalto, October 10, 1597, to Duke William of Bavaria, December 20, 1597, Arm. 44, t. 41, n. 227 and 326, Papal Secret Archives.

[2] See the *report of L. Cremaschi, January 17, 1598, Gonzaga Archives, Mantua.

[3] *" Nos quidem in ipso itinere chiragra et podagra aliquantulum tentati sumus " wrote the Pope from Fano on May 2, 1598, to the Duke of Mantua (original in Gonzaga Archives, Mantua). Cf. also BAUMGARTEN, loc. cit., 28.

[4] Clement VIII. repeatedly states in his briefs that the gout prevented him from writing with his own hand ; see *briefs to the Duke of Parma, March 18 and May 29, 1600, Arm. 44, t. 44, n. 90 and 148, Papal Secret Archives. Cf. also in Vol. XXIII. of this work, App. n. 43, the *letter to Sessa, December 3, 1603, Aldobrandini Archives, Rome.

[5] Cf. *report of G. C. Foresto, May 15, 1599, Gonzaga Archives, Mantua.

[6] See *Avviso of March 27, 1599, Urb. 1067, loc. cit.

[7] Cf. supra, p. 272 seq.

been discussing the approaching conclave.[1] " You would like to see me dead—he said in January 1601 to one of the ambassadors—but as you see, we are still alive."[2]

In September 1601, Barga, who had been Clement VIII.'s doctor for many years, and whom he greatly esteemed, died.[3] The new Papal physician prescribed a diet, and recommended the Pope to take more liquid, which did him good,[4] and during 1602 Clement VIII. seemed better than ever.[5] In November a more serious indisposition gave rise to all manner of rumours, but when the Pope again made his appearance in public he looked so well that it was said that he would yet survive[6] Cardinals Rusticucci and Galli, who during his illness had been taking a lively interest in the coming election. If during this year and the following one there were still attacks of arthritis Clement VIII. did not feel ill and was very cheerful.[7] The year 1604 opened less hopefully, and in January an attack of gout caused all the greater anxiety in that it was accompanied by want of appetite and insomnia,[8] and also because the seventy year old Pope refused to take any care of himself.[9] In March Clement himself thought

[1] Cf. *Avviso of January 27, 1601, Urb. 1069, loc. cit.

[2] See *report of G. C. Foresto, January 13, 1601, Gonzaga Archives, Mantua.

[3] See *Avviso of September 12, 1601, together with the contemporary *report of the envoy of Urbino, Urb. 1069, Vatican Library.

[4] See *Avvisi of October 17, 1601, and January 5, 1602, Urb. 1069, 1070, ibid.

[5] See *Avvisi of January 5 and August 7, 1602, Urb. 1070, ibid.

[6] See *Avvisi of November 13 and 19, 1602, ibid.

[7] For his jokes at the expense of " nano Pollacco " (named Trulla) see ORBAAN, Rome onder Clemens VIII., p. 34 ; *Avviso of July 26, 1603, Urb. 1071, loc. cit. and in Vol. XXIII., App. n. 33 ; for his health cf. the *reports of L. Arrigoni of January 4 and December 26, 1603, Gonzaga Archives, Mantua.

[8] See *Avviso of January 14, 1604, Urb. 1072, loc. cit.

[9] " Non ricusa fatticha ove va il servitio publico," Avviso of January 17, 1604, ibid.

that his end was at hand,[1] but soon afterwards he was again restored to health.[2] The strictness with which he observed the fast brought about another relapse in April,[3] but during the summer he once again felt so much stronger as to be able to adhere to his custom of himself carrying the Blessed Sacrament in the procession of Corpus Domini.[4] On the vigil of the Assumption he went fasting to St. Mary Major's, kept the fast of the vigil with all strictness and did a great deal of work, but this exertion, which had never before harmed him, this time had a serious effect upon him.[5] In September he was much worried by the anxieties occasioned by the rising of the Farnese,[6] but when he returned on October 5th from his beloved Frascati he felt so much better that he spoke of making a pilgrimage to Monte Cassino, from which however he was dissuaded.[7] The winter passed fairly well, but in January, 1605, the gout returned.[8] On January 19th the Pope unexpectedly paid a visit to the tomb which he had erected to his mother at the Minerva, and remained there for a full hour.[9] His state of health was still so good that Cardinal Aldobrandini was able to go to the archbishopric of Ravenna, which had recently been conferred on him, and where he intended to hold a synod.[10]

[1] *Avviso of March 10, 1604, *ibid.*

[2] *Avviso of March 17, 1604, *ibid.*

[3] *Avviso of April 24, 1604, *ibid.* *Cf.* Bijdragen tot de geschied. v. Brabant, VII. (1908), 365.

[4] *Avviso of June 19, 1604, Urb. 1072, *loc. cit.*

[5] *Avviso of August 18, 1604, *ibid.*

[6] *Cf.* Vol. XXIII. of this work, p. 261, n. 3, the *reports of Vialardo (September 17) and G. B. Thesis (October 23, 1604), Gonzaga Archives, Mantua.

[7] See the *reports of G. B. Thesis, October 9 and 15, 1604, Gonzaga Archives, Mantua, and *Avvisi of October 6 and 9, 1604, Urb. 1072, *loc. cit.*

[8] *Avvisi of January 8 and 12, 1605, Urb. 1073, *loc. cit.*

[9] *Avviso of January 19, 1605, *ibid.*

[10] *Avvisi of January 15, 19 and 22, 1605, *ibid.* For the preparations for the synod see the letter of Cardinal P. Aldobrandini

On the 21st the Pope presided at the congregation on the question of grace.[1] On January 30th Cardinal Palotta congratulated him in the name of the Sacred College on the beginning of a new year of his pontificate ; the Pope replied that he would like soon to be delivered from the labours and burdens of his high office.[2]

This desire was soon to be granted. On February 10th, 1605, during a session of the Inquisition, the old man had a slight apopletic stroke,[3] and a courier was at once sent to Aldobrandini bidding him return immediately.[4] In order to prevent alarm in Rome the carnival festivities were permitted, and it was given to be understood that the Pope was only suffering from a chill.[5] Clement VIII. knew that his end was come, and had Extreme Unction administered.[6] As there was then a slight improvement, those about him once more began to hope, but this was nullified by further attacks of apoplexy during the night between the Saturday and Sunday, February 20th, 1605. In the evening of that day Cardinal Aldobrandini arrived, but the sick man had lost consciousness. The Pope then revived, and recognized his nephew with joy, but his mental faculties were completely enfeebled. His strong constitution still resisted for a time, until on March 5th, a further stroke caused his death.[7]

---

to Caligari, Rome, October 2, 1604, in *Scelta di curiosita lett.*, CXCVIII., 250 *seq.*

[1] *Avviso of January 2, 1605, Urb. 1073, *loc. cit.*

[2] *Avviso of February 2, 1605, *ibid.*

[3] *Avvisi of February 12 and 16, 1605, *ibid.* *Cf.* SCORRAILLE, Fr. Suarez, I., 443 *seq.*

[4] *Avviso of February 16, 1605, *ibid.*

[5] *Avviso of February 19, 1605, *ibid.*

[6] See SCORRAILLE, *loc. cit.*

[7] For the last days and death of Clement VIII. see the *Avvisi of February 19, 23, 26, March 2 and 5, 1605, Urb. 1073, *loc. cit.* *Cf.* the *reports of G. B. Thesis of February 19 and 26, and March 5, 1605 ; the *report of Giov. Magno, February 25, 1605, and the very detailed *report of G. C. Foresto, February 19, 1605, all in Gonzaga Archives, Mantua. *Cf.* also *" Avvisi di Roma

In spite of a pontificate lasting thirteen years, the memory of Clement VIII., both from the ecclesiastical point of view and the political, had fallen into oblivion.[1]   If he did not meet with a worthy biographer, this was partly the fault of his relatives, who for too long timorously prevented access to the acta of his government.   But at last the return of these treasures to the Papal Secret Archives, due to the far-seeing

delli 21 febbraio 1605 " in the Boncompagni Archives, Rome, Cod. C. 20. *Ibid.* a detailed *relatione " della morte di Clemente VIII."   See also the *letter of Cardinal P. Aldobrandini to the nuncio in Venice, March 5, 1605, Aldobrandini Archives, Rome, 207, n. 5.   Among the doctors who attended Clement VIII. during his pontificate (see MARINI, I., 476 *seq.*) the most celebrated were Andrea Cesalpino (*cf. infra*, p. 450, n. 4) and Marsilio Cagnati (*cf.* ORBAAN in *Arch. d. Soc. Rom.*, XXXVI., 137, n. 2). See also HAESER, Gesch. der Medizin, II.[3], 12 ; ZAPPOLI, Medici celebri, 52.   From the letter of Cardinal P. Aldobrandini, published from *Carte Strozz.*, I., 2, 334 *seq.* it is evident that in the choice of doctors great importance was attached to their moral and religious conduct.   The fable spread by WOLF (Gesch. der Jesuiten, II., 308) that Clement VIII. was poisoned by the Jesuits, was exploded by DUHR (Jesuitenfabeln, 425 *seq.*, 735 *seq.*). Werminghoff too (in SCHIELE, Die Religion, I. [1908], 1838) rejects the poisoning as a fable unworthy of belief.   The body of Clement VIII. was first buried in St. Peter's (see CIACONIUS, IV., 268).   Paul V. in gratitude erected to him a splendid monument in St. Mary Major's, of which we shall speak in a future volume. The body was only translated to St. Mary Major's in 1646, see MORONI, XIV., 48.

[1] The " Vita et gesta Clementis VIII." in Inform. polit., XXXIX. of the State Library, Berlin (composed while Clement VIII. was still alive, and probably a work of Andrea Victorelli) is as unimportant as the *Dialogue by Mons. Malaspina in Cod. N. 17 of the Vallicella Library, Rome (*cf.* RANKE, III.[8], 89*, 96*).   Also the *Fragments of a Biography of Clement VIII. composed by Gius. Malatesta, a summary of which is preserved in Cod. K. 25, p. 294 *seq.*, 315 *seq.* of the Vallicelliana, give little that is new.   It is often quoted (*e.g.* by WALCH, Hist. der Päpste, 406).   L. WADDING, Vita Clementis VIII., Rome, 1723, but this work has never been found (see CIACONIUS, IV., 272).

care of Leo XIII., has been of great service to the memory of Clement VIII. Thus in his case too is verified the saying, that the best defence of the Popes is the knowledge of their lives, a thing that is no less true of the zeal displayed by Clement VIII. in the field of science and art.

CHAPTER XI.

CLEMENT VIII. AND LEARNING.—TORQUATO TASSO.

THE predilection for scholars and writers which Clement VIII. had already displayed while a Cardinal, was continued after he had become Pope. How highly he esteemed intellectual ability is shown by the preference for scholars which he displayed in conferring the highest ecclesiastical dignities. At his very first consistory the purple was conferred on Francisco Toledo, who was looked upon as the most learned man in Spain. So in subsequent creations men of learning were always taken into consideration : for example, in 1596 the Oratorian Francesco Maria Tarugi, the canonist Francesco Mantica, and the greatest historian of his time, Cesare Baronius. The most distinguished of the theologians of the day, Robert Bellarmine, received the red hat in 1599 ; at the same time there were admitted to the senate of the Church Silvio Antoniano and Domenico Toschi, who was well known everywhere as a canonist. In the conferring of the purple on Du Perron in 1604, a decisive factor were the scientific attainments of this man, who was called the Augustine of France.[1]

Among the men who formed the entourage of the Pope there were to be found men of distinction and great literary culture, such as Guido Bentivoglio and Giampietro Maffei. Clement VIII. liked to have scientific works read at table ; thus, for example, the works of the celebrated English theologian, Thomas Stapleton, who was looked upon as one

---

[1] For the above-mentioned *cf.* Vol. XXIII. of this work, pp. 36. 46, 170, 248, and *supra*, p. 193. *Cf.* also Vol. XXIII., App. n. 29.

of the best controversialists against the reformers whom the Church possessed.[1]

Clement VIII. took a prominent part in the activities of the intellectual life of the time, and a number of theologians were honoured by him with special briefs on account of their works.[2] Writers who had returned to the Church, after having hitherto employed their talents to the injury of the Catholic religion, were invited by him to labour on her behalf.[3] The Pope showed special interest in continuing the publication of the works of the great Doctors of the Church, begun under Sixtus V. Of the edition of St. Bonaventure, the third, fifth, sixth and seventh volumes appeared in 1596. The two last volumes of the works of St. Gregory the Great had already appeared in 1593.[4] The Pope caused study of the best manuscripts to be made with a view to a complete edition of the writings of St. Athanasius.[5] He also took a keen interest in the collection of General Councils suggested by Cardinal Santori in the time of Gregory XIV.[6] By his

---

[1] See HURTER, Nomenclator, I., 59.

[2] See *briefs to " Florim. Remundi senat. Burdigal," May 7, 1599 (in which he praises his work, *De anticristo*, against the innovators), Arm. 44, t. 43, p. 232, Papal Secret Archives ; to " Schillerius," April 14, 1601 (concerning his explanation of the psalms), *ibid.* t. 45, n. 108 ; to " Cornelius Scultingius theol. Colon.," February 9, 1602 (concerning his *Bibl. cath.*), t. 46, n. 54.

[3] *Brief to " Phil. Canaius," October 11, 1602, *ibid.* t. 46, n. 307.

[4] See BAUMGARTEN, Neue Kunde, 329 *seq.*

[5] *Cf. Arch. stor. ital.*, 5th ser. XIII., 463.

[6] See BAUMGARTEN, *loc. cit.* 333. *Cf.* also, besides the briefs of 1603 in FANTUZZI, IV., 170, the *briefs to the archbishop and chapter of Trêves (*cf. Serapeum*, 1863, 51), September 27, 1597, Arm. 44, t. 41, nn. 221-222, *loc. cit.* See App. n. 11. Significant of the interest taken by the Pope in learned works is the *brief to " Andr. Bacagliar, episc. Algarens," December 8, 1601, who had sent to Rome his Latin translation of the work by St. John Damascene, De fide orthodoxa, where it was compared with that of Stapleton and Billius ; the Pope in consequence said that he did not consider a new translation to be required, sending it back to Bacagliar. *Ibid.* t. 45, n. 418.

command Christopher Clavius published a defence of the Gregorian Calendar.[1] The Theatine Antonio Agellio was given the bishopric of Acerno in reward of the services which he had rendered as an exegetist.[2] Antonio Maria Graziani was made nuncio at Venice, and also honoured in other ways.[3] Giovanni Francesco Bordini, who had done good service to the memory of Sixtus V., received in 1597 the archbishopric of Avignon, while the Augustinian, Angelo Rocca, the founder of the Angelica Library, was appointed Bishop of Tagasta.[4]

Among all these scholars, after Antoniano, the dearest to the Pope were Baronius and Bellarmine; they were consulted in all matters of importance, and often had to preach before him.[5] Both were shining lights in the Sacred College, and were pioneers in the world of scholarship.

Robert Bellarmine,[6] " one of the most learned and outstanding theologians of his time,"[7] and above all of modern times, was born in 1542 at Montepulciano, and in 1560 entered the Society of Jesus. It was a decisive factor in his future intellectual activities when in 1569 his superiors sent him as preacher and professor to Louvain. Bellarmine thus found himself in surroundings where the struggle against Luther

---

[1] See Vol. XIX. of this work, pp. 259, 280.

[2] See RENAZZI, III., 53 ; HURTER, Nomenclator, I., 366.

[3] Cf. I. NICCII ERYTHRAEI Pinacotheca, I., 189.

[4] See RENAZZI, III., 148. Cf. CELANI, La Bibl. Angelica, Florence, 1911.

[5] See COUDERC, I., 293.

[6] Biography by GIACOMO FULIGATTI, trans. by Silvestro Petrasancta, Liège, 1626 ; BARTOLI in his Opere, XXII., Turin, 1836 ; J. B. COUDERC, Paris, 1893 ; X. M. LE BACHELET, Bellarmin avant son cardinalat, Paris, 1911 (there, pp. 438-466, the so-called autobiography, with note, also published by Döllinger and Reusch, 1887) ; the same : Auctarium Bellarminiarnum, Paris, 1913 ; J. DE LA SERVIÈRE, La théologie de Bellarmin, Paris, 1909 ; LE BACHELET in Dict. de théol. cath., II., 560-599 ; SOMMERVOGEL, Bibliothèque, I., 1151-1254, VIII., 1798-1807 ; RIVIÈRE, 11-13, 316 ; HURTER, Nomenclator, III., 678-695.

[7] K. A. MENZEL, Neuere Gesch. der Deutschen, V., Breslau, 1833, 309.

and Calvin played an all important part.   After his return
to the Eternal City in 1576 he was recognized as a man able
to give the students of the German and English Colleges the
necessary training for their intellectual struggle against the
heretics in their own countries.   For fifteen years Bellarmine
devoted himself to this work with all the thoroughness which
characterized him ;   copies of his lectures were very soon
much sought after in Germany and England, and from these
there gradually grew up his great work on the religious
controversies in which " the defence of the Roman Church
was at the same time made use of as a weapon of attack
against his adversaries, with greater power, exactitude and
skill than was done by others, both before and after him.
The assertions and arguments of the Protestants are used in
this very fully and in their own words ; to learning there is
added facility of expression, order and a pleasing style ; his
zeal is manifested with such well-weighed moderation that
the supreme disdain which the author feels for Protestantism
cannot be looked upon as an instrument of passion, but only
as the expression of his own convictions.   His work thus
afforded abundant materials for the weapons which, towards
the end of the last decade of the century, were employed
by the German Jesuits in their ever renewed attacks upon
the Protestant Church."[1]

When Bellarmine began the publication of his " Controversies " many champions had already arisen in defence
of the ancient faith.   In the treatment of individual questions
enough had already been done, especially in the countries
bordering on Germany, by the Polish Hosius and the Netherlander Lindanus,[2] while at Louvain the Englishman Stapleton,
leaving details aside, had struck at the roots of the differences
between the old and the new faiths, treating of them " in a
way not as yet surpassed "[3] in his masterpiece on the sources

---

[1] MENZEL, loc. cit. 309 seq., 313.

[2] Cf. HURTER, loc. cit. 44 seqq., 187 seqq.

[3] M. I. SCHEEBEN, Handbuch der Dogmatik, I., Freiburg, 1873,
447.   Cf. HURTER, loc. cit., 175 seqq.

and rules of faith. There was still needed, however, a work which should review all these special studies, and which should, concisely and clearly, gather together their final results. Bellarmine set himself to do this,[1] but he quickly realized that a mere collection of the works that had already been composed would not suffice, since, as he wrote later on,[2] " concerning the Word of God, the controverted points had been dealt with by many persons, but concerning the Church and the Pope by few, and concerning the remainder by hardly anyone." Many questions had therefore to be dealt with which so far had not been touched upon in controversial works. During the struggles of the XVIth century only this or that divergent doctrine had been dealt with ;[3] the fundamentals had been left on one side, and thus the whole doctrine of the faith had to some extent to be brought under discussion. " Thus Bellarmine includes almost the whole field of dogma, in a manner entirely in accordance with this particular purpose."[4] It is possible to gather from the very extent of the work how much it contains that is new ; in spite of its concise nature as far as details are concerned, it extends to three heavy folio volumes, the contents of which were afterwards divided into four.

Bellarmine realized well enough the difficulty of his undertaking ; in his opinion it called for almost unlimited learning ;[5] but he had the necessary equipment ; acuteness of intellect, soundness of judgment, knowledge of languages, together with an acquaintance with the Fathers of the Church and

[1] " Disputationes de controversiis christianae fidei adversus huius temporis haereticos," 3 vols., Ingolstadt, 1586, 1588, 1593. Ad Lectorem.

[2] To Greiser, October 19, 1607, Epist. familiares, 54.

[3] " Non uno aliquo errore, sed ipsa haeresum colluvione appetimur " (Dedication of the Disputationes to Sixtus V.). " Innumerabiles haereses Ecclesiam lacerant " (Preface Ad Lectorem).

[4] SCHEEBEN, loc. cit.

[5] Scientia prope infinita (Introductory lection of Bellarmine, 1576).

with more recent theologians, such as to excite constant wonder;[1] it seemed as though he retained indelibly in his memory everything that he had ever read.

An especially attractive characteristic of Bellarmine, both as a scholar and as a man, was his simple frankness. An episode belonging to the days of his studies is characteristic in this respect of the whole man ; at one of the disputations which were customary for the intellectual training in philosophical and theological studies, he could not find an answer to a certain objection, and the professor suggested that he might get out of the difficulty by calling upon his adversary to prove a thesis for which the latter was probably not prepared. But young Bellarmine would not hear of this, and made reply that the thesis was true, and preferred to take upon himself the humiliation of not being able to reply, than to make use of a means which did not seem to him quite honest.[2] Thus the simple frankness which characterized him was shown in his relations with others.[3] It was in a like spirit that he came forward in the world of learning ; he sometimes admitted that not everyone had been happy in their refutations of Calvin.[4] In no part of his great work does he look upon the struggle with his adversaries as easy ;

---

[1] The vast learning, clearness, energy and solidity of the work is even recognized by his adversaries (SCHEEBEN, *loc. cit.*, 447). In like manner KUHN in *Theol. Quartalschr.*, 1844, 282 *seqq.* His talent for teaching, his lucidity of thought, and his skill in disputation were beyond question (THIERSCH-HAUCK in Realenzykl., II.[3], 550). The judgment of earlier Protestants in BARTOLI, I., I, c. 13 (I., 115 *seq.*). MORHOF (Polyhistor., II.[4], Lübeck, 1747, 544).: " Est inter Pontificios quasi Hercules quidam Rob. Bellarminus, quo atlante coelum suum fulciunt." RANKE (Päpste I.[7], 328) calls Bellarmine the greatest controversialist of the Catholic Church. HASE (Kirchengesch.,[10] Leipzig, 1874, 494) says that the " most serious " attacks on Protestantism were made by Bellarmine.

[2] FULIGATTI, I., 2, c. 5 n.

[3] Bartoli, I., 2, c. 2 (II., 23).

[4] *Ibid.*, I., 2, c. 6, p. 64.

he always quotes their own words, and admits that part of them which is true, and allows himself no rest until he has clearly shown their weakness.[1] This very fact explains the extraordinary success of the work. In 1588 men wrote to the author from Mayence that at the Frankfort fair the second volume had been bought up as soon as it was published ; if the printer had had two thousand copies he would have sold them all down to the very last.[2] The three or four huge folio volumes had run through about thirty editions by the end of the XVIIth century ;[3] they formed the pivot upon which the controversy with the innovators turned, in a almost incalculable number of works on either side.[4] Many Protestants, convinced by the reasoning of Bellarmine, returned to the ancient Church.[5] Cardinal Du Perron, who, like Stapleton and Bellarmine, was one of the greatest controversialists against Protestantism, called Bellarmine and Baronius the two stars of the Church in his time, and was of opinion that the articles of Bellarmine concerning the Eucharist contained all that was best that had been written on the subject for the last five hundred years.[6] Baronius, in his Annals, twice, so to speak, went out of his way to extol

[1] The accounts given by Bellarmine of the opinions of the Protestants are complete and accurate (THIERSCH-HAUCK, loc. cit., 553).

[2] H. Thyräus to Bellarmine, September 29, 1588, in LE BACHELET, 219. Cf. Lessius to Bellarmine, December 10, 1588 : The first volume was read everywhere, even by the councillors and advocates. The copies that reached Louvain were at once bought up.

[3] SOMMERVOGEL, I., 1156.

[4] Index, ibid. 1165-1180. "For many years afterwards, Bellarmine was held by Protestant advocates as the champion of the Papacy, and a vindication of Protestantism generally took the form of an answer to his works'." Encyclop. Brit., III., 695.

[5] Testimony of the nuncio at Cologne, Antonio Albergati, in BARTOLI, I., 1, c. 13 (I., 124) ; of Cardinal Dietrichstein, ibid. I., 4, Testimoninanze n. 8 (IV., 21), etc.

[6] Du Perron to Bellarmine, February 10, 1605, in BARTOLI, I., 1, c. 15 (I., 144 seq.).

his friend Bellarmine.[1] The exegetist Cornelius a Lapide, was of the opinion that from the beginning of Christianity there had been no work comparable to that of this theologian.[2] It may be added that by his defence of the Papal authority he aroused the opposition, not only of the Protestants,[3] but also of the Gallicans. His first volume was prohibited in France.

[1] Ad a. 53, c. 32 (he praises the " nobilissimum opus " of the Controversies) ; ad a. 968, n. 93, " vir doctissimus ac religiosissimus Robertus Bellarminus, virtutum meritis toti christiano orbi conspituus."

[2] Opera, I., Antwerp, 1697, 10 n. 38. Certain objections were raised against the work by the Jesuits ; e.g. above all by Cardinal Toledo ; they collapsed when the General of the Order had them examined by two theologians. LE BACHELET, Bellarmin, 350, 412. For its inclusion in the Index by Sixtus V., and its removal by Urban VII. see Vol. XXI. of this work, p. 197, n. 3.

[3] The doctrines of Bellarmine were also little understood by Ranke. " In these assertions (of the plenitude of the power of the Pope) the opinion that the power of the king was also based upon divine right was closely approached. . . . The Jesuits had no scruple in making the power of the king come from the people. By their doctrine of Papal power they laid the foundations of the theory of the sovereignty of the people." (Päpste, II.[6], 123). But Bellarmine, on the contrary (De membris ecclesiae, I., 3 ; De laicis, c. 3 ; Controversiae, I., Prague, 1721, 298) expressly teaches that the civil power comes from God, proving its rights from the Sacred Scriptures (Prov. viii. 15 ; Matt. xxii. 21 ; Rom. xiii. 1). Therefore according to him it is not laid down by the will of God whether the form of government is to be monarchical or republican, or an hereditary or elective monarchy, or whether the sovereign must be chosen from this or that family. The people itself must decide as to this, and since it can transmit the sovereign power to certain persons, in this sense it must inhere in the people before it can be so conferred. But after the people has once transmitted this power, it is deprived of it, and cannot resume it at pleasure. In Bellarmine's theory nothing is said of the sovereignty of the people in the sense of Rousseau, or of any right of revolution. Particulars in DE LA SERVIÈRE, loc. cit. 244 seqq. ; SCHEEBEN in Staats lexikon, I.[3], (1908), 761 ; SCHNEEMANN in Stimmen aus Maria-Laach, II. (1872), 375 seqq.

After the completion of the second volume of the Controversies, Bellarmine gave up lecturing. In 1589 Sixtus V. appointed him theological adviser to Cardinal Errico Caetani, on his mission to France. After his return, the General, Aquaviva, employed him in the government of the Order ; he probably saw in him his own successor, and wished to give him an opportunity of acquiring experience in questions of administration. Thus in 1592 he was able to complete the third volume of the Controversies, but was then appointed rector of the Roman College, and soon after, in 1594, superior of the province of the Order in Naples. But Aquaviva's plans were never realized ; the Holy See had cast its eyes upon the clever scholar, and employed him in the preparation of the edition of the Vulgate, and in the work of the Inquisition. When the death of Toledo had left vacant the post of a Jesuit Cardinal, Clement VIII. conferred the red hat upon him in 1599. " We have chosen him—the Pope said on that occasion —because in the Church of God there is no one equal to him in doctrine, and because he is the nephew of Marcellus II."[1] How highly Clement VIII. esteemed him at that time may be seen from a treatise on the duties of a Pope, which he allowed Bellarmine to present to him, and in which he wrote replies to certain remarks.[2] A catechism which Bellarmine had drawn up for the instruction of the people was made obligatory by Clement VIII. for the whole of the States of the Church.[3] In 1602 he was appointed Archbishop of Capua ; the Pope himself consecrated him.[4] It was only natural that a Pope with such great knowledge of history as Pius XI. should

[1] BARTOLI, I., 2, c. 5 (II., 48). The mother of Bellarmine, Cinthia, was the sister of Marcellus II. In 1620 Bellarmine was given the titular church of Charles Borromeo, whom he greatly venerated (S. Prassede). *Avviso of September 2, 1620, Urb. 1088, Vatican Library.

[2] Cf. supra, p. 187, n. 5.

[3] Brief of July 15, 1598, Institutum Soc. Iesu, I., 123.

[4] The Pope wanted to remove him from Rome, on account of the controversies about grace (see supra, pp. 352, 354) for their opinions were divergent as to this.

have held up Bellarmine as a star of the first magnitude in the firmament of the Church, and as one of the most energetic champions of Catholic doctrine.[1]

How dear to Clement VIII. was Cesare Baronius, may be seen from the fact of his having chosen him as his confessor. Clement took a keen and active interest in Baronius' monumental work, the Annals of the Church. He summoned the learned Benedictine, Constantino Gaetano, to Rome[2] to assist him in his laborious task. Baronius showed his gratitude for the extraordinary interest taken by the Pope, a thing which he also showed in other ways, by dedicating to him the fourth, fifth and sixth volumes of his gigantic work,[3] which, drawing as it did upon an enormous treasury of documents, formed an entirely new basis for the history of the Church. The Catholic point of view was rigorously adhered to and courageously maintained against the attacks of the Protestants ; at the same time, however, Baronius did not shrink from frankness and even severity in his judgments ; his great work is still to-day of great value to scholars.[4] The fear which was expressed by some that his elevation to the cardinalate would hamper the great historian in his continuation of the Annals was fortunately not verified. The seventh volume appeared in 1596, which, like the eighth, published in 1599, was dedicated to Clement VIII. After the sudden death of the learned Cardinal Colonna, in May 1597, Baronius

---

[1] " A star of the first magnitude, and one of the most able controversialists of Catholic truth " (Allocution of April 15, 1923).

[2] Cf. RENAZZI, III., 135.

[3] See CALENZIO, Baronio, 348, 430. For the interest taken by Clement VIII. in Baronio see BAUMGARTEN, Neue Kunde, 126, 291 seq.

[4] Cf. the opinions of Reuter, Reumont, Böhmer, Lämmer and Mirbt, which I have collected under the title " Giudizi tedeschi intorno al Baronio " in the special work, Per Cesare Baronio nel terzo centenario della sua morte, Rome, 1911, 15 seq. See also BAUR, Die Epochen der kirchl. Geschichtschreibung (1852), 72 seq.

was able to thank the Pope for his appointment as head of the Vatican Library.[1]

The precious collection of manuscripts which Cardinal Sirleto had increased to a considerable number, now possessed, thanks to the care of Sixtus V., a magnificent home in the Papal palace ; united to them was also a part of the Papal Secret Archives. How much importance Clement VIII. attached to increasing these treasures may be seen from the invitation which he addressed to all the bishops of the Papal States to send to the Vatican Library all the manuscripts and documents which came to their knowledge, so that a selection maight be made of those which were of value.[2] Those which were preserved at the Vatican were not to be a buried treasure. By the order of Clement VIII., and under the superintendence of Baronius, the custodians of the Library, who belonged to the Rainaldi family, laboured with unwearied and altruistic zeal to render it available, and above all Domenico Rainaldi, who in the time of Clement VIII. worked with such delight in cataloguing the manuscripts and printed books, and the material in the archives, that in this respect as well the Vatican was able to take the first place among all the collections of manuscripts in the world.[3]

At the same time Domenico Rainaldi set in order the Archives of the Castle of St. Angelo,[4] for which Clement VIII., soon after his election, prepared as a resting place a special hall on the upper floor, which was richly decorated and furnished with valuable presses. With this measure, which was immortalized in a poem by Maffeo Barberini, was con-

---

[1] See CALENZIO, *loc. cit.*, 471, 517 ; BAUMGARTEN, *loc. cit.* 293, 299.

[2] See MERCATI, Biblioteca Apost., 22 *seq.* For the interest taken in the Acta of the Council, from the literary remains of Paleotto see *Röm. Quartalschr.*, IX., 396 *seq.*

[3] See EHRLE in *Hist. Jahrb.*, XI., 718 *seq.* ; MERCATI, *loc. cit.* 9 *seqq.*, 12 *seqq.*, 65 *seqq.*

[4] See KEHR in *Nachrichten der Gött. Gesellsch. der Wissensch.*, 1903, 509. *Cf.* also ORBAAN, Documenti, 138 n.

nected a plan for placing all the archival treasures of the Holy
See in this safe place.[1] Even though this plan was not fully
realized, nevertheless not a little was done to make the collection in the Castle of St. Angelo a real State Archivium.
Innumerable documents were removed thither from the
Guardaroba, accompanied by copies of documents on a large
scale. The Papal treasurer, Bartolomeo Cesi, who was the
real originator of this great and useful project, was appointed
prefect. After his appointment as Cardinal, on June 5th,
1596, Domenico Rainaldi took his place, which he filled with
great zeal. It is almost impossible to do justice to the
importance of the collection of documents and acta on the
most important questions of the day furnished by this
indefatigable worker for the purposes of the Secretariate of
State. They were of inestimable value, together with the
memorials attached to them, in the questions of the absolution
of Henry IV., the acquisition of Ferrara, the discussions
concerning the Papal election, and the controversies with
Spain. Again in 1604 the Pope caused documents to be
brought to Rome, so that copies might be made of
them.[2]

It was of highest importance for the Vatican Library
that the librarian of the Farnese, Fulvio Orsini, who
after the death of Muret held the first place in the

---

[1] The *Acta consist. on January 29, 1593, record : S.D.N.
" proposuit bullam faciendam super scripturis Sedis Apost.
custodiendis et adservandis in Archivio, quod mandavit extrui."
Order for the drawing up of the " formula bullae et de genere
scripturarum ibi servandarum et mittetur per manus ut quisque
admoneat " (Barb. lat. 2871, Vatican Library). The bull was
never published. Cf. MARINI, Archivi di S. Sede, Rome, 1825,
29 ; Cardinal Gasquet, British and allied Archives during the
war, in the Transactions of the R. Hist. Soc., 2, ser. II., London,
1920, 56.

[2] See MARINI, loc. cit., 27. Cf. LAEMMER, Anal. 58, Melet. 282 ;
CALENZIO, Baronio, 722 seqq. ; KEHR, loc. cit., 1900, 371, 375 ;
1903, 514 seq., and especially MERCATI, loc. cit., 78 seqq. See
also BAUMGARTEN Neue Kunde 119 seq.

world of letters, left a legacy in 1600 of his most precious
collection of manuscripts and books to the library of
the Pope.[1] The former custodian of the library,
Tommaso Sirleto, also gave his manuscripts to that
collection. The acquisition of the legacies of Aldus
Manutius and the learned Dominican Alphonsus Ciaconius
added to its wealth.[2] Some Persian manuscripts were also
acquired.[3]

Closely connected with the Vatican Library was the Vatican
Press, which was directed by Domenico Basa, and from 1596
by Bernardo Basa.[4] Sixtus V. had united several benefices
for the maintenance of the correctors of this institution, the
revenues of which, however, were employed in other ways by
Gregory XIV. Clement VIII. therefore took steps to remedy
the lack of skilled correctors of the press, by abolishing certain
posts in the library, and founding in their place five posts for
correctors of Latin and Greek works,[5] and on August 20th,
1593, he conferred these for life on the Benedictine Adriano
Cipriano, the Florentine priest Giovanni Battista Bandini,
the doctor in theology Francesco Lamata, a Spaniard, and
on Gerhard Vossius of the diocese of Liège. When this scholar,
who had done good service as editor of the works of the
Fathers of the Church, resigned, his place was taken by
Maurizio Bressio. There were also employed Federico Metio,
and lastly, as unpaid corrector, the Augustinian Angelo

[1] Cf. BLUME, III., 39 seq. ; Serapeum, VII. (1846), 318 seq. ;
BELTRAMI, I libri di F. Orsini nella Bibl. Vatic. Rome, 1886 ;
NOLHAC, La bibliothèque de F. Orsini, Paris, 1887. There too,
p. 29 seq., the marks of kindness shown by Clement VIII. to this
celebrated scholar.

[2] See MERCATI, loc. cit. 23. For the library of A. Manutius
see, besides PRINZIVALLI, Tasso, 103 n., BAUMGARTEN, Neue
Kunde, 145 seq.

[3] See HORN, Die pers. und türk. Handschriften der Vaticana
in Zeitschr. der morgenländ. Gesellsch., LI. (1897), 4.

[4] See BERTOLOTTI, Le tipografie orientali e gli orientalisti a
Roma nei secoli XVI. e XVII., Florence, 1878, 26 seqq.

[5] Cf. Bull. X., 81 seqq.

Rocca.[1] These six correctors were also to work in the library, as these two institutions were connected with each other.

Clement VIII. concerned himself in various ways with the Roman University ;[2] he confirmed the union established by Sixtus V. between the rectorate and the College of Proto-notaries, and carried on the new buildings of the university. In his pontificate the great hall, which was adorned with an artistic carved wooden ceiling and a magnificent pulpit, was completed.[3]

Clement VIII. did good service by summoning the cele-brated botanist and physiologist Andrea Cesalpino from Pisa to the Roman University, where that scholar also held the office of principal physician to Clement VIII., an office which he held with the greatest success until his death in 1603. Giulio de Angelis, who was also summoned by Clement VIII. to the medical faculty, was less celebrated than Cesalpino, but he too was one of the Pope's physicians and accompanied him to Ferrara.[4] A disciple of Cesalpino, Michele Mercati, had been since the time of Pius V. director of the botanical

---

[1] See BAUMGARTEN, Neue Kunde 137 *seqq.* *Ibid.* 132 *seq.* for Vossius. *Cf.* also POPPENS, Bibl. Belgica, I., Brussels, 1739, 362, and *Mededeel. v. h. Niederl. Hist. Institut.*, II. (1922), 100 *seq.*

[2] Of the *Ruoli* that of 1595 is published in RENAZZI, II., 224 *seq.* This enumerates 31 professors. In 1592 there were 29 ; in 1593 31, but in 1601 only 27 ; in 1603, 26 ; in 1605, 28 ; see the *report of Carlo Cartari in Cod. H. III. of the Chigi Library, Rome. For favours of Clement VIII. to the University of Perugia see Bull. X., 32 (*cf.* 71). For the University of Ferrara see *supra*, p. 400, for that of Würzburg see WEGELE, II., 52.

[3] See RENAZZI, III., 21 *seqq.*

[4] *Ibid.* 42 *seqq.* For A. Cesalpino *cf.* SACHS, Gesch der Botanik, 45 ; [AMATI] Bibliografia Rom., I., Rome, 1880, 81 *seq.* ; [A. ZAPPOLI], Illustraz. ai busti dei medici celebri posti nell'attico dell'arcispedale di S. Spirito, Rome, 1868 ; CICONE in *Riv. di storia d. scienze mediche*, 1912, 73-92. For the efforts, though fruitless, of Clement VIII. to obtain Thomas Stapleton for the university of Rome, see Corresp. de Frangipani, I., 65, 94, 99 *seq.*, 107.

gardens of the Vatican, and professor of botany at the Roman University. In 1593 he was succeeded by Andrea Bacci, then by Castore Durante, and lastly by the celebrated German scholar Johann Fabri of Bamberg.[1] The summoning of the Platonist, Fr. Patrizi to be professor of philosophy in the spring of 1592,[2] was not a success, as he passionately attacked Aristotle as an enemy of the faith.[3] The attitude adopted by the Pope in this dispute is clearly shown by the fact that after the death of Patrizi in February, 1597, he appointed his opponent Giacomo Mazzoni to his office at the Sapienza,[4] assigning to him the large annual stipend of 1,000 gold scudi. Great patrons of Mazzoni were the two Aldobrandini Cardinals, who also generously supported scholars and poets in other ways. The best known of the poets who entered the service of Pietro Aldobrandini was Giambattista Marini.[5] Cinzio Aldobrandini established an Academy in his palace, to which belonged the most distinguished scholars, such as Antonio Quarengho, Patrizi, Giovanni Battista Raimondi, and also the composer, Luca Marenzio, who was named " the most sweet swan " and who from 1595 was organist at the Papal Chapel;[6] later on there were Battista Guarino, the author

---

[1] See MARINI, Archiatri, I., 459 n. ; RENAZZI, III., 44 ; F. LADELCI, La storia d. botanica in Roma, Rome, 1884, 12 seqq. ; ZAPPOLI, loc. cit., 83 seq.

[2] See *Avviso of May 2, 1592, Urb. 1060, I., Vatican Library. Cf. SOLERTI, I., 730.

[3] See TIRABOSCHI, VII., 1, 359 seqq. Cf. QUERRINI, Di F. Patrizi e della rarissima edizione della sua Nova Philosophia, in Propugnatore, XII., 1-2 (Bologna, 1879). For an autobiography of Patrizi, though it does not include the time of Clement VIII., see Arch. stor. p. Trieste, l'Istria e il Trentino, III. (1884-1886), 275 seqq.

[4] See RENAZZI, III., 31 seqq. Cf. ZAZZERI, Sui codici d. Bibl. Malatest. 18 seqq.

[5] Cf. BORZELLI, Giambatt. Marini, Naples, 1898, 57 seqq.

[6] Marenzio lived at the Vatican ; see Ruolo 19. The privat-dozent, Dr. Johann Engel, of Munich, is preparing a monograph on Marenzio.

of the celebrated pastoral drama *Il pastor fido*, Guidobaldo
Bonarelli and Tasso.[1]

Just as was the case with Cardinals Pietro and Cinzio
Aldobrandini,[2] many works were dedicated to the Pope
himself. Among the prose works the greater number were
religious and ecclesiastical;[3] not a few were concerned with

---

[1] *Cf.* CIACONIUS, IV., 285 *seq.*, and SOLERTI, I., 736 *seqq.* It is
remarkable that Cardinal Cinzio Aldobrandini had manuscripts
sought for even in Moscow ; see PIERLING, II., 375 *seq.* ; *Poesie
di Mgr. Ciampoli in lode de SS[ri] Aldobrandini, in Barb. lat. 3671,
Vatican Library.

[2] *Cf.* PERSONENI, Notizie del cardinale Cinzio Personeni de
Ca' Passero Aldobrandini, Bergamo, 1786, 131 *seqq.*, and Osservaz.
sopra la epistolografia di Fr. Parisi, Bergamo, 1788, 54 *seqq.*
For the " Nautica " dedicated by Bartolomeo Crescenzi to
Cardinal P. Aldobrandini see CIAMPI, Viaggiatori Romani in
Nuova Antologia, August-September, 1874.

[3] The greater number of the printed works are enumerated in
CIACONIUS (IV., 271 *seq.*). To these may be added numerous
unpublished works : *e.g.* Vat. 3565 : *Sei discorsi di Giov. Paolo
Eustachio (with dedication of January 1, 1597), namely : 1. Della
necessità che fa N. S. alle religioni ; 2. Della ragion di stato
conforme alla s. scrittura ; 3. Della nobiltà et in particolare della
nobiltà d'Hebrei ; 4. Della causa che mantien l'Hebreo in
ostinatione ; 5. Che de iure divino non si può negare al penitente
d'esser ricevuto nel gremio di s. chiesa ; 6. Quel ch'ha da fare il
penitente per esser conosciuto per vero penitente ; Vat. 5512 :
Franc. a Sosa (ord. min.), *De iurisdictione et optimo genere
procedendi in causis regularium libri 6 ; Vat. 5452 : Philippi
Bocchii (Bonon.) *Diadema Dei in quo de principio, statu et fine
ecclesiae et totius mundi agitur ; Vat. 5490 : Petri Martyris
Felini de Cremona (ord. serv. B. M. V.) *Modus visitandi vel
faciendi scalas sanctas (also in Urb. 1511) ; Vat. 5512 :
Scipionis Iardini (Macerat.) *Tractatus de Romano Pontificatu ;
Vat. 5517 : Fra Arcangelo Agostino (Capuccino), *Epitalamio in
forma d'oration mentale sopra la s. casa di Loreto ; Vat. 6386 :
Petri Lombardi Hiberni *Comment. stromatic. de Hibernia
insula ; Vat. 6390 : Frat. Chrysostomi a Visitatione (ord. Cist.)
*Libri 5 de vero Mariae virg. partu contra opinionem Alf. Tostati

the Turkish peril,[1] and some of the acquisition of Ferrara.[2] The most important dedications, after the Controversies of Bellarmine,[3] was that of the Annals of Baronius. During one of his sojourns at Frascati the Pope obliged Bellarmine and Silvio Antoniano to engage in a poetical contest, in which the palm was to be given to the one who composed the most beautiful poem on the saint of that day, Mary Magdalen.

episc. Abulen. ; Reg. 1597 : Francesco Torina Bufalina (da Città di Castello), *Il Rosario sopra i misterii della vita di Cristo. Vatican Library.

[1] For example the discourses of G. Crispo (Rome, 1594) and of Scip. Ammirato (Florence, 1594). In the Vatican Library there are to be found the following, not yet printed : Vat. 5519 : Aurelii Marinatae Ravennatae *Tre ragionamenti della S. Lega che si doveria fare tra principi christ. contra i nemici della S. Chiesa ; Urb. 833, p. 509 : Pompei Floriani *Relazione sopra l'antica origine dei Turchi [also concerning the forces of the Turks and an offensive war against them, to prevent their coming to Italy] (Copy in Inform. polit., XVII. of the State Library, Berlin ; see RANKE, Osmanen[2], 452) ; Urb. 1492, p. 1 seqq. Tarquinio Pinaoro *Sopra una lega ad impresa che potriano fare i principi italiani contro il Turco in soccorso della M. Ces. e principe Transilvano l'a. 1596. Very widely spread in manuscript was a copy of the " Discorso di mons. Pietro Cedolini vescovo di Lesina fatto alla S^(ta) di N.S. Clemente VIII. per la difesa contro il Turco 1594 (January 28)," published in Tesoro Politico, III. (Turnoni, 1605), 85 seqq. ; manuscript copies in Rome : 1. Vat. 5485 ; 2. Urb. 836, p. 406 seqq., Vatican Library. In Berlin : State Library, Inform. polit. I. ; at Copenhagen : Library. Gl. K. S. fol. 523.

[2] Only some, such as ISABELLA CERVONI, Orazione a papa Clemente VIII. sopra l'impresa di Ferrara (Bologna, 1598), have been printed ; most are in manuscript, e.g. *Relazione della città e stato di Ferrara data per informat. a Clemente VIII., in Urb. 835, p. 216 seqq. (cf. Barb. 5356), the *Discorso storico del Francese Pietro Demarchis, in Vat. 5551, and ibid. Comitis Alexandri Randensis *Tractatus de s. pontificis iurisdictione et ducatus Ferrariae devolutione ad Sed. Apost. Vatican Library. Cf. also supra, p. 447 seq., for the labours of D. Rainaldi.

[3] See Autobiographia card. R. Bellarmini, c. 30.

This was the origin of Bellarmine's magnificent hymn, *Pater superni luminis*, which was afterwards inserted in the Breviary.[1]

As Clement VIII. had a great liking for poetry, very many poems were dedicated to him.[2] Among these were one by Maffeo Barberini on the Pope's gout, and another on the new archivium in the Castle of St. Angelo.[3] Mention must also be made of how Orlando di Lasso, who, with Palestrina[4] and Marenzio, was the most celebrated musician of the time, had in 1597, a short time before his death, dedicated to the Aldobrandini Pope his last composition, *Le Lagrime di san Pietro*.[5] To the Jesuit Pietro Maffei, who had made a name as an historical writer, Clement VIII. assigned an apartment in the Vatican, and charged him to write the history of his ponti-

---

[1] See COUDERC, I., 25.

[2] The printed ones in CIACONIUS, IV., 271 *seq.*, and in Cat. Bibl. Casanat., II., 156 ; unpublished ones by Ant. Vallius in Vat. 5515, p. 48 *seqq.* ; by Giov. Vinc. Passerino in Vat. 5502 ; by Girolamo Aleander in Ottob. 2431, p. 451 *seq.* ; by Gerundio Liberatorio in Barb. lat. 1780, Vatican Library. A *Carmen in reconciliationem cum ecclesia catholica Henrici Galliar. regis, *ibid.* Vat. 5514, p. 56, dedicated to Clement VIII. *Versi per l'unione de principi christiani sotto Clemente VIII. in the Aldobrandini Archives, Rome, 286, n. 2. The writer of satires, Trojano Boccalini, enjoyed the favour of Clement VIII. ; see *Archiv. für neuere Sprachen*, CIII. (1899), 110. For the honours bestowed upon the Polish poet Simon Szymonowicz (1558-1629) by Clement VIII. see HANISCH, Gesch. Polens, 229. For T. Boccalini *cf.* MEINECKE, Die Idee der Staatsraison in der neueren Geschichte, Munich, 1924 ; A. BELLONI, T. Boccalini (1924). *Cf. Nuova Riv. storica*, 1924.

[3] See Maphaei Barberini Card. nunc. Urbani P. VIII., Poemata, Rome, 1631, 203, 222 *seq.*

[4] Palestrina died on February 2, 1594. *Cf.* A. MERCATI, Melchiorre Major, l'autore del vibrante necrologio di P. da Palestrina, Gubbio, 1924. It has not been possible to find the tomb of Palestrina in St. Peter's, in spite of the researches of Mgr. Cascioli ; see *Rassegna Gregor.*, 1914.

[5] See JANSSEN-PASTOR, VI.[15-16], 172.

ficate, a task which unfortunately was never carried out, owing to the death of Maffei in 1603.[1]

The name of Clement VIII. is also connected with that of Torquato Tasso. The great poet had known the Pope as a Cardinal and had received various favours from him. From Naples, where he was then living, he had at once celebrated his election in a poem, in which he makes all the virtues from heaven descend upon him.[2] He composed an Italian sonnet for the anniversary of his coronation,[3] and a longer Latin poem in which he extols the ecclesiastical and civil power of the head of the Church.[4] In this he does not omit mention of the nephews of Clement VIII., to whom there are also addressed three other sonnets, probably composed on this occasion.[5] After this Tasso received an invitation to go to Rome, where he arrived at the beginning of May, 1592. As

---

[1] *Cf.* ORBAAN, Documenti, 55 n.

[2] See SOLERTI, I., 700, who calls the poem " soperba." It begins as follows :

> Questa fatica estrema al tardo ingegno
> Concedi, o Roma, e tu, che movi e reggi
> L'alto ciel, l'umil terra e'l mar profondo,
> A lui, che di tue sacre eterni leggi
> È vivo spirto, e del celeste regno
> Sostien le chiavi e porta il grave pondo,
> E quasi folce in Vaticano il mondo,
> Sacra la mente, il cor, la penna e i carmi.
> Questa è la meta eccelsa, a cui d'intorno
> Si volge notte e giorno
> Il mio pensier : nè di vittorie e d'armi
> Cantate, fama eguale e pregio attende ;
> Ma fine o meta a quel valor non miro
> Che fiammeggia fra noi con luce eterna.

[3] " Ecco l'alba, ecco il di ch'in sè ritorna." Opere, V., 3, 2, Pisa, 1822, 208.

[4] " Magne parens pastorque patrum, cui pascere greges," Carmina latina, *ed.* A. Martinius, Rome, 1895, 39.

[5] SOLERTI (I., 723) gives one of these ; the two others (Fra. il tuo splendore and Tra Fortuna e Virtù) in VATASSO, Rime inedite, Rome, 1915.

had been the case in the time of Sixtus V., he took up his abode with his former patron, Cardinal Scipione Gonzaga, in the Via della Scrofa ;[1] but as early as June he had removed to the palace of the Pope's nephew, in the Via dei Banchi, where there was an open house with scholars and poets. When in November, 1592, Cinzio Aldobrandini removed to the Vatican, Tasso was invited to follow him.[2] Then the poet took up his residence in the most beautiful palace in the world, where he was waited upon with all honour, invited to the tables of Cardinals and princes, and honoured and distinguished in every way.

If, with all this, a certain melancholy and restlessness, and a morbid desire for change did not leave him, this was an evident sign of his melancholia (periodical dementia), which, however—so closely akin are genius and madness—did not in any way interfere with his literary activity.[3] Cinzio Aldobrandini, who had a sincere veneration for the sorely tried poet, felt a sincere compassion for him. He efficaciously promoted the re-writing of Tasso's *Gerusalemme liberata*, giving him in the person of Angelo Ingegneri an amanuensis, who was able to decipher with facility the difficult handwriting of the poet.[4]

Besides his masterpiece Tasso also composed with feverish activity other poems in which he has given expression to his

[1] For the Palazzo Gonzaga, afterwards Negroni-Galitzin, see PRINZIVALLI, 46 *seqq.*, who however wrongly makes Tasso go to live with the Aldobrandini at once ; see *Giorn. stor. d. lett. ital.*, XXVII., 412.

[2] Cinzio Aldobrandini lived, as Prinzivalli shows (88-97) in the " Appartamento della contessa Matilde." Prinzivalli also tried to point out the poet's dwelling exactly, but was not successful ; see *Giorn. stor. d. lett. ital.*, XXVII., 413. ORBAAN (Documenti, 457 n.) however found a second *Ruolo* in which the situation of Tasso's three rooms is indicated.

[3] *Cf.* A. CORRADI, Le infermità di T. Tasso, in *Mem. dell'Ist. Lomb.*, XIV. (1881), 301 *seqq.* ; L. RONCORONI, Genio e pazzia di T. Tasso, Turin, 1896 ; BONFIGLI in *Arch. p. le malattie nervose*, 1887, fasc. 3.

[4] See SOLERTI, I., 741.

deep sense of religion. Thus there were written at that time
the pathetic verses on the *Santa Croce* and *Le lagrime della
beatissima Vergine*. The inspiration for the last named was
drawn from a picture attributed to Albert Dürer, which was
in the possession of Cinzio Aldobrandini.[1]

To this exalted patron Tasso dedicated the new version
of the Gerusalemme liberata, which was at last completed
in May, 1593, and was given the title of *Gerusalemme conquistata*. The printing was begun in July ; the expenses
were borne by Cinzio Aldobrandini, while the profits were
all to go to the author.[2] Cinzio, who became a member of
the Sacred College on September 17th, 1593, saw to it that he
received the necessary privileges to protect his rights as
author.[3] The first copies of the work, from which there had
been removed all the tributes to the House of Este, originally
in connexion with the character of Rinaldo, but which were
now replaced by others to the Cardinal nephews and the Pope,
were able to be issued in the early days of December. Of
greater importance than these external changes were the
internal ones, by which the new poetical work was intended
to be distinguished from the former one, as the heavenly
Jerusalem from the earthly one. In conformity with this
idea the religious character of the Crusades was emphasized,
by means of a dream of Godfrey de Bouillon, with the purpose
of introducing a magnificent description of heaven, and un-
folding a grandiose prophetic vision of the future development
of Christendom. The episode of Olindo and Sophronia was
omitted, but in so doing Tasso was rather influenced by
literary considerations, since a long digression such as this
did not seem opportune, especially at the beginning of the
poem. Literary considerations also led to the curtailing of
the romance of Rinaldo and Armida, as well as that of Tancred.
If the work thus received unity and harmony, on the other
hand it suffered by the omission of certain beautiful passages,

[1] *Ibid.* I., 752 *seqq.*
[2] *Ibid.* 760 *seqq.*
[3] *Ibid.* 761 *seqq.*

such as the magnificent description of the sea vogaye of the two heroes, when seeking for Rinaldo on the enchanted island. How unfortunate was such a change from the original form of this " first daring outburst of genius " was proved by the wretched success of the *Gerusalemme conquistata*, which was unable to overshadow the *Gerusalemme liberata*, which was entirely permeated by the enthusiasm of youth.[1]

Stricken once more at the beginning of 1594 by illness, Tasso resolved to seek repose at Naples, whither he was also drawn by a long-standing law-suit concerning the inheritance of his mother. He passed the summer and autumn at the Benedictine convent of S. Severino, engaged, despite his bad state of health, in constant literary activity.[2] While he was still in Rome he had already completed a long Latin poem on Clement VIII.[3] Cardinal Cinzio Aldobrandini, to whom Tasso dedicated his *Discorsi del poema eroico*, insisted in September on his return to the Eternal City ;[4] Tasso agreed to do so, but only after his law-suit had been happily ter- minated by means of a compromise. On November 10th he wrote from Rome : " I have returned ; alive it is true, but very ill." A week later he expressed the wish that all his works might be printed at Venice, eithei before or after his death.[5] The poet, who was at that time once again living at the Vatican, finished during that time a religious poem on the *Creazione del Mondo*, and composed two sonnets for the

[1] See BAUMGARTNER, VI., 385 *seq.*, 416 *seq.* ; SOLERTI, I., 754 *seqq.* DEJOB, 155 *seq.*, who shows that the few strophes in the *Gerusalemme liberata*, which Tasso himself described at the time as *lascive* (Lettere, *ed.* GUASTI, I., 144), and which might have scandalized a strict critic, remained in the *Gerusalemme conquistata*.

[2] See SOLERTI, I., 776 *seqq.*

[3] The poem does not commence, as was long thought, and as even Martini (Carmina lat. 35) thought, with the words : " O Deus Europae," but " O decus Europae " ; see *Giorn. stor. d. lett. ital.*, XXVII., 433.

[4] See Lettere, *ed.* GUASTI, V., 184.

[5] *Cf.* SOLERTI, I., 790 *seqq.*, 796 *seqq.*

anniversary of the Pope's coronation.[1] The latter was so
enthusiastic about these poems that he assigned to the author,
out of his privy purse, an annual pension of 200 scudi, which
was afterwards followed by other gifts of money.[2] For a long
time past a special honour had been projected for him, namely
his coronation at the Capitol, a thing that had not been done
in the case of any poet since the time of Petrarch. The news of
this had been so widely spread that it was spoken of as an
accomplished fact.[3] The ceremony was probably to take
place after Easter, which in 1595 fell on March 26th. In the
meantime the poet was constantly harassed by the thought
of death. On March 15th Cardinal Altemps died, and the
sonnet which he composed on this Prince of the Church was
probably the last of Tasso's poems.[4] When his health became
worse after Easter he addressed a touching letter of farewell
to his friend Antonio Costantini at Mantua : " What will
Signor Antonio say—this states—when he hears of the death
of his Tasso ? I do not think that the news will be long delayed,
for I feel myself at the end of my life, and have not been able
to find any remedy for my wretched indisposition, which has
supervened upon my many usual ailments, like a swift stream
by which, without being able to find any foot-hold, I plainly
find myself being carried away. There is no longer any time
for me to speak of my hapless fortune, to say nothing of the
ingratitude of the world, which has willed to triumph over
me by bringing me to a beggar's grave, when I had thought
that the glory which, despite those who do not so desire,
the world will have from my writings, would not leave me in
some way without guerdon. I have had myself brought

[1] The first sonnet begins : " Mentre fulmina il Trace, e i monti
e i campi," in Opere, V., 3, 2, Pisa, 1822, 308 ; the second begins :
" Ecco l'alba " (see *supra*, p 455, n. 3), *ibid*. For the poem
" Mondo creato " see MAZZONI in the Opere minori (of Tasso), II.,
Bologna, 1892, and FLAMINI, Cinquecento, 508 *seq*.

[2] See GUASTI, Lettere di Tasso, V., Florence, 1855, n. 1526.
Cf. SOLERTI, I., 802 n. 4 ; II., 260, 353 *seqq*., 390.

[3] *Cf.* SOLERTI, I., 762, 765, 797.

[4] *Cf. ibid*. 803.

to this monastery of S. Onofrio, not only because its air is praised by the doctors above that of any other part of Rome, but as it were to begin in that sublime eminence, and helped by the conversation of these pious fathers, my own conversation in heaven. Pray to God for me, and rest assured that if I have always loved and esteemed you in this life, I will still do so in that other more true life, where veritable and not feigned charity is to be found. And I recommend you as well as myself to the divine grace."[1]

Cardinal Aldobrandini did all that lay in his power to preserve this precious life, or at anyrate to alleviate the sufferings of the poet, who was not only racked by fever, but by attacks of melancholy. The Cardinal gave him two servants and sent to him his own physician and that of the Pope, but all was in vain.[2] The few days that still remained to the sick man were passed by him in prayer and pious meditation. It is not possible to visit without deep emotion the simple room,[3] in which the poet passed his last days ; later on it was transformed into the " Museo del Tasso." The poet left to the convent of S. Gregorio as well as to that of S. Onofrio money for the celebration of masses for his soul, while to the latter he left the bronze crucifix which had been given him by the Pope.[4] On April 24th he received Holy Viaticum and Extreme Unction with touching piety ; on hearing of this Cardinal Aldobrandini hastened to the Pope to ask for a blessing and absolution for his dying friend. Deeply grieved, Clement VIII. granted the request of his nephew, who then went in person to S. Onofrio to give the dying man, in proof of the favour of the head of the Church, this last consolation. " This is the coach—exclaimed Tasso—

---

[1] Lettere, ed. GUASTI, V., n. 1535. For S. Onofrio see CATERBI, La chiesa di S. Onofrio, Rome, 1858 ; CARRAROLI in La Fanfulla, XI. (Turin, 1887), nn. 1, 2, 4, 5 ; BAFFICO, ibid. XXII. (October, 1892), 25 seq.

[2] See SOLERTI, I., 806.

[3] Cf. PRINZIVALLI, 152 seq.

[4] See SOLERTI, I., 807.

in which I shall go, not as a poet to the Capitol, but as one of the blessed to heaven." Ever praying, and meditating on his last moments, the poet felt the approach of death on the morning of April 26th. Kissing the cross, he began to repeat the words of Christ : " Into Thy hands, O Lord . . ." but his words went no further, and without any agony he breathed forth his noble soul.[1]

His burial, according to Italian usage, took place the same evening. After a cast of his face had been taken in plaster,[2] his body was taken with princely pomp to the parish church of S. Spirito in Sassia, and in the cortège were to be seen the retinues of the Cardinal nephews, many members of the Papal court, the professors of the University, and many other scholars, nobles, priests and religious. All of them, after the obsequies, followed the dead poet to S. Onofrio, where the burial took place.[3] Tasso's brow was girt with the coveted laurels, while in his joined hands he held the sign of the Redemption, of which he had once sung :

> To the Cross my heart I consecrate, and hymns ;
> Victory's great standard, and the sign
> In which weak men still triumph over death.[4]

Tasso died a fervent Catholic, as he had always lived. He had dedicated magnificent poems, filled with the deepest feeling, to the Queen of Heaven.[5] All the ardour of his faith found most heartfelt expression in the sonnet in which he

[1] See *ibid.* 808 *seqq.*, where the anecdotes of Manso concerning the last days of Tasso are refuted.

[2] Still preserved at S. Onofrio ; see SOLERTI, III., 92. *Cf.* also *Jahrb. der kunst-hist. Samml. des österr. Kaiserhauses*, XXIX., 216, 218.

[3] See SOLERTI, I., 809 ; III., Doc. L., LI., LII. For the tomb of Tasso, with his portrait, erected by Cardinal Bevilacqua, see TOTTI, 47.

[4] " Rime spirituali del signor Torquato Tasso (sonnet to the Holy Cross), Bergamo, 1597, p. 1. See BAUMGARTNER, VI., 390.

[5] *Cf.* La Madre di Dio nella vita e negli scritti di T. Tasso, new edition, Rome, 1903.

venerated the Most Holy Sacrament.[1] His most celebrated
work, *La Gerusalemme liberata*, is entirely penetrated with
Catholic sentiment.[2]   This was already clearly shown in the
first draft of the poem, which was intended to describe the
struggle between Christendom and Islam, in its most sublime
chivalrous achievement :

> Arms, and the chief I sing, whose righteous hands
> Redeem'd the tomb of Christ from impious bands ;
> Who much in council, much in field sustain'd,
> Till just success his glorious labours gained ;
> In vain the powers of hell opposed his course,
> And Asia's arms, and Libya's mingled force ;
> Heaven bless'd his standards, and beneath his care
> Reduc'd his wandering partners of the war.
>
> (Hoole's Tasso.)[3]

[1] The sonnet is little known :

"NELLA COMUNIONE."

> Gia fui tronco infelice in queste sponde,
>   Che da radice amara ha doglia, e lutto :
>   M'inesta hor sacro ramo, e dolce in tutto,
>   Per divina virtù, ch'in se nasconde.
>
> E del tuo sangue il santo fiume, e l'onde
>   Giungono al cor quasi in terreno asciutto :
>   Talch'egli se n'irriga, e novo frutto
>   Fà di giustizia, e non sol fiori, e fronde.
>
> Era un deserto ancor l'alma dogliosa,
>   Hor che 'l tuo corpo è l'onbra, e 'l lume un Sole
>   Signor l'hai fatto un Paradiso adorno.
>
> Ove di carità vermiglia rosa
>   Hà di pura humiltà bianche viole,
>   E di sua castitate i gigli intorno.

(*Rime Spirituali* [vedi *supra*, p. 461, n. 4], p. 17).

[2] See G. SPERA, Il sentimento religioso nella Gerusalemme, in the
special work, Torquato Tasso, XXV. (Rome, 1895, April), 65 *seqq.*,
and DEJOB, 290 *seqq.*

[3] T. Tasso, Gerusalemme liberata, critical edition, by A.
SOLERTI, II., 3, Florence, 1895 (BAUMGARTNER, VI., 397).

It has been rightly pointed out to what a high degree the revival of Catholic consciousness was reflected in Tasso's immortal poem.[1] Like Petrus Angelus Bargaeus,[2] he too was of the opinion that it is better " to treat of an historical event in a Christian manner, than to seek by deceit for a glory that is unchristian." Therefore he did not draw his heroes from mythology, but from Christian history. It was the great Christian epoch that attracted him ; and he gave his hero the impress of a true Christian. Blameless, brave, wise, humble, generous, careless of earthly glory, filled with the true faith and a deep love for Christ and his Church, Godfrey de Bouillon is put before us almost in the guise of a saint. By placing this hero in the forefront of his poem, Tasso fulfilled in a high degree the task of composing a Christian epopee.[3] He completely turned his back on ancient pagan mythology, except for a few passages of secondary importance. In his poem he accepted prodigies in the Christian sense as an indispensable part of epic poetry, but out of deference for Italian taste adopted a prudent middle course. Entirely Christian in sentiment is the struggle of Godfrey de Bouillon with his fanatical Mohammedan adversaries, which was willed by God, for which reason the paladins of God on earth must have by their side the great spirits of heaven, though they too must experience the operations of the enemies of God and of their followers. The whole power of hell is enlisted to turn aside the crusaders from their sublime goal, and it

---

[1] RANKE, Päpste I.[7], 323. For the way in which these descriptions of Ranke were entirely misrepresented by Voigt and Sauer, *cf.* BAUMGARTNER, VI., 364, n. 1. In like manner what is said by HETTNER (Ital. Studien, Brunswick, 1879, 300 *seq.*) of the relations of Tasso with the counter-reformation, is faulty.

[2] For the poem on the Crusades, " Svrias " by BARGÄUS, see Vol. XXII., of this work, p. 194.

[3] *Cf.* for what follows the excellent chapters in BAUMGARTNER, VI., 408 *seq.*, 412 *seq.* ; for the Christian character of the epic see also RANKE, Ital. Poesie 57 *seq.* ; NORRENBERG, *loc. cit.*, II., 98 *seq.*, 114 ; FLAMINI, Cinquecento, 518 *seq.*

can find no better weapon than an abandoned woman, to confound the noblest heroes with the pleasures of sense, until the strength of the enemy should be so increased as to render the conquest of Jerusalem impossible. But however great is the part played in the epic by the most powerful of all the passions, Love, by which the heroic song of the holy war is to a great extent transformed into a romance of chivalry, yet it is conceived and developed in an absolutely moral way. The transgressions of Rinaldo are not extolled in a single verse, and the latter abandons the beautiful she-devil Armida, who is depicted in the most vivid colours, and cleanses his conscience by confession to Peter the Hermit :

> But think not yet, impure with many a stain,
> In his high cause to lift thy hand profane.

All the Christian combatants too prepare themselves by confession and communion for the decisive attack. The assault begins : victory follows the standards of the Christian army : Armida herself, held back from her intended suicide by Rinaldo, is converted, and the poem, suddenly cut short, concludes with the celebrated strophe of the entry into Jerusalem :

> Thus conquer'd Godfrey, and as yet the day
> Gave from the western waves the parting ray :
> Swift to the walls the glorious victor rode,
> The domes where Christ had made His blest abode ;
> In sanguine vest, with all his princely train,
> The chief of chiefs then sought the sacred fane ;
> There o'er the hallowed tomb his arms display'd,
> And there to heaven his vow'd devotions paid.

In spite of its numerous episodes, the classical unity of the epic remains inviolate, for the recovery of the Sepulchre of the Saviour shines forth throughout as the dominant idea of the poem. The strong relief into which the religious aspect of the Crusade is thrown is not indeed in accordance with history, but rather with the new spirit of religion which had become predominant in Italy.

When the inspired poet sang his song of *Gerusalemme liberata*, founded upon a great act of Christian heroism, he bestowed the aureole of poetry upon one of the most sublime aspects of the Catholic restoration, and upon the idea fostered by all the Popes of the time, the defence of Christendom against Islam. Tasso had been living as a young man in Rome on the glorious day of Lepanto, the greatest success ever won by Christian arms, and his celebrated poem reflects the jubilee that filled the Catholic world on that day.[1] The triumph that it met with was fully deserved, for it contained immortal beauties. Few creations of secular literature equal it in depth of conception, in the intensity and variety of its episodes, in the magnificent and impressive animation of its characters, in the strength and veracity of its descriptions of scenery, in its delicate touch of true lyric life, and in irresistible charm of style. It holds an eminent place in the splendid culture of the epoch of Catholic restoration.[2] It is no longer the worldly Ariosto, but the grave Tasso, so profoundly religious, who was the chosen poet of that time. Even in the XVIIth century the *Gerusalemme liberata* became the popular epic, and was printed and sung in all the principal dialects of Italy.[3] It

[1] See CIAN in *Giorn. stor. d. lett. ital.*, LXXVIII., 164. For the influence of the Gerusalemme liberata of Tasso on the part taken by Duke Vincenzo Gonzaga in the war against the Turks, see *Arch. stor. Lomb.*, XLII. (1915), 80 *seq.*

[2] *Cf.* TROELTSCH in *Hist. Zeitschr.*, CX., 548 *seq.*, who says : '' It was the Catholic culture of the counter-reformation which was the basis of the modern scientific-philosophical, juridical and aesthetic-artistic development, and not Protestantism." This view is opposed to Ranke, who maintains that the spiritual awakening of the Church helped indeed to elevate art, but had a repressive effect upon learning (Päpste, I.[7], 321), with which view the *Hist. polit. Blätter*, XXXVI., 1019 n. may also be compared.

[3] *Cf.* SALVIONI, La Divina Commedia, l'Orlando Furioso e la Gerusalemme liberata nelle versioni e nei travestimenti dialettali Bellinzona, 1902.

also became the inspiration of the music[1] and art[2] of the time.

[1] *Cf.* D'Angeli, La Gerusalemme liberata nel melodramma, in *La cronaca musicale*, 1909, nn. 4, 5.

[2] The drawings of Bernardo Castelli (see Baglione, 384, 395 *seq.*) for Tasso's Gerusalemme liberata were engraved by Agostino Caracci and Giovanni Fontana for the edition printed in 1590 at Genoa, see Thieme, VI., 147. The Caracci, Guido Reni and Guercino had a special predilection for the work of Tasso ; *cf.* Solerti in the periodical *Emporium*, III. (1896), n. 16, where is dealt with, and in part reproduced the interesting series of frescoes by the disciples of the Caracci, of scenes of the Gerusalemme liberata in the Palazzo Rossi at Bologna (Via Mazzini, 29). F. Malaguzzi Valeri treats in the *Rassegna d'arte*, VIII., 10 of the paintings of Tiepolo drawn from the Gerusalemme liberata.

CHAPTER XII.

CLEMENT VIII. AND ART.

JUST as was the case with religion and politics, the long pontificate of Clement VIII. was a period of transition in the field of art, during which the older tendencies gradually gave way to new ones. Clement VIII. himself was inclined to the former, and among architects, besides Giovanni Fontana, he at first employed almost exclusively Giacomo della Porta ; it was only when the latter died, in the autumn of 1602, that Carlo Maderna took his place.

In painting the Pope favoured, in the person of Giuseppe Cesari, known as the Cavaliere d'Arpino, the traditional classical school, while the naturalist Caravaggio was just beginning his career.[1] D'Arpino enjoyed the Pope's favour to such an extent that the painters whom he recommended, no matter how mediocre they were, received innumerable orders. It is still a mystery why Clement VIII. neglected to avail himself of the services of Caracci, whose talent was greater than that of all the rest. It is supposed that the strained relations between the Pope and the Farnese prejudiced him in this respect.[2] A contributory factor may have been that Clement VIII., unlike Sixtus V., was not a man with much initiative, so that even in artistic matters he always took into account the predominant greatness of his predecessor.

Immediately at the beginning of his pontificate Clement VIII declared his intention of completing all the constructions

---

[1] In 1592 Caravaggio began to paint the Contarelli Chapel in the left-hand nave of S. Luigi de' Francesi ; see *Jahrb. der preuss. Kunstsamml.*, XLIV., 90 *seq.* ; Voss, Malerei, 435, 441.

[2] So thinks ORBAAN (Rome onder Clemens VIII., p. 206).

begun under Sixtus V.[1] Among these the first place was
taken by the bridge over the Tiber near Borghetto, which was
of the greatest importance for the communications of Rome
with the north. It is known that in connexion with this the
enemies of Domenico Fontana accused the latter of irregular-
ity in his account of the expenses.[2] In May, 1592, it was
reported that a revision of all the accounts of the celebrated
and favourite architect of Sixtus V. had been ordered, and
it was asserted that many of Fontana's constructions, in
order to gain money, had been badly carried out.[3] Sixtus V.
too was undoubtedly responsible for certain defects of construction, as he was always urging haste. It is easy to
understand how it was that Fontana, who was deeply offended,
retired, and then left Rome in order to go in 1596 to Naples.[4]
His place, as the real architect of the new Pope, was taken
by Giacomo della Porta, who in the time of Sixtus V. had
successfully completed the cupola of St. Peter's, and had
thus acquired a great reputation.

One of the principal cares of Clement VIII. was the completion of the basilica of St. Peter's. It was characteristic of
the skilled jurist that the Pope should have set his hand to
the reorganization of the commission of the Fabbrica di S.

---

[1] *" N.S^re ha dato parola che si finischino tutte le fabriche
incominciate da Sisto V. tra le quali si finisce hora il ponte del
Borghetto et certe altre strutture." Avviso of February 12,
1592, Urb. 1060, I., Vatican Library.

[2] *Cf.* ORBAAN in *Bollet. d'arte*, 1915. For the bridge see *infra*,
p. 489.

[3] *" Si riveggono i conti al cavalier Fontana di fabriche e
strutture, che si pretende siano state malfatte di materie vili et
poco utile et per avanzare spesa." Avviso of May 13, 1592,
loc. cit.

[4] See ORBAAN, Sixtine Rome, 230, who corrects the account of
BAGLIONE (p. 80). *Ibid.* a reproduction of the sepulchral
monument to Fontana, erected in 1627, twenty years after his
death, in S. Anna dei Lombardi at Naples, the inscription on
which extolls him as " Summus Romae architectus—magna
molitus maiora potuit."

Pietro,[1] set up by Clement VII. for the administration of the revenues of the basilica. As the clumsy system of a college of sixty members had not been found practicable,Clement VIII. dissolved it, and following the example of the Congregation created by Sixtus V., he set up a special " Congregazione della rev. Fabbrica di S. Pietro," which was given judicial powers for carrying out its duties.[2]

After the lantern of the cupola of St. Peter's had been placed in position in the time of Gregory XIV., Clement VIII., before anything else, had the whole of the immense construction covered, in order to protect it from the weather, with strips of lead, joined at the edges by bands of gilt bronze.[3]

Sebastiano Torrigiani, who from the time of Gregory XIII. had superintended the Papal foundry, was ordered to cast the colossal metal ball, in which there is room for sixteen persons, and the great cross connected with it, which, richly gilt, was to crown the summit of the cupola of St. Peter's.[4] This work was completed in the autumn of 1593. According to the original intention of the Pope, the sign of the triumph of Christianity was to have been erected on the feast of the Exaltation of the Holy Cross (September 14th),[5] but in the end Clement VIII. decided upon the day of the Dedication of the basilica (November 18th). On that memorable morning the Pope, accompanied by Cardinals Gesualdo, Medici, Toledo and Cinzio Aldobrandini, went to St. Peter's. After a prayer before the altar of the Blessed Sacrament, and at the Confession, he went to the Gregorian Chapel, where the bronze cross had been erected at the Gospel side of the high altar. There he first consecrated two caskets intended for the arms

[1] Cf. Vol. X. of this work, p. 352.

[2] See Bull. bash. Vatic. III., 333. Cf. PHILLIPS, VI., 675 ; HINSCHIUS, I., 482. The bull itself has not so far been found, not even in the archives of the Fabbrica, it was already missing in the time of Benedict XIV.

[3] See ROCCA, Bibl. Vatic., App. 416 ; ORBAAN, Documenti, 48 n.

[4] See BAGLIONE, 324. Cf. O. POLLAK in the supplement to the Jahrb. der preuss. Kunstsamml., XXXVI. (1915), 80 seq.

[5] See *Avviso of September 15, 1593, Urb. 1060, I., loc. cit.

of the cross, containing relics and Agnus Dei, and then blessed the cross itself with the prayers of the ritual. He then celebrated mass. After the Pope had retired to his own apartments, the workmen set to work on erecting the cross. When towards evening the work was completed, all the bells were rung and the roar of the cannon of the Castle of St. Angelo burst forth. In the piazza of St. Peter's, where the Capella Giulia intoned hymns, 'he canons and all the other clergy of the basilica were assembled. The singing of the Te Deum completed the ceremony.[1]

The internal decoration of the dome had at first been assigned by the members of the Fabbrica of St. Peter's to Cristofano Roncalli, but Clement VIII. entrusted it to the Cavaliere d'Arpino.[2] The latter had already been in the service of Sixtus V., and after the death of that Pope in that of Cardinal Santori. With Clement VIII. his period of celebrity began ; the Pope conferred many distinctions on him and took him with him to Ferrara.[3] D'Arpino designed for the interior of the dome of St. Peter's a scheme of decoration that was as beautiful as it was suitable. The sixteen spaces of the dome, which rise in diminishing width between the great gilt ribs, were each divided into four large rectangular spaces, and two smaller round ones ; these were filled with mosaic pictures on a gold ground, the subjects of which form a magnificent " Sursum corda." In the topmost ring there are beautiful heads of angels ; in the next, angels in adoration ; then more heads of angels, and then angels with the instruments of the Passion of Our Lord ; below these, on a larger scale, are Christ, the Blessed Virgin, St. John the Baptist, and the choir of the Apostles, and lastly half-figures of the Popes and saints whose relics are preserved in St. Peter's. In the vault of the lantern is the figure of God the Father in the act of benediction, and on the ring which completes the dome the

[1] See in App. n. 1 the *report of Alaleone. *Cf.* also *Avviso of November 20, 1593, Urb. 1061, *loc. cit.*

[2] See BAGLIONE, 290.

[3] See Sobotka in THIEME, VI., 310. *Cf.* also Voss, II., 578.

inscription : S. PETRI GLORIAE SIXTUS P.P. V. ANNO 1590, PONTIFICATUS V.[1]

It is a striking proof of the strong sense of justice of Clement VIII., that though he was as a rule keenly anxious to immortalise his own name,[2] in this case he left to his predecessor the honour that belonged to him ; this he also did in another way ; the ribs, which are covered with gold stars on a blue ground, end in a lion's head in bronze, the arms of Sixtus V.

Quite a large number of artists, among them Francesco Zucchi, Cesare Torelli, Paolo Rossetti, and Marcello Provenzale were employed in executing the mosaics designed by d'Arpino,[3] a work which was only completed under Paul V. Cartoons by Giovanni de'Vecchi and Cesare Nebbia served as models for the enormous mosaic pictures of the Evangelists in the angles of the four pilasters.[4] To all this there was added, as a completion of the dome, as dignified as it was huge, on the gold ground of a frieze two metres in height, and in letters of dark blue mosaic, the words of institution of the Papacy : TU ES PETRUS ET SUPER HANC PETRAM AEDIFICABO ECCLESIAM MEAM.

Contemporaneously with the decoration of the cupola, the pavement of the new basilica was raised, thus forming the crypt, or the so-called " Grotte Vaticane."[5]

From the autumn of 1592 work was in progress on the erection of a new altar under the dome, and over the tomb of St. Peter. Giacomo della Porta employed ancient marbles for this,[6] and the consecration took place with great solemnity. This was on June 26th, 1594, after the old and the new basilica

---

[1] See BAGLIONE, 372 ; PISTOLESI, II., 256 ; LETAROUILLY-SIMIL, I., tav. 30 (coloured) ; cf. tav. 22 and 28.

[2] Cf. Avviso of November 10, 1604, in ORBAAN, Documenti, 47 n.

[3] See BAGLIONE, 102, 129, 170, 349. Cf. POLLAK, loc. cit. 72 seq., 75.

[4] See ORBAAN, loc. cit. 46 n.

[5] See BAGLIONE, 324.

[6] See LANCIANI, IV., 181. Cf. ORBAAN, loc. cit. 47 n.

had been richly adorned. All the Cardinals assisted and a great part of the Roman clergy, together with the confraternities of the city. The Pope himself consecrated the altar, in which was enclosed that erected in 1123 by Calixtus II., and granted a plenary indulgence on that occasion.[1] On the feast of St. Peter and St. Paul he celebrated high mass at the new altar.[2]

During the course of the work on the new pavement, archæological discoveries of great interest were made near the Confession. Some ancient inscriptions were found,[3] as well as some ancient Christian memorials. The vague statement of Francesco Maria Torrigio, that in 1594 the Pope and several Cardinals had seen, through an opening made by chance, the bronze tomb of St. Peter with the gold cross above it, is quite improbable.[4] But what was seen at that time was quite another matter ; at the altar of Calixtus II. openings were made beyond which there was another still older altar, enclosed within it, which was ascribed to St. Sylvester. Clement VIII. had these openings closed, so reports the contemporary writer, Giacomo Grimaldi.[5]

A monument that undoubtedly belonged to the ancient Christian era came to light in October, 1597, when, under the new altar, it was intended to erect another still deeper down, in the Confession, which was to open directly upon the tomb of the Prince of the Apostles. On this occasion an ancient

---

[1] See *Diarium P. Alaleonis, Barb. lat. 2871, Vatican Library ; *Liber rerum memorab. basil. Vatic. ; extract in *Miscell.*, VII., 45, p. 194, Papal Secret Archives ; *Avvisi of June 11 and 29, 1594, Urb. 1062, *loc. cit* The simple inscription on the altar, still preserved, in BARBIER, II., 439.

[2] See *Avviso of June 29, 1594, Urb. 1062, *loc. cit.*

[3] See LANCIANI, IV., 181 *seq.*

[4] See DUCHESNE in Mél. d'archéol., 1915, 9 *seqq.*, where however the consecration of the altar is wrongly placed on July 26. Wilpert (La tomba di san Pietro, 1922) follows (p. 30) the opinion of Duchesne.

[5] See CERRATI, Tiberii Alpharani de basil. Vatic. structura liber, p. 27 *seq.* ; *cf.* DUCHESNE, *loc. cit.*

sarcophagus in Parian marble, richly adorned with sculpture, was discovered. This contained the bones of the Prefect of the City, Junius Bassus, who, according to the inscription, " went to God while still a neophyte under the consulate of Eusebius and Hypatius " namely in the year 359.[1]

Clement VIII. followed with the greatest interest the works in St. Peter's. So as to be able to visit the Confession undisturbed and pray there, a subterranean passage was excavated from the Vatican, which was afterwards walled up.[2] In the spring of 1595 he twice visited the works in St. Peter's. In June, 1598, the wood-work of the roof of the ancient basilica, which was still standing, and which threatened to fall over the chapel of the Blessed Sacrament, was repaired. The Pope went to see the completion of this work in October, 1601.[3]

The large lateral chapel in the right hand nave, facing the Gregorian Chapel, was richly adorned at this time with marbles, mosaic and stucco, and given the name of Clement VIII. Giacomo della Porta superintended the work, to the satisfaction of the Pope, whose arms in mosaic appear in the vaulting of the cupola there. The mosaic figures were designed by Christofano Roncalli.[4] These works were substantially completed in the Holy Year, 1600 ;[5] in the mosaic of the pavement may be read the year 1601.[6]

[1] See the report of the discovery in the *Röm. Quartalschr.*, XVII., 77 *seq.* *Cf. ibid.* XXI., 121 *seq.*, and 1914, 5 *seq.* ; also GRISAR, I., 432 *seq.*, and DE WAAL, Der Sarkophag des Iunius Bassus in den Grotten von St. Peter, Rome, 1900. In 1597 Clement VIII. gave Torquato Conti a portrait in mosaic of his ancestor Innocent III., which was in St. Peter's, and is now in the Villa Catena near Poli ; see *Arte cristiana*, 1916, 116 *seq.*

[2] See ORBAAN, Documenti, 48 n.

[3] See *ibid.* 46 n., 47 n.

[4] See BAGLIONE, 81, 290 (*cf.* 114) ; also D'ACHILLE, I sepolcri dei Romani Pontefici, Rome, 1867, 18, 21 *seqq.* ; MIGNANTI, II., 50. *Cf.* the periodical *Roma*, 1925, 519.

[5] See BENTIVOGLIO, Memorie, 119. *Cf.* POLLAK, *loc. cit.*, 111 *seq.*

[6] See FORCELLA, VI., 118.

Later on the Pope had the idea of translating the relics of
St. Clement to the Clementine Chapel, which, like that corresponding to it, is as large as an imposing church.[1] At the
beginning of 1596 he had given another precious relic to the
basilica of St. Peter's, namely the head of St. Damasus.[2]

The Aldobrandini Pope, under whom the regular meetings
of the Accademia of painting of St. Luke had been begun on
November 14th, 1593,[3] must also be given the credit of
having begun the decoration of the basilica of St. Peter's
with altar-pieces. Cardinal Baronius, who appears to have
been the artistic adviser of Clement VIII., suggested the
subjects for these. In order to obtain works worthy of the
size and dignity of the place, the various painters of Rome
and central Italy were consulted. None of these, however,
were able to equal the simple and grandiose art with which
Muziano had discharged his task in the two gigantic paintings
in the Gregorian Chapel.[4] Cristofano Roncalli depicted the
punishment of Ananias, Francesco Vani the fall of Simon
Magus, Domenico Passignano the crucifixion of St. Peter,
Lodovico Cigoli the lame man cured by St. Peter, Bernardo
Castelli St. Peter leaving the ship and adoring the Redeemer,
Giovanni Baglione the raising to life of Tabitha.[5] All these
pictures were later on replaced by copies in mosaic.

[1] See Orbaan, Documenti, 47 n.

[2] See *Diarium P. Alaleonis, *loc. cit.* ; *Avviso of November 3,
1596, Urb. 1064, *loc. cit.* *Cf.* Forcella, VI., 116 ; Cancellieri,
De secret., 1673.

[3] See Missirini, Mem. d. Accad. di S. Luca, Rome, 1823,
27 *seqq.* ; Hoogewerff, Bescheiden en Italie, 's Gravenhage,
1913, 61. Other associations of native artists formed the little
academy of Fed. Zuccaro, in the latter's house, and the confraternity of the " Virtuosi al Pantheon," which held its meetings
high up under the roof of the Pantheon ; see Vol. XII. of this
work, p. 574, and Orbaan in *Repert. f. Kunstwissensch.*, XXXVII.
(1915), 17 *seq.*

[4] See Voss, II., 433 *seq.*

[5] See Baglione, 110 *seq.*, 153, 284, 290 *seq.* *Cf.* Thieme, II.,
356 ; Voss, II., 404, 514.

It was a serious loss to the Pope when in 1602 Giacomo della Porta died, the master who had opened out the way to the earliest baroque. Then Giovanni Fontana and his nephew Carlo Maderno,[1] became the architects of the basilica of St. Peter's. Maderno, who soon afterwards appears as the official state architect, did not follow the severe and rather harsh taste of his uncle and master, but continued to develop the style of Giacomo della Porta.[2]

After the basilica of St. Peter's, it was above all that of the Lateran to which Clement VIII. devoted his attention. It is a matter for congratulation that Giacomo della Porta, to whom this task was entrusted, proceeded with such careful consideration for architectural forms that these were still preserved.[3] The work was begun in the summer of 1592.[4] With this restoration was connected also a sumptuous decoration of the basilica. First of all the chapel of the Confession was constructed in 1594, the altar of which was decorated.[5] In the same year the ceiling of the transverse nave was gilt.[6] In July, 1596, still grander plans for the decoration of the basilica were under consideration, on which 40,000 scudi were to be expended.[7] In 1597 the decoration of the transverse nave with paintings, gilding and statues was begun ; the appearance of that part of the church was, however, so greatly changed that it was henceforward known as the " Nave Clementina."[8] The supreme direction was in the hands of d'Arpino.

[1] See BAGLIONE, 131, 308 seq.

[2] See ibid. 309 seq. Cf. MUÑOZ, C. Maderno, Rome, 1922.

[3] See LAUER, Latran, 326.

[4] See *Avviso of June 24, 1592, according to which the cost was divided between the Pope and the chapter, Urb. 1060, I., loc. cit.

[5] See RASPONI, 49 ; FORCELLA, VIII., 46.

[6] *Contract between the Apostolic Camera and the gilders Giulio di Giov. Batt. Caporali Perugino and Camillo di Bernardo Spallucci Fiorentino, dated June 28, 1594, Not. L. Calderinus, 1594, p. 478. Notarial Archives, Rome.

[7] See Avviso of July 3, 1596, in ORBAAN, Documenti, 130 n.

[8] Cf. LANCIANI, Wanderings through ancient Roman Churches, Boston, 1924, 210.

The view of contemporaries as to the position of this artist is characterized by an anecdote left to us by Joachim Sandrart. This states that the Pope, having once received as a gift from a Dutch merchant a barrel of beer, offered his protégé a glass of this beverage, then almost unknown in Italy. After a few sips d'Arpino refused the glass with thanks, whereupon Clement VIII. finished it at a draught.[1]

The monumental frescoes with which the transverse nave was decorated were planned in the form of tapestries, the walls below being decorated with plastic figures in small niches surmounted by a tympanum. Everywhere may be seen the name and arms of Clement VIII. D'Arpino employed very second-rate painters to execute the frescoes. Christofano Roncalli painted the Baptism of Constantine, Giovanni Baglione the Donation of that Emperor, Giovan Battista da Novara the laying of the first stone of the basilica. D'Arpino himself, in addition to other decorations and the putti with garlands of fruit near the figures between the windows, painted on the south wall of the transverse nave, on a gigantic scale, the Ascension of Jesus Christ.[2]

In the place of the doorway leading into the cloister, there was erected from the designs of Pier Paolo Olivieri, the majestic altar of the Blessed Sacrament.[3] It was in February, 1598, soon after the Te Deum in thanksgiving for the acquisition of Ferrara had been sung in the ancient basilica, that the Pope gave orders for the construction of this work of art, which was to be great and imposing.[4] He insisted on its being speedily completed. Already by the middle of March, one of the gigantic fluted columns of gilt bronze, which were to support the tympanum, which was also of metal, had been

[1] See ORBAAN, Rome onder Clemens VIII., p. 30 seq.

[2] See BAGLIONE, 60, 89, 102, 117, 147, 149, 290, 371, 401 ; CIACONIUS, IV., 266 ; SCHUDT, Mancini, 71. More recent restorations have to some extent considerably altered the frescoes ; 130, 151 ; ORTOLANI, loc. cit. 56 seq. Cf. VOSS, II., 566, 586.

[3] See BAGLIONE, 60, 76. Cf. RASPONI, 59, 107, and the accounts in LAUER, 617 seqq.

[4] See *Avviso of February 7, 1598, Urb. 1066, loc. cit.

erected.[1] These columns had originally stood between the
apse and the high altar, and it was said that they had been
erected by the Emperor Constantine.   They were in any case
very ancient, though the statement given in an inscription
of the time of Nicolas IV., that they had been brought to
Rome with the rest of the booty taken from the Holy Land
by Titus, is not proved.[2]

The altar of the Blessed Sacrament is itself composed of
precious marbles ; the two columns at the sides are of verde
antique, and the tabernacle being very richly decorated.   The
designer of the whole was the Roman, Pompeo Targone.[3]
Clement VIII., with significant symbolism, had the niches
at the sides of the altar filled with statues of Melchisedech,
Moses, Aaron and Elias, as " types " of the Most Holy Sacra-
ment of the Altar.   The two first named were executed by
Dutch artists,[4] and the statute of Elias, which was begun by
Pier Paolo Olivieri, was completed by Camillo Mariani.[5]
Above the niches were placed reliefs of scenes from the Old
Testament, also relating to the Holy Eucharist.

At the beginning of 1599 all was completed, but the Pope
was not entirely satisfied, a proof that he was not lacking
in artistic perception.   He found fault with the architectural
construction, and with the fact that the altar was placed at
the south end of the transverse nave, so that it was not possible
to see it on entering the church.   He also made other critic-
isms, rightly seeing that the variegated and busy background

[1] *" Il Papa sollecita che sia finita la nuova capella in S.
Giovanni Laterano per il Santissimo, ove si trasferi domenica per
vederne la riuscita restando sodisfatto si della architettura come
delle vaghezze che già si vede con tutto che non si sia drizzata se
non una di quelle colonne di bronzo tutta dorata."   Avviso of
March 14, 1598, Urb. 1066, *loc. cit.*

[2] See GRISAR, I., 786.

[3] See BAGLIONE, 329 *seq.*

[4] Niccolò d'Arras and Egidio Fiammingo ; see BAGLIONE, 67,
69. *Cf.* ORBAAN, Documenti, 312 n. ; LAUER, 618.

[5] See BAGLIONE, 113 *seq.* *Cf.* BERTOLOTTI, Art. Veneziani,
26.

of the marbles killed the effect of the magnificent structure of the columns.[1]

The decoration of the altar of the Blessed Sacrament was completed by placing in a niche above it a much venerated relic of the earliest times. This was a table in cedar wood, which it was believed had been used by Our Divine Redeemer at the Last Supper.[2] In front of the relic was placed a bas-relief in silver representing that event, and supported by two angels.[3] This work, in which a thousand pounds of silver were used, was completed in the April of the Holy Year, 1600.[4]

A bull of February 12th, 1600, arranged for the establishment of certain chaplaincies, the patronage of which was reserved to the Aldobrandini family.[5] Two commemorative coins recorded this foundation,[6] by which the Pope gave expression to his veneration for the Holy Eucharist.

The transverse nave of the Lateran Basilica was also furnished with a new pavement in coloured marbles by Clement VIII. In this, as in the rest of the decorations, the material was supplied by the old structure.[7]

In order to balance the altar of the Blessed Sacrament, at the other end of the transverse nave, over the entrance door, Clement VIII. caused to be built, by the Perugian Luca Blasio, a new organ, which surpassed in size and magnificence all others in Rome. The Milanese Giovan Battista Mantano executed the gallery, with artistic decorations and rich gilding.

---

[1] Cf. *Avviso of January 6, 1599, Urb. 1067, loc. cit. Cf. ORTOLANI, loc. cit. 61.

[2] See LAUER, 326 n. Cf. BARBIER, II., 345 seq.

[3] This masterpiece, which cost 12,000 gold scudi (see CIACONIUS, IV., 266) was stolen by the French at the beginning of the XIXth century. The bas-relief is by Curzio Vanni ; see MARTINELLI, 151.

[4] See *Avviso of April 22, 1600, Urb. 1068, loc. cit.

[5] See LAUER, 639.

[6] See BONANNI, II., 464 seq.

[7] See RODOCANACHI, Les monuments de Rome, 75. Cf. *Avviso of July 23, 1597, in App. n. 10.

This rested upon two antique columns, between which was
the entrance door, adorned with the arms of Clement VIII.
Over the two side doors were placed half busts of David and
Ezechias, executed by another Milanese artist, Ambrogio
Buonvicino.[1]

The Pope contributed to all the expenses from his privy
purse. The ceiling of the canons' sacristy was also adorned
with frescoes by Giovanni Alberti, who endeavoured to relieve
the gloomy character of that place.[2] Yet another decoration
of the Lateran Basilica which was projected by Clement VIII.,
according to what we are told by Baglione, was prevented
by the slowness with which the paintings in the transverse
nave progressed.[3] The Pope showed great delight with the
Ascension of Christ by d'Arpino, which was finished in the
summer of 1600, and gave expression to this by the gifts
which he bestowed upon the artist.[4] A gold coin and other
medals immortalized the decoration of the Lateran Basilica,[5]
which was further supplied with costly sacred vessels.[6] As
a mark of their gratitude the canons set up a bust of the
Pope in bronze, which is still preserved.[7]

[1] See BAGLIONE, 60, 111, 171. *Cf.* LAUER, 617 *seqq.* ; BONANNI,
II., 465 ; ORBAAN, Rome onder Clemens VIII., p. 123 ;
BERTOLOTTI, Art. Lomb., I., 344 *seq.*

[2] See BAGLIONE, 60, 70. *Cf.* VOSS, II., 529 ; POSSE in *Jahrb.
der preuss. Kunstsamml.*, XI., 134. Ciampelli painted on the
walls the miracle of the water and the martyrdom of Clement I.
See TITI, 216. Over the entrance to the sacristy are the arms
and a bronze bust of Clement VIII. *Cf.* ORTOLANI, *loc. cit.*, 62, 67.

[3] See BAGLIONE, 60, 356. The Lateran basilica was seriously
damaged in May, 1602, by a thunderbolt, which necessitated
costly repairs ; see *Avviso of May 14, 1602, Urb. 1070, loc. cit.
The accounts in LAUER, 617 *seq.*, cover the period from 1597 to
1601. The inscriptions on the altar of the Blessed Sacrament
and the organ are of 1598 (see FORCELLA, VIII., 48).

[4] See BAGLIONE, 371.

[5] See BONANNI, II., 464 *seq.* ; MARTINORI, 6. For the other
works in the Lateran Basilica *cf.* also ORTOLANI, *loc. cit.*, 55.

[6] See CIACONIUS, IV., 266.

[7] See BAGLIONE, 326. The inscription in FORCELLA, VIII., 48.

Inscriptions and coats of arms show that Clement VIII. also devoted his attention to the restoration and embellishment of the two side chapels in the Lateran Baptistery, erected by Pope Hilary, and dedicated to St. John the Baptist and St. John the Evangelist. Fortunately the mosaics were still intact. The decoration in grotesque was carried out by Giovanni Alberti. D'Arpino supplied the two pictures for the altars, taking their subjects from the history of St. John the Evangelist.[1]

At St. Mary Major's Clement VIII. restored the mosaics in the principal nave, and the organ, and to balance this had the wall of the church, above the tomb of Nicolas IV., decorated.[2] He also gave the ancient picture of the Madonna, attributed to St. Luke, a crown of brilliants, which was placed there in his presence.[3]

In 1600 he restored to the ancient cardinalitial deaconry of S. Cesareo, called *in Palatio* from the neighbouring Baths of Caracalla, the titular dignity which had been taken away by Sixtus V.[4] This church was in such a ruinous condition that Clement VIII. had almost entirely to reconstruct it, as is attested by the inscription in an ornate frame placed over the entrance.[5] The canonical visitation of the churches of Rome,[6] and later on the Holy Year, prompted the restoration of S. Maria della Rotonda

[1] See BAGLIONE, 70, 371 (*cf.* 321) ; FORCELLA, VIII., 46 *seq.* ; LAUER, 326.

[2] See BAGLIONE, 60 ; ADINOLFI, II., 162.

[3] See *Avviso of July 5, 1597, Urb. 1065, *loc. cit.*

[4] See FORCELLA, XII., 253 ; *Inventario*, I., 258 ; BAGLIONE (Nove chiese, Rome, 1639, 63) mentions works executed by Clement VIII. at St. Paul's outside the Walls. For the restoration of S. Maria in Monticelli see AZZURRI, S. Maria in Monticelli, Rome, 1860, 29 ; for those at S. Michele in Sassia see TOTTI, 38.

[5] See FORCELLA, XII., 254. *Cf.* BAGLIONE, 60 ; *Inventario*, I., 258 ; *Payments of 1597, 1601, and 1602, in Depos. gen., State Archives, Rome.

[6] *Cf.* CAVAZZI, S. Maria in Via Lata, Rome, 1908, 198.

(the Pantheon),[1] S. Angelo in Pescheria,[2] S. Nicolò de' Lorenesi,[3] and SS. Cosma e Damiano,[4] which was done at the expense of the Pope, who also provided the endowment for the monastery of the Carthusians in Rome.[5]

The church of the Dominicans, S. Maria sopra Minerva, was adorned with a beautiful work of filial piety. In the fifth chapel of the left-hand nave were buried the parents of Clement VIII., and in the spring of 1600 the Pope formed the plan of adorning this tomb more richly.[6] The direction of the work, in which were employed many coloured marbles taken from ancient monuments, was entrusted to Giacomo della Porta,[7] who also designed the beautiful monument which Clement VIII. erected at S. Maria sopra Minerva to his " old friend " Emilio Pucci, commandant of the Papal fleet, who died in 1595.[8] Painters were also employed for

---

[1] See ORBAAN, Documenti, 129, 130. Cf. *Avviso of July 23, 1597, in App. n. 10, ADINOLFI, II., 412 seq. In the museum of the Pantheon there is an inscription recording the restoration, with the arms of Clement VIII. and the date 1600 ; ibid. an inscription of Cardinal Aldobrandini.

[2] See ORBAAN, Documenti, 332.

[3] See ibid.

[4] *Payments of 1601 and 1602 in Depos. gen., State Archives, Rome. This restoration was made in order to repair the damage done by a thunderbolt ; see *Avviso of December 25, 1599, Urb. 1067, loc. cit.

[5] Cf. the *Reply to a letter of thanks from the General of the Order, August 9, 1604, which states : " Loci amoenitas multas habet delectationes : Aptae dispositae res, aedificii amplitudo, opus elegans praeclarumque animum oblectant maxime. Sed haec humana. Illud Nos christiana afficit voluptate, quod illic coetus angelorum existimamus, solitudinem esse pro frequentia, silentium instar vocum suavissimarum, ad similitudinem denique coelestis patriae prope accedere omnia " (Arm. 44, t. 46, p. 298b, Papal Secret Archives). Cf. also LANCIANI, II., 147 seq.

[6] See *Avviso of April 22, 1600, Urb. 1068, loc. cit.

[7] See BAGLIONE, 81.

[8] See FORCELLA, L., 477 ; BERTHIER, Minerve, 147 (with wrong date 1590). An *Avviso of February 19, 1597, says :

the decoration of the family chapel : Cherubino Alberti represented in the vaulting of the ceiling the triumph of the Holy Cross,[1] while Federico Barocci painted the altar-piece, the Last Supper. In the niches at the side of the altar were placed statues of the Princes of the Apostles, executed by Camillo Mariani of Vicenza.[2]

The tombs of the Pope's parents were executed by Guglielmo della Porta, a son of the architect. These show a like composition, though without repeating each other. Four precious columns, which support an architrave adorned with figures of angels, form the frame, and in the middle the sarcophagus with the half recumbent figures of the deceased ; at the base there are inscriptions inspired by filial piety, and between the columns on either side a statue symbolizing one of the virtues.[3] The figure of the Pope's mother, Luisa Deti, represents a venerable matron, holding in one hand a prayer book, and in the other a rosary. It was a sculptor from Lorraine, Nicolas Cordier, who created this masterpiece. He too was responsible for the statue of Love, with charming children. The corresponding statue, Religion, the extraordinary beauty of which is extolled by Baglione, is the work of Camillo Mariani.[4] Opposite, on the right-hand side, is the tomb of Silvestro Aldobrandini, a work of art worthy of standing beside that of his wife, together with whom he had brought up his five sons so successfully.[5] Cordier has represented him as a grave old man with a long beard, holding in

---

" Si è scoperto nella chiesa della Minerva un bellissimo deposito fatto fare da N.S. di finissima pietra al morto commendatore Pucci," Urb. 1065, *loc. cit.*

[1] See BAGLIONE, 132. *Cf.* BERTHIER, 110 *seqq.* ; VOSS, II., 529, 530. A *payment to Cherubino Alberti, January 10, 1605, in Depos. gen. State Archives, Rome.

[2] See BAGLIONE, 113. *Cf.* SCHMERBER, Ital. Malerie, 179.

[3] See BERTHIER, 114, where there are reproductions of the sepulchral monuments. *Cf.* also LITTA, fasc. 66, and MUÑOZ, Roma barocca, 56.

[4] See BAGLIONE, 113, 115. For N. Cordier *cf.* THIEME, VII., 401.

[5] *Cf.* FORCELLA, I., 454, 455.

his right hand a written scroll, while his left arm rests upon two cushions placed upon folio volumes, in allusion to the legal attainments of Silvestro ; at the sides are representations of the two virtues which distinguished the life of this hard-working man, Prudence and Fortitude. The author of these magnificent statues was probably Nicolas Cordier. The heads of the angels in the tympanum were executed by Stefano Maderno,[1] while the statue of the Pope placed in the niche on the wall, to the left of the altar, was the work of Ippolito Buzzi.[2] Clement VIII. is represented standing, with his right hand raised blessing the tombs of his dear ones ; the tiara lies at his feet. This statue is balanced on the other side of the altar by that of St. Sebastian, the patron of the Aldobrandini family, also executed by Cordier.[3]

Clement VIII. took the livliest interest in the decoration of the chapel to his parents. First in June, and again in October, 1602,[4] he visited the works, which, after the death of Giacomo della Porta, were directed by Carlo Maderno. The first visit which he made, after a serious illness, in March, 1604, was to this chapel ;[5] he personally gave directions for the placing of the statues,[6] which he had already inspected in Cordier's studio.[7] In December he returned once more.[8] Six weeks before his death the Pope was to be seen praying in tears for an hour at his mother's tomb,[9] which was not yet quite finished.[10]

[1] See BAGLIONE, 345 ; THIEME, VII., 403.

[2] See BAGLIONE, 341. Reproduction in BERTHIER, 110. For Buzzi see THIEME, V., 313.

[3] See BAGLIONE, 115 ; BERTHIER, 113.

[4] See *Avvisi of June 13 and October 23, 1602, Urb. 1070, *loc. cit.*

[5] See *report of Giov. Batt. Thesis, March 20, 1604, Gonzaga Archives, Mantua. *Cf.* ORBAAN, Documenti, 208 n.

[6] See *Avviso of August 7, 1604, Urb. 1072, *loc. cit.*

[7] See BAGLIONE, 116.

[8] See *Avviso of December 8, 1604, Urb. 1072, *loc. cit.*

[9] See *Avviso of January 19, 1605, Urb. 1073, *loc. cit.* The chapel was completely finished in 1611 ; see ORBAAN, Documenti, 187.

[10] See the inscription in FORCELLA, I., 454, according to which Cardinal Pietro Aldobrandini finished the tomb, as well as that of

Two colleges in Rome owe their foundation to Clement VIII.; that of the Scots and the " Clementinum." The former, a national college for the training of priests, was established in the Holy Year, 1600.[1] The establishment of the " Collegium Clementinum " which was intended for the education of youths of the aristocracy, took place in 1595. The first rector of this institution, which was entrusted to the Somaschi, who in 1600 were given a house of their own in the Piazza Nicosia, was the Neapolitan Giulio Cesare Volpino, at that time the Pope's confessor.[2]

Of the other works carried out in Rome by the Pope, mention must also be made of the column commemorating the return of Henry IV. to the Church,[3] the restoration of the beautiful fountain in front of S. Maria in Trastevere,[4] various works at the Castle of St. Angelo,[5] the erection of a larger building for the Monte di Pietà,[6] as well as the restoration of the Ponte S. Angelo and the Ponte Molle.[7]

It was only natural that Clement VIII. should have given orders, soon after the beginning of his pontificate, for the completion of the Vatican Palace begun by Sixtus V.[8] The

Cardinal M. Bonelli (see *ibid.* 486). P. M. FELINI (Trattato di cose mem. di Roma, 1610) speaks of the Aldobrandini Chapel as " unfinished " ; in the edition of 1615, p. 93, it is spoken of as " just finished."

[1] The college was originally situated facing S. Maria in Costantinopoli ; after 1604 in its present site facing the Palazzo Barberini ; see MORONI, XIV., 212.

[2] See O. M. PALTRINIERI, L'elogio del Collegio Clementino, Rome, 1795 ; G. DONNINO, I convittori illustri del Collegio Clementino, Rome, 1898, 11 *seqq.* *Cf.* MORONI, XIV., 156. The inscription, removed since 1870, in CIACONIUS, IV., 267.

[3] *Cf.* Vol. XXIII. of this work, p. 137.

[4] See BAGLIONE, 61 ; CIACONIUS, IV., 274.

[5] See BAGLIONE, 325 ; RODOCANACHI, St. Ange, 189 ; LANCIANI. IV., 84 ; ORBAAN, Documenti, 138 n. *Cf.* FORCELLA, XIII., 147,

[6] See the inscription in FORCELLA, XIII., 177.

[7] *Payments for this in Depos. gen. 1599, State Archives, Rome. *Cf.* CIACONIUS, IV., 267.

[8] *Cf.* FONTANA, Trasportatione, II., 11 and tav. 11. *Cf.* EHRLE, La grande veduta Maggi-Mascardi del tempio e palazzo

history of this imposing building can still to-day be reconstructed from its external appearance. The windows with their coats of arms recall the Pope who planned it, while under the cornice are those of the one who completed it.[1] The ceiling and the roof itself were, according to an inscription, finished in 1595.[2] Since the work of furnishing this five-storeyed edifice, which included eighty-five large halls, lasted until the end of 1596, at first the older parts of the palace had to be used to live in ; of these the rooms of Pius IV. in the Belvedere were especially adorned.[3]

By the advice of his doctors, and also for the convenience of the Curia, Clement VIII. passed the first two summers of his pontificate at the palace of S. Marco, which, however, in

Vaticano, Rome, 1914, 12 *seq.* The *Conventiones super fabrica palatii Vaticani, dated August 25, 1593, in Arch. dei segret. di Camera (Protoc. 369, Anno 1593, Not. L. Carderini, Notarial Archives, Rome) covenanted between the " Thesaurarius Barth. Caesius " and the " Magister Ant. del Puteo in urbe murator."

[1] See ORBAAN, Sixtine Rome, 206.

[2] See TAJA, 494.

[3] *S.B. fa abbellire le stanze di Pio IV. in Belvedere per andarvi tal volta a ricreatione (Avviso of March 18, 1592, Urb. 1060, I., *loc. cit.*). *Cf.* the accounts in ORBAAN, Documenti, 52. Near the sacristy of the Sixtine Chapel is the following inscription, adorned with the arms of the Pope :

Clemens VIII P.M.

Tria cubicula

infimum medium et superum

ambo totidemque ambulatiunculas

cochlides et otriolum

Apostolico sacrario adiecit.

F. Ang. Rocca Camerte Ep. T.

Eiusdem sacrarii praefecto

Postulante

Anno Dom. MDCIV.

The treasure chamber of the Sixtine Chapel still preserves a magnificent chasuble of Clement VIII., a gift from the Grand Duke of Tuscany, the only vestment which was not looted by the French.

its neglected state, was but ill adapted for the purpose.[1]
Therefore the summers of 1594 to 1596 were to a great extent
passed at the Quirinal, whither the Pope had already gone to
live for a time in February, 1593, so that he might rest a little.[2]
He there carried on the new building, which he had adorned
with paintings by Cherubino Alberti and Paul Bril.[3]   In the
gardens, grottos, fountains and hydraulic devices were constructed, the latter being greatly in vogue at that time, and
among which an hydraulic organ especially attracted attention.
Sometimes the Pope received the ambassadors and persons
of distinction in the garden, and on those occasions the best
musicians of the day performed their compositions.[4]

In February, 1595, Clement VIII. gave orders for the hasten-
ing of the works at the new Vatican Palace ;[5] he wished to
see these finished by Easter, but this did not prove possible.[6]
The halls there gave him the greatest satisfaction,[7] but it
was not until the end of October, 1596, that the palace could
be made use of as a winter residence.[8] Since, during the

[1] See DENGEL, Palazzo di Venezia, 113.

[2] See PARUTA, Dispacci, I., 113.   In July, 1594, Clement VIII.
removed to the palace of SS. Apostoli, as the heat was oper-
powering even at the Quirinal ; see *Avviso of July 20, 1594.
Urb. 1062, loc. cit. Cf. PARUTA, II., 373.

[3] Cf. ORBAAN, Documenti, 153 ; HOOGEWERFF, Nederl.
Schilders, 247.

[4] Cf. PARUTA, I., 202 ; BAGLIONE, 61 ; LANCIANI, IV., 99 ;
GOTHEIN, I., 314 ; HÜLSEN, Antikengarten, 93 ; ORBAAN,
Documenti, 153 n., 159 n. Mededeel. v.h. Nederl. Hist. Institut.,
II. (1922), 118. For the fountain of the Nicchione, with its
fairly well preserved hydraulic organ, see DAMI, 41 ; BAGLIONE,
edit. 1642, p. 61 ; MORONI, L., 233, and for its frescoes of the
Old and New Testaments cf. also DAMI in Bollett. d'arte XIII.
(1919), 114 seq. Ibid. for the Fontana del Nano, to be seen on
Maggi's plan. Cf. also G. B. DE ROSSI and A. D. TANI, Le
fontane di Roma, Rome, s.d.

[5] See *Avviso of February 4, 1595, Urb. 1063, loc. cit.

[6] See *Avviso of March 1, 1595, ibid.

[7] See *Avviso of July 8, 1595, ibid.

[8] See *Avvisi of October 30, 1596, and January 7, 1597, in
ORBAAN, Documenti, 52 n.

summer of 1596 many members of the Pope's entourage had
fallen seriously ill with fever, it became necessary to return
once more to the palace of S. Marco during the hot weather,
though, in order to enjoy the magnificent gardens, frequent
visits were paid to the Quirinal.[1] In 1599 the Pope intended
to spend the whole of the summer at the Vatican, but in
August all those who were not living on the sunny side fell ill,
among them Baronius.   The Pope therefore went in September
to the Quirinal, but only remained there until the end of
October, which he also did in the following years, since the
doctors had told him that residence at the Vatican suited him
better than anywhere else.[2] The latter then became the
principal palace,[3] and visits to the Lateran were only rarely
made.[4]

Two of the halls in the Vatican are still preserved in the
same state as when they were decorated by Clement VIII.
One of these is the Hall of Consistories,[5] finished in November,
1603, which was given a richly gilded ceiling, with the arms
of the Aldobrandini Pope, and paintings on the frieze.   Paul
Bril there represented the most celebrated hermitages of
Italy, among them Camaldoli, La Verna and Monte Cassino ;
Giovanni Alberti painted the saints who had lived in those
places.[6] The spaces between these charming landscapes
are adorned with the star of the Aldobrandini.

[1] See, besides DENGEL, *loc. cit.* 114 ; ORBAAN, *loc. cit.* 153 n.

[2] See ORBAAN, Rome onder Clemens VIII., p. 25 *seq.*

[3] Many particulars of the Vatican under Clement VIII. are to
be found collected in ORBAAN, Documenti, 50-56, among the notes.
Clement VIII. spent 8000 scudi on the baldacchino, throne and
decoration of the altar of the Pauline Chapel ; see *Avviso of
December 4, 1596, Urb. 1064, *loc. cit.*

[4] See besides the Avvisi mentioned by ORBAAN, Documenti
45 n., *that of June 25, 1597, Urb. 1067, *loc. cit.*   P. Bril also
painted some pictures in the Lateran Palace ; see HOOGEWERFF,
loc. cit.

[5] *Cf.* Avvisi of November 5 and 8, 1603, in ORBAAN, Documenti,
52 n.

[6] See BAGLIONE, 59 ; TAJA, 496 ; BARBIER DE MONTAULT,
Oeuvres, II., 30.

The other, called the Sala Clementina, which still serves as the antecamera to the apartments of the head of the Church, was decorated with incomparably greater splendour. For the ornamentation of this magnificent hall, which rises through two floors as far as the roof, various painters were employed ; above all Giovanni Alberti, who was assisted by his brother Cherubino, and the Netherlander, Paul Bril. A master of perspective, Giovanni Alberti was able to transform the flat vaulting into a marvellous scenic effect, the first example of this illusionary decorative art, afterwards carried to the pitch of perfection by Pietro da Cortona, the Jesuit del Pozzo, Luca Giordano and Tiepolo.[1] With masterly illusion he placed above the cornice a balustrade broken by colossal brackets, and above these graceful colonnades which uphold the vaulting, while in the middle appears the blue sky, in which, surrounded by a circle of angels, and supported on clouds, the saintly Pope Clement ascends to heaven. Resting on a plinth of half the height, highly decorated in colours, the side walls are treated in very simple architectural form, painted on two levels, broken by niches containing allegorical figures, by painted landscapes and real windows. The entrance wall is covered in all its width, and in the upper half of its height by a gigantic fresco by Paul Bril, which is made to look like a picture hanging in a broad gilt frame. This represents the martyrdom of the first Pope of the name of Clement. The spectator sees on the vast stretch of sea a ship with swelling sails, from which the Pope is being thrown into the water. The long waves of the stormy sea break upon the rocky crags of a promontory crowned by a temple, and on which are assembled many witnesses of the cruel spectacle. In the foreground the beach is filled by a magnificent group of trees, to the right of some storks. In the middle may be read the opening words of the prayer of David. Through the grey clouds with which the sky is covered, the sun breaks, illuminating the whole scene. An inscription at the bottom of the fresco tells how Clement VIII. had this painting carried

[1] See Voss, II., 131 seq. (cf. 528).

out in the year 1595. The corresponding picture, which is smaller, on the narrower side wall, represents the baptism of Constantine. Under the majestic chimney-piece there is another inscription which tells how Clement VIII. finished in 1595 the building of the palace which had been begun by Sixtus V.[1] On the walls are repeated again and again the devices and arms of the Aldobrandini,[2] balls with rays and indented bends. In the middle of the mosaic pavement, in coloured marbles, is inlaid the coat-of-arms of the family, with the inscription round it : " Clemens VIII. P.M. Pontif. Nostri anno XII." Baglione extols the whole work as one of the best productions of the art of that time.[3]

Outside Rome, too, Clement VIII. turned his attention to the completion of the works begun by Sixtus V. His first care, as we have already said, was the great bridge over the Tiber near Borghetto, the construction of which involved such vast sums that the city of Rome had to contribute towards it. On this work were employed masters who later on attained to a great reputation : Carlo Maderno, Taddeo Landini, C. Lambardi and G. Fontana, the brother of Domenico.[4] To the latter, who was an expert in hydraulic construction, was entrusted the supreme direction. Although the Pope interested himself in the completion of the construction of the

[1] See TAJA, 494. FORCELLA (VI., 116) gives the inscription inexactly. See also the description of the Sala Clementina in CHATTARD, II., 153 seq. ; ibid. 174 seq. for the ceiling. Cf. also EGGER, Architektonische Handzeichnungen, 9.

[2] See BARBIER DE MONTAULT, II., 28 seq.

[3] Cf. BAGLIONE, 59, 70 ; LANCIANI, IV., 184 seq. ; POSSE in Jahrb. der preuss. Kunstsamml., XL., 133. See also ORBAAN, Documenti, 54 n. ; MAYER, M. u. P. Brill, 44 seq. and tav. 23 ; OZZOLA in Ausonia, II., 308, 310. Reproductions in HOOGEWERFF Nederl. Schilders, 245 and (unfortunately too small) in Voss, II., 527. BAGLIONE (112) mentions the paintings of Pasquale Cati, " nelle loggie non finite e nei fregi delle stanze passata la Sala Clementina." *Payments for the paintings to P. Cati in Depos. gen., State Archives, Rome.

[4] See ORBAAN, Documenti, 460 n. For Giov. Fontana cf. THIEME, XII., 179 seq.

bridge,[1] the work dragged on until the beginning of the new century.[2] A work of no less importance was the bridge over the Nera, begun in 1602.[3]

Of the towers erected for the protection of the sea-coasts, Clement VIII. completed the two that had been begun by Sixtus V.[4] He also gave orders for the continuation of the construction of the harbour at Terracina,[5] begun by Gregory XIII. and continued by Sixtus V. In 1595 the construction of a harbour at Nettuno was projected, an unfortunate scheme, as the place was not fitted for the purpose.[6] The Pope therefore decided instead to spend considerable sums on improving the harbour at Civitavecchia,[7] and went there at the end of April, 1597, accompanied by Cardinals Pietro and Cinzio Aldobrandini, Farnese, Montalto, Baronius, Cesi and Monte, on his way to Viterbo,[8] also on that

[1] Cf. besides the Lettres d'Ossat, I., 452, the *Avviso of January 11, 1595 : In court circles it was thought that the Pope would go to Borghetto " per vedere, in che stato si trova il lavoro di quel ponte magnificatole grandemente dall' Illmo di Camerino, che sarebbe memoria eterna di laudi et gloria di S.B. da tutto il mondo per commodo universale di quelli, che d'ogni stati vengono a venerar questi santi vestigi, il tirarlo a perfettione." Urb. 1063, loc. cit. Cf. also App. n. 12.

[2] See Handschriften des württemberg Baumeisters H. Schickhardt, Stuttgart, 1892, 165. Cf. MORONI, LXVII., 106.

[3] Completed by Paul V. in 1619.

[4] See BAGLIONE, 130.

[5] *The Pope gave orders, so it is reported, that " si facci il porto di Terracina dove già siano state incaminate calci ed altre materie per si santa et necessaria opera, poichè in detto porto farebbero scala tante mercantie et vascelli che per necessità si fermano in Genova, Livorno et altri porti di quella spiaggia." Avviso of January 13, 1593, Urb. 1061, loc. cit. Cf. the reply to the memorial of Albergati cited infra, p. 491, n. 3.

[6] See *Avvisi of August 21, 1594, January 10, February 17 and 24, and March 2, 1596, Urb. 1062 and 1064, I., loc. cit.

[7] See *Avviso of March 2, 1596, ibid.

[8] See the valuable article by ORBAAN, Un viaggio di Clemente VIII. nel Viterbese in Arch. d. Soc. Rom., XXXVI., 113 seqq. ;

occasion paying a visit to the bridge over the Tiber at Borghetto. The Pope wished to see for himself the progress of the works on the harbour, which were absorbing exhorbitant sums, and were continued until the end of his pontificate.[1] Clement VIII. frequently tried to revive the trade of the beautiful and convenient harbour of Ancona, which had become greatly diminished,[2] but the measures taken by the officials were not, in the opinion of the inhabitants, sufficient. The jealous anxiety with which the Duke of Urbino and Venice followed these attempts, was therefore proved to be groundless.[3]

and Documenti, 455 *seq.* See also ORBAAN, Rome, 161 *seq.* Among the copious notes of Orbaan there is missing an *Inscription in the atrium of the church of S. Maria at Città Castellana (text in App. n. 12) ; at Civitavecchia Clement VIII. reviewed the Papal fleet which he had reorganized ; see GUGLIELMOTTI, Squadra, 92, 171 ; BONANNI, II., 151 ; CALISSE, Civitavecchia, 443-445. Civitavecchia also owes to Clement VIII. the fountain of S. Pietro, not far from the Lazzaretto. Mention must also be made of the care of Clement VIII. for the Apostolic Palace at Loreto, where there is an inscription concerning him at the Holy House, of 1595 ; see KEYSSLER, II., 425. The *Avviso of September 26, 1598, Urb. 1066, *loc. cit.* makes mention of a silver ornament intended for Loreto. The Pope also restored the Rocca at Spoleto, where an inscription with his arms records the fact.

[1] See GUGLIELMOTTI, Squadra, 130 *seq.* ; CALISSE, 443 *seq.* On the mole at Civitavecchia there are still to be seen three coats-of-arms of Clement VIII. with his name ; the inscriptions in CALISSE, 445.

[2] *Cf.* Bull. X., 104 *seq.*, 235 *seq.*

[3] See PARUTA, Dispacci, II., 237, 252 *seq.*, 329 *seq.*, 348 *seq.*, 352 *seq.*, 365, 381 *seq.*, 394 *seq.* ; *cf. Relazione*, 386. See also *" Discorso di Fabio Albergati a P. Clemente VIII. a nome del duca d'Urbino sopra il raddirzzare il commercio d'Ancona," in Cod. G. 63, pp. 3-25, Vallicella Library, Rome. *Ibid.* pp. 25-56, *Risposta alla suddetta scrittura dell'Albergati, which completely refutes his arguments : " Si vede in effetto," says the author, " che (Albergati) ha preso a fare più tosto quella parte che potessi

In the spring of 1592 the Pope sent Giovanni Fontana to Cervia to re-establish the salt mines there, which had fallen into such a state of neglect that instead of 40,000 scudi they only brought in 10,000. With this was connected the repairing of the harbour of Cervia.[1]

After Giovanni Fontana had successfully accomplished the regulation of the Teverone near Tivoli, the Pope in 1596 appointed him his principal architect.[2] In this capacity he was entrusted with the very difficult task of regulating the Velino. This very chalky stream was constantly depositing strata of lime in its bed, which caused floods, and consequently created marshes in the valleys of Rieti and Terni. As early as the year 271 B.C. the Romans had attempted to avert this danger by means of the drain constructed by Manlius Curius Dentatus. More recently Paul III. had turned his attention to the regulation of the Velino.[3] In 1598 Clement VIII. once more opened up the drain of Dentatus. This work, which had the effect of draining 35,000 rubbi of cultivatable land, was recorded by a special commemmorative medal.[4]

The journey to the northern districts of the Papal States in the spring of 1597 was an exception ; generally the Pope

farsi da un Venetiano per il suo proprio interesse, siccome è verisimile che il detto suo discorso non sia stato fatto senza participatione d'alcuno d'essi, i quali difendendo il commercio di Venetia vengono insieme a difendere l'intento del signor duca d'Urbino."

[1] See besides BAGLIONE, 130, the *Avviso of March 21, 1592 : " Si è mandato l'architetto Gio. Fontana a Cervia per ridurre al pristino stato l'artificio delle saline scadute et rovinate, che di 40m sc. l'anno, che rendevano prima, hora non fruttano 10^m." Urb. 1060, *loc. cit.*

[2] See BAGLIONE, 130.

[3] See Vol. XII. of this work, p. 591.

[4] See BONANNI, II., 497 ; BAGLIONE, 131 ; LANZI-ALTEROCCA, Guida di Terni (1899), 134. ORBAAN, Documenti, 464 n., 466 n. ; Vat. 7031, p. 1 *seqq.* contains *Considerazioni sulle acque del fiume Velino dirette al card. Aldobrandini, Vatican Library.

sought his recreation in the pleasant hills of Albano, for which Gregory XIII. had been the first to show a great predilection.[1] Under Sixtus V. all this had been changed ; only once, when he went to see the Acqua Felice, had that Pope spent a night at the Villa Mondragone. It was very different with Clement VIII., who stayed nowhere so gladly as at Frascati, which was so easily accessible from Rome. This opened out a new period of prosperity for the ancient Tusculum, whose pleasant heights, charming vineyards and olive-groves, and incomparable view of Rome and the wide Campagna, stretching to the silver band of the sea and the imposing range of the Sabine Hills, had long since enchanted the ancient Romans. Indeed, there were few places in the neighbourhood of the Eternal City so well fitted to refresh the mind in the clear mountain air after the bustle and suffocating heat of the dusty capital. Business, which never came to an end, could easily be discharged at Frascati by means of couriers, while it was possible there quietly to think over difficult problems. Baronius, who retired to a small villa at Frascati to devote himself undisturbed to his Annals, had already realized this. Besides the advice of Cardinal Altemps[2] and the physicians,[3] it was probably this scholar, who was so highly esteemed by Clement VIII., who decided him to seek a refuge among the heights of Tusculum. This he did for the first time in the autumn fo 1592, when, on September 26th the Pope repaired to that pleasant little city, and took up his residence at the Rocca. At first he had only intended to remain there for eight days, but as the air proved extraordinarily beneficial to him, he prolonged his stay until the middle of October, since, as he told his friends, he found more rest in a single night at Frascati, than in many in Rome. Every morning he made excursions on foot or on horseback to the churches and villas in the neighbourhood ; on returning home he gave audiences with youthful vigour, and in the evening

---

[1] See Vol. XIX. of this work, p. 42 *seq.*

[2] See the Avviso in GROSSI-GONDI, 221.

[3] See *Avviso of October 7, 1592, Urb. 1060, II., *loc. cit.*

generally visited some church, preferably that of the Capuchins.[1]

In May, 1593, the Pope again stayed for eight days at Frascati, where he first took up his residence at the episcopal palace, and afterwards at the Villa Mondragone. The anxieties of the French question and the Turkish peril kept Clement VIII. in Rome during the whole of 1594, and it was only in the autumn of 1595 that a three weeks' holiday became possible, which was spent at the Villa Mondragone. The Pope's confessor, Baronius, Cardinal Toledo and both the nephews were also invited.[2]

A great part of October, 1596, was also devoted to a holiday at Frascati, but this was made impossible in the following autumn by the gout from which the Pope was suffering. In 1598, from May to October, the court was at Ferrara.[3] In February, 1599, the Pope spent the days of carnival at Frascati,[4] and again in May, accompanied by Cardinals Baronius, Silvio Antoniano and Bellarmine, he again went for fourteen days to this place that he loved so much, where he resided at first at the Rocca and then in the Villa Mondragone. He also stayed at the latter place, with a few breaks, during the whole of October.[5] During the Holy Year he gave up all thought of a holiday, but in May and October, 1601, the Pope again went to rest at Frascati.[6] He resided alternately at the Rocca and the Villa Mondragone, but the work on the construction of a villa of his own had already been begun.

---

[1] See *Avvisi of September 23, 26 and 30, October 10 and 14, 1592, Urb. 1060, loc. cit. partly in GROSSI-GONDI, 221 seq. Cf. also PARUTA, I., 206 ; III., 321, and the *reports of Giulio del Carretto of September 26 and October 10, 1592, Gonzaga Archives, Mantua.

[2] See the reports in GROSSI-GONDI, 223 seqq.

[3] Cf. supra, p. 398 seq.

[4] See *Avviso of February 20, 1599, Urb. 1067, loc. cit.

[5] See the reports in GROSSI-GONDI, 227 seqq.

[6] See ibid. 228 seqq.

This project had been brought forward for the first time in 1592,[1] and its carrying out was made possible when in 1598 the inheritance of Monsignor Paolo Capranica came to the Apostolic Camera. The Pope was left a small villa, called Belvedere on account of its magnificent view, situated to the west of Frascati. As a reward for what he had done in connexion with the acquisition of Ferrara, Cardinal Pietro Aldobrandini had assigned to him, on October 16th, the whole of the hereditaments, including many pictures and some statues.[2] But it was necessary, if the Pope was to live there, that the villa should be rebuilt. Giacomo della Potra drew the designs; this was destined to be the last work of that architect, whom Clement VIII. had always employed by preference.[3] On September 4th, 1602, the Cardinal went with the architect to see the works, but on his return Giacomo had a fit of apoplexy, which caused his death.[4] It was only in September, 1604, that the building, which had been continued

---

[1] See *Avviso of September 30, 1592, in GROSSI-GONDI, 222.

[2] See " *Istrumento pubblico della donazione della villa di Belvedere, case, mobili e altri beni esistenti della villa fatto da Mgr. Tesoriere di ordine di Clemente VIII. al card. Pietro Aldobrandini per gli atti di Lodovico Martini, not. di Camera," dated Ferrara, October 16, 1598. There is cited the *Chirografo (dated " nel nostro castello di Ferrara, 1598, Ottobre 14 ") in which it is stated : " Habbiamo deliberato di donare al card. Pietro Aldobrandini la villa detta Belvedere posta nel territorio della nostra città di Frascati compreso nello spoglio di detto Mons. Paolo Capranica," Aldobrandini Archives, Rome. *Ibid.* n. 3 : " *Istrumento del possesso preso di villa Belvedere dal card. P. Aldobrandini unitamente all'inventario dei mobili di essa, 5 Novembre 1598 "; " *Breve di Clemente VIII. al card. P. Aldobrandini confirmatorio dell'istrumento della donazione delle villa Aldobrandini," dated Romae up. s. Marcum, 1601, September 28 (orig.).

[3] See BAGLIONE, 82.

[4] See the report in GROSSI-GONDI, 229. *Cf.* BAGLIONE, 82, and ORBAAN, Rome onder Clemens VIII., p. 59 *seqq.*

by Carlo Maderno, reached a point when the Pope could
go and live there.[1]

The Villa Aldobrandini, which was extolled by the
contemporary poets,[2] still enjoys to-day the reputation,
although some of its beauties have disappeared, of being
the queen among the villas of Frascati.[3] It covers a considerable area,[4] and is traversed by paths with high hedges,

[1] See the report in GROSSI-GONDI, 81 ; TOMASSETTI, IV., 456 seq.
Giovannoni in his dissertation, otherwise so valuable (in L'Arte,
XVI. [1913] 81 seqq.) wrongly places the death of Giacomo in 1604.

[2] The best known are the poems of Ciampoli (see BELLORI,
Seicento, 54) and Marrini (printed in Propugnatore, N.S. I., 5-6,
1888). Cf. EBERING in Anz. f. roman. Sprachen, N.S. I. [1889]
433, and BORZELLI, Marini, 63 seqq.) as well as the detailed
description of the beauties of the villa by Alessandro Donati, S.I.
in his Tusculanum Aldobrandinum (Carmina, I., Rome, 1625,
319-370).

[3] For what follows cf. BARRIÈRE, Villa Aldobrandini Tusculana,
Rome, 1647 ; FALDA (Rossi), Le fontane nei giardini di Frascati,
II., Rome, 1691, 1-11 ; PERCIER ET FONTAINE, Choix des plus
célèbres maisons de plaisance de Rome et ses environs (1809),
51-54, pl. 64-66 ; MAGNI, Barrocco a Roma tav. 12-15 ; GURLITT,
74 seqq. ; GOTHEIN, I., 332 seqq. See also DURN, Renaissance in
Italien, 215 ; O. RAGGI, I Colli Albani, e Tusculani, Rome, 1879,
392 seqq. ; A. GUIDI, I paesi dei colli Albani, Rome, 1880, 124 seqq. ;
NOHL, Tagebuch, 306 ; SCHRADER, Röm. Campagna, Leipzig,
1910 ; E. DE FONSECA, I castelli Romani, Florence, 1904, 104
seqq. ; GUIDI, Fontane, 35 seqq., 63 seqq. ; P. MISCIATELLI in
Vita d'Arte, IX. (1912), 58 seqq. ; E. v. KERCKHOFF, Oud.
Italienesche Villa's, Rotterdam, 1923, x-xi. ; DAMI, 27 seq. and
clvii seq. ; A. COLASANTI, Le fontane d'Italia, Milan, 1926,
67 seq. ; WÖLFFLIN, Renaissance und Barock, 162 seq., 176, 178.

[4] Cf. " *Bolla dell'affrancazione di villa Belvedere dall'abbadia
di Grottaferrata in favore del card. Pietro Aldobrandini," dated
Rome, 1603, September 20 ; " *Acquisto di una vigna unita alla
villa Belvedere, comprata dal cardinal P. Aldobrandini," dated
November 20, 1602 ; " *Compra di un pezzo di terra unito alla
villa Belvedere acquistato della compagnia del S. Sacramento di
Frascati," dated March 27, 1602, Aldobrandini Archives, Rome,
24, n. 6, 10, 13.

so as to conceal the plantations of olives, vines and other trees, thus giving the illusion of being in a park.   The building, which is of the true villa type, is of three storeys, and gives a majestic impression of size, although it has little depth.   Its site, half-way up the hill, is chosen with great skill.   Visible even from Rome, its façade and high roof rise above a green base of oak trees.   A shady avenue, and extensive terraces, which conceal the domestic offices,[1] lead to the summit.   On the upper terrace, on both sides of the villa, there are small plantations of oaks, and on the right a large flower garden with a graceful basin in the shape of a boat, which was a favourite form for fountains ever since Leo X. had reproduced an ancient ship in marble on Monte Celio, in front of the church of S. Maria in Domnica.

The interior of the building gives the impression of a house much larger than the majority of edifices of the kind.   Over the hearth of the great hall on the ground floor is the bust of the founder in bronze.   D'Arpino painted scenes from the Old Testament on the ceilings of the lower rooms.[2]

Behind the building, Giovanni Fontana, the greatest hydraulic artist of those times, employed all his skill in creating an enchanted poetic scene,[3] combining gems of architecture, sculpture and natural sylvan beauties.   From the wooded heights of the hill, against which there stands a nymphaeum in the form of a great semicircular portico with two lateral wings, there leaps a cascade breaking into smaller ones.   Statues, busts and pilasters give life to this strange construction.   Ionic pillars divide it into niches adorned

---

[1] The chimneys of the kitchens at the end of the terraces are camouflaged as ornamental towers.

[2] See BAGLIONE, 370.

[3] See ibid. 131.   Cf. TOMASSETTI, IV., 458 seq.   H. Rose says : " Aldobrandini must be given the special credit for having gathered together the experience of Roman construction of waterfalls and of having combined it in a single work, which may be said to be the culminating point of constructions of the kind (Spatbarock, 60) ; " in the Aldobrandini cascade this architectural style reaches its highest point " (ibid. 62).

with fountains and mythological statues ; in the central one
an Atlas with a terrestrial globe surmounts the fountain ;
above jets of water gush from the star of the arms of the
Aldobrandini.[1] This central group is balanced above by
the cascades of the waterfall which appears to gush forth
from the ancient walls, and which is flanked by two columns
pouring out water ; at the two sides are magnificent groups
of oaks which were originally surrounded by high hedges.
On the frieze of the nymphaeum a Latin inscription[2] records
how Cardinal Pietro Aldobrandini, nephew of Clement VIII.,
after he had restored peace to Christendom and re-acquired
the Duchy of Ferrara for the Papal States, had erected this
villa as a place of repose after the fatigues of Rome, in 1603,
and that the water had been brought from Monte Agido.

The works for the hydraulic effects had proved extraordinarily difficult,[3] and had involved larger expenditure than the
construction of the building itself, as it was necessary to
indemnify the losses entailed upon the landowners, and to
carry the water underground.[4]

[1] Cf. LEGHETTI, Frascate nella natura, 324 ; see also
TOMASSETTI IV., 457.

[2] The text of the inscription was long deliberated. In the
Aldobrandini Archives, Rome (174 n. 2), there are seven different
texts. One reads : " *Petrus card. Aldobrandinus S.R.E.
camerarius | locum prospectum coelo, collibus | ambulatione |
salubrem et gratum substructione commoda gratiorem fecit."
Another draft reads : " *Petrus Aldobrandinus cardinalis
camerarius Aedes in Tusculano extruxit | Ut naturae bona artis
ope augeretur."

[3] See LANCIANI, III., 55.

[4] " *Il Papa ha donato 50,000 scudi a Aldobrandini per la caduta
dell'acqua della villa di Frascati. La villa non vale tanto quanto
l'acqua," reports Fr. Maria Vialardo, January 1, 1604, Gonzaga
Archives, Mantua. Cf. " *Chirografo di Clemente VIII. diretto
al Pro-Tesoriere generale col quale gli ordina di pagare non solo
le spese per la conduttura dell'acqua della Molara a villa Belvedere
ma ben anchi i danni che deriverranno ai particolari di tale
operazione," dated Frascati, October 1, 1603, Aldobrandini
Archives, Rome, 29 n. 31. Ibid. n. 2, the *document in which

In one of the lateral wings of the nymphaeum there is a chapel with frescoes representing the saints of the Aldobrandini family.[1]   Another open space, the Sala del Parnasso, attained celebrity in 1608, when it had been decorated by a great master.

Here was represented in stucco the mountain of the Gods : on the summit Apollo, and before him the nine muses with musical instruments, while below was an organ worked by water power.   The deeds of the god, around whom melodies seemed to echo marvellously, were illustrated by Domenichino in ten fine frescoes of exquisite workmanship, which were given, by means of borders and painted fringes, the appearance of tapestries.   The backgrounds, carried out by Gian Battista Viola from the sketches of Domenichino, show landscapes harmonizing with the gay rural character of the villa.   In this work Domenichino created a new idyllic style, which formed an important stage towards the development of the classical landscape painting of Poussin.[2]

Clement VIII. " concede al card. P. Aldobrandini la proprietà et il dominio dell'acqua detta Giulia " for the villa Belvedere, dated January 19, 1604 ;   *ibid.* n. 3 : " *Istrumento col quale la communità di Monte Campatri approva et conferma la donazione dell'acqua della Molara, territ. di detto comune, fatta da Clemente VIII. al card. P. Aldobrandini per motu proprio d. 19 gennaio 1604," dated August 21, 1605.

[1] The frescoes are unfortunately so damaged by the damp that it is not possible to form an opinion of them.

[2] See TIETZE, Ausgewahlte Kunstwerke der Sammlung Lanckoronski, Vienna, 1918, 71 *seq.*   When the Borghese went bankrupt, there came into the possession of the Count, a connoisseur of art, by an acquisition in 1892 (see *Arch. stor. dell'arte*, 1892, 143) of the ten frescoes of Domenichino, six of which adorn the gallery of antiquities in the Lanckoronski palace, and four another place.   Two others, representing Apollo killing the Python, and the picture of Orpheus have been lost, and are only preserved in the fine engravings published by La Barrière in 1647 (*cf. supra*, p. 496, n. 3).   *Cf.* also SERRA, Domenichino, 17 *seqq.* ;   GERSTENBERG, Die ideale Landschaftsmalerei. Ihre Begründung und Vollendung in Italien, Halle, 1923, 59.

From the majestic hall which occupies the whole width of the principal building of the Villa Aldobrandini, may be seen on one side the enchanting creation of this nymphaeum, and on the other the grand panorama of the Campagna as far as the sea, with Rome enthroned in its midst.

When from this vantage point Clement VIII. looked at the capital of the world, he must have been filled with satisfaction at seeing how greatly it had developed. The Florentine painter, Antonio Tempesta,[1] the pupil of the celebrated Stradanus (Ian van Straet),[2] in his plan of the city has shown with great exactness and artistic taste the appearance of Rome at the time of the accession of Clement VIII.[3]

A glance at this panorama, which is taken from the Janiculum, is enough to show how sparsely inhabited, in spite of the efforts of Sixtus V., the district of the Monti still was. Still, as in the past the life of the city was concentrated in the level ground between the Tiber on one side, the Pincio, the Capitol and the Quirinal. The principal piazzas were all there : Campo di Fiori, the Piazza Navona, the Piazza del Duca (Farnese), the Piazza della Trinità and the Piazza Colonna ; smaller piazzas were to be found in front of the churches and some of the palaces. The central part of the old city, divided into two by the Tiber, still shows its medieval density and irregular arrangement. From this labyrinth, which had an indescribably picturesque fascination, and from the mass of the houses of the old city, there arose supreme

---

[1] For Tempesta *cf.* ORBAAN, Documenti lxxix *seqq.*, and Rome onder Clemens VIII., p. 119 *seqq.*

[2] See ORBAAN, Stradanus te Florence, 1553-1605, Rotterdam, 1903.

[3] Preserved in a single copy at Stockholm, discovered by J. Collijn (*cf.* J. COLLIJN, Magnus Gabriel de la Gardie Samling af alde Stadsoyer, Stockholm, 1915, 6 *seqq.* ; HÜLSEN, Saggio, 24) and published by H. SCHÜCK, Nagra ämmärkningar till A. Tempesta's Urbis Romae prospectus 1593, Upsala, 1917. Orbaan had already given a small reproduction of it in his Documenti. The labours of this scholar (*ibid.* lxxxvi *seq.*) have served as the basis of my own work.

the majestic Rotonda of the Pantheon, and the palaces of
the Altemps, Monte Giordano, the Cancelleria, Farnese,
S. Marco (Venezia), and the Capitol.   The campanili which
had been erected in the Middle Ages were still to a great
extent preserved ; while of the towers of the palaces, besides
that delle Milizie, there were the Torre Argentina and the
Torre Millina, as well as the Torre del Capocci.   The clock-
tower on the Palazzo Orsini near the Campo di Fiori may
also clearly be seen.   The Gothic campanili of the Anima
and S. Agostino are dwarfed by the many cupolas of the
churches of the Renaissance.   The columns of Trajan and
Antoninus stand out clearly by reason of the gilt statues
of the Princes of the Apostles which crown them.   New
prospects are provided by the obelisks erected by Sixtus V.,
while the Lateran Palace appears exactly in its present form,
and that of the Quirinal substantially so.

As in the past, the Leonine City forms an ensemble of its
own.[1]   On its periphery there stands on one side the Castle
of St. Angelo, as well as the imposing hospital and church
of S. Spirito ; on the other the mass of the " Palace of the
Popes," with the new Sixtine addition already covered with
its roof, and in a strange medley new and old St. Peter's,
with the dome now at last completed.

Special districts are formed, besides the Borgo, by Trastevere
with its numerous convents, the Island with its mills, and the
Ghetto, strictly enclosed within walls and gates, and indicated
by Tempesta as " La Giudea."

On the plan there are also clearly shown, besides the new
streets of Sixtus V., the old arteries, the so-called Via Papale
and the celebrated Via Giulia.

Ever more sparsely covered with buildings as its periphery
is approached, the Eternal City still shows, within the circle
of the Aurelian Walls, many uninhabited spaces and vast
gardens.   The Villa Medici, which still ranked as the most
celebrated villa of Rome, is marked on the plan as the garden

---

[1] *Cf.* M. BORGATTI, Borgo e S. Pietro nel 1300, nel 1600 e nel
1925, Rome, 1925.

of the Grand Duke of Tuscany (Viridarium magni ducis
Hetruriae), while the villa of Sixtus V. has no name. The
gardens of the Quirinal were still in their elementary state,
and the Farnese gardens on the Palatine are clearly marked.
The Palazzo de' Riarii on the Lungara adjoins a vast garden,
and there is a smaller one at the Farnesina, which from its
first owner bears the name of Palazzo Chigi.

While Tempesta was recording the transformation of Rome
by means of a drawing, others, Netherlands and Germans,
who were living there either permanently or temporarily,
were also devoting themselves to that work. Drawings
published in engravings show the many-coloured whirlpool
of public life with its ecclesiastical and secular festivals,
and its variegated street scenes. Productions of great historical interest are given us among others by Brambilla in his
folio " cries of itinerary vendors in Rome," by Giacomo
Franco, who depicts Clement VIII. on a journey, by Villamena
with his typical Roman beggar, and lastly by Bril, with his
illustrations to the " Dolce far niente." Sadeler, Willem
van Nieulandt, and one of the young Breughels give us good
topographical material in their engravings ; Valckenborch,
De Vries and Sebastian Vrancz in their paintings.[1]

The guide-books and books of travel[2] form a useful supplement to the illustrations. Among the most sought for guides
for tourists and pilgrims in the Holy Year were the itineraries
of Hieronymus Johanninus Campugnanus (died 1604) and
Franz Schott (died 1622), which appeared in various editions
after the Holy Year of 1600.[3] The *Deliciae Italiae* of Cyprian

---

[1] See ORBAAN, Rome onder Clemens VIII., p. 97 *seq.* ; *cf.*
Documenti, 475 n., and *Mededeel. v. h. Nederl. Hist. Institut*, V.
(1925), 128 *seq.* The picture by F. de Vries, of about 1595,
showing the Piazza of St. Peter's and the Vatican, in the possession
of Count Lanckoronski at Vienna, is deserving of publication.

[2] Dr. Schudt is about to publish a collection of all the guides,
as the result of prolonged research.

[3] For the Itinerarium Italiae (Antwerp, 1600) by Schott, the
Baedeker of those times, see SCHLOSSER, Kunstliteratur, Vienna,
1924, 473, 493.

Eichhov was also in great demand.[1] A learned and exhaustive work was the book *Romanae Urbis topographiae et antiquitates cum tab. a Theod. de Bry in aere incisis* by the celebrated French archaeologist Jean Jacques Boissard,[2] in which he collected inscriptions with special interest.[3]

The accounts of illustrious travellers who came from the north also described the splendour of Rome and its art treasures. Besides the Netherlanders Arend van Buchel[4] and Pieter Corneliszoon Hooft,[5] mention must also be made above all of the state architect of the Duchy of Würtemberg, Heinrich Schickhardt, which is of special importance on account of his artistic appreciation of works of art.[6] All the visitors to Rome at that time, not only the many artists, among them Mander and Rubens, but the princes as well

[1] For Eichhov see A. KAUFFMANN in *Zeitschr. f. Kulturgesch.*, N.S., II., 674 *seq.*

[2] I. I. BOISSARD, Romanae Urbis topographiae et antiquitates cum tab. a Theod. de Bry in aere incisis, 6 vols., Frankfort, 1597-1602 (*ibid.* 1603, also in German).

[3] Drawings by Boissard in the Bibliothèque Nationale, Paris ; see *Kunstchonik*, N.F., XVII., 71.

[4] See Diarium van Arend van Buchell uitgegeven door G. BROM in L. A. van Langeraad, Amsterdam, 1907. *Cf.* also *Mededeel. v. h. Nederl. Hist. Institut.*, II. (1922), 113 *seq.* ; IV. (1924), 153 *seq.*, 261 *seq.*

[5] Van Vloten has published the description of this journey by Hooft in the 2nd volume of Hooft's letters.

[6] The description of his journey by Schickhardt, to the importance of which LÜBKE especially draws attention (Gesch. der Renaissance in Deutschland, I., 44 *seq.*, 395 *seq.*) appeared for the first time in 1602 at Mömplegard, in 1603 at Tübingen. W. HEYD, Handschriften u. Handzeichnungen des H. Sch., Stuttgart, 1902, published a new and accurate edition of it, collated with the manuscript (Stuttgart Library, Cod. Hist. Q. 148, tasc. B.C.). HÜLSEN published in his Antikengarten (Heidelberg, 1917), p. 90, Schickhardt's description of the Quirinal Gardens, and his notes on Florence in *Mitteil. des Kunsthist. Instituts zu Florenz*, II. (1917).

showed a special interest in the gardens and incomparable villas of the Eternal City and its environs.[1]

Even in 1595 the revival of the Papal capital filled the Venetian ambassador, Paolo Paruta, with admiration.[2] The great development in building works led to the discovery of many antiquities, and from the many accounts of excavations we learn in what abundance the inexhaustible soil of Rome continued to reveal marbles and sculptures.[3] It was especially on the Esquiline that a rich harvest was gathered.[4] There, near the Arch of Gallienus, was discovered the ancient fresco known as the Nozze Aldobrandine, which was bought

---

[1] *Cf.* ORBAAN, Documenti, 475 n. Ernstlingers Reisebuch (Stuttgarter Liter. Verein. nn. 134-35, 1877, deals on p. 93 *seq.* with Rome in 1593. Interesting accounts of Rome in 1597 are to be found in the letters of Conradus Baro de Bemelberg et Hohenburg Junior ; see G. LUMBROSO, Viaggio di un giovane tedesco in Italia, in *Rendiconti dei Lincei*, V. 3 (1896). Very interesting is the *Description of Rome in 1601 by a young Moravian nobleman of the celebrated name of Waldstein, who at Florence met Prince Ludwig von Anhalt (the description by L. von Anhalt of his journey in Italy is to be found in *Access. hist. Anhalt.*, Zerbst, 1733, 261 *seqq.*, of BECKMANN) in Regin. 666 (Vatican Library). From Waldstein's description of his travels Orbaan has published the parts relating to Holland and Belgium in *Bescheiden in Italië omtrent Nederlandsche Kunstenaars en Geleerden*, 's Gravenhage, 1911, 170 *seqq.*, and those relating to the artistic German cities and art collections in *Museumskunde*, 1917, 43 *seqq.* For the method of travelling in those days *cf.* besides HASSEL in *Zeitschr. f. Kulturgesch.*, N.S., I., 407 *seq.*, E. S. BATES, Touring in 1600. A Study of the development of travel as a means of Education, London, 1911. Reise des Barons F. Eulenburg, published by SOMMERFELDT in *Lit. Gezellschaft zu Lotzen*, part 18 (1913).

[2] See PARUTA, Relazione, 422.

[3] *Cf.* REUMONT, III., 2, 765 *seq.* ; LANCIANI, IV., 186 *seqq.* ; ORBAAN, Documenti, 129 *seqq.*, n. The *Avviso of December 11, 1602, Urb. 1070, *loc. cit.* mentions the excavations near the Colosseum.

[4] See ORBAAN, Documenti, 131.

by Cardinal Cinzio Aldobrandini.[1] His brother Cardinal Pietro issued an edict as Camerlengo for the protection of antiquities in April, 1600. Ordinances of 1599 and 1604 were directed to the preservation of the catacombs, in which an ever increasing interest was being taken, thanks to Baronius, Chacon, Bosio and Philip von Winghen.[2]

The use of ancient materials for new buildings continued, as has been said, in the pontificate of Clement VIII.[3] Permission from the government, however, was required, both for excavations and for the exportation of works of art.[4] In spite of this prohibition so many antiquities were sent abroad, especially to the courts of Florence[5] and Mantua, that the representatives of the city as well as the Pope himself complained that Rome was being robbed of its best treasures.[6]

---

[1] *Cf.* Bartoli in FEA, Miscell. I. ccxlix ; LANCIANI IV., 207 *seqq.* ; NOGARA, Le Nozze Aldobrandine, Milan, 1907 ; HELBIG, I.[3], 267 *seq.*, where the special literature is cited. See also ORBAAN, Rome onder Clemens VIII., p. 226 *seqq.*

[2] See ORBAAN, Documenti, 131 n., 133 *seq.* n. (*cf.* 463 n.). *Cf.* also ORBAAN, Rome onder Clemens VIII., p. 229 *seqq.* ; VALERI, Bosio, Rome, 1900. Not without interest is the following *Avviso of March 5, 1603, Urb. 1071, *loc. cit.* : Per le gran pioggie, che furono la passata settimana al Coliseo, caderno alquante di quelle muraglie, che stavano più sconcie, con infiniti sassi bellissimi e bonìssimi et perchè alcuni andavano facendo cavare di là intorno per trovar sassi, et si dice sia il cav[r] Clemente, la Compagnia del sant[mo] Salvatore ha fatto far inhibitione, che nissuno ardischi toccar de detti sassi, et ho inteso, come detta Compagnia intra in questo, perchè ho inteso, che da Alessandro VI fu fatto dono di questo Coliseo alla sudetta Compagnia.

[3] See ORBAAN, Rome onder Clemens VIII. p. 221.

[4] LANCIANI, IV., 180

[5] See BERTOLOTTI, Esportazione di oggetti di belle arte da Roma nella Toscana, in *Riv Europ.*, 1877, II., 716. BERTOLOTTI in *Giorn. Ligust.*, 1876, 117 *seq.*

[6] *Cf.* especially the *reports of the Mantuan envoy, G. C. Foresto. On October 14, 1600, he reports that he has bought a statue of Antinous, which Cardinal Cinzio Aldobrandini would have been very glad to have acquired. Foresto explains the

Among art lovers and collectors there was a veritable rivalry in acquiring antiquities ; besides the Aldobrandini Cardinals, Ciriaco Mattei was especially an ardent collector.[1] As in the past, so now ancient statues were repaired and often copied in bronze.[2]

Many pictures were also exported, not a few of which went to Mantua ; if the originals could not be acquired, they had perforce to be satisfied with copies, which were specially made, from works of art which hitherto had not been allowed to be copied.[3]

Like the Duke of Mantua, Rudolph II. also sought to obtain

reason why the *licenza* to export it was still being waited for on January 27 (see *report of January 20, 1601) ; on January 27 he says : " Può anch'esser, che il popolo Romano si sia lasciato intendere che si lascia spogliare Roma delle migliori cose che si siano et cose simili oltre che la natura di S.S^{tà} tenacissima non fa più gratia di sorte alcuna che vaglia un soldo " (Gonzaga Archives, Mantua). For the difficulties which continued to arise *cf.* in App. nn. 18, 19, the *reports of December 30, 1600, and February 10, 1601. Leave to export was only granted in the case of certain of the statues acquired by Foresto (see *report of March 10, 1601). Finally on January 5, 1602, Lelio Arrigoni was able to report : " *Laudato il Signore, habbiamo ricuperato il possesso delle statue et questa sera l'hanno portato l'Antinoo a casa insieme con gli altri pezzi di più stima." From the *reports of Arrigoni of 1603 it appears that statues were once again being taken to Mantua at that time. Gonzaga Archives, Mantua.

[1] *Cf.* *report of G. C. Foresto, January 27, 1601, Gonzaga Archives, Mantua.

[2] *Cf.* BURCKHARDT, Beiträge, 496 *seq.* ; ORBAAN, Documenti, 133 n.

[3] See, besides the reports of Arrigoni for 1601-1602 published in LUZIO, La galleria dei Gonzaga, Milan, 1913, 91 *seq.*, the further *reports of the same of March 1, 1602 " quadro della Maddalena," April 4, August 17, August 31, October 5 and 12, copies of celebrated pictures, among them " 16 pezzi tutti cavati da disegni di Raffaelo " (Gonzaga Archives, Mantua). *Cf.* also BERTOLOTTI, Artisti in relazione coi Gonzaga di Mantova, Modena, 1885.

works of art from Rome, a thing in which he was not successful, owing to his want of money.[1]

The exportation of works of art was to some extent compensated by those which arrived in the Eternal City, either by way of purchase or donation.

Princes and nobles wished to show their gratitude to their hosts by giving them pictures, while others were collected by prelates who were travelling.[2]

Some of the Cardinals, as for example Sfondrato and Bonelli, had valuable collections of pictures.[3] The collection of important engravings on wood and copper, especially by Dürer, which Cardinal Scipione Gonzaga had acquired during a space of thirty years, was very celebrated.[4] In Rome almost all private men of wealth possessed antiquities, and rooms, court-yards and gardens were everywhere adorned with them.[5]

Of great importance to the Eternal City, especially from the point of view of health, was the care which Clement VIII. devoted to the maintenance of the streets. In the frescoes of the time of Sixtus V. we can see how the profitable swine, which were to be found in every country house in Italy, were pastured in the piazzas and streets of Rome. An ordinance of 1599 put an end to this abuse, and it was forbidden to keep swine in the inhabited part of the city.[6] At the same time a weekly cleansing of the streets was ordered.[7] Other edicts related to the paving of the Piazza Navona,[8] and the

---

[1] *Cf.* the report of Dr. Rudolf Corradus, published in *Blätter. f. Literatur. Kunst. u. Gesch.*, 1847, n. 33.

[2] *Cf.* URLICHS in *Zeitschr. f. bild. Kunst.*, 1870, 47 *seq.*

[3] See ORBAAN, Documenti, 489 *seqq.*

[4] See LUZIO, Galleria Gonzaga, 273 *seqq.*

[5] *Cf.* the report in BURCKHARDT, Beiträge, 495.

[6] See ORBAAN, Documenti, 263.

[7] See *Avviso of July 24, 1599, Urb. 1067, *loc. cit.*

[8] Editto of July 10, 1600, in *Editti*, V., 74, p. 156, Papal Secret Archives.

maintenance of the water channels and the fountains.[1]
Some new streets were also constructed.[2]

The long period of peace was extremely favourable for the
material development of Rome, and the consequence was
that splendour and luxury increased to an extraordinary
degree. The Venetian Paolo Paruta noticed this even in
1595. The sumptuous manner of life, which had hitherto
been the exclusive privilege of some of the more prominent
Cardinals and barons, he wrote, had spread in a surprising
way ; he lays special stress upon the luxury of apartments[3]
and their extraordinarily sumptuous furniture. The envoy
of Urbino, Battista Ceci, also mentions this development
in his report of 1605. He describes how the aristocracy
dressed with the greatest splendour, and kept large numbers
of retainers in elaborate liveries and many horses and carriages;
he tells how all the nobles lived beyond their means, and how
the citizens tried to follow this bad example. He complains
how the merchants dressed their wives as gentlewomen, and
permitted themselves all pleasures, no matter what they cost ;
what wonder then that their profits, even though they sold
everything at a high price, were not sufficient for their extrava-
gant expenditure ?[4]　It is not surprising therefore that in these

[1] See the *Bando of January 22, 1600, concerning the Acqua
Felice, in *Editti*, V., 51, p. 4, *loc. cit. Ibid.* p. 69, a *Bando of
February 2, 1600, concerning the fountains of the Acqua
Vergine.

[2] *Cf.* the inscription in the *Inventario*, I., 274, concerning the
road leading to S. Onofrio. *Cf.* also *Arch. d. Soc. Rom.*, V., 656.
An *Editto per fare la strada fuora della Porta di S. Pancrazio al
S^{mo} Crocifisso, July 27, 1601, in *Editti*, V., 74, p. 386, *loc. cit.*
A list of expropriations of buildings below the Aracoeli as far as
Macel de' Corvi for the construction of the principal street starting
from the Capitol, in the year 1601, in DENGEL, Palast u. Basilika
S. Marco, n. 55.

[3] See PARUTA, Relazione, 422.

[4] See " *Relatione delle qualità et governo della città di Roma
e dello stato eccles. l'a. 1605 di Battista Ceci da Urbino," Urb.
837, p. 468b *seqq.*, Vatican Library. *Cf.* also the *Relazione

circumstances moral conditions left a great deal to be desired.[1]
This state of affairs was also contributed to by the fact that
foreigners of all nations flocked to the capital of the world,
so that the real Romans formed a minority.[2]

Even though Ceci dwells upon these darker aspects of the
times, he also clearly brings out the brighter side of the picture,
and above all the rivalry in building magnificent churches,
and the activity in works of charity.[3] He points out how the
Pope took the lead by his example in the last-named ; every
month he distributed 400 scudi among the secret poor, and
the convents and hospitals ; at Christmas and Easter, on
the feast of St. Peter and St. Paul, and on the anniversary of
his coronation, 2,000 scudi, and another 1,000 for extraordinary alms. He also maintained the ancient custom of
feeding the poor at the Campo Santo near St. Peter's every
Friday. Ceci describes in detail the innumerable charitable
institutions in Rome, which were all excellently organised
and served by the confraternities.[4] These cared for every
class and for the sick of every kind. The lepers had a special
hospital outside the city, while the others were so skilfully
distributed that help was nowhere lacking. Those institutions
which did not enjoy ample means, like the ancient hospital

distintissima di Roma, anime [1593 altogether 99,627] entrate,
chiese, palazzi, casali con molte piante di ville e altre minuzie
particolari, in Cod. Strozz. 721, State Archives, Florence.

[1] Cf. supra, p. 427.

[2] Ceci says in his *Relazione (see supra, p. 508, n. 4) : " La
città può fare 100,000 in circa anime, i due terzi e più forestieri."

[3] *Dall'altra parte se si considera ella è una città santa : gran
carità e grand'opere pie vi si fanno ; gran concorso si vede di chi
fa quasi a gara per potere più splendidamente e con più magnifi-
cenza erigere tempii e chiese al culto di Dio e luoghi e monasteri
a beneficio del prossimo et oltre all'esservi una infinità di chiese
e capelle ornate con tant'oro e pietre pretiose, vi sono anche
tanti spedali et si fanno giornalmente innumerabili elemosine.
Urb. 837, p. 469[le], loc. cit.

[4] See the *relazione of Ceci, ibid, 470-474. Cf. Vol. XXIII.
of this work, p. 34, for the Pope's almsgiving.

of S. Spirito, the annual revenues of which amounted to
100,000 scudi, were maintained by abundant alms. It is
worthy of record that the lunatics maintained at the Madonna
della Pietà were very well treated, which was not the case
at that time in any other asylum of the kind.[1]

The civic hospitals were accessible to all foreigners, but
besides these there had been from remote times many national
hospices for foreign visitors to Rome, where pilgrims received
gratuitously for three days lodging and food, and in case of
illness help of other kinds. Those institutions, too, such as
the Bohemian and Swedish hospices, which owing to the
religious schism no longer had many coming to them, were
also maintained.[2] The number of hospitals and hospices
was forty in all.[3]

However worthy of condemnation the luxury was, it was
very advantageous for art. Among the Cardinals who were
conspicuous as lovers of art, besides Frederick Borromeo,
Bonelli and Colonna, Odoardo Farnese held the first place. Not
content with his magnificent family palace, which was richly
adorned with profane and religious paintings, antique statues,
medals and a valuable library,[4] he caused a splendid pictorial
work to be carried out between the years 1595 and 1603. On
the first floor, on the side facing the Tiber, the ceiling and
walls of the so-called gallery were adorned with magnificent
frescoes by Annibale Caracci, assisted by his brother, Agostino
and Domenichino, the subjects of which were drawn exclusively

[1] *Qui si tengono tutti quelli che sono scemi di cervello e pazzi
raccolti in Roma e fuor di Roma di qualunque sesso e natione di
maniera che con la cura che li si fa molti tornano in buon sentimento, e se pure non possono guarire li tengono perpetuamente
con carità nello spedale, ove sono custoditi, governati e proveduti
di tutte le cose necessarie standovene continumente oltre a 80
con molti ufficiali e ministri che per servizio loro si tengono.
Ceci, *loc. cit.*

[2] See *ibid.*

[3] *Cf.* FANUCCI, Opere pie di Roma, 1601.

[4] See NAVENNE, Rome et le Palais Farnèse, I., 29 *seqq.*

from pagan mythology.[1]   Of the three central pictures, one,
the triumph of Bacchus and Ariadne, was intended to portray
the reign of love upon the earth, the second, Aurora and
Cephalus, its power in the air, and the third, a Nereid embraced by a Triton, the dominion of love in the waters, just
as Guarini had sung in the prologue to his *Pastor fido.*[2]   This
masterpiece of the Caracci is of the highest importance in the
history of culture.   Men realized the paradox of a great prince
of the Church, just as though he were still living in the days
of Leo X., having his palace adorned with such erotic subjects,
and at the same time trying to make those subjects more
acceptable to the most rigid censors by means of allegories
and interpretations, attempting thus to reconcile the Christian
conscience with representations of scenes of loves of the gods
and pagan heroes, which went beyond all due limits.[3]   Moreover this is a crushing retort to the unfounded assertions that
the artists of the period of the Catholic restoration were
hampered in their freedom and activities ;[4] in fact they were
free to select their subjects from ancient mythology as before.

[1] See the beautiful dissertation by H. TIETZE : A. Carraccis
Galerie im Palazzo Farnese u. seine Werkstatte, in *Jahrb. der
Kunstsamml. des österr. Kaiserhauses*, XXVI., 71 *seqq.* Cf. also
SCHMERBER, Ital. Malerei (1906), 187 *seq.* ; *Jahrb. der preuss.
Kunstsamml.*, XI. (1919), 140 *seq.* ; MUÑOZ, Roma barocca,
22 *seqq.* ; NAVENNE, *loc. cit.* I., 65-98 ; Voss, Malerei, 493 *seq.*

[2] See TIETZE, *loc. cit.* 94.

[3] See *ibid.* Cf. also VOGEL, Aus Goethes röm. Tagen, Leipzig,
1905, 223 *seq.*, and ROUCHÈS, La peinture Bolognaise 1575-1619,
Paris, 1911, 175. NAVENNE (*loc. cit.* 95) thinks that O. Farnese
himself had certain scruples : Comparez la Galatée parcourant
les mers avec le carton en grandeur d'exécution de la National
Gallery, vous noterez qu'une légère draperie se dessine dans la
fresque sous la main du Triton et que le carton en est affranchie.
L'adjonction fut-elle imposée au moment de l'exécution ou
intervint-elle après l'achèvement des peintures ? Cela import
peu. Ce qu'il faut retenir, c'est qu'il y eut correction au profit
de la bienséance.

[4] See Voss, I., 24. Cf. ROUCHÈS, *loc. cit.*, 176.

Even in the matter of the representation of the nude in profane art they were by no means restricted. The rigorous principles which were applied after the Council of Trent,[1] only referred to pictures in churches, as is shown by an edict of the Cardinal Vicar, Borghese, in 1603.[2] Even the man who had ordered the frescoes of Caracci conformed to these enactments ; in 1595 Cardinal Odoardo Farnese had the nude figure of Justice on the tomb of Paul III. covered with a garment of thin metal.[3]

The increase of luxury was also shown in the fact that the Aldobrandini, in addition to their orginal house in the Via de' Banchi, which the Pope had given to Olimpia Aldobrandini in 1601,[4] also possessed other palaces in Rome ; one in the Piazza Colonna (afterwards the Palazzo Chigi),[5] another near S. Luigi de' Francesi,[6] and a third, with a garden, on the southern slope of the Quirinal (the Villa Aldobrandini of to-day). In 1601 Clement VIII. also acquired for Olimpia the palace of the Duke of Urbino in the Corso (afterwards the Palazzo Doria), the chapel of which was decorated by Annibale

[1] See SCHLOSSER, Materialien z. Kunstgesch., VI., Vienna, 1919, 97 *seqq.* *Cf.* also A. FORATTI in the periodical *L'Archiginnasio,* IX. (Bologna, 1914), 15 *seqq.,* and *Repert. f. Kunstwissensch.,* XXXVII., 36 *seq.* As early as 1582 Possevino suggested that the nude statues and images should be covered for the Russians who came to Rome ; see PIERLING, La Russie, II., 202.

[2] See *Repert. f. Kunstwissensch.,* XXXVII., 34 *seq.* ; WEISSBACH Der Barock als Kunst der Gegenreformation, Berlin, 1921, 12.

[3] See *Mel. d'archéol.,* IX., 68 ; *Jahrb. der preuss. Kunstsamml.,* XXXIX., 178, 196 ; NAVENNE, Rome et le Palais Farnèse, I., 564.

[4] See PRINZIVALLI, T. Tasso, 67.

[5] Constructed by Giacomo della Porta, completed by Maderno ; see MUÑOZ, Maderno, 6. The frescoes of the life of Clement VIII., which adorn the frieze of the large hall on the first floor, are deserving of a closer examination ; as far as I am aware they have been entirely overlooked.

[6] By C. Maderno, now the Palazzo Patrizi ; see FREY, Architettura barocca, Rome, 1926, xxii ; see G. ZUCCA, Gli orti pensili Aldobrandini, in the periodical *Capitolium,* I. (1927), 742 *seq.*

Caracci and his pupils, among them Albani, with frescoes of the life of the Madonna.[1]

During the pontificate of Clement VIII. there was at last undertaken, as the result of his insistence, the carrying out of Michelangelo's plans for the Capitoline palaces. A young architect, Girolamo Rinaldi, constructed the façade of the Senators, so that this was given the character of severe grandeur which distinguished the design of the great master. All this was done on the initiative of Clement VIII. so that he deserves the place of honour that is assigned to him in the great inscription of 1598, placed over the principal door and enumerating all the outstanding events of his pontificate.[2] Girolamo Rinaldi also directed the works on the third palace designed by Michelangelo on the Capitol, of which the Pope laid the first stone on June 27th, 1603.[3] He did not live to see its completion, but on the other hand was able to delight in the decoration of the Palace of the Conservatori with monumental frescoes of the ancient history of Rome. On these the president of the Academia S. Luca, Tommaso Laureti, and the Pope's favourite, d'Arpino, were employed. Among the frescoes by the latter mention must be made of the battle between the Horatii and the Curiatii as a valuable work of art.[4]

The artistic activity which prevailed during the pontificate

[1] See CANCELLIERI, Possessi, 505 ; PRINZIVALLI, 62 ; TIETZE in *Jahrb. der Kunstsamml. des österr. Kaiserhauses*, XXVI., 155 *seq.* ; ORBAAN, Documenti, 41, 66 *seqq*, 157.

[2] See FORCELLA, I., 48. *Cf.* BAGLIONE, 73 ; LANCIANI, II., 75 *seqq.* ; RODOCANACHI, Capitole, 95 *seqq.*, 99 *seqq.* ; MICHAELIS in *Zeitschr. f. bild. Kunst.*, N.S. II., (1891), 193 *seq.* ; THODE, Michelangelo, V., 193.

[3] See CIACONIUS, IV., 261 ; BONANNI, I., 455 ; RODOCANACHI, Capitole, 95. An *Avviso of June 28, 1603, reports : Yesterday the Pope went to the Capitol " per veder la nuova fabrica, che fanno o voglion fare li Conservatori dalla banda di Araceli, essendoci S.S. andata per buttar come fece il primo sasso nel fondamento, nel qual sasso non era altro motto che il nome di S.B." Urb. 1071, Vatican Library.

[4] See Voss, II., 572, 585.

of Clement VIII. was of great advantage to the churches, to which greater attention was now paid, partly on account of the canonical visitations and partly because of the Holy Year. Although the number of existing churches was already very large, several new ones were built ; for example, S. Maria della Scala in Trastevere,[1] S. Niccolò da Tolentino,[2] S. Giuseppe a Capo le Case,[3] and S. Bernardo alle Terme.[4] The national church of the Florentines, S. Giovanni de' Fiorentini, the masterpiece of Jacopo Sansavino, was finally completed in 1600,[5] only the façade being left unfinished. The church of the Sicilians, S. Maria in Constantinopoli, was also completed in 1593.[6]

The church of the Theatines, S. Andrea della Valle, promised to become a splendid edifice of the first rank, worthy to rival the Gesù. Cardinal Gesualdo had since 1596 expended 40,000 scuid in this church,[7] the first stone of which was laid on March 12th, 1591.[8] After his death in 1603 Cardinal Peretti undertook the expense.[9] The superintendence of the building was in the hands of Pietro Paolo Olivieri, who had also made the designs : a nave in the form of a Latin cross, with four deep chapels on either side.[10] When Olivieri died

[1] See *Avviso of February 5, 1597, Urb. 1065, loc. cit.

[2] Cf. FORCELLA, XI., 457. According to the *Avviso of July 29, 1600, Clement VIII. granted the church to the " natione Marchegiana " as their national church. Urb. 1068, loc. cit.

[3] Cf. FORCELLA, X., 175.

[4] Cf. ibid., IX., 171 ; ORTOLANI, S. Bernardo alle Terme, Rome, s.d.

[5] See the hitherto unnoticed remark of BENTIVOGLIO, Memorie, 198.

[6] See GALLETTI, S. Maria di Costantinopoli, Rome, 1889.

[7] See *Avviso of July 17, 1596, which says : " La fabrica in vero sara non men bella di quella del Gesù." Urb. 1064, II., loc. cit.

[8] See [A. BONI] La chiesa di S. Andrea della Valle in Roma, Rome, 1907.

[9] See *Avviso of March 1, 1603, Urb. 1071, ibid.

[10] See BAGLIONE, 76 seq.

on July 6th, 1599, his place was taken by Carlo Maderno ; he carried out the tribune and the dome, the largest in Rome after St. Peter's, and drew a design for the façade.[1] This large and spacious temple, almost the only one of the Roman churches of the XVIth century which has retained its original appearance, was until 1902 a perfect example of the Renaisances.[2] The restoration undertaken in that year has greatly impaired the grave, tranquil and solemn effect of the interior, as the vaulting of the central nave was covered with stucco and paintings, the plain pilasters fluted, and the capitals gilt.

Not far from this, in the great church of the Oratorians, S. Maria in Vallicella, great activity was shown under Clement VIII. in carrying on the decoration of the interior, and a noble rivalry with the church of the Jesuits in constructing altars and chapels of a like magnificence.[3] A richly decorated chapel was prepared to receive the body of Philip Neri,[4] and another was founded by Cardinal Silvio Antoniano[5]. The solemn consecration of this third great church belonging to religious communities was made by Cardinal Medici on May 23rd, 1599.[6]

[1] See *ibid.* 308. An *Avviso of November 1, 1595, reports : Li Padri Barnabiti detti qua di S. Biagio dell'Anello, perchè li Padri Teatini di S. Andrea con la fabrica loro, che tuttavia fanno molto magnifica et bella, arriveranno al loro convento, necessitati però a cercar altro luoco, hanno comprate le case poste in faccia della Piazza Colonna, che son contigue a Pazzarelli, ove disegnano fabricar una bella chiesa et un amplo convento, il quale sopra detta Piazza farà bellissima vista. Urb. 1063, *loc. cit.*

[2] See GURLITT, 197.

[3] We have information as to the construction of the altars in the *Avviso of January 31, 1596, Urb. 1064, I., *loc. cit.*

[4] See *Avviso of November 27, 1602, Urb. 1070, *ibid.* Cf. CAPECELATRO, St. Philip Neri, p. 585. [Engl. ed., 1926.]

[5] Cf. CIACONIUS, IV., 329.

[6] See *Diarium P. Alaleonis, Barb. 2815, Vatican Library. In 1592 Cardinal Galli ordered the building of S. Maria della Scala, whither in 1597 Clement VIII. summoned the discalced Carmelites in order to make better provision for pastoral work in the Trastevere ; see TOTTI, 71.

By the command of Cardinal Rusticucci Carlo Maderno turned his attention to S. Susanna, and gave it a noble façade.[1] Other Cardinals as well restored and adorned churches, as for example, Giustiniani S. Prisca,[2] Albert of Austria S. Croce in Gerusalemme,[3] Madruzzo S. Onofrio,[4] Salviati S. Giacomo degli Incurabili and S. Gregorio in Celio,[5] Cesi S. Maria in Portico, Medici and Caetani S. Pudenziana.[6] Just as Caetani erected in the latter church a magnificent sepulchral chapel,[6]

---

[1] See BAGLIONE, 73, 308.   Cf. GURLITT, 331 ; MUÑOZ, Maderno, 8.

[2] See CIACONIUS, IV., 169 ; FORCELLA, XI., 173. For the " Amore divino ed amore profano " painted by Giov. Baglione to accompany the " Amore vincitore " of Caravaggio see BERTOLOTTI, Art. Lomb., II., 63 ; Voss in *Berliner Museen*, 1922, 60 *seq.*, and Malerei, 127, 467.

[3] *Cf.* besides ORTOLANI, S. Croce in Gerusalemme, 19, the *Reisebericht von* 1598 in *Mitteil. des Hist. Ver. f. Steiermark*, XLVIII. (1900), 64.

[4] See TIETZE in *Jahrb. der Kunstsamml. des österr. Kaiserhauses*, XXVI., 143. *Cf. Arch. per l'Alto Adige*, IX., 56 *seqq.*

[5] See BAGLIONE, 308 ; MUÑOZ, Maderno, 6.

[6] An *Avviso of August 16, 1597, reports that : " S. Maria in Portico è già del tutto abbelita con molta spesa di figure et altri ornamenti dalla molta pietà et zelo del card. Cesi suo titolare, et cosi anche quelle di S. Pudentiana et di S. Susanna dalli card. Caetano et Rusticucci, che veramente si scuoprono in si sant'opre molto affettuosi et zelanti " (Urb. 1065, *loc. cit.*). *Cf.* B. ODESCALCHI, Mem. d. Accad. dei Lincei, Rome, 1806, 7.

[7] The transformation of the ancient oratory, known as " Titulus Pastoris " into the richly decorated Caetani chapel, had been begun under Sixtus V. (see FORCELLA, XI., 138) ; according to the *Avviso of September 13, 1595, the works were still being carried on at that time (Urb. 1063, *loc. cit.*). On December 9, 1599, Cardinal Caetani went to see the place of his burial (see *Avviso of December 11, 1599, Urb. 1067, *loc. cit.*) ; he died on the 13th ; on the 14th he was buried in his " capella che ha fatto fare bellissima et sopra ogni altra bella, se bene non è ancora finita." (*Avviso of December 15, 1599, *loc. cit.*). Cardinal Radziwill, who died on January 21, 1600, was buried in front of

so did Santori in Lateran Basilica.[1] Cardinal Bernerio at S. Sabina founded a chapel to St. Hyacinth, the altar of which was consecrated on May 23rd, 1600.[2] Cardinal Domenico Pinelli restored the paintings in the upper part of the central nave of S. Maria Maggiore.[3] Some relics which were discovered at S. Bartolomeo all Isola[4] gave Cardinal Tarugi an opportunity for erecting a magnificent altar. The officials of the Curia, too, such as Gabriele Bombasio and Tiberio Cerasa, founded chapels and altars. The chapel of S. Diego, of the Spaniard Enrico d'Errera at S. Giacomo degli Spagnuoli, was decorated by Francesco Albani with frescoes of the life of the saint.[5]

An important work of that period was the restoration carried out by Cardinal Baronius in his titular church, which was in a very dilapidated state, of SS. Nereo and Achilleo, at a cost amounting to 7,000 scudi.[6] This learned expert and admirer of antique Christian art ordered that as far as possible the original character of the building should be preserved. In an inscription he prayed his successor to leave in its ancient condition this little church dedicated to the holy eunuchs

---

Cardinal Caetani ; he had left a legacy of 20,000 scudi for the chapel (*Avviso of January 22, 1600, Urb. 1068, *lo. cit.*). *Cf.* also the *Reisebericht, loc. cit.*, p. n. 362.

[1] When Santori died on June 7, 1602, his chapel was not yet finished ; see *Avviso of June 13, 1602, Urb. 1070, *loc. cit.* For the Santori Chapel built by Onorio Lunghi see BAGLIONE, 147 ; PASCOLI, II., 513. The tomb of Santori by Giuliano Finelli (see PASCOLI, II., 57 ; PASSERI, 260) has a fine bust of the dead man.

[2] See MUÑOZ, S. Sabina, Rome, 1919, 40. *Cf.* *Diarium P. Alaleonis, Barb. lat. 2816, Vatican Library.

[3] See WILPERT, Mosaiken, 418 n. 1. *Cf.* BAGLIONE, 139, 148 ; VOSS, I., 30. *Cf.* also EGGER, Architekten Handzeichungen, 9-10.

[4] *Avviso of August 29, 1601, Urb. 1069, *loc. cit.*

[5] See TIETZE in *Jahrb. der Kunstsamml. des österr. Kaiserhauses*, XXVI., 133, 134, 172 *seq.* Caterina Nobili Sforza, Contessa di S. Fiora, built S. Bernardo alle Terme between 1598 and 1600 ; see S. ORTOLANI, S. Bernardo alle Terme, Rome, s.d.

[6] See CALENZIO, Baronio, 467 *seq.* *Cf.* BAGLIONE, 104.

of Flavia Domitilla, a relative of the Emperor Domitian.[1]
The translation by Cardinal Baronius to his titular church
of the relics of these saints, which had been discovered in
S. Adriano a Campo Vaccino, took place with great solemn'ty
on May 12th, 1597.[2]   Three new altars, for which C. Roncalli
painted a picture, were not finished for another three years.[3]
    Baronius also restored the two venerable chapels at
S. Gregorio, and adorned them with paintings by Antonio
Viviano and with statues of St. Gregory I., and his mother
St. Sylvia, executed by Nicholas Cordier.[4]   In the actual
church of St. Gregory Cardinal Salviati founded a beautiful
chapel and a magnificent altar, adorned with a picture by
Domenichino, the Prayer of Gregory I., for the miraculous
and much venerated image of the Blessed Virgin which had
spoken to St. Gregory.[5]   Giovan Battista Ricci of Novara
represented in the vaulting of the dome the triumph of Mary.[6]
A new chapel of the Madonna was erected in S. Lorenzo in
Lucina,[7] one of the many proofs of the fervent veneration of
the Mother of God in Rome at that time.[8]   When in January,
1594, the Pope visited the church of the Gesù, he suggested to
Cardinal Rusticucci that he should build a chapel to match
that of the Savelli.[9]   Towards the end of the pontificate of
Clement VIII. we are told of the grandiose plans being entertained by Cardinals Sandoval and Peretti for S. Anastasia

---

[1] FORCELLA, XI., 423 ; BAUMGARTEN, Neue Kunde, 297.

[2] See the description in the *Avviso of May 14, 1597, Urb.
1065, loc. cit.   Cf. FORCELLA, III., 53.

[3] See BAGLIONE, 290.   The inscriptions in FORCELLA, XI., 424 ;
ORBAAN, Rome onder Clemens VIII., n. 46.

[4] See BAGLIONE, 103, 115 ; FORCELLA, II., 122 seqq. ; Voss, II.,
500 seqq. ; GIBELLI (note 6 infra), 22 seqq.   Cf. V. MOSCHINI,
S. Gregorio al Celio, Rome, s.d. 11 seq.

[5] See TIETZE, loc. cit., 161 seq.

[6] See A. GIBELLI, Mem. d. chiesa dei santi Andrea e Gregorio
al Clivo Scauro, Siena, 1888, 20.

[7] Cf. *Avviso of August 28, 1596, Urb. 1064, II., loc. cit.

[8] Cf. *Avviso of August 21, 1604, Urb. 1072, loc. cit.

[9] See *Avviso of January 8, 1594, Urb. 1062, loc. cit.

and the SS. Apostoli.[1] Cardinal Peretti had already shown
his interest in art by his erection of the great sepulchral
monument to his uncle Sixtus V. at St. Mary Major's[2]

We are not surprised to learn that Cardinal Pietro Aldobrandini too did not allow himself to be outdone in this rivalry.
At S. Maria in Via he had a chapel painted by d'Arpino ;[3]
at Avignon he ordered the restoration of the church of
S. Chiara, which had been founded by one of his ancestors ;
in Rome he gave orders for the restoration and decoration of
his titular church, S. Niccolò in Carcere.[4] But his principal
attention was devoted to his abbey of Tre Fontane.[5] The
third of the churches on that spot, S. Paolo alle Tre Fontane,
owed its erection to the Cardinal ; this was a simple building
in the form of a portico, exactly adapted to the site of the
three recently discovered springs, and which stood upon the
site of the more ancient church built in memory of the place
where the Apostle of the Gentiles had been beheaded.[6] The
façade, adorned with Doric pilasters bears the arms of the
Cardinal ; on the attic may be seen those of Clement VIII.
Inscriptions on the façade and in the interior mention 1599

[1] See *Avviso of October 9, 1604, which states : " Il cardinal
Montalto anco si va dicendo sia rissoluto di rifar la chiesa de
SS[ti] Apostoli, opra che doveva fare Sisto V., et dicono voglia
spendere da 200[m] scudi con assegnarli per la fabrica 20[m] scudi
l'anno, si che sarà una bellissima et gran fabrica, et competerà
et supererà quella del Gesù." Urb. 1072, *loc. cit.*

[2] *Cf.* Vol. XXII. of this work, p. 289.

[3] See BAGLIONE, 370.

[4] *Cf. ibid.* 359, 401 ; FORCELLA, IV., 115.

[5] *Cf.* CIACONIUS, IV., 283 *seqq.*

[6] *Cf.* GRISAR, I., 615 ; E. LOVATELLI in the *Nuova Antologia,*
CLXXXII. (1914), 11 *seqq.* Dr. Stein reports in his *Reisebericht
that the springs which had once again been enclosed in marble by
Aldobrandini had the reputation of being very salutary in diseases
of body and soul : " soletque populus matutino tempore nudis
pedibus excurrere et ex devotione hanc aquam ad salutem animae
potare corallisque vel rosariis columnam attingere." Cod. 1751,
the Library, Königsburg.

as the year of the building ; a third, on the pavement, mentions 1601.[1] Giacomo della Porta made the designs both for this and for the second church,[2] a rotunda, which, in accordance with a vision of St. Bernard, bears the name of S. Maria Scala Coeli ; this had been begun by Cardinal Farnese.[3] Pietro Aldobrandini undertook its completion, and gave the high altar and the mosaics in the tribune, which show the Madonna being crowned by angels, surrounded by St. Bernard and other saints, and with Clement VIII. and the founder kneeling before them. This splendid work was executed by the Florentine, Francesco Zucchi, from the designs of Giovanni de' Vecchi.[4] The Pope was so greatly interested in the building of S. Paolo alle Tre Fontane, begun in February, 1599,[5] that he twice paid a visit to it during the following year.[6]

Clement VIII. also took an active part in the discoveries which Cardinal Sfondrato, who was living a life of strict asceticism, devoted solely to works of piety and charity,[7] had made in Trastevere during the restoration of his titular church of S. Cecilia.[8] There, on October 20th, 1599, during

[1] See FORCELLA, XII., 329 seq.

[2] See BAGLIONE, 81.

[3] See in FORCELLA, XII., 335, the inscription in the interior of the cupola of 1584.

[4] See BAGLIONE, 102, 128.

[5] *" Il card. Aldobrandini rissolto di risarcire la chiesa della sua abbadia di tre fontane vi si trasferì la settimana passata con l'architetto per effectuarla." *Avviso of February 20, 1599, Urb. 1067, loc. cit.

[6] See the *Avvisi of April 12 and October 18, 1600, Urb. 1068, ibid.

[7] An *Avviso of July 23, 1597, reports that the Cardinal fasts and prays continually. Cf. an *Avviso of March 1, 1600. For the great munificence of Sfondrato see the *Avvisi in Urb. 1065, 1067, 1068, 1071, loc. cit.

[8] Cf. the accounts of BARONIUS (Annales ad a. 821, n. 13 seqq.) and BOSIO (Historia passionis S. Caeciliae, Rome, 1600, 153 seqq.) with which may be read the *Avvisi of October 23 and 30, November 10, 17 and 27, and December 1, 1599 (Urb. 1067, loc. cit.). During this year there were discovered in the course

the course of the works near the high altar, two white marble sarcophagi came to light, in which the Pope, on the strength of an inscription of Paschal I. in the church, came to the conclusion that they had discovered the bones of St. Cecilia and of SS. Valerian, Tiburtius and Maximus, who had been converted by that noble Roman lady and martyred with her. Sfondrato had the sarcophagi opened in the presence of witnesses. When the cover was removed, there was seen the cypress-wood casket, still in a good state of preservation, in which Paschal I. in 821 had had the virgin martyr translated from the catacomb of St. Callixtus. The Cardinal himself opened it. The mortal remains of the martyr were found in the same position in which they had been placed eight centuries before. Through the silk gauze veil there shone the dress of the saint, embroidered in gold ; at her feet were the small cloths stained with blood, mentioned by Paschal I. The Cardinal resolved at once to inform the Pope, who was at Frascati, of his discovery. When he got there he found Clement VIII. confined to his bed with a bad attack of gout, so that the Pope, who would have liked to have gone at once to Rome, sent Cardinal Baronius instead. The latter's report, and that of Antonio Bosio, the indefatigable explorer of the catacombs, tell us what happened. It may be clearly seen from their accounts how deeply they were moved when Sfondrato opened the casket of cypress wood, and they saw the reverently covered body. Cecilia's stature was extraordinarily small, and as nothing could be seen of her head, it was thought that the face was turned towards the ground ; but from a holy reverence no further investigations were made. Bosio expresses the opinion that the saint was found in the same position as when she had yielded her last breath, but Baronius says nothing as to this.[1]

of the repairs necessitated by the inundation of the Tiber at S. Bartolomeo all'Isola, the casket containing the bones of SS. Exuperantius and Marcellus ; see *Avviso of December 30, 1600, Urb. 1068, loc. cit.

[1] See the criticism of the accounts of the excavations by L. DE LACGER in Bull. de litt. ecclés. p. p. l'Institut Cath. de Toulouse, XXIV. (1923), 218 seqq.

The casket was taken to a chapel in the right nave used for the confessions of the adjoining convent of nuns ; there the relics were quite safe, and could be seen through a window by the faithful who flocked thither from all parts of Rome. The relics were to remain exposed there, so Clement VIII. ordered, until the feast of St. Cecilia (November 22nd). As soon as his health permitted the Pope came to Rome, and immediately upon his arrival, on November 10th, he went to show his veneration for the relics of the martyr.[1] He gave further proof of this by having a silver covering placed over the cypress wood casket, at a cost of more than 4,000 gold scudi.[2] The Pope refused to allow a more detailed examination,[3] and the body was to be buried in the same place where it had been found ; all that was taken out was a small piece of the gold-embroidered dress and of blood-stained linen, together with a splinter of bone from the skull, which, with the heads of SS. Valerian, Tiburtius and Maximus, taken from the other sarcophagus, were preserved in precious reliquaries.[4]

In the meantime Sfondrato had made further excavations, in the course of which a third sarcophagus was discovered ; it was believed, from the inscription of Paschal I., that this contained the bones of Popes Urban and Lucius.

Now it was evident what a change of sentiment had taken place. When, a century before, the body of a girl belonging to the days of antiquity, had been found on the Appian Way

[1] See *Avvisi of November 6 and 10, 1599, Urb. 1067, *loc. cit.*

[2] Bosio, *loc. cit.*, 168 ; 4392. It is entered in the *Depos. gen.* of the State Archives, Rome, on January 8 : *" E scudi 2000 di moneta pagati per chirografo di Nostro Signore a Curtio Vanni orefice a sui conti, dissero che hanno da servire per la cassa d'argento per riporre il corpo di santa Cecilia ritrovato ultimamente, che fu fino a conque di novembre passato."

[3] See Baronius, *loc. cit.* n. 16.

[4] *Cf.* Bosio, *loc. cit.* 163, 180. The Archduchess Maria wrote on March 29, 1604, from Graz to Cardinal Sfondrato to ask for a relic of St. Cecilia ; see letter in Cod. Chig. L. III. 66. Vatican Library.

the Romans of the Renaissance had been filled with so great enthusiasm that Innocent VIII. had thought it necessary to interfere.[1] Now Clement VIII. could not do enough to satisfy the cultus of St. Cecilia. The youthful martyr was celebrated in poetry,[2] the casket containing her relics was adorned with candles and flowers, and the Romans flocked thither incessantly to venerate Cecilia and to implore her intercession. The crowds were so great that it was necessary to call in the assistance of the Swiss Guard. Cardinal Sfondrato remained the greater part of the day in the church, where the solemn burial took place on November 22nd, 1599. So as to prevent any accident among the vast throng of people, the passage of vehicles was forbidden in the Trastevere that morning. At the appointed hour the Pope appeared, accompanied by all the dignitaries of the court and the Roman Senate. There were also present all the Cardinals, forty-two in number, as well as the diplomatic representatives of France, Venice and Savoy. The Pope went first to the chapel where the cypress wood casket was exposed and blessed the silver coffer which he had had made for the purpose, and which was adorned with a short inscription and his arms. The casket was then taken to the high altar, where Clement VIII. celebrated high mass. The burial took place after the communion. The Cardinal Deacons, Farnese, Aldobrandini and Cesi, assisted by the Pope himself, carried the casket to the small confession below.[3] There it was placed in the silver coffer, and this

[1] *Cf.* Vol. V. of this work, p. 331 *seq.*

[2] *In divam Caeciliam virginem martyremque (Barb. 2092, p. 23b, Vatican Library) dated October 31, 1601, perhaps composed by P. Angelo Galuzzi. The poem of Urban VIII. to St. Cecilia, printed in ALEX. DONATI SENEN. S.J. Carminum volumen primum, Rome, 1625, 147 *seqq.* probably belongs to this period. After the discovery of the body of St. Cecilia a "compagnia" was established in her honour at S. Andrea, which accompanied the Blessed Sacrament to the sick ; the members wore the image of the saint on their hats ; see TOTTI, 86.

[3] See BOSIO, *loc. cit.* 164 *seqq.* *Cf.* the *Avviso of November 27, 1599, Urb. 1067, *loc. cit.*, and *Diarium P. Alaleonis, Barb. lat. 2816, *ibid.*

was lowered into a new and larger sarcophagus of marble,[1] which was closed by the Pope himself. After a short prayer Clement VIII. returned to the altar, where the mass was continued. The Romans flocked thither until dusk, to pray at the new tomb, to the decoration of which, as well as to the further adornment of the church, Cardinal Sfondrato, who was so fond of art, continued to devote himself.

After the restoration of the roof, Sfondrato intended to introduce a ceiling in gilt wood, but gave up this project when the architects declared that the central nave, which was very broad but rather low, would appear too heavy. He therefore contented himself with adorning the old ceiling with paintings. The walled-up windows of the central nave were re-opened, and the frescoes which were found there were restored, their ancient and venerable character being carefully respected. On the other hand the two ancient ambos were removed, and the side naves were adorned with pictures and new marble altars, containing pictures by Roman and foreign artists.[2]

The Netherland master, Paul Bril, decorated the corridor leading to the second chapel on the right with representations of the saints : Francis, Sylvia, Mary Magdalene, Mary of Egypt, Paul the Hermit, Jerome, Antony, Onofrio, Spiridion, Eulogius and Hilary. As these were shown among rocks and crags, Bril was able to introduce landscapes of romantic ruggedness, which revealed that painter's great understanding of the beauties of nature, and at the same time a change of style.[3] This elaborate decoration was chosen for this corridor, because it led to one of the most celebrated sanctuaries of Rome. Here were to be found the remains, already carefully preserved by Paschal I., of an ancient Roman bathroom, in

---

[1] Cf. CABROL, Dict. d'archéol., II., 2, 2772.

[2] See BOSIO, loc. cit., 171 seqq. Cf. also BAGLIONE, 60, 93, 111, 168, and L'Arte, X. (1907), 305.

[3] See MAYER, M. e P. Brill, 29 seq. and tav. 17-22. Cf. GERSTENBERG, Die ideale Landschaftsmalerei in Italien, Halle, 1923, 73.

which it was supposed that St. Cecilia had triumphantly survived her first martyrdom (suffocation by hot steam). Cardinal Sfondrato carefully preserved all these remains ; the pipes from which the steam came, and the leaden channels for the draining of the water and restored the ancient chapel,[1] for which Guido Reni, who came to Rome in 1602, painted as an altar-piece, the martyrdom of the saint.[2]

The Gothic marble tabernacle over the high altar of S. Cecilia, the work of Arnolfo di Cambio, was also preserved, as well as the medieval candlestick for the Paschal candle. Both of these were carefully restored. The Cardinal also sumptuously decorated the confession in front of the high altar with many-coloured marbles, onyx, lapislazuli, and ornaments in gilt bronze. The altar itself was richly decorated by Stefano Maderno with candelabra, vases, lamps, six statues of saints and two bronze angels.[3] The angels are holding up a crown over the white marble statue of St. Cecilia, which lies in a niche of black marble immediately in front of the high altar, as though in an open sarcophagus. In this Maderno created a new form of altar, which was often imitated later on.[4] The statue of the saint, carved in the finest marble, and almost transparent, is one of the most celebrated and best known of Italian works of art. The master drew his inspiration from the legend that the saint expired in her bath-room, three days after receiving the mortal blow of the axe. Maderno did not therefore represent her lying as one who was dead, but reclining on her right side, with her knees drawn up, her hands half folded, her head covered with a veil, and her face turned

[1] See BOSIO, *loc. cit.* 176 *seqq.*

[2] See PASSERI, 62. *Cf.* EISLER in the *Burlington Magazine,* 1905, 318, and TIETZE in *Jahrb. der Kunstsamml. des österr. Kaiserhauses,* XXVI., 139.

[3] A. MUÑOZ, St. Maderno, in *Atti e Mem. d. R. Accad. di S. Luca, Annuario,* 1913-14, Rome, 1915, 6 *seqq.*

[4] *E.g.* C. Menghini for St. Martina in SS. Luca e Martina, Antonio Giorgetti at St. Sebastian's, Ercole Ferrata at S. Anastasia, and Giambattista Marini for St. Anne at S. Andrea della Fratte ; *cf.* MUÑOZ, *loc. cit.* 9.

towards the ground, her neck showing the stroke of the executioner's axe. Cecilia lies in the noblest simplicity, a picture of virginal purity, like a flower that has been plucked.[1] If in the catacombs the spirit of the first centuries of Christianity appeals directly to the heart of the visitor, it has nowhere found a more sublime artistic expression than here.[2]

Cardinal Sfondrato, who at the end of 1600 had already expended more than 25,000 scudi on the restoration and decoration of the church of S. Cecilia,[3] visited it almost every

[1] The common view, that Maderno represented the statue in this way, because it was as he had seen the saint at the opening of the cypress-wood casket, is not probable. In his remarks on the accounts of the discovery Quentin says : " On voit par ces textes combien il serait exagéré de regarder, par example, la statue de Maderno comme un document ; elle n'est qu'une artistique restitution Le Cardinal Sfondrati n'a evidemment permis à qui que se fut d'ouvrir en son absence la chasse provisoire, ou il avait enfermé et scellé le coffre de cyprès contenant le corps de sainte Cécile, et, lui présent, personne ne s'est permis de soulever les voiles qui recouvraient et peut-être même enveloppaient ce corps. Personne n'a pu se rendre compte de son état de conservation sauf dans les grandes lignes, et l'on ignore si les ossements seuls se sont conservés ou si les chairs desséchées y sont restées adhérentes." (CABROL, Dict. d'archéol., II., 2, 2736). L. DE LACGER (loc. cit. 221 seqq.) rightly agrees with this view. The view that in 1599 the body of St. Cecilia was found, quite intact with the three wounds on the neck, was expressed as quite certain in the Reisebericht of the abate Marchstaller in 1625, printed in Carinthia, LXXI. (1881), 307.

[2] Cf. MOLITOR-WITTMER, 155. See also CANTALAMESSA in Arch. stor. dell'arte, V., 200 seq. Observations against the article by REYMOND in the Gaz. des beaux-arts, 1892. The full value of Maderno's work may be seen by comparing it with the painting in which Fr. Vanni represented the finding of the saint in the " confessio " underneath ; see VOSS, II., 514 (with illust.) ; BRINKMANN, Barockskulptur, II., 222.

[3] An *Avviso of November 25, 1600, reports that : on Wednesday the Pope said mass at S. Cecilia and greatly praised Sfondrato for having expended more than 25,000 scudi on the

day, and chose it for his place of burial.[1]   Clement VIII. too,
had a special predilection for it.   In the latter years of his
life he regularly offered the Holy Sacrifice at the tomb of the
martyr on St. Cecilia's feast.[2]   It is easy to understand this
predilection, because among the countless tombs of the saints
there is hardly any other so graceful and so touching as that
of this noble Roman scion of the family of the Cecilii.

It was no mere coincidence that, at the moment when
Baronius was reviving the study of Christian antiquity, and
when Bosio, Philip von Winghen and Ciaconius were exploring
the subterranean sepulchral city from which the universal
kingdom of the Church had sprung,[3] a great-hearted Cardinal
and a Pope should have set before the eyes of the faithful
of the period of Christian restoration, in the revival of the
cultus of one of the most noble martyrs of Christ, an idea
drawn from the heroic days of Christendom, thus pointing out
the way by which the Church, purified in the fires of tribulation,
has ever attained to her greatest triumphs.

restoration and decoration of the church, " havendo anch'animo
di volergliene spendere dell'altri per maggiore decoro." Urb.
1068, *loc. cit.*

[1] See Bosio, *loc. cit.* 182.

[2] See *Avvisi of November 22, 1603, and November 24, 1604,
Urb. 1071 and 1072, *loc. cit.*

[3] *Cf.* Cabrol, Dict. d'archéol., II., 1, 1085 *seqq.* ; III., 2801 *seq.*

APPENDIX

OF

UNPUBLISHED DOCUMENTS

AND

EXTRACTS FROM ARCHIVES

APPENDIX.

1. DIARY OF THE MASTER OF CEREMONIES PAOLO ALALEONE
OF THE 18TH NOVEMBER, 1593.[1]

Feria V^a chè 18 novembris 1593. In festo die dedicationis
basilicae SS. Apostolorum Petri et Pauli S.D.N.D. Clemens
Papa VIII. crucem aeneam magnam auratam, quae posita et
collocata est supra pallam magnam auratam in cacumine
S. Petri cum sacris reliquiis et Agnis Dei intus inclusis solemni
ritu benedixit intus sacellum Gregorianum praesentibus
quinque dd. cardinalibus cum mantellettis et rochettis,
videlicet ill^{mis} dd. Alphonso Gesualdo episcopo Ostiensi,
Alexandro Medices de Florentia nuncupato tit. S. Petri ad
Vincula, Francisco Toleto tit. S. Mariae Transpontinae
presbyteris, Petro Aldobrandino S. Nicolai in Carcere et
Cynthio Aldobrandino S. Georgii nuncupato diaconis, ac
multis episcopis, praelatis et aliis sanctis caeremoniis praece-
dentibus. Papa a suis cameris descendit per scalas sacristiae
ad sacellum Gregorianum, in quo benedicta fuit crux, indutus
stola supra mozzettam, cruce praecedente, et in porta
Gregoriani aspersit se et alios cardinales de aqua benedicta,
de more ministrante aspersorium ill^{mo} d. cardinale Gesualdo.
Deinde fecit orationem ante altare dicti sacelli Gregoriani,
supra quod altare capsula argentea erat et intus reliquiae in
cruce includendae et Agni Dei et duae capsalue plumbeae,
quarum in una erant includendae reliquiae, in altera Agni
Dei. Papa facta oratione accessit ad altare et visis omnibus
supradictis in altare positis deposito bireto benedixit duas
capsulas plumbeas, prout dicitur in libro Pontificali, indutus
stola supra mozzettam. Benedictis capsulis inclusit reliquias
intus unam ex capsulis plumbeis videlicet de ligno s^{mae} crucis
D. N. Iesu Christi, de reliquiis S. Andreae Apostoli, S. Iacobi
maioris Apostoli, S. Clementis Papae et Martyris, S. Callisti
Papae et Martyris, S. Sixti Secundi Papae et Martyris, S.
Ioannis I Papae et Martyris cum tribus granis incensi. Deinde

inclusit in altera capsula Agnos Dei. Hoc confecto Papa discendens ab altare venit ante crucem collocatam extra altare a cornu Evangelii in angulo, quam benedixit, prout in libro Pontificali habetur, cum eisdem caeremoniis notatis et descriptis in dicto libro Pontificali. Benedicta cruce Papa suis manibus collocavit capsulam plumbeam cum reliquiis intus inclusis in brachio dextero crucis et capsulam plumbeam cum Agnis Dei intus inclusis in brachio sinistro crucis. Deinde Papa genuflexus adoravit crucem et illam lacrimando osculatus est. Post Papam adorarunt crucem ill^{mi} dd. cardinales supradicti, episcoli, praelati et alii. Demum Papa apud altare deposita stola ac mozzetta lavit manus et accepit paramenta pro missa lecta dicenda, quam dixit in altare dicti sacelli Gregoriani de die festo dedicationis, praesentibus omnibus supradictis. Absoluta missa oravit ante altare maius S^{ti} Petri sub quo condita sunt corpora SS. Apostolorum Petri et Pauli. Deinde ascendit superius ad suas cameras per eandem viam, qua venit. Indulgentia non fuit concessa, quia in basilica S. Petri hodie est plenaria. De libro servivit in benedictione capsularum et crucis r^{mus} d. archiepiscopus Montis Regalis et de candela episcopus Cassanensis induti mantellettis et rochettis. Crux benedicta fuit collocata supra pallam in cacumine cuppae magnae S. Petri circa horam 21 et fuerunt pulsatae campanae dictae basilicae S. Petri sonarunt tubycines et timpanistae et fuerunt exoneratae bombardae in arce S. Angeli et in platea S. Petri, et canonici et capitulum basilicae S. Petri cantarunt hymnum, *Vexilla Regis prodeunt*, dum superius crux ferebatur et trahebatur, et deinde hymnum, *Te Deum*, etc. Quos hymnos cantores dictae basilicae cantarunt praesente toto clero S. Petri.

[*Barb.* 2815, p. 326 ss. Vatican Library.]

2. STATEMENT FROM SIGISMUND, KING OF POLAND, TO POPE CLEMENT VIII.[1]

1594, March 8, Upsala.

Sedis Ap^{ae} autoritati tanto nos plus debere fatemur, quanto maioribus beneficiis prae caeteris orbis christ. principibus ab ea auctos nos esse cognoscimus ; etenim cum in turbulentum regni Poloniae statum nostri initium imperii incidisset subditisque nostris factionibus misere distractis summa rei in

---

[1] See *supra*, pp. 97, 98, 100.

lubrico versaretur, irritatis praesertim tot potentissimorum
principum animis, id tandem Sedis Ap. beneficio, prudentia et
dexteritate S^{tis} V. consecuti sumus, ut sublatis turbis atque
discordiis, pacato atque tranquillo regni statu potiremur ;
longum vero esset recensere, quae ac quanta beneficia postmodum officia ab eadem S. Sede per legatos in nos derivata
sunt.

For this reason he looks upon it as his duty to defend the
Holy See and the Faith. He has not shrunk from the difficult
journey, and it makes no difference to him that he has not
accomplished more, and this he wishes to tell you. Quamprimum in hoc nostrum regnum appulimus, deprehendimus
inter praecipuos regni ordines non dubitanter coniuratum,
mortem se omnes malle appetere, quam publicum cath.
religionis usum atque exercitium admittere, quod temporis
progressu semper magis magisque apparuit. Cum vero rem
serio essemus aggressi, non solum de regnis sed etiam de vita
cepimus periclitari, enimvero aperte nobis denunciarunt,
nisi eorum postulatis satisfieret, se unanimes ab obedientia
et fide nostra discessuros ac nobis regressum Stockholmiam
prohibituros, et si dux Carolus, quem auctorem suorum con-
siliorum et incensorem habuerunt omnes, nostrum Stockholmiam reditum antevertere non posset, facile tamen futurum
tum propter anni tempus, tum propter religionis nostrae
insectationem, nos omni commeatu prohibere, neque hic fuit
modus seu meta audaciae, verum in eo processerunt perfidia,
ut carceres et vincula nobis, Polonis quos nobiscum adduximus
interitum, catholicis Suecis extremum supplicium minitaren-
tur. Inter haec tamen parum regni iacturam maerebamus
neque tanti aestimabamus vitae periculum, quin conscientiam
nostram haberemus potiorem, sed multa ac varia animo nostro
obversabantur. Explicatum nobis imprimis fuit a Polonis
publicum regni Poloniae detrimentum atque vicinam cladem
propter intestinas factiones et circumfusas tot barbarorum
copias, consortis nostrae reginae aetate, sexu, vitae periculo
non potuimus non commoveri, legati apost^{ci}, quem propter
S^{tem} V. et ipsius in nos merita unice diligimus, certissimum
vitae discrimen ob oculos versabatur aliaque non spernen-
darum rerum momenta, suis quae ponderibus examinavimus,
ob quae consultius videbatur tempori tantisper cedere, donec
Deo volente opportunior occasio rei gerendae oblata fuerit.

Quam ob rem petimus a S^te V^a diligenter et obnixe, ut nos habeat excusatos et simul apud omnes christ. principes excuset atque defendat ; remedia nonnulla quae huic malo opportune adhiberi poterunt, excogitavimus, quae iudicio et censurae S^tis V. libenter submittimus, et imprimis quidem an ea quae vi et minis totque propositis periculis extorserunt, quamprimum mare navigationi apertum fuit nec amplius propter anni tempus hic inclusi et ab omni externo auxilio exclusi erimus, revocanda sint ; deinde an quod auctoritate nostra et accurata tractatione effici non potuit, id vi et armis in reditu nostro tentare debeamus, quod quidem si S^tis V^ae placuerit, obnixe petimus, ut nobis sua auctoritate et opera praesto esse velit, quo necessaria auxilia ad hoc perficiendum a regno Poloniae obtinere possimus ; praeterea anne hic aliquid moliendum, antequam denuo reversi sedem nostram atque imperium magis stabiliremus, nam interea illorum impetus facile defervescet et aditum nobis ad rem opportune gerendam muniemus. In hisce omnibus ad consilium et auctoritatem S^tis V^ae recurrimus. . .

Interea si in tractatione pacis cum Moscis ad opem et auxilium Polonorum recurrerint Sueci, quod facturi videntur, denegabitur illis omnino, nisi prius liberum atque publicum religionis exercitium se inter regnum admissuros spoponderint. Curabimus etiam summo studio et contentione, ut nemo ad regni administrationem admittatur, qui non prius sancte receperit se permissurum introduci religionis nostrae exercitium. Iuvenes praeterea aliquot e nobilitate melioris spei e regno emittemus, ut in pura fide educentur ad cath. religionis messem, quam aliquando uberem et copiosam speramus ; iis vero qui iam hic sunt catholici, non modo praesidio erimus, sed etiam auxilio, ut nihil ad convenientem vitae sustentationem desiderare possint ; dedimus iam illis assicurationem religionis catholicae, cuius exemplar S^ti V^ae misimus una cum exemplari protestationis, quam contra haereticos fecimus.—Egli si raccomanda al Papa.

[Orig. Doria Archives, Roma.]

3. Germanico Malaspina to Cardinal Cinzio Aldobrandini.[1]

1594, March 8, Upsala.[2]

Hanno finalmente li heretici estorto da S. M^tà l'assicuratione intorno al negotio della religione, et è così impia et

[1] See *supra*, p. 99.
[2] Deciphered on April 20th.

esorbitante, come V. S. ill^{ma} vederà dalla copia di essa segnata
con la lettera A, che, se bene è poi seguita la coronatione,
et che perciò molti giudicando che sia stabilito il dominio
politico, stimano assai che per mezzo di essa coronatione si
siano rotti li disegni che con le antecedenti mie insinuai a
V. S. ill^{ma}, del duca Carlo et delli senatori; et tengono per
fermo che non vi era altro modo, si per evitare la libidine
del dominare dell'uno e dell'altri, come anco per assicurare
questo regno in persona cattolica; et si persuadeno che
confirmato che sarà l'imperio di questa Maestà, sia per essere
la sollevatione del Cattolicismo tanto maggiare quanto hora
è stata tal oppressione e tanto maggiore il resentimento di
questo Seren^{mo} contro li heretici quanto è stata maggior la
violenza e per conseguenza l'ingiuria; et che puoco si è
potuto perdere dove niente si può, et sia per aportare notabile
sollevamento all'affetto et turbolento stato della Christianità.
Tuttavia havendo S. M^{tà} fatta un'attione, della quale non
se ne può adurre essempio alcuno, et essendo però stato lo
scandalo grande et il pregiuditio della nostra santa religione
non inferiore, pare a me che Sua M^{tà} non possa restar sicura
di non haver irritata l'ira et indignatione di Dio contro di se
et che essendo illeciti et condennati li mezzi tenuti per assi-
curarsi del politico, sia per essere puoco stabile et durabile un
dominio confirmato di questa maniera, et che, havendo levata
l'anima al corpo, sia per restare un cadavere fetente et sottoposto a corruttione . . .

There then follows a detailed account of events, which will
lead to this effect; the principal point states:

. . . Il giorno seguente poi, radunatosi insieme tutti li
Ordini, mandorno due de più favoriti familiari di Sua Maestà,
nobili Svedesi, ad intimare a S. M^{tà} che, se lei non si risolveva
a sottoscrivere a tutte le petitioni loro, che fra tre hore sarebbono venuti tutti li Ordini a levarle la obedienza, et se bene li
mandati non soggiongevano altro, tuttavia non mancavano
di quelli che minacciavano a S. M^{tà} che non solamente ella
non potrebbe ritonar a Stocolmo, ma che la sarebbe stata
incarcerata; per il che Sua M^{tà} chiamati li tre senatori
Pollacchi, li mandò dalli padri Giesuiti, a quali proposero il
caso tanto pericoloso, che, se bene il confessore della regina
era sempre stato del mio parere, non dimeno, vedendo così
risoluto il confessore del re, non ardi di opponersi al suo parere;
onde non solamente in viva voce il confessore di Sua M^{tà}

disse che poteva fare ciò che gli heretici dimandavano, ma
diede anco in scritto il voto suo et ciò fu fatto senza mia
participatione, anzi stetti due giorni senza saper cosa alcuna di
quello che era seguito. Dopò il confessore del re si è scusato
meco, dicendo che non gli fu dato se non tre hore di tempo a rispondere. Io, come quello che, havendo in Germania osservato
il stile delli heretici, non ho conosciuto pericolo di qualità
havrei desiderato che Sua M^{tà} havesse risposto alli due mandati, che Sua M^{tà} non voleva in modo alcuno fare attione così
di diretto contro la sua conscienza, et che li Ordini fussero
venuti a lor posta, perchè forsi non sarebbono andati, o,
quando pure fussero andati, Sua Maestrà era a tempo a far
pur quello che fece ; ma perchè è difficile in simili casi far
certo giuditio, io non ardisco di condennare nè riprendere
alcuno, e mi consolo di non essere stato nè autore nè promotore
nè consapevole de simili consigli. Segui poi il primo del
corrente la coronatione fatta da uno di questi vescovi, insieme
coll'untione fatta con il semplice balsamo ungendo il fronte et
polsi di S. M^{tà} ; ma la seren^{ma} regina non volse esser unta.
Permise S. M^{tà} d'esser coronata et unta per mano d'un ministro
heretico, perchè fu avertita che Carlo voleva subito o dopo la
partita, secondo li fosse tornato commodo, far dichiarare dalli
ministri nullo l'atto della coronatione ; ma siccome noi siamo
restati afflitti, così esso è restato chiarito, perchè non si poteva
mai persuadere che Sua M^{tà} fosse per accettar la corona con
simili conditioni. Hora egli ha totalmente deposta ogni
speranza ; quelle resolutioni, che Sua M^{tà} ha prese, V. S. ill^{ma}
le vedrà dalla lettera sua a N^{ro} Sig^{re}, et dalle proteste et
dechiarationi fatte pure dalla M^{tà} Sua, le quali perchè con-
tengono cose di molta qualità e conseguenze per li affari di
quà, essendo necessaria secretezza grande, mi ha Sua M^{tà}
ricercato che io le faccia mettere in cifra, il che ho fatto
volentieri. Si starà aspettando il conseglio che Nostro
Signore darà a Sua M^{tà} et acciò V. S. ill^{ma} pegga le promesse
che Sua M^{tà} fece, quando parti di quà per Polonia, et furono
accettate et sottoscritte dalli Ordini del regno, invio la scrittura che sarà con questa alla lettera M, per la quale si potrà
comprendere, che, quanto al particolare della Polonia, si è
guadagnato, poichè della Estonea non se n'è fatta mentione,
et d'altre cose di non poca consideratione.

[Borghese III., 91 A B, p. 54, Papal Secret Archives.]

4. Cardinal Cinzio Aldobrandini to the Nuncio Malaspina.[1]

1594, April 30, Rome.

" . . . Le dico che essendo S. M^{tà} del re stata indotta da evidente necessità alle cose seguite, N. S^{re} con le viscere di vero amore paterno non solo la scusa et la benedice, ma la compassiona grandemente et confida nella divina misericordia che non havendo peccato la volontà sarà facile l'ottener perdono. La costanza della ser^a regina in non volersi lasciar ungere in quella profana maniera et le lagrime sparse per dolore dell'offese che vedava fare a Dio, meritano lode grandissima et haveranno dal cielo li debiti premii."

[Copy, Borghese II., 68, Papal Secret Archives.]

5. Cardinal Cinzio Aldobrandini to the Cardinal-Legate Madruzzo.[2]

1594, May 2, Rome.

La divina misericordia va moltiplicando i servi della religione cattolica in Olanda di maniera che se ne sperano ogni dì progressi maggiori, massime che già pare che gli heretici stessi, confuse nelle loro discordie et dalla christiana patienza de nostri, attentino quel rigore di persecutione che solevano usar contro sacerdoti che secretamente andavano pascendo l'anime con i santissimi sacramenti, se bene in niun tempo si è veduta quivi la fierezza che s'è provata in altre nationi più prive d'humanità.

Hora quelli che travagliano in quella vigna, tornano a ricordare il bisogno che hanno d'un vescovo che secretamente versasse fra di loro. Nè N. S. resteria di consolari purchè si trovasse soggetto a proposito, poichè D. V. Cauchio, che pareva idoneo, ricusò di sopporsi a quelle fatiche. Se a lei occorrerà consiglio o persona atta, ce ne scriva ; qua intendono il parere di mons. di Tricarico, per le cui mani sono passate quelle faccende . . .

In the meantime we send as catechist " Padre Fra Pietro Hestelio," a Fleming of the order of St. Dominic " versato nel paese et et nell'opera medesima." He displays zeal, he has received faculties from the Inquisition ; the Cardinal recommends him.

[Orig. Cod. Campori, 214, Este Library, Modena.]

[1] See *supra*, p. 99.
[2] See *supra*, p. 4.

6. Germanico Malaspina to Cardinal Cinzio Aldobrandini.[1]

1594, August 15, Di Nave.

Illmo et rev^{mo} sig$_r$ patron mio col^{mo}.

Le infermità di questo regno nel politico et spirituale si sono andate successivamente scoprendo tali che, come suol alle volte accadere nelli corpi ripieni di humori che il rimedio che si usa per provedere a una parte ne genera delli altri più perniitiosi et di maggior pericolo, così quelle medicine che questo ser^{mo} re è andato applicando hora per conservare il politico, hora per introdurre il spirituale, non hanno sempre fatta quella operatione in bene che il zelo et la prudenza di Sua M^{tà} ricercava, anzi quel rimedio così commendato da alcuni politici Polacchi, di concedere le cose desiderate intorno al negotio della religione, non ha sminuito, ma accresciuto li disegni dell'heretici nel politico.   Onde è degno di molta lode questo Ser^{mo} havendo stabilito in assai buona forma il politico et sollevato in qualche parte l'afflitto stato della religione, come nel foglio a parte V. S. ill^{ma} intenderà.   Ma è bene stato in questa trattatione cosa notabile et degna di posterità il vedere questo buon re, difeso solamente dalla maestà regia, rimanere per ogni altro rispetto esposto all'ambitione d'un zio potente et di natura temeraria et fascinato da quel condennato et seditioso seme di Calvino, et alla discretione d'una nobiltà che a guisa di fiera selvaggia usa ad essere ritenuta in un serraglio, uscitane fuori recalcitra per non ritornarvi et il resto de sudditi, se bene di natura pacati, agitati però de queste furie infernali de predicanti, non hanno mai dato argumento alcuno di ricognoscere se non in parole per loro vero signore questa Maestà, et perciò, si come quanto più è stata ardua questa negotiatione et per rispetto di questo regno hereditario, dove la massa è tutta corrotta et tutti gli ordini alieni dal loro re, et per causa dell'elettivo sottoposto a varie pratiche, il quale per haver prefisso, se bene ragione volmente, il tempo del ritorno in Polonia, ha in un certo-moda suministrato armi a questo altro, con le quali potesse offendere questo ser^{mo} re, così a questo tempo et nelle con-giontture che si ritrova lo stato della Christianità, niuna cosa era più preclara nè più gloriosa, quanto conservare l'elettivo et acquistare questo altro senza strepito nè tumulto, et con

[1] See *supra*, p. 98, 102.

la patienza et con la industria et particolarmente con la pietà
rendere vani li conati delli adversarii. Et in vero deve essere
desiderato da questa Maestà l'accrescimento della presente
grandezza, che conservarà con l'aiuto di Dio volontariamente,
che quella che hanno mantenuta li suoi predecessori con la
violenza. Et se bene non rimangono qua gli huomini con-
sideratori delle cose future liberi dal sospetto, che nell'absentia
di Sua M^{tà} le cose si siano per mutare in peggio, tuttavia
voglio sperare che la opinione del cancelliere di Polonia sia
per verificarsi, cioè che Sua M^{tà} sarà più obedita et stimata
resedendo in Polonia che non è stata mentre si è fermata quà,
perchè, se bene sarebbe temerità il negare che simil attione
non sia sottoposta a varii pericoli, nondimeno non credo che
sia degna di riprensione questa Maestà, se non la ha regolata
come se tutti li pericoli havessero a succedere, sperando nella
Providenza Divina che non verrà innanzi tutto quello di male
che può accadere, anzi teniamo per cosa indubitata che non
saranno così congionti questi suditi a una ribellione manifesta,
come sono stati congionti con consegli et machinationi occulte.
Questo ho voluto con ogni humiltà significare a V. S. ill^{ma}
acciochè lei veda avanti quello che scrivo in altra forma che
Sua M^{tà} crede di haver data tal direttione al governo di questo
regno et havere incominato il negotio della religione di tal
maniera, et havere misurato et calculato quello che a lei
conveniva quanto al temporale et spirituale, che intorno al
primo tiene che la ritentione de l'uno et l'altro regno seguirà ;
et nel secondo si persuade Sua M^{tà} d'havere gettati così buoni
fondamenti che Sua Beat^{ne} può restare consola·a per l'augu-
mento che sotto il suo pontificato vedrà dell'honore et gloria
di Dio.   Io, Illmo Sig^{re}, se ben conosco che si deve suspendere
l'intelletto nel fare giuditio della racolta del seminato da noi
insin'tanto che un'altra volta si apra il mare, essendo peri-
colosa cosa il fidarsi della fede di coloro che non l'hanno
osservata a Dio, nondimeno non posso contenermi di non
sentire molta consolatione et di non rendere alla Divina
Maestà gratie infinite per il favore ricevuto d'havere, senza
incorrere in tragedie, sostentata la carica di questa mia fontione
aquilonare con dignità, et che nella promotione et direttione
di così difficile, varia et odiosa trattatione la confidentia di
queste Maestà verso di me, non solo non si sia sminuita, ma
augumentata, et che li signori Polacchi habbino a conoscere

che quanto al ritorno di Sua Maestà si sia proceduto con loro bona fide, per il che, non come vittorioso di questa, dirò così, guerra d'heretici, ma come reconoscitore in qualche parte delli beneficii divini, ho eretto il vessillo di s^ta Chiesa et le armi di N^ro Sig^re in questo mar Baltico, acciochè, havendomi questo Ser^mo consignata la nave generale dell'armata, in essa risplendesse quel stendardo che meritamente in ogni, luogo deve essere preposto a tutti gli altri . . .

Di nave il giorno dell'Assuntione 15 agosto 1594.

[Address :]   Al sig^r Card^le S. Giorgio.   Ger^co vescovo di S, Severo.

[Borghese III., 91 A B, p. 152, Papal Secret Archives.]

7. INSTRUCTION BY L. TAVERNA FOR HIS SUCCESSOR IN THE VENETIAN NUNTIATURE, ANTONIO MARIA GRAZIANI.[1]

1596, March 30, Venice.

. . . Una delle più importanti cure che habbi il Nuntio qua è il tribunal della s. Inquisizione . . . Si rauna tre volte la settimana cioè il martedì, il giovedì, il sabato ; in esso sono capi et giudici il Nuntio, il Patriarca et l'Inquisitore.   V'intervengono però l'auditore del Nuntio, il vicario del Patriarca et il commissario del s. Officio, ch' è frate eletto dall'Inquisitore et hanno voto consultivo.   Vi assistono anche tre senatori principali nominati dall'ecc. senato per dar il braccio secolare quando bisogna fare qualche cattura o altra esecutione.   Io per l'ordine espresso datomi da N. S^re prima che partessi di Roma non ho mai mancato d'andare a questo tribunale se non il sabato per essere quel giorno ordinariamente occupato in scrivere, se ben anco in esso si è atteso ordinariamente ad esaminare i rei o testimonii riservandosi poi il fare il decreto et le risolutioni martedì et giovedì acciò vi fossimo tutti presenti importando assai la presenza del Nuntio per l'autorità dell' offitio, per il rispetto che gl'hanno li clarissimi assistenti et per esser li Nuntii per il più di professione legale, della quale non sono il Patriarca et l'Inquisitore.   Però sarà gran servitio di Dio benedetto o di S. Sta che V. S. R. ci vada quanto più spesso potrà et procuri con la prudenza et destrezza sua di mantenere la giurisdittione et autorità di detto tribunale in che li bisognerà essere oculatissima.   Gioverà anco assai il tenere buona intelligenza con il p. Inquisitore essendo vigilante,

---

[1] See *supra*, pp. 153, 156, 214, 222.

assiduo, di grande integrità, molto intelligente et prattico in questi negotii oltra la notitia che potrà dare delle cose di Venetia, delle quali è molto informato per esservi stato lungo tempo . . .

Quando s'ha da sententiare diffinitivamente in qualche cosa d'importanza si sogliono chiamare quattro altri consultori, due canonisti et due theologi ch'habbino però notitia de'canoni et doppo esservi uditi tutti li voti consultivi il Nuntio, il Patriarca et l'Inquisitore pronuntiano come li pare che ricerchi il giusto et l'honesto. In tempo mio non mi ricordo che sia mai stata differenza tra noi tre, mas se vi nascesse li voti di due prevaleriano . . .

Quando venni a Venetia li regolari vivevano con tanta licenza et dissolutione ch'era grandissima vergogna et scandalo. I have attempted a reform, but it is necessary to carry it on. By order of the Pope I have driven out two apostates of the "minimi conventuali, Fra Paolo della Pergola et un Fra Fabritio Napolitano," they are now living as exiles and have vainly tried to stir up the government against the Pope. Fra Paolo is still in " questi contorni," he hopes after my departure to be able to remain : the nuncio must see that Fra Paolo is punished.

There continue " differenze di giurisdittione " between the bishops and the magistrates. I have always upheld ecclestical jurisdiction.

[Copy. Istruzioni I., 11 *seq.*, Graziani Archives, Città di Castello.]

8. Lelio Arrigoni to the Duke of Mantua.[1]

1596, June 29, Rome.

. . . Nelle riforme che d'ordine di N. S. si vanno tuttavia facendo d'infinite cose, et particolarmente intorno alla stampa, annullando molte opere et altre sottomettendo a nuova corretione, come appare per il nuovo indice, intendo che si habbia a sospendere l'opera di Merlino[2] la quale per l'honore che apporta a cotesta città di onde è venuta et per esser anco stata fatica assai virtuosa, potrebbe forsi essere desiderata viva da V. A., et perchè in tal caso l'autorità sua appresso S. B^ne et questi riformatori sarebbe potente a sostenerla che

---

[1] See *supra*, p. 217.
[2] " Folengo " : see Reusch, Index, I., 394.

non fosse lacerata affatto, ho voluto scriverlene affine se nell'
A. V. fusse pensiero che perciò se ne facesse qualche ufficio,
resti servita di comandarlo . . .

[Orig. Gonzaga Archives, Mantua.]

9. POPE CLEMENT VIII. TO THE INQUISITOR ANTONIO DE MATOS DE NORONHA, BISHOP OF ELVAS.[1]

1596, September 19, Rome.

Almost every day there came to Rome Portuguese, so-called
neo-Christians converted from Judaism, who witness to the
diversity of these neo-Christians ; some keep the faith inviolate and in its entirety, while others call themselves
Christians hypocritically, but adhere to the superstitions
of their forefathers ; they hate the true Christians, their
fellow-countrymen, and seek by calumnies to involve them
in their own condemnation when they are punished by the
Inquisition. The true Christians complain that besides being
thus thrown into prison, and examined by the Inquisition
" per interrogatoria suggestiva," being thus trapped they
are compelled to admit things which they have not done.
We warn you to admonish the inquisitors and the judges of
the Inquisition to proceed in accordance with legitimate
evidence, and not upon false depositions, and that " omnino
a suggestionibus ac captiosis interrogationibus abstineant."

[Brevia, Arm. 40, t. 40, n. 379, Papal Secret Archives.]

10. AVVISO DI ROMA OF 23 JULY, 1597.[2]

The Pope goes almost every morning to a church, thus on
Sunday to the Rotonda, where the canons showed him " le
molte necessità, in che si trova quella machina et particolarmente la cuppola, la quale è talmente dall'antichità disfatta,
che quando piove, tutta la chiesa si riempie d'acqua, suppli-
candola però a voler compatire alla lor'povertà, onde la
S. S. si mostrò prontissimo a un'opra tanto pia havendovi di
già destinato un'architetto, che vegga il bisogno, et in somma
dicesi, che si ricoprirà la cuppola di piombo, et si abbellirà
dentro de bellissime cappelle, et di fuori alla porta si farà
un'cancello di ferro et molte pietre di fino marmo, che stavano
sotterrate in quel porticale, son state discavate per condurle a

[1] See *supra*, p. 199.
[2] See *supra*, pp. 478, 481.

S. Gio. Laterano in servitio della nova cappella, che S. S. fa fare in quella basilica con notabilissima spesa."

(Orig. Urb. 1065, p. 439, Vatican Library.]

11. POPE CLEMENT VIII. TO THE PRINCE-ELECTOR OF TRÊVES, JOHANN VON SCHÖNENBERG.[1]

1597, September 27, Rome.

Venerabilis frater, salutem et apostolicam benedictionem. Catholicae Ecclesiae, cui divina bonitas nullis Nostris meritis infirmitatem Nostram praeesse voluit, prodesse etiam quacunque ratione, Deo iuvante, possumus, valde cupientes, hanc quoque cogitationem suscepimus ut vetera oecumenica concilia in Nostra Vaticana typographia quam emendatissime imprimantur ; quorum quanta sit in eadem Ecclesia Dei auctoritas atque utilitas, fraternitas Tua non ignorat, et iam prima illa quattuor, quibus tamquam quattuor Evangeliis venerationem adhibendam esse, magnum Ecclesiae Romanae lumen, sanctus Gregorius summus pontifex et doctor egregius docuit, non mediocri piorum et literatorum hominum labore emendata sunt, undique tam graecis quam latinis conquisitis ac collatis libris, et eodem studio in aliorum eiusmodi conciliorum emendatione diligenter iussu Nostro incumbetur. Interea relatum Nobis est in bibliotheca nobilis istius metropolitanae ecclesiae vetustos aliquot conciliorum codices manuscriptos inveniri, qui magno usui esse poterunt ad hanc quam molimur editionem, in primis vero sextam synodum integram grandioribus litteris in membrana scriptam, synodum item Chalcedonensem eadem forma, volumen etiam conciliorum diversorum et decretales epistolas Romanorum Pontificum priscorum. Ex quorum sane codicum collatione multa ad publicam ultilitatem depromi posse speramus. Quare a Tua fraternitate petimus, ut eosdem libros ad Nos transmittendos cures, quod Te et dilectos filios canonicos et capitulares eiusdem metropolitanae ecclesiae, ad quos etiam litteras damus, libenter facturos confidimus, quod vestra erga hanc Sanctam Sedem perspecta pietas et devotio Nostraque erga vos paterna caritas merito postulat. Hac quidem in re quid spectemus vides : solam Dei gloriam et catholicae fidei, quam sacra concilia, rite convocata, Spiritu Sancto auctore docuerunt, propagationem quaerimus. At tam praeclarum opus

---

[1] See *supra*, p. 438.

et fraternitatem Tuam et canonicos convenire, vobis et
ecclesiae isti honorificum est et Nobis pergratum erit, quemadmodum Tibi copiosius exponet venerabilis frater episcopus
Auxerensis,[1] Nuntius Noster Apostolicus, cui ut fidem
cumulate habeas a Te petimus.

Datum Romae apud S. Marcum sub annulo piscatoris, die
27 Septembris 1597, pontificatus Nostri anno sexto.

[Brevia, Arm. 44, t. 41, n. 22, Papal Secret Archives.]

12. Inscription at the Portico of the Cathedral of S. Maria in Civita Castellana.[2]

Clemens VIII P. O. M., qui octo praecipuis S. R. E. cardinalibus comitatus pontis molem super Tiberim inter Veyentes
et Sabinos a Sixto V fe. rec. olim deliberatam modo suo iussu
et aere constructam oculata fide exploraturus ad Veyos
divertit et in arce a Petro Aldobrandino eiusdem Smi ex
frate nepote card. ampliss. eiusdem civitatis gub. splen-
didissime receptus semel et iterum tranquille pernoctavit ;
interea cum summa lenitate magistratus ad iustitiam colendam
patritiosque ad rite et recte vivendum adhortatus proventibus
archivi et damni dati nuncupatis officiis communitati con-
donatis pia loca eleemosinis fovit superque nonnullos cives
carceribus et exilio in caput mancipatos paterne misertus
omnes libertate facile donavit, cathedralem porro ecclesiam
re sacra ad aram maiorem mira cum pietate peracta bis
illustravit et plenaria indulgentia in festo d. Georgii adventus
sui die auspicatissima quotannis cumulatissime ditavit,
populum tandem pre [sic] illius recessu moestum et solicitum
pia cum benedictione complexus itinere in pace sumpto
foelix recessit a. d. 1597.

Sim. Petronio I. U. D. Io. D. Bu. et Blu. Caio conservatori-
bus curan.

13. Report of G. Malaspina on the situation in Sweden.[3]

Relatione dello stato spirituale e ploitico del regno di Svetia
di ciò che segui quando di re andò a pigliare il possesso di
esso regno, et come di nuovo vi si rimpiantò la fede cattolica
del beneficio che può ricevere la Christianità della congiuntione

---

[1] Coriolano Garzadoro, bishop of Ossero.
[2] See *supra*, pp. 490, 491.
[3] See *supra*, pp. 88, 97, 98, 100, 104, 105, 106.

della Svetia con la Polonia, della provincia della Finlandia a'confini del Mosco, del porto di Calmar chiave del mar Baltico, del porto di Elsburg fuori dello stretto di Dania.

Gustavo che fu avo del ser^mo re di Polonia, doppo di havere con molto valore et gloria liberato il regno di Svetia, patria sua, dalla tirannide di Cristerno re di Dania, et fattosi di privato cittadino sebene d'antica et nobile famiglia, di consenso et applauso de'popoli re di Svetia, et ridotto il regno di elettivo hereditario, oscurò lo splendore delle sue gloriose operationi con una nota d'infamia perpetua, poichè mosso non tanto da depravata coscienza quanto da timore di non poter sostenere con le tenue entrate che alli re eletti di Svetia,erano assignate la dignità del grado dentro del regno et di fuori difendersi da Cristerno, emulo et inimico suo, applicò a se tutte l'entrate ecclesiastiche del suo regno, et perchè se i suoi sudditi fossero rimasti cattolici, non havrebbono permesso che havesse violato il giuramento che fece quando come cattolico fu ricevuto per re, di conservare et protegere l'ordine eccl^co et regolare, per potere esseguire questo suo depravato desiderio apostatò dalla fede catt^ca et abbracciò la dannata setta di Lutero, et con diverse diaboliche arti, indusse la semplice plebe (dalla quale dipendono in gran parte le deliberationi che in quel regno si prendono) a seguire i vestigi suoi, di modo ch'egli potè sicuramente occupare i beni ecclesiastici. Successe a Gustavo Enrico suo figlio primogenito il quale fu anch'esso infetto di heresia, ma non già di moderati costumi come Gustavo poichè fu superbo, crudele et precipitoso. Per impietà faceva un'asino carico di sale a piedi d'una montagna erta et senza via per salirvi sopra et egli era distinto con un bastone in mano che batteva il detto asino et interpretava detta sua impresa nella seguente forma, che l'asino cennò i sudditi, il sale le gravezze, la montagna significava che il suddito deve essere forzato a fare anco quello che haveva dell'impossibile per mezzo del bastone. Costui carcerò Giovanni suo fratello duca di Finlandia et stando prigione insieme con la moglie, sorella del re Sigismondo Augusto et figliuolo della regina Bona, dotata di singolar pietà et prudenza, nacque il presente re di Polonia et in povertà tale che non havendo la madre con che fasciarlo, fece di una camisa fascie. Suoleva Enrico andare alla carcere con animo di far morire Giovanni suo fratello insieme con la moglie et figlio, ma gionto ad essa carcere non solo non effettuava la sua mala intentione, ma si raccomandava al fratello dicendo : So, che tu sarai re et io tuo prigione, habbimi per raccomandato. Et non fu falso profeta perchè Giovanni con l'aiuto di Carlo terzo fratello et duca di Sudermania uscì di carcere et fece prigione Enrico et esso fu creato re morendo poi Enrico in carcere. Fu Giovanni di natura incostante et varia, ma ingenuo et regendo esso in Svetia fu eletto il figliuolo re di Polonia, et perchè egli era in secreto cattolico sicome al Nuntio l'a affirmato il re suo figliuolo, usò ogni industria perchè il figliuolo ritornasse mentre esso viveva in Svetia, affine di dichiararsi apertamente cattolico et ridurre il regno ad abbracciare essa fede, ne inclinava che il figliuolo ritenesse la Polonia, ma stimava essere più spediente preferire l'hereditario regno all'elettivo. Et perchè quando il ser^mo re di Polonia si abboccò in Revaglia col padre, i senatori Svedesi che havevano havuto odore di questa intentione di Giovanni, furono causa che il re di Polonia non passasse in Svetia, sdegnato li privò della dignità, confiscò loro le facoltà et li mandò in esilio. Morse poi il re Giovanni et con estremo dolore del figliuolo morse hereticamente. Afferma la M^tà Sua che s'essa si fosse ritrovata presente haverebbe la M^tà di suo padre fatto fine cattolico et il regno si sarebbe ridotto alla cognitione della vera fede. Diede il ser^mo re parte alli senatori di Polonia della morte del padre, del desiderio che mostravano i sudditi che la M^tà Sua si trasferisse in Svetia, della proteste che facevano, caso che non passasse et della necessità in che era costituito di passare in quelle parti. Furono intimati i comitii et volevano alcuni che S. M^tà andasse armata, altri disarmata, ma prevalse l'opinione di coloro che consigliorno che non andasse armato, quali giudicorno che l'andarvi armato era andare come nemico et che non conveniva andare a pigliare il possesso della sua heredità con violenza et forza, tanto più che tutto il regno l'aspettava, l'invitava per mezzo di ambasciatori. Haveva inviato l'armata navale a Dansico, ove i più principali signori erano comparsi per incontrare et condurre la M^tà Sua, ma il tempo fece conoscere poi che il sopradetto consiglio non fu buono, poichè dall'essere il re comparso disarmato, ne risultò che andò a ricevere, non a dar legge, perchè gli Ordini si unirono contra la M^tà Sua sotto pretesto della religione et pretendevano che per vigore del testamento di Gustavo, i posteri di esso Gustavo, dovessero essere heretici se volevano essere capaci della successione, dimodo che il duca Carlo, la matrigna del re et la nobiltà prosupponevano che gli Ordini non fussero tenuti di prestar giuramento di fedeltà ad un re cattolico, et Carlo nella propria persona, la matrigna del re nella persona del figliolo, fratello da lato di padre del re aspiravano alla corona, et li nobili riducendosi a memoria la libertà che godevano quando il regno era elettivo et la tirannide usata con essi dopo che è fatto hereditario, desideravano di togliersi il duro giogo da dosso. Carlo si fondava nelle clientele che haveva dentro et fuori del regno et nel favore de' Calvinisti et per facilitare maggiormente le sue pretensioni comparve armato nella dieta che si fece in Upsalia, città dove sogliono coronarsi li re, et perchè dubitava che gli Ordini non haverebbono escluso due chiamati prima di lui nella successione, cioè il re di Polonia et il fratello da lato di padre, si scoperse che disegnava di essere dichiarato governatore del fratello del re et procedessero, come già si fece in Milano in un caso non molto dissimile. Li senatore poi alienissimi di animo dalla familia di Gustavo stavano aspettando che le discorde tra il duca et il re di Polonia et la matrigna aprissero loro via di potersi estinguere. Per il che il ser^mo re, trovandosi disarmato et duca Carlo armato et li heretici uniti contra di esso et essendo il cuor dell'inverno et agghiaciato il mare non potendo pensare a ritirarsi, si trovava circondato da molte angustie, perchè da un canto gli heretici non volevano venire all'atto della coronatione et di prestarle giuramento di fedeltà se non confirmava il loro essercitio et non excludeva totalmente il cattolico et non dichiarava inhabili detti cattolici da ogni officio et dignità del regno, et dall'altra parte essendo S. M^tà di timorata coscienza, vedeva che il candore d'essa si saria grandemente denigrato se condescendeva a così inique con- ditioni. Si mostrò però animoso nel principio et risoluto di voler piutosto perdere il regno, che macular la coscientia et estimatione sua. Onde gli heretici attribuendo al ministro Apost^co la renitenza del re, mandarono dal Nuntio quattro nobili ad invitarlo che dovesse uscire del regno, protestando che sarebbono succeduti de' grandi inconvenienti, caso che non l'havesse fatto. A che rispose il Nuntio ch'egli era entrato publicamente nel regno et era stato ricevuto come ministro di S.S. et non poteva ne voleva uscirne, non havendo

egli commesso cosa per la quale meritasse che si violasse il
ius gentium seco. Mandorno quasi nello stesso tempo ad
intimare a S.M^{tà} per due suoi familiari et parenti che se la
M^{tà} Sua non giurava le loro petitioni, che gli haverebbono
levata l'obbedientia et messo la corona del regno in capo del
duca Carlo, et che in tal caso la M^{tà} Sua haverebbe fatto
esperienza delle pernitiose conseguenze che haverebbe portato
seco simile loro deliberatione. Et in spetie si lasciarono
intendere che il primo mestiere che disegnavano fare era di
assaltare la casa del ministro del Papa, per il che S. M^{tà} mandò
dal Nuntio il palatino Laschi a significarli che se la M^{tà} Sua
non consentiva alle petitioni degli heretici, che nello spatio di
tre hore gli heretici haverebbono ammazzato il Nuntio et la
familia sua et che a Sua M^{tà} più dispiacerebbe la morte di esso
Nuntio che quasi la sua propria. Al che rispose il Nuntio, che
Sua M^{tà} haveva occasione buonissima di chiarirsi se le minacce
degli heretici erano verbali et semplicemente per atterrire
Sua M^{tà} o pure d'altra qualità con sospendere (come il Nuntio
lo supplicava) di concedere alli heretici cosa alcuna per lo
spatio di quelle tre hore in detrimento della religione cattolica
et se in detto spatio havessero ammazzato esso Nuntio, sicome
all'hora si sarebbe chiarito, che si procedeva da essi non per
atterrire con parole, ma col far dei fatti, così in tal caso S. M^{tà}
concedesse o non concedesse, secondo che più le fosse piaciuto ;
ma dato che non succedesse la morte del Nuntio, che in tal
caso S. M^{tà} haverebbe conosciuto essere verbali le minacce
degli heretici et che però haveva potuto astenersi di far così
gran detrimento alla religione. Et perchè il Nuntio dubitò
che il palatino non riferisse l'ambasciata, mandò un suo
familiare ad esporla a S. M^{tà} et insieme a farle una protesta
che in eterno non haveria prestato consenso alcuno che
potesse denigrare quella purità, che sempre haveva conservato
nelle cose della fede la Sede Apostolica et la simile protesta si
fece anche con la ser^{ma} regina. Et perchè S. M^{tà} era risoluta
di non volere consentire alle petitioni degli heretici senza
consenso del Nuntio, che così era restato di concerto con esso
Nuntio, quando lo condusse seco di Polonia. Però quando
Sua M^{tà} si chiarì essere impossibile di persuadere al Nuntio di
consentire, mandò alcuni senatori Polacchi da dui padri
Gesuiti ch'erano venuti con la M^{tà} Sua a darli parte dello
stato delle cose con le sue circostanze et conseguenze et detti

padri dichiarorno che pur supposta la necessità et pericolo nel quale era costituita la M.^{tà} Sua la potesse senza offendere Dio concedere alli heretici ciò che ricercavano et la M.^{tà} Sua per sua giustificatione ne volle uno scritto da detti padri. Et perchè era disposto il Nuntio di volere nelli publici comitii comparire et protestare, si tenne segreta al detto Nuntio la risposta data dalli detti padri al re, et a notitia del Nuntio non pervenne tal concessione se non doppo tre giorni che le fu concessa et subito che n'hebbe odore, volle partire del regno per la via di Dania, dove quella M.^{tà} lo aspettava con desiderio, et voleva trattarlo humanissimamente per insegnare (come diceva) alli barbari Svedesi in che maniera si trattano gli ambasciatori de' principi. Ma S. M.^{tà} come quella che vedeva volentieri che il Nuntio facesse le sopradette dimostrationi per quello che potesse col tempo succedere, non volle che partisse, anzi fece ordinare che non fossero dati cavalli al Nuntio, et così fu necessitato a restare. Hora fatta la coronatione et concessione, pose ogni studio il Nuntio per applicare qualche rimedio al disordine seguito, onde operò per sicurezza della coscienza di S. M.^{tá} ch'ella facesse una protesta in scritto, come ella non con la volontà, ma per pura forza si era indotto a concedere ciò che haveva concesso. Et perchè non bastava cercare di assicurare per questo mezzo solo la coscienza, ma bisognava sollevare l'afflitto stato delle reliquie de' catolici, quali restavano et senza essercitio et privi delle dignità et uffici del regno, persuase il Nuntio al ser^{mo} re che concedesse da parte a cattolici altretanto quanto haveva conceduto alli heretici, di modo che a guisa dell'Imp^{re} et del re di Polonia restasse la M^{tà} Sua giurata utrique parti. S. M^{tà} si contentò di farlo et immediate mise in esecuzione le dette concessioni, perchè avanti la sua partenza diede uffici et dignità a cattolici et lasciò in quattro luoghi l'essercitio della religione et fece giurare a quattro governat^{ri} (se bene erano heretici) quali lasciò nel regno, che haverebbero protetto la religione et li cattolici. Et il Nuntio esercitò tutte le funtioni episcopali publicamente et successe che havendo lavato li piedi a dodici poveri in chiesa con grandissimo concorso di popoli, et essendosi quei poveri dichiarati cattolici, furono poi banditi dalli heretici. Tenne anco il Nuntio in luogo publico uno stendardo alzato, da una parte del quale era una nave con l'immagine di s. Pietro sopra l'acque con tali parole : fluctuat non mergitur, et dall'altra vi era l'arma di S.S^{tà} et a piedi di essa questo motto : fugantur tenebrae tantis irradiatae fulgoribus, et s'introdusse et mise in uso la forma di sepellire cattolicamente con candele accese, croci et con tutto il resto secondo il rito cattolico. Ma doppo la partita di S. M^{tà} il duca Carlo, quale non haveva voluto accettare il governo del regno in compagnia coi senatori et pretendea non concreta, ma suprema et assoluta autorità et che i senatori servissero per consiglieri et non havessero ne autorità ne voto, si usurpò con la forza tutto questo che gli era stato negato, levando l'esercitio cattolico et il governo alli quattro governatori et ridusse lo stato di quel regno a tale che a S. M^{tà} non rimaneva altro che il nudo titolo di re, et la licenza et insolenza sua procedette tant'oltre che S. M^{tà} giudicò havere il duca violato il giuramento prestato, onde S. M^{tà} è stata forzata a trasferirsi di nuovo in quel regno, ma in differente forma della prima volta, cioè in modo che la potesse prescrivere ad altri la legge et non ricerverla, et pensa di lasciare tali presidii che al duca non verrà fatto quello che l'altra volta fece, havendo condotto seco assai buon numero di soldati, et tanto più ha speranza che le cose siano per succedere felicemente, quantochè Carlo ha governato così tirannicamente il regno che ha alienato da se la nobiltà et con haver cercato di levare l'elevatione dell'hostia alli Luterani ha commossi contra di lui tutti li contadini, quali sono divotissimi di detta elevatione, perchè per mezzo d'essa d'idolatri si fecero cristiani. Il che passò nella seguente forma : L'arcivescovo Cantaranense in Inghilterra radunato il suo clero con li suffraganei propose la missione al regno di Svetia per ridurlo alla fede christiana, et rispondendo tutti che se voleva andare che andasse et egli si risolse di farlo, et navigando per quella volta smontò ad un'isoletta di detto regno et celebrando messa, alcuni pastori mentre facevano l'elevatione videro un bambino nell'hostia et subito chiamorno li compagni li quali havendo anch'essi veduto lo stesso, subito lo fecero sapere al governatore nella provincia, quale dopo haver riputati per pazzi detti pastori finalmente crescendo il numero di quelli che affermavano ciò essere verissimo, si dispose di chiarirsene, et ritrovò anch'egli esser vero tutto quello che da pastori gli era stato riferito ; onde si risolse darne parte al re, quale trasferendosi anch'esso nel detto luogo vide il medesimo et misso dal miracolo si fece christiano

insieme con tutti li suoi sudditi. Per il che i contadini che
sono quasi tutti arditissimi et inclinatissimi alla religione
cattolica non hanno mai permesso che sia levata loro la detta
elevatione. Però havendo il duca come Calvinista cercato di
farlo, tumultuorono, et sicome si alienorno da esso, così si
congiunsero d'animo col ser^{mo} re.

Oltra di questo successe anco un'altro caso mirabile, et
ciò fu che havendo il duca ordinato che si levassero le imagini
delle chiese si trovava in una chiesa parrochiale una imagine di
legno del beato Enrico re di Svetia quale levata fuori di chiesa
et esposta in luogo publico, un soldato voltato alla persona
del detto santo disse : Enrico, Enrico, tu devi haver commesso
qualche gran peccato poichè non vogliono che tu stii in chiesa
et dicendo queste parole scaricò l'archibugio et la palla
miracolosamente doppo di havere percossa la statua, senza
lesione alcuna, ritornò indietro et ammazzò il soldato. Li
sopradetti accidenti non hanno come di sopra ho detto deterio-
rata, ma migliorata la conditione di S. M^{tà}. Oltrachè le scel-
leratezze enormi congiunte con una grandissima ignoranza che
commettono li predicanti heretici, sono tali che pare impossibile
che li popoli siano per sopportarli più lungo tempo, et per ogni
buon rispetto il Nuntio fece cavare li processi formati contra
detti predicanti atti pubblici delle communità et si lessero
eccessi non uditi commessi da detti predicanti, de'quali se ne
riferirà solamente uno.

Un predicante haveva insegnato a parlare ad un corvo et
amando detto corvo grandemente, cominciò a dolersi ch'esso
corvo fosse escluso dal paradiso, onde acciò si salvasse s'indusse
a battezzarlo, servata la vera forma del battesimo. È ancor
cosa degna di pervenire a notitia della posterità che dopo che
l'heresia è intrata in Svetia, ne il mare ha prodotti pesci in
tanta quantità come faceva prima, et la terra ha persa la sua
fertilità et gli uccelli de quali era abbondanza grandissima,
hanno fatta trasmigratione in altri paesi. La M^{tà} Sua come
quella che è dotata di singolar pietà et zelo et è di timorata
coscienza attribuisce alle concessioni fatte da lei agli heretici
l'haverli Dio levata la moglie et mandatile altri travagli et con
molta effusione di lacrime significò al Nuntio questo suo
timore, dicendo ch'ella doveva piuttosto morire che concedere
cosa che potesse maculare il candore della sua coscienza. Onde
trovarà mons^r Nuntio buona dispositione in Sua M^{tà} di

sollevare l'afflitto stato della religione, ma è ben vero ch' è
necessario che Sua M^{tà} stabilisca prima bene il politico dominio,
et che in questo mezzo alimenti liberalmente li poveri cattolici
fatti esuli dal duca.

Questo è quello che mi è occorso di dire circa la religione,
non pretermettendo però di dire che si come il re Gustavo fu
riputato uno de'più savi, sagaci et valorosi principi del suo
tempo, così in esso più che in niun altro si scoperse quanto
siano incerte le providenze et timidi li pensieri humani, poichè
egli per stabilire il regno nella sua persona et posteri suoi, tenne
più conto di detto stabilimento che della salute dell'anime,
ma non li bastò atteso che non previde che della sua maculata
radice, doveda nascere un suo descendente alieno della sua
religione, quale non haverebbe potuto risiedere ne'regni ; onde
fu insieme con li suoi figli più intento ad acquistare de facto
et mantener con violenza ciò che si usurpava contra le leggi
et in pregiuditio della nobiltà che sollecito a stabilirlo con
consenso de'popoli, et perchè quando il regno di elettivo
fu ridotto ad hereditario, furono ben corrette le leggi del
regno in tutto quello che aspettava alla successione et altre
preminenze che toccano a principi hereditarii, ma non già
emendate in quella parte che concerne i privilegi, essentioni
et immunità della nobiltà, però la nobiltà Svedese ricercava
sapere dalla M^{tà} Sua, s'ella pretendea di reggere tirannicamente come haveano fatto i suoi antecessori overo secondo
le leggi, che se doveano havere un re di aliena religione et
absente, pretendeano ch'esso re havesse nel governo rispetto
alle leggi, in quello che sono favorevoli alla nobiltà, petitioni
che quando alli Svedesi fossero fatte buone, sarebbono stati
più liberi che non sono li Polacchi, et il re più ristretto di
autorità. Per il che veniva la M^{tà} Sua consigliata a conservarsi in quel possesso ch'erano i suoi maggiori, ma la
M^{tà} Sua rispose, che la si contentava di osservar le leggi,
purchè i sudditi anch'essi le osservassero, et che condannando
le leggi ogni altro esercito eccetto il cattolico et disponendo
che l'ordine ecclesiastico havesse le sue preminenze et in spetie
l'arcivescovo primate, che però le cose si riducessero a quello
stato qual presuppone la legge, che Sua M^{tà} nel resto haverebbe
loro dato soddisfattione. A che non seppero rispondere
altro se non che Gustavo, avo del re gli haveva indotti a mutar
religione. Ma lasciando da parte le cose concernenti la

religione, trattaremo di cose politiche subordinate ad essa religione, cioè della utilità che alli vicini regni et a tutta la christianità può apportare il regno di Svetia.

Tre cose sono in quel regno di grandissima consideratione, prima la provincia di Finlandia, 2° il porto di Calmar, 3o quello di Elsburgo.

La Finlandia confina col Mosco, et non è dubbio che se i Polacchi seguendo la norma di Stefano applicassero l'animo a soggiogare il Mosco, che la impresa si renderebbe facile con l'aiuto di detta provincia perchè oltre al sito d'essa la Svetia abbonda di fanteria assai buona, di che la Polonia ha penuria, et se il re Stefano con solo le forze Polacche ridusse il Mosco in grandi angustie, che sarebbe se aggiungessero alle Polacche le forze Svedesi? Et quando anche la Santità di N. S^{re} perseverasse in quel concetto che già hebbe di unire Svedesi, Moschi et Polacchi, non fu mai migliore occasione di quella che è hora, atteso che in mano del re di Polonia stà, senz'anco muover guerra al Mosco, di levarli il commercio et nel mar Baltico et fuor di esso mare, impedendoli la navigatione allo stretto di Dania col mezzo della Finlandia et di Calmaro. Et perchè il Mosco non ha ne rendite ne miniere, et le sue entrate consistono in pelli et altre merci, ne le può smaltire se non per il mar Baltico et per terra verso Polonia, levatoli ta'commercio restarebbe povero et infelice principe.

Quanto al porto di Calmar è la chiave del mar Baltico et capace per ogni armata, et chi è padrone di esso porto, può dire di esser padrone anco del mare et di poter tenere in freno tutte le città aggiacenti ad esso mare come Danzico, Elbinga, Riga et altre per impedire che non entrino le mercantie nello stretto di Dania, et così ridurre quel re ad estrema povertà ; et mentre S. M^{tà} possiede quel porto non è pericolo che perda la Svetia, perchè per esso può mandare di Polonia quanta gente vuole in quel regno. Vi è poi il porto di Elsburgo in Vestergotia, provintia del regno di Svetia, quale è fuori dello stretto di Dania et posto sul mare Oceano capacissimo di qualsivoglia armata, sicuro et che ha comodità di selve, dove è copia di varii legnami per fabricare ogni sorte di vascelli. Dalla parte del mar Oceano ha vicino il regno di Norovegia, quello di Inghilterra et di Scotia et delli Paesi Bassi. Non è lontano dalla Francia et ha facile navigatione alli regni di Spagna et a quello di Portogallo. Dall'altra parte ha lo

stretto di Dania, et passato esso il mar Baltico nel quale
entrano di Polonia, di Russia, di Pomerania, di Livonia et di
Moscovia non solo grani, ma anco tutte le cose pertinenti alla
militare, et sono portate fuori di esso stretto in diverse parti.
Li Svedesi stimano molto esso porto per la qualità del sito et
capacità sua, et tanto più quanto che in Svetia è copia grande
di periti marinari di artigliaria di ferro et d'ogni altra cosa
che si ricerca per la marinaresca, et affermano che se il Cattolico havesse havuto questo porto non sarebbe andato a
traverso l'armata destinata alla impresa d'Inghilterra, et che
è molto opportuno per li Paesi Bassi et per tenere in officio la
regina Inglese, et di più che chi tenesse armata nel detto porto,
potrebbe vietare che niun vascello entrasse ne uscisse dello
stretto di Dania, le quali cose se ciano vere, ognuno può far
giuditio di che importanza sia esso porto et quanto importi
alla Cristianità che si conservi in potere di principe cattolico,
perchè essendo in mano di cattolici può apportare utilità
grandissima, et essendo in potestà di persone aliene dalla
nostra santa religione può apportare altrettanto detrimento,
imperochè potendo impedire il transito dello stretto di Dania,
può ridurre quel re et li Polacchi et altri che sono al lato del
mar Baltico in estrema necessità et privare i regni fuori di
esso stretto di Dania delle cose pertinenti al vitto. Il che se
si usasse per reprimere la petulantia degli heretici, saria bene,
ma se contra cattolici saria male. Hora si può considerare
(si come quando fui in Svetia, alcune persone di qualità mi
posero in consideratione) l'utile che la Maestà Cattolica et
suoi regni et il ser^{mo} re di Svetia et di Polonia cavarebbono
ogni volta che a S. M^{tà} Catt^{ca} fosse permesso di fabricare,
mantenere et alimentare un'armata in quel porto et servirsi
delle persone et di tutto quello che il detto regno di Svetia
può dare pertinente alla marinaresca ; perchè se bene gli
Ordini di Polonia a contemplatione di S. M^{tà} Catt^{ca} destinorno
ambasciatori alla reina et alli Paesi Bassi protestando loro
che se non permettevano che la navigatione fosse libera
haveriano fatta rappresaglia degli navigli loro, nondimeno
essendo l'autorità regia ristretta et essendo parte della popola-
rità appresso la quale è tutta l'autorità infetta dello con-
dannato seme d'heresia, si ritruoveranno delli intoppi per
indurli a far l'essecutione reale. Et però il vero modo sarebbe
di tenere una armata nel detto porto, perchè oltre le sudette

utilità, se la M^{tà} Catt^{ca} havesse esso porto, si potrebbe servire
con minore suò dispendio di soldati Polacchi et Svedesi che di
Tedeschi, poichè etiam si condurebbono con maggior prestezza
et facilità, oltre che alla cavalleria Polacca non si paga più
che sei fiorini al mese, et alla fateria Svedese si dà parimente
stipendio molto tenue. Ne deve credere che la regina
d'Inghilterra quando havesse un'inimico così vicino qual
potrebbe pervenire nel suo regno, nello spatio di tre giornate,
s'inducesse a convertire le forze sue in paesi così lontani come
sono l'Indie essendo certa che allontanandosi la sua armata
haverebbe nelle parti cordiali quella del re di Spagna.

Circa poi alle utilità che ne verrebbono ai re di Polonia et
di Svetia sono le infrascritte. La Maestà del re di Polonia,
con la sponda et amicitia del Cattolico reprimerebbe li heretici
di Svetia, levarebbe loro il modo di condurre gente fuorastiera
nel detto regno, come sogliono fare servendosi dell'oppor-
tunità di quel porto, chiusa del detto regno dalla parte dell'
Oceano, si come il porto di Calmar è chiave di quello del mar
Baltico. Et se bene gli heretici del detto regno di Svetia
quando il porto di Calmar fosse in loro podestà, potrebbono
impedire il disbarco delle genti Polacche, tuttavia però
agevolmente potrebbe questo succedere loro, ogni volta che
l'altro porto di Elsburgo fosse a dispositione della Maestà del
re, atteso che privi di esterno soldato mancherebbono loro
le forze. Oltra di questo col mezzo del sopradetto porto di
Elsburgo potrebbe accrescere la sua autorità hora così ristretta
con Polacchi, perchè sostentandosi essi col mezzo del traffico
del mar Baltico ogni volta che fosse in mano di S. S^{tà} di
impedire esso traffico, non è dubbio che stimarebbono la
Maestà Sua, la quale conseguirebbe questo intento con via
più facile che non fece il re Stefano col procurare di impadro-
nirsi di Danzico, impresa che non gli riuscì.

Hora havendo discorso delle utilità che risultarebbono alle
M^{tà} del re di Spagna et di Polonia et ai dominii loro, è necessario di proporre i mezzi per conseguire il fine. Il primo
mezzo è che il re di Polonia ponga il porto in potestà di
soggetto cattolico, cosa che non sarà molto difficile et giovarà
per facilitare la trattatione ; che S. M^{tà} sia assicurata che
entrando gente fuorastiera in quel porto non sia in loro mano
il levarglielo, et però si è pensato che a spese del Cattolico si
mantenga un presidio nella fortezza che guarda il porto sopra

la quale niuna superiorità habbia il Cattolico ma consegni lo
stipendio per esso presidio al re di Polonia ; et quanto da
assicurare il Cattolico che il porto restarà per uso della sua
armata, forse assai assicuramento sarebbe il potersi ritenere
l'entrate Napolitane ogni volta che venisse mancato al Cattolico. Se bene sicome della fede del re di Polonia non si deve
dubitare così anco si può havere sicurezza delli sudditi suoi,
per l'utile et commodo che risultava loro di smaltire ciò che
produce il regno di Svetia.

Et perchè il re di Polonia dice che dubita che soprastia al
porto una torre del re di Diana, la quale possa impedire non
l'ingresso ad esso porto, ma far danno alle navi quando saranno
entrate, et dall'altra parte i Svedesi affermano che non vi è
impedimento alcuno, si potrebbe visitate il sopradetto porto,
et essendo tale qual viene dipinto dalli Svedesi et quale altre
volte ha riputato il re Cattolico, quando già quindici anni fa
mandò in Svetia un ambasciatore per causa del detto porto,
si potrà all'hora con fondamento dar principio a trattare nella
forma predetta et quando anco fosse vero che il re di Dania
havesse quella torre si potrebbe forse indurlo a qualche intelligenza col Cattolico et col re di Polonia et dominii suoi. Del
che se ne può concepire qualche speranza si per haver egli
ricusato d'entare nella lega stabilita fra la regina d'Inghilterra
et li Paesi Bassi, si anco perchè havendo inteso il poco rispetto
che il duca Carlo porta al re di Polonia, senza essere ricercato,
si è mosso a protestarli, ch'ogni volta ch'esso non sia obediente
al re, egli per vigore delli compatenti tra il regno suo et quello
di Svetia, sarà forzato a risentirsene.

A Polacchi ancora non potrebbe se non piacere che il detto
porto fosse in podestà del re Cattolico, perchè cessando dopo
la morte del presente duca di Prussia la linea di quei marchesi
Brandeburgensi che sono chiamati nella investitura della
ducal Prussia, et pretendendo l'elettore per alcuni privilegi
ottenuti dalli antecessori del presente re a quali il corpo della
nobiltà non ha consentito di dover succedere al duca, et
essendo risoluti gli Ordini di Polonia, di non volerlo permettere
et il duca di voler conservare nella famiglia sua detto ducato
di grandissima importanza et di rendita di 60^m et più talleri,
si come si prevede che la cosa ha da riuscire all'armi, così alla
familia elettorale Brandeburgense la quale ha collocato (per
essere detta Prussia ducale così circondata dai dominii Poloni,

che non ponno venirle soldati di Germania o d'altrove) ogni speranza nel soccorso del mare per la commodità che essa Prussia ducale ha di porti nel mar Baltico, si verrebbe per mezzo d'un'armata a levarle et impedirle il suddetto soccorso marittimo, onde resterebbono essi Brandeburgensi con le sole forze della ducal Prussia, le quali non sarebbono sufficienti a resistere a quelle de Polacchi, congiunte con quelle di Svetia, per il che i Polacchi, se ben poco esperimentati nel mare, per haver fatto professione i loro maggiori che bastasse loro di haver tanta giurisditione nel mar Baltico, quanto potesse un huomo a cavallo entrarvi et camminar dentro, come quei che riputavano esser più gloriosa occupatione di militare per terra contra Turchi, Moscoviti et Tartari, formarebbono nondimeno essercito per terra, et li Svedesi con la commodità della Finlandia, assaltarebbono li Brandeburgensi con armata navale, et così bisognarebbe che quel ducato venisse totalmente sotto l'imperio della corona di Polonia.

Ma quando per li peccati medesimi le cose di Svetia camminassero di male in peggio (il che Dio non voglia per sua misericordia), niun altro rimedio si è giudicato essere più opportuno quanto che S. M^{tà} unischi et incorpori la Estonia, provincia di Livonia et la Finlandia al regno di Polonia con conditione ch'essi Polacchi siano tenuti ad eleggere sempre per re il primogenito di S. M^{tà} et di porgerli aiuto a ricuperare il resto del regno. Di questa maniera S. M^{tà} per un regno mezzo perso ne assicurarebbe due, ne ella ha tanto obligo al fratello da lato di padre o al duca Carlo, ch'essendo sicura che durante la sua posterità conservarebbe per essa posterità li dominii di detti suoi regni, che dovesse premerle molto, la consideratione che se mancasse la linea di S. M^{tà} ne restarebbono privi il fratello e lo zio, essendo massime heretici et inimici della M^{tà} Sua. Et sopra questo particolare scrisse già S. M^{tà} alla Santità ni N. S^{re} proponendoli questo pensiero, caso che le cose andassero affatto a traverso. Et acciò questo potesse in tal caso succedere sarà necessario che monsig^r Nuntio faccia ufficio con Sua M^{tà} che ponghi soggetti cattolici per governatori della Estonia et della Finlandia, o almeno tali che della fede loro non possa dubitare.

[Copia. Cod. N. 33, p. 144 s. of the Vallicelliana Library, Rome, Urb. 858, p. 547 ss., Vatican Library, Malaspina is here expressly mentioned as the author A 3rd copy in Cod. H 155, p. 1 s. of the Ambrosian Library, Milan.]

14. POPE CLEMENT VIII. TO THE CLERGY AND PEOPLE
OF ROME.[1]

Beginning of 1599.

Clemens PP. VIII.

Clero et populo almae Urbis Nostrae.

Dilecti filii salutem et apostolicam benedictionem. Manus
Domini, manus Patris, manus illa potens et salutaris, quae
sola, dum iuste vulnerat, pie medetur, ipsa tetigit nos, filii
dilectissimi. Fluvius Tiberis, extra alveum ripasque suas
diffusus, tanta aquarum copia Urbem, suburbia, prata et agros
inundavit, neque in planis solum, sed in editioribus etiam
locis in tantam crevit altitudinem, quantum neque nos neque
parentes nostri meminerunt. Quae Urbis facies, quis aspectus
per hos dies fuerit, plane luctuosus et miserabilis, quae hominum, pecorum, aedificiorum et earum rerum, quae ad vitam
victumque quotidianum necessariae sunt, pernicies et iactura
extiterit, nec sine acerbissimo doloris sensu commemorari
potest, nec certe commemorare est necesse ; vos ipsi oculis
vestris cuncta perspexistis et passi estis, et Nos etiam vidimus
et omnium miserias paterno et miseratione complexi oculis et
manibus in coelum elevatis, cum prae doloris magnitudine
cor Nostrum disrumperetur et quasi cera colliquefactum esset.
Sed huius tantae eluvionis et calamitatis causae non ex
principiis naturalibus curiose nimis inquirendae sunt et ex
eorum opinionibus, qui, dicentes se esse sapientes, stulti facti
sunt, tamqum si gentes essemus quas ignorant Deum, sed
potius, ut christianos decet, in timore et tremore veriorem
magisque intimam harum aerumnarum originem intra nosmet
ipsos pervestigemus, ac nisi nos ipsos fallere et decipere velimus,
peccata nostra respondebunt nobis et iniquitates nostrae,
quae multiplicatae sunt nimis coram Deo. Abyssus enim
peccatorum abyssum aquarum evocavit et inundatio inundationem peperit ; nam maledictum et mendacium et furtum et
adulterium inundaverunt et sanguis sanguinem tetigit. Ne
tamen, filii, pusillo animo sitis, neve, quod absit, cor vestrum
obduretis, ut indomiti et obstinati peccatores solent, qui plagis
Dei deteriores fiunt, quorum miseram et miserandam con-
ditionem exprimit Ieremias verbis illis : ' Domine, percussisti
eos, et non doluerunt ; attrivisti eos, et noluerunt accipere
disciplinam ; induraverunt facies suas supra petram, et

[1] See *supra*, p. 411.

noluerunt reverti.' Vos autem, filii, non sic, sed revertimini
ad Dominum in toto corde vestro, in ieiunnio et fletu et
planctu, et poenitentiae salutaris tabulam apprehendite, nec
pereatis in diluvio aquarum multarum irae Des et iusti iudicii
eius. Deus enim noster pius est et misericors et praestabilis
super malitia, qui non vult mortem peccatoris, sed magis ut
convertatur et vivat. Plaga haec, si sapitis, si intelligitis, si
novissima providetis, non est ad mortem, sed ad salutem.
Corripuit nos Dominus, sed non in furore suo, immo vero in
visceribus misericordiae suae, ut pater, qui hic in hac brevi et
caduca vita filiis flagella adhibet, ut in aeternum parcat.
Quem enim diligit Dominus castigat, et flagellat omnem filium
quem recipit. Ecce Deus noster, qui dives est in misericordia,
tanquam filiis offert se vobis : surgite et vos cum filio prodigo
et ite ad Patrem, qui vos vocat, qui apertis brachiis vos
expectat et ad complexum et pacem et reconciliationem invitat.
Clamate ad Dominum in fortitudine et ex intimo corde verba
illa pronuntiate : ' Omnia quae fecisti nobis, Domine, in vero
iudicio fecisti, quia peccavimus tibi et mandatis tuis non
obedivimus ; sed da gloriam nomini tuo et propitius esto
peccatis nostris propter nomen tuum.' Denique, filii in Christo
dilecti, convertatur unusquisque a vita sua mala et qui
Ninivitas peccantes imitati estis, imitamini poenitentes ; ite
ad matrem gratiarum, ad advocatam peccatorum, ad beatissi-
mam semper Virginem Dei genitricem Mariam et illius opem
atque auxilium implorate, ite ad gloriosissimos apostolorum
principes, Petrum et Paulum, qui peculiares patroni huius
almae Urbis sunt, cui evangelii doctrinam cum sanguine
tradiderunt ; hi enim sunt gloriosi principes terrae et patres
et pastores tui, o Roma, qui te ad hanc gloriam provexerunt,
ut gens sancta, populus electus, civitas sacerdotalis et regia
per sacram beati Petri sedem, caput orbis effecta, latius
praesideres religione divina quam dominatione terrena . . .[1]
obite, filii, in spiritu humilitatis et animo contrito sacras
apostolorum basilicas et fortissimorum martyrum, quibus
veluti propugnaculis cincta est ; plorate coram Domino et
preces cum lacrimis fundite, ut per merita et intercessionem
sanctorum, qui cum Christo regnant, veniam atque indul-
gentiam impetremus. Pacem igitur cum fratribus habete ;
cessent odia et inimicitiae, ne si manus plenas sanguine

---

[1] Here is an omission in the MS.

extendatis, avertat Deus oculos suos a vobis ; libido, intemperantia, luxuries tollatur et caetera vitia, quibus Dei iracundia provocatur ; vigeat modestia, temperantia et misericordia in pauperes : nunc enim latissimus pietati propositus est campus, ut ii potissimum, qui ditiores sunt, peccata sua eleemosinis redimant et pauperum inopiam sua abundantia sublevent, quod ut faciant et omni cum alacritate faciant, illos quanta possumus cum efficacia hortamur. Nam propter omnium peccata haec plaga a Deo immissa est et ad omnes seu pauperes seu divites pertinere debet, sive per miseriam sive per commiserationem, ut, dum corporis nostri, quod unum est in Christo, membra quaedam patiuntur, caetera compatiantur. Sumite igitur, filii, arma militiae nostrae, non carnalia, sed potentia Dei, quibus ipse Deus exercituum fortissimus et omnipotens vincitur, poenitentiam, orationem, ieiunium et eleemosinam ; his enim placatur Deus, qui, si viderit opera vestra bona et quia conversi estis ab omni via mala in sinceritate cordis vestri, revertetur et ipse a furore irae suae, et non peribitis. Atque ut tanto ardentius ad divinorum sacramentorum medicinam accurratis, ut veterem hominem exuentes, ac mente et spiritu renovati ambuletis in novitate vitae, nos spirituales Ecclesiae thesauros, quorum dispensatores a Deo constituti sumus, ex apostolica benignitate aperientes, universis et singulis Christi fidelibus utriusque sexus in eadem alma Urbe Nostra locisque adiacentibus commorantibus etc.

[Brevia, Arm. 44, t. 43, n. 40, Papal Secret Archives.]

15. Giulio Cesare Foresto to the Duke of Mantua.[1]

1559, February 27, Rome.

. . . All'ufficio del sodetto s. ambas^re [of Savoy] N. S. rispose le seguenti parole, che li pareva cosa di meraviglia che li principi secolari li quali nel crearsi un loro consigliere vogliono così a pieno sodisfare a loro stessi, e che nella creatione de card^li li quali sono consiglieri de Pontefici, cerchino d'astringere gli stessi Pontefici a valersi in simile dignità di persone sopra le quali essi non disegnano. . . .

[Orig. Gonzaga Archives, Mantua.]

[1] See *supra*, p. 194.

16. LIST OF PRISONERS, TRIALS AND SENTENCES OF THE
ROMAN INQUISITION.[1]

1599, April 5.[2]

[Lista de carcerati nel S^{to} Officio a dì 5 Aprile 1599.]
Fra Giordano Bruni da Nola, a dì 27 di Febraro 1593: si
ha da proporre la sua causa.

Ercole Rota Bolognese, a dì 29 Luglio 1597 : fu risoluta la
causa coram S^{mo} a dì 19 Febraro 1598 : debet torqueri et
retineri in carceribus ; spora gli novi inditii sono stati repetiti
i testimonii, dimanda la copia.

Alessandro Musculeo, a 25 Giugno 1598 : ha havuto li
testimonii per repetiti ; si ha da deliberare, se deve farsi
riconoscere dalli testimonii.

Prete Pietro Orlandini, a dì 6 Luglio 1598 : la causa fu
riferita a dì 4 Novembre ; si hanno a vedere li testimonii
esaminati a sua difesa.

Francesco Maria Calvi alias Cavvilanuus di Alessandria, a dì
26 Ottobre 1598 : si ha da riferire la causa.

Prete Giovanni Solitto della Saponara, a dì 26 Ottobre
1598 : sono stati repetiti li testimonii e ha fatto le difese ; si
hanno a vedere.

Fra Bartolomeo Vite da Cantiana, a dì 18 Novembre 1598 :
si ha a riferire la causa.

Orinthio Acquarelli da Riete, a dì 20 Novembre 1598 : si
ha a riferire la causa.

Horatio Melillo da Vitulano, a dì 14 Decembre 1598 : si è
scritto per la repetitione de testimonii.

Fra Giovanni Bosso, a dì 25 Gennaro 1599 : fu risoluto a
16 Marzo quod torqueatur et abiuret de vehementi.

Claudio Giannardi Francese, a dì 28 Gennaro 1599 : confessa
di essere heretico ; si ha da riferire la causa.

Prete Giovanni Tabulario Greco, a dì 9 Febraro 1599 : è
visto il processo et si da riferire.

Prete Claudio Gailard di Lorena mandato dall' Inquisitore
di Malta, a dì 11 Febraro 1599 : si ha per matto.

Francesco Antonio Cerato da Napoli, a 15 Febraro 1599 : è

---

[1] See *supra*, pp. 200, 211. See also SPAMPANATO, Vita di G. Bruno 774 *seq.*
[2] On January 30, 1592, 32 accused were in the prison of the Inquisition.

stata riferita la causa et ha prodotte alcune scritture in sua difesa.[1]

Guglielmo Cochelles Inglese a dì 10 Marzo 1599.

Egidio Cambi Romano, a 17 Marzo 1599 : è stato esaminato et si ha da riferire la causa.

Prete Galeazzo Porta a dì 26 Marzo 1599
Francesco Bruno della Cava a 26 Marzo 1599
Fra Clemente Mancini da Napoli a 26 Marzo 1599   } complici della falsità delle lett. Apost. dispensationis.
Frate Antonio Carrara da Napoli a 26 Marzo 1599

Pompeo Florio di Radiano in Abruzzo a dì 2 Aprile 1599.

Lista de processati habilitati per Roma.

Giovanni Roa d'Avila habilitato per Roma lì 28 Nov. 1597.

Fra Tomaso da Picerno ; è visto il processo et si ha da riferire la sua causa.

Fra Domenico Andreasso da Ragusa ; sono venute le repetitioni et le difese ; si hanno a riferire.

Frate Arcangelo da Perugia habilitato nel monast. di S. Agostino li 31 Luglio 1598.

Giovanni Santi Palombo da Terani habilitato a 16 Nov. 1598.

Giov. Angelo Santini pittore habilitato li 23 Sett. 1598.

Ginevra Pina habilitato per la parrochia li 23 Sett. 1598.

Fulginio Berti di Casacastalda habilitato li 10 Marzo 1599.

Lorenzo Ursolino da Tossignano habilitato li 24 Marzo 1599.

Fra Ignatio da Lorena
Fra Francesco Hiberno   } cappuccini habilitati al p⁰ Aprile 1599.

Nota de condennati alle carceri nel S^to Offitio.

Don Giacomo Fabrone carcerato a 7 Giugno 1582.

---

[1] In the *Diario delle giustizie fatte in Roma di persone eretiche e religiose dall' a⁰ 1567 fino al 1657 (Papal Secret Archives, Arm. 3, t. 8, p. 365 seq.) the following are recorded :

1591. A dì 6 Febraro 1591, in Torre di Nona fra Andrea figlio del qᵐ Giovanni Angelo Forzati da Castellaccio diocesi di Capua, Flaminio del qᵐ Girolamo Fabrio da Mediolano, Francesco Serafino figlio del qᵐ Nicolò Venetiano, sacerdote professo et apostata di San Benedetto furono tutti appiccati et abbrugiati in Campo di Fiore.

1599. A dì 9 Novembre 1599 fra Clemente Mancini e D. Galeazzo Porta ambedue Milanesi furono in Ponte decapitati sopra un palco.

1600. A dì 9 Giugno 1600 D. Francesco Moreno da Minerbino diocesi di Bari fu appiccato e brugiato in Ponte.

1601. A dì 10 Aprile 1601 furono appiccati in Ponte D. Livio Palasto Modanese e D. Marcello de Conti da Melfi, il quale doppo morte fu anche abbrugiato.

Fra Francesco Fortunato a dì 4 Nov. 1584.

Francisco Quirico a dì 18 Luglio 1593 [sic].

David Vendelio a dì 28 Agosto 1592.

Don Clemente Serafino a 23 Giugno 1593.

[Copy : Cod. II., 49 50 (Raccolta di note, studii e diligenze di
P. Paolo V. mentre era cardinale in diverse materie), p. 32,
Borghese Library, Rome.]

17. POPE CLEMENT VIII. TO PHILIP III., KING OF SPAIN.[1]

1600, September 4, Rome.

Carissime in Christo fili Noster salutem et apostolicam
benedictionem. Nihil ardentius cupimus pro Nostro Apostolicae servitutis officio, quam divina adiutrice gratia animas
multas Christo lucrari, neque eos solum, qui Christiani et
Catholici sunt et ecclesiam unam, cui Nos immeritos Deus
praeesse voluit, matrem agnoscunt, libenter hortamur et
excitamus, ut quod fide profitentur, operibus comprobent,
sed eos etiam qui extra Ecclesiam sunt, ad eam adducere, et
gentibus quoque remotissimis, quae suave Christi iugum
ignorant, evangelii veritatem annuntiare ac promulgare,
avidissime expetimus. Regum autem catholicorum ea in
primis insignis est laus, summorum Pontificum studia, labores,
sollicitudines ad fidei propagationem omni ope et opera
adiuvare ac propterea Maiestatem Tuam potissimum, tanta
potentia, tantis viribus, tanta regnorum et ditionis ampli-
tudine extulit Deus, ut lux evangelii ab hac sancta Romana
ecclesia, omnium ecclesiarum matre et magistra, Te strenue
adiuvante, in nationes etiam a Nobis disiunctissimas quam
latissime diffundatur, neque enim dubitamus, Maiestatem
Tuam pro sua prudentia intelligere et pro sua praestanti
pietate velle, iure ac merito a Te Deum postulare, ut quae
Tibi ipse tribuit, ut ad eius gloriam et honorem praecipue
conferas et convertas. Sed quae nunc a Te petimus, nec
magna nec difficilia sunt, sed quae tamen benedicente Domino,
ad res plane maximas aditum aperire et viam munire facile
poterunt. Audivimus saepe, quod et Maiestatem Tuam
audisse arbitramur, regem Persarum multis ac non obscuris
indiciis prae se ferre, se animo sane propenso esse erga
Christianam religionem, sed nuper id multo certius cognovimus
ex Lusitano sacerdote Francisco Costa, qui ex India per

[1] See *supra*, pp. 247, 267.

praesidem [sic] Roman venit, quem vir nobilis dux Suessae, orator Tuus, ad Nos introduxit. Is mira quaedam, et quae vias Domini cogitanti lacrimas prae gaudio elicere possint, de rege illo narrat, habere eum apud se aulicos et viros primarios complures Christianos, quos ipsemet palam per occasionem Christianos esse cum multa voluptate indicat, sacerdotes et presbyteros a Nobis et a Romana ecclesia valde expetere, eius rei causa certam ad Nos legationem misisse, seque etiam amoris et amicitae Nostrae percupidum ostendere, ecclesiam praeterea aedificari iussisse, ut ibi christiano ritu Deo serviatur. Quae et alia complura cum attentius consideraremus, adhibitis etiam in consilium dilectis filiis cardinalibus congregationi fidei propagandae a Nobis praefectis, non minus piis quam prudentibus, memores a Christo Domino dictum esse beato Petro, et Nobis in eo : Duc in altum et laxate retia vestra in capturam, et denique scientes nullum verbum esse impossibile apud Deum, statuimus tantam occasionem, divinitus oblatam nullo modo esse praetermittendam, sed litteras ad regem Persarum dare, ita accurate scriptas, quemadmodum tanti negotii gravitas requirit, ac licet eiusdem regis legati nundum ad Nos pervenerint, ac propter viae longinquitatem et varia pericula valde incertum sit, an et quando sint venturi, placet at eum nihilominus celeriter presbyteros mittere, ne qua in Nobis mora sit, quominus semen divinae gratiae in magni illius regis corde, per evangelii praedicationem, ipso Deo dante incrementum coalescat, et populis illis, qui in tenebris et umbra mortis sunt, vita et veritas, si Deo omnipotenti placuerit, illucescat et denique cum tam potenti et Turcarum tyranno tam infenso principe ea amicitia et benevolentia concilietur, quae Christianae reipublicae universae et Tuae Maiestati atque inclytae domui vestrae Austriacae, ut Tu optime intelligis, multiplices utilitates est allatura. Cum igitur de presbyteris idoneis mittendis cogitaremus, statim oculos coniecimus in societatem Jesu, quae veluti perpetuum seminarium est fortium et fidelium operariorum vineae Domini, quique huic muneri ex Nostra et Apostolicae Sedis obedientia praecipue addicti, in ipso potissimum Oriente atque India magnam evangelicae praedicationis laudem sunt consecuti, itaque mandavimus dilecto filio Claudio, eiusdem societatis praeposito generali, ut ex ipsa India Orientali atque ex ea provintia, quae

Persarum regno propinquior est, aliquot presbyteros et
operarios mittat ad regem, qui, Spiritu Sancto auctore, regis
ipsius et populorum illorum corda, veluti agros ratione prae-
ditos, evangelico aratro proscindant et sementem verbi Dei
faciant ; potens est autem Dominus, eorum animos sic
praeparare et emollire, ut non solum semen accipiant, sed
fructum multum etiam ferant, quod divinae bonitatis et
potentiae proprium est, et Nos certe laboris et diligentiae
Nostrae numquam poenitebit ; optimum autem visum est
ex finitimis provintiis operarios accipere, qui praeter doctrinam
et zelum salutis animarum, multis aliis ad hanc missionem
necessariis adiumentis sunt instructi, nam et regionis, et
notitiam habent nationum et linguarum usum et diuturnam
etiam ad eiusmodi functiones obeundas exercitationem, tum
ex locorum propinquitate brevi quod summopere optamus
in Persidem et in ipsius Regis conspectum pervenient ;
summam enim quoad fieri poterit, celeritatem adhiberi
cupimus, ne antiquus humani generis hostis satanas, cuius
astutias non ignoramus, difficultates aliquas interponat et
opus Dei impediat. Quo magis Maiestatem Tuam hortamur
et efficacissime in Domino requirimus, ut ad viceregem Indiae
atque ad capitaneum Ormuzii regias suas det litteras quam
diligentissime scriptas, eisque serio mandet, ut huius missionis
promovendae omnem curam et cogitationem suscipiant, et
quae in navigiis parandis et ad iter et navigationem expedien-
dam opportuna aut necessaria erunt, omni alacritate et
celeritate curent, ut operarii illi, quos dilectus filius provin-
cialis Societatis in India ex sui generalis praescripto delegerit,
ut in Persidem proficiscantur, ipsius viceregis et capitanei
auxilio subleventur, ut nave quam primum conscensa Ormuz-
ium petant et deinde recta in Persidem atque adeo ad ipsius
regis aulam tuto, commode et expedite, quantum licuerit,
pergant, cum multum ommino in celeritate sit positum.
Postremo sic eos accendat Maiestas Tua, ut in re gravissima
quae ad Dei gloriam tantopere pertinet, se Catholici regis
catholicos ministros vere esse ostendant. Mandavimus autem
venerabili fratri archiepiscopo Sipontino Nostro Apostolico
Nuntio, ut de pluribus litteris eodem exemplo conscribendis
et ad Nos omni cum festinatione transmittendis et demum
de toto hoc negotio cum Maiestate Tua sic agat ut de re, quae
Nobis cordi est maxime, ut sane esse debet et Tibi quoque,

fili carissime, fore confidimus : nescit enim tarda molimina gratia Spiritus Sancti, quam Tibi copiosam a Deo precamur, et Maiestati Tuae Apostolcam Nostram benedictionem amantissime impartimur.

Dat. Romae apud sanctum Petrum sub annulo piscatoris die 4. septembris anno Iubilei 1600, pontificatus Nostri anno nono.

[Brevia Arm. 44, t. 44, n. 243.]

18. Giulio Cesare Foresto to the Duke of Mantua.[1]

1600, December 30, Rome.

. . . Hoggi mentre trattavo con l'ill^mo s. Giorgio, l'ill^mo s. Marcello che s'è trovato in compagnia et senza ch'io glie n'habbia data occasione, mi ha detto che innanzi che conceder la licenza dell'estratione delle dette statue, S. S^tà, la quale s'è ritenuta la lista, gl'ha ordinato che s'informi come si sono havute da diverse persone con longhezza di tempo o pure tutte da uno, et il s^r card^le S. Giorgio non aspettando ch'io rispondessi, non senza dimostrar un poco di passione, rispose che si erano havute tutte in un luogo et che è stato un colpo non più fatto in Roma da molti anni in quà, et io ho poi soggionto che le statue sono appresso di me, delle quali cose il s^r card^le S. Marcello disse che bisognava ne desse conto a S. S^tà, et se bene non metto difficoltà nella licenza, non vorrei però che venisse voglia a S. S^tà di veder parte di queste teste, perchè mi troveri in un labirinto così fatto se havessi da mandarlene a Palazzo, et particolarmente l'Antinoo, del quale il s^r card^le s. Giorgio ne parla come della più pretiosa statua che sia in Roma rispetto alla qualità della cosa, et però volontieri l'havrei veduto portar per terra sotta la condotta di persona fidata . . .

[Orig. Gonzaga Archives, Manuta.]

19. Giulio Cesare Foresto to the Duke of Mantua.[2]

1601, February 10, Rome.

. . . S. S^tà ha detto che non è conveniente che si lasci spogliar Roma di quelle cose che la fanno illustre per illustrare altre città, havendo di più saputo che queste sono delle più nobili antiquità di Roma, et tanto che non è stata senza

---

[1] See *supra*, p. 506.
[2] See *supra*, p. 506.

pensiero la S. S^tà di voler venire a vederle, se non che intese
che stanno incassate . . .

[Orig. Gonzaga Archives, Mantua.]

20. POPE CLEMENT VIII. TO THE SHAH OF PERSIA.[1]

1601, February 24, Rome.

Rex potentissime et illustris salutem, et oblatum a Deo
divinae gratiae lumen toto corde accipere. Magna est vis
virtutis, magna efficacitas, cuius pulchritudo mirabilem in
nobis amorem excitat, erga illos etiam quos nunquam vidimus ;
id re ipsa in Te amando experimur, nam etsi longissimo terrarum marisque intervallo a Te disiuncti simus, nec Te aliquando
viderimus, tamen quia a plerisque multa et praeclara accepimus de Tua praestanti virtute, de Tui regalis animi magnitudine, de insigni fortitudine aliisque naturae ornamentis,
quibus Te altissimus et bonorum omnium largitor Deus
cumulavit, haec de Te a nobis saepius audita, ut Te amemus
effecerunt, quin etiam ut a Te vicissim amari cupiamus,
quamquam et illud Nobis relatum est, magna Nostra cum
voluptate, iam Te erga Nos egregie affectum gratiam et
amicitiam Nostram expetere, legationem etiam misisse ad
Nos, multa cum amoris et reverentiae erga Nos significatione, quae tamen legatio si missa est, nondum ad Nos
pervenit, sed illud praeterea de Te audivimus, quod
Christianum nomen honorifice appelles et propensam prae
Te feras voluntatem erga Christianam religionem, quae
sola veram salutis et felicitatis viam docet et praestat,
narrant enim et personas Tibi coniunctissimas Christianas
esse, et in aula Tua regia complures esse fortes viros tibique
carissimos, qui se Christo addictos esse profiteantur, idque
ipsum Te iubente palam ostendant, signo salutaris et vivificae
crucis quae est gloria nostra, in qua ipse salvator mundi et
vitae auctor Iesus Christus, Dominus noster, aeterni patris
aeternus filius, carne nostra mortali indutus, salutem nostram
in medio terrae mirabiliter operatus est ; quae si vera sunt,
ut vera esse speramus et toto ex animo optamus, haec certe
tanto gaudio cor Nostrum complent, ut eiusdem gaudii
magnitudinem nullis verbis satis exprimere possimus ; Nos
autem scimus nullum verbum esse impossibile apud Deum
omnipotentem, qui solus est rex regum, per quem reges

[1] See *supra*, p. 247.

regnant et in cuius manu corda regum sunt, et quocumque
voluerit convertit illa, qui antiquissimis temporibus et in
saeculis a nostra memoria valde remotis, Cyri fortissimi regis
Persarum manum dexteram apprehendit et subiecit ante
faciem eius gentes et dorsa regum vertit, et gloriosos ac
potentes terrae humiliavit, et ipse rex Cyrus, multis victoriis
Dei auxilio clarissimus, populum Dei qui erat captivus in
Babilone, liberum dimisit, et divino instinctu permotus,
decrevit templum Domini a Chaldaeorum rege destructum
iterum aedificare in Hierusalem et vasa templi aurea atque
argentea, quae asportata fuerant, restitui iussit, quemadmodum sacrarum litterarum monumentis memoriae commen-
datum est. Nunc autem, o rex Persarum potentissime et
magni illius Cyri successor, audimus de Te, quod ecclesias
rito christiano, in regno Tuo aedificari cupias, aut fortasse
etiam aedificare iam ceperis, ut in eis Deus optimus assidue
laudetur et sacrosancta sacrificia offerantur et sanctum
Christi evangelium praedicetur in salutem omni credenti, et
ob eam causam narrant Te Christianos praesbyteros et
sacerdotes expetere, qui a Romana ecclesia mittantur. Magna
haec sunt, o rex, et maiorum rerum exordia, et plane maxi-
marum, ut in Dei summa clementia confidimus, cuius spiritu
cor Tuum ad tam praeclaras cogitationes moveri non dubitamus, nam si Nostram, hoc est Romani Pontificis et Christian-
orum regum patris, amicitiam vere appetis, si Christi fidem
in Tuis provintiis promulgari, ecclesias aedificari, evangelii
doctores et magistros apud Te habere, denique Christi nomen
et Christianam religionem in Tuo regno amplissimo vere
propagari desideras, esto bono animo, nam et Deus ipse Tibi
adiumento erit, et Nos quoque ipsius Dei adiutrice gratia his
desideriis Tuis libenter in primis suffragabimur. Recte autem
praesbyteros ad Te mitti cupis ab hac sancta Romana ecclesia,
quae omnium ecclesiarum, quae toto orbe terrarum sunt,
mater est et magistra, nam sicut unus est Deus, et una fides et
unum baptisma, ita una est ecclesia Catholica et Apostolica,
cuius caput est ecclesia Romana, magistra veritatis, firma-
mentum unitatis, domicilium Christianae religionis, in qua
beatissimus apostolorum princeps Petrus, quem Christus
dominus ovium suarum pastorem summum constituit, suam
Apostolicam Sedem divino consilio collocavit, in qua Sancta
Sede post tot aetatum curricula, post longam et nunquam

interruptam pontificum successionem, Nos hoc tempore,
humiles licet et indigni, Spiritu Sancto ita disponente prae-
sidemus. Ad Te vero presbyteros et sacerdotes Christi
libenter admodum mittemus, qui evangelicam veritatem Tibi
et populis Tuis annuntient, quam si corde humili audieris et
complexus fueris, et tandem Deo Te mirabiliter vocanti
perfecte obedire et Iesu Christo nostrae salutis auctori et
sempiternae vitae largitori nomen dare decreveris, tum
demum et ipse vere felix eris et regnis Tuis veram felicitatem
paries, et ad regum Persarum veterem famam tantum Tuae
gloriae cumulum adiicies, ut de Tuis meritis et laudibus nulla
posteritas conticescat ; sunt autem in Oriente presbyteri et
operarii Christi fideles ac strenui, filii Nostri in Christo dilecti
ex ea societate, quae a dulcissimo Iesu nomine nuncupatur,
quae sub Nostra et huius Sanctae Apostolicae Sedis peculiari
tutela Deo militat et in remotissimis etiam Orientis Indor-
umque regionibus victricem Christi crucem fixit et semen
evangelii in salutem credentium disseminavit, et Deo auxili-
ante disseminare studet, nullis parcen laboribus, ut verbo
salutaris doctrinae et vitae integerrimae exemplo, et denique
divino baptisimi lavacro et caelestibus sacramentis animas
Christo lucrifaciat, quemadmodum Tibi non inauditum neque
omnino ignotum esse arbitramur. Ex ea igitur societate et
ex iis orientalibus regionibus et locis, quae ad ditionem
pertinent potentissimi principis et filii Nostri in Christo
carissimi Philippi regis Catholici, quaeque loca a provintiis
tuis minus longe absunt, et ad commeandum opportuniorem
viam praebent, praesbyteros ad Te mitti curabimus, et eo
numero qui erit necessarius, et iam nunc ea de re mandata
dedimus, omnia denique quae Tua populorumque Tuorum
salus postulaverit, summo studio benedicente Domino
praestabimus, nihilque aliud expectamus, nisi ut de Tua tota
voluntate Nobis planius constet, et quae fama et multorum
relatu, ut diximus, accepimus, eadem ex Te ipso, hoc est ex
litteris Tuis Tuisque etiam Nuntiis multo certius multoque
cumulatius cognoscamus. Interea ut amoris erga Te Nostri
et desiderii sincerae amicitiae inter nos conciliandae illustrior
exstet significatio, has Nostras litteras ad Te dare placuit,
testes voluntatis in Te Nostrae et veluti pignus benevolentiae
eas autem tibi reddent hi duo dilecti filii Nostri, quos ad Te
nominatim mittimus, nimirum Franciscus Costa, religiosus

praesbyter ex eadem societate Iesu, doctrina et zelo Dei praestans, et vir industrius ac diligens Didacus de Miranda, ambo Lusitani, ambo rerum usu praediti Nobisque probati et valde grati, qui alias etiam in Perside fuerunt, Tuoque regio nomini sunt addictissimi, quin etiam Didacus Venetiis collocutus est cum Assandebechio familiari Tuo, eaque ab eo accepta de Te Nobis retulit, quae Nobis incunda valde fuerunt, ex iis igitur mentem Nostram, ubi ad Te, angelo Domini duce, incolumes pervenerint, multo apertius multoque copiosius intelliges, atque illud in primis, quam appetentes simus salutis Tuae, quam cupidi Tuae amplitudinis et gloriae. Quare a Te petimus, ut illis fidem plenissimam habeas perinde ac si Nos ipsi Tecum praesentes loqueremur ; confidimus autem, quod hos nuntios Nostros et Nobis dilectos, omi cum honore et humanitate excipies, nam et Nos erga Tuos quos ad Nos miseris, parem humanitatem adhibebimus, ut Noster inter Nos amor firmiores radices agat et in dies magis coalescat ; vere enim ex Nostra animorum et voluntatum coniunctione magnae et multiplices utilitates redundare poterunt, quas Te pro Tua prudentia satis perspicere non dubitamus, sed ea in primis, quae est de Tuo et Nostro et totius nominis Christiani perpetuo atque infensissimo hoste Turca coercendo, qui intolerabili superbia et insatiabili cupiditate dominandi omnia regna, omnes provintias sua tyrannide opprimere et durissimae servitutis iugo subiicere avidissime desiderat ; sed speramus in Dei clementia, quod humiliabit superbum et brachium eius et dentes eius conteret in ore eius et molas leonis confringet, cuius rei non obscura indicia annis proximis dedit Deus in Ungaria, et leonem illum immanissimum superari posse ostendit ; Nos vero pro Nostro pastorali officio praeter ea adiumenta, quae carissimo filio Nostro Rudolpho Imperatori electo adversus teterrimum hostem praebuimus et praebebimus, in ea cura maxime versamur, ut reges et principes Catholicos, filios Nostros in Christo carissimos, omni officii genere permoveamus, quo communem inimicum communibus studiis oppugnent, et magna spe sumus fore, ut id a divina miseracordia impetremus, quod si Tu quoque, iusta indignatione permotus, tam multas et tam graves Tibi a Turcis illatas iniurias aliquando ulcisci statueris, et avitae Persarum gloriae memor Tuaeque propriae virtutis, summa vi summoque animi ardore bellum non minus

Tibi gloriosum quam necessarium susceperis, profecto fera illa
et immanis bellua undique vulneribus confecta prosternetur,
quod tanto magis sperare Nobisque polliceri licet, quod
divinae motionis vim in Tuo corde videmur videre, dum erga
Christi nomen et Christianam religionem Te adeo propensum
esse audimus ; sic Deus et pater misericordiarum opus suum,
quod iam in Te incepit, ipse perficiat, ut unum Nobiscum et
cum principibus Christianis corpus efficiaris, ut Tecum
arctissime colligati, omnia Tua sua ducant tantoque vehemen-
tius contra communem inimicum pro communi salute et
gloria exardescant.   Deum autem exercituum, in cuius manu
sunt victoriae et triumphi, toto ex animo precamur, ut quemadmodum olim ante Cyrum, sic eat ante Te et portas aeneas
conterat et vectes ferreos confringat, Teque omnibus difficul-
tatibus superatis, victorem et triumphatorem efficiat.   Esto
igitur forti et excelso animo, atque ut Te decet magna meditare
et magna aggredere, ut maiorum Tuorum gloriam virtute et
magnitudine animi non solum sustineas, sed etiam adaugeas
et amplifices.   Dat Romae etc.

[Brevia Arm. 44, t. 45, n. 61, Papal Secret Archives.]

21. POPE CLEMENT VIII. TO THE SHAH OF PERSIA.[1]

1601, May 2, Rome.

Rex potentissime et illustris, salutem et oblatum a Deo
divinae gratiae lumen toto corde accipe.   Pervenerunt his
proximis diebus ad hanc almam Urbem nostram, arcem
Christianae religionis et portum nationum, quos ad Nos, ut
ipsi referunt, misisti, vir nobilis Antonius Scierleius et vir
honoratus Assandebechius, quorum adventus periucundus
Nobis fuit, cum a tanto rege et tantae potentiae principe, et
tam multis, ut audimus, animi et corporis ornamentis praedito,
ex tam longinquis et remotis regionibus ad Nos venerint,
Tuasque, quemadmodum ipsi affirmant, litteras Nobis
gratissimas attulerint, quas accepimus singulari cum voluptate ; ipsos, qui eas nobis Tuo nomine reddiderunt, oculis
vultuque hilari aspeximus omnique cum benignitate excepimus,
atque a Nostris quam humanissime tractari iussimus, quod
ipsi multo uberius Tuae Celsitudini referre poterunt et denique
ea benevole in primis attenteque audivimus, quae Tuo nomine
Nobis retulerunt.   Paria enim Tibi in amore reddimus, et

---

[1] See *supra*, p. 248.

quemadmodum Tu et litteris et viva Tuorum voce profiteris, Te gratiae et amicitiae Nostrae esse appetentem, ita Nos vicissim pari benevolentiae affectu Tibi respondemus, ex hac enim nostra amicitia et coniunctione, tamquam ex quodam fonte, magna bona redundare posse intell gimus, ad totius Christianae reipublicae, tum ad Tuam Tuaeque illustris coronae utilitatem et gloriam, quod Tu quoque pro Tua prudentia non ignoras, sed optime intelligis. Accedit, quod divinae potentiae et sapientiae proprium est, non secus atque ex parvo semine ingentes arbores procreantur, ita ex initiis exiguis res maximas efficere, non enim viae Dei sunt sicut viae hominum, sed omnia quaecumque vult facit in coelo et in terra. Ac sane sperandum es in summa Dei bonitate, si forti et excelso animo esse velimus, tempus advenisse, quo immanis-simus Turcarum tyrannus, cuius insatiabilis dominandi libido nullis terminis continetur, non solum coerceatur, sed plane superetur, cuius rei manifesta extant argumenta, cum per hos annos magnas clades terra marique a Christianis principibus acceperit. Unde tanto magis animi Tui magnitudo excitari atque inflammari debet adversus teterrimum et superbissimum hostem, qui Te ipsum et maiores etiam Tuos gravissimis iniuriis et detrimentis affecit, et Nos sane id Tecum agimus, quod Summi Romani Pontifices praedecessores Nostri cum patre et maioribus Tuis saepius egerunt, ut scilicet iusto dolore exardescas et inimicum infensissimum regum Persarum nomine, qui omnes quidem, sed Te potissimum durissimo servitutis iugo opprimere molitur, ne inultum abire patiaris, sed ita vehementer oppugnes, ut illum aliquando audaciae et superbiae suae poeniteat. Nam quod Te cupere significas, quodque ii, quos ad Nos misisti, coram etiam narrarunt, ut reges et principes Christiani Tecum contra Turcam foedus ineant, nos idem cupimus, partesque Nostrae pontificiae auctoritatis ad id interponemus, sed res magni momenti diligenti tracta-tione et non modico tempore indigent. Interea non desunt ex principibus Nostris, qui eum bello exerceant atque infestent, et praesertim carissimus filius Noster Rudolphus electus Imperator, qui continenter cum eo bellum gerit et iam nunc hac ipsa aestate gesturus est, et Nos quoque illi adiumento sumus et auxiliares Nostras copias contra Turcas mittimus et Catholicos principes filios Nostros ad eidem electo Imperatori opem ferendam omni officii genere permovemus ; itaque Tuae

est prudentiae et consilii uti hac opportunitate, et dum Turca
robur exercitus sui in Ungariam mittit et armis Christianis
distinetur, Tu illum invade et quasi illius nudatum latus ferro
aggredere, ut ille ancipiti bello distractus et pluribus in locis
oppugnatus, veluti quaedam ferox bellua multorum vena-
torum concursu vexata, telisque coniectis saucia, tandem ad
terram prosternatur ; nihil igitur procrastinandum, ne occasio
praetereat, sed quod Nostros ex sua parte facere vides, Tu
quoque ex Tua fac et Turcam eodem tempore oppugna quam
fortissime ; sic Tu Christianis et Chrisitani Tibi vicissim
adiumento erunt, et quod omnes spectamus, re ipsa efficietur,
ut communis hostis genuina oppugnatione delibitatus corruat
atque intereat, atque hoc ipsum ad foedus, quod desideras,
conciliandum maiorem et faciliorem aditum aperiet, Nosque
tanto efficacius de eo agemus, cum apud omnes constiterit,
Te summo studio, summo ardore totisque viribus in illius
hostis perniciem incumbere, quem ab aliis quoque invadi
atque opprimi concupiscis.   Quod principes Christiani complures, ut diximus, iam pro sua virili faciunt. Nos vero
utilitati et rationibus Tuis et gloriae Tuae valde ex animo
favemus et favebimus, quod ex eo facile perspicere potes, quod
antequam Tui, quos ad Nos misisti, Romam pervenissent, iam
Nos ad Te cum litteris Nostris, amantissime scriptis, duos
familiares Nostros miserimus, videlicet dilectos filios Francis-
cum Costam, sacerdotem Christi, et Didacum Mirandam,
ambos Lusitanos et nobis valde gratos, qui cum incolumes,
Deo duce, in conspectum Tuum venerint, quod supra quam
dici possit optamus, sane ex Nostri litteris atque ex eorum
sermone intelliges copiosius, quam praeclaram de Tua virtute
opinionem habeamus, et quam benevolo erga Te animo simus,
et quantopere cupiamus, non solum Te omni humana felicitate
esse florentissimum, sed sempiterna etiam illa in caelo felicitate
et beatitudine frui, quam nemo potest adipisci, nisi qui ex
aqua et spiritu regeneratus, Christianae fidei veritatem
susceperit et professus fuerit. Quamobrem incredibilem
voluptatem cepimus ex eo capite litterarum Tuarum et
colloquio eorundem duorum praestantium virorum, quod ad
Nos misisti, velle Te nimirum, ut Christianis et iis praesertim,
qui a Nobis mittentur, aditus pateat in regnum et provintias
Tuas, quodque Christianis et Persis libera sint commercia,
ipsique Christiani non solum immunitate multisque favoribus

et privilegiis a Te ample concessis gaudeant et potiantur, sed etiam ecclesias et templa christiano ritu Deo altissimo in Tuo regno et ditione aedificent, sacerdotes et presbyteros habeant, qui divina officia persolvant, sacramenta administrent, verbum Dei praedicent et lucem ac semen evangelii Christi in salutem omni credenti ubique disseminent atque diffundant, quibus rebus nihil Nobis gratius, nihil Deo acceptius, nihil Tibi salutarius et magnifiicentius potest accidere ; nam cum Tu vere et ex animo Dei gloriae servieris, ille etiam, per quem solum reges regnant, te gloriosum et de inimicis tuis Turcis victorem et triumphatorem efficiet ; quare brevi ad Te presbyteros mittemus doctores veritatis et magistros salutis, quemadmodum alteris Nostris litteris solliciti sumus, quas Francisco et Didaco supradictis ad Te perferendas dedimus, quos Tibi iterum et saepius commendamus, petimusque ut eos humaniter accipias laetosque ad Nos remittas, sicut Nos Tuos accepimus et ad Te remittimus multa cum amoris significatione et litteris Nostris, quibuscum de his ipsis rebus, de quibus ad Te scribimus, copiose locuti sumus, qui etiam ex ore et oculis Nostris Nostram in Te eximiam voluntatem Tuaeque gloriae desiderium perspicere potuerunt. Deus omnipotens qui Te in magni Cyri regis solio collocavit, det Tibi cor sapiens et corroboret Te ex alto virtute et fortitudine, ut vincas hostes Tuos Turcas, et lucem evangelii Christi in regnum Persarum, ubi olim late resplenduit, restituas, omnesque reges, qui ante Te in regno isto fuerunt, ita rerum gestarum magnitudine et gloria superes, ut nulla aetas nullaque posteritas famam Tuam ignoret, nec de Tuis unquam laudibus conticescat.— Dat. Romae apud sanctos Apostolos sub annulo piscatoris die secunda Maii 1601, pontificatus Nostri anno decimo.

[Brevia Arm. 44, t. 45, n. 124, Papal Secret Archives.]

22. POPE CLEMENT VIII. TO JUSTIN CALVIN.[1]

1601, December 12, Rome.

Clemens PP. VIII.

Dilecte fili salutem et apostolicam benedictionem. Litteras Tuas et apologiam de Tuo ad gremium catholicae ecclesiae reditu, quas ad Nos misisti, libenti animo accepimus, gratumque est Nobis, quod praeclara erga Te divinae misericordiae beneficia et pie agnoscis et magnifice praedicas et ad eandem

---

[1] See *supra*, p. 277.

veritatis lucem, quam Spiritu Sancto auctore invenisti, alios adhuc tenebris involutos perducere studes. Non erit, ut speramus, infructuosus labor Tuus, Deo ipso sementi Tuae incrementum dante, tuum Tibi certe meritum apud patrem misericordiarum constabit ac salvum erit. Quod venerabilis frater Noster archiepiscopus et princeps elector Moguntinus, et Nostra commendatione et Tua virtute adductus, benigne, ut scribis, Tecum agat Teque foveat, id Nobis pergratum est Nostraeque expectationi consentaneum, ad quem alteras nunc quoque Tui causa commendatitias litteras damus; ut Te tanto propensius complectatur; quin etiam et decano illius insignis capituli Te commendamus, ut plura Tibi praesidia paremus. Tu vero, si Roman venire statueris, gratus Nobis advenies et libenter in primis Te videbimus et Tibi adiumento erimus; amamus enim Te in Christo paterno affectu; ipse autem, qui Te vocavit in admirabile lumen suum, dona sua in te custodiat atque adaugeat, et Nos Tibi apostolicam benedictionem Nostram ex animo impartimur.

Datum Romae apud sanctum Petrum sub annulo piscatoris die 12 Decembris 1601, pontificatus Nostri anno decimo.

[Brevia, Arm. 44 t. 35, n. 421, Papal Secret Archives.]

23. FRANCESCO MARIA VIALARDO TO THE DUKE OF MANTUA.[1]

1604, December 11, Rome.

. . . Il card^le di Perone sarà qui questa sera. Gioiosa è ammalato di lieve puntura, il Papa fa sborsare 50^m duc^ti per il negotio dell'acqua di Ferrara, vuole che si rimetta la congregatione de propaganda fide. . . .

[Orig. Gonzaga Archives, Mantua.]

---

[1] See *supra*, p. 268.

INDEX OF NAMES IN VOL. XXIV.